Motives
for Writing

ROBERT KEITH MILLER
University of St. Thomas

SUZANNE S. WEBB
Texas Woman's University

Mayfield Publishing Company
Mountain View, California
London • Toronto

LIBRARY OF CONGRESS CATALOGING-IN-PUBLICATION DATA
Miller, Robert Keith, 1949–
    Motives for writing / Robert Keith Miller, Suzanne S. Webb.
        p.   cm.
    Includes index.
    ISBN 0-87484-974-8
    1. College readers.   2. English language — Rhetoric.   I. Webb,
Suzanne S.   II. Title.
PE1417.M4884   1991
808'.0427 — dc20   91-35832
                                                                            CIP

Manufactured in the United States of America
10 9 8 7 6 5 4 3 2 1

Mayfield Publishing Company
1240 Villa Street
Mountain View, CA 94041

Sponsoring editor, Thomas V. Broadbent; managing editor, Linda Toy; production editor, April Wells; text and cover designer, David Bullen; art director, Jeanne M. Schreiber; manufacturing manager, Martha Branch; cover image, Gary Overacre. The text was set in 10.5/12 Bembo and printed on 50# Finch Opaque by the Maple-Vail Book Manufacturing Group.

ILLUSTRATION CREDITS
p. 380 Walt Whitman, *Leaves of Grass,* frontispiece, 1855.
p. 382 "Front Porch, Elgin, Illinois: August, 1941," John Vachon.
p. 383 "Kashmir," © Henri Cartier-Bresson; reprinted by permission of
    Magnum Photos, Inc.
p. 383 "Ludmilla Tscherina," © Duane Michals; courtesy Sidney Janis
    Gallery, New York.
p. 384 "The World of H.C.B.," © Henri Cartier-Bresson; reprinted by
    permission of Magnum Photos, Inc.
p. 385 "Poverty," © Gilles Peress; reprinted by permission of Magnum
    Photos, Inc.
p. 386 Photograph of Kenneth Burke, courtesy of Elspeth Burke Hart.

Acknowledgments and copyrights continue at the back of the book on pages 535–537, which constitute an extension of the copyright page.

PREFACE

This book reflects our belief that helping students to discover and fulfill their motives for writing can motivate as well as empower them to write well. As its title suggests, *Motives for Writing* emphasizes the importance of the writer's purpose — the reason for composing and the ends that process should achieve. In focusing upon purpose, we have been influenced by the work of such theorists as James Britton, James Kinneavy, and James Moffett, all of whom have shown that understanding the aims of discourse can contribute to meaningful communication. We believe that an emphasis upon these aims can help students to develop the active minds that are essential for making sense of the world and conveying that sense to others.

Users of this book will find that it is designed to provide both instructors and students with flexibility. We frequently remind writers that the aims of discourse can be pursued by different means, and as we discuss different methods of planning and drafting we encourage writers to choose the methods that work best for them. The entire book reflects our awareness that not only do different writers work well in different ways but the same writer may work well by using different approaches at different times. We have seen in our own classrooms that providing students with choices can enable them to overcome the difficulties that writers encounter and to keep growing as writers.

Because of the importance we attach to flexibility, we have not tied the book to the work of any single theorist. But because we believe that the pentad of Kenneth Burke provides a useful means for helping students both to read and to write, we have drawn upon it at several points. Its presence is most noticeable within the headnotes that precede the selections in Chapters 1–10. Rather than write headnotes devoted to introducing the writer, we have used these notes to orient students to concerns of special importance in the selections that follow.

The selections themselves have been chosen to illustrate the various motives for writing and to provide examples of different writing styles and patterns of arrangement. We have included a number of familiar pieces both because they have proven records as classroom favorites and because we wanted to spare instructors the necessity of undertaking an entirely new preparation. Maya Angelou, Bruce Catton, Norman Cousins, Annie Dillard, Martin Luther King, Jessica Mitford, George Orwell, and Jonathan Swift are all represented by well-known works. But we wanted most of the readings to be new to the world of college readers. We hope that both teachers and students will find many pieces that will be a pleasure to read. Although the readings differ in length — with the longer, more challenging selections concentrated in the second half of the book — they all address issues that are likely to inspire good class discussion, and we have provided an alternative table of contents grouping selections on related topics for readers interested in pursuing a particular subject or theme.

To facilitate class discussion, every selection has its own apparatus. Although some of the "Questions for Discussion" are designed simply to gauge reading comprehension, most raise concerns that invite readers to think about what they have read and to formulate their own responses. Every reading is also followed by two "Suggestions for Writing." Individual readers may well identify other questions and suggestions; we did not attempt to exhaust the possibilities for any piece. Our goal was simply to encourage thoughtful responses to reading, and we recognize that such responses, when encouraged, can take any number of directions.

Most chapters begin with short, readily accessible readings and conclude with longer, more demanding pieces. And the motives themselves have been arranged according to the degree of difficulty inexperienced writers are likely to have with them. We begin with such writer-oriented motives as "Writing to Record a Memory" and "Writing to Discover Oneself" and then move on to motives that become increasingly reader oriented. But because every chapter is self-contained, the various motives can be studied in any sequence that seems appropriate for a specific class — just as the readings within any chapter can be read in a sequence determined by individual interests or needs.

A word here about the rhetorical modes: We teach that writing seldom involves conforming to a fixed pattern of organization, that a single piece usually involves several modes, and that no mode is limited to any one motive. In other words, we present the modes as means that writers can choose to employ when pursuing different aims, but we do not present them as models to which writers should make their thoughts conform. We believe that instruction based upon fixed patterns of arrangement can turn writing into an academic exercise that stresses product over process and bears little relation to the way writers write in the world beyond the classroom. A professional writer would be unlikely to begin with the intention of writing, say, an exposition to be organized along the lines of a definition, comparison, or classification. Although the writing produced may ultimately reflect one of these methods, the arrangement is more likely to grow out of writing than to be imposed upon it at the outset as a framework to which invention must be subordinate. Our book thus encourages students not only to use the modes when doing so would be useful but also to recognize that arrangement is simply one of the writers' tools and not an end in itself.

Teaching the motives in the order in which we have arranged them, however, would roughly parallel the sequence in which rhetorical modes are often taught. "Writing to Record a Memory" often employs narration and description; "Writing to Explain" often involves process; "Writing to Evaluate" may require comparison and contrast; and "Writing to Explore an Idea" may lead to definition. Instructors accustomed to teaching rhetorical modes will find that we have not abandoned these strategies. The book contains many examples of the modes, together with some discussion of them. We recognize that teachers of composition must be prepared to help students organize their thoughts, and the modes can be useful for this type of instruction. The Index by Rhetorical Strategy (Mode) beginning on page 539 is designed to be helpful in this regard.

In completing this book we are indebted to colleagues and friends with whom we have discussed our work. Ruth Dorgan, Warren Garitano, and Ozzie Mayers all provided good counsel. Marilyn Boroughs Keef, Donna Skeen Shelton, and Caroline Bloomfield Quigley have offered support as well as contributed ideas and research talent. We are especially grateful to Ellen Wynn, who not only helped us with the selection of photographs for Chapter 8 but also fed us Dungeness crab when we most needed it. We very much appreciate the support we received from April Wells, Julie Rovesti, and Pamela Trainer. Carol Beale, our manuscript editor, and David Bullen, our designer, deserve many thanks for their contributions. And finally, to Tom Broadbent, our editor, we both join in special thanks for the generosity with which he gave us friendship, advice, and attention to detail.

CONTENTS

     One of our best nature writers recalls Death Valley as "a hard place to love."

Mellix shares her journey from "the old me . . . , hugging to herself a disabling mistrust of a language she thought could not represent a person with her history and experience" to "a person who feels the consequences of her education, the weight of her possibilities. . . ."

If a "marathon with all those emaciated runners sprawled on the grass, tongues hanging out, wheezing, moaning, writhing, throwing up . . . is the way to happiness and a long life, pass . . . the cheesecake."

Allen offers his own version of "an imaginary . . . course bulletin that is more or less typical of them all."

Accusing his wife and neighbors of "rural literalism," Trillin determines to go back to the city where clichés are meant symbolically, "the way [they were] meant to be meant."

Goodman suggests that there is "one way in which the male sex is innately different from the female: Men are by their very nature congenitally unable to ask directions."

Speculating that men invented civilization because they "needed an excuse to get . . . out of doing the housework," Barry offers an unusual solution to the problem.

In addition to boiling the game down to its essentials, the final days of the baseball season also turn the game into "something more along the lines of *As the Bat Swings.*"

Defining "old friends" as people who "know each other so well that no one holds back," Rooney reports a number of comments his friend Quintin ought to have held back.

argues. But "increasing our capacity to punish retail drug dealers has . . . some hope of actually reducing the impact of drug dealing on our lives."

READINGS ARRANGED BY SUBJECT AND THEME

Family

Gender

Introduction

Writing for Your Life

Writing can change your life. It can help you to discover who you are and empower you to achieve the goals you set for yourself. It can help you to make sense of the information that assaults you daily and to present ideas so that others will take you seriously. And it can broaden your world by enabling you to communicate effectively with people you have never met.

But despite the tremendous advantages of writing well, many people persuade themselves that they can never learn to write because they believe that writing is a talent they were denied at birth. People who think in these terms are unlikely to write well, because they lack the motivation to take their writing seriously. It is true that some people learn to write more easily than others because they have a certain aptitude for it or because they have been encouraged by parents or good teachers. But to a very large extent writing is a skill that can be learned by anyone who is willing to take the trouble. Believe that you will fail, and you are likely to fail. Believe that you can succeed, and you will have begun to succeed. It will certainly take time and effort to write successfully, for writing involves hard work, but you will find that this investment will pay rich dividends.

You probably know more about writing than you realize, but you may not know how to use that knowledge to accomplish the full range of writing you need to do. You may have been discouraged by assignments that seemed silly and pointless. If so, you probably wondered "Why?" and, when you finished, "So what?" What you sensed was that real writing is done for a real purpose. Someone has a motive for writing — a motive that is stronger than simply wanting to complete an assignment. There are, as you will see, many motives for writing. Whatever the specific motive may be, however, writers write because they understand that writing is a way to satisfy a purpose that is important to them.

This book takes the position that successful writing begins with having a motive for writing and understanding how that motive can be fulfilled. The ten sections that follow this introduction discuss a number of these motives and show how various writers have realized them: to record a memory, to discover oneself, to amuse others, to move others, to persuade others, to convey information, to explain something, to evaluate something, and to explore an idea. The final section emphasizes writing to understand reading, but the entire book assumes that reading is intimately connected to writing. Recognizing, through reading, the motives of other writers can help you to discover your own sense of what you hope to accomplish when you write and to understand the principles likely to help you succeed.

THE RHETORICAL SITUATION

As a form of communication, writing (like speaking) involves five elements which together form what is called the rhetorical situation.

- Author (the writer or speaker)
- Audience (the reader or listener)
- Purpose (why the writer or speaker is communicating)
- Topic (what the writer or speaker wants to communicate)
- Occasion (when and where the communication takes place)

Because this is a book about writing, we will focus on writers and readers, even though much of what is said would be true of speakers and listeners.

As writers pursue different motives, they emphasize certain elements of the rhetorical situation over others. Recording a memory and discovering oneself focus mainly on satisfying the needs of the writer. Amusing, moving, and persuading others focus mainly on eliciting an appropriate response from the audience. Conveying information, explaining something, evaluating something, exploring ideas, and writing about reading focus in varying degrees on the subject matter or topic. But whatever your emphasis, you can seldom lose sight of the other elements for long. Thus, while you focus on subject matter when you want to convey information, you must still consider your audience in order to choose language that will help your readers understand the information you wish to convey. You must also try to convince readers that you are conveying the information reliably. Experienced writers understand that they can seldom focus on themselves alone.

Author

Some writers write slowly, and others write quickly. Some do their best work in the early morning, and others write best at night. Some need a quiet place, and others write happily with music playing and friends wandering around the room. In short, different writers write best in different environments — and you should consider the time and setting that are the most conducive to your own work.

But while writers have different habits and write in different ways, good writers all have at least one common characteristic: They are readers as well as writers. As readers, they are constantly acquiring new information — much of which they may never use, but some of which will help them to write. To put it simply: The more you know, the more you have to say, and the easier it is to discover ideas for writing.

But good writers are also readers in a different sense: They are readers of their own work. When they write — and especially when they revise — they consider their work not only from their own point of view (by asking, for example, "Have I said what I wanted to say?") but also from the point of view of readers (by asking, for example, "Is this point clear?"). Such writers understand that writing is a form of communication — usually a transaction between the writer and at least one other person.

One way of thinking about the variety of possible transactions between writers and readers is to envision them on a scale, or perhaps a spectrum, ranging from the personal and private at one end to the impersonal and public at the other, with an increasingly diverse range of motives brought into play as you move from the private toward the public. This is not to say that any one type of writing is necessarily better than another; but some choices work better than others when you are trying to satisfy a specific purpose. What marks experienced writers is the ability to analyze the rhetorical situation and make appropriate choices, adjusting the degree of personal expression accordingly. The more experience you gain in writing, the more readily you can make appropriate and deliberate choices.

Audience

Having a good sense of audience is one of the most important factors in writing well. Inexperienced writers often write as if they did not really expect anyone else to read what they have written. There are, without question, times when writers write solely for their own benefit — putting on paper words they have no intention of sharing with others. But most of the writing that we do in life involves communicating with other people. The "others" with whom we communicate can range from a single individual, whom we may or may not know, to a large group that includes people we have never met.

Chaim Perelman, a European legal philosopher, explored the idea of audience and concluded in his book *The Realm of Rhetoric* that there are basically two kinds: a particular audience, which may be composed of one person or many people, and a universal audience, which is a mental construct including "all those who are competent and reasonable." In other words, you might write a paper for your English instructor or to share with the other students in your English class, but you are guided in doing so not only by what you know about those specific individuals but also by a belief that on the whole they belong to — are in certain ways representative of — intelligent people of good will anywhere.

Some rhetoricians have even gone so far as to argue that writers mentally construct their audience and that readers then willingly play the part of the audience they sense that the writer envisioned. So, as you can see, the question of audience could be discussed at length, for it has inspired a number of different theories. But at this point we can offer two generalizations:

1. Whether audiences are particular or universal, imaginary or real, most rhetoricians agree that writers need to recognize the values and needs of readers and not rely too much on the patience and cooperation of these readers. If readers find that they have to work unnecessarily hard to figure out what a writer means, or if they feel that a writer is insulting their intelligence, they will often stop reading even if they have reason to believe that the material is important. You should almost always choose topics and language appropriate for whoever will actually be reading what you write. The exception would be writing for an audience that is for some reason different from your actual reader. For example: If you write a paper that will be read only by your English instructor but envision an audience of college freshmen, your instructor may assume the role of the audience you imagined if your paper clearly reveals the audience at which it is directed. In this case, the topic and language of the paper should be appropriate for college freshmen even if college freshmen will not actually be reading the paper.

2. Being able to imagine more than one type of audience can help you to write well. Dwell too much on a particular audience that has power and expertise, and you may end up feeling intimidated. In such circumstances you might benefit from constructing another audience in your mind. Doing so can help you to draft the first (and often most difficult) version of the work at hand, and you can always make adjustments for a particular audience as you revise. To take a simple example: Suppose you feel nervous when writing for an English instructor who will, you know, be putting a grade on your work. Focusing on the instructor may lead to

writer's block, but thinking in terms of a universal audience (all reasonable people of good will) or another particular audience (college freshmen at your school) can help you to generate a credible first draft. But because your instructor is also an important part of your audience, you can address some of his or her concerns (such as the length and variety of your sentences) as you revise your writing into something that you yourself feel good about.

Purpose

A writer's *purpose* is essentially the same as a writer's *motive;* both terms are used to describe what a writer hopes to accomplish. A good way to understand purpose is to ask yourself why a writer chose to approach a topic one way rather than another. When reading a humorous essay, you might immediately understand that the writer's motive was to amuse, but you can then enrich your understanding of the essay by considering why someone would want to be amusing on the topic this writer chose.

We have already identified a number of motives for writing, each of which will be discussed individually in the sections that follow this general introduction. Keep in mind, however, that writing often reveals an interplay among various motives. For example, although the primary purpose of an argument may be to persuade readers to accept some belief or undertake some action, an argument might easily include paragraphs devoted to informing, amusing, or moving readers. Having more than one purpose is fine as long as one purpose does not conflict with another in the same work. As a general rule, however, you should try to make one purpose prevail within any one work, for this will help make the work unified and coherent.

Topic

Although the terms *subject* and *topic* are often used interchangeably, a distinction can be made between them. *Subject* is often used to describe the general area that a writer has considered, while *topic* identifies the specific part of that subject that the writer has discussed. Writers often begin with a subject and then narrow it down to a topic suitable for the length of the work they have in mind. If you are interested in writing about the Second World War, you could not hope to discuss more than a small part of this subject in an essay of three or four pages. The subject contains many possible topics, and you might decide to write about the attack on Pearl Harbor or the firebombing of Tokyo—both of which topics could be narrowed even further.

By narrowing a subject to a specific topic, you focus attention on something that you want your readers to see in detail. To use an analogy: If you are watching a football game from a seat high up in a large stadium, you have a very large field of view, much of which is totally irrelevant to the game — thousands of spectators, the curve of the bleachers, the pitch of the ramps, and so on. Unless you find some way to narrow that field of view, you are going to be distracted by these irrelevancies, and you will not be able to get a clear view of exactly what is happening on the field. A pair of binoculars will help immensely, for you can train them on the players, and the binoculars will magnify the images of the players so that you can see more details of each play. However, you have to adjust the focus of the binoculars to see the players clearly. Just as you have too large a field of view from the top of the stadium, you may target too large an area to write about at first; and, as you proceed, you may discover that you are most interested in a much smaller part of it. Thus, just as you would at the ball game, you must shut out some details and focus on others.

Because choosing a topic is such an important part of writing well, we will offer additional advice on how to do so later in this introduction. For the moment, however, note that a good topic is not only suitable for the length of the paper in question; it will also lead to saying something worth saying. Some topics have been written about so extensively that you may find it difficult to communicate something to readers that they do not already know. A writer with an original topic, or a topic about which something new can be said, has a head start on maintaining the interest of readers.

Occasion

Writing is also influenced by where and when it occurs — what is called the *occasion* for writing (or sometimes the *context*). Writing an essay in class, for example, may be very different from writing an essay out of class even though the author, audience, purpose, and topic have remained the same. Or suppose you want to write a letter to a friend. If you are a thoughtful writer, your tone will reflect what you know of your friend's state of mind even though the basic elements of the rhetorical situation have remained the same: A light letter full of jokes might not be appropriate if you knew your friend had just sustained a serious loss.

In academic writing, occasion may involve a number of things, including how much technical language you are expected to use, the kind of organization that is expected of you, and the attitude you are expected to assume. For instance, your professor in a physics course might wonder if you knew what you were talking about if you substituted the word "doughnut" for the technical physics term "torus" in a report on fusion reaction; "doughnut" would be the wrong level of language for this occasion even though it can mean "torus" and might be used in an informal conversation between physicists. Or your political science instructor might expect you to demonstrate an objective attitude in a report summing up the results of a recent session of Congress. The nature of the assignment would influence content as well as vocabulary and tone. Or to choose another example: Writing a formal paper in the social sciences often requires a pattern of organization that would be inappropriate for writing in the humanities. A paper reporting the results of research in psychology might begin with a summary (or abstract) and then move on to separate sections devoted to research methods, results, and discussion. Such divisions, although commonly found in writing for the social sciences, would be unusual in a paper for an English or history course, where readers would normally expect each paragraph to flow smoothly into the next. Although each of these examples involves the expectations of certain readers (the audience), these expectations have been shaped by the conventions of different disciplines. A sense of occasion helps writers to satisfy these conventions.

THE WRITING PROCESS

How, exactly, do writers cope with all the demands made upon them? And how do some writers produce material that is a pleasure to read? The answer is that there are about as many ways that writers write as there are writers. Everyone has his or her own process, but experienced writers follow a process that includes finding a topic, planning, drafting, revising, and editing. There is no predetermined order in which these activities must occur, however; no obligation to complete one activity before beginning another. When we write, we loop back and forth over our own mental tracks time and again, rethinking, rearranging, restating, researching. We may not complete one loop before we're off in another direction with another loop. And we don't necessarily begin at the beginning; sometimes we finish at the beginning. All of this goes to say that writing is a fairly chaotic process. Still, we do know some things.

Writers need something to write about, and finding a topic is often the most difficult part of the writing process. Of course, writing goes best when we can write about something we are vitally interested in, but that is often not the case. Sometimes we are given our subject by a teacher, an employer, or even a friend or relative who expects a letter. In that case, the preliminary work becomes finding something to say about that subject (a task that we do almost unconsciously when we are enthusiastic about a subject). We also have to plan what to include and what to leave out as well as settle on some trial order for presenting our material. Much of this work goes on informally while we are actually doing other things — burrowing under the covers early in the morning, waiting at a traffic light, mowing the lawn. Some of it is more structured, however, as in the lists we may make to be sure we don't forget one of our important points.

When we have a pretty good idea of what we want to write about, we may begin *drafting,* writing it down. Here is where the "looping back" (or recursive) nature of writing is most readily apparent. We may draft several pages to discover what we want to say and decide to throw out all but two or three sentences. Or if we are more confident of what we mean to say, we may draft several pages before we are interrupted; then when we come back to the writing, we may start out by revising what we have written, or we may find ourselves starting over — but we'll save the writing we're not using because it may be useful later. We may also draft a part of the writing we feel most comfortable about first to warm up our brains in an effort to hit our intellectual stride for the more difficult parts. It doesn't matter if the piece of writing we do first will come near the end. We'll put it where it belongs when we have a clearer vision of the shape of what we are saying.

When we've developed all of these pieces of writing, we can weave them together — a process we may have begun earlier. If we begin to see, in the structure of the information, gaps which we have to fill with new writing, we're doing our job as writers. And if we haven't already done so, we have to find a way to begin and a way to conclude. We may have been revising all along, reshaping sentences that disappoint us as soon as we see them and rearranging paragraphs when we are only midway through our initial draft. But it is only after we can see the whole composition that we can really move into *revising,* testing everything we say against what we have already said or what comes later, seeking the greatest possible clarity, coherence, and concision, as well as correctness. Although there's no real order to the parts of the writing process, obviously we can't revise what never was written, and we've stopped all of the other parts of the process when we do final proofreading. It is within those boundaries that the writing process occurs.

Finding a Topic

So how do we know what we want to write about? Conventional wisdom tells new writers, "Write what you know," "Write about what you enjoy" — sound advice, but not terribly practical if you're not sure what you know and why what you know could interest other readers.

For most of us a choice of subject is seldom entirely free, and for everyone the subject for writing derives directly from the rhetorical situation. In this way college writing is not really very different from writing on the job. In college writing the choice of a subject is conditioned by the courses in which the writer is enrolled — by the academic discipline as well as by the dictates of the professor. In the working world the subject for writing depends on the constraints of employment — the employer's attitudes and requirements. However, insofar as we have choices, we are well advised to follow our interests, keeping in mind that the goal in both kinds of writing is to show competence as well as to fulfill a specific purpose for writing.

Consider the full rhetorical situation in which you are writing: What (in addition to showing competence) is your purpose? Precisely what are you to do, and what information do you need to do it? Ask yourself who will read your writing, bearing in mind that your audience may be larger than it seems: You might write a memo to your boss, but your boss may decide to distribute it to other people in the company. Workaday writing and academic writing require different approaches: For instance, an analysis of a firm's sales trends in the last quarter of the year will probably require more graphics than will an academic discussion of business cycles in the eighties. But different kinds of writing can also make use of the same techniques: trace the progress of a particular project or the influence of the printing press, report on employee performance or a lab experiment, classify a competitor's products or the types of sixteenth century naval vessels, explain why a valve failed or what a poem means.

CHAOTIC PROCESSES Ways of exploring a subject fall rather naturally into two groups: chaotic processes and structured processes. Among the chaotic processes for exploring subjects are those that rely on the subconscious knowledge we all have. They are time-tested techniques for encouraging that kind of knowledge to surface so that we can impose order on it. Depending upon your inclination and your topic, two of these techniques — *brainstorming* and *freewriting* — may be interchangeable; the other technique, *mapping,* places ideas in spatial relationships to each other. You may already be familiar with these methods; if they have worked for you in the past, by all means continue to use them. If you've never tried them, you may find them useful. But if they don't work for you, try something else, perhaps some of the structured processes which are described later.

Brainstorming For many years the business community has been using brainstorming — getting a small group of people together for unstructured discussion of an idea — as a way to increase creativity and productivity; but it can also be used successfully by one person looking for ideas about a subject. It involves listing everything that occurs to you (or that others say) about the idea as fast as possible in a limited period of time. You can do it over and over, checking your list at the end of each spurt of intensive thinking.

To try it out, get a pen or pencil and a sheet of paper. Set your alarm clock or the oven timer for fifteen or twenty minutes. Concentrate on your subject. Ask yourself what you know about it and jot down your answers. As ideas come crowding to the surface, write as fast as you can to jot them down. Don't worry about spelling or flow or anything except putting the ideas somewhere on that piece of paper. And don't worry about whether your answers seem worthwhile. You can evaluate them later. The point is to get as many thoughts as you can on paper. If you keep your mind working, a good idea may come only after a dozen that you'll later reject. Stop when the alarm goes off and take a few minutes to look over your jottings. Mark ideas you find useful or interesting. Colored markers ease the task of grouping those that seem to go together. If you think you still don't have enough to go on, you can brainstorm again, perhaps focusing on one of the ideas you wrote down or taking a new direction; but give yourself a rest between sessions.

Freewriting Like brainstorming, freewriting is done nonstop, it occurs intensely for a short period of time, and it is unselfconscious. The difference is that freewriting results in a kind of connected writing. Although freewriting may produce much that is unusable, it can also produce much that will be surprisingly important, attesting to the notion that our subconscious minds contain enormous amounts of valuable information. Freewriting is a way to get some use out of this information, and it may very well give you a focus for the rest of your work on the subject. Sometimes, when we find an approach to a subject through brainstorming, freewriting unlocks a wealth of ideas to pursue.

First, at the top of your sheet of paper jot down one or two sentences stating your idea. Some writers like to think informally about this idea before they put pen to paper. That's okay. Then, set your timer for ten or fifteen minutes. When you begin writing, don't worry if you can't think of something to write. Just write anything, even if it's "I feel silly." Don't stop for any reason: to figure out how to spell a word, to choose between two terms, or for any other reason. Don't worry if you find yourself straying from your guide sentence at the top of the page. The new direction may be useful. When your buzzer sounds, stop writing and look at what you have. Here, too, as in brainstorming, colored markers may be useful in identifying a good idea that is buried under a number of random thoughts. If you find a good idea, you may be able to flesh it out to make a completed draft, or you may have something that with shaping will become part of your finished work.

Mapping Mapping (sometimes called *clustering* or *webbing*) is a way of visually analyzing the parts of a subject. Write the subject in the middle of your paper and circle it. From the edges of the circle, draw lines radiating outward to nodes labeled to represent the main parts of the subject. Repeat this process for each of those nodes until you have exhausted all of the information you have. You will notice that some parts generate several levels, whereas others do not and that the interrelationships between parts of the idea are easy to see in this kind of graphic chart. Consider the illustration on page 11, but note that no two maps look just alike.

Brainstorming, freewriting, and mapping can be used together to bring some order to the chaotic information that surfaces from the unconscious. Try pulling some of the related ideas that surfaced during a brief brainstorming session into a single statement and jotting that statement at the top of your freewriting paper. When you are through freewriting, look at what you have produced and try to group related ideas. This activity will focus your efforts to find the vein of gold in the ton of sludge.

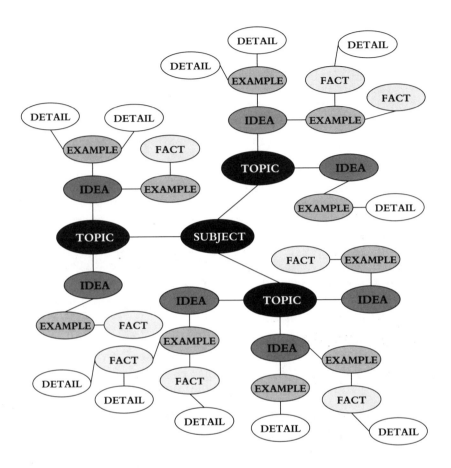

FIGURE 1. Mapping

STRUCTURED PROCESSES Structured processes are ways of prodding our minds to come up with information. They are conscious ways to encourage thinking along specific lines. To get below the surface of a subject, Aristotle provided thirty-two approaches called *topoi*, the word from which "topic" has been derived. In our own century, the philosopher Kenneth Burke offered an alternative way to explore a subject by using five elements called the *pentad*. A related method, *journalists' questions*, lists six aspects of a subject.

Classical Topics It is often useful to look at a subject from the perspectives originally developed by Aristotle to help people generate ideas.

Aristotle proposed that questions can be asked to define what something is and others to compare and contrast it with other things. Still other questions help in examining the relationships that are possible: cause, antecedent, contraries, contradictions. Questions about circumstances explore matters of possibility and factuality. And questions about testimony — authority, statistics, maxims, law, examples — can help writers support their points.

Originally designed as ways to discover proofs in persuasive writing, Aristotle's topics provided a foundation for the work of many other rhetoricians and have played an important role in education for more than two thousand years. One of the advantages of the topics is that they remind us to consider both the general qualities and particular features of any given subject. At least one of Aristotle's questions should always be appropriate, whatever we want to write about. The answers we provide help us to decide what we want or need to say.

Few people are able to keep a list of thirty-two approaches in mind. But, without memorizing a long list of topics, you can still benefit from classical rhetoric by asking yourself a series of questions when preparing to write. These questions can help you not only to generate ideas when you feel stymied but also to narrow and focus a subject so that you can choose an appropriate topic:

- Should I provide an *example* of what I mean?
- Should I *divide* this subject into parts, discuss each separately, or focus upon a single part?
- Can I *classify* this subject by putting it in a context of similar things?
- Would it be useful to *narrate,* or provide a short story?
- Would it be appropriate to see this subject as a *process* and explain how it takes place?
- Should I explain what *caused* this subject or what its *effects* will be?
- Should I *define* what I mean?
- Should I *describe* the features of my subject?
- Should I *compare* my subject to something similar or *contrast* it with something with which it might be confused?

Providing the answers to these questions has led some people to think that writing needs to be organized along the lines that the topics suggest. You may have already studied a book that taught you how to write a "description" or a "definition." Such assignments have a certain value, but it is much like the value that practicing scales has for a musician. Outside of classes in composition, a writer is unlikely to wake up some morning and decide, "Today I am going to write an essay of comparison and contrast." Writers are much more likely to begin with a motive or a topic and then decide upon a plan that best suits what they want to say. When you use classical topics or questions derived from them, think of them as a way to get started rather than as a formula that you are bound to follow.

Pentad Kenneth Burke believed that neither reading nor writing can be passive. Burke's pentad explains how this active response takes place. We'll be discussing it here as an aid to thinking about reading and writing and will draw upon it elsewhere to help you understand the reading selections in the sections that follow.

Burke defines five elements that are always present to some degree in a piece of writing:

Scene
Purpose
Act
Agent
Agency

For instance, a writer may concentrate attention on landscape, locale, or environment; on a particular moment in time; or even on spectacle or atmosphere. These are all a part of what Burke calls *scene*. Similarly, a writer may choose to emphasize a *purpose,* that is, a motive, rationale, or reason; a goal, aim, or objective; an intention or design; a mission or cause. And, of course, the writer may have chosen to focus on an event, an *act,* which may involve examining something that happens but may also include delving into the meaning of the event. Sometimes a writer chooses to spotlight an *agent,* which may be a person but might also be a force or power or a catalyst for producing an event. The other element the writer may examine is *agency,* which could be described as an instrument that caused something, the mechanism or vehicle by which something is accomplished.

But even if a writer has emphasized one element of the pentad, you should be able to find the others if you look for them. Burke's own analogy may help you to understand how the various elements of the pentad are related to one another. He compared them to the five fingers on a hand—separate, but ultimately joined. Tracing down one finger should help you make a path to another. We can, of course, cross our fingers or clench them together. Similarly, we can consider any element of the pentad in combination with any other to establish a relationship (what Burke called a *ratio*) among the elements. And these relationships expand meaning. For instance, an act can be examined in its relationship to the scene, the agent, the agency, and the purpose just as the scene can be examined in relationship to act, agent, agency, and purpose, and so on. These expanded perspectives from which to view the subject matter are useful to writers as well as readers. They help us to understand more fully and more clearly what we mean to say as well as what some other writer meant us to know. Two examples can illustrate how this method works. The first shows that the method is especially useful when we apply it to drama (hence the method is called *dramatistic*), and the second shows how suggestive it can be when we think about any subject.

This book includes a play called *Trifles,* in which the scene is a farmhouse, the act is a murder, and the agency is a piece of rope. When we consider the act in terms of the scene, we learn the agent and the agent's purpose — who killed the victim and why. An examination of the scene alone tells us that the farmhouse is old, cold, messy, and deserted. Examining the scene in the light of the act reveals much about the killer's motivation — what kind of a husband the victim was, that the couple had no children, and a number of other facts that lead us to deduce who committed the murder.

For the second example, suppose the subject is hot weather. We can examine what people do and how they feel in hot weather, when and where hot weather occurs and what the world looks like when it is hot, what causes hot weather, how hot weather develops, and what purpose it serves. And, as Burke argued, we will discover the most if we view each of these parts of the pentad in relation to every other part (the ratios).

This dramatistic method has been used to analyze all kinds of subjects and to reveal how the elements of which a subject is composed relate to each other. For example, what happens when we see the act in relation to the scene? In our example about hot weather, we could look at what people do (act) in certain cultures (scene) when it is hot. Or we can examine how people respond to hot weather in the South and in the North or how we lived with hot weather before air conditioning.

If you think about the pentad in this way, your understanding of an event changes as you combine and recombine the elements. This leads also to the idea Burke later advanced that the pentad is enriched and expanded by considering the combinations in the context of social concerns and economic processes. When we do that, we gain a new perspective on what we see. For instance, keeping the effects of rural isolation in mind when reading *Trifles* reveals that economic forces created a brutal and insensitive husband who emotionally abused his wife for years — an understanding that can lead us to see that neither agent nor agency in this play is as simple as it first appears.

How, then, can the pentad help you as a writer? If you use it as a tool to analyze what others have written, you discover that you have much to say about that piece. But you can also use it as a means for writing something entirely on your own. Burke himself described dramatism as "a generating principle." Suppose that you have been asked to write about a significant personal experience. Once you have identified that experience (or act, in Burke's terms), you have to decide where to begin your essay, how much to include, and what points to emphasize. In one case the pentad might lead you to discover the importance of scene, and much of the essay you write will then focus on how the scene contributed to the act. In another instance you may realize that you want to emphasize the means through which an act was done or the agents who committed that act.

Journalists' Questions Journalists' questions are similar to Burke's pentad, but they do not incorporate the relationships to the same extent.

They look only at *who* did *what* to whom, *when* and *where,* and *why* and *how.* Here is the first sentence of a news story from the business section of the *Dallas Times Herald* for January 30, 1991:

> Last week California-based Intel Corp. sold an early model of its new parallel-processing supercomputer to an arm of the Mitsubishi group, scoring a major American coup in a key high-tech field that the Japanese government has targeted for world domination.

Notice how much information the reader is given in this first sentence: who, what, when, where, and why. The only vital piece of information the reader is not given in this lead is *how* the event occurred — information that will follow shortly. The rest of the news story was devoted to developing and expanding the information given in this sentence.

> *Who:* "Intel Corp." We want to know more about Intel. What kinds of products does it make? Is it big or small? New or old?
>
> *What:* "sold an early model of its new parallel-processing super-computer to an arm of the Mitsubishi group." Is this new super-technology? What's a supercomputer? Why is it newsworthy to have sold this to a Japanese company?
>
> *When:* "last week." Exactly when did this sale happen? Had it been planned for a long time?
>
> *Where:* "California-based." We're interested in this story because it tells us that an American company made an important sale. But can we assume that Intel is American-owned simply because it is based in California?
>
> *Why:* "scoring a major American coup in a key high-tech field that the Japanese government has targeted for world domination." Now we know why the story is news. An American company has broken into a difficult overseas market.
>
> *How:* is presented in the next sentence of the article: "By success-fully marketing its iPSC-860 supercomputer. . . ."

These questions work well for exploring almost any kind of subject; and by answering each of them, you can discover interesting information that you can use for writing. Certainly not all of the questions will be suitable for every subject; but in general, this method always gives you something to say.

Dealing with Writer's Block

It is easy to get sidetracked in your writing at this point. You may even talk yourself into a case of writer's block. You know what you are going to write about and you know what the main points are, but you just can't seem to begin writing. There's that awful piece of blank paper staring back at you. How do you overcome writer's block? Many of the techniques useful for exploring ideas are also useful for getting over this snag, but you should consider, too, whether you are trying to write in a setting conducive for doing good work. You may be tensing up simply because you are trying to work in the wrong place or in the wrong clothes.

Make yourself as comfortable as you can, but don't get so comfortable that you will fall asleep. (Going to sleep is a particularly insidious way of avoiding writing.) Fish out your favorite sweatshirt, loosen your belt, clear your desk, sharpen your pencils or arrange your pens, provide yourself with a stack of paper, arrange the lighting, set a snack nearby, and sit down. Pull over a piece of paper, take up your pen or pencil, and begin to freewrite. At this point it doesn't matter what you write. You are just breaking through your block.

As soon as your ideas are flowing freely, you can begin to be more conscious of what you are saying and how the pieces are going together. Perhaps the piece you are working on isn't very congenial just at the moment. So change it; start on something else. You don't have to begin at the beginning. You can begin with something that will flow easily for you, and you can fit it into the whole later on. This method has been called *chunking*. Writers begin with a piece of writing they feel comfortable working on and develop that piece as far as it needs to go. Then they set it aside and take up another piece, sometimes at the same sitting, sometimes not. When all of the pieces have been written, they fit the pieces into a whole, linking them with appropriate transitional material and providing introductions and conclusions.

But if you are particularly susceptible to writer's block, it may be a good idea to do what Ernest Hemingway used to do and end each writing session at a point where you feel sure you know what will come next. That way you can pick up quickly where you left off. Other things you can do to stave off writer's block include talking into a cassette recorder and then transcribing what you have dictated, rereading or retyping on your typewriter or word processor material you have already written, writing on the backs of old drafts so that you don't really have a blank sheet of paper, writing on small pieces of paper so as not to be intimidated by a large one, writing letters to friends to exercise your writing muscles, writing in a journal, or using a "magic" pen or pencil—one that has already written a number of completed compositions or one that feels especially good in the hand. If none of these techniques helps, try anything you think will help. Exercise: Ride your bicycle, go for a walk, wash dishes, shovel snow, or do some other physical task that requires little concentration, during which a good idea may come to mind if you keep your mind receptive. You will come back to writing refreshed. If that doesn't seem fruitful, put the idea of writing aside for the time being; go to a movie, watch television for an hour, read a couple of chapters of a novel. But be alert for ways you may be fooling yourself out of, rather than into, writing. If you find a way to overcome a block, remember it and use it whenever you need it much as baseball players wear lucky socks or eat certain meals before games.

As you gain more experience and as you write more and more, you will have a stock of information that will help you get over future writing blocks. Some writers keep files of interesting material they find while reading for pleasure, just as they do when they are actually researching. Others, like Joan Didion, keep a journal in which they write down ideas and perceptions that may be useful in the future. When you feel like writing you can go to this material to find a subject to explore, and you can consult it to help you over a sterile time.

Planning

After you have generated a number of ideas, identified a topic for your paper, and feel ready to write, how can you arrange your ideas into an effective sequence? Some of your instructors may have advised you to make an outline or list the order in which you will present your main points. That's good advice if you can work that way. Unfortunately, many people can't. These people often find themselves going wherever the writing takes them. Even when they prepare an outline, they wind up not following it but rather going where the writing takes them. There is nothing intrinsically wrong with that; writing is, after all, one of the best ways to learn, and you will generally wind up with something that can be reworked into a worthwhile piece of writing. Writing often takes its own shape as you do it, and plans developed beforehand go out the window. That's all right, too. Planning and drafting can occur over and over until you feel that you have said exactly what you intended. The point is that some kind of plan needs to be evident in the writing when it is completed, whether or not the plan was there from the beginning.

Even experienced writers need to plan so that the writing they do will be organized. Some writers prepare a detailed outline before they even complete their search for ideas. Others barge ahead without having a very clear idea of where they're going; they let the writing lead them. Some writers work one way on one project and a different way on the next. The important thing to understand about planning is that your plans are not contracts. They can easily be changed. In fact, most writing plans do change during drafting and revision. So there's no single correct way to plan that will work every time you write. Any plan that works for you is the correct plan for that writing activity. With that in mind, let's look at a number of different methods.

DISCOVERY DRAFTS Your creative juices are flowing and the pieces of information are crowding each other to get out onto paper. It's all right to go ahead and let them flow; write them down as fast as you can. Writers frequently begin with only a general idea of what they want to discuss, and they simply let the ideas flow naturally until they have figured out what point or points they really want to make. If you write without any kind of formal plan, letting your ideas on a specific topic flow and take shape as you set them down, you are producing a discovery draft. Discovery drafts are different from freewriting in that you stick to a topic as you write. For this kind of draft, the end is usually signaled by the discovery of the point you want your essay to make.

The important thing to remember is that the discovery draft is only a beginning, a way to let ideas find their own shape, and that ultimately the writer will have to take charge to find the most effective plan and reshape the draft. In other words, a discovery draft can help you to define the thesis of the paper you are planning, making it easier for you to then write a draft that is more focused and orderly or to arrange your ideas into a plan that will guide your next draft.

OUTLINES The traditional way to organize writing has been to prepare an outline and then to fill it in, but that technique doesn't always mean the same thing. There are several kinds of outlines, each of which might suit a different kind of project or a different kind of writer. Some outlines are exceedingly detailed, presenting almost as much information as the completed project will (but certainly not everything). Other outlines are very sketchy, offering only a general road map of where to go next. The kind you need depends on a combination of your working habits, your style, and your project. But if you find that your readers frequently comment that they can't follow what you're writing about, you probably need to make your outline a little more detailed. Or when you finish drafting, you may need to outline your draft meticulously and compare the "before" outline with the "after" outline. At the very least you will see where you need to revise heavily, and at best you will be able to chart where the revision should go. Conversely, if your readers tell you that your writing is boring and mechanical, you need to loosen up some. Making your outline a little less formal may be one way to go about it.

Lists and Jottings The most informal kind of outline is a list you jot down on a scrap of paper or keep in your head. It may be as informal as listing two or three points you don't want to forget. Such a list for a paper on hunting elephants for ivory, say, may contain "environmental impact, human impact — esp. dangers, health hazards" and nothing else. Notice that two main ideas are listed: environmental impact and human impact. Under "human impact" two subheadings are listed: danger and health hazards. Nothing is indicated about other points that the writer may plan to include, nor is anything noted about the order the points will appear in. This kind of outline is for you only, and you don't need to worry about making it more comprehensive if it does its job for you. Many students find this kind of outline helpful in taking essay examinations because it is brief enough to occupy a very small space and it doesn't take much time to produce. But it can be suitable for other occasions as well.

Here is a somewhat more detailed list for the same writing project:

1. Place in endangered species lists
   Reasons, locations
2. Who hunts ivory
   Natives, poachers
3. Place in environmental chain
   Above and below in food chain
   Relationship to other animals
   Meaning for humans
4. Human Impact
   Physical dangers of elephant hunting — from elephants, from authorities
   Health hazards: food-related — rotting meat, loss of food; ivory-related: elephant anthrax

Formal Outlines A formal outline for the same paper would indicate the relationships between main points and details more clearly than a list.

Thesis: Hunting elephants for ivory has two negative effects: It causes environmental damage, and it is dangerous to humans.

  I. Environmental effects
    A. Endangered species
      1. Reasons
      2. Location
    B. Place in environmental chain
      1. Relationship of elephant to other animals
        a. Effect on food chain
        b. Maintenance of grasslands
      2. Importance of elephant for humans
 II. Human impact
    A. Physical dangers of elephant hunting
      1. Unpredictability of elephants
      2. Crackdown by governments on poachers
      3. Legal permits scarce
    B. Health hazards
      1. Food issues
        a. Carcasses left to rot
        b. Natives starving
      2. Disease issues
        a. Geographic connections
        b. Elephant anthrax
          (1) Conditions for infecting humans
          (2) Course of the disease

Notice that the formal outline is a graphic representation of the paper and that it shows balance and completeness. For this reason, some people insist that if there is an item 1, there must be an item 2, or if there is an item A, an item B must follow. Actually, there is no hard-and-fast rule, but common sense suggests that if there is only an item 1, say, either the writer has not pursued the subject far enough or the main heading and subheading can be combined. For example, if there were only a disease issue and no geographic connection in point 2 under "Health hazards," the idea should be expressed as "2. Elephant anthrax dangerous to humans."

Beginning with uppercase roman numerals, a formal topic outline relies upon indented uppercase letters of the alphabet, Arabic numbers, lowercase letters, Arabic numbers in parentheses, and so on to reflect various levels of relationships. Each topic should be grammatically parallel with other topics on the same level. Any topic outline can be easily turned into a sentence outline by stating all points as sentences. A sentence outline has the advantage of helping writers be specific. For instance, a sentence outline for the example above may have the item "B. Elephant hunting poses health hazards."

Formal outlines can be developed as plans for writing, but they are more common as revision tools and guides for readers. Most writers need flexibility in the plans they make to guide their writing, because the human mind often develops new insights during drafting. If you do make a formal outline before you write, don't let it become a straitjacket.

NUTSHELLS, ABSTRACTS, AND CAPSULES Another way to bring some order to writing is to use a summary paragraph (sometimes called a nutshell, abstract, or capsule) as a kind of microcosm for the whole piece of writing. Consider this paragraph, for example:

> Under the microscope we can see that blood is composed of a watery fluid called plasma, in which certain formed elements are suspended. The formed elements are different types of cells — red blood cells, white blood cells and platelets. — *Louis Faugeres Bishop*

It is easy to imagine how we can use this paragraph as a nutshell: The first group of paragraphs following this one will describe red blood cells, what they look like, how they are made, what their parts are; the next group of paragraphs will offer the same kind of information about white blood cells, and the final paragraphs will describe platelets. That is, indeed, how Bishop developed this piece of writing, and the technique works well for some situations. However, you may already have discovered that this method has a drawback: Although it is often taught in secondary schools because it has the advantage of ensuring that the writer does not stray from the topic at hand, it has the disadvantage of being predictable if it is used too much — and what is predictable can become boring.

CLASSIC ORATION The classic pattern for presenting information was in full use at least two thousand years ago, and that pattern continues to be useful today, especially in writing to persuade. People who gathered to listen to the great orators of classical times generally knew that right after they had been exhorted to pay attention, they would get background information on the subject which would be followed by a clear statement of what issues would be addressed and what position the speaker would take. Then, of course, they could expect to hear information that would confirm the speaker's point and that would refute the opposing viewpoint. And finally, they usually expected a summary of what had been said and sometimes even a call to act upon it. (A variation in the sequence could draw attention to a particular part of the oration and thereby divert attention from another part.) In other words, classic oration had the following outline:

- *Introduction:* Inform the audience of the goal and gain their attention and confidence.
- *Statement of issues, facts, or circumstances:* Give the relevant background information and description of present conditions.
- *Proof of the case:* Select and arrange the material collected during the exploring and planning stages.
- *Refutation of opposing viewpoints:* State the objections and any complications; then show why these points should not trouble the audience.
- *Conclusion:* Sum up, highlight important points, point out future directions, and give a call to action.

Originally developed for oral presentations, this sequence became well established because nearly everyone used the same pattern — thus making it easy for listeners to follow the speech. And if the sequence varied, the listeners could depend upon their experience to know which part they were listening to. Even today, we often expect written presentations to follow the same pattern or some variation of it.

Drafting

Drafting means writing a preliminary version of a work that you will later revise. If you think of drafting as "writing the paper," you put yourself at risk. Thinking in these terms can lead to writer's block by making drafting seem excessively important. And if you think "drafting" means "writing," you may be less likely to appraise your work critically before preparing another version of it. Experienced writers usually compose more than one draft of what they write. So drafting is simply one of several stages in the writing process.

Unlike planning and revision — both of which can be undertaken at various times throughout a busy day — drafting usually requires a block of uninterrupted time. If you have twenty minutes free between classes, you can brainstorm or refine a paragraph or two that are already drafted. But when you are ready to write the first draft of a paper, you should plan to set aside at least two or three hours when you can give undivided attention to this work. You may finish your draft much sooner, but knowing that you have a few hours at this point in the writing process will help you to avoid feeling tense. Providing yourself with adequate time for drafting can also protect you from being forced to stop prematurely just as your ideas have started to flow.

You may be thinking by now, "Don't these people know how busy I am? Where can I ever find two or three hours to draft a paper?" The answer is that busy people can usually find time to do the things that they genuinely want or need to do — even if it means getting up earlier, staying up later, or putting another activity aside. But no one expects you to invest an afternoon in everything you draft. The strategy we are recommending is for writing that matters to you. And as you become a more experienced writer, you may find that you need less time for drafting. Because experienced writers expect to revise their work, they often draft quickly — aware that they are only composing a preliminary version of their work.

Because writing a good introduction can be difficult, some writers draft by beginning in the middle and compose an introduction only after they have drafted several pages. But some writers draft most comfortably after they have composed an introduction that pleases them, and there are even some writers who need to write a good title before they can draft with any ease. Writers such as these like the sense of direction that they obtain from a title or an introduction, for a good title or introduction often reveals a writer's thesis. Follow the procedure that seems best suited to you.

Whether you begin by defining your thesis or draft in order to discover what you want to say, writing the first draft of your paper requires you to define your main point. As a reader, you may ordinarily expect to find a thesis stated pretty early in a piece of writing — probably in the first paragraph or two (or the first chapter of a book). And you ordinarily expect to find some version of that point stated again at the end.

But neither writing nor reading would be much fun if all writers had to work the same way. Although classical rhetoric emphasized the need to follow predetermined patterns, modern rhetorical theory has given writers much more freedom. Thus, a writer may state the main point early in an essay and restate it in the conclusion, or engage the attention of the reader by experimenting with introductions that seem at first unrelated to the topic. Moreover, writers are not always bound to a single main point. Sometimes, particularly in a long piece, a writer will develop two or more main points. And when pursuing some motives, a writer may not have a thesis as that concept is usually understood. When writing to explore an idea, for example, a writer's work may be unified by the search for meaning rather than by a central idea that can be stated within a sentence or two. (For an example of this kind of work, see "How to Build a Slaughterhouse" in Chapter 9.)

You should recognize, however, that writing without either a thesis or a clearly defined goal can leave readers feeling confused. When you read writing that seems pointless, you may feel that you missed something. As a reader, you may be willing to go back and reread; but as a writer, you should understand that some readers are not going to take the trouble. So if you are writing without a thesis, you should consider the expectations of your audience. You should also consider your motive for writing: If you are writing to discover yourself, then you may not need a thesis, but you will need a thesis for other motives such as writing to persuade. In short, ask yourself if you are following a strategy suitable for your rhetorical situation.

Revising

Revising is the professional writer's secret weapon. It is one of the things that distinguishes writing from speaking: Revision is a second (or third, or tenth) chance to get the meaning right. Donald Murray, a professional writer and writing teacher, explains that he always produces a "zero draft," a draft that is even rougher than a first draft. Then he feels he can get down to the business of writing as he reshapes those rough ideas into the first of many drafts. Many writers feel, as Murray does, that they aren't writing when they are drafting; they are only writing when they are revising.

Some people say that the attitude toward revising is what distinguishes good writers from poor writers. Good writers don't expect to get it right the first time. Poor writers think they have. For most people writing is a dynamic and unpredictable process: It doesn't begin with planning and proceed through drafting, then revision, then proofing. But each of those activities can occur or recur at any moment during the production of a finished piece of prose. You may even get an idea that you want to include in your paper just as you are typing the final word of the final draft. If that happens, don't be discouraged; and above all, don't throw that good idea away. Just work it into your paper and produce another final copy. Conversely, you may know from the very first moment you set pencil to paper what the final words of your piece will be. Go ahead, write them down. Let them stay there throughout your whole effort as a beacon to aim toward. There's no right or wrong way to go about writing, so be a pragmatist: If a technique works for you, then go ahead and use it.

Revising involves considerably more than fixing up the spelling and punctuation before passing the writing on to a reader. It is easier to understand what revising is if we break the word into its parts: *re-* meaning "again" and *vising* meaning "seeing." Revising is seeing again, taking another look. Even though writers often do some revising as they draft, revision is most productive when something written days or weeks ago can be viewed with "new" eyes, almost as another person would see it. (Days and weeks are desirable incubation periods for writing, but few students have that luxury. A practical length of time for students to let writing incubate is overnight.) When you revise in this way, if you are alert and keep your audience in mind, you will notice parts that are unclear, inaccurately phrased, carelessly organized, inadequately explained.

Think of revision as reentering the writing on at least three different levels to see what works and what might need changing: appraising the content, checking the organization, and refining the style. On the first, or deepest, level, you can look at whether you have conveyed the proper meaning, done what you promised the reader you would do, provided enough support, focused clearly enough on your main point. You can use several techniques to reenter and review your writing at this level. One good way to see whether you have said what you intended is to read your manuscript aloud, pretending to be your audience. If it helps, try to read your writing as if you were the person you most admire. You may immediately see where you have gone astray. You can also do the same exercise pretending that you have just received the manuscript in the mail.

Writing summaries for each major set of paragraphs in your paper may also help you when revising at this level. If you summarize each paragraph, try to boil the paragraph down into a single sentence. Then read the summaries through to see whether the abbreviated version makes sense. (Remember that the main idea of a paragraph will occasionally be implied rather than stated.) An exercise akin to this one is to try to outline your paper. That should help you discover whether you have maintained your focus throughout or strayed from the topic.

Another technique is to try to answer the following questions: Have you stressed the important issues? Have you made sure your point is clear? Have you dealt fairly with your audience? Did you promise anything that you could not deliver? Have you accounted for any objections that might be raised? Has your attitude been appropriate? That is, have you been condescending or arrogant? Have you apologized too much? Have you been overly friendly?

Revision at this level is not merely a way to fix problems that you can see on the page. It is also a way to identify where you need to say more. Play the audience role again, this time looking for what is not said. Are there any points that have not been made that should have been? Are examples needed to illustrate a point more clearly? Are there any unexplored consequences or loose ends? Have you taken anything for granted that readers may not understand?

When you have answered these questions as well as you can, you are ready to move on to a closer examination of structure, considering the unity of each paragraph and the organization of your essay as a whole. You may have already cut some sentences that didn't seem to fit and decided to move others to different paragraphs. But since your first level of revision may have led to major changes, including the addition of new material, you should now focus upon how well your essay flows.

Look at each paragraph to see if it is truly coherent and unified. Do you need to combine any paragraphs? Split others? Shift them around?

Have you provided transitions so that each paragraph seems to flow smoothly into the next? Do you need to delete irrelevant information? Do these changes require you to make any others?

Pay particular attention to the two paragraphs that will receive the most emphasis: the first and the last. These two paragraphs are emphasized because of their position; they are bordered on only one side, as opposed to being surrounded by other paragraphs. Recognizing the importance of these paragraphs, readers have certain expectations of them. A good introductory paragraph will capture the attention of readers and provide them with a sense of where the essay is going. And a good concluding paragraph will draw the essay together.

Although writers sometimes begin by drafting a strong introduction or conclusion, they may find that these paragraphs no longer fit the essay they have written: You can't be altogether sure what you are introducing until you have written what you want to introduce. And revision could also lead you to decide that you have begun before the beginning or ended after the ending. It is not unusual for a writer to get off to a slow start and write a paragraph or two that adds little to the paper; in this case, you might be able to begin with what is the second or third paragraph of your draft. Similarly, writers sometimes ramble on a bit after they have said what they needed to say; in this case the conclusion of your essay may be buried somewhere before the point where you stopped writing.

If you discover that you need to write a new introduction, you could write a nutshell paragraph that states the major points that the following paragraphs will discuss. But for variety, try beginning with an anecdote, example, quotation, unusual detail, or statement of the problem you hope to resolve. If you find that you need a conclusion, you can restate or summarize your major points. But this strategy often works best for long essays during which readers might lose sight of an idea. Repeating key points may be unnecessary within a short essay, and it may leave some readers feeling as if you doubt their intelligence. When trying to write an effective conclusion, you can often benefit from asking yourself, "Why have I told you all this?" or, as a reader might put it, "So what?" Thinking along these lines may lead you to take one last step that will make the significance of your paper clear. Another effective strategy is to repeat an element found in the introduction, thus framing the essay with two paragraphs that seem related to each other. You can also try either rephrasing your thesis or asking your readers to undertake an action that the essay seems to invite.

After studying the structure of your work as a whole, you should then check to see whether individual sentences can be improved. You will find a detailed discussion of style within a handbook or rhetoric, but here are a few basic points to bear in mind:

- Vary the length of your sentences. If too many sentences are short, your writing will be choppy. If too many of your sentences are long, your readers may grow tired and impatient. A mixture of different lengths usually works best, but note that short sentences receive more emphasis than long sentences, so use short sentences to make key points.

- Vary the structure of your sentences. If too many sentences follow a pattern of subject–verb–object, your writing may seem monotonous. Try beginning with an adverb, a phrase, or a subordinate clause. Check the rhythm of your sentences by reading them aloud and listening carefully to how they sound.

- If your sentences are often described as "too long," your problem may be wordiness. Wordiness refers to redundancy, padding, and unnecessary clutter. Look for unnecessary repetition. See also if you can reduce wordiness by eliminating qualifiers and intensifiers — such as *rather, very,* and *quite.* Look for such empty statements as *in the event that, on the part of, it seems to me that, as a matter of fact that, in view of, the point that I am trying to make* and delete them.

- Use the active voice, which means making the grammatical subject of a sentence the same as the doer of the action: *I broke your bowl* (active), as opposed to *Your bowl was broken by me* (passive). Note that the passive voice is wordier and also makes it possible to duck responsibility, reducing clarity: *Your bowl was broken.* As a general rule, use the passive voice only if the receiver of an action is more important than the doer or if the doer is unknown.

- Make sure that elements that should be parallel are parallel. That is, use the same pattern and the same grammatical forms to express words, phrases, and clauses that have the same function and importance. For example: I have learned how much water I am using whenever I *wash my car, water my lawn,* or *take a shower.*

- Check your sentences for clichés and jargon. Clichés are those tired expressions that show up in your paper without your ever thinking about them — such as *in today's society, at the crack of dawn,* or *hitting the books.* Jargon is language that is specific to a particular group or field. If you find yourself writing about *font managers* and *scalable outlines,* for example, you had better be sure that your audience consists only of computer experts; the average reader would be grateful for simpler language.

When you think you are finished, or after you have made several revision cycles through your writing, get a friend to read your draft aloud and listen for any weak spots. Then, ask your friend to read through it again and point out any weaknesses he or she notices. Professional writers seldom rely only upon their own judgment. They test what they have written by having others read it — family, friends, other authors, professional editors — to determine whether the writing communicates what the writer intended to say. And very often these early readers make suggestions that help the writer produce a more effective text. Try to make your own early readers understand that you are not just looking for praise.

When you review someone's writing, don't think it is a kindness *not* to criticize things you think need attention. Tactful, constructive criticism is always appropriate. Naturally, most of us have felt at some time or another as though we have put ourselves at risk when we showed our writing to another person. Writer Cynthia Ozick refers to this feeling of risk when she says that writing is "an act of courage." And Barbara Mellix, in an essay in this book, says, "Each experience of writing was like standing naked and revealing my imperfection, my 'otherness.'" So it is understandable if a writer feels hurt or defensive when his or her writing has elicited something other than a totally favorable response. Writing is intensely personal. We offer the world a part of ourselves, and we don't want to be rejected. But it is important to overcome undue sensitivity if you want to write well. Be honest with others and encourage others to be honest with you. You may find yourself wincing every now and again when criticism is directed to you, and you may get some unhappy looks when you offer criticism to others. But pleasure in a job well done ultimately outweighs any aches along the way.

Revision is the means by which we shift the writing from an act that satisfies our own need to express ourselves to one that satisfies the reader's need to understand. That is, when our writing is no longer writer based or focused on ourselves, but is focused on the communication of meaning to another person, it becomes reader-based. But that's a hard shift to make; it requires that the writer put on a different persona, that the writer become the reader. Soliciting help from well-disposed, thoughtful readers helps us gain a new perspective on what we have written. We can begin to recognize our own developing maturity as writers when we are able not only to accept and profit from constructive criticism but also to seek it out.

Editing

When you are certain that you have said what you want to say in the way you want to say it, you are ready to edit your paper. Begin by checking your grammar. Make sure that each sentence is complete, and check each subject-verb pair to make sure that they agree. Correct dangling modifiers and shifts in tense, person, or tone. Look for instances of mixed metaphors and faulty predication. Make sure that all your pronouns clearly refer to their antecedents.

As you begin to prepare your final draft, pay attention to spelling, mechanics, and punctuation. If you are using a word processor, this is the time to run your spelling checker. But don't expect a computer program to identify every problem. If you used *there* when you needed *their,* or mistyped *fro* (as in *to and fro*) instead of *for,* your spelling checker is unlikely to notice. Be picky about the final appearance of your paper. First impressions are just as important in writing as they are in social relationships. But don't confuse good typing with good writing. A beautifully printed essay on thick, expensive paper may be a pleasure to see and to hold. What ultimately matters, however, is what you have written and how well you have written it. Consider the presentation of your final draft as a symbol rather than a disguise. It should look good because it is good.

Finally, don't be overwhelmed by the advice in this introductory section, or elsewhere in this book. Remember that no one is expecting you to become a perfect writer by the end of the semester. Writing well is a lifelong challenge. The immediate challenge, the one confronting you in the weeks ahead, is to understand the principles that can help you to become the best writer you can be. Although these principles can be studied in the abstract, they are best understood through examples and through practice. If you want to write well, you must be prepared to write often and to appraise your work critically. You must also be prepared to read often and to think critically about what you read. The essays, stories, and poems collected in this book offer you an opportunity to exercise your reading and thinking skills, and they will introduce you to authors and topics that you may want to read more of in the future.

1

Writing to Record a Memory

The wish to record a memory is one of the most common motives inspiring people to write. In her memoir *An American Childhood* Annie Dillard records how her own motive for writing can be traced to a wish to rescue the beauty of experience from the destructiveness of change. Describing an early ideal, she writes:

> As a life's work, I would remember everything—everything, against loss. I would go through life like a plankton net. I would trap and keep every teacher's funny remark, every face on the street, every microscopic alga's sway, every scrap of overhead cloud. . . .
>
> Some days I felt an urgent responsibility to each change of light outside the sunporch windows. Who would remember any of it, any of this our time, and the wind thrashing the buckeye limbs outside? Somebody had to do it, somebody had to hang on to the days with teeth and fists, or the whole show had been in vain.

Dillard's youthful ideal is impossible to fulfill. Some alga will sway unseen, and some changes of light will pass unnoticed while we're talking on the telephone. But even if it is impossible to remember *everything,*

Dillard understands a basic truth about writing: Writers need to have memories, and memories need to be preserved from loss.

In addition to inspiring memoirs and journals, this motive can also prompt something as simple as a list. To remember passing thoughts, we scribble "Call George" or "Buy milk" on whatever paper is close at hand. In doing so, we demonstrate a fundamental connection between the written word and how we conduct our lives: By writing things down, no matter how small or insignificant, we can bring order to experience.

KEEPING A JOURNAL

Like the lists we make to organize our days, a journal is written for ourselves. The difference, of course, is that a journal allows us to record in detail whatever we have in mind — what happened, for example, when we called George (or why we decided to postpone that call, since George is starting to get on our nerves). Many writers find this kind of writing to be highly satisfying. Because we write journals for ourselves, we can write whatever we want without worrying about grammar, style, or whatever someone else might think of us. While recording our memories, we may sometimes have other motives as well — writing to discover ourselves, for example, or writing to explore an idea. But the initial impulse that leads most people to keep a journal is the need to record memories before they become lost beneath the ever-growing accumulation of experience as each day slips into the next.

Strictly speaking, the difference between a journal and a diary is that a diary is simply a record of what happens every day, whereas a journal includes reflections and observations. Some diaries offer little more than weather reports, meals eaten, and bedtimes. Journals, on the other hand, often pass over the surface details of life and focus instead upon how the writer reacts to experience: A journal is less likely to note what the writer ate for breakfast than to record how the writer responded to a novel, a sunset, or a quarrel. To put it simply, journals are often more personal and more reflective than diaries. But the distinction between the two should not be overemphasized. When writing to record memories, writers often move back and forth between entries that list events and those that explore their significance.

Keeping some type of daily record of your life — whatever you choose to call it — offers a number of advantages. By making writing a normal part of every day, you can protect yourself from the anxiety some people feel when they are forced to write. As a general rule, the more writing you do, the more natural it seems to write. Another advantage is that you can explore experience that you would be reluctant to discuss with anyone, believing it to be too trivial, too personal, or too confusing for sharing with others. A final advantage is that a written record of your life can jog your memory when you undertake other types of writing. No matter how much experience a writer may have, it is not unusual to feel, at times, that there's "nothing to write about." Most people know much more than they realize, and reviewing the entries in a journal can often help writers recall events and ideas that they had somehow lost sight of— thus generating topics for further writing.

But you should not let the prospect of some future advantage obscure the immediate benefits of keeping a written record of your life. If you feel as if you are writing for posterity or are obliged to be sensitive and profound whenever you write in your journal, you may very well deprive yourself of the principal pleasure of writing to record a memory: the freedom to write what you choose. You will profit the most from this writing experience if you are willing to devote some time to it, but time will vary from day to day. On some days you may have a lot to say; on others you may not. The main thing is to write something every day without worrying about a specific quota—and to feel free to let the words come tumbling out whenever you have something in particular on your mind.

Journal writing can be a form of freewriting, with one sentence leading to another that you had not anticipated when you began to write. When you are writing what you have seen, heard, read, or felt, you will write some entries that are stronger than others. But it would be a mistake to try to edit yourself as you write, attempting to write a consistent series of well-crafted passages, each of the same length. As in freewriting, you shouldn't worry about repeating yourself or wandering off the point. The point is anything you want it to be, for you are your own audience.

Writing of this sort is analogous to taking snapshots. If you like to take pictures of the people you know and the places you've been, you've probably taken some that you like very much and others that didn't turn out the way you expected. On most rolls of film there are pictures that are similar to other pictures—and perhaps a few in which someone has been caught in an awkward position. You might not consider entering any of these pictures in a photography contest, but the pictures have value for you because of the associations you bring to them. "Oh, look at the food on Scott's plate!" you might exclaim. "Wasn't that the day he ate so much that he got sick?" If you asked strangers to look at the same picture (and the other seventy-one shots you took at the family picnic), they probably wouldn't enjoy them as much as you do. Except for those exceptional photographs that are works of art, most pictures have value because they are visual records of memory. By looking at them, we can recover part of our past.

Writing our memories down on paper offers the same advantage. As writers, you shouldn't be afraid to waste film. People who manage to make a single roll of film last three years (convinced that they see nothing worth photographing or determined to wait for the perfect shot) may find that the film is spoiled by the time it gets out of the camera. Experienced photographers snap lots of pictures, in part because they know that some will not turn out, but also in part because an unplanned shot can sometimes prove to be the best on the roll. Think along these lines when you are writing in your journal: The more you write, the more likely you are to produce something that will one day give you great pleasure to reread. As for the shots that don't turn out, take comfort in the knowledge that no one else has to see them.

Although it is the work of a professional writer and has been edited for publication, Edward Abbey's "Death Valley" illustrates how recording memories in a journal helps a writer preserve details that might otherwise be lost. Within his first three paragraphs Abbey records the altitude (4,317 feet) from which he descended into Death Valley and the temperature (114 degrees) he found there at ten o'clock on a June morning. It's hard to remember specific numbers, and these details are useful enough as far as they go. But the record of a trip that limited itself to numbers would not take anyone far into the experience of that trip. Memory, like understanding, is clearest when we see what we are looking at and when we can give names to what we see. Because Abbey was a trained observer of the natural world, he records the vegetation he sees — arrowweed, creosote shrubs, and mesquite trees. He also notes that creosote bushes secrete a poison that kills other plants. When writing to record your own memories, realize that it is better to describe a creosote bush when you see it than to settle for the obvious and general: "There weren't many trees around." But the first step is to see the bush. You will have more memories to record if you keep your eyes and ears open.

If you are observant, you will note things that other people miss. These unexpected details are often the most interesting for both writers and readers. Consider what happens to Abbey when he stops at a gas station for a cold drink:

> Sipping cold drinks, we watch through the window a number of desert sparrows crawl in and out of the grills on the front of the parked automobiles. The birds are eating tourists — bugs and butterflies encountered elsewhere and smashed, baked, annealed to the car radiators. Like the bears of Yellowstone, the Indians of Arizona, and roadside businessmen everywhere, these birds have learned to make a good thing off passing trade. Certainly they provide a useful service; it's a long hot climb out of here in any direction and a clean radiator is essential.

Where an inexperienced writer might have only noted, "Stopped for a soda," Abbey records a glimpse of birds eating bugs, and that in turn leads him to reflect upon the relationship between the natural world and the people who drive through it. Think how much is conveyed because Abbey remembered these birds: We learn that there are birds in Death Valley, what kind of birds they are, how difficult it must be for them to survive, and how nature seems able to accommodate at least some of the incursions of humans. As readers, we can be pleased that Abbey took the trouble to record that memory in his journal, for it is precisely the sort of small but illuminating moment that most people would either fail to note or fail to remember.

As this excerpt from "Death Valley" suggests, journal writing often involves a combination of narration and description. The anecdote about the birds is a story told within a few sentences. As in any narrative, we find all the elements of Kenneth Burke's pentad (pp. 11–14): The *scene* is a gas station/store in Death Valley, the *act* is the eating of bugs, the *agents* are the birds, the *agency* is the cars that have brought the insects into the Valley, and the *purpose* is survival. But if we can see all this happening, it is because of Abbey's descriptive detail. The bugs aren't simply some-where outside the window; they are "smashed, baked, annealed to the car radiators." The birds must be small if they can crawl in and out of the grills to reach the radiators, and, as already noted, they must be hungry if they are willing to go to the trouble. There are only two additional details that we might ask for. What kind of a cold drink was Abbey sipping? (Was it a beer or a Diet Pepsi?) And whom does that "we" include?

You will find additional information on narration and description later in this introduction. For the moment, it is enough to make these observations:

- Narration and description go together naturally when we write to record a memory.
- Details are essential for making memories come alive upon the page.
- Writers select the details they report and do not have the respon-sibility of reporting everything they see and do.

Even in a journal, when you are writing only for yourself, you don't have to tell what you were drinking if you don't feel like it.

WRITING A MEMOIR

In a memoir writers can decide on the extent to which they focus on themselves. The only fixed requirement of memoir (from *memoria,* Latin for "memory") is that the writer must address an aspect of the past about which she or he has personal knowledge. A memoir can focus upon events (in which case narration will prevail) or upon a person or place (in which case description will prevail).

The memories that we record can take varied forms. When writing about the things that have happened to you, you need to decide whether to report a series of related events or to focus upon a single episode that is somehow significant. Essayists usually focus upon something specific, because they are working on a small canvas. In "Taking the Test," for example, David Groff confines himself to remembering his test for AIDS and what it was like to wait for the results. There are probably many stories he could tell from his life before that test, but Groff wisely recognized that there is a limit to how much he could cover in a short essay. Other writers summarize an overall situation and then dramatize it with a close-up or two. At the heart of "Finishing School" is the moment when Maya Angelou deliberately breaks some dishes. But before Angelou narrates that specific afternoon in an Alabama kitchen, she builds up to it by providing readers with necessary background information. Similarly, Primo Levi helps readers to understand his life in a concentration camp by combining background information with a detailed account of fixing a bicycle in exchange for a hard-boiled egg and four lumps of sugar.

All of these writers made good strategic decisions. Groff could safely assume that most readers today would understand why taking an AIDS test would be stressful. He doesn't need to provide information on AIDS or discuss his sexual history in detail. On the other hand, without some background, readers would probably have trouble understanding why someone would deliberately break dishes or risk his life for a little courtesy and a hard-boiled egg. What you should note about all three of these examples, however, is that close-ups are usually more dramatic than overviews. When writing an essay of your own, try to make the focus specific, and include background information only to the extent that it is necessary for your audience to understand what you want the heart of your essay to convey.

As an essay like Marilyn Schiel's "Levi's" suggests, a writer with a well-chosen focus can say a lot within a few pages. In this case the focus is on a pair of used jeans. Most people would think, "What could be simpler than that?" And inexperienced writers might not even consider writing on such an apparently simple topic because they have convinced themselves that writers need extraordinary material in order to be interesting. But interest is something the writer creates. Some writers are capable of making the extraordinary seem boring; others help us to see what is wonderful about the ordinary. In Schiel's hands the memory of a pair of jeans becomes a vehicle for understanding the author's life. We can see what she was like, what her brother was like, and what her mother was like. We also come away understanding something of what it meant to grow up in the 1950s.

Although the essay includes some narration (girl wants jeans, girl is denied jeans, girl gets jeans), the focus is on an object rather than an event, so description prevails. By the time we finish Schiel's essay, we learn about triple-roll cuffs with sidewalk burns, real pockets marked with metal rivets, and a difficult-to-manage button fly. Details combine to re-create through words a specific pair of jeans. As you search among your own memories for a writing topic, you might try thinking of something that you once felt privileged to possess and then try writing about it so that other people can understand why it mattered to you.

Recording one memory can sometimes lead to another. You see something, or go someplace, and it brings back the memory of an earlier experience. When this happens, you should feel free to tie one memory to another. Some forms of writing (like writing a journal or writing to discover oneself) can become voyages of exploration that take us far away from where we began. A short memoir, however, does not afford room for every memory that occurs to the writer. If you find yourself wanting to move from one memory to another, ask yourself if they are closely related or if you are being lured away from your original focus by material that might best be saved for another writing occasion.

Two of the essays in this section demonstrate how writers can include more than one memory without losing their focus. In "When Father Doesn't Know Best" Andrew Merton shares the memory of taking his four-year-old son to his first baseball game, but he includes within it the memory of his own first ball game. Although thirty years separate the two memories, they are naturally related to one another because, as the author reveals, he was using his son to try to re-create an aspect of his own childhood. The essay is unified by a consistent focus upon fathers, sons, and baseball. Similarly, Geoffrey Norman's "Gators" also moves between the recent and distant past. In this essay Norman begins by narrating his experience with an alligator "a couple dozen years ago" and then moves on to record a recent experience with alligators. The transition between these memories occurs midway through the essay, when the author observes, "I had not seen one for years until the other day." Although Norman does not come out and tell us what motivated him to write about alligators, it is likely that his experience "the other day" triggered the earlier memory with which the essay began. The essay as a whole is unified — but not just because both of the stories it includes are about alligators. As in the baseball essay, an older memory helps provide the background for understanding a recent memory.

The sequence of the events remembered in "Gators" is chronological, which means that they are presented in the order in which they occurred. This is the easiest and most common way of recording a memory of events, but variation is often possible. In "When Father Doesn't Know Best," for example, Merton includes a paragraph about the distant past in the middle of his memory of the recent past. And Maya Angelou begins with the memory of a recent conversation that leads her back to the older memory that is the focus of "Finishing School." In an essay of your own you might begin in the middle of a story — if the middle provides an opening that would attract the attention of readers — and then go back to the start before finishing with the conclusion.

There is no single method of organization that works all the time. But there are two principles that you should try to keep in mind when planning how to share a memory with readers:

1. Whether you are writing chronologically or moving backward and forward in time for dramatic effect, try to save a strong scene for the ending so that your essay does not trail off after reaching an early climax.
2. Remember to give readers a clear indication of where your memories are located in time.

Merton locates his essay in July 1983 and his earlier memory in 1952; Angelou lets us know that she is recalling events that happened when she was ten, and Levi uses transitions such as "A short time before" and "A few days later" to help readers follow his memory of Christmas at Auschwitz.

A memoir can easily end with what is simply the final event of the story — as when Angelou concludes with the dramatic moment when she breaks some valued dishes or Levi concludes with his unusual Christmas dinner. This strategy works best when you are recalling a memory that has a clear ending built right into it. At other times you may end with a paragraph or two reflecting upon the significance of what you have remembered. This does not mean tacking some kind of moral onto the end of the story, but it does mean giving readers an additional clue about why you found this memory worth writing about. Groff, Merton, and Norman all conclude by offering a brief comment upon the memories they have recorded.

As should be clear by now, writing a memoir is different from recording memories in a journal. Because memoir is aimed at an audience beyond the writer, it must be more focused and shaped than journal writing. Although you can include anything in a journal (and the more the better), you need to be selective about what to include in a memoir. Whether you are emphasizing an event, a person, a place, or an object from your past, you must try to convey a sense of why this memory is significant. In many memoirs this significance is achieved through a conflict between the writer and the writer's world. Angelou is in conflict with her employer, Schiel with her mother, Merton with his son, and Levi with the Nazis who imprisoned him. Conflict not only heightens the reader's sense of "What's going to happen?" but also shows the writer being tested — and how that test is met may well be significant. In some cases conflict may be only implied, and it need not necessarily involve the writer directly. In "Gators," for example, Geoffrey Norman suggests a conflict between alligators and encroaching civilization. In another memoir — such as the memory of a wonderful restaurant that no longer exists — the conflict may simply be between the present and the past.

Do not think that memoir must focus upon the turning point of your life, an encounter with an extraordinary person, a visit to an exotic land, or the discovery of a rare object. Memoir can certainly include these possibilities, but it can just as easily be a record of Levi's, baseball, and broken dishes. You are the best judge of what is significant to you. The challenge of memoir is to convey that significance to others.

DEATH VALLEY
Edward Abbey

Death Valley is considered one of the most inhospitable places on earth, but this selection comes from a work called The Journey Home — *a title that suggests the author found satisfaction of some sort in visiting this place. Edward Abbey was a professional writer who wrote many works about the American West. Look for clues that indicate how Abbey felt about Death Valley. Learn what you can about this place, and consider why it was important to Abbey.*

SUMMERTIME

From Daylight Pass at 4,317 feet we descend through Boundary Canyon and Hell's Gate into the inferno at sea level and below. Below, below . . . beneath a sea, not of brine, but of heat, of shimmering simmering waves of light and a wind as hot and fierce as a dragon's breath.

The glare is stunning. Yet also exciting, even exhilarating — a world of light. The air seems not clear like glass but colored, a transparent, tinted medium, golden toward the sun, smoke-blue in the shadows. The colors come, it appears, not simply from the background, but are actually present in the air itself — a vigintillion microscopic particles of dust reflecting the sky, the sand, the iron hills.

On a day in June at ten o'clock in the morning the thermometer reads 114 degrees. Later in the day it will become hotter. But with humidity close to zero such heat is not immediately unpleasant or even uncomfortable. Like the dazzling air, the heat is at first somehow intoxicating — one feels that grace and euphoria that come with just the right ration of Old Grandad, with the perfect allowance of music. Sunlight is magic. Later will come. . . . Yes, out of the car and standing hatless under the sun, you begin to feel the menace in this arid atmosphere, the malignancy within that silent hurricane of fire.

We consider the dunes, the sea of sand. Around the edges of the dunes grow clumps of arrowweed tall as corn shocks, scattered creosote shrubs bleached out and still, a few shaggy mesquite trees. These plants can hardly be said to have conquered the valley, but they have in some way made a truce — or found a point of equilibrium in a ferocious, inaudible struggle between life and entropy. A bitter war indeed: The creosote bush secretes a poison in its roots that kills any other plant, even its own offspring, attempting to secure a place too near; in this way the individual creosote preserves a perimeter of open space and a monopoly of local moisture sufficient for survival.

We drive on to the gas station and store at Stovepipe Wells, where a few humans huddle inside beneath the blast of a cold-air blower. Like other mammals of the valley, the human inhabitants can endure its summer only by burrowing deep or by constructing an artificial environment — not adaptation but insulation, insularity.

Sipping cold drinks, we watch through the window a number of desert sparrows crawl in and out of the grills on the front of the parked automobiles. The birds are eating tourists — bugs and butterflies encountered elsewhere and smashed, baked, annealed to the car radiators. Like the bears of Yellowstone, the Indians of Arizona, and roadside businessmen everywhere, these birds have learned to make a good thing off passing trade. Certainly they provide a useful service; it's a long hot climb out of here in any direction and a clean radiator is essential.

The Indians of Death Valley were cleverest of all. When summer came they left, went up into the mountains, and stayed there until it was reasonable to return — an idea too subtle in its simplicity for the white man of today to grasp. But we too are Indians — gypsies anyhow — and won't be back until September.

FURNACE CREEK, SEPTEMBER 17. Again the alarming descent. It seemed much too hot in the barren hills a mile above this awful sinkhole, this graben (for Death Valley is not, properly understood, a valley at all), this collapsed and superheated trench of mud, salt, gravel, and sand. Much too hot — but we felt obliged to come back once more.

A hard place to love, Death Valley. An ugly place, bitter as alkali and rough, harsh, unyielding as iron. Here they separate the desert rats from the mice, the hard-rock prospectors from the mere rock hounds.

Cactus for example. There is none at all on the floor of the valley. *10* Too dry or too brackish or maybe too hot. Only up on the alluvial fans and in the side canyons 1,000 feet above sea level do we find the first stunted and scrubby specimens of cholla and prickly pear and the pink-thorned cottontop — poor relation of the barrel cactus.

At first glance, speeding by car through this valley that is not a valley, one might think there was scarcely any plant life at all. Between oases you will be impressed chiefly by the vast salt beds and the immense alluvial fans of gravel that look as hostile to life as the fabled seas of the moon.

And yet there is life out there, life of a sparse but varied sort — salt grass and pickleweed on the flats, far-spaced clumps of creosote, saltbush, desert holly, brittlebush, and prickly poppy on the fans. Not much of anything, but a little of each. And in the area as a whole, including the surrounding mountains up to the 11,000-foot summit of Telescope Peak, the botanists count a total of 900 to 1,000 different species, ranging from microscopic forms of algae in the salt pools to limber pine and the ancient bristlecone pine on the peaks.

But the first impression remains a just one. Despite variety, most of the surface of Death Valley is dead. Dead, dead, deathly — a land of jagged salt pillars, crackling and tortured crusts of mud, sunburnt gravel bars the color of rust, rocks and boulders of metallic blue naked even of lichen. Death Valley is Gravel Gulch.

TELESCOPE PEAK, OCTOBER 22. To escape the heat for a while, we spend the weekend up in the Panamints. (Summer still baking the world down below, far below, where swirls of mud, salt, and salt-laden streams lie motionless under a lake of heat, glowing in lovely and poisonous shades of auburn, saffron, crimson, sulfurous yellow, dust-tinged tones of white on white.)

Surely this is the most sterile of North American deserts. No matter how high we climb it seems impossible to leave behind the influence of aridity and anti-life. At 7,000 feet in this latitude we should be entering a forest of yellow pine, with grassy meadows and freshwater brooks. We are farther north than Santa Fe or Flagstaff. Instead there are only the endless barren hills, conventional in form, covered in little but shattered stone. A dull monotonous terrain, dun-colored, supporting a few types of shrubs and small, scattered junipers.

From 7,000 to 9,000 feet we pass through a belt of more junipers and a fair growth of pinyon pines. Along the trail to Telescope Peak — at 10,000 feet — appear thin stands of limber pine and the short, massive, all-enduring bristlecone pine, more ancient than the Book of Genesis. Timberline.

There is no forest here. And fifty or sixty airline miles to the west stands the reason why — the Sierra Nevada Range blocking off the sea winds and almost all the moisture. We stand in the rain shadow of that still higher wall.

I walk past three wild burros. Descendants of lost and abandoned prospectors' stock, they range everywhere in the Panamints, multiplying freely, endangering the survival of the native bighorn sheep by trespassing on the latter's forage, befouling their springs. But the feral burros have their charm too. They stand about 100 feet from the trail watching me go by. They are quite unafraid, and merely blink their heavy eyelashes like movie starlets when I halt to stare at them. However they are certainly not tame. Advance toward them and they trot off briskly.

The bray of the donkey is well known. But these little beasts can make another sound even more startling because so unexpected. Hiking up some arid canyon in the Panamints, through what appears to be totally lifeless terrain, you suddenly hear a noise like a huge dry cough behind your shoulder. You spring ten feet forward before daring to look around. And see nothing, nothing at all, until you hear a second cough and scan the hillsides and discover far above a little gray or black burro looking down at you, waiting for you to get the hell out of its territory.

I stand by the cairn on the summit of Telescope Peak, looking out on a cold, windy, and barren world. Rugged peaks fall off southward into the haze of the Mojave Desert; on the west is Panamint Valley, the Argus Range, more mountains, more valleys, and finally the Sierras, crowned with snow; to the north and northwest the Inyo and White mountains; below lies Death Valley — the chemical desert — and east of it the Black Mountains, the Funeral Mountains, the Amargosa Valley and farther mountains, wave after wave of wrinkled ridges standing up from the oceanic desert sea until vision gives out somewhere beyond the curving rim of the world's edge. A smudge hangs on the eastern horizon, suggesting the presence of Death Valley's counterpart and complement, the only city within 100 miles: Las Vegas: Glitter Gulch West.

ECHO CANYON, NOVEMBER 30. A hard place to love. Impossible? No, there were a few — the prospectors, the single-blanket, jackass prospectors who wandered these funeral wastes for a century dreaming of what? Sudden wealth? Not likely. Not Shorty Borden, for example, who invested eight months of his life in building by hand a nine-mile road to his lead and silver diggings in Hanaupah Canyon. Then discovered that even with a road it would still cost him more to transport his ore to the nearest smelter than the ore itself was worth.

Echo Canyon. We are deep into the intricacies of the Funeral Mountains. Named not simply for their proximity to Death Valley, but also for shape and coloration: lifeless escarpments of smoldering red bordered in charcoal, the crags and ridges and defiles edged in black and purple. A primeval chaos of faulted, uplifted, warped, and folded dolomites, limestones, fanglomerates of mud, sand, and gravel. Vulcanism as well: vesiculated andesite, walls embellished with elegant mosaics of rose and yellow quartz. Fool's gold — pyrite — glittering in the black sand, micaceous shales glinting under back light, veins of pegmatite zigzagging and intersecting like an undeciphered script across the face of a cliff: the writing on the wall: "God Was Here." Shallow caves, holes in the rock, a natural arch, and the canyon floor littered with boulders, deep in coarse gravel.

Nowhere in Echo Canyon can I find the slightest visible trace of water. Nevertheless, it must be present under the surface, at least in intermittent or minute amounts, for here and there stand living things. They look dead but are actually dormant, waiting for the resurrection of the rain. I mean the saltbush, the desert fir, the bladderweed, a sprinkling of cottontop cactus, the isolated creosote bush. Waiting.

You may see a few lizards. In sandy places are the hoofprints of bighorn sheep, where they've passed through on their way from the high parts of the range to the springs near Furnace Creek. Sit quite still in one spot for an hour and you might see a small gray bird fly close to look you over. This is the bird that lives in Echo Canyon.

The echoes are good. At certain locations, on a still day, one clear shout will create a series of overlapping echoes that goes on and on toward so fine a diminuendo that the human ear cannot perceive the final vibrations.   *25*

Tramp far enough up Echo Canyon and you come to a ghost town, the ruins of a mining camp — one of many in Death Valley. Deep shafts, a tipple, a rolling mill largely intact, several cabins — one with its inside walls papered with pages from the *Literary Digest*. Half buried in drifted sand is a rusted model-T Ford without roof or motor, a child's tricycle, a broken shovel.

Returning through twilight, I descend the narrow gorge between flood-polished walls of bluish andesite — the stem of the wineglass. I walk down the center of an amphitheater of somber cliffs riddled with grottoes, huge eyesockets in a stony skull, where bats hang upside down in the shadows waiting for night.

Through the opening of the canyon I can see the icy heights of Telescope Peak shining under the cloud-reflected light of one more sunset. Scarlet clouds in a green sky. A weird glow pervades the air through which I walk; it vibrates on the canyon walls, revealing to me all at once a vision of the earth's slow agony, the convulsive grinding violence of a hundred thousand years. Of a million years. I write metaphorically, out of necessity. And yet it seems impossible to believe that these mountains, old as anything on the surface of the planet, do not partake in some dim way of the sentience of living tissue. Genealogies: From these rocks struck once by lightning gushed springs that turned to blood, flesh, life. Impossible miracle. And I am struck once again by the unutterable beauty, terror, and strangeness of everything we think we know.

Questions for Discussion

1. Abbey describes Death Valley as a "hard place to love." How would you characterize his attitude toward this place?
2. What role do human beings play in Death Valley? What is the implication of comparing people to "other mammals" and describing bugs as "tourists"?
3. According to Abbey, Las Vegas is the "counterpart and complement" of Death Valley. What do you think he means by this? What could a growing American city, famous for gambling casinos, have in common with "the most sterile of North American deserts"?
4. In paragraph 28 Abbey claims, "I write metaphorically, out of necessity." A metaphor is a comparison between unlike things that does not use either *like* or *as*. An example is describing grottoes as "huge eyesockets in a stony skull." Identify at least three other metaphors in this work, and be prepared to discuss why Abbey found it necessary to use them.
5. Although "Death Valley" is set up like a journal and may have originated as a journal, Abbey almost certainly revised his original notes before publishing them. His language is polished, there are no loose ends, and the longer work from which this selection has been excerpted even includes a footnote at one point. In writing what could be described as an essay, why do you think Abbey chose to build his work from a series of journal-like entries? What advantage is there to this form? Are there any disadvantages?

Suggestions for Writing

1. Experiment with keeping a written record of your life, varying entries between those that record events and those that record thoughts and feelings. Try to write at least a hundred words a day.
2. Try to discover beauty where someone else might miss it. Visit a specific spot at least twice, preferably at different times of day or under different weather conditions. Record details and impressions in a journal, and draw upon these entries to write a description that reveals a clear point of view.

FINISHING SCHOOL

Maya Angelou

As you read this chapter from Angelou's first volume of autobiography, I Know Why the Caged Bird Sings, *think about the relationship between the setting, a small Southern town during the 1930s, and the events that happened there to a ten-year-old African-American girl — Angelou herself. At a time when many people questioned the value of higher education for women, young women were sometimes sent to "finishing schools"; their brothers went to college. Finishing schools offered a limited curriculum that emphasized such skills as giving parties and writing thank-you notes. Angelou's finishing school is the kitchen of a middle-class white woman who takes her social position seriously. Think about what Angelou learned when working there, and ask yourself if these lessons are still being taught today.*

Recently a white woman from Texas, who would quickly describe herself as a liberal, asked me about my hometown. When I told her that in Stamps my grandmother had owned the only Negro general merchandise store since the turn of the century, she exclaimed, "Why, you were a debutante." Ridiculous and even ludicrous. But Negro girls in small Southern towns, whether poverty-stricken or just munching along on a few of life's necessities, were given as extensive and irrelevant preparations for adulthood as rich white girls shown in magazines. Admittedly the training was not the same. While white girls learned to waltz and sit gracefully with a tea cup balanced on their knees, we were lagging behind, learning the mid-Victorian values with very little money to indulge them. (Come and see Edna Lomax spending the money she made picking cotton on five balls of ecru tatting thread. Her fingers are bound to snag the work and she'll have to repeat the stitches time and time again. But she knows that when she buys the thread.)

We were required to embroider and I had trunkfuls of colorful dish-towels, pillowcases, runners and handkerchiefs to my credit. I mastered the art of crocheting and tatting, and there was a lifetime's supply of dainty doilies that would never be used in sacheted dresser drawers. It went without saying that all girls could iron and wash, but the finer touches around the home, like setting a table with real silver, baking roasts and cooking vegetables without meat, had to be learned elsewhere. Usually at the source of those habits. During my tenth year, a white woman's kitchen became my finishing school.

Mrs. Viola Cullinan was a plump woman who lived in a three-bedroom house somewhere behind the post office. She was singularly unattractive until she smiled, and then the lines around her eyes and mouth which made her look perpetually dirty disappeared, and her face looked like the mask of an impish elf. She usually rested her smile until late afternoon when her women friends dropped in and Miss Glory, the cook, served them cold drinks on the closed-in porch.

The exactness of her house was inhuman. This glass went here and only here. That cup had its place and it was an act of impudent rebellion to place it anywhere else. At twelve o'clock the table was set. At 12:15 Mrs. Cullinan sat down to dinner (whether her husband had arrived or not). At 12:16 Miss Glory brought out the food.

It took me a week to learn the difference between a salad plate, a bread plate and a dessert plate. 5

Mrs. Cullinan kept up the tradition of her wealthy parents. She was from Virginia. Miss Glory, who was a descendant of slaves that had worked for the Cullinans, told me her history. She had married beneath her (according to Miss Glory). Her husband's family hadn't had their money very long and what they had "didn't 'mount to much."

As ugly as she was, I thought privately, she was lucky to get a husband above or beneath her station. But Miss Glory wouldn't let me say a thing against her mistress. She was very patient with me, however, over the housework. She explained the dishware, silverware and servants' bells. The large round bowl in which soup was served wasn't a soup bowl, it was a tureen. There were goblets, sherbet glasses, ice-cream glasses, wine glasses, green glass coffee cups with matching saucers, and water glasses. I had a glass to drink from, and it sat with Miss Glory's on a separate shelf from the others. Soup spoons, gravy boat, butter knives, salad forks and carving platter were additions to my vocabulary and in fact almost represented a new language. I was fascinated with the novelty, with the fluttering Mrs. Cullinan and her Alice-in-Wonderland house.

Her husband remains, in my memory, undefined. I lumped him with all the other white men that I had ever seen and tried not to see.

On our way home one evening, Miss Glory told me that Mrs. Cullinan couldn't have children. She said that she was too delicate-boned. It was hard to imagine bones at all under those layers of fat. Miss Glory went on to say that the doctor had taken out all her lady organs. I reasoned that a pig's organs included the lungs, heart and liver, so if Mrs. Cullinan was walking around without those essentials, it explained why she drank alcohol out of unmarked bottles. She was keeping herself embalmed.

When I spoke to Bailey° about it, he agreed that I was right, but he also informed me that Mr. Cullinan had two daughters by a colored lady and that I knew them very well. He added that the girls were the spitting image of their father. I was unable to remember what he looked like, although I had just left him a few hours before, but I thought of the Coleman girls. They were very light-skinned and certainly didn't look very much like their mother (no one ever mentioned Mr. Coleman). 10

Bailey: Identified earlier in the work from which this selection is excerpted; Bailey is the author's brother.

My pity for Mrs. Cullinan preceded me the next morning like the Cheshire cat's smile. Those girls, who could have been her daughters, were beautiful. They didn't have to straighten their hair. Even when they were caught in the rain, their braids still hung down straight like tamed snakes. Their mouths were pouty little cupid's bows. Mrs. Cullinan didn't know what she missed. Or maybe she did. Poor Mrs. Cullinan.

For weeks after, I arrived early, left late and tried very hard to make up for her barrenness. If she had had her own children, she wouldn't have had to ask me to run a thousand errands from her back door to the back door of her friends. Poor old Mrs. Cullinan.

Then one evening Miss Glory told me to serve the ladies on the porch. After I set the tray down and turned toward the kitchen, one of the women asked, "What's your name, girl?" It was the speckled-faced one. Mrs. Cullinan said, "She doesn't talk much. Her name's Margaret."

"Is she dumb?"

"No. As I understand it, she can talk when she wants to but she's 15 usually quiet as a little mouse. Aren't you, Margaret?"

I smiled at her. Poor thing. No organs and couldn't even pronounce my name correctly.

"She's a sweet little thing, though."

"Well, that may be, but the name's too long. I'd never bother myself. I'd call her Mary if I was you."

I fumed into the kitchen. That horrible woman would never have the chance to call me Mary because if I was starving I'd never work for her. I decided I wouldn't pee on her if her heart was on fire. Giggles drifted in off the porch and into Miss Glory's pots. I wondered what they could be laughing about.

Whitefolks were so strange. Could they be talking about me? Every- 20 body knew that they stuck together better than the Negroes did. It was possible that Mrs. Cullinan had friends in St. Louis who heard about a girl from Stamps being in court and wrote to her. Maybe she knew about Mr. Freeman.°

My lunch was in my mouth a second time and I went outside and relieved myself on the bed of four-o'clocks. Miss Glory thought I might be coming down with something and told me to go on home, that Momma would give me some herb tea, and she'd explain to her mistress.

I realized how foolish I was being before I reached the pond. Of course Mrs. Cullinan didn't know. Otherwise she wouldn't have given me the two nice dresses that Momma cut down, and she certainly wouldn't have called me a "sweet little thing." My stomach felt fine, and I didn't mention anything to Momma.

That evening I decided to write a poem on being white, fat, old and

---

Mr. Freeman: He had sexually abused the author during an earlier scene set in St. Louis, and she testified against him in court.

without children. It was going to be a tragic ballad. I would have to watch her carefully to capture the essence of her loneliness and pain.

The very next day, she called me by the wrong name. Miss Glory and I were washing up the lunch dishes when Mrs. Cullinan came to the doorway. "Mary?"

Miss Glory asked, "Who?"

Mrs. Cullinan, sagging a little, knew and I knew. "I want Mary to go down to Mrs. Randall's and take her some soup. She's not been feeling well for a few days."

Miss Glory's face was a wonder to see. "You mean Margaret, ma'am. Her name's Margaret."

"That's too long. She's Mary from now on. Heat that soup from last night and put it in the china tureen and, Mary, I want you to carry it carefully."

Every person I knew had a hellish horror of being "called out of his name." It was a dangerous practice to call a Negro anything that could be loosely construed as insulting because of the centuries of their having been called niggers, jigs, dinges, blackbirds, crows, boots and spooks.

Miss Glory had a fleeting second of feeling sorry for me. Then as she handed me the hot tureen she said, "Don't mind, don't pay that no mind. Sticks and stones may break your bones, but words . . . You know, I been working for her for twenty years."

She held the back door open for me. "Twenty years. I wasn't much older than you. My name used to be Hallelujah. That's what Ma named me, but my mistress give me 'Glory,' and it stuck. I likes it better too."

I was in the little path that ran behind the houses when Miss Glory shouted, "It's shorter too."

For a few seconds it was a tossup over whether I would laugh (imagine being named Hallelujah) or cry (imagine letting some white woman rename you for her convenience). My anger saved me from either outburst. I had to quit the job, but the problem was going to be how to do it. Momma wouldn't allow me to quit for just any reason.

"She's a peach. That woman is a real peach." Mrs. Randall's maid was talking as she took the soup from me, and I wondered what her name used to be and what she answered to now.

For a week I looked into Mrs. Cullinan's face as she called me Mary. She ignored my coming late and leaving early. Miss Glory was a little annoyed because I had begun to leave egg yolk on the dishes and wasn't putting much heart in polishing the silver. I hoped that she would complain to our boss, but she didn't.

Then Bailey solved my dilemma. He had me describe the contents of the cupboard and the particular plates she liked best. Her favorite piece was a casserole shaped like a fish and the green glass coffee cups. I kept his instructions in mind, so on the next day when Miss Glory was hanging out clothes and I had again been told to serve the old biddies on the porch,

I dropped the empty serving tray. When I heard Mrs. Cullinan scream, "Mary!" I picked up the casserole and two of the green glass cups in readiness. As she rounded the kitchen door I let them fall on the tiled floor.

I could never absolutely describe to Bailey what happened next, because each time I got to the part where she fell on the floor and screwed up her ugly face to cry, we burst out laughing. She actually wobbled around on the floor and picked up shards of the cups and cried, "Oh, Momma. Oh, dear Gawd. It's Momma's china from Virginia. Oh, Momma, I sorry."

Miss Glory came running in from the yard and the women from the porch crowded around. Miss Glory was almost as broken up as her mistress. "You mean to say she broke our Virginia dishes? What we gone do?"

Mrs. Cullinan cried louder, "That clumsy nigger. Clumsy little black nigger."

Old speckled-face leaned down and asked, "Who did it, Viola? Was   40
it Mary? Who did it?"

Everything was happening so fast I can't remember whether her action preceded her words, but I know that Mrs. Cullinan said, "Her name's Margaret, goddamn it, her name's Margaret." And she threw a wedge of the broken plate at me. It could have been the hysteria which put her aim off, but the flying crockery caught Miss Glory right over her ear and she started screaming.

I left the front door wide open so all the neighbors could hear.

Mrs. Cullinan was right about one thing. My name wasn't Mary.

Questions for Discussion

1. Why does Mrs. Cullinan call the author Mary when her name is Margaret? Why did Angelou resent this (even she herself eventually changed her name)?
2. In a house stocked with so many glasses, why did Angelou and Miss Glory have their own drinking glasses on a separate shelf?
3. According to Angelou, Mrs. Cullinan's kitchen became her "finishing school." What exactly did she learn there?
4. Although Miss Glory is patient with Angelou and even sticks up for her at one point, she ultimately sides with Mrs. Cullinan. What is Miss Glory's function in this narrative? How is she different from Angelou?
5. When this work is reprinted in anthologies, editors usually omit the line "I decided that I wouldn't pee on her if her heart was on fire." Now that you have read this selection as originally published, consider the effect of omitting paragraph 19. Which version do you prefer and why?

Suggestions for Writing

1. Have you ever been the victim of an unkind employer or been trapped in a relationship that seemed difficult to break? Write about a time when you felt frustrated enough to drop dishes on the floor.

2. Narrative often involves a "turning point" — a point when a character changes in some fundamental way. Such a change can be caused by almost anything. But whether the cause is something big or something small, it seems significant within the narrative. Write an essay that will show a turning point in your own life.

LEVI'S

Marilyn Schiel

> *In "Levi's" Marilyn Schiel paints a picture of the past that focuses on a pair of blue jeans. Think about how the clothes people wear help determine what acts they perform — what they can and cannot do. As you read, ask yourself why the Levi's were so important to Schiel. What would they enable her to do? If you have seen reruns of such TV series as "Leave It to Beaver" or "Father Knows Best," you have some knowledge of American values in the fifties and early sixties. Draw upon what you know of that era so that you can locate Schiel's memoir within a context of time and place.*

They weren't boot cut, or spiked leg, or 501. They weren't stone washed, or acid bleached, or ice black. They weren't Guess, or Zena, or Jordache. They were just blue jeans — old, worn Levi's.

My ten-year-old brother wore blue jeans. I wore slacks. In summer, cotton pastel pants with embroidered bunnies or ducks. In winter, grey-corduroys with girl-pink flannel lining. I wanted to wear blue jeans.

As a five-year-old I didn't understand the difference between cause and coincidence. My brother's jeans meant he could wander his two-wheel bike blocks from home after school; he could, with a crew of blue-jeaned boys, build a tree house in the oak in the vacant lot next door; he could carry a BB gun all the way to the cemetery to shoot at squirrels. I had to be content triking my embroidered bunnies up and down the driveway; I had to settle for building domino houses on the living room floor; I could shoot only caps at imaginary black-hatted cowboys in the basement. I wanted to wear blue jeans.

But little girls in my 1950 world didn't wear blue jeans. Big girls didn't wear them either. Big girls didn't even wear pastel cotton slacks or winter corduroys. At least my mother, the big girl I knew best, didn't. When the family gathered for breakfast, seven days a week sharp at 7:30, Mom was already in uniform, a shirtwaist dress garnished with a colored, beaded necklace that matched clip-on earrings. By the 1960s June Cleaver may have been an anachronism, but in the early 1950s she lived at my house.

Mothers stayed home. Unlike dads, mothers didn't work. Mothers made the beds, cooked the meals, cleaned the house, baked the cookies, tended the garden, canned the vegetables, squeezed the clothes through the wringer-washer, hung washed clothes to dry on lines strung through the basement, ironed everything — including sheets and towels — scrubbed the floors while kneeling on pink rubber pads, walked seven blocks pulling an empty Red-flyer wagon to buy groceries, struggled seven blocks home with a week's worth of carefully budgeted supplies, and picked out the clothes their children would wear. My brother got blue jeans. I got embroidered bunnies. 5

Then, in 1953, my world changed. Elvis took us all to Heartbreak Hotel; Eisenhower brought us home from Korea; and my mother went to work. The hardware store Dad bought pulled Mom from the home to the business. Her transition from the breadbaker to a breadwinner taught my mother that women, big or little, didn't have to wear embroidered bunnies anymore.

The change was more evolutionary than revolutionary. She still wore the housewife uniform — but now she wore it to work. She still did the laundry, but now with an automatic washing machine and electric dryer. We still ate breakfast together at 7:30, but now cereal and milk replaced eggs and bacon. The ironing went out every Tuesday night to a house on the hill behind the railroad tracks and came back folded every Wednesday evening. And as a businesswoman, my mother discovered that sometimes function was more important than fashion, at least for little girls.

Those old, worn Levi's of my brother's met the expectations of the advertisements. They survived an entire season of his hard wear and, unlike most of his clothes, were outgrown before worn out. And as mother used to say about anything that might be salvaged for use, "These old pants still have a little life left in them."

Not only did they have some life left in them, but they were going to give that life to me. A year earlier they would have been boxed with other we-don't-want-them-anymore clothes for the "naked children" of some foreign country I'd never heard of or, if the postage wasn't too expensive, shipped off to my poor cousins in South Dakota. With her newfound economic acumen and with her slowly evolving awareness of a woman's place, my mother looked at those blue jeans differently than she would have the year before. Maybe she looked at me a little differently, too.

"Marilyn, come here," she called from my brother's room. That in itself tripped anticipation. Now that Bob was approaching adolescence, his room held the mystery earned of secrecy. The door to his room was open; my mother leaned over the bed folding and sorting boy-clothes. Shirts in one stack, pants in another, worn to see-through-thin garments in still a third pile. But smoothed out full length along the edge of Bob's bed were a pair of old, worn Levi's.

"Here, try these on." She held them up against my seven-year-old middle. "I think these will fit you if you roll up the legs."

And fit they did, more like a gunnysack than a glove, but they were blue jeans and they were my brother's — and they were now mine. Cinched tightly with an Indian-beaded belt scrounged from my brother's dresser, the chamois-soft denim bunched in unplanned pleats at my waist. No more sissy elastic for me. Triple-roll cuffs still scuffed the ground by my shoe heels when I walked — my excuse for the swaggering steps those Levi's induced. After a time sidewalk burns frayed the bottom edge, finally denoting my singular ownership. Metal rivets marked the pockets and seam overlaps. Gone were the telltale girl-white overstitching outlines.

And those pockets. Real pockets. Not that patch pocket pretend stuff of girl-pants, but deep inside pockets of white, soft, gather-in-my-fist material that could be pulled inside out in search of the disappeared dime.

But those Levi's marked more than my move from little-girl clothes to big-brother clothes. Indeed, they were the only hand-me-downs ever handed down. Instead, those old ratty pants marked my move to freedom, freedom from the conventional girl-stuff my mother had so carefully fostered only one year earlier. Maybe my mother — who was learning the difference between roofing nails and wood screws, who was learning to mix paint in the vise-gripping shake-machine bolted to the floor in the back room of the hardware store, who would later teach me to cut glass, make keys, and clean Surge milk pumpers — wanted me to know what she was learning about women's work and men's work. I don't know. I just know that those Levi's — old, worn, with a difficult-to-manage button fly — meant the world to me, at least the limited world offered by my neighborhood.

The next summer I got my first two-wheeled bike, a full-size, blue, fat-tire Schwinn off the store's showroom floor. It was mother who convinced Dad that I didn't need training wheels. "If you want her to learn to ride, put her on it and let her ride." Oh, I dented the fenders some that summer and suffered some scars from the inescapable tip-overs, but I learned to ride as well as the boys. And by the end of the summer, Mom was packing peanut butter sandwiches for me to take on fishing expeditions down at the Chippewa River below the railroad trestle.

Along with the traditional dolls and play cookware, Christmas Eve brought chemistry kits and carpenter tools. Even my brother acknowledged my newfound worldliness. Better than any gift were the after-school hours spent helping him rebuild an old auto engine in the basement. I didn't do much, but watching him work and occasionally fetching wrenches taught me where pistons went and what they did, and that my big brother didn't mind having me around.   15

By junior high, I had my own .22. Our family Sundays in the fall found three of us in the woods searching the squirrel. My brother elected to hunt a more dangerous game, senior high school girls. Dad wore that goofy brown billed hat with cold-weather earflaps; I wore wool side-zipping slacks from the juniors department at Daytons, topped by a crew-neck matching sweater — style in a seventh-grade girl mattered even in the woods; Mom wore a turtleneck under one of Dad's wool shirt-jacs pulled out to hang over her blue jeans — old, worn Levi's.

Questions for Discussion

1. How does Schiel characterize her mother in this piece? What causes her mother to change? Does Schiel approve of this change?
2. Why did Schiel want to wear jeans when she was a little girl? What details in this essay help you to understand her point of view?

3. The first three sentences in this essay begin with the same two words, and the fourth provides only a minor variation. What is the effect of paragraph 1? Do you note any other examples of repetition in this essay? What does repetition contribute to the essay as a whole?
4. Consider the third sentence in paragraph 5. What is the effect of conveying so much information within a single sentence?
5. In the last glimpse of herself that she provides here, Schiel remembers wearing a pair of slacks from a fashionable department store rather than the jeans that once meant so much to her. What is this meant to show?

Suggestions for Writing

1. Remember a favorite possession of yours when you were young. Write about that item in enough detail for readers to understand why it mattered to you.
2. Write about a time when you were denied the chance to do something because other people considered it unsuitable for your gender.

WHEN FATHER DOESN'T KNOW BEST
Andrew Merton

In this essay by a professor at the University of New Hampshire, you will recognize two settings or "scenes" — a ball park and a museum. Look for any connection between these places and the conflict this memoir records. Consider what you learn about Merton and his son from the way they respond to the places they visit. As you read, keep yourself open to memories of times when your own interests differed from someone older or younger than you.

On Nov. 25, 1983, the prizefighter Marvis Frazier, 23 and inexperienced, was knocked out by the heavyweight champion of the world, Larry Holmes, after 2 minutes and 57 seconds of the first round. Frazier was sucker-punched. Holmes faked a left jab and Frazier went for it, leaving himself open for the decisive punch, a right. Frazier managed to stay on his feet while Holmes pummeled him with 19 consecutive punches. Finally, with three seconds left in the round, the referee stopped the fight. At that moment, Marvis Frazier's father and manager, the former heavyweight champion Joe Frazier, embraced his son and repeated over and over: "It's all right. It's all right. I love you."

Later, responding to criticism that he had overestimated his son's abilities, Joe Frazier said, "I knew what I was doing." In the face of indisputable evidence to the contrary, Joe Frazier was unable to give up the notion that Marvis would succeed him as champion, that he would continue to reign through his son.

It is an insidious business, this drive for immortality, usually much more subtle than thrusting one's son naked into the ring. Often it is simply a matter of expecting the boy to repeat one's own boyhood, step for step.

In July 1983, my son Gabriel was 4 and extremely conscious of it. In fact, he defined and justified much of his behavior by his age: "Four-year-olds can buckle their own sandals." Or "I can run faster than Mike. That's because I'm 4 and he's only 3." A 4-year-old, I thought, was ready for a major-league baseball game. So on Saturday, July 16, I drove him to Boston to see the Red Sox play the Oakland A's.

It was a clear, hot day — very hot, in fact, setting a record for Boston on that date at 97 degrees — but, rare for Boston, it was dry. A good day for hitters. Jim Rice, Tony Armas, Carl Yastrzemski and Wade Boggs had been on a tear. I expected a slugfest. I had packed a bag with fruit and vegetables. Gabe slept through the entire 90-minute drive to Boston, a good sign; he'd be fresh for the game. Another good sign: I found a free, legal parking space. And as we entered the ball park, Gabe seemed excited. Gravely he heeded my advice to go to the bathroom now, so we would not have to move from our seat during the action.

As we walked through the catacombs beneath the stadium, I remembered my own first game, in Yankee Stadium in 1952. My only previous view of major-league baseball had come via the flickering images of black-and-white television. As my father and I emerged into the sun, I was overwhelmed by the vast, green expanse of the outfield. A stubble-faced pitcher named Vic Raschi fired strike after strike, a Yankee first baseman named Joe Collins hit a home run and the Yankees won, 3-2. The opponent had been the old Philadelphia Athletics, direct ancestors of the Oakland team. I felt joy and anticipation as Gabe and I now emerged into the sun for his first look at the left-field wall at Fenway, the Green Monster. Gabe said nothing, but he must have felt the excitement.

We found our seats, on the right-field side of the park halfway between first base and the foul pole. Good seats, from which we could see every part of the playing field. We were about a half-hour early, and we settled down to watch the end of batting practice. Then, as the ground crew manicured the infield, Gabe said he was hungry. I gave him a carrot stick, which he munched happily. When he finished that, he asked what else I had in the bag. I gave him some grapes, then an apple. Within 15 minutes he had polished off most of the contents of the bag. And then he said: "I think I've had enough baseball. I want to go home now."

"But the game hasn't started yet," I said. "You haven't seen any baseball."

"Yes, I have. And I want to go home."

"That was only batting practice. Don't you want to see the real   10 game?"

"No."

I considered staying anyway. It was *my* day with my son that was being ruined here, wasn't it?

But I knew better. I knew now that if I insisted on staying, it would be *his* day that would be ruined so Dad could watch a ball game. Submitting to the logic of this, I gritted my teeth. In a foul mood, I carried him out of the park on my shoulders just as the Red Sox took the field. I was muttering to myself, almost audibly, "It's *his* day, dammit."

"Daddy? Can I have an ice-cream cone?"

Without much grace, I bought him an ice-cream cone. Then we got   15 in the car, and I drove away from my precious parking space, still fuming. He was well aware that I was upset; I could see the tentative look on his face, a combination of fear and pain. I hated that look. But I could not shake my mood. I was not looking forward to the drive back to New Hampshire.

Then on Storrow Drive, I spotted the Boston Museum of Science, just across the Charles River. Gabe had been there before, and he had loved it, although he still referred to it, quite seriously, as the "Museum of Silence." Still angry, I managed to say, "Gabe, would you like to go to the museum?"

"Yeah," he said.

We had the museum nearly to ourselves. As we walked through the wonderfully cool exhibition halls, I acknowledged to myself how much I wanted Gabe to be like me. He was supposed to like the baseball game, not for his sake, but for mine, and I had gotten angry at him when he didn't measure up to my expectations. It was those expectations, and not Gabe's actions, that were out of line. And it was those expectations that had to change.

I also thought about the competition between us: what had happened at the ball park was, after all, a battle of wills. He had won. He had prevailed because he was persistent and stubborn and stood up for what he thought was right.

We spent three quick hours at the museum, viewing the life-sized   20
tyrannosaurus rex from different angles, trying out the space capsule, making waves and viewing exhibits on everything from centrifugal force to probability. Each time Gabe made a discovery, he called me over to share his excitement. And I *was* excited.

Son and father, together, had saved the day — he by holding out for something he enjoyed and I by having the sense, finally, to realize that he was right, and to let go of my dream of how things should be.

This time, anyway.

And then I remembered something else. When my own father took me to Yankee Stadium, I was 6 years old, not 4.

Maybe in a couple of years. . . .

Questions for Discussion

1. The first two paragraphs describe a prizefight that had occurred seven years before this essay was first published. Why do you think Merton chose to begin with this example? How does it relate to the essay that follows?
2. Why does Merton get so angry with his son? How does he manage to salvage what seems to be turning into a bad day?
3. What is Gabe like? Is he simply a typical four-year old, or does he seem to have a personality of his own?
4. What is the effect of the second-to-last paragraph?
5. Although focused upon the memory of a day Merton spent with his son, this essay includes some other memories as well: the memory of the author's first ball game in 1952, the memory of an earlier trip to the Boston Museum of Science, and the final memory of being six upon first visiting Yankee Stadium. How closely related are these memories to one another, and what do they show about the nature of memory?

Suggestions for Writing

1. Remember a time in your childhood when your wishes differed from the expectations of a parent or someone else who had authority over you. Tell the story of how that conflict was resolved.
2. Write about attending a public event at two different points in your life. Focus primarily upon one memory, but use the second to show how you have changed.

GATORS

Geoffrey Norman

As you read the following essay, bear in mind that time is part of any scene: A place can seem different at different times of the year, and some places change as time passes. "Gators" take place in Florida, but the scene shifts from Florida in the 1950s to Florida in 1980, when this essay was first published. Consider why this shifting scene is important. As you read about Norman's experience with alligators, it might help you to know that they were on the endangered-species list when he wrote.

One of my jobs a couple dozen years ago was to haul the garbage from our family's summer place. It was good training for a boy. It taught me humility and reminded me to wash my hands. And though the job had its disciplinary aspect, it was just about the only chore I looked forward to. Because of the alligator.

The summer house was on a beach so remote that we had no electricity. There was no garbage pickup, either, so at first we buried the stuff. The boys in the family were reminded to dig deep holes for the garbage, meaning six feet, at least — deep enough to decently bury a dead man, which was one of the few things we never actually put in those holes.

Ours was a big house and a big family, and there was a lot of garbage. We caught and cleaned all our own seafood, so there were fish heads and shrimp shells by the pound. We also buried all the road kills, which were frequent, probably because the blacktop was new and the animals had not yet learned to fear it. Every day there was a dead possum, armadillo, or snake to dispose of. Burying those bodies and all that garbage became the grimmest part of my day — worse, even, than baths or bedtime or Sunday school.

Then, about three hundred yards from the house, we discovered the slough and the gator. The slough was a depression full of dark water, lily pads, cattails, and frogs. It was perhaps as big as a football field. One day an alligator appeared there.

It was not a large gator like those ten- or twelve-footers you see in dirty concrete pits at the cheap Florida roadside attractions. But it was not a toy or a pet, either. This was a mature alligator, six or seven feet long. At first, we tried out its appetite on a few simple things: leftover fish, stale bread, overripe fruit. Whatever we offered, it ate greedily, which may be the only way an alligator ever eats. Then we made it tougher, tossing the gator crab scraps and dead raccoons, watermelon rinds and coffee grounds. Suddenly there were no more tedious pits and smelly funerals; when we boys were called on to take out the garbage, it was an adventure. Now we gladly took the short walk to the slough, hoping all the way that the gator would be in sight once we got there. About half the time, it would be out where we could get a good look.

5

It was something I never got over. Although I did not fear the alligator with a trembling, cold-fleshed fear, I knew when I saw it that I was looking at the *other*. This was a creature governed by the oldest, most irreducible urges, and they seemed almost visible on him. No other creature so clearly displays its origins and, in some fashion, its essence. An alligator is not mean; it is merely primitive.

We all understood that, even though we were just boys, and we watched the gator through three or four summers without ever trying to touch it or feed it with our hands or wrestle with it. We respected that alligator and appreciated the job it did.

One night, as the cold-blooded gator lay on the road enjoying the residual warmth of the blacktop, a carful of drunks came along. They stopped their car, got out, and beat the alligator to death with tire irons. Then they sped off in the night, whooping it up. They were called rednecks then, and that was their style. We heard the whole thing, but there wasn't enough time to get to the road and stop it.

The next morning, we buried the alligator and went back to burying the garbage. We watched the slough to see if another gator would move in and claim the vacant turf. When that didn't happen, I thought about going back to the swamp and catching a small one, which was easy and safe enough to do if you used a snare or a net. I never caught one for the slough, though. There was no need. Electricity came to town. The road was improved. We got a telephone. And somebody started hauling garbage.

As civilization arrived, the alligators disappeared. Soon a golf course 10 was built on the black-water lake they used to inhabit, and I could not have found one to transplant even if I'd wanted to.

The problem, of course, was not just local, and the alligator made the endangered-species list several years ago. Women — and some men, no doubt — liked alligator-skin belts, boots, and bags so much that it was possible to make a living by killing them and selling the hides. What the Army Corps and the developers had started, fashion and the poachers threatened to finish.

The alligators' turnaround since that time has made national news. Protection and strict controls on interstate shipment of gator hides have worked: the animals have come back strong. Every so often, one will eat a poodle or take up residence in the water hazard on the sixteenth hole. Fish-and-game people are then called out to lasso the uncomprehending reptile and move it to an out-of-the-way place. There is even some limited commerce again in the skins. At least one entrepreneur is ranching alligators, just as though they were cattle or mink. Not long ago, someone in Florida was killed by an alligator in what I suspect must have been a well-deserved attack.

But to survive is not necessarily to thrive, and although the gator is back from the jaws of extinction, I had not seen one for years until the other day. I was coming home with my daughter from a prosaic errand, driving along the old winding blacktop instead of on the straight new highway. It was late in the afternoon. The earth glistened from a thunderstorm that had built up all day and had then climaxed in a wild discharge of lightning and sheets of driving rain. Now the air was cool, and the low country had come to life.

The road ran through a flat, desolate marsh, where blackbirds darted across meaty cattail pods. Seven bobwhite chicks marched behind their mother like nervous recruits. A water moccasin lay dead in the road where an automobile tire had flattened it. I remembered a time when I had watched an alligator devour a big moccasin. The snake had struck repeatedly and futilely at the gator's head, but mere fangs had no chance against that hide. The alligator swallowed the snake with primitive nonchalance, swam back to a clear stretch of bank, crawled out of the pond, and disappeared in the saw grass.

In the midst of recalling that scene, I noticed a characteristic profile — nose, then eyes — and a slight disturbance on the surface of the water above a massive body. There was an alligator in the drainage pond just off the shoulder of the road. I stopped the car and walked to the water's edge with my daughter, who had never seen an alligator except in books. I pointed to the low profile, not really expecting her to appreciate it for what it was. It looked like a log. They always do.   15

The gator turned. I expected it to dive and swim away. Instead, it swam right for us, stopping when it reached the water's edge, its snout less than a yard from our feet. My daughter was delighted and slightly concerned. She held my hand tightly and willingly. We had nothing to feed the gator except a piece of bubble gum that the bank clerk had given us. I unwrapped it and tossed it to the gator, which took it down with a single swallow.

We told that story for a day or two, then returned, with my wife and a bag of marshmallows, to the little pond. When we walked to the bank, the gator swam over to meet us. We threw marshmallows, but they were ignored. Instead of eating, the alligator hissed at us, the air making a rattling sound as it escaped the gator's throat. My daughter was frightened. We put the marshmallows down and stood there. The alligator looked up at us with vacant eyes and a reptilian grin, like a captured creature trapped in some zoo. I felt terrible for all of us.

Then my daughter pointed and said, "Another one."

I looked, and, indeed, another gator had materialized about thirty feet from the bank. This one was about five feet long, a little smaller than the one that lay unblinking at our feet.

I threw a marshmallow, and it landed four feet from the alligator's nose. The large mouth opened in what looked like an exaggerated yawn. The marshmallow disappeared. For my daughter's amusement I threw half a dozen more of them at the cruising gator, feeling worse all the time.   20

Then the alligator at our feet slid back into the water and swam for the middle of the pond. We assumed that he was after marshmallows and, for some reason, would not eat them at the bank. We watched as the two alligators glided closer together, graceful and silent. Then the larger alligator attacked. It was deliberate and swift. There was no damage, only a sudden noisy swirl of dark water and a splashy retreat by the smaller alligator. The first gator then returned to his station at our feet and hissed at us rudely.

"What was that all about?" my wife asked.

"No telling," I said.

In a few minutes, the second alligator reappeared. The marshmallows must have been irresistible. I threw a few more out on the surface of the pond, where they were snapped up. Then the gator at our feet backed off the bank, swam effortlessly to the middle of the pond, and attacked again.

"I don't get it," my wife said. . . .   *25*

"I don't know," I said. I felt much better, though.

That night, we decided that the first gator must have been a nesting female and the second a transient male. The first had come to warn us off and to defend her nest. The second was hungry and couldn't pass up easy food. The first did not approve of the invasion of her nest. It was a plausible theory, though I did not try to verify it by locating the nest. Happy as I was to see an alligator after all those years, I knew that if I had stepped into the pond or reached too close with one of those marshmallows, the primeval imperative would have taken over, and that gator would have taken off my arm.

Questions for Discussion

1. Norman claims that he never got over his boyhood experience with an alligator. What did the alligator represent for him?
2. Much of paragraph 3 is devoted to road kills. What connection is there between these dead animals and the alligators that are the focus of this essay?
3. Norman reports that he was "feeling worse all the time" when feeding marshmallows to the alligator. After watching another alligator attack, he reports that he felt much better. Why did he have these responses?
4. In paragraphs 11 and 12, Norman departs from recording memories to offer background information on the status of alligators. Are these paragraphs worth including, or do they distract attention from the memories that come before and after them?
5. Is there anything admirable about the alligators described in this essay? Why should anyone care that alligators have been rescued from what Norman aptly calls "the jaws of extinction"?

Suggestions for Writing

1. Norman remembers a chore that became an adventure. Write about one of your own childhood chores if you can remember a time when performing that chore was especially interesting or difficult.

2. Write about some aspect of your childhood that has been lost or endangered by "civilization." Describe an environment that now seems at risk, and show what has caused it to change.

TAKING THE TEST

David Groff

As its title suggests, the focus of this essay is on an act: taking a test. The test in question is the test for HIV-positive antibodies that indicate infection with the AIDS virus. The author takes the test because he is gay and considers himself at risk. As you read, try to imagine what it would be like to wait for your test results if you knew that you might have been exposed to AIDS. Think about why Groff chose to write about this experience and then publish what he wrote.

The time had come for me to take the Test, as we gay men call it. "The Test" is part of our succinct new vocabulary of non-words — PCP, DDI, KS, DHPG, CMV, AZT — all representing either opportunistic infections or treatments for that acronym looming in so many of our lives: AIDS. For years I had wondered which non-word might ambush me and which series of non-words could prolong my life. Now I sat on an examining table, my left hand a fist, as the doctor's latexed fingers drew my purple blood into a vial. For years — practically ever since the HIV antibody test had been released in 1985 — I had avoided this moment, avoided knowing whether or not I was antibody-positive and therefore more likely to develop immunosuppression, which could lead to AIDS. Along with my friends, I could justify avoiding the Test. It seemed better to be surprised by AIDS than to live paralyzed by a prospect I was powerless to alter.

That isn't true anymore. Or, as my doctor put it, "Two years ago, if you took the Test and you were positive, all I could do would be to send you to a shrink. Now if you're positive, we still send you to a shrink — but we can intervene."

My rational self agreed with my doctor. If I was positive and if my level of helper cells was suppressed, I could go on AZT, the very toxic drug that seems to counter the virus in some people and that remains the only antiviral approved by the government for widespread and standard use. But watching my blood enter the vial still panicked me. I had made the first of a series of decisions that could change forever how I lived my life — if not how long my life might be.

The doctor withdrew the needle, capped the vial, and labeled the tube. On a little form he checked off half the risk groups listed: gay or bisexual male, sexual partner of persons at risk, and "other." He scrawled something on an envelope and shoved the vial and form inside. Then he explained where to drop it off, told me a bad joke, bandaged my arm, patted it, and left.

Minutes later I was on the subway from my doctor's office on the Upper East Side, heading down to the Department of Public Health at

5

Twenty-sixth and First Avenue. They would test the blood not confiden-tially but anonymously — I was identified only by number — and in two weeks I would visit my doctor again to find out the results face to face.

The vial balanced on top of the papers in my shoulder bag. I imag-ined the blood rolling out and smashing onto the floor amid the evening rush-hour commuters. I imagined them leaping back, wondering — just as I wondered — whether the blood was infected. I almost wanted the vial to crash and break; then I wouldn't have to deliver it and I would never know. Even though I intended to keep private the fact of my taking the Test, a part of me wanted to appall the commuters — just as I was appalled.

It was after hours, and the lobby to the building was deserted. I asked the guard where Room 102 was, feeling obvious, feeling infected. With a nearly imperceptible and perhaps contemptuous nod he directed me the right way. My question, and my situation, were ordinary for him.

Room 102 was a refrigerator in a closet. I had expected a bustling clinic of white-coated lab technicians testing the city's blood day and night. Inside the refrigerator, envelopes with vials of blood lay on the trays, each one labeled with a series of medical abbreviations unfamiliar to me. There were hundreds of vials. I laid my blood in gently among them and thought for a long moment before I shut the refrigerator door and left.

When I turned around I found a woman in front of me, tall, dressed in sleek black, her hair hidden under a black scarf and her face dead white. She was holding an envelope identical to mine. I met her blue eyes for an instant and then we both looked away. I made my way around her, spec-ulating a little on what brought her here — marriage, prospective preg-nancy, a boyfriend, a tragedy. For a moment we were a two-person community of the worried well, eyes averted just like regular New York-ers. Someone knew my secret; someone knew hers.

When I got outside, the city was beautiful, even this unphotogenic *10* section of First Avenue. The gray lines of buildings and sky seemed like a riot of subtle colors, the horns and headlights a vigorous party. I felt acutely aware of my possibly infected body, how it took up space, how the muscles worked in my legs and how, as a result, I moved. I wouldn't be moving forever, I knew that; someday I would be still. I turned around and saw the woman in black hurrying the opposite way. I wondered if she felt about her body the way I felt about mine.

For the next two weeks I ate bacon cheeseburgers almost daily, a series of last meals. Every time the phone rang, at home or at the office, I felt an electric anxiety. My doctor had promised he would not call, but I kept hoping he'd break our agreement and phone to say I was negative. That way I could sleep at night. He didn't call.

I grew more obsessed daily. Even though for hours at a time I'd forget to anticipate my test results, my fear would ambush me like a bowel-loosening punch in the gut. I told myself that I wouldn't die the very day the doctor told me the bad news. My HIV-positive friends, and those who had been diagnosed with AIDS, were still alive — mostly. They'd coped. I'd cope too. Cold comfort.

I'd wake up in the middle of the night trying to remember the details of every sexual experience I'd ever had, however minimal the risk of infection might have been. I went so far as to get up at 2 A.M. and scour the phone book to locate those men I'd lost contact with. One name was absent. That was unnerving, because I knew he had been listed and that he owned his apartment and thus wasn't likely to leave New York. Probably he was just unlisted now. But I lay awake the rest of the night wondering if Peter was still alive.

Two weeks later, my body feeling oddly light, as if I could still sense the ounce of blood I'd lost, I was sitting on that same examining table, hearing my doctor's low voice from the next room. He was running late. I told myself I'd know how to react, but I knew I wouldn't. I let my eyes focus on a bad watercolor above the sink: a beached sailboat lying coyly on its side in the sand. The pastels were fey but they seemed brilliant to me.

The door opened and my doctor's face appeared, sweaty at the end   15 of the workday, as bemused as usual.

Forgive me, but I will not tell you what my doctor told me.

Imagine for yourself the immense relief, the knot of tension sliced through, the light-headed desire to hug the doctor and laugh. But imagine also the doctor's pronouncement, his optimistic droning about prolonged longevity and further T-cell tests, the spit in the stomach forming a big sickening ball, the disbelief, the thousands of self-steelings. Imagine that different sort of light-headedness.

My antibody status does not matter to you. Certainly it matters — with absolute enormity — to me. But what I'd like you to remember is the blood on the subway, the click of the refrigerator door, the woman in black so elegant and uneasy, First Avenue at gritty, gorgeous dusk, the brilliance of that bad art in the examining room, the pores of the doctor's face — all of them declaring, by their very existence: As long and as well as you can, live, live.

Questions for Discussion

1. AIDS is not restricted to gay men, and Groff could have written about being tested for this disease without revealing his sexual preference. But he makes this revelation in the opening sentence of his essay, and repeats it in paragraphs 4 and 13. What do you think motivated this candor? How would the essay change if the author did not disclose his sexual preference?
2. What does the fantasy in paragraph 6 reveal about Groff's state of mind?
3. In his conclusion Groff writes that he wants us to remember the woman in black. What is her role in the essay?

4. Why does Groff find the city beautiful after he leaves the Department of Public Health? Did the city change or did Groff?

5. Consider Groff's decision to withhold the results of his AIDS test. How would the essay change if you knew he had tested either positive or negative?

Suggestions for Writing

1. Recall situations in which you suffered from anxiety waiting for the results of a medical test, a job interview, an examination at school — or any other time when news of your future seemed only a phone call away. Focus upon one specific memory and write about it so that others can understand how you felt.

2. Write about a time when you did something against your will because you believed this action was necessary.

THE LAST CHRISTMAS OF THE WAR
Primo Levi

> *Writing about concentration camps usually focuses upon death — and with good reason. In our century many millions of people have been killed in these camps. But in writing about a part of Auschwitz, the huge camp that was designed by the Nazis for killing on a massive scale and that functioned like a small city, Primo Levi chose to focus upon what life was like for prisoners who were not immediately sent to the gas chamber. Levi writes about several people he knew in Auschwitz, and each does something that can give you a little window through which to see how the author, who was a skilled chemist, managed to go on living while under a constant threat of death.*

In more ways than one, Monowitz, a part of Auschwitz, was not a typical Camp. The barrier that separated us from the world — symbolized by the double barbed-wire fence — was not hermetic, as elsewhere. Our work brought us into daily contact with people who were "free," or at least less slaves than we were: technicians, German engineers and foremen, Russian and Polish workers, English, American, French and Italian prisoners of war. Officially they were forbidden to talk to us, the pariahs of KZ (*Konzentrations-Zentrum°*), but the prohibition was constantly ignored, and what's more, news from the free world reached us through a thousand channels. In the factory trash bins we found copies of the daily papers (sometimes two or three days old and rain-soaked) and in them we read with trepidation the German bulletins: mutilated, censored, euphemistic, yet eloquent. The Allied POWs listened secretly to Radio London, and even more secretly brought us the news, and it was exhilarating. In December 1944 the Russians had entered Hungary and Poland, the English were in the Romagna, the Americans were heavily engaged in the Ardennes but were winning in the Pacific against Japan.

At any rate, there was no real need of news from far away to find out how the war was going. At night, when all the noises of the Camp had died down, we heard the thunder of the artillery coming closer and closer. The front was no more than a hundred kilometers away; a rumor spread that the Red Army was already in the West Carpathians.° The enormous factory in which we worked had been bombed from the air several times with vicious and scientific precision: one bomb, only one, on the central power plant, putting it out of commission for two weeks; as soon as the damage was repaired and the stack began belching smoke again, another bomb and so on. It was clear that the Russians, or the Allies in concert with the Russians, intended to stop production but not destroy the plants.

Konzentrations-Zentrum: German for "Concentration Center."
West Carpathians: A range of mountains in central Europe, the Carpathians are less than twenty miles from Auschwitz.

These they wanted to capture intact at the end of the war, as indeed they did; today that is Poland's largest synthetic rubber factory. Active anti-aircraft defense was nonexistent, no pursuing planes were to be seen; there were guns on the roofs but they didn't fire. Perhaps they no longer had ammunition.

In short, Germany was moribund, but the Germans didn't notice. After the attempt on Hitler in July, the country lived in a state of terror: a denunciation, an absence from work, an incautious word, were sufficient to land you in the hands of the Gestapo as a defeatist. Therefore both soldiers and civilians fulfilled their tasks as usual, driven at once by fear and an innate sense of discipline. A fanatical and suicidal Germany terrorized a Germany that was by now discouraged and profoundly defeated.

A short time before, toward the end of October, we'd had the opportunity to observe a close-up of a singular school of fanaticism, a typical example of Nazi training. On some unused land next to our Camp, a *Hitlerjugend*—Hitler Youth—encampment had been set up. There were possibly two hundred adolescents, still almost children. In the mornings they practiced flag-raising, sang belligerent hymns, and, armed with ancient muskets, were put through marching and shooting drills. We understood later that they were being prepared for enrollment in the Volkssturm, that ragtag army of old men and children that, according to the Führer's mad plans, was supposed to put up a last-ditch defense against the advancing Russians. But sometimes in the afternoon their instructors, who were SS veterans, would bring them to see us as we worked clearing away rubble from the bombings, or erecting slapdash and useless little protective walls of bricks or sandbags.

They led them among us on a "guided tour" and lectured them in ⁵ loud voices, as if we had neither ears to hear nor the intelligence to understand. "These that you see are the enemies of the Reich, *your* enemies. Take a good look at them: would you call them men? They are *Untermenschen,* submen! They stink because they don't wash; they're in rags because they don't take care of themselves. What's more, many of them don't even understand German. They are subversives, bandits, street thieves from the four corners of Europe, but we have rendered them harmless; now they work for us, but they are good only for the most primitive work. Moreover, it is only right that they should repair the war damages; these are the people who wanted the war: the Jews, the Communists, and the agents of the plutocracies."

The child-soldiers listened, devout and dazed. Seen close up, they inspired both pain and horror. They were haggard and frightened, yet they looked at us with intense hatred. So we were the ones guilty for all the evils, the cities in ruins, the famine, their dead fathers on the Russian front. The Führer was stern but just, and it was just to serve him.

At that time I worked as a "specialist" in a chemical laboratory inside the plant: these are things that I have written about elsewhere, but, strangely, with the passing of the years these memories do not fade, nor do they thin out. They become enriched with details I thought were forgotten, which sometimes acquire meaning in the light of other people's memories, from letters I receive or books I read.

It was snowing, it was very cold, and working in that laboratory was not easy. At times the heating system didn't work and at night, ice would form, bursting the phials of reagents and the big bottle of distilled water. Often we lacked the raw materials or reagents necessary for analyses, and it was necessary to improvise or to produce what was missing on the spot. There was no ethyl acetate for a colorimetric measurement. The laboratory head told me to prepare a liter of it and gave me the needed acetic acid and ethyl alcohol. It's a simple procedure; I had done it in Turin in my organic preparations course in 1941. Only three years before, but it seemed like three thousand. . . . Everything went smoothly up to the final distillation, but at that point suddenly the water stopped running.

This could have ended in a small disaster, because I was using a glass refrigerator. If the water returned, the refrigerating tube, which had been heated on the inside by the product's vapor, would certainly have shattered on contact with the icy water. I turned off the faucet, found a small pail, filled it with distilled water, and immersed in it the small pump of a Höppler thermostat. The pump pushed the water into the refrigerator, and the hot water fell into the pail as it came out. Everything went well for a few minutes, then I noticed that the ethyl acetate was no longer condensing; almost all of it was coming out of the pipe in the form of vapor. I had been able to find only a small amount of distilled water (there was no other) and by now it had become warm.

What to do? There was a lot of snow on the windowsills, so I made   10
balls with it and put them into the pail one by one. While I was busy with my gray snowballs, Dr. Pannwitz, the German chemist who had subjected me to a singular "state examination" to determine whether my professional knowledge was sufficient, came into the lab. He was a fanatical Nazi. He looked suspiciously at my makeshift installation and the murky water that could have damaged the precious pump, but said nothing and left.

A few days later, toward the middle of December, the basin of one of the suction hoods was blocked and the chief told me to unplug it. It seemed natural to him that the dirty job should fall to me and not to the lab technician, a girl named Frau Mayer, and actually it seemed natural to me too. I was the only one who could stretch out serenely on the floor without fear of getting dirty; my striped suit was already completely filthy. . . .

I was getting up after having screwed the siphon back on when I noticed Frau Mayer standing close to me. She spoke to me in a whisper with a guilty air; she was the only one of the eight or ten girls in the lab — German, Polish, and Ukrainian — who showed no contempt for me. Since my hands were already dirty, she asked, could I fix her bicycle, which had a flat? She would, of course, give me something for my trouble.

This apparently neutral request was actually full of sociological implications. She had said "please" to me, which in itself represented an infraction of the upside-down code that regulated our relationships with the Germans. She had spoken to me for reasons not connected with work; she had made a kind of contract with me, and a contract is made between equals; and she had expressed, or at least implied, gratitude for the work I had done on the basin in her stead. However, the girl was also inviting me to break the rules, which could be very dangerous for me, since I was there as a chemist, and by repairing her bike I would be taking time away from my professional work. She was proposing, in other words, a kind of complicity, risky but potentially useful. Having a human relationship with someone "on the other side" involved danger, a social promotion, and more food for today and the day after. In a flash I did the algebraic sum of the three addends: hunger won by several lengths, and I accepted the proposal.

Frau Mayer held out the key to the padlock, saying that I should go and get the bicycle; it was in the courtyard. That was out of the question; I explained as best I could that she must go herself, or send someone else. "We" were by definition thieves and liars: if anybody saw me with a bicycle I'd really be in for it. Another problem arose when I saw the bicycle. In its tool bag there were pieces of rubber, rubber cement, and small irons to remove the tire, but there was no pump, and without a pump I couldn't locate the hole in the inner tube. I must explain, incidentally, that in those days bicycles and flat tires were much more common than they are now, and almost all Europeans, especially young ones, knew how to patch a tire. A pump? No problem, said Frau Mayer; all I had to do was get Meister Grubach, her colleague next door, to lend me one. But this too wasn't so simple. With some embarrassment I had to ask her to write and sign a note: *"Bitte um die Fahrradpumpe.°"*

I made the repair, and Frau Mayer, in great secrecy, gave me a hard-boiled egg and four lumps of sugar. Don't misunderstand; given the situation and the going rates, it was a more than generous reward. As she furtively slipped me the packet, she whispered something that gave me a lot to think about: "Christmas will soon be here." Obvious words, absurd actually when addressed to a Jewish prisoner; certainly they were intended to mean something else, something no German at that time would have dared to put into words. 15

In telling this story after forty years, I'm not trying to make excuses for Nazi Germany. One human German does not whitewash the innumerable inhuman or indifferent ones, but it does have the merit of breaking a stereotype.

Bitte um die Fahrradpumpe: Colloquial German meaning "Request for the bicycle pump."

It was a memorable Christmas for the world at war; memorable for me too, because it was marked by a miracle. At Auschwitz, the various categories of prisoners (political, common criminals, social misfits, homosexuals, etc.) were allowed to receive gift packages from home, but not the Jews. Anyway, from whom could the Jews have received them? From their families, exterminated or confined in the surviving ghettos? From the very few who had escaped the roundups, hidden in cellars, in attics, terrified and penniless? And who knew our address? For all the world knew, we were dead.

And yet a package did finally find its way to me, through a chain of friends, sent by my sister and my mother, who were hidden in Italy. The last link of that chain was Lorenzo Perrone, the bricklayer from Fossano, of whom I have spoken in *Survival in Auschwitz,* and whose heartbreaking end I have recounted . . . in "Lorenzo's Return." The package contained ersatz chocolate, cookies, and powdered milk, but to describe its real value, the impact it had on me and on my friend Alberto, is beyond the powers of ordinary language. In the Camp, the terms eating, food, hunger, had meanings totally different from their usual ones. That unexpected, improbable, impossible package was like a meteorite, a heavenly object, charged with symbols, immensely precious, and with an enormous momentum.

We were no longer alone: a link with the outside world had been established, and there were delicious things to eat for days and days. But there were also serious practical problems to resolve immediately: we found ourselves in the situation of a passerby who is handed a gold ingot in full view of everyone. Where to put the food? How to keep it? How to protect it from other people's greediness? How to invest it wisely? Our year-old hunger kept pushing us toward the worst possible solution: to eat everything right then and there. But we had to resist that temptation. Our weakened stomachs could not have coped with the abuse; within an hour, it would have ended in indigestion or worse.

We had no safe hiding places so we distributed the food in all the regular pockets in our clothes, and sewed secret ones inside the backs of our jackets so that even in case of a body search something could be saved. But to have to take everything with us, to work, to the washhouse, to the latrine, was inconvenient and awkward. Alberto and I talked it over at length in the evening, after curfew. The two of us had made a pact: everything either one of us managed to scrounge beyond our ration had to be divided into two exactly equal parts. Alberto was always more successful than I in these enterprises, and I often asked why he wanted to stay partners with anyone as inefficient as I was. But he always replied: "You never know. I'm faster but you're luckier." For once, he turned out to be right.

Alberto came up with an ingenious scheme. The cookies were the biggest problem. We had them stored, a few here, a few there. I even had some in the lining of my cap, and had to be careful not to crush them when I had to yank it off fast to salute a passing SS. The cookies weren't all that good but they looked nice. We could, he suggested, divide them into two packages and give them as gifts to the Kapo and the barracks Elder. According to Alberto, that was the best investment. We would acquire prestige, and the two big shots, even without a formal agreement, would reward us with various favors. The rest of the food we could eat ourselves, in small, reasonable daily rations, and with the greatest possible precautions.

But in Camp, the crowding, the total lack of privacy, the gossip and disorder were such that our secret quickly became an open one. In the space of a few days we noticed that our companions and Kapos were looking at us with different eyes. That's the point: they were looking at us, the way you do at something or someone outside the norm, that no longer melts into the background but stands out. According to how much they liked "the two Italians," they looked at us with envy, with understanding, complacency, or open desire. Mendi, a Slovakian rabbi friend of mine, winked at me and said *"Mazel tov,"* the lovely Yiddish and Hebrew phrase used to congratulate someone on a happy event. Quite a few people knew or had guessed something, which made us both happy and uneasy; we would have to be on our guard. In any case, we decided by mutual consent to speed up the consumption: something eaten cannot be stolen.

On Christmas Day we worked as usual. As a matter of fact, since the laboratory was closed, I was sent along with the others to remove rubble and carry sacks of chemical products from a bombed warehouse to an undamaged one. When I got back to Camp in the evening, I went to the washhouse. I still had quite a lot of chocolate and powdered milk in my pockets, so I waited until there was a free spot in the corner farthest from the entrance. I hung my jacket on a nail, right behind me; no one could have approached without my seeing him. I began to wash, when out of the corner of my eye I saw my jacket rising in the air. I turned but it was already too late. The jacket, with all its contents, and with my registration number sewed on the breast, was already out of reach. Someone had lowered a string and hook from the small window above the nail. I ran outside, half undressed as I was, but no one was there. No one had seen anything, no one knew anything. Along with everything else, I was now without a jacket. I had to go to the barracks supplymaster to confess my "crime," because in the Camp being robbed was a crime. He gave me another jacket, but ordered me to find a needle and thread, never mind how, rip the registration number off my pants and sew it on the new jacket as quickly as possible. Otherwise *"bekommst du fünfundzwanzig"*: I'd get twenty-five whacks with a stick.

We divided up the contents of Alberto's pockets. His had remained unscathed, and he proceeded to display his finest philosophical resources. We two had eaten more than half of the food, right? And the rest wasn't completely wasted. Some other famished man was celebrating Christmas at our expense, maybe even blessing us. And anyway, we could be sure of one thing: that this would be our last Christmas of war and imprisonment.

Questions for Discussion

1. What is the function of paragraph 2? What do you think motivated Levi to describe the nature of Allied bombing at Auschwitz? What has he left unstated but implied?
2. Why does Levi include his glimpse of a Hitler Youth tour in October within an essay that is supposed to be about Christmas?
3. What is the significance of Levi's encounter with Frau Mayer? Explain why it was risky for Levi to fix Frau Mayer's bicycle tire and why he was motivated to take the risk. What did this woman mean when she whispered, "Christmas will soon be here"?
4. What has this essay taught you about survival in a concentration camp? How did Levi survive at Auschwitz when millions of other prisoners were killed?
5. Levi writes that his Christmas package was "like a meteorite, a heavenly object, charged with symbols, immensely precious, and with an enormous momentum." Why did this gift mean so much to him?
6. Does Levi receive any gifts besides food? Consider his relationship with Alberto. Why is the last paragraph an appropriate conclusion for a memory about Christmas?

Suggestions for Writing

1. Write about a time when someone treated you with unexpected kindness.
2. Have you ever been part of a system that treated you as if you were less than human? If so, write an essay showing how you were made to feel bad.

2

Writing to Discover Oneself

Self-discovery is one of the most rewarding activities we can engage in, because understanding who we are can help us to lead the lives we want to have. Although there are some similarities between writing to discover oneself and writing to record a memory—the subject of the previous chapter—the emphasis is different. All of the writers in this chapter make use of memories to some extent; but memory is a means to an end rather than an end in itself, and it is not the only means to self-discovery. To discover who you are, you can look not only to your past but also to your present or future; you can examine your social, cultural, and racial heritage; you can interpret your experiences; you can explore your relationships to your world and to the people around you; and you can simply meditate upon your feelings and your hopes. The writers in this section explore many of these avenues as they seek a deeper knowledge and understanding of themselves.

Most people spend some time trying to figure out reasons for things they have done or felt. For instance, suppose that you normally conduct yourself fairly sedately in public. But one evening, feeling particularly joyous and full of zest for living, you begin to tap dance down the street and swing around lampposts—as Gene Kelly did in the movie classic *Singing in the Rain*. The next day, you are probably going to wonder not only who saw you do it but also, more significantly, why you did it. Attempting to answer these questions can motivate writing to discover yourself—or, more accurately, a part of yourself, for there are usually many sides to what is commonly called the "self."

The answer to the first question, "Who saw you swing on the lamp-post?" leads to the kind of writing in which you discover yourself by trying to see through the eyes of others. Scott Russell Sanders gives us an example of this kind of approach when he speculates about another customer in the restaurant he is leaving:

> She might figure me for a carpenter, noticing my beard, the scraggly hair down over my collar, my banged-up hands, my patched jeans, my flannel shirt the color of the biscuits I just ate, my clodhopper boots. Or maybe she'll guess mechanic, maybe garbageman, electrician, janitor, maybe even farmer.

Imagining yourself through another pair of eyes can lead to some insight about yourself. Although he does not do so, because he is pursuing another concern, Sanders could easily have gone on to reflect upon why he wears the clothes he describes here and what his "scraggly hair" says about him.

The other kind of writing for self-discovery is more common. In this kind we look inside ourselves to discover why we feel the way we do, why we think what we think, and why we do what we have done; in all, we ask why we have, perhaps, swung on lampposts. The most straight-forward way to do this is the way Linda Bird Francke tells a story from her life and explores the mixed feelings she has about her experience. She gives us a context for the precipitating event—the scene at the bar with her husband; she narrates the event—an abortion; and she asks a question that reveals her motive for writing:

> How could it be that I, who am so neurotic about life that I step over bugs rather than on them, who spend hours planting flowers and vegetables in the spring even though we rent out the house and never see them, who make sure the children are vaccinated and inoculated and filled with vitamin C, could so arbitrarily decide that this life shouldn't be?

Her essay is an attempt to answer this question.

Linda Bird Francke, Richard Rodriguez, Scott Russell Sanders, and Barbara Mellix all examine the influence external forces have exerted upon them. You might write an essay along these lines by considering how something (or someone) outside of you has helped shape the person you have become—or led you to do something that you might not otherwise have done. Other writers examine the internal forces that lead them to behave in certain ways. For instance, Joan Didion records observations and events about other people in her notebook, much as you might if you were to follow the advice in the previous chapter on recording a memory. But although her mother gave her her first notebook, no one makes Didion write. She describes her impulse to write as a "compulsion" that "begins or does not begin in the cradle." In her essay Didion then writes about what follows from that compulsion in order to understand her motive for keeping a notebook. Still other writers seek to discover themselves by looking for parallels between what they see in the world around them and how they perceive themselves. Annie Dillard, for example, approaches her search for self-discovery by meditating on the death of a moth at a time when she was unsure of her purpose in life.

You may have felt, upon occasion, that you would like to write something down to express the way you feel about things that have happened to you. Although it can be satisfying at times to write down whatever comes first to mind — as you might, for example, when keeping a journal — you can achieve a higher degree of satisfaction by using writing as a way to understand the significance of what you are writing about. Achieving this understanding requires time and effort. Few people know immediately after an experience occurs what the implications for the future will be or even why they acted in a particular way when caught off guard. Certainly, Linda Bird Francke's account reveals that she has some perspective on having had an abortion, although some people may question whether she really had enough distance to completely understand her decision and its consequences. Distance is essential. That is why writing about a current romance is often difficult. You might write more successfully about a former romance, because there is a better chance you will have the distance necessary for understanding why it worked for a time and why it ultimately broke down. Writing for self-discovery relies upon thought and reflection more than emotion and confession. Thinking can be difficult when your heart is full.

GETTING STARTED

So how should you begin? As always, you have to explore to find something to write about. In this case your motive is clear: You are going to write to discover something about yourself, rather than report something you know before you begin to write. Insight will be generated by the acts of writing. Do not think that writing to discover yourself means revealing a truth that is conveniently stored somewhere in your head. Thinking in these terms can lead you to believe that there is only one truth about your life, some sort of magic key that makes sense of everything. Self-discovery can always lead to new perceptions. There is no single "right answer."

To see how to proceed, you can look at the beginnings of the essays in this chapter — though by no means do they represent all of the ways you can get started. For example, Scott Russell Sanders tells us he was inspired by a newspaper report that Indiana leads the nation in fat; Joan Didion is motivated to write by rereading her notebook. Perhaps something you read — newspaper, magazine, novel, even a textbook — will unlock reflections for you, too.

Conversations may also lead to self-discovery. If you've ever said something you later regretted, or continued a conversation in your mind in an attempt to figure out what was really being said, you may be able to write an essay that resolves a puzzling exchange of words. Barbara Mellix, for example, begins her essay with words she spoke to her daughter. Or think about some event that has left you feeling a little uneasy. Writing to understand your response may lead to a good essay.

Many people have physical attributes they would like to change, such as being too fat or too thin, and some they cannot change, such as being tall or short. Richard Rodriguez uses one of these, the color of his skin, as a catalyst for writing about how he sees himself. You might write an essay on how you feel about your own complexion or some other physical attribute, be it the feel of your hair or the shape of your nose. Or you might write about a habit you would like to change. Have your friends told you they wish you would stop drumming your fingers on the table? You might want to explore that behavior to see why you do it, when you began it, if it has ever bothered anyone before, and so on. An alternative approach is to explore the significance of behavior with which you are perfectly content. For instance, if you enjoy getting up earlier than most people, you might explore how early rising affects you.

However you choose to proceed, recognize that there are many ways to express what you know about yourself without becoming confessional. And you may feel more comfortable writing about something that is already "public," in that it involves an attribute or behavior that other people can see, rather than trying to write about a private concern that you are not likely to talk about.

Search through your memories to see whether you can find some that are particularly significant for having made you the way you are. Perhaps you can pull those together to show, for instance, the development of an interest in art or the ways travel made you more tolerant of other people's customs. Still another direction you might take involves seeing yourself in various relationships with others — family, friends, and so on. How do you think those people see you? Is there a difference in how they see you and how you know yourself to be? Or perhaps you have tested yourself against a current issue and noted some inconsistency in your behavior. For example, if you are a supporter of animals' rights, do you still eat meat? Should this be the case, you might write about why you eat meat or, perhaps, how you are able to reconcile your conflicting values.

Find something in the way you think about other people that makes you uncomfortable with yourself, and examine the implications carefully to see what your attitudes say about yourself. You are a vast repository of information that you can draw upon simply by deciding to do so.

When you have a focus, begin to write in whatever way seems most comfortable for you. But remember that you don't have to have all the answers. Your discovery of yourself can be a work in progress. Be honest, and let your reader see you take some risks; but don't feel as though you have to confess all. If you think certain revelations would be too embarrassing, don't bring them up. What ultimately matters is the degree of insight that you have achieved through writing, not the degree of intimacy with which you have reported your personal life. As Joan Didion's essay shows, a thoughtful writer can discover important things about herself when writing about why she writes. Another writer could address much more personal material without reaching a better understanding of herself. To a large extent, the topic matters less than what you do with it.

WRITING THE ESSAY

The organization of your discovery essay can be fairly flexible. Think of your essay as a quest for understanding the significance of your topic. Some writers like to state this significance as a thesis early in the essay, as Barbara Mellix does; others, like Joan Didion, leave it until the end; and some, like Richard Rodriguez and Annie Dillard, never state a thesis directly.

Wherever you put the thesis, and whether or not you state one at all, you will need to make sure your reader understands your focus and what you have discovered. You can explore important events, ideas, or people to flesh out your account. If a person is a significant part of your discovery, create a portrait to help your reader understand your relationship. Be sure to provide concrete details that will show the image you want your readers to have. Details will make your picture more vivid. But this does not mean that you should lose your focus. A portrait can be created in a line or two when you write about a topic in which a person is only part of the background. Consider, for example, how Scott Russell Sanders makes a waitress come alive before going on to discover why he's chosen to eat certain foods:

> Her permed hair is a mat of curls the color of pearls. Stout as a stevedore, purple under the eyes, puckered in the mouth, she is that indefinite age my grandmother remained for the last twenty years of her long life.

Thinking of his grandmother subsequently helps Sanders achieve a degree of self-discovery that readers can share.

In addition to using narration and description (pp. 33–35), you will probably want to analyze your material to see whether the events you present had specific results or whether they were the inevitable result of some other incident. Many writers find this technique—often called "cause and effect"—particularly useful for self-discovery. For instance, Scott Russell Sanders traces his love of fattening foods back to his farm heritage, and Richard Rodriguez points out how he had incorrectly matched causes and effects when he was a child. Barbara Mellix constructs a causal chain (a sequence in which one cause triggers another) as she probes her past to discover the effects language had on her development as a person and a writer. Linda Bird Francke and Steve Tesich also explore their reasons for significant personal actions.

Think about your audience. Will you be writing mainly for your own enlightenment, or will you be communicating your discovery to someone else? When you write entirely for yourself, sometimes you can take shortcuts in explaining exactly what you mean; but even then, you may want to consider what it would be like to reread your writing next year. Doing so may lead you to write further. If your audience consists of other people, such as your instructor and your editing group, you will need to be careful about what you share with your readers. Honesty is important, but you may regret revealing embarrassing details. Such revelations can make your readers uncomfortable and diminish their ability to respond to your work. Do not confuse self-discovery with self-exposure. Understanding something about yourself, be it large or small, matters more than confessing the intimate details of your private life.

Finally, if you expect to share your essay with other people, try to find a way to help your readers connect your experience and discovery with their own. A poster picturing a bored child sitting in a crowded school room offers this advice:

> Tell me and I forget.
> Show me and I remember.
> Involve me and I understand.

Make clear the significance for your newfound understanding of yourself through the details you select and the conclusion you reach.

As you prepare to write your own essay of self-discovery, remember that you have a unique perspective on yourself and on your world. No one else can know exactly what you know, because it is inside you. What you discover and how much you tell is your choice.

GRUB

Scott Russell Sanders

The following essay includes many details about the author and a cafe where he goes for breakfast. Look for connections between the scene and Sanders himself so that you can understand what he is doing there — and what he learns about himself by reflecting upon his meal. If you are surprised that a writer could discover something about himself by considering why he eats "slithery eggs and gummy toast," ask yourself if what you eat and where you eat it says anything about who you are.

The morning paper informs me that, once again, Indiana leads the nation in fat. The announcement from the Centers for Disease Control puts it less bluntly, declaring that in 1989 our state had the highest percentage of overweight residents. But it comes down to the same thing: on a globe where hunger is the rule, surfeit the exception, Indiana is first in fat.

I read this news on Saturday morning at a booth in Ladyman's Cafe, a one-story box of pine and brick wedged between the Christian Science Reading Room and Bloomington Shoe Repair, half a block from the town square. It is a tick after 6 A.M. My fellow breakfasters include a company of polo-shirted Gideons clutching Bibles, a housepainter whose white trousers are speckled with the colors of past jobs, two mechanics in overalls with "Lee" and "Roy" stitched on their breast pockets, three elderly couples exchanging the glazed stares of insomniacs, and a young woman in fringed leather vest and sunglasses who is browsing through a copy of *Cosmopolitan*. Except for the young woman and me, everyone here is a solid contributor to Indiana's lead in fat. And I could easily add my weight to the crowd, needing only to give in for a few weeks to my clamorous appetite.

I check my belt, which is buckled at the fourth notch. Thirty-two inches and holding. But there are signs of wear on the third and second and first notches, tokens of earlier expansions.

The lone waitress bustles to my booth. "Whatcha need, hon?" Her permed hair is a mat of curls the color of pearls. Stout as a stevedore, purple under the eyes, puckered in the mouth, she is that indefinite age my grandmother remained for the last twenty years of her long life.

"What's good today?" I ask her.

"It's all good, same as every day." She tugs a pencil from her perm, drums ringed fingers on the order pad. Miles to go before she sleeps. "So what'll it be, sugar?"

I glance at the smudgy list on the chalkboard over the counter. Tempted by the biscuits with sausage gravy, by the triple stack of hotcakes

5

slathered in butter, by the twin pork chops with hash browns, by the coconut cream pie and glazed doughnuts, I content myself with a cheese omelet and toast.

"Back in two shakes," says the waitress. When she charges away, a violet bow swings into view among her curls, the cheeriest thing I have seen so far this morning.

I buy breakfast only when I'm on the road or feeling sorry for myself. Today — abandoned for the weekend by my wife and kids, an inch of water in my basement from last night's rain, the car hitting on three cylinders — I'm feeling sorry for myself. I pick Ladyman's not for the food, which is indifferent, but for the atmosphere, which is tacky in a timeless way. It reminds me of the truck stops and railroad-car diners and jukebox cafés where my father would stop on our fishing trips thirty years ago. The oilcloth that covers the scratched Formica of the table is riddled with burns. The seat of my booth has lost its stuffing, broken down by a succession of hefty eaters. The walls, sheathed in vinyl for easy scrubbing, are hung with fifty-dollar oil paintings of covered bridges, pastures, and tree-lined creeks. The floor's scuffed linoleum reveals the ghostly print of deeper layers, material for some future archaeologist of cafés. Ceiling fans turn overhead, stirring with each lazy spin the odor of tobacco and coffee and grease.

There is nothing on the menu of Ladyman's that was not on the   10
menus I remember from those childhood fishing trips. But I can no longer order from it with a child's obliviousness What can I eat without pangs of unease, knowing better? Not the eggs, high in cholesterol, not the hash browns, fried in oil, not the fatty sausage or bacon or ham, not the salty pancakes made with white flour or the saltier biscuits and gravy, not the lemon meringue pies in the glass case, not the doughnuts glistering with sugar, not the butter, not the whole milk.

Sipping coffee (another danger) and waiting for my consolatory breakfast, I read the fine print in the article on obesity. I learn that only thirty-two states took part in the study. Why did the other eighteen refuse? Are they embarrassed? Are they afraid their images would suffer, afraid that tourists, knowing the truth, would cross their borders without risking a meal? I learn that Indiana is actually tied for first place with Wisconsin, at 25.7 percent overweight, so we share the honors. For Wisconsin, you think of dairies, arctic winters, hibernation. But Indiana? We're leaders in popcorn. Our hot and humid summers punish even the skinny, and torture the plump. Why us? There's no comment from the Indiana Health Commissioner. This gentleman, Mr. Woodrow Myers, Jr. (who is now on his way to perform the same office in New York City), weighed over three hundred pounds at the time of his appointment. He lost more than a hundred pounds in an effort to set a healthy example, but has since gained most of it back. He doesn't have much room to talk.

My platter arrives, the waitress urging, "Eat up, hon," before she hustles away. The omelet has been made with processed cheese, anemic and slithery. The toast is of white bread that clots on my tongue. The strawberry jelly is the color and consistency of gum erasers. My mother reared me to eat whatever was put in front of me, and so I eat. Dabbing jelly from my beard with a paper napkin as thin as the pages of the Gideons' Bibles, I look around. At six-thirty this Saturday morning, every seat is occupied. Why are we all here? Why are we wolfing down this dull, this dangerous, this terrible grub?

It's not for lack of alternatives. Bloomington is ringed by the usual necklace of fast food shops. Or you could walk from Ladyman's to restaurants that serve breakfast in half a dozen languages. Just five doors away, at the Uptown Cafe, you could dine on croissants and espresso and quiche.

So why are we here in these swaybacked booths eating poorly cooked food that is bad for us? The answer, I suspect, would help to explain why so many of us are so much bigger than we ought to be. I sniff, and the aroma of grease and peppery sausage, frying eggs and boiling coffee, jerks me back into the kitchen of my grandparents' farm. I see my grandmother, barefoot and bulky, mixing biscuit dough with her blunt fingers. Then I realize that everything Ladyman's serves she would have served. This is farm food, loaded with enough sugar and fat to power a body through a slogging day of work, food you could fix out of your own garden and chicken coop and pigpen, food prepared without spices or sauces, cooked the quickest way, as a woman with chores to do and a passel of mouths to feed would cook it.

"Hot up that coffee, hon?" the waitress asks.   15

"Please, ma'am," I say, as though answering my grandmother. On those fishing trips, my father stopped at places like Ladyman's because there he could eat the vittles he knew from childhood, no-nonsense grub he never got at home from his wife, a city woman who had studied nutrition, and who had learned her cuisine from a Bostonian mother and a Middle Eastern father. I stop at places like Ladyman's because I am the grandson of farmers, the son of a farm boy. If I went from booth to booth, interviewing the customers, most likely I would find hay and hogs in each person's background, maybe one generation back, maybe two. My sophisticated friends would not eat here for love or money. They will eat peasant food only if it comes from other countries — hummus and pita, fried rice and prawns, liver pâté, tortellini, tortillas, tortes. Never black-eyed peas, never grits, never short ribs or hush puppies or shoofly pie. This is farm food, and we who sit here and shovel it down are bound to farming by memory or imagination.

With the seasoning of memory, the slithery eggs and gummy toast and rubbery jam taste better. I lick my platter clean.

Barely slowing down as she cruises past, the waitress refills my coffee once more, the oil-slicked brew jostling in the glass pot. "Need anything else, sugar?"

My nostalgic tongue wins out over my judgment, leading me to say, "Could I get some biscuits and honey?"

"You sure can." 20

The biscuits arrive steaming hot. I pitch in. When I worked on farms as a boy, loading hay bales onto wagons and forking silage to cows, shoveling manure out of horse barns, digging postholes and pulling barbed wire, I could eat the pork chops and half a dozen eggs my neighbors fed me for breakfast, eat corn bread and sugar in a quart of milk for dessert at lunch, eat ham steaks and mashed potatoes and three kinds of pie for supper, eat a bowl of hand-cranked ice cream topped with maple syrup at bedtime, and stay skinny as a junkyard dog. Not so any longer. Not so for any of us. Eat like a farmer while living like an insurance salesman, an accountant, a beautician, or a truck driver, and you're going to get fat in a hurry. While true farmers have always stored their food in root cellars and silos, in smoke shacks and on canning shelves, we carry our larders with us on haunches and ribs.

The Gideons file out, Bibles under their arms, bellies over their belts.

With the last of my biscuits I mop up the honey, thinking of the path the wheat traveled from Midwestern fields to my plate, thinking of the clover distilled into honey, of grass become butter, the patient industry of cows and bees and the keepers of cows and bees. Few of us still work on the land, even here in Indiana. Few of us raise big families, few of us look after herds of animals, few of us bend our backs all day, few of us build or plow or bake or churn. Secretaries of Agriculture tell us that only four percent of our population feeds the other ninety-six percent. I have known and admired enough farmers to find that a gloomy statistic.

I am stuffed. I rise, stretch, shuffle toward the case register. The woman in the fringed vest looks up from her *Cosmopolitan* as I pass her booth. She might figure me for a carpenter, noticing my beard, the scraggly hair down over my collar, my banged-up hands, my patched jeans, my flannel shirt the color of the biscuits I just ate, my clodhopper boots. Or maybe she'll guess mechanic, maybe garbageman, electrician, janitor, maybe even farmer.

I pluck a toothpick from a box near the cash register and idly chew 25 on it while the waitress makes change. "You hurry back," she calls after me.

"I will, ma'am," I tell her.

On the sidewalk out front of Ladyman's, I throw my toothpick in a green trash barrel that is stenciled with the motto "Fight Dirty." I start the car, wincing at the sound of three cylinders clapping. I remember yesterday's rainwater shimmering in the basement, remember the house empty of my family, who are away frolicking with relatives. Before letting out the clutch, I let out my belt a notch, to accommodate those biscuits. Thirty-three inches. One inch closer to the ranks of the fat. I decide to split some wood this morning, turn the compost from the right-hand bin to the left, lay up stones along the edge of the wildflower bed, sweat hard enough to work up an appetite for lunch.

Questions for Discussion

1. Why is Sanders eating breakfast in a restaurant? Why has he chosen Ladyman's when he could be dining on "croissants and espresso and quiche"?
2. Why is it that Sanders hesitates to eat food that he enjoys? How has his life changed since he was a young man?
3. The essay begins with what turns out to be an exaggeration about Indiana. Why do you think Sanders waits for several paragraphs before reporting more about the study first cited in paragraph 1?
4. What role does the waitress play in this essay? How does she help Sanders enjoy a bad meal?
5. Consider the description of himself that Sanders provides in paragraphs 3 and 24. Why is it misleading? What is the woman reading *Cosmopolitan* unlikely to realize?

Suggestions for Writing

1. Are there any foods that you enjoy even though you know they are not good for you? Of all the things you eat, is there any food that you are most likely to eat when you are alone? Write an essay about eating that will reveal something about yourself.
2. Visit a place that reminds you of your past. Write a description of it that will make readers understand what you see and feel when you visit there.

COMPLEXION

Richard Rodriguez

Born and raised in California and holding a bachelor's degree from Stanford University and a doctorate in English Renaissance literature from the University of California at Berkeley, Richard Rodriguez is a professional writer and lecturer. "Complexion," from his autobiography Hunger of Memory: The Education of Richard Rodriguez, *refers to the color and condition of skin, but it also suggests a pun on the word* complex. *Consider how Rodriguez explores* complexion *as a way of understanding himself in relation to his heritage. You might also ponder what he means his readers to understand when he says he saw his "dark self, lit by chandelier light, in a tall hallway mirror." Ask yourself if you have a "dark self," whatever the color of your skin may be.*

Regarding my family, I see faces that do not closely resemble my own. Like some other Mexican families, my family suggests Mexico's confused colonial past. Gathered around a table, we appear to be from separate continents. My father's face recalls faces I have seen in France. His complexion is white — he does not tan; he does not burn. Over the years, his dark wavy hair has grayed handsomely. But with time his face has sagged to a perpetual sigh. My mother, whose surname is inexplicably Irish — Moran — has an olive complexion. People have frequently wondered if, perhaps, she is Italian or Portuguese. And, in fact, she looks as though she could be from southern Europe. My mother's face has not aged as quickly as the rest of her body; it remains smooth and glowing — a cool tan — which her gray hair cleanly accentuates. My older brother has inherited her good looks. When he was a boy people would tell him that he looked like Mario Lanza, and hearing it he would smile with dimpled assurance. He would come home from high school with girl friends who seemed to me glamorous (because they were) blonds. And during those years I envied him his skin that burned red and peeled like the skin of the *gringos*. His complexion never darkened like mine. My youngest sister is exotically pale, almost ashen. She is delicately featured, Near Eastern, people have said. Only my older sister has a complexion as dark as mine, though her facial features are much less harshly defined than my own. To many people meeting her, she seems (they say) Polynesian. I am the only one in the family whose face is severely cut to the line of ancient Indian ancestors. My face is mournfully long, in the classical Indian manner; my profile suggests one of those beak-nosed Mayan sculptures — the eaglelike face upturned, open-mouthed, against the deserted, primitive sky.

"We are Mexicans," my mother and father would say, and taught their four children to say whenever we (often) were asked about our ancestry. My mother and father scorned those "white" Mexican-Americans who tried to pass themselves off as Spanish. My parents would never have thought of denying their ancestry. I never denied it: My ancestry is Mexican, I told strangers mechanically. But I never forgot that only my older sister's complexion was as dark as mine.

My older sister never spoke to me about her complexion when she was a girl. But I guessed that she found her dark skin a burden. I knew that she suffered for being a "nigger." As she came home from grammar school, little boys came up behind her and pushed her down to the sidewalk. In high school, she struggled in the adolescent competition for boyfriends in a world of football games and proms, a world where her looks were plainly uncommon. In college, she was afraid and scornful when dark-skinned foreign students from countries like Turkey and India found her attractive. She revealed her fear of dark skin to me only in adulthood when, regarding her own three children, she quietly admitted relief that they were all light.

That is the kind of remark women in my family have often made before. As a boy, I'd stay in the kitchen (never seeming to attract any notice), listening while my aunts spoke of their pleasure at having light children. (The men, some of whom were dark-skinned from years of working out of doors, would be in another part of the house.) It was the woman's spoken concern: the fear of having a dark-skinned son or daughter. Remedies were exchanged. One aunt prescribed to her sisters the elixir of large doses of castor oil during the last weeks of pregnancy. (The remedy risked an abortion.) Children born dark grew up to have their faces treated regularly with a mixture of egg white and lemon juice concentrate. (In my case, the solution never would take.) One Mexican-American friend of my mother's, who regarded it a special blessing that she had a measure of English blood, spoke disparagingly of her husband, a construction worker, for being so dark. "He doesn't take care of himself," she complained. But the remark, I noticed, annoyed my mother, who sat tracing an invisible design with her finger on the tablecloth.

There was affection too and a kind of humor about these matters. *5* With daring tenderness, one of my uncles would refer to his wife as *mi negra*.° An aunt regularly called her dark child *mi feito* (my little ugly one), her smile only partially hidden as she bent down to dig her mouth under his ticklish chin. And at times relatives spoke scornfully of pale, white skin. A *gringo's* skin resembled *masa* — baker's dough — someone remarked. Everyone laughed. Voices chuckled over the fact that the *gringos* spent so many hours in summer sunning themselves ("They need to get sun because they look like *los muertos*.°")

I heard the laughing but remembered what the women had said, with unsmiling voices, concerning dark skin. Nothing I heard outside the house, regarding my skin, was so impressive to me.

---

mi negra: My negress.
los muertos: The dead.

In public I occasionally heard racial slurs. Complete strangers would yell out at me. A teenager drove past, shouting, "Hey, Greaser! Hey, Pancho!" Over his shoulder I saw the giggling face of his girl friend. A boy pedaled by and announced matter-of-factly, "I pee on dirty Mexicans." Such remarks would be said so casually that I wouldn't quickly realize that they were being addressed to me. When I did, I would be paralyzed with embarrassment, unable to return the insult. (Those times I happened to be with white grammar school friends, *they* shouted back. Imbued with the mysterious kindness of children, my friends would never ask later why I hadn't yelled out in my own defense.)

In all, there could not have been more than a dozen incidents of name-calling. That there were so few suggests that I was not a primary victim of racial abuse. But that, even today, I can clearly remember particular incidents is proof of their impact. Because of such incidents, I listened when my parents remarked that Mexicans were often mistreated in California border towns. And in Texas. I listened carefully when I heard that two of my cousins had been refused admittance to an "all-white" swimming pool. And that an uncle had been told by some man to go back to Africa. I followed the progress of the southern black civil rights movement, which was gaining prominent notice in Sacramento's afternoon newspaper. But what most intrigued me was the connection between dark skin and poverty. Because I heard my mother speak so often about the relegation of dark people to menial labor, I considered the great victims of racism to be those who were poor and forced to do menial work. People like the farmworkers whose skin was dark from the sun.

After meeting a black grammar school friend of my sister's, I remember thinking that she wasn't really "black." What interested me was the fact that she wasn't poor. (Her well-dressed parents would come by after work to pick her up in a shiny green Oldsmobile.) By contrast, the garbage men who appeared every Friday morning seemed to me unmistakably black. (I didn't bother to ask my parents why Sacramento garbage men always were black. I thought I knew.) One morning I was in the backyard when a man opened the gate. He was an ugly, square-faced black man with popping red eyes, a pail slung over his shoulder. As he approached, I stood up. And in a voice that seemd to me very weak, I piped, "Hi." But the man paid me no heed. He strode past to the can by the garage. In a single broad movement, he overturned its contents into his larger pail. Our can came crashing down as he turned and left me watching, in awe.

"*Pobres negros°,*" my mother remarked when she'd notice a headline   10
in the paper about a civil rights demonstration in the South. "How the *gringos* mistreat them." In the same tone of voice she'd tell me about the mistreatment her brother endured years before. (After my grandfather's

Pobres negros: Poor negroes. *Pobre* can also mean "poor man," as it does later in this paragraph.

death, my grandmother had come to America with her son and five daughters.) "My sisters, we were still all just teenagers. And since *mi pápa* was dead, my brother had to be the head of the family. He had to support us, to find work. But what skills did he have! Twenty years old. *Pobre*. He was tall, like your grandfather. And strong. He did construction work. 'Construction!' The *gringos* kept him digging all day, doing the dirtiest jobs. And they would pay him next to nothing. Sometimes they promised him one salary and paid him less when he finished. But what could he do? Report them? We weren't citizens then. He didn't even know English. And he was dark. What chances could he have? As soon as we sisters got older, he went right back to Mexico. He hated this country. He looked so tired when he left. Already with a hunchback. Still in his twenties. But old-looking. No life for him here. *Pobre*."

Dark skin was for my mother the most important symbol of a life of oppressive labor and poverty. But both my parents recognized other symbols as well.

My father noticed the feel of every hand he shook. (He'd smile sometimes — marvel more than scorn — remembering a man he'd met who had soft, uncalloused hands.)

My mother would grab a towel in the kitchen and rub my oily face sore when I came in from playing outside. "Clean the *grasa* off of your face!" (*Greaser!*)

Symbols: When my older sister, then in high school, asked my mother if she could do light housework in the afternoons for a rich lady we knew, my mother was frightened by the idea. For several weeks she troubled over it before granting conditional permission: "Just remember, you're not a maid. I don't want you wearing a uniform." My father echoed the same warning. Walking with him past a hotel, I watched as he stared at a doorman dressed like a Beefeater. "How can anyone let himself be dressed up like that? Like a clown. Don't you ever get a job where you have to put on a uniform." In summertime neighbors would ask me if I wanted to earn extra money by mowing their lawns. Again and again my mother worried: "Why did they ask *you*? Can't you find anything better?" Inevitably, she'd relent. She knew I needed the money. But I was instructed to work after dinner. ("When the sun's not so hot.") Even then, I'd have to wear a hat. *Un sombrero de* baseball.

(*Sombrero*. Watching gray cowboy movies, I'd brood over the meaning of the broad-rimmed hat — that troubling symbol — which comically distinguished a Mexican cowboy from real cowboys.) 15

From my father came no warnings concerning the sun. His fear was of dark factory jobs. He remembered too well his first jobs when he came to this country, not intending to stay, just to earn money enough to sail on to Australia. (In Mexico he had heard too many stories of discrimination in *los Estados Unidos*. So it was Australia, that distant island-continent, that loomed in his imagination as his "America.") The work my father found in San Francisco was work for the unskilled. A factory job. Then a cannery job. (He'd remember the noise and the heat.) Then a job at a warehouse. (He'd remember the dark stench of old urine.) At one place there were fistfights; at another a supervisor who hated Chinese and Mexicans. Nowhere a union.

His memory of himself in those years is held by those jobs. Never making money enough for passage to Australia; slowly giving up the plan of returning to school to resume his third-grade education — to become an engineer. My memory of him in those years, however, is lifted from photographs in the family album which show him on his honeymoon with my mother — the woman who had convinced him to stay in America. I have studied their photographs often, seeking to find in those figures some clear resemblance to the man and the woman I've known as my parents. But the youthful faces in the photos remain, behind dark glasses, shadowy figures anticipating my mother and father.

They are pictured on the grounds of the Coronado Hotel near San Diego, standing in the pale light of a winter afternoon. She is wearing slacks. Her hair falls seductively over one side of her face. He appears wearing a double-breasted suit, an unneeded raincoat draped over his arm. Another shows them standing together, solemnly staring ahead. Their shoulders barely are touching. There is to their pose an aristocratic formality, an elegant Latin hauteur.

The man in those pictures is the same man who was fascinated by Italian grand opera. I have never known just what my father saw in the spectacle, but he has told me that he would take my mother to the Opera House every Friday night — if he had money enough for orchestra seats. ("Why go to sit in the balcony?") On Sundays he'd don Italian silk scarves and a camel's hair coat to take his new wife to the polo matches in Golden Gate Park. But one weekend my father stopped going to the opera and polo matches. He would blame the change in his life on one job — a warehouse job, working for a large corporation which today advertises its products with the smiling faces of children. "They made me an old man before my time," he'd say to me many years later. Afterward, jobs got easier and cleaner. Eventually, in middle age, he got a job making false teeth. But his youth was spent at the warehouse. "Everything changed," his wife remembers. The dapper young man in the old photographs yielded to the man I saw after dinner: haggard, asleep on the sofa. During "The Ed Sullivan Show" on Sunday nights, when Roberta Peters or Licia Albanese would appear on the tiny blue screen, his head would jerk up alert. He'd sit forward while the notes of Puccini sounded before him. ("Un bel dí.")

By the time they had a family, my parents no longer dressed in very fine clothes. Those symbols of great wealth and the reality of their lives too noisily clashed. No longer did they try to fit themselves, like paper- *20* doll figures, behind trappings so foreign to their actual lives. My father no longer wore silk scarves or expensive wool suits. He sold his tuxedo to a second-hand store for five dollars. My mother sold her rabbit fur coat to the wife of a Spanish radio station disc jockey. ("It looks better on you than it does on me." she kept telling the lady until the sale was completed.) I was six years old at the time, but I recall watching the transaction with complete understanding. The woman I knew as my mother was already physically unlike the woman in her honeymoon photos. My mother's hair was short. Her shoulders were thick from carrying children. Her fingers were swollen red, toughened by housecleaning. Already my mother would admit to foreseeing herself in her own mother, a woman grown old, bald and bowlegged, after a hard lifetime of working.

In their manner, both my parents continued to respect the symbols of what they considered to be upper-class life. Very early, they taught me the *propio*° way of eating *como los ricos*. And I was carefully taught elaborate formulas of polite greeting and parting. The dark little boy would be invited by classmates to the rich houses on Forty-fourth and Forty-fifth streets. "How do you do?" or "I am very pleased to meet you," I would say, bowing slightly to the amused mothers of classmates. "Thank you very much for the dinner; it was very delicious."

I made an impression. I intended to make an impression, to be invited back. (I soon realized that the trick was to get the mother or father to notice me.) From those early days began my association with rich people, my fascination with their secret. My mother worried. She warned me not to come home expecting to have the things my friends possessed. But she needn't have said anything. When I went to the big houses, I remembered that I was, at best, a visitor to the world I saw there. For that reason, I was an especially watchful guest. I was my parents' child. Things most middle-class children wouldn't trouble to notice, I studied. Remembered to see: the starched black and white uniform worn by the maid who opened the door; the Mexican gardeners—their complexions as dark as my own. (One gardener's face, glassed by sweat, looked up to see me going inside.)

"Take Richard upstairs and show him your electric train," the mother said. But it was really the vast polished dining room table I'd come to appraise. Those nights when I was invited to stay for dinner, I'd notice that my friend's mother rang a small silver bell to tell the black woman when to bring in the food. The father, at his end of the table, ate while wearing his tie. When I was not required to speak, I'd skate the icy cut of crystal with my eye; my gaze would follow the golden threads etched onto the rim of china. With my mother's eyes I'd see my hostess's manicured nails and judge them to be marks of her leisure. Later, when my schoolmate's father would bid me goodnight, I would feel his soft fingers

propio: Proper; that is, the "proper way of eating" is the way the upper-class people eat.

and palm when we shook hands. And turning to leave, I'd see my dark self, lit by chandelier light, in a tall hallway mirror.

Questions for Discussion

1. How does Rodriguez see himself compared with the rest of his family? Do you think he would change his complexion if he could?
2. How did Rodriguez acquire his concern about having dark skin?
3. Consider the "symbols" in paragraph 14. Why would someone worry about wearing a uniform or earning money by mowing lawns?
4. Rodriguez writes that his father once loved going to the opera but suddenly stopped. What do you think these evenings represented to him, and why do you think he never returned after a certain point in his life?
5. What is Rodriguez saying about himself in the last three paragraphs of this essay? What does he mean when he writes that he was "my parents' child"?

Suggestions for Writing

1. Write about some aspect of yourself that made you feel self-conscious when growing up. Try to show what caused you to feel as you did.
2. How do you present yourself when you are meeting new people? Are you yourself or are you someone else? If you show different sides of yourself to different people, write an essay contrasting two different versions of yourself.

AN AMATEUR MARRIAGE
Steve Tesich

Have you ever worried that you weren't feeling what you were supposed to feel? That something was wrong because you couldn't get excited about some event that seemed to matter to other people? Steve Tesich, the author of Breaking Away *and other screenplays, writes about a number of occasions when, as he puts it, "Nothing happened." As you read his essay, consider the way he presents himself and whether or not he can be taken at his word.*

Everyone told me that when I turned sixteen some great internal change would occur. I truly expected the lights to go down on my former life and come up again on a new, far more enchanting one. It didn't work. Nothing happened. When asked by others, I lied and said yes, I did feel a great change had taken place. They lied and told me they could see it in me.

They lied again when I turned eighteen. There were rumors that I was now a "man." I noticed no difference, but I pretended to have all the rumored symptoms of manhood. Even though these mythical milestones, these rituals of passage, were not working for me, I still clung to the belief that they should, and I lied and said they were.

My twenty-first birthday was the last birthday I celebrated. The rituals weren't working, and I was tired of pretending I was changing. I was merely growing — adding on rooms for all the kids who were still me to live in. At twenty-one, I was single but a family man nevertheless.

All these birthday celebrations helped to prepare me for the greatest myth of all: marriage. Marriage comes with more myths attached to it than a six-volume set of ancient Greek history. Fortunately for me, by the time I decided to get married I didn't believe in myths anymore.

It was a very hot day in Denver, and I think Becky and I decided to   5
get married because we knew the city hall was air-conditioned. It was a way of hanging around a cool place for a while. I had forgotten to buy a wedding ring, but Becky was still wearing the ring from her previous marriage, so we used that one. It did the job. She had to take it off and then put it back on again, but it didn't seem to bother anyone. The air-conditioners were humming.

I felt no great change take place as I repeated our marriage vows. I did not feel any new rush of "commitment" to the woman who was now my wife, nor did I have any plans to be married to her forever. I did love her, but I saw no reason why I should feel that I had to love her forever. I would love her for as long as I loved her. I assumed she felt the same way. The women I saw on my way out of city hall, a married man, did not look any less beautiful than the women I saw on my way in. It was still hot outside. We walked to our car carrying plastic bags containing little samples of mouthwash, toothpaste, shampoo and aspirin, gifts from the Chamber of Commerce to all newlyweds.

And so my marriage began — except that I never really felt the beginning. I had nothing against transforming myself into a married man, but I felt no tidal pull of change. I assumed Becky had married me and not somebody else, so why should I become somebody else? She married a family of kids of various ages, all of them me, and I married a family of kids of various ages, all of them her. At one time or another I assumed some of them were bound to get along.

Marriage, I was told, required work. This sounded all wrong to me from the start. I couldn't quite imagine the kind of "work" it required, what the hours were, what the point was. The very idea of walking into my apartment and "working" on my marriage seemed ludicrous. My apartment was a place where I went to get away from work. The rest of life was full of work. If marriage required "work," I would have to get another apartment just for myself where I could go and rest. Since I couldn't afford that at the time, I said nothing to Becky about working on our marriage. She said nothing about it herself. We were either very wise or very lazy.

We were led to believe that the harder we try, the better we get. This aerobic-dancing theory of life may apply to certain things, but I don't think marriage is one of them. You can't go to a gym and pump marriage. It can't be tuned up like a car. It can't be trained like a dog. In this century of enormous scientific breakthroughs, there have been no major marriage breakthroughs that I know of.

Progress junkies find this a frustrating state of affairs. They resist the notion that marriage is essentially an amateur endeavor, not a full-time profession, and they keep trying to work on their marriages and make them better. The only way to do that is to impose a structure on the marriage and then fiddle and improve the structure. But that has nothing to do with the way you feel when the guests have left the house and it's just the two of you again. You are either glad you're there with that person or you're not. I've been both.

This need to improve, the belief that we can improve everything, brings to mind some of my friends who are constantly updating their stereo equipment until, without being aware of it, they wind up listening to the equipment and not to the music. You can do the same thing to friendship, to marriage, to life in general. Let's just say I have chosen to listen to the music, such as it is, on the equipment at hand.

The best trips that I have taken were always last-minute affairs, taken as a lark. When I've sent off for brochures and maps, the trips always turned into disappointments. The time I invested in planning fed my expectations, and I traveled to fulfill my expectations rather than just to go somewhere I hadn't been. I consider my marriage one of those trips

10

taken as a lark. I have become rather fond of the sheer aimlessness of the journey. It's a choice. I know full well that people do plan journeys to the Himalayas, they hire guides, they seek advice, and when they get there, instead of being disappointed, they experience a kind of exhilaration that I never will. My kind of marriage will never reach Mount Everest. You just don't go there as a lark, nor do you get there by accident.

I'm neither proud nor ashamed of the fact that I've stayed married for thirteen years. I don't consider it an accomplishment of any kind. I have changed; my wife has changed. Our marriage, however, for better or worse, is neither better nor worse. It has remained the same. But the climate has changed.

I got married on a hot day a long time ago, because it was a way of cooling off for a while. Over the years, it's also become a place where I go to warm up when the world turns cold.

Questions for Discussion

1. Although the topic of this essay is the author's marriage, he devotes his first four paragraphs to writing about birthdays. What is the point of this opening? Is it appropriate for the essay that follows?
2. What does Tesich mean when he writes that his wife "married a family of kids of various ages"?
3. Why does Tesich believe that marriage is "an amateur endeavor," not something that can be worked at? Do you agree?
4. Does writing about his marriage lead Tesich to discover anything about himself?

Suggestions for Writing

1. Write about how you felt when you passed an important milestone such as graduating from high school or turning eighteen. Was it what you expected it to be?
2. Have you ever worked at a relationship only to have it fail — or believed that you could have preserved a past relationship by working harder at it? If so, write about a typical evening with that person and try to show what went wrong.

THE DEATH OF A MOTH: TRANSFIGURATION IN A CANDLE FLAME

Annie Dillard

You will find that this essay can be divided into three sections. If the divisions startle you at first, think about how the various parts of the essay fit together. And as you read, keep the essay's subtitle in mind: "Transfiguration in a Candle Flame." Transfiguration means "a change in form or appearance, especially a spiritual change." Dillard includes so many details that you should have little difficulty seeing the death of a moth, but understanding the significance of that death will be more challenging. The subtitle provides a clue. Ask yourself what it refers to, and look for similarities between Dillard and the moth. What could an insect have in common with an author whose nonfiction has been awarded a Pulitzer Prize?

I live alone with two cats, who sleep on my legs. There is a yellow one, and a black one whose name is Small. In the morning I joke to the black one. Do you remember last night? Do you remember? I throw them both out before breakfast, so I can eat.

There is a spider, too, in the bathroom, of uncertain lineage, bulbous at the abdomen and drab, whose six-inch mess of web works, works somehow, works miraculously, to keep her alive and me amazed. The web is in a corner behind the toilet, connecting tile wall to tile wall. The house is new, the bathroom immaculate, save for the spider, her web, and the sixteen or so corpses she's tossed to the floor.

The corpses appear to be mostly sow bugs, those little armadillo creatures who live to travel flat out in houses, and die round. In addition to sow-bug husks, hollow and sipped empty of color, there are what seem to be two or three wingless moth bodies, one new flake of earwig, and three spider carcasses crinkled and clenched.

I wonder on what fool's errand an earwig, or a moth, or a sow bug, would visit that clean corner of the house behind the toilet; I have not noticed any blind parades of sow bugs blundering into corners. Yet they do hazard there, at a rate of more than one a week, and the spider thrives. Yesterday she was working on the earwig, mouth on gut; today he's on the floor. It must take a certain genius to throw things away from there, to find a straight line through that sticky tangle to the floor.

Today the earwig shines darkly, and gleams, what there is of him: a dorsal curve of thorax and abdomen, and a smooth pair of pincers by which I knew his name. Next week, if the other bodies are any indication, he'll be shrunk and gray, webbed to the floor with dust. The sow bugs beside him are curled and empty, fragile, a breath away from brittle fluff. The spiders lie on their sides, translucent and ragged, their legs drying in knots. The moths stagger against each other, headless, in a confusion of

5

arcing strips of chitin like peeling varnish, like a jumble of buttresses for cathedral vaults, like nothing resembling moths, so that I would hesitate to call them moths, except that I have had some experience with the figure Moth reduced to a nub.

Two summers ago I was camped alone in the Blue Ridge Mountains of Virginia. I had hauled myself and gear up there to read, among other things, *The Day on Fire*, by James Ullman, a novel about Rimbaud° that had made me want to be a writer when I was sixteen; I was hoping it would do it again. So I read every day sitting under a tree by my tent, while warblers sang in the leaves overhead and bristle worms trailed their inches over the twiggy dirt at my feet; and I read every night by candle-light, while barred owls called in the forest and pale moths seeking mates massed round my head in the clearing, where my light made a ring.

Moths kept flying into the candle. They would hiss and recoil, reel-ing upside down in the shadows among my cooking pans. Or they would singe their wings and fall, and their hot wings, as if melted, would stick to the first thing they touched—a pan, a lid, a spoon—so that the snagged moths could struggle only in tiny arcs, unable to flutter free. These I could release by a quick flip with a stick; in the morning I would find my cooking stuff decorated with torn flecks of moth wings, ghostly triangles of shiny dust here and there on the aluminum. So I read, and boiled water, and replenished candles, and read on.

One night a moth flew into the candle, was caught, burnt dry, and held. I must have been staring at the candle, or maybe I looked up where a shadow crossed my page; at any rate, I saw it all. A golden female moth, a biggish one with a two-inch wingspread, flapped into the fire, dropped abdomen into the wet wax, stuck, flamed, and frazzled in a second. Her moving wings ignited like tissue paper, like angels' wings, enlarging the circle of light in the clearing and creating out of the darkness the sudden blue sleeves of my sweater, the green leaves of jewelweed by my side, the ragged red trunk of a pine; at once the light contracted again and the moth's wings vanished in a fine, foul smoke. At the same time, her six legs clawed, curled, blackened, and ceased, disappearing utterly. And her head jerked in spasms, making a spattering noise; her antennae crisped and burnt away and her heaving mouthparts cracked like pistol fire. When it was all over, her head was, so far as I could determine, gone, gone the long way of her wings and legs. Her head was a hole lost to time. All that was left was the glowing horn shell of her abdomen and thorax—a fraying, partially collapsed gold tube jammed upright in the candle's round pool.

And then this moth-essence, this spectacular skeleton, began to act as a wick. She kept burning. The wax rose in the moth's body from her soaking abdomen to her thorax to the shattered hole where her head should have been, and widened into flame, a saffron-yellow flame that robed her to the ground like an immolating monk. That candle had two wicks, two

---

Rimbaud: Arthur Rimbaud (1854–1891), a French poet.

winding flames of identical light, side by side. The moth's head was fire. She burned for two hours, until I blew her out.

She burned for two hours without changing, without swaying or *10* kneeling — only glowing within, like a building fire glimpsed through silhouetted walls, like a hollow saint, like a flame-faced virgin gone to God, while I read by her light, kindled, while Rimbaud in Paris burnt out his brain in a thousand poems, while night pooled wetly at my feet.

So. That is why I think those hollow shreds on the bathroom floor are moths. I believe I know what moths look like, in any state.

I have three candles here on the table which I disentangle from the plants and light when visitors come. The cats avoid them, although Small's tail caught fire once; I rubbed it out before she noticed. I don't mind living alone. I like eating alone and reading. I don't mind sleeping alone. The only time I mind being alone is when something is funny; then when I am laughing at something funny, I wish someone were around. Sometimes I think it is pretty funny that I sleep alone.

Questions for Discussion

1. As the title reveals, this essay is about the death of a moth. Yet it begins and ends with paragraphs focused upon how the author lives and sleeps alone with two cats. How do these paragraphs relate to the story of the moth that flew into the candle?
2. In paragraph 1 Dillard jokes with one of her cats. "Do you remember last night?" she asks. Can you explain this joke — and why it is appropriate for the essay?
3. Why did Dillard go camping in Virginia? What does her reading reveal about her?
4. Consider the reference to "angels' wings" in paragraph 8. What does it imply about the moth? Are there any other religious references within the essay?
5. Dillard reports that the moth that burns for two hours was a female, and paragraphs 8–10 include several references to "she" and "her." How would the essay change if Dillard wrote about a male moth?
6. According to Dillard, "I believe I know what moths look like, in any state." Do you believe her? Why do you think this might be worth knowing?

Suggestions for Writing

1. Study the behavior of an animal that you can observe firsthand. Consider whether it reminds you of yourself in any way. Write a description of the animal's behavior that will accurately report the details of what you have seen and, if possible, suggest a parallel with human behavior.
2. Experiment with writing by composing a narrative essay framed, like Dillard's, with paragraphs that seem unrelated to your main story but that are nevertheless related to that story on some level.

ON KEEPING A NOTEBOOK
Joan Didion

Although she has written both novels and screenplays, Joan Didion is best known for personal essays. "On Keeping a Notebook" comes from Slouching Towards Bethlehem, *the 1966 collection that won her a national audience. This essay is built around a series of brief passages that Didion quotes from a notebook she had kept several years earlier and is now trying to decipher. "I have already lost touch with a couple of people I used to be," she writes. One way of approaching her essay is to read it as Didion's attempt to renew acquaintance with the person she once was. As you read it, try to understand what the author is saying about herself.*

"'That woman Estelle,'" the note reads, "'is partly the reason why George Sharp and I are separated today.' *Dirty crepe-de-Chine wrapper, hotel bar, Wilmington RR, 9:45 A.M. August Monday morning.*"

Since the note is in my notebook, it presumably has some meaning to me. I study it for a long while. At first I have only the most general notion of what I was doing on an August Monday morning in the bar of the hotel across from the Pennsylvania Railroad station in Wilmington, Delaware (waiting for a train? missing one? 1960? 1961? why Wilmington?), but I do remember being there. The woman in the dirty crepe-de-Chine wrapper had come down from her room for a beer, and the bartender had heard before the reason why George Sharp and she were separated today. "Sure," he said, and went on mopping the floor. "You told me." At the other end of the bar is a girl. She is talking, pointedly, not to the man beside her but to a cat lying in the triangle of sunlight cast through the open door. She is wearing a plaid silk dress from Peck & Peck, and the hem is coming down.

Here is what it is: the girl has been on the Eastern Shore, and now she is going back to the city, leaving the man beside her, and all she can see ahead are the viscous summer sidewalks and the 3 A.M. long-distance calls that will make her lie awake and then sleep drugged through all the steaming mornings left in August (1960? 1961?). Because she must go directly from the train to lunch in New York, she wishes that she had a safety pin for the hem of the plaid silk dress, and she also wishes that she could forget about the hem and the lunch and stay in the cool bar that smells of disinfectant and malt and make friends with the woman in the crepe-de-Chine wrapper. She is afflicted by a little self-pity, and she wants to compare Estelles. That is what that was all about.

Why did I write it down? In order to remember, of course, but exactly what was it I wanted to remember? How much of it actually happened? Did any of it? Why do I keep a notebook at all? It is easy to deceive oneself on all those scores. The impulse to write things down is a peculiarly compulsive one, inexplicable to those who do not share it, useful only accidentally, only secondarily, in the way that any compulsion tries to justify itself. I suppose that it begins or does not begin in the cradle. Although I have felt compelled to write things down since I was five years old, I doubt that my daughter ever will, for she is a singularly blessed and accepting child, delighted with life exactly as life presents itself to her, unafraid to go to sleep and unafraid to wake up. Keepers of private notebooks are a different breed altogether, lonely and resistant rearrangers of things, anxious malcontents, children afflicted apparently at birth with some presentiment of loss.

My first notbook was a Big Five tablet, given to me by my mother   5 with the sensible suggestion that I stop whining and learn to amuse myself by writing down my thoughts. She returned the tablet to me a few years ago; the first entry is an account of a woman who believed herself to be freezing to death in the Arctic night, only to find, when day broke, that she had stumbled onto the Sahara Desert, where she would die of the heat before lunch. I have no idea what turn of a five-year-old's mind could have prompted so insistently "ironic" and exotic a story, but it does reveal a certain predilection for the extreme which has dogged me into adult life; perhaps if I were analytically inclined I would find it a truer story than any I might have told about Donald Johnson's birthday party or the day my cousin Brenda put Kitty Litter in the aquarium.

So the point of my keeping a notebook has never been, nor is it now, to have an accurate factual record of what I have been doing or thinking. That would be a different impulse entirely, an instinct for reality which I sometimes envy but do not possess. At no point have I ever been able successfully to keep a diary; my approach to daily life ranges from the grossly negligent to the merely absent, and on those few occasions when I have tried dutifully to record a day's events, boredom has so overcome me that the results are mysterious at best. What is this business about "shopping, typing piece, dinner with E, depressed"? Shopping for what? Typing what piece? Who is E? Was this "E" depressed, or was I depressed? Who cares?

In fact I have abandoned altogether that kind of pointless entry; instead I tell what some would call lies. "That's simply not true," the members of my family frequently tell me when they come up against my memory of a shared event. "The party was *not* for you, the spider was *not* a black widow, *it wasn't that way at all*." Very likely they are right, for not only have I always had trouble distinguishing between what happened and what merely might have happened, but I remain unconvinced that the distinction, for my purposes, matters. The cracked crab that I recall having for lunch the day my father came home from Detroit in 1945 must certainly be embroidery, worked into the day's pattern to lend verisimilitude; I was ten years old and would not now remember the cracked crab. The day's events did not turn on cracked crab. And yet it is precisely that fictitious crab that makes me see the afternoon all over again, a home movie run all too often, the father bearing gifts, the child weeping, an exercise in family love and guilt. Or that is what it was to me. Similarly, perhaps it never did snow that August in Vermont; perhaps there never were flurries in the night wind, and maybe no one else felt the ground hardening and summer already dead even as we pretended to bask in it, but that was how it felt to me, and it might as well have snowed, could have snowed, did snow.

How it felt to me: that is getting closer to the truth about a notebook. I sometimes delude myself about why I keep a notebook, imagine that some thrifty virtue derives from preserving everything observed. See enough and write it down, I tell myself, and then some morning when the world seems drained of wonder, some day when I am only going through the motions of doing what I am supposed to do, which is write — on that bankrupt morning I will simply open my notebook and there it will all be, a forgotten account with accumulated interest, paid passage back to the world out there: dialogue overheard in hotels and elevators and at the hat-check counter in Pavillon (one middle-aged man shows his hat check to another and says, "That's my old football number"); impressions of Bettina Aptheker and Benjamin Sonnenberg and Teddy ("Mr. Acapulco") Stauffer; careful *aperçus*° about tennis bums and failed fashion models and Greek shipping heiresses, one of whom taught me a significant lesson (a lesson I could have learned from F. Scott Fitzgerald, but perhaps we all must meet the very rich for ourselves) by asking, when I arrived to interview her in her orchid-filled sitting room on the second day of a paralyzing New York blizzard, whether it was snowing outside.

I imagine, in other words, that the notebook is about other people. But of course it is not. I have no real business with what one stranger said to another at the hat-check counter in Pavillon; in fact I suspect that the line "That's my old football number" touched not my own imagination at all, but merely some memory of something once read, probably "The Eighty-Yard Run." Nor is my concern with a woman in a dirty crepe-de-Chine wrapper in a Wilmington bar. My stake is always, of course, in the unmentioned girl in the plaid silk dress. *Remember what it was to be me:* that is always the point.

It is a difficult point to admit. We are brought up in the ethic that others, any others, all others, are by definition more interesting than ourselves; taught to be diffident, just this side of self-effacing. ("You're the least important person in the room and don't forget it," Jessica Mitford's governess would hiss in her ear on the advent of any social occasion; I copied that into my notebook because it is only recently that I have been able to enter a room without hearing some such phrase in my inner ear.)

aperçus: French for "sketches."

Only the very young and the very old may recount their dreams at breakfast, dwell upon self, interrupt with memories of beach games and favorite Liberty lawn dresses and the rainbow trout in a creek near Colorado Springs. The rest of us are expected, rightly, to affect absorption in other people's favorite dresses, other people's trout.

And so we do. But our notebooks give us away, for however dutifully we record what we see around us, the common denominator of all we see is always, transparently, shamelessly, the implacable "I." We are not talking here about the kind of notebook that is patently for public consumption, a structural conceit for binding together a series of graceful *pensées;*° we are talking about something private, about bits of the mind's string too short to use, an indiscriminate and erratic assemblage with meaning only for its maker.

And sometimes even the maker has difficulty with the meaning. There does not seem to be, for example, any point in my knowing for the rest of my life that, during 1964, 720 tons of soot fell on every square mile of New York City, yet there it is in my notebook, labeled "FACT." Nor do I really need to remember that Ambrose Bierce liked to spell Leland Stanford's name "£eland $tanford" or that "smart women almost always wear black in Cuba," a fashion hint without much potential for practical application. And does not the relevance of these notes seem marginal at best?:

> In the basement museum of the Inyo County Courthouse in Independence, California, sign pinned to a mandarin coat: "This MANDARIN COAT was often worn by Mrs. Minnie S. Brooks when giving lectures on her TEAPOT COLLECTION."

> Redhead getting out of car in front of Beverly Wilshire Hotel, chinchilla stole, Vuitton bags with tags reading:

> > MRS LOU FOX
> > HOTEL SAHARA
> > VEGAS

Well, perhaps not entirely marginal. As a matter of fact, Mrs. Minnie S. Brooks and her MANDARIN COAT pull me back into my own childhood, for although I never knew Mrs. Brooks and did not visit Inyo County until I was thirty, I grew up in just such a world, in houses cluttered with Indian relics and bits of gold ore and ambergris and the souvenirs my Aunt Mercy Farnsworth brought back from the Orient. It is a long way from that world to Mrs. Lou Fox's world, where we all live now, and is it not just as well to remember that? Might not Mrs. Minnie S. Brooks help me to remember what I am? Might not Mrs. Lou Fox help me to remember what I am not?

pensées: French for "thoughts or reflections."

But sometimes the point is harder to discern. What exactly did I have in mind when I noted down that it cost the father of someone I know $650 a month to light the place on the Hudson in which he lived before the Crash? What use was I planning to make of this line by Jimmy Hoffa: "I may have my faults, but being wrong ain't one of them"? And although I think it interesting to know where the girls who travel with the Syndicate have their hair done when they find themselves on the West Coast, will I ever make suitable use of it? Might I not be better off just passing it on to John O'Hara?° What is a recipe for sauerkraut doing in my notebook? What kind of magpie keeps this notebook? *"He was born the night the Titanic went down."* That seems a nice enough line, and I even recall who said it, but is it not really a better line in life than it could ever be in fiction?

But of course that is exactly it: not that I should ever use the line, but that I should remember the woman who said it and the afternoon I heard it. We were on her terrace by the sea, and we were finishing the wine left from lunch, trying to get what sun there was, a California winter sun. The woman whose husband was born the night the *Titanic* went down wanted to rent her house, wanted to go back to her children in Paris. I remember wishing that I could afford the house, which cost $1,000 a month. "Someday you will," she said lazily. "Someday it all comes." There in the sun on her terrace it seemed easy to believe in someday, but later I had a low-grade afternoon hangover and ran over a black snake on the way to the supermarket and was flooded with inexplicable fear when I heard the checkout clerk explaining to the man ahead of me why she was finally divorcing her husband. "He left me no choice," she said over and over as she punched the register. "He has a little seven-month-old baby by her, he left me no choice." I would like to believe that my dread then was for the human condition, but of course it was for me, because I wanted a baby and did not then have one and because I wanted to own the house that cost $1,000 a month to rent and because I had a hangover.

It all comes back. Perhaps it is difficult to see the value in having one's self back in that kind of mood, but I do see it; I think we are well advised to keep on nodding terms with the people we used to be, whether we find them attractive company or not. Otherwise they turn up unannounced and surprise us, come hammering on the mind's door at 4 A.M. of a bad night and demand to know who deserted them, who betrayed them, who is going to make amends. We forget all too soon the things we thought we could never forget. We forget the loves and the betrayals alike, forget what we whispered and what we screamed, forget who we were. I have already lost touch with a couple of people I used to be; one of them, a seventeen-year-old, presents little threat, although it would be of some interest to me to know again what it feels like to sit on a river levee drinking vodka-and-orange-juice and listening to Les Paul and Mary Ford

John O'Hara: American novelist (1905–1970).

₁₅

and their echoes sing "How High the Moon" on the car radio. (You see I still have the scenes, but I no longer perceive myself among those present, no longer could even improvise the dialogue.) The other one, a twenty-three-year-old, bothers me more. She was always a good deal of trouble, and I suspect she will reappear when I least want to see her, skirts too long, shy to the point of aggravation, always the injured party, full of recriminations and little hurts and stories I do not want to hear again, at once saddening me and angering me with her vulnerability and ignorance, an apparition all the more insistent for being so long banished.

It is a good idea, then, to keep in touch, and I suppose that keeping in touch is what notebooks are all about. And we are all on our own when it comes to keeping those lines open to ourselves: your notebook will never help me, nor mine you. *"So what's new in the whiskey business?"* What could that possibly mean to you? To me it means a blonde in a Pucci bathing suit sitting with a couple of fat men by the pool at the Beverly Hills Hotel. Another man approaches, and they all regard one another in silence for a while. "So what's new in the whiskey business?" one of the fat men finally says by way of welcome, and the blonde stands up, arches one foot and dips it in the pool, looking all the while at the cabaña where Baby Pignatari is talking on the telephone. That is all there is to that, except that several years later I saw the blonde coming out of Saks Fifth Avenue in New York with her California complexion and a voluminous mink coat. In the harsh wind that day she looked old and irrevocably tired to me, and even the skins in the mink coat were not worked the way they were doing them that year, not the way she would have wanted them done, and there is the point of the story. For a while after that I did not like to look in the mirror, and my eyes would skim the newspapers and pick out only the deaths, the cancer victims, the premature coronaries, the suicides, and I stopped riding the Lexington Avenue IRT because I noticed for the first time that all the strangers I had seen for years — the man with the seeing-eye dog, the spinster who read the classified pages every day, the fat girl who always got off with me at Grand Central — looked older than they once had.

It all comes back. Even that recipe for sauerkraut: even that brings it back. I was on Fire Island when I first made that sauerkraut, and it was raining, and we drank a lot of bourbon and ate the sauerkraut and went to bed at ten, and I listened to the rain and the Atlantic and felt safe. I made the sauerkraut again last night and it did not make me feel any safer, but that is, as they say, another story.

Questions for Discussion

1. Consider the questions with which paragraph 4 begins. Where else does Didion ask questions? Why does she raise questions instead of simply giving answers?

2. According to Didion, how does keeping a notebook differ from keeping a diary? Why isn't she interested in keeping a diary? What use is a notebook to her?

3. Why does Didion find it difficult to admit her motive in keeping a notebook?

4. What is the "significant lesson" that Didion learns when she interviews a Greek shipping heiress?

5. In paragraph 13 Didion contrasts two entries about women. How does Mrs. Minnie S. Brooks differ from Mrs. Lou Fox? Why does Didion find them worth remembering?

6. How does Didion present herself in this essay? What have you learned about her?

Suggestions for Writing

1. For a period of at least a week, keep both a diary and a notebook. Consider which type of journal you find the most satisfying. Write an essay in which you contrast these two exercises and reveal your preference.

2. Didion believes, "we are well advised to keep on nodding terms with the people we used to be, whether we find them attractive company or not." Study a journal, letter, or essay that you wrote when you were younger. Consider how you sounded then and whether you now find yourself different in any way from the person who wrote what you have just reread. Have you lost a quality that you once valued or overcome a limitation that you now find irritating? Define an aspect of yourself that makes for attractive or unattractive company.

THE AMBIVALENCE OF ABORTION

Linda Bird Francke

First published anonymously in the New York Times *in 1976, the following essay tells the story of an abortion — the author's abortion. As you read it, notice how Francke uses details to give readers a sense of her husband and to convey the scene at the clinic. Try to understand why Francke chose to have an abortion and how she felt afterward. Compare how she sees herself at the end of the essay with how she sees herself at the beginning. What does Francke discover about herself?*

We were sitting in a bar on Lexington Avenue when I told my husband I was pregnant. It is not a memory I like to dwell on. Instead of the champagne and hope which had heralded the impending births of the first, second and third child, the news of this one was greeted with shocked silence and Scotch. "Jesus," my husband kept saying to himself, stirring the ice cubes around and around, "Oh, Jesus."

Oh, how we tried to rationalize it that night as the starting time for the movie came and went. My husband talked about his plans for a career change in the next year, to stem the staleness that fourteen years with the same investment-banking firm had brought him. A new baby would preclude that option.

The timing wasn't right for me either. Having juggled pregnancies and child care with what freelance jobs I could fit in between feedings, I had just taken on a full-time job. A new baby would put me right back in the nursery just when our youngest child was finally school age. It was time for *us*, we tried to rationalize. There just wasn't room in our lives now for another baby. We both agreed. And agreed. And agreed.

How very considerate they are at the Women's Services, known formally as the Center for Reproductive and Sexual Health. Yes, indeed, I could have an abortion that very Saturday morning and be out in time to drive to the country that afternoon. Bring a first morning urine specimen, a sanitary belt and napkins, a money order or $125 cash — and a friend.

My friend turned out to be my husband, standing awkwardly and ill at ease as men always do in places that are exclusively for women, as I checked in at nine A.M. Other men hovered around just as anxiously, knowing they had to be there, wishing they weren't. No one spoke to each other. When I would be cycled out of there four hours later, the same men would be slumped in their same seats, locked downcast in their cells of embarrassment.

The Saturday morning women's group was more dispirited than the men in the waiting room. There were around fifteen of us, a mixture of races, ages and backgrounds. Three didn't speak English at all and a fourth, a pregnant Puerto Rican girl around eighteen, translated for them.

There were six black women and a hodgepodge of whites, among them a T-shirted teenager who kept leaving the room to throw up and a puzzled middle-aged woman from Queens with three grown children.

"What form of birth control were you using?" the volunteer asked each one of us. The answer was inevitably "none." She then went on to describe the various forms of birth control available at the clinic, and offered them to each of us.

The youngest Puerto Rican girl was asked through the interpreter which she'd like to use: the loop, diaphragm, or pill. She shook her head "no" three times. "You don't want to come back here again, do you?" the volunteer pressed. The girl's head was so low her chin rested on her breastbone. "*Si,*" she whispered.

We had been there two hours by that time, filling out endless forms, giving blood and urine, receiving lectures. But unlike any other group of women I've been in, we didn't talk. Our common denominator, the one which usually floods across language and economic barriers into familiarity, today was one of shame. We were losing life that day, not giving it.

The group kept getting cut back to smaller, more workable units, and finally I was put in a small waiting room with just two other women. We changed into paper bathrobes and paper slippers, and we rustled whenever we moved. One of the women in my room was shivering and an aide brought her a blanket.

"What's the matter?" The aide asked her. "I'm scared," the woman said. "How much will it hurt?" The aide smiled. "Oh, nothing worse than a couple of bad cramps," she said. "This afternoon you'll be dancing a jig."

I began to panic. Suddenly the rhetoric, the abortion marches I'd walked in, the telegrams sent to Albany to counteract the Friends of the Fetus, the Zero Population Growth buttons I'd worn, peeled away, and I was all alone with my microscopic baby. There were just the two of us there, and soon, because it was more convenient for me and my husband, there would be one again.

How could it be that I, who am so neurotic about life that I step over bugs rather than on them, who spend hours planting flowers and vegetables in the spring even though we rent out the house and never see them, who make sure the children are vaccinated and inoculated and filled with vitamin C, could so arbitrarily decide that this life shouldn't be?

"It's not a life," my husband had argued, more to convince himself than me. "It's a bunch of cells smaller than my fingernail."

But any woman who has children knows that certain feeling in her taut, swollen breasts, and the slight but constant ache in her uterus that signals the arrival of a life. Though I would march myself into blisters for a woman's right to exercise the option of motherhood, I discovered there in the waiting room that I was not the modern woman I thought I was.

When my name was called, my body felt so heavy the nurse had to help me into the examining room. I waited for my husband to burst through the door and yell "stop," but of course he didn't. I concentrated on three black spots in the acoustic ceiling until they grew in size to the shape of saucers, while the doctor swabbed my insides with antiseptic.

"You're going to feel a burning sensation now," he said, injecting Novocain into the neck of the womb. The pain was swift and severe, and I twisted to get away from him. He was hurting my baby, I reasoned, and the black saucers quivered in the air. "Stop," I cried. "Please stop." He shook his head, busy with his equipment. "It's too late to stop now," he said. "It'll just take a few more seconds."

What good sports we women are. And how obedient. Physically the pain passed even before the hum of the machine signaled that the vacuuming of my uterus was completed, my baby sucked up like ashes after a cocktail party. Ten minutes start to finish. And I was back on the arm of the nurse.

There were twelve beds in the recovery room. Each one had a gaily 20
flowered draw sheet and a soft green or blue thermal blanket. It was all very feminine. Lying on these beds for an hour or more were the shocked victims of their sex, their full wombs now stripped clean, their futures less encumbered.

It was very quiet in that room. The only voice was that of the nurse, locating the new women who had just come in so she could monitor their blood pressure, and checking out the recovered women who were free to leave.

Juice was being passed about, and I found myself sipping a Dixie cup of Hawaiian Punch. An older woman with tightly curled bleached hair was just getting up from the next bed. "That was no goddamn snap," she said, resting before putting on her miniskirt and high white boots. Other women came and went, some walking out as dazed as they had entered, others with a bounce that signaled they were going right back to Bloomingdale's.

Finally then, it was time for me to leave. I checked out, making an appointment to return in two weeks for an IUD insertion. My husband was slumped in the waiting room, clutching a single yellow rose wrapped in a wet paper towel and stuffed into a Baggie.

We didn't talk the whole way home, but just held hands very tightly. At home there were more yellow roses and a tray in bed for me and the children's curiosity to divert.

It had certainly been a successful operation. I didn't bleed at all for 25
two days just as they had predicted, and then I bled only moderately for another four days. Within a week my breasts had subsided and the tenderness vanished, and my body felt mine again instead of the eggshell it becomes when it's protecting someone else.

My husband and I are back to planning our summer vacation and his career switch.

And it certainly does make more sense not to be having a baby right now — we say that to each other all the time. But I have this ghost now. A very little ghost that only appears when I'm seeing something beautiful, like the full moon on the ocean last weekend. And the baby waves at me. And I wave at the baby. "Of course, we have room," I cry to the ghost. "Of course, we do."

Questions for Discussion

1. Why is it significant that Francke told her husband about her pregnancy in a bar? Why does she report the street name and mention her husband stirring his ice cubes?
2. What reasons led Francke to have an abortion? Was it her decision? How did the experience reported here lead Francke to reflect upon her values?
3. Consider the repetition at the end of paragraph 3. What does it imply?
4. *Irony* describes a deliberate difference between what is said and what is meant or between what happens and what is expected to happen. An example of verbal irony is, "It had certainly been a successful operation." Can you detect any other examples of irony in this essay?
5. Why was it necessary to divert the children's curiosity when Francke and her husband returned home from Women's Services?
6. How effective is the scene with the little ghost that Francke uses for her conclusion?

Suggestions for Writing

1. Without feeling as if you have to write about something as personal as Francke did, tell the story of something you did and later came to regret.
2. Write about a personal experience that gave you insight into what had previously been only an abstract issue — something that you had heard about but that had never before touched your own life.

FROM OUTSIDE, IN

Barbara Mellix

> *Barbara Mellix teaches writing at the University of Pittsburgh. By re-counting events in her own life, she shows how language is a means to an end—an agency that can be used for different acts. As you read the following essay, notice how Mellix uses narrative to convey the person she once was and the person she became by learning how to write. When trying to understand how Mellix has changed, consider what she means by her title.*

Two years ago, when I started writing this paper, trying to bring order out of chaos, my ten-year-old daughter was suffering from an acute attack of boredom. She drifted in and out of the room complaining that she had nothing to do, no one to "be with" because none of her friends were at home. Patiently I explained that I was working on something special and needed peace and quiet, and I suggested that she paint, read, or work with her computer. None of these interested her. Finally, she pulled up a chair to my desk and watched me, now and then heaving long, loud sighs. After two or three minutes (nine or ten sighs), I lost my patience. "Looka here, Allie," I said, "you too old for this kinda carryin' on. I done told you this is important. You wronger than dirt to be in here haggin' me like this and you know it. Now git on outta here and leave me off before I put my foot all the way down."

I was at home, alone with my family, and my daughter understood that this way of speaking was appropriate in that context. She knew, as a matter of fact, that it was almost inevitable; when I get angry at home, I speak some of my finest, most cherished black English. Had I been speaking to my daughter in this manner in certain other environments, she would have been shocked and probably worried that I had taken leave of my sense of propriety.

Like my children, I grew up speaking what I considered two distinctly different languages—black English and standard English (or as I thought of them then, the ordinary everyday speech of "country" coloreds and "proper" English)—and in the process of acquiring these languages, I developed an understanding of when, where, and how to use them. But unlike my children, I grew up in a world that was primarily black. My friends, neighbors, minister, teachers—almost everybody I associated with every day—were black. And we spoke to one another in our own special language: *That sho is a pretty dress you got on. If she don' soon leave me off I'm gon tell her head a mess. I was so mad I could'a pissed a blue nail. He all the time trying to low-rate somebody. Ain't that just about the nastiest thing you ever set ears on?*

Then there were the "others," the "proper" blacks, transplanted relatives and one-time friends who came home from the city for weddings, funerals, and vacations. And the whites. To these we spoke standard English. "Ain't?" my mother would yell at me when I used the term in the presence of "others." "You *know* better than that." And I would hang my head in shame and say the "proper" word.

I remember one summer sitting in my grandmother's house in Gree- 5
leyville, South Carolina, when it was full of the chatter of city relatives who were home on vacation. My parents sat quietly, only now and then volunteering a comment or answering a question. My mother's face took on a strained expression when she spoke. I could see that she was being careful to say just the right words in just the right way. Her voice sounded thick, muffled. And when she finished speaking, she would lapse into silence, her proper smile on her face. My father was more articulate, more aggressive. He spoke quickly, his words sharp and clear. But he held his proud head higher, a signal that he, too, was uncomfortable. My sisters and brothers and I stared at our aunts, uncles, and cousins, speaking only when prompted. Even then, we hesitated, formed our sentences in our minds, then spoke softly, shyly.

My parents looked small and anxious during those occasions, and I waited impatiently for our leave-taking when we would mock our relatives the moment we were out of their hearing. "Reeely," we would say to one another, flexing our wrists and rolling our eyes, "how dooo you stan' this heat? Chile, it just too hy*ooo*-mid for words." Our relatives had made us feel "country," and this was our way of regaining pride in ourselves while getting a little revenge in the bargain. The words bubbled in our throats and rolled across our tongues, a balming.

As a child I felt this same doubleness in uptown Greeleyville where the whites lived. "Ain't that a pretty dress you're wearing!" Toby, the town policeman, said to me one day when I was fifteen. "Thank you very much," I replied, my voice barely audible in my own ears. The words felt wrong in my mouth, rigid, foreign. It was not that I had never spoken that phrase before—it was common in black English, too—but I was extremely conscious that this was an occasion for proper English. I had taken out my English and put it on as I did my church clothes, and I felt as if I were wearing my Sunday best in the middle of the week. It did not matter that Toby had not spoken grammatically correct English. He was white and could speak as he wished. I had something to prove. Toby did not.

Speaking standard English to whites was our way of demonstrating that we knew their language and could use it. Speaking it to standard-English-speaking blacks was our way of showing them that we, as well as they, could "put on airs." But when we spoke standard English, we acknowledged (to ourselves and to others—but primarily to ourselves) that our customary way of speaking was inferior. We felt foolish, embarrassed, somehow diminished because we were ashamed to be our real selves. We were reserved, shy in the presence of those who owned and/or spoke *the* language.

My parents never set aside time to drill us in standard English. Their forms of instruction were less formal. When my father was feeling particularly expansive, he would regale us with tales of his exploits in the outside world. In almost flawless English, complete with dialogue and flavored with gestures and embellishment, he told us about his attempt to get a haircut at a white barbershop; his refusal to acknowledge one of the town merchants until the man addressed him as "Mister"; the time he refused to step off the sidewalk uptown to let some whites pass; his airplane trip to New York City (to visit a sick relative) during which the stewardesses and porters — recognizing that he was a "gentleman" — addressed him as "Sir." I did not realize then — nor, I think, did my father — that he was teaching us, among other things, standard English and the relationship between language and power.

My mother's approach was different. Often, when one of us said,   10 "I'm gon wash off my feet," she would say, "And what will you walk on if you wash them off?" Everyone would laugh at the victim of my mother's "proper" mood. But it was different when one of us children was in a proper mood. "You think you are so superior," I said to my oldest sister one day when we were arguing and she was winning. "Superior!" my sister mocked. "You mean I'm acting 'biggidy'?" My sisters and brothers sniggered, then joined in teasing me. Finally, my mother said, "Leave your sister alone. There's nothing wrong with using proper English." There was a half-smile on her face. I had gotten "uppity," had "put on airs" for no good reason. I was at home, alone with the family, and I hadn't been prompted by one of my mother's proper moods. But there was also a proud light in my mother's eyes; her children were learning English very well.

Not until years later, as a college student, did I begin to understand our ambivalence toward English, our scorn of it, our need to master it, to own and be owned by it — an ambivalence that extended to the public-school classroom. In our school, where there were no whites, my teachers taught standard English but used black English to do it. When my grammar-school teachers wanted us to write, for example, they usually said something like, "I want y'all to write five sentences that make a statement. Anybody git done before the rest can color." It was probably almost those exact words that led me to write these sentences in 1953 when I was in the second grade:

> The white clouds are pretty.
> There are only 15 people in our room.
> We will go to gym.
> We have a new poster.
> We may go out doors.

Second grade came after "Little First" and "Big First," so by then I knew the implied rules that accompanied all writing assignments. Writing was an occasion for proper English. I was not to write in the way we spoke to one another: The white clouds pretty; There ain't but 15 people in our room; We going to gym; We got a new poster; We can go out in the yard. Rather I was to use the language of "other"; clouds *are*, there *are*, we *will*, we *have*, we *may*.

My sentences were short, rigid, perfunctory, like the letters my mother wrote to relatives:

> *Dear Papa,*
> How are you? How is Mattie? Fine I hope. We are fine. We will come to see you Sunday. Cousin Ned will give us a ride.
>
> > Love,
> > Daughter

The language was not ours. It was something from outside us, something we used for special occasions.

But my coloring on the other side of that second-grade paper is different. I drew three hearts and a sun. The sun has a smiling face that radiates and envelopes everything it touches And although the sun and its world are enclosed in a circle, the colors I used — red, blue, green, purple, orange, yellow, black — indicate that I was less restricted with drawing and coloring than I was with writing standard English. My valentines were not just red. My sun was not just a yellow ball in the sky.

By the time I reached the twelfth grade, speaking and writing standard English had taken on new importance. Each year, about half of the newly graduated seniors of our school moved to large cities — particularly in the North — to live with relatives and find work. Our English teacher constantly corrected our grammar: "Not 'ain't,' but 'isn't'." We seldom wrote papers, and even those few were usually plot summaries of short stories. When our teacher returned the papers, she usually lectured on the importance of using standard English: "I *am*; you *are*; he, she, or it *is*," she would say, writing on the chalkboard as she spoke. "How you gon git a job talking about 'I is,' or 'I isn't' or 'I ain't'?"

In Pittsburgh, where I moved after graduation, I watched my aunt   15 and uncle — who had always spoken standard English when in Greeley-ville — switch from black English to standard English to a mixture of the two, according to where they were or who they were with. At home and with certain close relatives, friends, and neighbors, they spoke black English. With those less close, they spoke a mixture. In public and with strangers, they generally spoke standard English.

In time, I learned to speak standard English with ease and to switch smoothly from black to standard or a mixture, and back again. But no matter where I was, no matter what the situation or occasion, I continued to write as I had in school:

Dear Mommie,
How are you? How is everybody else? Fine I hope. I am fine. So are Aunt and Uncle. Tell everybody I said hello. I will write again soon.

Love,
Barbara

At work, at a health insurance company, I learned to write letters to customers. I studied form letters and letters written by co-workers, memorizing the phrases and the ways in which they were used. I dictated:

Thank you for your letter of January 5. We have made the changes in your coverage you requested. Your new premium will be $150 every three months. We are pleased to have been of service to you.

In a sense, I was proud of the letters I wrote for the company: they were proof of my ability to survive in the city, the outside world—an indication of my growing mastery of English. But they also indicate that writing was still mechanical for me, something that didn't require much thought.

Reading also became a more significant part of my life during those early years in Pittsburgh. I had always liked reading, but now I devoted more and more of my spare time to it. I read romances, mysteries, popular novels. Looking back, I realize that the books I liked best were simple, unambiguous: good versus bad and right versus wrong with right rewarded and wrong punished, mysteries unraveled and all set right in the end. It was how I remembered life in Greeleyville.

Of course I was romanticizing. Life in Greeleyville had not been so very uncomplicated. Back there I had been—first as a child, then as a young woman with limited experience in the outside world—living in a relatively closed-in society. But there were implicit and explicit principles that guided our way of life and shaped our relationships with one another and the people outside—principles that a newcomer would find elusive and baffling. In Pittsburgh, I had matured, become more experienced: I had worked at three different jobs, associated with a wider range of people, married, had children. This new environment with different prescripts for living required that I speak standard English much of the time, and slowly, imperceptibly, I had ceased seeing a sharp distinction between myself and "others." Reading romances and mysteries, characterized by dichotomy, was a way of shying away from change, from the person I was becoming.

But that other part of me—that part which took great pride in my ability to hold a job writing business letters—was increasingly drawn to the new developments in my life and the attending possibilities, opportunities for even greater change. If I could write letters for a nationally known business, could I not also do something better, more challenging, more important? Could I not, perhaps, go to college and become a school teacher? For years, afraid and a little embarrassed, I did no more than imagine this different me, this possible me. But sixteen years after coming north, when my youngest daughter entered kindergarten, I found myself unable—or unwilling—to resist the lure of possibility. I enrolled in my first college course: Basic Writing, at the University of Pittsburgh.

For the first time in my life, I was required to write extensively about 20 myself. Using the most formal English at my command, I wrote these sentences near the beginning of the term:

> One of my duties as a homemaker is simply picking up after others. A day seldom passes that I don't search for a mislaid toy, book, or gym shoe, etc. I change the Ty-D-Bol, fight "ring around the collar," and keep our laundry smelling "April fresh." Occasionally, I settle arguments between my children and suggest things to do when they're bored. Taking telephone messages for my oldest daughter is my newest (and sometimes most aggravating) chore. Hanging the toilet paper roll is my most insignificant.

My concern was to use "appropriate" language, to sound as if I belonged in a college classroom. But I felt separate from the language—as if it did not and could not belong to me. I couldn't think and feel genuinely in that language, couldn't make it express what I thought and felt about being a housewife. A part of me resented, among other things, being judged by such things as the appearance of my family's laundry and toilet bowl, but in that language I could only imagine and write about a conventional housewife.

For the most part, the remainder of the term was a period of adjustment, a time of trying to find my bearings as a student in a college composition class, to learn to shut out my black English whenever I composed, and to prevent it from creeping into my formulations; a time for trying to grasp the language of the classroom and reproduce it in my prose; for trying to talk about myself in that language, reach others through it. Each experience of writing was like standing naked and revealing my imperfection, my "otherness." And each new assignment was another chance to make myself over in language, reshape myself, make myself "better" in my rapidly changing image of a student in a college composition class.

But writing became increasingly unmanageable as the term progressed, and by the end of the semester, my sentences sounded like this:

> My excitement was soon dampened, however, by what seemed like a small voice in the back of my head saying that I should be careful with my long awaited opportunity. I felt frustrated and this seemed to make it difficult to concentrate.

There is a poverty of language in these sentences. By this point, I knew that the clichéd language of my Housewife essay was unacceptable, and I generally recognized trite expressions. At the same time, I hadn't yet mastered the language of the classroom, hadn't yet come to see it as belonging to me. Most notable is the lifelessness of the prose, the apparent absence of a person behind the words. I wanted those sentences — and the rest of the essay — to convey the anguish of yearning to, at once, become something more and yet remain the same. I had the sensation of being split in two, part of me going into a future the other part didn't believe possible. As that person, the student writer at that moment, I was essentially mute. I could not — in the process of composing — use the language of the old me, yet I couldn't imagine myself in the language of "others."

I found this particularly discouraging because at midsemester I had been writing in a much different way. Note the language of this introduction to an essay I had written then, near the middle of the term:

> Pain is a constant companion to the people in "Footwork." Their jobs are physically damaging. Employers are insensitive to their feelings and in many cases add to their problems. The general public wounds them further by treating them with disgrace because of what they do for a living. Although the workers are as diverse as they are similar, there is a definite link between them. They suffer a great deal of abuse.

The voice here is stronger, more confident, appropriating terms like "physically damaging," "wounds them further," "insensitive," "diverse" — terms I couldn't have imagined using when writing about my own experience — and shaping them into sentences like, "Although the workers are as diverse as they are similar, there is a definite link between them." And there is the sense of a personality behind the prose, someone who sympathizes with the workers: "The general public wounds them further by treating them with disgrace because of what they do for a living."

What caused these differences? I was, I believed, explaining other people's thoughts and feelings, and I was free to move about in the language of "others" so long as I was speaking *of* others. I was unaware that I was transforming into my best classroom language my own thoughts and feelings about people whose experiences and ways of speaking were in many ways similar to mine.

The following year, unable to turn back or to let go of what had become something of an obsession with language (and hoping to catch and hold the sense of control that had eluded me in Basic Writing), I enrolled in a research writing course. I spent most of the term learning how to prepare for and write a research paper. I chose sex education as my subject and spent hours in libraries, searching for information, reading, taking notes. Then (not without messiness and often-demoralizing frustration) I organized my information into categories, wrote a thesis statement, and composed my paper — a series of paraphrases and quotations spaced between carefully constructed transitions. The process and results felt artificial, but as I would later come to realize I was passing through a necessary stage. My sentences sounded like this:

> This reserve becomes understandable with examination of who the abusers are. In an overwhelming number of cases, they are people the victims know and trust. Family members, relatives, neighbors and close family friends commit seventy-five percent of all reported sex crimes against children, and parents, parent substitutes and relatives are the offenders in thirty to eighty percent of all reported cases.[12] While assault by strangers does occur, it is less common, and is usually a single episode.[13] But abuse by family members, relatives and acquaintances may continue for an extended period of time. In cases of incest, for example, children are abused repeatedly for an average of eight years.[14] In such cases, "the use of physical force is rarely necessary because of the child's trusting, dependent relationship with the offender. The child's cooperation is often facilitated by the adult's position of dominance, an offer of material goods, a threat of physical violence, or a misrepresentation of moral standards."[15]

The completed paper gave me a sense of profound satisfaction, and I read it often after my professor returned it. I know now that what I was pleased with was the language I used and the professional voice it helped me maintain. "Use better words," my teacher snapped at me one day after reading the notes I'd begun accumulating from my research, and slowly I began taking on the language of my sources. In my next set of notes, I used the word "vacillating"; my professor applauded. And by the time I composed the final draft, I felt at ease with terms like "overwhelming number of cases," "single episode," and "reserve," and I shaped them into sentences similar to those of my "expert" sources.

If I were writing the paper today, I would of course do some things differently. Rather than open with an anecdote—as my teacher suggested—I would begin simply with a quotation that caught my interest as I was researching my paper (and which I scribbled, without its source, in the margin of my notebook): "Truth does not do so much good in the world as the semblance of truth does evil." The quotation felt right because it captured what was for me the central idea of my essay—an idea that emerged gradually during the making of my paper—and expressed it in a way I would like to have said it. The anecdote, a hypothetical situation I invented to conform to the information in the paper, felt forced and insincere because it represented—to a great degree—my teacher's understanding of the essay, *her* idea of what in it was most significant. Improving upon my previous experiences with writing, I was beginning to think and feel in the language I used, to find my own voices in it, to sense that how one speaks influences how one means. But I was not yet secure enough, comfortable enough, with the language to trust my intuition.

Now that I know that to seek knowledge, freedom, and autonomy means always to be in the concentrated process of becoming — always to be venturing into new territory, feeling one's way at first, then getting one's balance, negotiating, accommodating, discovering one's self in ways that previously defined "others" — I sometimes get tired. And I ask myself why I keep on participating in this highbrow form of violence, this slamming against perplexity. But there is no real futility in the question, no hint of that part of the old me who stood outside standard English, hugging to herself a disabling mistrust of a language she thought could not represent a person with her history and experience. Rather, the question represents a person who feels the consequence of her education, the weight of her possibilities as a teacher and writer and human being, a voice in society. And I would not change that person, would not give back the good burden that accompanies my growing expertise, my increasing power to shape myself in language and share that self with "others."

"To speak," says Frantz Fanon, "means to be in a position to use a certain syntax, to grasp the morphology of this or that language, but it means above all to assume a culture, to support the weight of a civilization."* To write means to do the same, but in a more profound sense. However, Fanon also says that to achieve mastery means to "get" in a position of power, to "grasp," to "assume." This, I have learned — both as a student and subsequently as a teacher — can involve tremendous emotional and psychological conflict for those attempting to master academic discourse. Although as a beginning student writer I had a fairly good grasp of ordinary spoken English and was proficient at what Labov calls "code-switching" (and what John Baugh in *Black Street Speech* terms "style shifting"), when I came face to face with the demands of academic writing, I grew increasingly self-conscious, constantly aware of my status as a black and a speaker of one of the many black English vernaculars — a traditional outsider. For the first time, I experienced my sense of doubleness as something menacing, a built-in enemy. Whenever I turned inward for salvation, the balm so available during my childhood, I found instead this new fragmentation which spoke to me in many voices. It was the voice of my desire to prosper, but at the same time it spoke of what I had relinquished and could not regain: a safe way of being, a state of powerlessness which exempted me from responsibility for who I was and might be. And it accused me of betrayal, of turning away from blackness. To recover balance, I had to take on the language of the academy, the language of "others." And to do that, I had to learn to imagine myself a part of the culture of that language, and therefore someone free to manage that language, to take liberties with it. Writing and rewriting, practicing, experimenting, I came to comprehend more fully the generative power of language. I discovered — with the help of some especially sensitive teach-

Black Skin, White Masks (1952; rpt. New York: Grove Press, 1967), pp. 17–18.

ers — that through writing one can continually bring new selves into being, each with new responsibilities and difficulties, but also with new possibilities. Remarkable power, indeed. I write and continually give birth to myself.

Questions for Discussion

1. Is there a difference between standard English and proper English?
2. How does context determine the language that Mellix uses? In what sort of "other environments" would she be reluctant to use the language she grew up speaking?
3. How does Mellix feel about black English? Does she think it is inferior to the language she learned in school? What obstacles did she have to overcome in learning to speak and write in a public voice?
4. In paragraph 9 Mellix realizes something that she did not realize as a child. What does she mean when she writes that her father had tried to teach her "the relationship between language and power"?
5. What does Mellix mean by "the generative power of language"? How can writing lead someone to "continually bring new selves into being"?

Suggestions for Writing

1. What would happen if you always spoke the same way, regardless of what you were speaking about, where you were speaking, and whom you were speaking to? Write an essay that shows you using language in different ways depending upon context.
2. Mellix reports that her first experiences with college writing made her feel "like standing naked and revealing my imperfection." Write an essay about how you feel when you show your writing to someone else.

3

Writing to Amuse Others

Both writing to record a memory and writing to discover oneself—
the subjects of the two previous chapters—can be done simply for your
own satisfaction. Writing to amuse, however, requires that you focus upon
readers other than yourself.

THINKING ABOUT THE AUDIENCE

If you find pleasure in writing to amuse, it will come from knowing
that you succeeded in bringing pleasure to others. Consider what happens
when you tell a joke. If people laugh, you feel pleased that you told the
joke—and told it well. On the other hand, if no one laughs, you'll probably feel disappointed or embarrassed but not pleased. An egotist might be
so caught up in himself that he doesn't notice that others are not amused
by his efforts at humor, but that may explain why he is not funny: He is
focusing upon himself rather than his audience.

Of course, an audience might be amused even if it is not laughing—
although this is unlikely in the case of a good joke. In telling some stories,
and writing some essays, you may hope only to inspire a wry smile that

seems to say, "I know what you mean; something like that happened to me too." It is a rare and wonderful piece of writing that can make us laugh out loud. More common, but not necessarily less valuable, is writing that makes us smile at aspects of life about which we have mixed feelings — things that we can enjoy making fun of but would hesitate to abandon altogether. Woody Allen, for example, can make us smile at the absurdities of a college catalog without necessarily making us feel that it is ridiculous to go to college. And Mike Royko's essay on fitness can make us laugh without requiring us to believe that exercise is truly silly.

From this observation we can understand a basic principle about writing to amuse: Whether designed to produce belly laughs or merely to bring a twinkle of recognition to someone's eye, humor has an element of tension within it. Despite the great range of material that can be considered "comic," one constant feature is that humor always sends a double message: "Take me seriously, but don't take me seriously." People often laugh because of a sudden and surprising shift between the two parts of this message.

Laughter, however, is not always a sign of amusement, any more than amusement is always indicated by laughter. To release an excess of good spirits, you might laugh when you are having fun, even when no one has said or done anything funny. Strictly speaking, laughter is physiological — a motor and intellectual response that can be produced by many situations. And these situations are not necessarily amusing. Laughter can be inspired in ways that are essentially mean-spirited attempts to deprive other people of their humanity — as, for example, in the once common practice of laughing at dwarfs. It can also signal anxiety, as in a nervous laugh, or hysteria, as when someone is emotionally overwrought and cannot stop laughing.

When writing to amuse, your primary object is to make readers enjoy themselves. You may be funny, but you should also be good-humored. This means having a sympathetic understanding of human frailty rather than a contempt for anyone or anything that seems different from what you are accustomed to. Ridicule is not genuinely amusing, and it easily lends itself to abuse. You should try to laugh *with* rather than *at,* since your purpose is to give pleasure through reconciliation. By helping readers to laugh about their failures (such as the failure to stay on a diet), you may help them to fail less frequently. But by reminding people that failure is not unique, you can make them feel part of a larger community. Humor thus reconciles people to human imperfection.

THINKING ABOUT THE SUBJECT

You are probably wondering by now what types of material lend themselves most readily to humor. Answering this question is like trying to explain why a joke is funny. Part of the problem is that different people laugh at different things, and circumstances can determine whether or not something seems amusing to the same person on any given day. What seems funny in the morning could be annoying in the afternoon. Another problem is that much humor is topical, related closely to a specific cultural context; so that what amused people in the past (and inspired various theories about the comic) can provide only a general sense of what is likely to amuse people today. The humor of Woody Allen's "Spring Bulletin" depends upon readers' having some experience with American higher education in the late twentieth century. Someone from another era or another culture may be altogether baffled by it and wonder how anyone could have found it funny.

Yet Allen's work reflects one of the oldest theories of humor. In his *Poetics* Aristotle wrote that comedy — like poetry — springs from the pleasure people find in imitation. Aristotle argued that this pleasure is instinctive. Whether or not this is true, we can observe young children already delighting in imitation when they see someone mimic another person or when they mimic someone themselves. One way to approach "Spring Bulletin" is to consider it an imitation of a college catalog. And in a broader sense the other selections in this part of the book also involve "imitation" in that their humor depends upon the portrayal of experience that readers can recognize. "Farewell to Fitness," for example, does not imitate a specific form, but Royko "imitates" or re-creates a common situation: wanting to have your cake and diet too.

THE WRITER'S PERSONA

Both Allen and Royko also demonstrate another feature frequently found in writing to amuse. These writers establish a nonthreatening *persona,* a first-person narrator who conveys a particular voice and point of view that may or may not be the authors' own. From the Latin word for the masks used in the classical theater, persona is usually associated today with fiction, but the creation of a literary self (that may be an imagined self) is also useful when you are writing to amuse. One way to create a persona is to make yourself seem like an average but nevertheless engaging person who is faintly bewildered by whatever you want readers to be amused by. During the 1930s Will Rogers achieved great fame by cultivating this kind of voice. More recently, Garrison Keillor and Andy Rooney have succeeded with a similar voice. Professional writers, like professional comics, choose how they want to present themselves to their audience. Although Woody Allen claims to be "an uneducated, unextended adult," he is by no means as helpless as he pretends to be — any more than Mike Royko, a syndicated columnist for a major newspaper, sits around all day eating pork shanks and drinking beer.

In presenting themselves as flawed somehow — uneducated or out of shape — writers like Allen and Royko also draw upon another Aristotelian principle: that comedy concerns characters who have a "defect." According to Aristotle, "Comedy is . . . an imitation of persons inferior — not, however, in the full sense of the word bad. . . . It consists of some defect or ugliness which is not painful or destructive." Like the characters in a comedy, comic writers often seem to have some flaw we ourselves may have. But they do not truly suffer as the result of it, and this is one reason we can afford to laugh. Andy Rooney may be mildly embarrassed that his house needs painting and his lawn chairs need new webbing, but the laziness he attributes to himself seems reassuring. He is willing to drink from the jelly glass when there aren't enough wine glasses to go around, and he remains marvelously patient with some pretty dreadful house guests. We know that he is not "in the full sense of the word bad," and we find comfort in knowing that Rooney is managing to get by all right despite an exaggerated version of our own bad habits.

By creating an engaging persona, writers can make readers laugh with them rather than against them. We may smile at the way Allen, Royko, and Rooney present themselves, but the principal source of amusement is some problem outside themselves that they find hard to take: academic prose, diet-conscious athletes, and irritating house guests. This leads to another important aspect of writing to amuse; although not didactic, it is often designed as a corrective. The assumption behind much comic writing is that if you can make people laugh, they will change their behavior. For instance, although Calvin Trillin does not preach about avoiding clichés, his humor in "Literally" could make people a little more careful about the language they use.

THINKING ABOUT PURPOSE

Writing to amuse can, at times, take less friendly forms. In satire, for example, the corrective aspect of writing to amuse is readily apparent. The writer of a satire has usually withdrawn from the text; we no longer have the sense of a flawed but affable persona. The satirist usually directs attention to the flaws of other people with the purpose of making people laugh at those flaws. The result can be very funny, but it can also be cruel. A basic bond between writer and audience exists even in satire, however. The satirist assumes that someone or some group has departed from behavior that is recognized as acceptable; this presumes that recognized standards exist and that the audience of a satire (if not its butt) believes in the standards that have been violated.

In keeping with its role as a social corrective, writing to amuse often reinforces traditional standards (such as marriage, which provides the happy ending that resolves so many comedies written for the stage). Beneath much humor is the message that people should grow up and stop acting silly, a conservative and responsible message made palatable through laughter.

But humor can also be subversive. As Mikhail Bakhtin, a Russian critic, has argued, comedy records "the defeat . . . of all that oppresses and restricts." The restrictions that oppress may be the very conventions that a satirist would like to restore. For example, the Marx brothers often amuse people by disrupting a very proper and pompous socialite. Or to take an example close at hand: Ellen Goodman challenges conventional gender roles even as she uses them as a source for humor. Although "In the Male Direction" seems based upon the idea that men are men and women are women, the essay as a whole invites men to reconsider what Goodman presents as typical male behavior. While writing ostensibly about housework and baseball, Dave Barry and Anna Quindlen also poke fun at common gender roles.

The disruptive potential of humor may be one reason why some people are suspicious of it. Convinced that comedy inspires social rebellion, Plato proposed banning comedians from his ideal republic, and Aristotle argued that comedy is like a strong wine and, as such, unsuitable for the young. Once people have begun to laugh about authority, the credibility of that authority is undermined. Dictators do not take kindly to jokes at their expense.

It would seem, then, that humor involves a certain amount of tension, because it encourages people to laugh at what, on some level, they think is no laughing matter. Hence, humor can seem to work simultaneously toward both reconciliation and rebellion. The rebellion is against rigid and artificial authority, rules, or behavior; the reconciliation is aimed at restoring a natural sense of community. To take a simple example: Mike Royko assumes that rules governing the way people are expected to behave have become too rigid. He is rebelling against authorities that insist he eat sensibly and exercise frequently. But he is also attempting to reconcile people to what, in fact, many people want to do — enjoy themselves and not worry so much about what seems socially correct.

PATTERNS

The humor of Royko's piece depends upon people recognizing a pattern that has been frequently repeated. This essay would not seem funny if the author were the only person worried about being overweight, or the only person who had to deal with an aggressively healthy colleague. In other cases comic writers exploit the idea of a repeated pattern much more directly. According to Henri Bergson, a French theorist who wrote what critics agree is an important work on laughter, one of the principal sources of humor is a situation in which people behave mechanically, repeating the same motion or saying the same thing. Once we begin to notice this repetition, it becomes predictable — and we are inclined to laugh when our expectations are fulfilled. Students may laugh after noticing that their professor always says "One last thing" at least twice in every class. Cartoons often depend heavily upon this principle of predictable repetition: We know that the Roadrunner will always outmaneuver the Coyote, and the Coyote will always be back in action no matter how many times he falls off a cliff.

Among the readings that follow, Andy Rooney's "Old Friends" provides the clearest sense of what Bergson called "automatism": By the time we are halfway through the essay, we know that Quintin and Barbara can be counted on to always find fault with the home they are visiting. What would be annoying if it happened only once or twice becomes amusing when reduced to mechanical behavior that we can safely predict and thus, to a degree, dismiss.

WRITING TIPS

How, then, can you go about writing an amusing essay of your own? Although there is no formula that is guaranteed to succeed, the following guidelines may help you to get started.

1. *Choose your topic.* Your own experience, or the readings that follow, may suggest a variety of topics. But if you are stuck for an idea, try to identify a flaw in the behavior of people you know. The flaw you choose should be easy to observe so that you can count upon its being recognized by your audience.

2. *Cultivate an appropriate voice.* Address your readers as members of a community who share the same values and have suffered the same problems. Be careful not to make yourself sound superior to your readers or to sound as if you would do anyone a real injury.

3. *Experiment with wordplay.* One of the great sources of humor is the pleasure people derive from unexpected combinations of words. Surprise readers with a pun or a playful variation of a cliché. (An actress of questionable virtue once described herself as being "pure as the fresh-driven slush.") Or you can invent words that are delightful simply because of the way they sound.

4. *Use repetition.* Although deliberate repetition can serve many rhetorical ends, it can be especially useful when you are trying to amuse. The repetition may take the form of someone's always saying the same thing or always reacting in a predictable way — such as Gracie Allen, who, like Trillin's wife (as he portrays her), could always be counted upon to take things literally.

5. *Test your choice.* A good way to measure your success in writing to amuse is to read a draft of your paper aloud to friends. But you should also ask yourself if there is anyone in whose presence you would be embarrassed to read the paper. A good-humored paper should be suitable for many audiences. It should produce a smile rather than a sneer. If you feel worried that your paper might give offense, you may be writing to ridicule rather than to amuse.

FAREWELL TO FITNESS
Mike Royko

> *During the last twenty years it has been fashionable to be concerned about health and fitness — and almost anything that becomes fashionable is likely to attract the eye of a humorist. There is, after all, a difference between being genuinely concerned about one's health and mindlessly following the crowd headed to the nearest gym. Deciding that working out is no longer for him, Mike Royko, a columnist for the* Chicago Tribune, *declares, "pass me the cheesecake." As you read "Farewell to Fitness," consider the way Royko presents himself to readers, and be alert for signs that he may be exaggerating.*

At least once a week, the office jock will stop me in the hall, bounce on the balls of his feet, plant his hands on his hips, flex his pectoral muscles and say: "How about it? I'll reserve a racquetball court. You can start working off some of that. . . ." And he'll jab a finger deep into my midsection.

It's been going on for months, but I've always had an excuse: "Next week, I've got a cold." "Next week, my back is sore." "Next week, I've got a pulled hamstring." "Next week, after the holidays."

But this is it. No more excuses. I made one New Year's resolution, which is that I will tell him the truth. And the truth is that I don't want to play racquetball or handball or tennis, or jog, or pump Nautilus machines, or do push-ups or sit-ups or isometrics, or ride a stationary bicycle, or pull on a rowing machine, or hit a softball, or run up a flight of steps, or engage in any other form of exercise more strenuous than rolling out of bed.

This may be unpatriotic, and it is surely out of step with our muscle-flexing times, but I am renouncing the physical-fitness craze.

Oh, I was part of it. Maybe not as fanatically as some. But about 15   5
years ago, when I was 32, someone talked me into taking up handball, the most punishing court game there is.

From then on it was four or five times a week — up at 6 A.M., on the handball court at 7, run, grunt, sweat, pant until 8:30, then in the office at 9. And I'd go around bouncing on the balls of my feet, flexing my pectoral muscles, poking friends in their soft guts, saying: "How about working some of that off? I'll reserve a court," and being obnoxious.

This went on for years. And for what? I'll tell you what it led to: I stopped eating pork shanks, that's what. It was inevitable. When you join the physical-fitness craze, you have to stop eating wonderful things like pork shanks because they are full of cholesterol. And you have to give up eggs benedict, smoked liverwurst, Italian sausage, butter-pecan ice cream, Polish sausage, goose-liver pate, Sara Lee cheesecake, Twinkies, potato chips, salami-and-Swiss-cheese sandwiches, double cheeseburgers with fries, Christian Brothers brandy with a Beck's chaser, and everything else that tastes good.

Instead, I ate broiled skinless chicken, broiled whitefish, grapefruit, steamed broccoli, steamed spinach, unbuttered toast, yogurt, eggplant, an apple for dessert and Perrier water to wash it down. Blahhhhh!

You do this for years, and what is your reward for panting and sweating around a handball-racquetball court, and eating yogurt and the skinned flesh of a dead chicken?

- You can take your pulse and find that it is slow. So what? Am I a   *10*
  clock?
- You buy pants with a narrower wasitline. Big deal. The pants don't cost less than the ones with a big waistline.
- You get to admire yourself in the bathroom mirror for about 10 seconds a day after taking a shower. It takes five seconds to look at your flat stomach from the front, and five more seconds to look at your flat stomach from the side. If you're a real creep of a narcissist, you can add another 10 seconds for looking at your small behind with a mirror.

That's it.

Wait, I forgot something. You will live longer. I know that because my doctor told me so every time I took a physical. My fitness-conscious doctor was very slender — especially the last time I saw him, which was at his wake.

But I still believe him. Running around a handball court or jogging   *15* five miles a day, eating yogurt and guzzling Perrier will make you live longer.

So you live longer. Have you been in a typical nursing home lately? Have you walked around the low-rent neighborhoods where the geezers try to survive on Social Security?

If you think living longer is rough now, wait until the 1990s, when today's Me Generation potheads and coke sniffers begin taking care of the elderly (today's middle-aged joggers). It'll be: "Just take this little happy pill, gramps, and you'll wake up in heaven."

It's not worth giving up pork shanks and Sara Lee cheesecake.

Nor is it the way to age gracefully. Look around at all those middle-aged jogging chicken-eaters. Half of them tape hairpieces to their heads. That's what comes from having a flat stomach. You start thinking that you should also have hair. And after that comes a facelift. And that leads to jumping around a disco floor, pinching an airline stewardess and other bizarre behavior.

I prefer to age gracefully, the way men did when I was a boy. The   *20* only time a man over 40 ran was when the cops caught him burglarizing a warehouse. The idea of exercise was to walk to and from the corner tavern, mostly to. A well-rounded health-food diet included pork shanks, dumplings, Jim Beam and a beer chaser.

Anyone who was skinny was suspected of having TB or an ulcer. A fine figure of a man was one who could look down and not see his knees, his feet or anything else in that vicinity. What do you have to look for, anyway? You ought to know if anything is missing.

A few years ago I was in Bavaria, and I went to a German beer hall. It was a beautiful sight. Everybody was popping sausages and pork shanks and draining quart-sized steins of thick beer. Every so often they'd thump their magnificent bellies and smile happily at the booming sound that they made.

Compare that to the finish line of a marathon, with all those emaciated runners sprawled on the grass, tongues hanging out, wheezing, moaning, writhing, throwing up.

If that is the way to happiness and a long life, pass me the cheesecake.

May you get a hernia, Arnold Schwarzenegger. And here's to you,   25
Orson Welles.

Questions for Discussion

1. One of the ways Royko achieves humor in this piece is to surprise the expectations of readers. What would someone normally expect to hear after "No more excuses" in a discussion of physical fitness? Where else does the essay take a surprising twist?
2. Depending upon context and purpose, exaggeration can either undermine or enhance the impact of what we write. Where does Royko exaggerate in this essay? Is he using exaggeration effectively?
3. In paragraph 5 Royko reveals that he was in his late forties when he wrote this piece. Why is that significant? Would the essay be as funny if the author were nineteen?
4. How would Royko like to age? Why does he claim to be unconcerned about living longer?
5. Does Royko have a purpose in this piece aside from being amusing? What is he making fun of besides his own appetite?

Suggestions for Writing

1. Identify a current fad and write an essay explaining why you, for one, have no intention of following the crowd.
2. Royko comments on "middle-aged jogging chicken-eaters" who try to seem younger than they are. What about people who try to seem older than they are? Write a humorous essay about teenagers who work at seeming sophisticated.

SPRING BULLETIN
Woody Allen

> *You may have seen Woody Allen in movies such as* Bananas, Radio
> Days, *and* Hannah and Her Sisters. *But in addition to being a widely
> admired actor and director, Allen is also a writer. Hired as a staff writer for
> NBC when he was only seventeen, Allen has written numerous short stories
> and essays. As you read "Spring Bulletin," notice how Allen achieves humor
> by making surprising shifts between the serious and the mundane.*

The number of college bulletins and adult-education come-ons that
keep turning up in my mailbox convinces me that I must be on a special
mailing list for dropouts. Not that I'm complaining; there is something
about a list of extension courses that piques my interest with a fascination
hitherto reserved for a catalogue of Hong Kong honeymoon accessories,
sent to me once by mistake. Each time I read through the latest bulletin of
extension courses, I make immediate plans to drop everything and return
to school. (I was ejected from college many years ago, the victim of
unproved accusations not unlike those once attached to Yellow Kid Weil.)
So far, however, I am still an uneducated, unextended adult, and I have
fallen into the habit of browsing through an imaginary, handsomely
printed course bulletin that is more or less typical of them all:

SUMMER SESSION

ECONOMIC THEORY: A systematic application and critical evaluation of the basic analytic concepts of economic theory, with an emphasis
on money and why it's good. Fixed coefficient production functions, cost
and supply curves, and nonconvexity comprise the first semester, with the
second semester concentrating on spending, making change, and keeping
a neat wallet. The Federal Reserve System is analyzed, and advanced
students are coached in the proper method of filling out a deposit slip.
Other topics include: Inflation and Depression—how to dress for each.
Loans, interest, welching.

HISTORY OF EUROPEAN CIVILIZATION: Ever since the discovery of a fossilized eohippus in the men's washroom at Siddon's Cafe-
teria in East Rutherford, New Jersey, it has been suspected that at one time
Europe and America were connected by a strip of land that later sank or
became East Rutherford, New Jersey, or both. This throws a new perspective on the formation of European society and enables historians to
conjecture about why it sprang up in an area that would have made a much
better Asia. Also studied in the course is the decision to hold the Renaissance in Italy.

INTRODUCTION TO PSYCHOLOGY: The theory of human behavior. Why some men are called "lovely individuals" and why there are others you just want to pinch. Is there a split between mind and body, and, if so, which is better to have? Aggression and rebellion are discussed. (Students particularly interested in these aspects of psychology are advised to take one of these Winter Term courses: Introduction to Hostility; Intermediate Hostility; Advanced Hatred; Theoretical Foundations of Loathing.) Special consideration is given to a study of consciousness as opposed to unconsciousness, with many helpful hints on how to remain conscious.

PSYCHOPATHOLOGY: Aimed at understanding obsessions and phobias, including the fear of being suddenly captured and stuffed with crabmeat, reluctance to return a volleyball serve, and the inability to say the word "mackinaw" in the presence of women. The compulsion to seek out the company of beavers is analyzed.

PHILOSOPHY I: Everyone from Plato to Camus is read, and the following topics are covered:

> Ethics: The categorical imperative, and six ways to make it work for you.
> Aesthetics: Is art the mirror of life, or what?
> Metaphysics: What happens to the soul after death? How does it manage?
> Epistemology: Is knowledge knowable? If not, how do we know this?
> The Absurd: Why existence is often considered silly, particularly for men who wear brown-and-white shoes. Manyness and oneness are studied as they relate to otherness. (Students achieving oneness will move ahead to twoness.)

PHILOSOPHY XXIX-B: Introduction to God. Confrontation with the Creator of the universe through informal lectures and field trips.

THE NEW MATHEMATICS: Standard mathematics has recently been rendered obsolete by the discovery that for years we have been writing the numeral five backward. This has led to a re-evaluation of counting as a method of getting from one to ten. Students are taught advanced concepts of Boolean Algebra, and formerly unsolvable equations are dealt with by threats of reprisals.

FUNDAMENTAL ASTRONOMY: A detailed study of the universe and its care and cleaning. The sun, which is made of gas, can explode at any moment, sending our entire planetary system hurtling to destruction; students are advised what the average citizen can do in such a case. They are also taught to identify various constellations, such as the Big Dipper, Cygnus the Swan, Sagittarius the Archer, and the twelve stars that form Lumides the Pants Salesman.

MODERN BIOLOGY: How the body functions, and where it can usually be found. Blood is analyzed, and it is learned why it is the best   *10* possible thing to have coursing through one's veins. A frog is dissected by students and its digestive tract is compared with man's, with the frog giving a good account of itself except on curries.

RAPID READING: This course will increase reading speed a little each day until the end of the term, by which time the student will be required to read *The Brothers Karamazov* in fifteen minutes. The method is to scan the page and eliminate everything except pronouns from one's field of vision. Soon the pronouns are eliminated. Gradually the student is encouraged to nap. A frog is dissected. Spring comes. People marry and die. Pinkerton does not return.

MUSICOLOGY III: The Recorder. The student is taught how to play "Yankee Doodle" on this end-blown wooden flute, and progresses rapidly to the Brandenburg Concertos. Then slowly back to "Yankee Doodle."

MUSIC APPRECIATION: In order to "hear" a great piece of music correctly, one must: (1) know the birthplace of the composer, (2) be able to tell a rondo from a scherzo, and back it up with action. Attitude is important. Smiling is bad form unless the composer has intended the music to be funny, as in *Till Eulenspiegel*,° which abounds in musical jokes (although the trombone has the best lines.) The ear, too, must be trained, for it is our most easily deceived organ and can be made to think it is a nose by bad placement of stereo speakers. Other topics include: The four-bar rest and its potential as a political weapon. The Gregorian Chant: Which monks kept the beat.

WRITING FOR THE STAGE: All drama is conflict. Character development is also very important. Also what they say. Students learn that long, dull speeches are not so effective, while short, "funny" ones seem to go over well. Simplified audience psychology is explored: Why is a play about a lovable old character named Gramps often not as interesting in the theatre as staring at the back of someone's head and trying to make him turn around? Interesting aspects of stage history are also examined. For example, before the invention of italics, stage directions were often mistaken for dialogue, and great actors frequently found themselves saying, "John rises, crosses left." This naturally led to embarrassment and, on some occasions, dreadful notices. The phenomenon is analyzed in detail, and students are guided in avoiding mistakes. Required text: A. F. Shulte's *Shakespeare: Was He Four Women?*

INTRODUCTION TO SOCIAL WORK: A course designed to instruct the social worker who is interested in going out "in the field." Topics covered include: how to organize street gangs into basketball teams, and vice versa; playgrounds as a means of preventing juvenile crime, and how to get potentially homicidal cases to try the sliding pond;

15

Till Eulenspiegel: A composition by Richard Strauss (1864–1949) inspired by the story of a prankster.

discrimination; the broken home; what to do if you are hit with a bicycle chain.

YEATS AND HYGIENE, A COMPARATIVE STUDY: The poetry of William Butler Yeats is analyzed against a background of proper dental care. (Course open to a limited number of students.)

Questions for Discussion

1. Allen describes himself as "an uneducated, unextended adult." Does he intend readers to take this description at face value? What would an *extended* adult be like?
2. What aspects of this imaginary catalog seem recognizable to you? What is Allen exaggerating?
3. Does this essay reinforce any stereotypes about college education? Who is likely to enjoy it more: an audience of people who have never gone to college or an audience of people who have attended college long enough to be familiar with course descriptions?
4. What do you think motivated Allen to write this piece? Is he making fun of college education?

Suggestions for Writing

1. One way of describing Allen's essay is to say that it is a humorous imitation of a college catalog. Try writing an imitation of a text that you have found annoying: hard-to-follow instructions, a long-winded business memo, or a form letter attempting to sell you something.
2. Write an imaginary description of someone who thinks that any college course is a waste of time. Make your description humorous if you wish, but try not to be mean-spirited.

LITERALLY

Calvin Trillin

"Literally" is set in the country and exploits a time-honored comic theme: the misadventures of city people in the countryside. As you read this essay by a former staff writer for The New Yorker, *consider how Calvin Trillin presents himself and how he characterizes his wife. Note how Trillin creates a humorous conflict marked by different responses to language. The language in question is inspired by the essay's rural scene. But ask yourself if Trillin is making a point from which readers can benefit whether they live in the city, the country, or someplace in between.*

My problem with country living began innocently enough when our well ran dry and a neighbor said some pump priming would be necessary.

"I didn't come up here to discuss economics," I said. Actually, I don't discuss economics in the city either. As it happens, I don't understand economics. There's no use revealing that, though, to every Tom, Dick and Harry who interrupts his dinner to try to get your water running, so I said, "I come up here to get away from that sort of thing." My neighbor gave me a puzzled look.

"He's talking about the water pump," Alice told me. "It needs priming."

I thought that experience might have been just a fluke — until, on a fishing trip with the same neighbor, I proudly pulled in a fish with what I thought was a major display of deep-sea angling skill, only to hear a voice behind me say, "It's just a fluke."

"This is dangerous," I said to Alice, while helping her weed the   5 vegetable garden the next day. I had thought our problem was limited to the pump-priming ichthyologist down the road, but that morning at the post office I had overheard a farmer say that since we seemed to be in for a few days of good weather he intended to make his hay while the sun was shining. "These people are robbing me of aphorisms," I said, taking advantage of the discussion to rest for a while on my hoe. "How can I encourage the children to take advantage of opportunities by telling them to make hay while the sun shines if they think that means making hay while the sun shines?"

"Could you please keep weeding those peas while you talk," she said. "You've got a long row to hoe."

I began to look at Alice with new eyes. By that, of course, I don't mean that I actually went to a discount eye outlet, acquired two new eyes (20/20 this time), replaced my old eyes with the new ones and looked at Alice. Having to make that explanation is just the sort of thing I found troubling. What I mean is that I was worried about the possibility of

Alice's falling into the habit of rural literalism herself. My concern was deepened a few days later by a conversation that took place while I was in one of our apple trees, looking for an apple that was not used as a *dacha* by the local worms. "I just talked to the Murrays, and they say that the secret is picking up windfalls," Alice said.

"Windfalls?" I said. "Could it be that Jim Murray has taken over Exxon since last time I saw him? Or do the Murrays have a natural-gas operation in the back forty I didn't know about?"

"Not those kinds of windfalls," Alice said. "The apples that fall from the tree because of the wind. They're a breeding place for worms."

"There's nothing wrong with our apples," I said, reaching for a   10
particularly plump one.

"Be careful," she said. "You may be getting yourself too far out on a limb."

"You may be getting yourself out on a limb yourself," I said to Alice at breakfast the next morning.

She looked around the room. "I'm sitting at the kitchen table," she said.

"I meant it symbolically," I said. "The way it was meant to be meant. This has got to stop. I won't have you coming in from the garden with small potatoes in your basket and saying that what you found was just small potatoes. 'Small potatoes' doesn't mean small potatoes."

"Small potatoes doesn't mean small potatoes?"   15

"I refuse to discuss it," I said. "The tide's in, so I'm going fishing, and I don't want to hear any encouraging talk about that fluke not being the only fish in the ocean."

"I was just going to ask why you have to leave before you finish your breakfast," she said.

"Because time and tide wait for no man," I said. "And I mean it."

Had she trapped me into saying that? Or was it possible that I was falling into the habit myself? Was I, as I waited for a bite, thinking that there were plenty of other fish in the sea? Then I had a bite — then another. I forgot about my problem until after I had returned to the dock and done my most skillful job of filleting.

"Look!" I said, holding up the carcass of one fish proudly, as Alice   20
approached the dock. "It's nothing but skin and bones."

The shock of realizing what I had said caused me to stumble against my fish-cleaning table and knock the fillets off the dock. "Now we won't have anything for dinner," I said.

"Don't worry about it," Alice said. "I have other fish to fry."

"That's not right!" I shouted. "That's not what that means. It means you have something better to do."

"It can also mean that I have other fish to fry," she said. "And I do. I'll just get that other fish you caught out of the freezer. Even though it was just a fluke."

I tried to calm myself. I apologized to Alice for shouting and offered   *25*
to help her pick vegetables from the garden for dinner.

"I'll try to watch my language," she said, as we stood among the
peas.

"It's all right, really," I said.

"I was just going to say that tonight it seems rather slim pickings,"
she said. "Just about everything has gone to seed."

"Perfectly all right," I said, wandering over toward the garden shed,
where some mud seemed to be caked in the eaves. I pushed at the mud
with a rake, and a swarm of wasps burst out at me. I ran for the house,
swatting at wasps with my hat. Inside, I suddenly had the feeling that
some of them had managed to crawl up the legs of my jeans, and I tore the
jeans off. Alice found me there in the kitchen, standing quietly in what the
English call their smalls.

"That does it," I said. "We're going back to the city."

"Just because of a few stings?"

"Can't you see what happened?" I said. "They scared the pants
off me."

Questions for Discussion

1. *Pump priming* is a phrase often used to describe attempts to stimulate
   the economy by either lowering interest rates or increasing the money
   supply. Consult a dictionary, if necessary, to identify at least two meanings of *fluke* that make sense within the context of paragraph 4.
2. Why is the rhetorical effect of using *dacha,* a Russian word meaning a
   country house, instead of simply saying *cottage*? What is this word
   meant to establish? How does the humor of this essay depend, in part,
   upon the way Trillin presents himself?
3. How many clichés were you able to identify in this piece? How does
   Trillin make these commonly used expressions seem amusing?
4. What point about language is Trillin making in this essay?

Suggestions for Writing

1. Using dialogue, write an essay designed to call humorous attention to
   some form of language that you frequently hear.
2. At the end of his essay Trillin vows to go back to the city. Follow
   Trillin's example and write another humorous essay focused upon the
   misadventures of city people in the country or, if you prefer, country
   people in the city. Try to emphasize attitudes and expectations without
   using negative stereotypes.

IN THE MALE DIRECTION
Ellen Goodman

Have you ever driven aimlessly with someone who refused to ask for directions? This is the situation that Ellen Goodman chose to write about in the following essay, one of the many columns she has written for the Boston Globe — *columns that are now syndicated in almost four hundred newspapers. As you read "In the Male Direction," notice how Goodman writes about a common human flaw — a flaw that she attributes to men. Consider Goodman's tone, and ask yourself whether this essay could be enjoyed equally by men and women.*

There was a time in my life, I confess, when I thought that the only inherent differences between men and women were the obvious ones.

In my callous youth, I scoffed at the mental gymnastics of sociobiologists who leaped to conclusions about men and women from long years spent studying bugs. I suspected the motives of brain researchers who split the world of the sexes into left and right hemispheres.

But now, in my midlife, I can no longer deny the evidence of my senses or experiences.

Like virtually every woman in America who has spent time beside a man behind a wheel, like every woman in America who has ever been a lost passenger outward bound with a male driver, I know that there is one way in which the male sex is innately different from the female: Men are by their very nature congenitally unable to ask directions.

The historical record of their unwillingness was always clear. Con- 5
sider, for example, the valiant 600 cavalrymen who plunged into the Valley of Death . . . because they refused to ask if there wasn't some other way around the cannons.

Consider the entire wagon train that drove into the Donner Pass . . . because the wagon master wouldn't stop at the station marked Last Gas before the Disaster.

Consider even my own childhood. My father — a man with a great sense of humor and no sense of direction — constantly led us on what he referred to as "scenic routes."

But for centuries we assumed that this refusal was a weird idiosyncrasy. We never dreamed that it came with the testosterone.

In recent years, I have from time to time found myself sitting beside men who would not admit they were lost until I lit matches under their fingertips in an attempt to read maps in a box canyon.

One particular soul would consult an astronomical chart for his 10
whereabouts before he would consult a police officer. Another would use a divining rod or a compass before he would use a gas station attendant.

In the 1970s, people believed in roles instead of genes, and I assumed that this behavior came from growing up male in America. I figured that males were taught that being lost was a challenge and seeking help was a cop-out. I assumed that the lost highwayman thought of himself as the Daniel Boone of Route 66.

Finally, however, the new breed of scientists are offering us new insights, not into upbringing but into biology and brains.

The male brain, according to researchers, is organized differently than the female. Men have better spatial abilities; women have better verbal abilities. Thus, we see the problem: Men read maps and women read people. The average man uses instruments. The average woman uses the voice.

Due to this fact, the husband who is able to adequately drive into a toll booth and roll down the car window is handicapped with the inability to then ask the question: "Where is Route Twenty?" A man who can stick-shift and double-clutch, using his right hemisphere, is handicapped by his left hemisphere when it comes to asking, "Do we take a right here?"

It isn't his fault, you understand. It has to do with our Darwinian roots (what doesn't these days?). The primeval hunter couldn't ask a highway patrolman which way the antelopes were running. He had to shut up and follow the tracks. A good berry picker, on the other hand, could follow advice. 15

These primitive differences have all the value of the appendix. They are likely to rupture in modern life. In my own life, the differences between the sexes has led to all sorts of misunderstandings and midnight hysterics. In other cases, they have led to deserted roadways, and divorce instead of doorsteps.

It is time for the female who finds herself in the passenger seat on a scenic tour to take the wheel or to be more understanding. After all, anatomy may not be destiny — but it has a lot to do with destination.

Questions for Discussion

1. Why do you think Goodman begins her essay by claiming that she once thought that men and women were basically the same? Does this strategy give her any advantage?
2. Consider the sequence of examples in paragraphs 5–7. Why does Goodman cite her own father last?
3. What exaggerations suggest that we should not take this essay literally?
4. According to Goodman, what is the difference between the male and female brain?
5. Has Goodman succeeded in calling humorous attention to a basic difference between men and women, or is she simply exploiting a questionable stereotype?

Suggestions for Writing

1. Can you identify another difference between the way men and women typically act? If so, write an essay illustrating that difference in an amusing manner.

2. If you've ever been the passenger of a driver who made traveling more difficult than it had to be, write the story of that trip. Feel free to exaggerate, if necessary, to achieve a comic effect.

A SOLUTION TO HOUSEWORK

Dave Barry

> *According to columnist Dave Barry, "People have been avoiding house-*
> *work for millions of years." To illustrate his point, he describes his own*
> *habits — which include cleaning with a shovel and acid after he lets a bathroom*
> *shower go uncleaned for several months. But as you read "A Solution to*
> *Housework," ask yourself whether Barry's humor is directed only at the*
> *tedium of housework or whether he has other targets as well.*

Almost all housework is hard and dangerous, involving the insides of ovens and toilets and the cracks between bathroom tiles, where plague germs fester. The only housework that is easy and satisfying is the kind where you spray chemicals on wooden furniture and smear them around until the wood looks shiny. This is the kind of housework they show on television commercials: A professional actress, posing as the Cheerful Housewife (IQ 43), dances around her house, smearing and shining, smearing and shining, until before she knows it her housework is done and she is free to spend the rest of the afternoon reading the bust-development ads in *Cosmopolitan* magazine. She never cleans her toilets. When they get dirty, she just gets another house. Lord knows they pay her enough.

Most of us would rather smear and shine than actually clean any-thing. For example, our house has a semifinished basement, which means it looks too much like a finished room to store old tires in, but too much like a basement to actually live in. Our semifinished basement has a semi-bathroom, and one time, several years ago, a small woodland creature crept into the house in the middle of the night and died in the shower stall. This is common behavior in the animal world: many animals, when in danger, are driven by instinct to seek refuge in shower stalls.

Since we hardly ever go down to our semifinished basement, we didn't discover the dead woodland creature until several weeks after it crept in, at which time it was getting fairly ripe. Now obviously, the correct thing to do was clean it up, but this is the hard kind of housework. So instead we stayed upstairs and went into an absolute frenzy of smearing and shining, until you could not walk into our living room without wear-ing sunglasses, for fear of being blinded by the glare off the woodwork. Eventually, we managed to block the woodland creature out of our minds.

Several months later, our friend Rob, who is a doctor, came to visit. He stayed in our semifinished basement, but we noticed that he came upstairs to take showers. One of the first things they teach you in medical school is never to take a shower with a dead woodland creature. We were so embarrassed that we went down and cleaned up the shower stall, with a shovel and acid. But I doubt we'd have done it if Rob hadn't been there.

Our behavior is not unique. People have been avoiding housework   5
for millions of years. Primitive man would stay in one cave until the floor
was littered with stegosaurus bones and the walls were covered with
primitive drawings, which were drawn by primitive children when their
parents went out to dinner, and then the family would move to a new
cave, to avoid cleaning the old one. That's how primitive man eventually
got to North America.

In North America, primitive man started running out of clean caves,
and he realized that *somebody* was going to have to start doing housework.
He thought about it long and hard, and finally settled on primitive
woman. But he needed an excuse to get himself out of doing the housework, so he invented civilization. Primitive woman would say: "How
about staying in the cave and helping with the housework today?" And
primitive man would say: "I can't, dear: I have to invent fire." Or: "I'd
love to, dear, but I think it's more important that I devise some form
of written language." And off he'd go, leaving the woman with the
real work.

Over the years, men came up with thousands of excuses for not
doing housework — wars, religion, pyramids, the United States Senate —
until finally they hit on the ultimate excuse: business. They built thousands of offices and factories, and every day, all over the country, they'd
get up, eat breakfast, and announce: "Well, I'm off to my office or factory
now." Then they'd just *leave*, and they wouldn't return until the house
was all cleaned up and dinner was ready.

But then men made a stupid mistake. They started to believe that
"business" really *was* hard work, and they started talking about it when
they came home. They'd come in the door looking exhausted, and they'd
say things like "Boy, I sure had a tough meeting today."

You can imagine how a woman who had spent the day doing housework would react to this kind of statement. She'd say to herself: "Meeting?
He had a tough *meeting*? I've been on my hands and knees all day cleaning
toilets and scraping congealed spider eggs off the underside of the refrigerator, and he tells me he had a tough *meeting*?"

That was the beginning of the end. Women began to look into   10
"business," and they discovered that all you do is go to an office and
answer the phone and do various things with pieces of paper and have
meetings. So women began going to work, and now nobody does housework, other than smearing and shining, and before long there's going to
be so much crud and bacteria under the nation's refrigerators that we're all
going to get diseases and die.

The obvious and fair solution to this problem is to let men do the
housework for, say, the next six thousand years, to even things up. The
trouble is that men, over the years, have developed an inflated notion of
the importance of everything they do, so that before long they would turn
housework into just as much of a charade as business is now. They would

hire secretaries and buy computers and fly off to housework conferences in Bermuda, but they'd never clean anything. So men are out.

But there is a solution; there is a way to get people to willingly do housework. I discovered this by watching household-cleanser commercials on television. What I discovered is that many people who seem otherwise normal will do virtually any idiot thing *if they think they will be featured in a commercial*. They figure if they get on a commercial, they'll make a lot of money, like the Cheerful Housewife, and they'll be able to buy cleaner houses. So they'll do *anything*.

For example, if I walked up to you in the middle of a supermarket and asked you to get down and scrub the floor with two different cleansers, just so I could see which one worked better, you would punch me in the mouth. But if I had guys with cameras and microphones with me, and I asked you to do the same thing, you'd probably do it. Not only that, but you'd make lots of serious, earnest comments about the cleansers. You'd say: "I frankly believe that New Miracle Swipe, with its combination of grease fighters and wax shiners, is a more effective cleanser, I honestly do. Really. I mean it." You'd say this in the same solemn tone of voice you might use to discuss the question of whether the United States should deploy Cruise missiles in Western Europe. You'd have no shame at all.

So here's my plan: I'm going to get some old cameras and microphones and position them around my house. I figure that before long I'll have dozens of people just *dying* to do housework in front of my cameras. Sure, most of them will eventually figure out that they're not going to be in a commercial, but new ones will come along to replace them. Meanwhile, I'll be at work.

Questions for Discussion

1. What is Barry's opinion of housewives as portrayed on television commercials? Do you think it justified by the commercials you have seen?
2. What does Barry mean by "smear and shine"?
3. Although he is writing about housework from a man's point of view, has Barry confined himself to an audience of men? Are any parts of this essay especially likely to appeal to women?
4. Is Barry making fun of housework in this piece, or is he really drawing attention to something else?
5. Consider the last sentence of this essay. How are we meant to respond to it? What does it say about how Barry is presenting himself?

Suggestions for Writing

1. Identify a job that you try to avoid, and write an essay about how you go about doing so.
2. Poke fun at television commercials by writing about advertisements that you find unrealistic.

A BASEBALL WIMP

Anna Quindlen

> *To set the stage for writing about her own response to baseball, Anna Quindlen describes how Americans behave during the World Series. The scene is New York City, where Quindlen is a columnist for the* New York Times. *Consider whether the scene has any influence upon Quindlen. And as you read her essay, ask yourself whether you would react differently to it if the author were a man.*

It was during the thirteenth inning, with it all tied up at 3–3, that I found myself hanging over the partition inside a Checker cab, my back end in the back seat, my front end in the front, twisting the dials of the radio to find the playoff game between the Mets and the Astros. My driver, who had been tuned to so-called easy-listening music, was a Thai immigrant who seemed to think that what he was witnessing was exactly what you could expect of indigenous Americans. His English was spotty, but moments before I finally picked up the game amid a ribbon of relentless static, he did manage to say feelingly, "You big fan."

Well, no. Actually, I am what is known in the vernacular as a baseball wimp. I ignore the whole season until, each year at this time, during the playoffs and the World Series, I became terribly interested in baseball. You've heard Reggie Jackson called Mr. October? I am Ms. October. Someone very nicely described it the other night as eating the whipped cream off the sundae. At home, not nicely at all, I am described as a disgrace to a noble sport, a fair-weather fan, a Joanie-come-lately.

I've always liked baseball, even as a child, when tradition dictated that I should be prohibited from playing, and my three brothers should be egged on. I like the sense of both the camaraderie and the aloneness of it, the idea of nine men working together in a kind of grand pavane — pitcher to catcher, shortstop to second baseman to first baseman — and the idea of one man looking down the loaded barrel of a pitcher's arm and feeling the nice clean solid thunk as he hits a ball that will fly into the bleachers. (I like basketball, too. I do not like football, which I think of as a game in which two tractors approach each other from opposite directions and collide. Besides, I have contempt for a game in which players have to wear so much equipment. Men play basketball in their underwear, which seems just right to me.)

But I like other things, too. I like the sense of drama, and I have to admit that I just don't find the question of whether someone is out at the plate in the third inning of the forty-eighth game of the season that inherently dramatic. I like a sense of continuity, and in today's baseball you don't get much. As soon as I take a shine to a player, he's gone — to another team or to run a car dealership somewhere in the Middle West. I have never fully recovered from the disappearance of a player from the Yankees called Chicken Stanley, for whom I developed an unwarranted affection some years back, not because of his playing or even his funny name, but because he looked somehow vulnerable and pathetic in pinstripes.

I like a sense of community, and in the early months of the baseball season it always seems to me that the community consists mainly of solitary men staring glassy-eyed at television sets and occasionally saying to befuddled three-year-olds, "Shortstop! That's a good position for you. Shortstop!" On the occasions when I try to join this community, I always blow it by doing something stupid, like screaming when Reggie Jackson hits a triple because I still think he plays for New York, or saying, when a player comes up to bat, "Boy, he's cute," which can throw a pall on the whole afternoon. Playoff games produce real community. I monitored the final National League playoff game in stages: first with an entire office full of people clustered around a television in midtown Manhattan; then in the cab with the radio; next in a commuter bus in which two people were listening to Walkman radios and reporting to all assembled, saying things like "They've tied it up" (groans) and "The Astros just struck out" (cheers), and then to a street being patrolled by a man in a white Pinto who kept leaning out and yelling, "Top of the sixteenth, still tied." I made it home to watch the last inning with my husband.

Baseball at this stage of the game offers just about everything I want. With only a handful of teams in contention, I can keep track of who's who and what they do best, of who can't run and who can't hit and who can't field. Each play is fraught with meaning, each loss a joy or a disaster. And each game is played before great communities of people, in bars, in rec rooms, even in offices, the ranks of the faithful swelled by those who have a passing interest and those who have no interest at all in baseball, but know a good cliffhanger when they see one — the same kind of people who watched the first episode this season of *Dallas* to see what happened to Bobby and then forgot about it. In fact, at this time of year baseball becomes a different kind of spectacle for me, something more along the lines of *As the Bat Swings*. Will Keith lose his temper? Will Lenny be a hero? Will Davey show emotion? Now we get down to the soap operas, and Chicken Stanley or no Chicken Stanley, I love soap operas.

Questions for Discussion

1. What does Quindlen mean when she describes herself as a "baseball wimp"? How well does she seem to know baseball? How typical of other fans are the reasons that draw her to the game?
2. Consider the anecdote with which this essay opens. Why does Quindlen picture herself in such an undignified position? Why does she report that the cabdriver was Thai?
3. In paragraph 5 Quindlen claims that when she watches a baseball game, she sometimes says things "which can throw a pall on the whole after-

noon." What evidence in this essay suggests that she intends readers to be amused rather than irritated by her attitude toward sports?

4. What does end-of-the-season baseball have in common with soap opera? Can you identify the allusion implicit in calling a baseball game *As the Bat Swings*?

Suggestions for Writing

1. Write an enthusiastic account of a football game from the point of view of someone who is watching the game for the first time and not altogether understanding what is happening on the field.

2. Have you ever taken the field but wished you had stayed on the sidelines? If you can make it seem amusing in retrospect, tell the story of a game that went wrong.

OLD FRIENDS

Andy Rooney

> *Andy Rooney is a writer for CBS who achieved a national following through the wry commentaries that he delivers at the end of "60 Minutes." In the following essay he invites readers to laugh at his troubles when entertaining guests who think friendship entitles them to give unsolicited advice. As you read "Old Friends," try to identify with Rooney by thinking of a time when you were tempted to trade an old friend in for a newer model.*

The next time we have friends at the house over a weekend, I'm going to make sure it isn't *old* friends. I want our next house guests to be friends we don't know well enough to be perfectly at ease with — not that I didn't enjoy having Barbara and Quintin, mind you. It's just that we all know each other so well that no one holds back.

"Boy, you got a lot of work to do around this place," Quintin said.

Well I *know* I have a lot of work to do and I *know* I'm not going to do a lot of it, and I don't need a good friend telling me about it.

"I drove up to Montreal to get my paint," Quintin said, "They can still make paint with lead in it up there, and it lasts a lot longer. That's why all the paint is peeling on your house. Paint made in the U.S. isn't good anymore."

He thinks perhaps I haven't *noticed* the house needs painting? 5

"I nearly broke my neck on those stone steps out by the back porch," he said. "That slab of stone on top is rocking. Can't you jam another little stone or something under there so it doesn't rock? Someone's going to get killed."

Quintin thinks perhaps I haven't been meaning to stabilize that stone for four years now since the frost heaved it?

"That's a good aerial you've got on your television set," he said. "Of course, you're on high ground here so you get a good picture. Why don't you get yourself a decent-sized television set so you can see it?"

Saturday night we had some other friends over for a drink and dinner. Barbara and Quintin wanted to help.

"Sure," I said. "You can put the glasses and the ice and the bottles 10 out on the table on the front lawn."

"Which glasses?" Barbara said.

I told her where the glasses were and she started taking things out.

"There are only seven of these glasses and there are going to be eight of us," Barbara said.

"I know, I know," I said. "We used to have twelve of them. You have to use one jelly glass. I'll drink out of that one."

"Don't fall on that loose stone step as you go out," Quintin said to 15 Barbara. "What about chairs for out front?" he asked me.

I told him there were some old ones up in the garage if he wanted to get a couple of those.

Quintin is a willing helper. He went out to the garage and he was gone for about ten minutes before he returned carrying two aluminum chairs with broken webbing.

"You mean *these*?" he asked incredulously.

Those were the ones I meant. I knew the webbing was broken. If the webbing hadn't been broken they wouldn't have been in the garage in the first place.

"Boy," he said, as he put the chairs down, "I thought my garage was   *20* a mess. How do you ever get a car in there? You got stuff hanging all over. You ought to have a garage sale . . . and sell the garage." He laughed. Friends can be so cruel.

"Why don't I make the salad dressing," Barbara said to my wife. "Is this the only vinegar you have?" she asked, holding up a bottle of super-market house brand, El Cheapo vinegar. "I guess I'll use lemon instead of vinegar," she said.

"Here comes the first guests," Quintin said. "There sure isn't much space for them to park in that driveway of yours."

"I'll go greet the guests," Barbara said.

"Don't break your neck on that stone step as you go out," Quintin yelled after her.

Questions for Discussion

1. The scene of this essay is a house in which the author has evidently lived for several years. How much of the dialogue depends upon the scene?
2. What is the difference between old friends and new friends? Explain what Rooney means by the first line in his essay.
3. Do you think Barbara and Quintin are real friends of the author's? If so, how would they feel upon reading this essay? If not, what are they meant to represent?
4. Why has Rooney relied so heavily upon dialogue in this piece?
5. Why do you think Rooney lets us know that he is willing to drink from a jelly glass? Does he expect readers to sympathize with him?

Suggestions for Writing

1. Has an old friend ever gotten on your nerves? Or have you ever taken a trip with friends only to find yourself liking them less each day? Write a humorous essay about a time when friendship seemed like hard work.
2. Imagine someone difficult to please taking a tour of your home. Write the story of that visit, using dialogue where appropriate.

4

Writing to Move Others

The desire to move an audience has been a major motive of rhetoric since ancient times. *Ceremonial speech,* as conceived by classical rhetoric, did not need to inspire a specific decision or action; its purpose was simply to strengthen beliefs that were already held. The ancient Greeks even had contests in which speakers were judged by how successful they were in moving their audience. Such contests are rare today and are more likely to feature students than professional speakers, but it is still useful to think of "writing to move" as a type of public performance.

THINKING ABOUT THE AUDIENCE

You have probably already heard examples of ceremonial speech if you have ever been addressed as part of a crowd that has something in common — the shared values that writing to move assumes. Graduation speeches usually attempt to inspire loyalty to one's old school and to exhort graduates to live productive lives. The eulogy at a funeral is usually designed to inspire admiration or respect for the dead. And churches offer sermons aimed at reinforcing beliefs that are, in theory at least, already held. In each of these cases the audience has a common bond: graduation from the same school, acquaintance with the same person, or membership in the same church. Without that common tie ceremonial speech would be less appropriate than other types of discourse—such as writing to persuade or writing to inform.

Consider, for example, the purpose of a keynote speech at a political convention. Everyone at the convention already belongs to the same party; they don't need to be persuaded to join or to be informed about what the party stands for. The speaker can usually assume that the audience will support the party's candidates in the next election and that this support will be given with varying degrees of enthusiasm. Some people at the convention probably favor candidates who were not nominated; others may be feeling hot, tired, and eager to get back home where they have other obligations to fulfill—obligations that may take precedence over helping the party win the election. The primary purpose of this keynote speech is to inspire enthusiasm—to make the delegates forget their other concerns, rise to their feet, and feel certain that they are part of a noble cause. The speaker in this case may benefit from reinforcement unavailable to writers; at key moments carefully selected video images may flash across screens surrounding the podium, as red, white, and blue balloons fall from the ceiling. But this speech began as a written speech employing rhetorical strategies that we can adopt for other occasions.

PURPOSE AND STYLE

Martin Luther King's "I Have a Dream" provides an example of political exhortation at its very best. The words on the page, and the care with which they are arranged, make it a moving piece of prose without the benefit of our hearing King's voice or being present at the scene where this speech was delivered. Visualizing the situation for which this speech was designed, however, can help you understand King's purpose—and how a writer can be moving. The occasion was the hundredth anniversary of the Emancipation Proclamation; the scene was the steps of the Lincoln Memorial from which King faced an audience of more than two hundred thousand people who had marched to Washington on behalf of civil rights for African Americans. King did not need to persuade that audience that African Americans deserved civil rights. If they didn't already believe this, they would not have come to Washington. What King needed to do was to reinforce the beliefs his audience already held—to vindicate whatever hardships they had endured and to help them lift up their hearts.

Although the entire speech deserves close reading, a short excerpt illustrates a number of points essential to our understanding of writing to move. Here are paragraphs 9 and 10 from the eighteen-paragraph-long speech:

> I am not unmindful that some of you have come here out of great trials and tribulations. Some of you have come fresh from narrow jail

cells. Some of you have come from areas where your quest for freedom left you battered by the storms of persecution and staggered by the winds of police brutality. You have been the veterans of creative suffering. Continue to work with the faith that unearned suffering is redemptive.

Go back to Mississippi, and go back to Alabama. Go back to South Carolina. Go back to Georgia. Go back to Louisiana. Go back to the slums and ghettos of our Northern cities, knowing that somehow this situation can and will be changed. Let us not wallow in the valley of despair.

When we look closely at these paragraphs, we see that King is not attempting to persuade his audience to undertake a specific action. It is true that he advises his listeners to go back home and keep on working, but the promise that "somehow this situation can and will be changed" is short on details and unlikely to satisfy someone who has not been moved by the speech as a whole.

A paraphrase of these two paragraphs might read: "I know you've all had a rough time, but go back home and cheer up. Things are going to get better." Reducing King's prose to this paraphrase is grotesque but illuminating. Focusing only upon content, we have stripped these paragraphs of their beauty and their power to move — deprived them of their reason for being. What is it, then, that makes King's prose moving?

In the first place, King was a gifted stylist with a fine ear for prose rhythm; his sentences are so nicely cadenced that they can engage the attention of an audience by the quality of their music. The short excerpt reprinted above uses two techniques that can be found in much of King's work. When he writes "trials and tribulations," he is using a simple form of *parallel construction,* which means putting similar ideas in similar form for the sake of balance. In this case a plural noun is balanced with a plural noun.

The third sentence in the first paragraph provides another example of parallelism: "battered by the storms of persecution and staggered by the winds of police brutality." "Battered" is balanced against "staggered," "storms" against "winds," and "persecution" against "police brutality" — as can be easily seen when we reformat these lines:

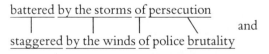

Only "police" keeps this example from being perfectly parallel. It is being used here as an adjective describing "brutality," but there is no equivalent adjective describing "persecution."

From this example we can conclude two things:

1. Parallelism does not necessarily require a word-for-word balance — although the more words that are balanced, the stronger the parallel will be.

2. A word or phrase that does not fit within a parallel will receive
   increased emphasis, because it interferes with the prevailing
   rhythm.

In this case it is quite possible that King wanted "police" to have this extra
emphasis. His original audience would have believed that the police were
interfering with much more than parallel construction.

The first four sentences of the second paragraph can also be described
as parallel. The second, third, and fourth sentences are perfectly parallel
with one another; and the first sentence harmonizes with them because its
two independent clauses repeat the prevailing pattern. But these lines also
illustrate another rhetorical device: *anaphora,* or deliberate repetition at the
beginning of sentences or clauses. King emphasizes *Go back* to such an
extent here that the words no longer seem as simple as they would in
another context (e.g., "Go back to your room and get a sweater."). As the
*Go back*s accumulate, they become a type of song in which the words
mean more than they say. Behind these *Go back*s is a meaning that can be
felt even though it is unstated. *Go back* becomes "Go back and don't give
up; go back and keep on fighting."

The rhetorical use of repetition for emphasis can be thought of as a
more sophisticated version of how a cheerleader uses repetition ("*Go* team
go; fight team *fight*") when trying to move a crowd. Unlike the simple
chants you can hear at a pep rally, King's prose draws upon a variety of
techniques and does so for a serious end. Nevertheless, one way of reading
"I Have a Dream" is to read it as a type of rallying cry. King's purpose,
after all, was to move the crowd to continued struggle by reaffirming the
importance of their common cause.

Neither parallel construction nor deliberate repetition are limited to
exhortation, and you will find examples of them in works that have other
motives behind them. But because writing to move has strong links to
oratory, it is especially likely to draw upon strategies like these that make
sentences easy to read and easy to remember. When you read "I Have a
Dream," you will find that King uses both parallelism and repetition
repeatedly. You will also find that he keeps his diction simple. With the
possible exception of two words ("tribulations" and "redemptive"), the
words of the passage quoted above could be understood by almost any
English-speaking person. An experienced speaker, King understood that
this was an occasion on which eloquence required simplicity. We cannot
be moved by what we do not understand.

Style, however, is only one of the factors that explain why King's
prose is so much more effective than our paraphrase of it. Writing to move
requires creating a bond between the writer and the reader. It is one thing
to say "I know you've had a rough time." It is something else to show that
you mean it and to leave your audience feeling personally addressed. Many
of the people in King's audience would have been touched personally by
the sympathetic reference to "narrow jail cells." And almost everyone in
that audience would have had some experience with "persecution" and

"police brutality." King then makes specific references to five southern states and a more general reference to northern cities. Anyone from Mississippi, Alabama, South Carolina, Georgia, or Louisiana would have felt as if King were addressing him or her as an individual. Furthermore, the list of five is long enough to be understood as examples representing other states that pass unmentioned. And references to different states remind the entire crowd that they are part of a nationwide struggle with friends and allies in other states.

As "I Have a Dream" suggests, writing to move requires more than eloquent phrasing. It also requires a strong sense of audience, which, in turn, ultimately depends upon understanding human nature and the types of experience that evoke different emotions.

WRITING TIPS

When analyzing "I Have a Dream" and the other readings in this section, you can benefit from principles laid down in the eighteenth century by Hugh Blair, a professor at the University of Edinburgh, to determine what makes language moving. He offers seven principles that can help you understand the work of other writers and to write moving essays of your own.*

1. *Choose a topic that is suitable for writing to move.* In the pages that follow, Martin Luther King addresses the subject of social injustice, George Orwell writes about an execution, Judy Syfers protests against the exploitation of women, Alice Walker reflects upon the treatment of an animal, and both Randall Williams and Jonathan Swift write about poverty. Depending upon how a writer proceeds, topics such as these can inspire a number of emotions — including anger, indignation, pity, or grief. There are, of course, many other topics suitable for this type of writing. On the other hand, there are also topics (such as how the brain functions or how automobiles are manufactured in Japan) that would be inappropriate for writing to move. If you try to inspire an emotion that seems unrelated to the topic, your prose may seem overwrought rather than moving.

2. *Get right into the topic without warning readers of your intention.* If you begin by writing, "I am going to tell you a sad story" (or words to that effect), you are weakening your work in at least two ways. By telling readers how you want them to respond — as opposed to letting the response grow naturally out of the work — you are giving people a ready-made standard for evaluating your work; and you may find someone responding by saying, "Well, I didn't think that was so sad." Moreover, by putting readers on guard, you lose the strategic advantage of a surprise

*These principles are adapted from Blair's *Lectures on Rhetoric and Belles Lettres,* first published in 1783. A modern edition is available, edited by Harold F. Harding (Carbondale: Southern Illinois University Press, 1965).

attack. Readers alerted in advance to "a sad story" could brace themselves against feeling sad or decide to put your work aside in order to read something more cheerful. When you read "A Hanging," for example, you will find that Orwell never tells us how he wants us to feel about the execution he describes. And anyone reading "A Modest Proposal" for the first time may find it shocking at first, because Swift conceals his intention for several paragraphs.

3. *Include details that can evoke the response you intend.* Although supporting detail is important in almost all types of writing, it is especially important when writing to move. And the details that you choose should have emotional appeal. For example, a specific description of a homeless person sleeping on a sidewalk is likely to be more moving than several paragraphs of statistics. Consider, in this regard, how Randall Williams makes us see his childhood through concrete detail: "I have seen my Daddy wrap copper wire through the soles of his boots to keep them together in the wintertime." His essay "Daddy Tucked The Blanket" includes many other details about growing up poor, but the copper wire is the detail with which his childhood first comes alive.

4. *Be moved yourself.* Although there are many rhetorical situations in which writers need to keep their feelings to themselves, writing to move requires that you yourself feel the emotion that you want others to share. This does not mean that you have to come out and tell how you feel; on the contrary, you should try to keep your focus on your subject rather than upon yourself. It happens that all of the writers in this chapter use the first person at some point. In an essay like "I Want a Wife," it's hard not to notice that the author is angry. But even if you never mention yourself, readers should be able to tell how you feel about your subject. The main thing is to avoid insincerity. If you really don't care about poverty, but think it would be proper to sound as if you do, you are unlikely to succeed at moving others. Write about what you care about, and don't try to fake emotion.

5. *Write simply and directly.* When you feel something strongly, you are likely to use language that is simple, direct, and bold. Formal diction and long, complicated sentences will seem artful rather than direct, thus diminishing the sense that you are moved by the subject you are writing about. Here, for example, is Alice Walker describing her response to eating meat: "I am eating misery, I thought, as I took the first bite. And spit it out." These two sentences may be the result of several drafts, for the words that first occur to writers are not necessarily those that are the simplest and most direct. But the apparent simplicity of these sentences helps to convey emotion. The force of "And spit it out" would be lost if, afraid to use a word like *spit,* we consulted a thesaurus and tried using something like *expectorated.* Because of the directness necessary for writing to move, you should find all of the selections in this chapter easy to read, with the possible exception of "A Modest Proposal." Swift's essay is the most difficult to read—in part because words written more than two

hundred fifty years ago often seem less natural than those written last year, and in part because Swift deliberately violates the rule in question here as part of his strategy to surprise readers with a proposal that turns out to be anything but modest.

6. *Be faithful to your purpose.* When writing to move, you need to avoid any digression that would interrupt the flow of feeling you are trying to inspire. Had Martin Luther King paused in the middle of "I Have a Dream" to offer an analysis of congressional legislation affecting civil rights, he would have weakened the emotional power of his speech. King knew a great deal about his topic, but the occasion of "I Have a Dream" was an occasion that called for inspiration rather than information. As you revise an essay designed to move, be prepared to cut not only digressions but also any sentence that seems too fancy. As Blair put it, "Sacrifice all beauties, however bright and showy, which would divert the mind from the principal object, and which would amuse the imagination, rather than touch the heart."

7. *Know when to stop.* As a general rule, writing designed to move needs to be kept fairly short. It is difficult to sustain intensity of feeling at any great length, and if you write too much about your subject, you run the risk of readers deciding that you are making too much of a fuss. Most of the readings in this chapter are only four pages long. But "knowing when to stop" cannot be measured by word count alone. It is also a matter of understanding where you can afford to linger and where it is best to let a few carefully chosen words convey a sense of things unsaid. When your material is strong, you can often benefit from handling it with restraint, letting the imagination of your readers fill in gaps along lines that you have merely suggested. Here, for example, are two paragraphs from Randall Williams:

> Later that night everyone was in bed and I heard Daddy get up from the couch where he was reading. I looked out from my bed across the hall into their room. He was standing right over Mama and she was already asleep. He pulled the blanket up and tucked it around her shoulders and just stood there and tears were dropping off his cheeks and I thought I could faintly hear them splashing against the linoleum rug.
>
> Now they're divorced.

What is remarkable about these paragraphs, taken from an essay describing the effects of poverty, is how they involve a combination of showing and suggesting. The first paragraph is full of detail. We know when this happened, where everyone was, what Daddy had been doing, and exactly what happened after he tucked a blanket around his wife's shoulders. The second paragraph, by contrast, confronts us with a single piece of information. But the simplicity with which that information is conveyed is more dramatic than a paragraph spelling out all the reasons that led to the divorce. Within the context of the essay we can imagine those details for ourselves. We are less likely to imagine the sound of tears upon linoleum — hence the author's decision to provide that detail. Moreover, the starkness of the second paragraph serves as a corrective to a potentially sentimental scene: One sentence about Daddy's tears is moving; a second could be maudlin. Williams wisely recognized that his material called for a mixture of intimacy and restraint.

Of course, writing to move cannot be mastered by simply memorizing a few rules. For whatever reason you may want to move people, you should not only practice the techniques outlined here but also watch and listen to other people. You may already know how to touch the hearts of people who are close to you. By reading the work of other writers and practicing the techniques of writing to move, you can ultimately learn to touch people you have not met. The ability to inspire emotion is one of the most useful achievements of rhetoric. But like any other type of writing, it takes study and practice.

I HAVE A DREAM
Martin Luther King, Jr.

"I Have a Dream" is the text of a speech King delivered in 1963 upon the hundredth anniversary of the Emancipation Proclamation. Consider how this occasion may have reinforced what King had to say, and try to imagine the scene where this speech was delivered: the Lincoln Memorial in Washington, D.C. As you read "I Have a Dream," think about why its author would be honored with the Nobel Peace Prize a year after giving this speech — and assassinated only a few years later.

I am happy to join with you today in what will go down in history as the greatest demonstration for freedom in the history of our nation.

Five score years ago, a great American, in whose symbolic shadow we stand today, signed the Emancipation Proclamation. This momentous decree came as a great beacon of light of hope to millions of Negro slaves who had been seared in the flames of withering injustice. It came as a joyous daybreak to end the long night of their captivity. But one hundred years later, the Negro still is not free. One hundred years later, the life of the Negro is still sadly crippled by the manacles of segregation and the chains of discrimination. One hundred years later, the Negro lives on a lonely island of poverty in the midst of a vast ocean of material prosperity. One hundred years later, the Negro is still anguished in the corners of American society and finds himself in exile in his own land. And so we have come here today to dramatize a shameful condition.

In a sense we have come to our nation's capital to cash a check. When the architects of our republic wrote the magnificent words of the Constitution and the Declaration of Independence, they were signing a promissory note to which every American was to fall heir. This note was the promise that all men — yes, Black men as well as white men — would be guaranteed the inalienable rights of life, liberty, and the pursuit of happiness.

It is obvious today that America has defaulted on this promissory note insofar as her citizens of color are concerned. Instead of honoring this sacred obligation, America has given the Negro people a bad check, a check which has come back marked "insufficient funds." But we refuse to believe that the bank of justice is bankrupt. We refuse to believe that there are insufficient funds in the great vaults of opportunity of this nation; and so we have come to cash this check, a check that will give us upon demand the riches of freedom and the security of justice.

We have also come to this hallowed spot to remind America of the fierce urgency of *now*. This is no time to engage in the luxury of cooling off or to take the tranquilizing drug of gradualism. *Now* is the time to make real the promises of democracy. *Now* is the time to rise from the dark and desolate valley of segregation to the sunlit path of racial justice. *Now* is the time to lift our nation from the quicksands of racial injustice to the solid rock of brotherhood. *Now* is the time to make justice a reality for all of God's children.

It would be fatal for the nation to overlook the urgency of the moment. This sweltering summer of the Negro's legitimate discontent will not pass until there is an invigorating autumn of freedom and equality. Nineteen sixty-three is not an end, but a beginning. And those who hope that the Negro needed to blow off steam and will now be content will have a rude awakening if the nation returns to business as usual. There will be neither rest nor tranquility in America until the Negro is granted his citizenship rights. The whirlwinds of revolt will continue to shake the foundations of our nation until the bright day of justice emerges.

But there is something that I must say to my people who stand on the warm threshold which leads into the palace of justice. In the process of gaining our rightful place, we must not be guilty of wrongful deeds. Let us not seek to satisfy our thirst for freedom by drinking from the cup of bitterness and hatred. We must forever conduct our struggle on the high plane of dignity and discipline. We must not allow our creative protest to degenerate into physical violence. Again and again we must rise to the majestic heights of meeting physical force with soul force. And the marvelous new militancy which has engulfed the Negro community must not lead us to a distrust of all white people; for many of our white brothers, as evidenced by their presence here today, have come to realize that their destiny is tied up with our destiny, and they have come to realize that their freedom is inextricably bound to our freedom.

We cannot walk alone. And as we walk we must make the pledge that we shall always march ahead. We cannot turn back. There are those who are asking the devotees of civil rights, "When will you be satisfied?" We can never be satisfied as long as the Negro is the victim of the unspeakable horrors of police brutality. We can never be satisfied as long as our bodies, heavy with the fatigue of travel, cannot gain lodging in the motels of the highways and the hotels of the cities. We cannot be satisified as long as the Negro's basic mobility is from a smaller ghetto to a larger one. We can never be satisfied as long as our children are stripped of their selfhood and robbed of their dignity by signs stating "For Whites Only." We cannot be satisfied as long as the Negro in Mississippi cannot vote and a Negro in New York believes he has nothing for which to vote. No, no, we are not satisfied, and we will not be satisfied until justice rolls down like waters and righteousness like a mighty stream.

I am not unmindful that some of you have come here out of great trials and tribulations. Some of you have come fresh from narrow jail cells. Some of you have come from areas where your quest for freedom left you battered by the storms of persecution and staggered by the winds of police brutality. You have been the veterans of creative suffering. Continue to work with the faith that unearned suffering is redemptive.

Go back to Mississippi, and go back to Alabama. Go back to South Carolina. Go back to Georgia. Go back to Louisiana. Go back to the slums and ghettos of our Northern cities, knowing that somehow this situation can and will be changed. Let us not wallow in the valley of despair.

I say to you today, my friends, even though we face the difficulties of today and tomorrow, I still have a dream. It is a dream deeply rooted in the American dream. I have a dream that one day this nation will rise up and live out the true meaning of its creed: "We hold these truths to be self-evident, that all men are created equal." I have a dream that one day, on the red hills of Georgia, sons of former slaves and the sons of former slave owners will be able to sit down together at the table of brotherhood. I have a dream that one day even the state of Mississippi, a state sweltering with the heat of injustice, sweltering with the heat of oppression, will be transformed into an oasis of freedom and justice. I have a dream that my four little children will one day live in a nation where they will not be judged by the color of their skin, but by the content of their character.

I have a dream today. I have a dream that one day down in Alabama — with its vicious racists, with its governor's lips dripping with the words of interposition and nullification — one day right there in Alabama, little Black boys and Black girls will be able to join hands with little white boys and white girls as sisters and brothers.

I have a dream today. I have a dream that one day every valley shall be exalted and every hill and mountain shall be made low, the rough places will be made plain and the crooked places will be made straight, and the glory of the Lord shall be revealed, and all flesh shall see it together.°

This is our hope. This is the faith that I go back to the South with. And with this faith we will be able to hew out of the mountain of despair a stone of hope. With this faith we will be able to transform the jangling discords of our nation into a beautiful symphony of brotherhood. With this faith we will be able to work together, to play together, to struggle together, to go to jail together, to stand up for freedom together, knowing that we will be free one day.

And this will be the day — this will be the day when all of God's children will be able to sing with new meaning:

My country, 'tis of thee,
Sweet land of liberty,
    Of thee I sing;
Land where my fathers died,
Land of the Pilgrims' pride,

---

every valley shall be . . . see it together: A quotation from the Old Testament, Isaiah 40: 4–5.

From every mountainside
Let freedom ring.

And if America is to be a great nation, this must become true.

And so let freedom ring from the prodigious hilltops of New Hampshire. Let freedom ring from the mighty mountains of New York. Let freedom ring from the heightening Alleghenies of Pennsylvania. Let freedom ring from the snow-capped Rockies of Colorado. Let freedom ring from the curvaceous slopes of California.

But not only that. Let freedom ring from Stone Mountain of Georgia. Let freedom ring from Lookout Mountain of Tennessee. Let freedom ring from every hill and molehill of Mississippi. "From every mountainside let freedom ring."

And when this happens — when we allow freedom to ring, when we let it ring from every village and every hamlet, from every state and every city — we will be able to speed up that day when all of God's children, Black men and white men, Jews and Gentiles, Protestants and Catholics, will be able to join hands and sing in the words of the old Negro spiritual: "Free at last! Free at last! Thank God Almighty. We are free at last!"

Questions for Discussion

1. Why was the Lincoln Memorial an appropriate setting for this speech? Can you identify any references within the speech that link it to the setting in which it was originally presented?
2. Why does King begin paragraph 2 with "Five score years ago" instead of simply saying "one hundred years ago"?
3. *Anaphora*, as noted earlier, is a term describing the use of repetition at the beginning of sentences, clauses, or verses for rhetorical effect. Examples are the three sentences beginning "One hundred years later" in paragraph 2. Can you identify any other examples?
4. What do you think King meant by "the tranquilizing drug of gradualism" in paragraph 5?
5. Paragraph 13 concludes with a quotation from the Bible. Why was it appropriate for King to use the Bible within the context of this speech?
6. What evidence in this essay suggests that King recognized that he was speaking to an audience already committed to the importance of racial equality?

Suggestions for Writing

1. A *metaphor* is a figure of speech that makes a comparison between two unlike things without using *like* or *as*. When King writes, "we have come to our nation's capital to cash a check," he does not mean these words to be taken literally. Instead, he is making an implied comparison between an uncashed check and unfulfilled promises to African

Americans. Reread "I Have a Dream" identifying other metaphors King uses. Then paraphrase any five successive paragraphs, eliminating all metaphors and all anaphora.

2. Using both anaphora and metaphor, write a short speech that calls attention to a current social problem that concerns you.

A HANGING

George Orwell

You may already know Orwell as the author of novels such as 1984 *and* Animal Farm, *but you may not know that he served, as a young man, as a police officer in Burma when that country was part of the British Empire. "A Hanging" is one of several works that Orwell wrote about his experience in Burma. As you read, observe the details Orwell uses to convey the scene. Be alert, in particular, for details that inspire sympathy for the victim.*

It was Burma, a sodden morning of rains. A sickly light, like yellow tinfoil, was slanting over the walls into the jail yard. We were waiting outside the condemned cells, a row of sheds fronted with double bars, like small animal cages. Each cell measured about ten feet by ten and was quite bare within except for a plank bed and a pot for drinking water. In some of them brown silent men were squatting at the inner bars, with their blankets draped round them. These were the condemned men, due to be hanged within the next week or two.

One prisoner had been brought out of his cell. He was a Hindu, a puny wisp of a man, with a shaven head and vague liquid eyes. He had a thick, sprouting moustache, absurdly too big for his body, rather like the moustache of a comic man on the films. Six tall Indian warders were guarding him and getting him ready for the gallows. Two of them stood by with rifles and fixed bayonets, while the others handcuffed him, passed a chain through his handcuffs and fixed it to their belts, and lashed his arms tight to his sides. They crowded very close about him, with their hands always on him in a careful caressing grip, as though all the while feeling him to make sure he was there. It was like men handling a fish which is still alive and may jump back into the water. But he stood quite unresisting, yielding his arms limply to the ropes, as though he hardly noticed what was happening.

Eight o'clock struck and a bugle call, desolately thin in the wet air, floated from the distant barracks. The superintendent of the jail, who was standing apart from the rest of us, moodily prodding the gravel with his stick, raised his head at the sound. He was an army doctor, with a grey toothbrush moustache and a gruff voice. "For God's sake hurry up, Francis," he said irritably. "The man ought to have been dead by this time. Aren't you ready yet?"

Francis, the head jailer, a fat Dravidian° in a white drill suit and gold spectacles, waved his black hand. "Yes sir, yes sir," he bubbled. "All iss satisfactorily prepared. The hangman iss waiting. We shall proceed."

Dravidian: A member of a race of people living in southern India and Ceylon.

"Well, quick march, then. The prisoners can't get their breakfast till   *5*
this job's over."

We set out for the gallows. Two warders marched on either side of
the prisoner, with their rifles at the slope; two others marched close against
him, gripping him by arm and shoulder, as though at once pushing and
supporting him. The rest of us, magistrates and the like, followed behind.
Suddenly, when we had gone ten yards, the procession stopped short
without any order or warning. A dreadful thing had happened—a dog,
come goodness knows whence, had appeared in the yard. It came bound-
ing among us with a loud volley of barks, and leapt round us wagging its
whole body, wild with glee at finding so many human beings together. It
was a large woolly dog, half Airedale, half pariah. For a moment it pranced
round us, and then, before anyone could stop, it had made a dash for the
prisoner and, jumping up, tried to lick his face. Everyone stood aghast,
too taken aback even to grab at the dog.

"Who let that bloody brute in here?" said the superintendent angrily.
"Catch it, someone!"

A warder, detached from the escort, charged clumsily after the dog,
but it danced and gambolled just out of his reach, taking everything as
part of the game. A young Eurasian jailer picked up a handful of gravel
and tried to stone the dog away, but it dodged the stones and came after us
again. Its yaps echoed from the jail walls. The prisoner, in the grasp of the
two warders, looked on incuriously, as though this was another formality
of the hanging. It was several minutes before someone managed to catch
the dog. Then we put my handkerchief through its collar and moved off
once more, with the dog still straining and whimpering.

It was about forty yards to the gallows. I watched the bare brown
back of the prisoner marching in front of me. He walked clumsily with
his bound arms, but quite steadily, with that bobbing gait of the Indian
who never straightens his knees. At each step his muscles slid neatly into
place, the lock of hair on his scalp danced up and down, his feet printed
themselves on the wet gravel. And once, in spite of the men who gripped
him by each shoulder, he stepped slightly aside to avoid a puddle on
the path.

It is curious, but till that moment I had never realized what it means   *10*
to destroy a healthy, conscious man. When I saw the prisoner step aside to
avoid the puddle I saw the mystery, the unspeakable wrongness, of cutting
a life short when it is in full tide. This man was not dying, he was alive
just as we are alive. All the organs of his body were working—bowels
digesting food, skin renewing itself, nails growing, tissue forming—all
toiling away in solemn foolery. His nails would still be growing when he
stood on the drop, when he was falling through the air with a tenth-of-a-
second to live. His eyes saw the yellow gravel and the grey walls, and his
brain still remembered, foresaw, reasoned—reasoned even about puddles.

He and we were a party of men walking together, seeing, hearing, feeling, understanding the same world; and in two minutes, with a sudden snap, one of us would be gone — one mind less, one world less.

The gallows stood in a small yard, separate from the main grounds of the prison, and overgrown with tall prickly weeds. It was a brick erection like three sides of a shed, with planking on top, and above that two beams and a crossbar with the rope dangling. The hangman, a grey-haired convict in the white uniform of the prison, was waiting beside his machine. He greeted us with a servile crouch as we entered. At a word from Francis the two warders, gripping the prisoner more closely than ever, half led half pushed him to the gallows and helped him clumsily up the ladder. Then the hangman climbed up and fixed the rope round the prisoner's neck.

We stood waiting, five yards away. The warders had formed in a rough circle round the gallows. And then, when the noose was fixed, the prisoner began crying out to his god. It was a high, reiterated cry of "Ram! Ram! Ram! Ram!" not urgent and fearful like a prayer or cry for help, but steady, rhythmical, almost like the tolling of a bell. The dog answered the sound with a whine. The hangman, still standing on the gallows, produced a small cotton bag like a flour bag and drew it down over the prisoner's face. But the sound, muffled by the cloth, still persisted, over and over again: "Ram! Ram! Ram! Ram! Ram!"

The hangman climbed down and stood ready, holding the lever. Minutes seemed to pass. The steady, muffled crying from the prisoner went on and on. "Ram! Ram! Ram!" never faltering for an instant. The superintendent, his head on his chest, was slowly poking the ground with his stick; perhaps he was counting the cries, allowing the prisoner a fixed number — fifty, perhaps, or a hundred. Everyone had changed color. The Indians had gone grey like bad coffee, and one or two of the bayonets were wavering. We looked at the lashed, hooded man on the drop, and listened to his cries — each cry another second of life; the same thought was in all our minds: oh, kill him quickly, get it over, stop that abominable noise!

Suddenly the superintendent made up his mind. Throwing up his head he made a swift motion with his stick. "Chalo°!" he shouted almost fiercely.

There was a clanking noise, and then dead silence. The prisoner had vanished, and the rope was twisting on itself. I let go of the dog, and it galloped immediately to the back of the gallows; but when it got there it stopped short, barked, and then retreated into a corner of the yard, where it stood among the weeds, looking timorously out at us. We went around the gallows to inspect the prisoner's body. He was dangling with his toes pointed straight downwards, very slowly revolving, as dead as a stone.

15

Chalo: Hindi for "Let's go."

The superintendent reached out with his stick and poked the bare brown body; it oscillated slightly. "*He's* all right," said the superintendent. He backed out from under the gallows, and blew out a deep breath. The moody look had gone out of his face quite suddenly. He glanced at his wrist-watch. "Eight minutes past eight. Well, that's all for this morning, thank God."

The warders unfixed bayonets and marched away. The dog, sobered and conscious of having misbehaved itself, slipped after them. We walked out of the gallows yard, past the condemned cells with their waiting prisoners, into the big central yard of the prison. The convicts, under the command of warders armed with lathis, were already receiving their breakfast. They squatted in log rows, each man holding a pannikin, while two warders with buckets marched round ladling out rice; it seemed quite a homely, jolly scene, after the hanging. An enormous relief had come upon us now that the job was done. One felt an impulse to sink, to break into a run, to snigger. All at once every one began chattering gaily.

The Eurasian boy walking beside me nodded towards the way we had come, with a knowing smile: "Do you know, sir, our friend (he meant the dead man) when he heard his appeal had been dismissed, he pissed on the floor of his cell. From fright. Kindly take one of my cigarettes, sir. Do you not admire my new silver case, sir? From the boxwalah, two rupees eight annas. Classy European style."

Several people laughed—at what, nobody seemed certain.

Francis was walking by the superintendent, talking garrulously: "Well, sir, all hass passed off with the utmost satisfactoriness. It was all finished—flick! like that. It iss not always so—oah, no! I have known cases where the doctor wass obliged to go beneath the gallows and pull the prissoner's legs to ensure decease. Most disagreeable!" *20*

"Wriggling about, eh? That's bad," said the superintendent.

"Ach, sir, it iss worse when they become refractory! One man, I recall, clung to the bars of hiss cage when we went to take him out. You will scarcely credit, sir, that it took six warders to dislodge him, three pulling each leg. We reasoned with him. 'My dear fellow,' we said, 'think of all the pain and trouble you are causing to us! But no, he would not listen! Ach, he wass very troublesome!"

I found that I was laughing quite loudly. Everyone was laughing. Even the superintendent grinned in a tolerant way. "You'd better all come out and have a drink," he said quite genially. "I've got a bottle of whiskey in the car. We could do with it."

We went through the big double gates of the prison into the road. "Pulling at his legs!" exclaimed a Burmese magistrate suddenly; and burst into a loud chuckling. We all began laughing again. At that moment Francis' anecdote seemed extraordinarily funny. We all had a drink together, native and European alike, quite amicably. The dead man was a hundred yards away.

Questions for Discussion

1. Consider the scene Orwell describes in his opening paragraph. How does his description of the weather and the cells contribute toward inspiring sympathy for the prisoner who is about to be executed?
2. Around what type of contrast has Orwell constructed his second paragraph?
3. What role does the dog play in this essay? Why does Orwell describe its presence at the execution as "dreadful"?
4. Why does Orwell consider it significant that the condemned man stepped aside to avoid a puddle?
5. Orwell describes the prisoner's prayer as "steady, rhythmical, almost like the tolling of a bell." Why is he calling attention to the prayer? Do you recognize an allusion in the reference to the bell?
6. How has witnessing this execution affected the men in the essay? How has it affected you?
7. Some critics have claimed that Orwell never witnessed the execution described in this selection. In that case, what is usually considered an "essay" would become a "story." Would that limit its effectiveness? Would your own response change if you considered the piece fiction?

Suggestions for Writing

1. If you have ever witnessed a disturbing event that you were powerless to stop, narrate the story of that event so that other people will feel as you do about what you saw.
2. For many people capital punishment is simply an abstract social issue, but an essay or story focused upon a specific execution can make people see the issue differently. Identify a social issue that concerns you, and then dramatize it through the use of narration.

I WANT A WIFE

Judy Syfers

> *Widely reprinted since its first publication in 1971, "I Want a Wife" is often used to illustrate such strategies as definition and classification. As you read it, note how Syfers defines the function of a wife and how she classifies a wife's duties. But above all, consider her motive in writing this essay. What do you think Syfers hoped to accomplish through a public expression of anger and frustration?*

I belong to that classification of people known as wives. I am A Wife. And, not altogether incidentally, I am a mother.

Not too long ago a male friend of mine appeared on the scene fresh from a recent divorce. He had one child, who is, of course, with his ex-wife. He is looking for another wife. As I thought about him while I was ironing one evening, it suddenly occurred to me that I, too, would like to have a wife. Why do I want a wife?

I would like to go back to school so that I can become economically independent, support myself, and if need be, support those dependent upon me. I want a wife who will work and send me to school. And while I am going to school I want a wife to take care of my children. I want a wife to keep track of the children's doctor and dentist appointments. And to keep track of mine, too. I want a wife to make sure my children eat properly and are kept clean. I want a wife who will wash the children's clothes and keep them mended. I want a wife who is a good nurturant attendant to my children, who arranges for their schooling, makes sure that they have an adequate social life with their peers, takes them to the park, the zoo, etc. I want a wife who takes care of the children when they are sick, a wife who arranges to be around when the children need special care, because, of course, I cannot miss classes at school. My wife must arrange to lose time at work and not lose the job. It may mean a small cut in my wife's income from time to time, but I guess I can tolerate that. Needless to say, my wife will arrange and pay for the care of the children while my wife is working.

I want a wife who will take care of *my* physical needs. I want a wife who will keep my house clean. A wife who will pick up after my children, a wife who will pick up after me. I want a wife who will keep my clothes clean, ironed, mended, replaced when need be, and who will see to it that my personal things are kept in their proper place so that I can find what I need the minute I need it. I want a wife who cooks the meals, a wife who is a *good* cook. I want a wife who will plan the menus, do the necessary grocery shopping, prepare the meals, serve them pleasantly, and then do the cleaning up while I do my studying. I want a wife who will care for me when I am sick and sympathize with my pain and loss of time from school. I want a wife to go along when our family takes a vacation so that someone can continue to care for me and my children when I need a rest and change of scene.

I want a wife who will not bother me with rambling complaints   *5* about a wife's duties. But I want a wife who will listen to me when I feel the need to explain a rather difficult point I have come across in my course of studies. And I want a wife who will type my papers for me when I have written them.

I want a wife who will take care of the details of my social life. When my wife and I are invited out by my friends, I want a wife who will take care of the babysitting arrangements. When I meet people at school that I like and want to entertain, I want a wife who will have the house clean, will prepare a special meal, serve it to me and my friends, and not interrupt when I talk about things that interest me and my friends. I want a wife who will have arranged that the children are fed and ready for bed before my guests arrive so that the children do not bother us. I want a wife who takes care of the needs of my guests so that they feel comfortable, who makes sure that they have an ashtray, that they are passed the hors d'oeuvres, that they are offered a second helping of food, that their wine glasses are replenished when necessary, that their coffee is served to them as they like it. And I want a wife who knows that sometimes I need a night out by myself.

I want a wife who is sensitive to my sexual needs, a wife who makes love passionately and eagerly when I feel like it, a wife who makes sure that I am satisfied. And, of course, I want a wife who will not demand sexual attention when I am not in the mood for it. I want a wife who assumes the complete responsibility for birth control, because I do not want more children. I want a wife who will remain sexually faithful to me so that I do not have to clutter up my intellectual life with jealousies. And I want a wife who understands that *my* sexual needs may entail more than strict adherence to monogamy. I must, after all, be able to relate to people as fully as possible.

If, by chance, I find another person more suitable as a wife than the wife I already have, I want the liberty to replace my present wife with another one. Naturally, I will expect a fresh, new life; my wife will take the children and be solely responsible for them so that I am left free.

When I am through with school and have a job, I want my wife to quit working and remain at home so that my wife can more fully and completely take care of a wife's duties.

My God, who *wouldn't* want a wife?   *10*

Questions for Discussion

1. Consider the title of this essay. Upon what does its effectiveness depend?
2. Why does Syfers repeat "I want" so often in this essay?

3. Do you think Syfers really wants someone else to take over all the responsibilities listed in this essay? If so, is anyone likely to volunteer? Or is her purpose something different?
4. How would you characterize the tone of her essay? Does Syfers sound angry or does she sound as if she is feeling sorry for herself?
5. Does this essay seem dated to you? How many men still expect a wife to perform the duties Syfers lists in this essay? Have relations between the sexes undergone a significant change?

Suggestions for Writing

1. If you have ever felt that too much was expected of you, write an essay designed to make readers sympathize with your situation.
2. Syfers defines *wife* according to what she believes a wife is expected to do. Use this technique to define an occupation that you consider praiseworthy.

AM I BLUE?

*"Ain't these tears in these eyes tellin' you?"**

Alice Walker

> *Alice Walker writes about a stallion named Blue, who lives in a pasture near her home, and how his life changed when he was given a companion — a mare who is subsequently taken away from him. But as her title suggests, Walker is not interested in the horse alone. Looking at the way Blue is treated leads the author to identify with him. As you read this essay by the author of* The Color Purple, *be alert for how Walker inspires sympathy for Blue and links this sympathy to other concerns.*

For about three years my companion and I rented a small house in the country that stood on the edge of a large meadow that appeared to run from the end of our deck straight into the mountains. The mountains, however, were quite far away, and between us and them there was, in fact, a town. It was one of the many pleasant aspects of the house that you never really were aware of this.

It was a house of many windows, low, wide, nearly floor to ceiling in the living room, which faced the meadow, and it was from one of these that I first saw our closest neighbor, a large white horse, cropping grass, flipping its mane, and ambling about — not over the entire meadow, which stretched well out of sight of the house, but over the five or so fenced-in acres that were next to the twenty-odd that we had rented. I soon learned that the horse, whose name was Blue, belonged to a man who lived in another town, but was boarded by our neighbors next door. Occasionally, one of the children, usually a stocky teen-ager, but sometimes a much younger girl or boy, could be seen riding Blue. They would appear in the meadow, climb up on his back, ride furiously for ten or fifteen minutes, then get off, slap Blue on the flanks, and not be seen again for a month or more.

There were many apple trees in our yard, and one by the fence Blue could almost reach. We were soon in the habit of feeding him apples, which he relished, especially because by the middle of summer the meadow grasses — so green and succulent since January — had dried out from lack of rain, and Blue stumbled about munching the dried stalks half-heartedly. Sometimes he would stand very still just by the apple tree, and when one of us came out he would whinny, snort loudly, or stamp the ground. This meant, of course: I want an apple.

It was quite wonderful to pick a few apples, or collect those that had fallen to the ground overnight, and patiently hold them, one by one, up to his large, toothy mouth. I remained as thrilled as a child by his flexible dark lips, huge, cubelike teeth that crunched the apples, core and all, with such finality, and his high, broad-breasted *enormity*; beside which, I felt small indeed. When I was a child, I used to ride horses, and was especially friendly with one named Nan until the day I was riding and my brother deliberately spooked her and I was thrown, head first, against the trunk of a tree. When I came to, I was in bed and my mother was bending worriedly over me; we silently agreed that perhaps horseback riding was not the safest sport for me. Since then I have walked, and prefer walking to horseback riding — but I had forgotten the depth of feeling one could see in horses' eyes.

I was therefore unprepared for the expression in Blue's. Blue was   5
lonely. Blue was horribly lonely and bored. I was not shocked that this should be the case; five acres to tramp by yourself, endlessly, even in the most beautiful of meadows — and his was — cannot provide many interesting events, and once rainy season turned to dry that was about it. No, I was shocked that I had forgotten that human animals and nonhuman animals can communicate quite well; if we are brought up around animals as children we take this for granted. By the time we are adults we no longer remember. However, the animals have not changed. They are in fact *completed* creations (at least they seem to be, so much more than we) who are not likely *to* change; it is their nature to express themselves. What else are they going to express? And they do. And, generally speaking, they are ignored.

After giving Blue the apples, I would wander back to the house, aware that he was observing me. Were more apples not forthcoming then? Was that to be his sole entertainment for the day? My partner's small son had decided he wanted to learn how to piece a quilt; we worked in silence on our respective squares as I thought . . .

Well, about slavery: about white children, who were raised by black people, who knew their first all-accepting love from black women, and then, when they were twelve or so, were told they must "forget" the deep levels of communication between themselves and "mammy" that they knew. Later they would be able to relate quite calmly, "My old mammy was sold to another good family." "My old mammy was —————." Fill in the blank. Many more years later a white woman would say: "I can't understand these Negroes, these blacks. What do they want? They're so different from us."

And about the Indians, considered to be "like animals" by the "settlers" (a very benign euphemism for what they actually were), who did not understand their description as a compliment.

And about the thousands of American men who marry Japanese, Korean, Filipina, and other non-English-speaking women and of how happy they report they are, *"blissfully,"* until their brides learn to speak English, at which point the marriages tend to fall apart. What then did the men see, when they looked into the eyes of the women they married, before they could speak English? Apparently only their own reflections.

I thought of society's impatience with the young. "Why are they playing the music so loud?" Perhaps the children have listened to much of the music of oppressed people their parents danced to before they were born, with its passionate but soft cries for acceptance and love, and they have wondered why their parents failed to hear.

I do not know how long Blue had inhabited his five beautiful, boring acres before we moved into our house; a year after we had arrived — and had also traveled to other valleys, other cities, other worlds — he was still there.

But then, in our second year at the house, something happened in Blue's life. One morning, looking out the window at the fog that lay like a ribbon over the meadow, I saw another horse, a brown one, at the other end of Blue's field. Blue appeared to be afraid of it, and for several days made no attempt to go near. We went away for a week. When we returned, Blue had decided to make friends and the two horses ambled or galloped along together, and Blue did not come nearly as often to the fence underneath the apple tree.

When he did, bringing his new friend with him, there was a different look in his eyes. A look of independence, of self-possession, of inalienable *horse*ness. His friend eventually became pregnant. For months and months there was, it seemed to me, a mutual feeling between me and the horses of justice, of peace. I fed apples to them both. The look in Blue's eyes was one of unabashed "this is *it*ness."

It did not, however, last forever. One day, after a visit to the city, I went out to give Blue some apples. He stood waiting, or so I thought, though not beneath the tree. When I shook the tree and jumped back from the shower of apples, he made no move. I carried some over to him. He managed to half-crunch one. The rest he let fall to the ground. I dreaded looking into his eyes — because I had of course noticed that Brown, his partner, had gone — but I did look. If I had been born into slavery, and my partner had been sold or killed, my eyes would have looked like that. The children next door explained that Blue's partner had been "put with him" (the same expression that old people used, I had noticed, when speaking of an ancestor during slavery who had been impregnated by her owner) so that they could mate and she conceive. Since that was accomplished, she had been taken back by her owner, who lived somewhere else.

Will she be back? I asked.

They didn't know.

Blue was like a crazed person. Blue *was*, to me, a crazed person. He galloped furiously, as if he were being ridden, around and around his five beautiful acres. He whinnied until he couldn't. He tore at the ground with his hooves. He butted himself against his single shade tree. He looked always and always toward the road down which his partner had gone. And then, occasionally, when he came up for apples, or I took apples to him, he looked at me. It was a look so piercing, so full of grief, a look so *human,* I almost laughed (I felt too sad to cry) to think there are people who do not know that animals suffer. People like me who have forgotten, and daily forget, all that animals try to tell us. "Everything you do to us will happen to you; we are your teachers, as you are ours. We are one lesson" is essentially it, I think. There are those who never once have even considered animals' rights: those who have been taught that animals actually want to be used and abused by us, as small children "love" to be frightened, or women "love" to be mutilated and raped. . . . They are the great-grandchildren of those who honestly thought, because someone taught them this: "Women can't think," and "niggers can't faint." But most disturbing of all, in Blue's large brown eyes was a new look, more painful than the look of despair: the look of disgust with human beings, with life; the look of hatred. And it was odd what the look of hatred did. It gave him, for the first time, the look of a beast. And what that meant was that he had put up a barrier within to protect himself from further violence; all the apples in the world wouldn't change that fact.

And so Blue remained, a beautiful part of our landscape, very peaceful to look at from the window, white against the grass. Once a friend came to visit and said, looking out on the soothing view: "And it *would* have to be a *white* horse; the very image of freedom." And I thought, yes, the animals are forced to become for us merely "images" of what they once so beautifully expressed. And we are used to drinking milk from containers showing "contented" cows, whose real lives we want to hear nothing about, eating eggs and drumsticks from "happy" hens, and munching hamburgers advertised by bulls of integrity who seem to command their fate.

As we talked of freedom and justice one day for all, we sat down to steaks. I am eating misery, I thought, as I took the first bite. And spit it out.

Questions for Discussion

1. Consider the opening paragraph of this essay, a paragraph that sets the scene but does not mention the horse that provides the focus for the paragraphs that follow. Why does Walker write that the mountains were farther away than they seemed and that an unseen town intervened?
2. Why is it significant that the horse is named Blue? How has Walker attempted to make readers sympathize with him?
3. The title of this essay, which comes from a song popular in the 1920s, can be read in more than one way. How do you interpret it?

4. Walker refers to her "companion" and "partner"; later, she refers to Blue's "friend." Why do you think she has chosen these words when there are other alternatives?

5. Walker writes that she looked into Blue's eyes and found them lonely, grief-stricken, and, eventually, filled with hatred. Do you think an animal can express these emotions? Or do you think that Walker is projecting her own feelings upon the horse?

6. Consider the transition between paragraphs 6 and 7, where Walker moves temporarily away from the story of Blue in order to reflect upon other types of oppression. How successfully has she managed this transition? How would the essay change if she kept Blue's story together and added social commentary only in her final paragraphs?

7. Explain the last paragraph of this essay. Is Walker bothered by eating meat? Or is it something else that is upsetting her?

Suggestions for Writing

1. Write about a neglected or abandoned animal so that people can begin to understand what happens to an animal that has been mistreated.

2. Write an essay comparing Walker's essay with Annie Dillard's "The Death of a Moth." Both Dillard and Walker have looked closely at a member of another species. How does their point of view differ?

DADDY TUCKED THE BLANKET

Randall Williams

> *"I was ashamed of where I lived," writes Randall Williams in this essay about growing up in poverty. But although he was too ashamed as a teenager to bring friends to his house, he subsequently chose to describe it in the* New York Times, *where "Daddy Tucked the Blanket" was first published. As you read this essay, try to understand the author's purpose. What could motivate him to share such personal material with readers? The painfully embarrassing scene with which Williams concludes may provide you with a clue.*

About the time I turned 16, my folks began to wonder why I didn't stay home any more. I always had an excuse for them, but what I didn't say was that I had found my freedom and I was getting out.

I went through four years of high school in semirural Alabama and became active in clubs and sports; I made a lot of friends and became a regular guy, if you know what I mean. But one thing was irregular about me: I managed those four years without ever having a friend visit at my house.

I was ashamed of where I lived. I had been ashamed for as long as I had been conscious of class.

We had a big family. There were several of us sleeping in one room, but that's not so bad if you get along, and we always did. As you get older, though, it gets worse.

Being poor is a humiliating experience for a young person trying   5 hard to be accepted. Even now — several years removed — it is hard to talk about. And I resent the weakness of these words to make you feel what it was really like.

We lived in a lot of old houses. We moved a lot because we were always looking for something just a little better than what we had. You have to understand that my folks worked harder than most people. My mother was always at home, but for her that was a full-time job — and no fun, either. But my father worked his head off from the time I can remember in construction and shops. It was hard, physical work.

I tell you this to show that we weren't shiftless. No matter how much money Daddy made, we never made much progress up the social ladder. I got out thanks to a college scholarship and because I was a little more articulate than the average.

I have seen my Daddy wrap copper wire through the soles of his boots to keep them together in the wintertime. He couldn't buy new boots because he had used the money for food and shoes for us. We lived like hell, but we went to school well-clothed and with a full stomach.

It really is hell to live in a house that was in bad shape 10 years before you moved in. And a big family puts a lot of wear and tear on a new house, too, so you can imagine how one goes downhill if it is teetering when you move in. But we lived in houses that were sweltering in summer and freezing in winter. I woke up every morning for a year and a half with plaster on my face where it had fallen out of the ceiling during the night.

This wasn't during the Depression; this was in the late 60's and early 70's.

When we boys got old enough to learn trades in school, we would try to fix up the old houses we lived in. But have you ever tried to paint a wall that crumbled when the roller went across it? And bright paint emphasized the holes in the wall. You end up more frustrated than when you began, especially when you know that at best you might come up with only enough money to improve one of the six rooms in the house. And we might move out soon after, anyway.

The same goes for keeping a house like that clean. If you have a house full of kids and the house is deteriorating, you'll never keep it clean. Daddy used to yell at Mama about that, but she couldn't do anything. I think Daddy knew it inside, but he had to have an outlet for his rage somewhere, and at least yelling isn't as bad as hitting, which they never did to each other.

But you have a kitchen which has no counter space and no hot water, and you will have dirty dishes stacked up. That sounds like an excuse, but try it. You'll go mad from the sheer sense of futility. It's the same thing in a house with no closets. You can't keep clothes clean and rooms in order if they have to be stacked up with things.

Living in a bad house is generally worse on girls. For one thing, they traditionally help their mother with the housework. We boys could get outside and work in the field or cut wood or even play ball and forget about living conditions. The sky was still pretty.

But the girls got the pressure, and as they got older it became worse. Would they accept dates knowing they had to "receive" the young man in a dirty hallway with broken windows, peeling wallpaper and a cracked ceiling? You have to live it to understand it, but it creates a shame which drives the soul of a young person inward.

I'm thankful none of us ever blamed our parents for this, because it would have crippled our relationships. As it worked out, only the relationship between our parents was damaged. And I think the harshness which they expressed to each other was just an outlet to get rid of their anger at the trap their lives were in. It ruined their marriage because they had no one to yell at but each other. I knew other families where the kids got the abuse, but we were too much loved for that.

Once I was about 16 and Mama and Daddy had had a particularly violent argument about the washing machine, which had broken down.

Daddy was on the back porch — that's where the only water faucet was — trying to fix it and Mama had a washtub out there washing school clothes for the next day and they were screaming at each other.

Later that night everyone was in bed and I heard Daddy get up from the couch where he was reading. I looked out from my bed across the hall into their room. He was standing right over Mama and she was already asleep. He pulled the blanket up and tucked it around her shoulders and just stood there and tears were dropping off his cheeks and I thought I could faintly hear them splashing against the linoleum rug.

Now they're divorced.

I had courses in college where housing was discussed, but the soci-   20
ologists never put enough emphasis on the impact living in substandard housing has on a person's psyche. Especially children's.

Small children have a hard time understanding poverty. They want the same things children from more affluent families have. They want the same things they see advertised on television, and they don't understand why they can't have them.

Other children can be incredibly cruel. I was in elementary school in Georgia — and this is interesting because it is the only thing I remember about that particular school — when I was about eight or nine.

After Christmas vacation had ended, my teacher made each student describe all his or her Christmas presents. I became more and more uncomfortable as the privilege passed around the room toward me. Other children were reciting the names of the dolls they had been given, the kinds of bicycles and the grandeur of their games and toys. Some had lists which seemed to go on and on for hours.

It took me only a few seconds to tell the class that I had gotten for Christmas a belt and a pair of gloves. And then I was laughed at — because I cried — by a roomful of children and a teacher. I never forgave them, and that night I made my mother cry when I told her about it.

In retrospect, I am grateful for that moment, but I remember want-   25
ing to die at the time.

Questions for Discussion

1. Describing what it was like to be poor as a child, Williams writes of the difficulty he has finding "words to make you feel what it was really like." How well does he succeed? Is it true that "you have to live it to understand it"? Or can reading lead to understanding when a writer finds the right words?
2. Trained as a journalist, Williams writes in short paragraphs, but some of his paragraphs are shorter than others. Consider paragraphs 3, 10, and 19. What is the effect of making these paragraphs unusually short?
3. What is the function of paragraphs 6–8?

4. Why does Williams believe that poverty is harder on girls than boys?

5. To what does Williams attribute his parents' divorce? Does he take a side in the dispute between his parents?

6. Consider the anecdote with which this essay concludes. Why would Williams be "grateful for that moment"?

Suggestions for Writing

1. If you have ever been upset by a fight between people you loved, describe what you witnessed, and try to show why it happened.

2. As this essay reveals, children can be cruel to one another, and teachers can be insensitive. Write an essay about betrayal on the playground or in the classroom.

A MODEST PROPOSAL
FOR PREVENTING THE CHILDREN OF
POOR PEOPLE IN IRELAND FROM
BEING A BURDEN TO THEIR PARENTS
OR COUNTRY, AND FOR MAKING
THEM BENEFICIAL TO THE PUBLIC

Jonathan Swift

> *As you read "A Modest Proposal," you may find it useful to know that Ireland was ruled as an English colony during Swift's lifetime — and that the English enacted a number of laws that resulted in great hardship. Irish trade and industry were suppressed, and religious conflicts were intensified. Swift's parents were English colonists in Ireland, and he was a member of the Protestant ruling class, but it would be a mistake to assume that he was indifferent to the suffering he saw around him. Consider the act Swift proposes, and think about why he, a clergyman, would make such a proposal.*

It is a melancholy object to those who walk through this great town° or travel in the country, when they see the streets, the roads, and cabin doors, crowded with beggars of the female sex, followed by three, four, or six children, all in rags and importuning every passenger for an alms. These mothers, instead of being able to work for their honest livelihood, are forced to employ all their time in strolling to beg sustenance for their helpless infants: who as they grow up either turn thieves for want of work, or leave their dear native country to fight for the Pretender° in Spain, or sell themselves to the Barbadoes.°

I think it is agreed by all parties that this prodigious number of children in the arms, or on the backs, or at the heels of their mothers, and frequently of their fathers, is in the present deplorable state of the kingdom a very great additional grievance; and, therefore, whoever could find out a fair, cheap, and easy method of making these children sound, useful members of the commonwealth, would deserve so well of the public as to have his statue set up for a preserver of the nation.

But my intention is very far from being confined to provide only for the children of professed beggars; it is of a much greater extent, and shall take in the whole number of infants at a certain age who are born of

---

great town: Dublin.   *Pretender:* James Stuart, son of James II and a Catholic. In 1688 the throne had gone to his sister Mary, a Protestant who ruled with her husband William of Orange. *Barbadoes:* To get out of Ireland, many people went as indentured servants to Barbados and other British colonies.

parents in effect as little able to support them as those who demand our charity in the streets.

As to my own part, having turned my thoughts for many years upon this important subject, and maturely weighed the several schemes of our projectors, I have always found them grossly mistaken in their computation. It is true, a child just dropped from its dam may be supported by her milk for a solar year, with little other nourishment; at most not above the value of *2s.,* which the mother may certainly get, or the value in scraps, by her lawful occupation of begging; and it is exactly at one year old that I propose to provide for them in such a manner as instead of being a charge upon their parents or the parish, or wanting food and raiment for the rest of their lives, they shall on the contrary contribute to the feeding, and partly to the clothing, of many thousands.

There is likewise another great advantage in my scheme, that it will   5
prevent those voluntary abortions, and that horrid practice of women murdering their bastard children, alas! too frequent among us! sacrificing the poor innocent babes I doubt more to avoid the expense than the shame, which would move tears and pity in the most savage and inhuman breast.

The number of souls in this kingdom being usually reckoned one million and a half, of these I calculate there may be about 200,000 couple whose wives are breeders; from which number I subtract 30,000 couple who are able to maintain their own children (although I apprehend there cannot be so many, under the present distress of the kingdom); but this being granted, there will remain 170,000 breeders. I again subtract 50,000 for those women who miscarry, or whose children die by accident or disease within the year. There only remain 120,000 children of poor parents annually born. The question therefore is, how this number shall be reared and provided for? which, as I have already said, under the present situation of affairs, is utterly impossible by all the methods hitherto proposed. For we can neither employ them in handicraft or agriculture; we neither build houses (I mean in the country) nor cultivate land; they can very seldom pick up a livelihood by stealing, till they arrive at six years old, except where they are of towardly parts; although I confess they learn the rudiments much earlier; during which time they can, however, be properly looked upon only as probationers; as I have been informed by a principal gentleman in the country of Cavan, who protested to me that he never knew above one or two instances under the age of six, even in a part of the kingdom so renowned for the quickest proficiency in that art.

I am assured by our merchants, that a boy or a girl before twelve years old is no saleable commodity; and even when they come to this age they will not yield above *3l.* or *3l. 2s. 6d.*° at most on the exchange; which

---

3l, 2s. 6d.: Three pounds, two shillings, and six pence.

cannot turn to account either to the parents or kingdom, the charge of nutriment and rags having been at least four times that value.

I shall now therefore humbly propose my own thoughts, which I hope will not be liable to the least objection.

I have been assured by a very knowing American of my acquaintance in London, that a young healthy child well nursed is at a year old a most delicious, nourishing, and wholesome food, whether stewed, roasted, baked, or broiled; and I make no doubt that it will equally serve in a fricassee or a ragout.

I do therefore humbly offer it to public consideration that of the 120,000 children already computed, 20,000 may be reserved for breed, whereof only one-fourth part to be males; which is more than we allow to sheep, black cattle, or swine; and my reason is, that these children are seldom the fruits of marriage, a circumstance not much regarded by our savages; therefore one male will be sufficient to serve four females. That the remaining 100,000 may, at a year old, be offered in sale to the persons of quality and fortune through the kingdom; always advising the mother to let them suck plentifully in the last month, so as to render them plump and fat for a good table. A child will make two dishes at an entertainment for friends; and when the family dines alone, the fore or hind quarter will make a reasonable dish, and seasoned with a little pepper or salt will be very good boiled on the fourth day, especially in winter.

I have reckoned upon a medium that a child just born will weigh 12 pounds, and in a solar year, if tolerably nursed, will increase to 28 pounds.

I grant this food will be somewhat dear, and therefore very proper for landlords, who, as they have already devoured most of the parents, seem to have the best title to the children.

Infant's flesh will be in season throughout the year, but more plentiful in March, and a little before and after: for we are told by a grave author, an eminent French physician, that fish being a prolific diet, there are more children born in Roman Catholic countries about nine months after Lent than at any other season; therefore, reckoning a year after Lent, the markets will be more glutted than usual, because the number of popish infants is at least three to one in this kingdom: and therefore it will have one other collateral advantage, by lessening the number of papists among us.

I have already computed the charge of nursing a beggar's child (in which list I reckon all cottagers, laborers, and four-fifths of the farmers) to be about 2s. per annum, rags included; and I believe no gentleman would repine to give 10s. for the carcass of a good fat child, which, as I have said, will make four dishes of excellent nutritive meat, when he has only some particular friend or his own family to dine with him. Thus the squire will learn to be a good landlord, and grow popular among the tenants; the mother will have 8s. net profit, and be fit for work till she produces another child.

Those who are more thrifty (as I must confess the times require) may *15*
flay the carcass; the skin of which artificially dressed will make admirable
gloves for ladies, and summer boots for fine gentlemen.

As to our city of Dublin, shambles° may be appointed for this purpose in the most convenient parts of it, and butchers we may be assured
will not be wanting: although I rather recommend buying the children
alive, and dressing them hot from the knife as we do roasting pigs.

A very worthy person, a true lover of his country, and whose virtues
I highly esteem, was lately pleased in discoursing on this matter to offer a
refinement upon my scheme. He said that many gentlemen of this kingdom, having of late destroyed their deer, he conceived that the want of
venison might be well supplied by the bodies of young lads and maidens,
not exceeding fourteen years of age nor under twelve; so great a number
of both sexes in every country being not ready to starve for want of work
and service; and these to be disposed of by their parents, if alive, or
otherwise by their nearest relations. But with due deference to so excellent
a friend and so deserving a patriot, I cannot be altogether in his sentiments;
for as to the males, my American acquaintance assured me from frequent
experience that their flesh was generally tough and lean, like that of our
schoolboys by continual exercise, and their taste disagreeable; and to fat-
ten them would not answer the charge. Then as to the females, it would,
I think, with humble submission be a loss to the public, because they soon
would become breeders themselves: and besides, it is not improbable that
some scrupulous people might be apt to censure such a practice (although
indeed very unjustly), as a little bordering upon cruelty; which, I confess,
has always been with me the strongest objection against any project, how
well soever intended.

But in order to justify my friend, he confessed that this expedient
was put into his head by the famous Psalmanazar, a native of the island
Formosa, who came from thence to London about twenty years ago: and
in conversation told my friend, that in his country when any young person
happened to be put to death, the executioner sold the carcass to persons of
quality as a prime dainty; and that in his time the body of a plump girl of
fifteen, who was crucified for an attempt to poison the emperor, was sold
to his imperial majesty's prime minister of state, and other great mandar-
ins of the court, in joints from the gibbet, at 400 crowns. Neither indeed
can I deny, that if the same use were made of several plump girls in this
town, who without one single groat to their fortunes cannot stir abroad
without a chair, and appear at the playhouse and assemblies in foreign
fineries which they never will pay for, the kingdom would not be the
worse.

Some persons of a desponding spirit are in great concern about that
vast number of poor people, who are aged, diseased, or maimed, and I

shambles: Slaughterhouses.

have been desired to employ my thoughts what course may be taken to ease the nation of so grievous an encumbrance. But I am not in the least pain upon that matter, because it is very well known that they are every day dying and rotting by cold and famine, and filth and vermin, as fast as can be reasonably expected. And as to the young laborers, they are now in as hopeful a condition: they cannot get work, and consequently pine away for want of nourishment, to a degree that if at any time they are accidentally hired to common labor, they have not strength to perform it; and thus the country and themselves are happily delivered from the evils to come.

I have too long digressed, and therefore shall return to my subject. I *20* think the advantages by the proposal which I have made are obvious and many, as well as the highest importance.

For first, as I have already observed, it would greatly lessen the number of papists, with whom we are yearly overrun, being the principal breeders of the nation as well as our most dangerous enemies; and who stay at home on purpose to deliver the kingdom to the Pretender, hoping to take their advantage by the absence of so many good Protestants, who have chosen rather to leave their country than stay at home and pay tithes against their conscience to an Episcopal curate.

Secondly, the poor tenants will have something valuable of their own, which by law may be made liable to distress and help to pay their landlord's rent, their corn and cattle being aleady seized, and money a thing unknown.

Thirdly, whereas the maintenance of 100,000 children from two years old and upward, cannot be computed at less than *10s.* a-piece per annum, the nation's stock will be thereby increased £50,000 per annum, beside the profit of a new dish introduced to the tables of all gentlemen of fortune in the kingdom who have any refinement in taste. And the money will circulate among ourselves, the goods being entirely of our own growth and manufacture.

Fourthly, the constant breeders, beside the gain of *8s.* sterling per annum by the sale of their children, will be rid of the charge of maintaining them after the first year.

Fifthly, this food would likewise bring great custom to taverns, *25* where the vintners will certainly be so prudent as to procure the best receipts for dressing it to perfection, and consequently have their houses frequented by all the fine gentlemen, who justly value themselves upon their knowledge in good eating; and a skillful cook, who understands how to oblige his guests, will contrive to make it as expensive as they please.

Sixthly, this would be a great inducement to marriage, which all wise nations have either encouraged by rewards or enforced by laws and penalties. It would increase the care and tenderness of mothers toward their children, when they were sure of a settlement for life to the poor babes, provided in some sort by the public, to their annual profit instead of expense. We should see an honest emulation among the married women, which of them would bring the fattest child to the market. Men would become as fond of their wives during the time of their pregnancy as they are now of their mares in foal, their cows in calf, their sows when they are ready to farrow; nor offer to beat or kick them (as is too frequent a practice) for fear of a miscarriage.

Many other advantages might be enumerated. For instance, the addition of some thousand carcasses in our exportation of barreled beef, the propagation of swine's flesh, and improvement in the art of making good bacon, so much wanted among us by the great destruction of pigs, too frequent at our table; which are no way comparable in taste or magnificence to a well-grown, fat, yearling child, which roasted whole will make a considerable figure at a lord mayor's feast or any other public entertainment. But this and many others I omit, being studious of brevity.

Supposing that 1,000 families in this city would be constant customers for infants' flesh, besides others who might have it at merry-meetings, particularly at weddings and christenings, I compute that Dublin would take off annually about 20,000 carcasses; and the rest of the kingdom (where probably they will be sold somewhat cheaper) the remaining 80,000.

I can think of no one objection that will possibly be raised against this proposal, unless it should be urged that the number of people will be thereby much lessened in the kingdom. This I freely own, and it was indeed one principal design in offering it to the world. I desire the reader will observe, that I calculate my remedy for this one individual kingdom of Ireland and for no other that ever was, is, or I think ever can be upon earth. Therefore let no man talk to me of other expedients: of taxing our absentees at 5s. a pound: of using neither clothes nor household furniture except what is of our own growth and manufacture: of utterly rejecting the materials and instruments that promote foreign luxury: of curing the expensiveness of pride, vanity, idleness, and gaming in our women: of introducing a vein of parsimony, prudence, and temperance: of learning to love our country, in the want of which we differ even from Laplanders and the inhabitants of Topinamboo: of quitting our animosities and factions, not acting any longer like the Jews, who were murdering one another at the very moment their city was taken: of being a little cautious not to sell our country and conscience for nothing: of teaching landlords to have at least one degree of mercy toward their tenants: lastly, of putting a spirit of honesty, industry, and skill into our shopkeepers; who, if a resolution could now be taken to buy only our native goods, would immediatly unite to cheat and exact upon us in the price, the measure, and the goodness, nor could ever yet be brought to make one fair proposal of just dealing, though often and earnestly invited to it.

Therefore I repeat, let no man talk to me of these and the like expedients, till he has at least some glimpse of hope that there will be ever some hearty and sincere attempt to put them in practice. *30*

But as to myself, having been wearied out for many years with offering vain, idle, visionary thoughts, and at length utterly despairing of success, I fortunately fell upon this proposal; which, as it is wholly new, so it has something solid and real, of no expense and little trouble, full in our own power, and whereby we can incur no danger of disobliging England. For this kind of commodity will not bear exportation, the flesh being of too tender a consistence to admit a long continuance in salt, although perhaps I could name a country which would be glad to eat up our whole nation without it.

After all, I am not so violently bent upon my own opinion as to reject any offer proposed by wise men, which shall be found equally innocent, cheap, easy, and effectual. But before something of that kind shall be advanced in contradiction to my scheme, and offering a better, I desire the author or authors will be pleased maturely to consider two points. First, as things now stand, how they will be able to find food and raiment for 100,000 useless mouths and backs. And secondly, there being a round million of creatures in human figure throughout this kingdom, whose subsistence put into a common stock would leave them in debt 2,000,000*l*. sterling, adding those who are beggars by profession to the bulk of farmers, cottagers, and laborers, with the wives and children who are beggars in effect; I desire those politicians who dislike my overture, and may perhaps be so bold as to attempt an answer, that they will first ask the parents of these mortals, whether they would not at this day think it a great happiness to have been sold for food at a year old in the manner I prescribe, and thereby have avoided such a perpetual scene of misfortunes as they have since gone through by the oppression of landlords, the impossibility of paying rent without money or trade, the want of common sustenance, with neither house nor clothes to cover them from the inclemencies of the weather, and the most inevitable prospect of entailing the like or greater miseries upon their breed for ever.

I profess, in the sincerity of my heart, that I have not the least personal interest in endeavoring to promote this necessary work, having no other motive than the public good of my country, by advancing our trade, providing for infants, relieving the poor, and giving some pleasure to the rich. I have no children by which I can propose to get a single penny; the youngest being nine years old, and my wife past child-bearing.

Questions for Discussion

1. At what point in this essay did you first become aware that Swift is being ironic?
2. What steps has Swift taken to make his proposal seem "modest" and his voice reasonable?
3. Why does the speaker in this essay believe that his proposal would be unsuitable for adolescents? Why isn't he worried about the problem of the elderly poor?

4. What does this essay reveal about Ireland under British domination?

5. Does Swift offer any alternative to eating the children of the poor? If there are alternatives to cannibalism, why devote so many paragraphs to a proposal that most people would quickly reject?

6. What is the function of the concluding paragraph?

7. Writers of textbooks often reprint this essay as an example of writing to persuade, and the essay does incorporate such persuasive strategies as anticipating and responding to points that might be raised by one's opponents (see pp. 182–83). How would you define Swift's purpose? Is he writing to persuade readers to adopt the proposals outlined in paragraph 29? Or is he writing primarily to shock people out of complacency?

Suggestions for Writing

1. Use irony to write a "modest" solution to a contemporary social problem.

2. Would you be willing to sell your child on the black market? Imagine yourself to be desperately poor, and write a response to someone who has offered to buy your child.

5

Writing to Persuade Others

As the previous chapter has shown, writers are sometimes motivated to move readers simply for the sake of producing an emotion from which some unspecified good may follow. Judy Syfers, for example, does not tell her readers what they should do to change their lives. She simply expresses her anger and frustration, assuming that many other women would share those feelings and enjoy seeing them get public recognition. The evocation of feeling may be necessary when working for change — be it rights for women or the elimination of poverty. But when we want to argue for a specific change, we must do more than move our audience. We must persuade them to support a proposal or undertake an action.

Persuasion ranges from advertising to scholarly arguments. Between these extremes are dozens of situations in which persuasion is fundamental to everyday life. When you apply for a job, propose a marriage, try to borrow money, or ask your landlord to fix the plumbing, you are using persuasion in an attempt to get someone to do something you want. At other times you use persuasion to achieve benefits for others — as in trying to raise money for the victims of a famine or in trying to persuade the government to protect an endangered species of wildlife. What all of these examples have in common is that they presume the need to change someone's mind. We need to persuade others only when differences of opinion exist. Persuasion is unnecessary when widespread agreement already exists, and it is inappropriate when questions allow for only one correct answer.

Classical rhetoric recognized that persuasion was accomplished through three means: the credibility of the writer/speaker (*ethos*), the logic of the argument (*logos*), and the skill with which appropriate feelings are inspired (*pathos*). This threefold approach to persuasion prevailed in the West for almost two thousand years, but its practitioners vary in what they emphasize and what strategies they recommend. Aristotle, for example, believed that ethos is the most important aspect of persuasion and that we make ourselves believable by how we present ourselves in what we say and write. But Aristotle defined *ethos* as something created within the work (from which it would follow that a bad person could seem to be credible because of his skill in arguing). Other rhetoricians have argued that ethos cannot be created artificially and that only good people (or people who are actively trying to be good) can write arguments that are truly persuasive. Still others have emphasized the role of pathos. Cicero, one of the greatest speakers of the ancient world, argued that nothing is more important than to be able to move an audience: "For men decide far more problems by hate, or love, or lust, or rage, or sorrow, or joy, or hope, or fear, or illusion, or some other inward emotion, than by reality, or authority, or any legal standard, or judicial precedent, or statute."

In short, there has been — and there is still — no universal agreement about how to persuade others. Different opinions prevailed in the classical world, and the debate is still going on. But at this point we can offer some basic principles.

- Your strategy may vary depending upon the topic and your audience. But you should always consider the extent to which you have employed ethos, pathos, and logos. As a general rule, an argument depending upon only one of these methods probably won't be as persuasive as an argument using more than one.
- Although people sometimes make decisions upon impulse, and some forms of persuasion (like television commercials) are designed to inspire unreasoned decisions, the most persuasive arguments are those that still make sense after we have thought about them for a while. It follows that persuasion should appeal to the mind as well as to the heart.

USING LOGIC

Appealing to the mind requires at least some familiarity with logic. Classical rhetoric teaches two types of logic, inductive and deductive reasoning. Modern rhetoric has explored alternative forms of reasoning designed to complement traditional approaches. Whatever type of logic you decide best suits your needs, you should realize that you can move freely among the various options outlined below.

Inductive Reasoning

To reason inductively means using examples to discover what seems to be true. In an inductive argument a writer presents a series of examples (or pieces of evidence) and draws a conclusion from their significance. Reaching this conclusion means going beyond the accumulated evidence and making a reasonable guess, the *inductive leap*. Induction is persuasive when the evidence is sufficient to justify the conclusion. Writers who make the inductive leap from insufficient evidence are said to be jumping to conclusions, a failure in reasoning so common that it has become a cliché.

When you use induction carefully, you will reach a conclusion that is probably true. But you should recognize that your conclusion is probable rather than absolute. It is always possible that other evidence, which you haven't considered, could lead to a conclusion different from your own. For example, suppose that it is the first week of classes and you are taking a math class from a professor you have never worked with previously. At each of the first three classes the professor arrives late and lectures in a disorganized manner that is difficult to understand. Tomorrow is the last day you can drop the class and still add a new one in its place. Concluding that your math teacher is a bad teacher, you decide to drop his course and substitute another course in its place. Within the constraints of daily life, which often require us to make decisions quickly, you have used induction to make a decision that seems reasonable under the circumstances. On the other hand, it is possible that the math professor had a bad week because he was staying up all night with sick children and that his performance will improve dramatically in the weeks that follow.

As a rule, your conclusions will be the strongest when they rest upon a foundation built of many separate pieces of evidence. When a serious conclusion is arrived at inductively, it will almost certainly have extensive information behind it. The scientific method illustrates induction at its best. Researchers conduct hundreds and sometimes thousands of experiments before arguing for a new type of medical treatment, and after publication of these results other researchers seek to verify them independently. But however solid these conclusions seem to be, they are often challenged by new studies that take a different approach. (See Lewis Thomas's essay, "The Art of Teaching Science," in Chapter 9.) So no matter how many examples support an inductively derived conclusion, you can never be certain that you have somehow managed to discover an absolute truth.

Deductive Reasoning

To reason deductively means to identify propositions that are already believed to be true and to discover an additional truth that follows from these propositions. A deductive argument reflects the logic of a syllogism in which a major and a minor premise lead to a conclusion that is necessarily true.

Major Premise:	All men have hearts.
Minor Premise:	Bill is a man.
Conclusion:	Bill has a heart.

In this case the reasoning is both valid and true. It is *valid* because it follows the conventions of logic: If we accept the major and the minor premise, then we must recognize that the conclusion follows logically from them.

Occasionally, however, you will find syllogisms that are valid but *untrue:*

Major Premise:	All chemistry professors are boring.
Minor Premise:	Veronica is a chemistry professor.
Conclusion:	Veronica is boring.

Although this syllogism follows the same pattern as the previous syllogism and is valid, it is untrue because it rests upon a highly questionable major premise. For a syllogism to be true as well as valid, both the major and the minor premise must be unquestionably true.

Unfortunately, there are relatively few propositions that everyone accepts as true — or "self-evident," as Thomas Jefferson declares at the beginning of "The Declaration of Independence." And the number seems to be decreasing. Consider what happens if we modify our first example.

Major Premise:	All men have functioning kidneys.
Minor Premise:	Bill is a man.
Conclusion:	Bill has functioning kidneys.

A hundred years ago, this syllogism would have been both valid and true; today, it is valid but untrue, since dialysis machines allow people to live without functioning kidneys. Conceivably, the day may come when people can function without hearts. (We have already seen several attempts to support life with artificial hearts.)

Consider, also, that different readers have different responses to language and that language is dependent upon social context. To put it simply, words can (and do) change in meaning. The major premise of our first example ("All men have hearts") is already more questionable than it would have been fifty years ago. A writer beginning with this statement could face such questions as "What do you mean by *men?* Does that include women?" and "What about *hearts?* Do you mean a body organ or a capacity for feeling emotion?"

But writing an essay is not the same as writing a syllogism: You have more than three sentences to make your case. If you want to organize an essay deductively because your position derives from a fundamental principle that you are confident your audience will share, you should pace yourself according to the needs of the situation. On some topics, for some audiences, you may need to spend several paragraphs establishing your premise. At other times you may be able to take your premise for granted and offer what is called an *enthymeme,* or two-part deductive argument from which the major premise has been omitted. Abbreviating an argument in this way does not necessarily mean that it will be shorter; it just means that you have omitted one step in order to emphasize other aspects of your case.

Substantive Reasoning

Over the years deductive reasoning has been favored by philosophers because it seemed the type of logic most likely to lead to truth. But many writers find it ill suited for argumentation, and philosophers increasingly acknowledge other forms of reasoning. After spending many years analyzing arguments in practical fields such as politics and law, Chaim Perelman concluded that formal logic is seldom appropriate, since argument is more concerned with winning the adherence of an audience than with demonstrating the truth of abstract propositions.

> What are we to think of this reduction to two forms of reasoning of all the wide variety of arguments that men use in their discussions and in pleading a cause or in justifying an action? Yet, since the time of Aristotle, logic has confined its study to deductive and inductive reasoning. . . . As a result, an argument that cannot be reduced to canonical form is regarded as logically valueless. (*The New Rhetoric and the Humanities* [Dordrecht, Holland: Reidel, 1979], 26)

Perelman showed that when we actually examine arguments that we find persuasive, we realize that many of them seem reasonable even though they do not conform strictly to the conventions of induction or deduction.

At about the same time as Perelman was conducting his research in Belgium, the British philosopher Stephen Toulmin was reaching a similar conclusion. Analyzing arguments made within various fields, Toulmin discovered that they had certain features in common. This discovery led him to offer a new model of argument that is easy for writers to use. *Substantive logic* was the term he preferred for his system, a working logic suitable for the needs of the diverse range of arguments identified by Perelman and other theorists.

According to Toulmin, every argument includes a *claim,* which is the assertion or conclusion the argument is trying to prove. The claim is supported by *data,* which describes the various types of evidence (such as facts, personal experience, or appeals to authority) that lead an audience to decide that the claim is reasonable. Both the claim and the data are stated explicitly in the argument. Underlying them, however, and not necessarily made explicit (although they can be) are what Toulmin called *warrants*. He described warrants as "bridges [that] authorize the sort of step to which our argument commits us." Warrants may be directly stated, but very often (especially when they are obvious), they are not.

Here is one of the examples that Toulmin used to illustrate his model.

Claim: Harry is a British subject.
Data: Harry was born in Bermuda.
Warrant: A man born in Bermuda will be a British subject.

As you can see from this example, the claim is based directly upon its data. The warrant is simply explanatory; its function is to show *why* the claim follows from the data. A good way to understand the warrant, especially when it has not been explicitly stated, is to imagine a statement beginning with either *since* or *because*. In the example cited above the data supports the claim, since people born in Bermuda are British subjects. If you were making this argument in Bermuda or in England, you could probably assume that your audience would understand the warrant even if you did not state it. On the other hand, if you were making this argument in Tibet, you would probably need to make sure that the warrant was clearly understood.

Behind any warrant is what Toulmin called *backing*. The backing, or grounds, for a warrant will vary from argument to argument and from field to field. For the example cited above, the backing consists of the specific pieces of legislation that govern the citizenship of people born in British colonies. Like the warrant, backing may be either explicit or implicit in an argument. But unlike the warrant, which is a generalization, backing consists of facts. If you use Toulmin's model for writing persuasive essays, you should always ask yourself if you could come up with backing for your warrant if someone questioned its legitimacy.

For writers, one of the advantages of Toulmin's model is that it does not require a fixed pattern of organization. You can arrange your ideas in whatever sequence seems best suited for your work, as long as you are careful to provide data for any claim you make and are able to explain why the data supports the claim when the link between them is not immediately clear. Another advantage of Toulmin's model is that it easily incorporates *qualifiers,* such as *probably* or *unless,* that protect the overall integrity of your arguments from exceptions that could be used to challenge what you are arguing. When arguing about Harry's citizenship, for example, you could point out that the data supports the claim unless Harry's parents were aliens in Bermuda or unless he has become a naturalized citizen of another country.

LOGICAL FALLACIES

Whatever type of reasoning you use, you should try to be alert for certain errors that can undermine your case. The detailed study of logic reveals many different ways arguments can break down. Dwelling upon these *logical fallacies,* as they are called, can sometimes make writers feel that writing to persuade is more difficult than it really is. Nevertheless, having some familiarity with a few of the most common fallacies can help you evaluate the arguments you read and revise those that you write.

Ad Hominem Argument

Latin for "to the man," an *ad hominem* argument is a personal attack upon someone whose view differs from that of the arguer. Writers who make *ad hominem* arguments undermine their credibility in at least two ways. To attack an opponent, rather than what an opponent has argued, is to ignore the real issues under consideration. Personal attacks also appear to be mean-spirited, which can alienate an impartial audience. When a writer arguing for gun control attacks members of the National Rifle Association as "macho men who don't understand the definition of a civilized society," she is offending the people she most needs to persuade and probably making unbiased readers sympathize with the opponents she just attacked.

There are, of course, some situations in which it can be legitimate to question the personal integrity of an opponent. In a political campaign, for example, voters might decide that a candidate who has cheated on his income tax cannot be trusted to govern, no matter how appealing his positions are on various issues. But even in politics, where personal attacks can sometimes be justified, people quickly tire of a campaign that seems to consist of nothing but *ad hominem* arguments. As a general rule, it is more honorable to focus argument upon ideas rather than personalities.

Appeal to False Authority

A good way to support an argument is to cite testimony from authorities in the field you are writing about. If you are writing about child care, for instance, you may wish to incorporate the views of a respected pediatrician. But knowledge in one field does not make someone expert in another. Citing the pediatrician in an argument on the space program is an appeal to a false authority. Advertisements offer many examples of this fallacy by attempting to persuade us to buy products that have been endorsed by well-known actors or athletes who probably know no more about the product than we do.

But appeals to false authority also occur in written arguments — in part because well-known people sometimes enjoy making public statements on anything that happens to interest them. In "What Is Vulgar?"

(Chapter 9) Joseph Epstein describes a prominent writer who was asked during a television interview to give his views on the war in Vietnam. "I am a writer," the author answered, "and that doesn't mean I have to have an opinion on everything. I'd rather discuss literature." Such self-restraint is admirable and worth remembering. Quote a novelist on writing novels and you will have appealed to a legitimate authority. Quote that same novelist on the conduct of a war and, unless the novelist happens to be an expert on warfare as well, you will have appealed to a false authority.

Begging the Question

Writers beg the question when they begin an argument by assuming what they actually need to prove. At its most obvious, begging the question takes the form of a statement that leads nowhere, since it goes around in a circle: "College is too expensive because it costs more than it is worth." This statement simply makes the same point two ways. An argument could be written to show that college is too expensive, but it would need to be supported with evidence rather than repetition. Begging the question can also take more subtle forms, such as introducing a word (like *unfair*) that expresses an unsupported value judgment.

Jumping to Conclusions

This fallacy, sometimes called "hasty generalization," occurs when a writer makes a conclusion based upon insufficient evidence. Consider, for example, a personnel director who decides, "I don't think we should hire any other graduates of that school; we hired Randy, and he couldn't do anything right." To judge all of the graduates of a school by one person is to jump to a conclusion. People often jump to conclusions in daily life, especially when decisions are influenced by feeling: "I know you two are going out together. I saw you talking after class today!"

Writers sometimes jump to conclusions because they lack evidence or because they are anxious to complete an assignment. Rather than jumping to a conclusion your argument has not supported, you should either search for additional evidence or modify your claim in such a way that your evidence does support it.

Post Hoc, Ergo Propter Hoc

The name of this fallacy is Latin for "after this, therefore because of this." *Post hoc* arguments, as they are called for short, confuse cause with coincidence. Examples of *post hoc* reasoning are often found in discussions of large social questions: "Since MTV began broadcasting, the number of teenage pregnancies has risen sharply." This statement assumes that MTV is causing teenagers to get pregnant. Although the lyrics of rock music and the sensual imagery of rock videos may contribute to an atmosphere that encourages sexual activity, there are almost certainly many causes for the rise of teenage pregnancy during the same period that MTV happened to be broadcasting.

Superstitions can embody a type of *post hoc* reasoning: "I failed the quiz because I walked under a ladder yesterday." It is important to realize that every event is preceded by many unrelated events: The sun may come up shortly after the rooster crows, but that doesn't prove that the rooster is making the sun come up.

Slippery Slope

Although it is reasonable to consider the probable effects of any change that is being argued for, it is fallacious to base one's opposition to that change entirely upon the prediction of some future result that is, at best, a guess. Writers who use slippery slope arguments are using what is almost always a type of fear tactic: "Give them an inch, and they will take a mile." An argument like this shifts attention away from the issue at hand. Because the future is hard to predict, and one change does not necessarily have to lead to another, it is wiser to consider the immediate effects of what is being debated than to draw frightening pictures of what could happen someday.

RESPONDING TO OPPOSITION

Although writers need to avoid logical fallacies, doing so does not in itself guarantee that their arguments will be persuasive. Because persuasion assumes the existence of an audience that has views different from our own, it is essential to recognize these differences and respond to them fairly. One-sided arguments are almost never convincing. To be persuasive, writers must show that they have given consideration to views that differ from their own. After anticipating the arguments most likely to be advanced by opponents, you can respond to these arguments by either refuting them or conceding that they have merit.

Of these two strategies, refutation has been traditionally emphasized in rhetoric. By introducing an opposition argument into your own essay, and then showing why that argument is faulty, you demonstrate good credibility, or ethos, as you respond fairly to that view. You also improve the logos of your case by resolving concerns that readers may be wondering about. Although there are no fixed rules governing where and when you refute the views of opponents, you should usually try to do so relatively early in an argument. If you wait until the end of your argument, some readers may have already decided that you are too one-sided, and some may have even stopped reading.

Many writers find that the easiest way to introduce opposition arguments without obscuring their own position is to begin a paragraph with an argument offered by opponents and then devote the rest of the paragraph to providing a counterargument. By following this method, they get the chance to have the last word. In "Death and Justice" Edward Koch organized his entire argument according to this plan, but it is more common for writers to devote only a few paragraphs to refutation and reserve other paragraphs for advancing their own position.

When you consider opposition arguments, you may very well find that there is one that you cannot refute. Controversy usually exists because there is at least one good argument that can be made on different sides. If you want to be persuasive, you should be prepared to concede any point that you cannot refute. By admitting that you see merit in one of the arguments made by your opponents, you show that you are fair-minded and make it easier for opponents to recognize merit in your own case. Telling people "I am completely right, and you are completely wrong" is more likely to annoy them than to persuade them. But when you say, in effect, "I admit that you have a good point there," you create a bridge over which people can cross to your side.

By attempting to overcome the differences that exist between you and your opponents, you are using what Kenneth Burke called *identification*. According to Burke, identification is the necessary corrective to the divisions that exist between people. Even though individuals are distinct and may disagree strongly about a particular issue, they can be united by some principle that they share. Persuasion is achieved by identifying your cause with the interests of your audience. You can make a simple form of identification by declaring a common bond with your audience. When speaking to a group of children, for example, you might say, "I know how you feel. When I was a child, I used to feel that way too." But the principle of identification goes far beyond such overt statements. Once we begin to think about what we have in common with others, including our opponents, we can often detect ties that we had not previously recognized.

Writing to persuade thus becomes a means of overcoming division and drawing people together. At its crudest levels persuasion may draw people together superficially through means that are manipulative rather than honest: A successful advertising campaign can convince thousands of people to buy a product they really don't need. But when we write about ideas and treat our opponents with respect, we open the way for long-lasting agreements built upon shared beliefs.

Persuasion should thus be conducted honorably. You should never overlook important evidence that operates against your conclusion. And you should never exaggerate or misrepresent views that differ from your own. Show that you are fair-minded, but be sure your own position is clear and well supported.

DOWN WITH MOTHER'S DAY
Estelle Gilson

> *In making an argument against Mother's Day, Estelle Gilson runs the risk of making readers think she has something against motherhood — which, we have often been told, is as American as apple pie. Why would she run this risk? As you read her essay — which was first published in* Newsweek *a few days before Mother's Day in 1990 — consider Gilson's purpose. Would she be satisfied if readers voted to abolish Mother's Day, or is she really bothered by something else?*

Mother's Day has got to go. . . .

This treacly, anachronistic celebration was proposed by Anna M. Jarvis to commemorate her mother's death in May 1905. It became an officially recognized American occasion by congressional resolution, proclaimed by President Woodrow Wilson in 1914.

Why?

Because in 1914 there was no widespread birth control and no legal abortion; no baby food, no formula, no disposable diapers, no washing machines, no dishwashers, no frozen foods, no takeout food, no microwaves, blenders, or food processors, no pizzas, no workout tapes, no family cars and no midwinter flights to the Caribbean. The average mother washed, rinsed, wrung and ironed, shopped, chopped, cooked and baked, shoveled, cleaned, scoured and scrubbed in her winter-cold, summer-hot home to enable the head of her household and their offspring to look presentable at work and at school, respectively. How Mother felt or looked didn't matter. Where did she go anyway, except to church once a week, and everybody knows she had one good dress for that. And in 1914 the earning power of mothers was nil. Who wouldn't give such pathetic creatures candy or flowers once a year?

By Mother's Day's "anagram" year, 1941, with the celebration a   5 regular and reliable event, mothers had changed. They had a new sense of their worth, but still lacked economic and political power. The puniest and most impoverished of all human creatures, the baby, demanded and received more care and attention than the average mother. By then, however, to compensate for self-denial, exploitation and dependency, American mothers, though still ostensibly submissive, had evolved a method of controlling their husbands and children. They promulgated the canon that motherhood is "sacred," and developed insidious and artful techniques to support the new theology which became known as momism. According to writer Philip Wylie, who exposed the whole shoddy business, momism depended on threats, seduction, deception and bribery to succeed. And succeed it did. For generations, "megaloid momworship," in Wylie's

words, enabled America's women to dominate its most powerful men.

Alas, Wylie-moms are still with us. Female life expectancy has increased with the decades, and motherhood has been parlayed into a highly
cost-efficient profession. Don't laugh. Though mothering's early rewards
may not equal those of good left-handed pitching, it guarantees a longer
career.

For an investment of seven, eight, maybe 10 years of mothering, plus
a nine-month carrying charge, sons and daughters are not only expected
to provide mothers with yearly tributes of cards, candy, flowers, scarves,
pins, theater tickets and turkey dinners on Mother's Day *and* birthdays,
anniversaries and sundry other occasions. The children find themselves in
indentured servitude for the rest of dear old Mom's life. This peonage,
which often lasts 60 or 70 years, may include shopping trips, checkbook
balancing, visits to doctors, phone calls in the middle of the night, searches
for lost keys, to say nothing of listening to constant reports about how
other people's children send them to Florida.

It is time to end this bondage. However much these paragons sob
and sigh, however real some of their problems may be, they are no longer
the powerless, pathetic creatures of yore. There has, after all, been a wom-
en's movement and vast changes in what is expected of mothers and how
they live. The home-based mother in a two-parent family has a range of
gadgets and services that, for the first time in history, includes a father
who can boil water and deal with diapers. She has time to go shopping
with her own mother, go bowling, study Greek or indulge other personal
fancies.

The single working mother does not need programmed adulation.
She knows exactly what she's doing and why. If she's giving her children
an allowance out of a borderline income, she doesn't want it wasted on
five-and-dime trinkets.

The working mother with a working husband and a higher standard   *10*
of living doesn't have to wait for the second Sunday in May for her reward,
either. She can buy herself precisely what she wants, when she wants it.

As for the woman (currently invisible to polite society) who heaps
AIDS, addictions, physical and sexual abuse on her children, there's the
fact that sometimes, birthing is not the same as mothering.

Wake up, America! Mother's Day's time has come and gone. It served
its purpose. It recognized the importance of mothers in the male-dominated family, when there was such a thing as the male-dominated family.
Along with apple pie and the Brooklyn Dodgers, motherhood formed the
sacred trinity, belief in which sustained us through the second world war.

But apple pie has been replaced by yogurt, the Dodgers are long
gone to Los Angeles and motherhood has finally been demystified. The
truth is America's mothers don't need yearly handouts or propitiatory
offerings. Their relationships to their husbands, to their sons and daugh-

ters are more open, more honest and more direct. And that's the way it should be.

Besides, American free enterprise being what it is, Mother's Day has gotten too commercial. I say let's get rid of it. Let's export it along with rock music, farm machinery and bank loans to Eastern Europe where budding young capitalists and their overworked mothers will enjoy it. For a while.

Questions for Discussion

1. Gilson begins her essay by stating her claim. What is the advantage of this strategy? Are there any disadvantages?
2. According to Gilson, Mother's Day served a purpose in the past, but its "time has come and gone." Why does she believe that this holiday is "anachronistic"?
3. Consider the first two sentences in paragraph 4. Why does Gilson cram so much information into these sentences? Would she lose anything by breaking them up?
4. Gilson charges that women have used motherhood as a way to control husbands and children. Does this strike you as a reasonable generalization?
5. In paragraphs 8–11 Gilson recognizes that there are different types of mothers. How effectively has she responded to the lives of these women?
6. When this essay was first published, it was followed by the information that Gilson is "a daughter, mother, and grandmother." How does that information influence your response to the essay? Do you think a national magazine would have published this essay if it had been written by a man?

Suggestions for Writing

1. Are there any holidays that you object to? For example, how do you feel about New Year's Eve or Valentine's Day? Or how do you feel about birthdays? Write an argument against celebrating an occasion other people take for granted.
2. If you disagree with Gilson, write an argument on behalf of giving mothers the recognition that you think they deserve.

CLEAN UP OR PAY UP
Louis Barbash

> *Louis Barbash believes that college sports are a "mess," and he proposes a way to clean them up. If you are a fan of college sports, you may not like his proposal, but try not to let a love for sports keep you from evaluating this essay as an argument. Look at the data Barbash provides to support his case; and if the data does not persuade you to accept his proposal, consider whether you could raise any objections that the author has not anticipated.*

Tom Scates is one of the lucky ones. He has a bachelor's degree from Georgetown University, where he played basketball under the fabled John Thompson, one of the best college basketball coaches in the country, and one of the few who insist that their players go to class. Ninety percent of Thompson's players at Georgetown receive degrees, about three times the national average.

More than a decade after Tom Scates received his diploma, he has managed to parlay his Georgetown degree and education, his athletic skills, and the character he developed during his career in intercollegiate athletics, into a job as a doorman at a downtown Washington hotel.

Still, Scates *is* one of the lucky ones. He played for a good team at a good school, under a moral coach, and under a president, Father Timothy Healy, who believed that Georgetown was a school with a basketball team, not a basketball team with a school. He was not implicated in drug deals, shoplifting, violence, grade altering, point shaving, or under-the-table money scandals. He didn't have his scholarship yanked. He didn't emerge from school functionally illiterate. He got a job.

Many of the men Scates played against when he was at Georgetown, and their basketball and football counterparts at major colleges and universities, have not been so fortunate. Less than half the football and basketball scholarship athletes will graduate from college. And what education athletes do get is often so poor that it may be irrelevant whether they graduate or not.

In addition to corrupting the university's basic academic mission, big-time sports have been a lightning rod for financial corruption. College athletes are cash-poor celebrities. Although their performance on the field or court produces millions in revenue for the university, they receive in return only their scholarships — tuition, room, and board — and no spending money. They are forbidden from working part-time during the season. Athletes have been caught trying to make money by getting loans from coaches and advisers, selling the shoes and other gear they get as team members, taking allowances from agents, and getting paid for no-show summer jobs provided by jock-sniffing alumni — all violations of National Collegiate Athletic Association (NCAA) rules.

Things might be different if the NCAA would show some real inclination to clean up the college sports mess. But that organization has a well-developed instinct for the capillaries: instead of attacking the large-scale academic, financial, and criminal corruption in college sports, too often the investigators from Mission, Kansas, put their energies into busting athletes for selling their complimentary tickets and coaches for starting their practices a few weeks ahead of schedule. Meanwhile, the real problems of college athletics continue to fester.

Will the NCAA change? And if so, would that matter? Earlier this year, NCAA Executive Director Dick Schultz proposed new rules to stem college sports corruption. Schultz's reforms included "quality academic advising and career-counseling programs," restriction of recruiting, long-term contracts for coaches, reduced pressure and time demands on athletes, and the elimination of athletic dormitories to "make the athlete as indistinguishable from the rest of the student body as is humanly possible."

It's illegal to bet on sports except in Nevada, so bet on this instead: Schultz's proposals will not pass an NCAA dominated by college sports officials whose careers rest on winning games. Recall what has happened to much weaker suggestions. Even Georgetown's Coach Thompson boycotted his own team's games to protest as too severe the timid requirements of the NCAA's Proposition 48, which would have barred entering freshmen from athletic scholarships and competition if they did not have a 2.0 high school GPA and SAT scores totaling 700 points. Interested in even better odds? Take this to the bank: Even if Schultz gets every one of his proposals put in exactly as he outlined them, they—like everything else the NCAA has tried—will not work.

Well then, is there any way out of this mess? Yes. Actually, there are *two* ways out. Because the NCAA has so utterly failed, because in the present system the big-money pressures to cheat are so enormous, and because, like it or not, sports have such a widespread impact on the country's moral climate, there should be a federal law that requires schools *either* to return to the Ivy League ideal in which players are legitimate members of the student body, judged by the same standards as everybody else, *or* to let players on their teams be non-student professionals. All the trouble comes from trying to mix these two alternatives—from trying to achieve big revenues while retaining the veneer of purity.

The pure alternative doesn't have to ignore athletic ability among 10 prospective students—there were plenty of good football teams before today's double-standard disaster got firmly entrenched. You want to consider the athletic ability of college applicants for the same reason you want to consider musical or theatrical ability; a university should be a wonderfully diverse collection of talents that together stimulate people to develop in all sorts of positive ways. Athletic skill is one such talent—one that even academic purists ought to look at. But the key is that universities must consider athletic ability as only *part* of what they take into account when they accept a student. The fundamental mistake of today's college sports system is that it supposes a student could be at a university *solely* because of his athletic skill.

While the purely amateur option is probably the more desirable of the two, the professional one isn't nearly as horrible as it might seem at first. After all, coaches were originally volunteers, and now they're paid. (Army's first head coach, Dennis Michie, received no pay. Jess Hawley coached for free at Dartmouth from 1923-28. His 1925 team went undefeated and was the national champion.) So why not players?

Sweat Equity

How much would a salaried college athlete make? If the example of minor league baseball is anything to go on — and such authorities as Roger Meiners, a Clemson University economist who specializes in the economics of college sports, and Ed Garvey, the former head of the NFL Players Association, think that it is — college salaries would be enough for a young athlete to live on, but not so much as to bust college budgets. Minor league baseball players start at around $11,000 for their first full professional season and range upward to the neighborhood of $26,000 for players on AAA teams under major league option. So it seems fair to estimate a salary of about $15,000 for an average player on an average team.

The professional option's chief virtue is honesty. The current student-athlete system requires both students and universities to pretend that the young athletes are not full-time professionals, but rather full-time students who play sports in their spare time. But does anyone suppose that high school athletes reading four and five years below grade level would be considered for college admission, much less recruited and given full scholarships, if they were not football or basketball stars? Can the abuses of NCAA rules that have been uncovered at almost half of its biggest schools have any other meaning than that giving these athletes a real education is not what universities are trying to do?

The hypocrisy begins with the fundamental relationship between the players and the university: 18- to 20-year-olds, many of them poorly educated, inner-city blacks, coerced and deceived into playing four years of football or basketball without pay so that the university can sell tickets and television rights.

The coercion comes from the colleges' control of access to professional football or basketball: It is virtually impossible to go to the pros without playing college ball first. Colleges open that opportunity only to athletes who will agree to perform for the college for four years without getting a salary or even holding an outside part-time job. The athlete does receive a four-year scholarship and room and board while he is enrolled, a package the NCAA values at about $40,000. The deception lies in the fact 15 that the inducements held out to athletes by colleges — the chance to play pro ball and getting a college education — are essentially worthless, and the schools know it.

The athlete's first priority is to play pro ball. Forty-four percent of all black scholarship athletes, and 22 percent of white athletes, entertain hopes of playing in the pros. That's why they will play four years for nothing. But in fact, the lure of sports that keeps kids in school is a false hope and a cruel hoax. "The dream in the head of so many youngsters that they will achieve fame and riches in professional sports is touching, but it is also overwhelmingly unrealistic," says Robert Atwell, president of the American Council on Education. The would-be pro faces odds as high as 400-1: of the 20,000 "students" who play college basketball, for example, only 50 will make it to the NBA. The other 19,950 won't. Many of them will wind up like Tom Scates, in minimum wages jobs, or like Reggie Ford, who lost his football scholarship to Northwest Oklahoma State after he injured his knee, and now collects unemployment compensation in South Carolina.

The scholarships and promises of education are also worthless currency. Of every 10 young men who accept scholarships to play football at major schools, according to NCAA statistics, just 4 will graduate. Only 3 of every 10 basketball players receive degrees.

Not only are these athletes being cheated out of a promised education, but they and their universities are forced to erect elaborate, meretricious curricula to satisfy the student-athlete requirement, so of those who *do* get degrees, many receive diplomas that are barely worth the parchment they're printed on. Running back Ronnie Harmon majored in computer science at the University of Iowa, but took only one computer course in his three years of college. Another Iowa football player also majored in computer science, but in his senior year took only courses in billiards, bowling, and football; he followed up by getting a D in a summer school watercolor class. Transcripts of the members of the basketball team at Ohio University list credit for something called "International Studies 69B" — a course composed of a 14-day/10-game trip to Europe.

As things stand now, athletically gifted students who genuinely want an education are often steered away by eligibility-conscious advisers. Jan Kemp, the University of Georgia academic adviser for athletes who won a lawsuit after the university fired her for insisting on the athletes' right to be educated, recalls how a Georgia athlete was always placed in "dummy" classes despite his efforts to take "real" ones. "There's nothing wrong with his mind," says Kemp. "But the situation is magnified for athletes because there is so much money involved. There is too much control over who gets in and who takes what courses."

No case illustrates the cynicism that poisons big-time college sports better than that of former Washington Redskins star defensive end Dexter

20

Manley. Manley spent four years as a "student-athlete" at Oklahoma State University only to emerge, as he admitted years later, functionally illiterate. But OSU President John Campbell was not embarrassed: "There would be those who would argue that Dexter Manley got exactly what he wanted out of OSU. He was able to develop his athletic skills and ability, he was noticed by the pros, he got a pro contract. So maybe we did him a favor by letting him go through the program."

One scarcely knows where to start in on a statement like that. It's appalling that an accredited state university would admit a functional illiterate, even recruit him, and leave him illiterate after four years as a student. It's shocking that it would do all this in order to make money from his unpaid performance as an athlete. And it is little short of grotesque that an educator, entrusted with the education of 20,000 young men and women, would argue that the cynical arrangement between an institution of higher learning and an uneducated high school boy was, after all, a fair bargain.

The infection of hypocrisy spreads from the president's office to the athletic department and coaching staff. This may be the saddest betrayal in the system. These are 17-year-olds, dreaming of a lucrative career in sports. They have placed their faith in the coaches who have visited their homes, solicited their trust, and gotten to know their parents. But those coaches, as Robert Atwell points out, "may have a vested interest in perpetuating the myth rather than pointing out its inherent fallacy." That vested interest, of course, is that if they do not produce winning teams, at whatever cost, they will lose their jobs.

So instead, to recruit highly sought-after high-school athletes, coaches promise playing time, education, and exposure to national TV audiences and professional scouts. But once the player arrives on campus, coaches are under strong pressure to treat him like what he is: an employee, whose needs must be subordinated to the needs of the enterprise, i.e., winning.

Sports Without Strings

Gary Ruble, a former scholarship football player at the University of North Carolina, told a House subcommittee investigating college athletics that North Carolina "came to me and offered me, basically, the world. They came to me and said come to our school. Be a student athlete. We will guarantee that you graduate. We will promise you to be a star, et cetera, et cetera, et cetera." But once in Chapel Hill, Ruble found himself riding the bench. "You go in as an offensive lineman, which I was, at 240 pounds, and you go into a system where you have offensive linemen who are 285 and they are telling you that you are going to play. That's an impossibility," Ruble told the subcommittee. After three years, "my position coach called me into his office and stated that I should consider either transferring to another school or dropping out gracefully. I was no longer to be considered in their plans for our team," Ruble says. When he reported back to school anyway, he was told "I had no option of whether to stay or go. They were not allowing me to retain my scholarship."

A system of sports without strings — releasing college athletes and their universities from the pretense that they are students, and instead paying them for their services — would cure the student-athlete system's chief vices: its duplicity and its exploitiveness.

Athletes who want to get started on careers in sports, including those whose only way out of the ghetto may be the slam dunk and the 4.4-40, would find paying jobs in their chosen field. Overnight, thousands of new jobs as professional football and basketball players would be created. Players with the ability to get to the NFL and NBA would get paid during their years of apprenticeship. For those of lesser abilities, playing for college teams would be a career in itself, a career they could start right out of high school and continue as long as skills and bodies allowed. And as they matured and their playing careers drew to a close, the prospect of a real college education might seem more inviting than it did at 17.

Releasing athletes from having to be students would, ironically, make it easier for those who want an education to get it. Even with the best intentions, today's college athletes have little hope of being serious students. Basketball practice, for instance, begins October 15, and the season does not end for the most successful teams until after the NCAA championships in early April; in other words the season starts one month after school begins and ends one month before school is out. During the season, athletes spend six or more hours a day, 30 to 40 hours a week, on practice, viewing game-films, at chalk talks, weight lifting, conditioning, and attending team meetings. The best-prepared students would have difficulty attending to their studies while working 34 hours a week — and these are not the best-prepared students.

But under no-strings sports, athletes who want educations will fare better than they do now, because the pace of their education need not be governed by their eligibility for athletic competition. A football player could play the fall semester and study in the spring. Basketball players, whose season spans the two semesters, might enroll at schools with quarter or trimester systems, or study summers and after their sports careers are over. Instead of being corralled into courses rigged to provide high grades like "Theory of Volleyball," "Recreation and Leisure," "Jogging," and "Leisure Alternatives," athletes would be in a position to take only the courses they want and need. This would be even more likely if, as part of the pro option, universities were still required to offer full scholarships to athletes, to be redeemed whenever the athletes wanted to use them.

Under these changes, those athletes who end up going to college would be doing so because they were pursuing their own educational goals. This reform would replace today's phony jock curriculum with the kind of mature academic choices that made the G.I. Bill such a success.

Such considerations make it clear that it's time for schools to choose   30
between real amateurism and real professionalism. They can't have a little of both. From now on, in college sports, it's got to be either poetry or pros.

Questions for Discussion

1. Consider the introduction to this essay. Why does Barbash begin his argument by providing information about Tom Scates? Why does he wait until the end of paragraph 2 before revealing that Scates is a hotel doorman?
2. Barbash charges that the NCAA concerns itself with only minor rules infractions while "the real problems of college athletics continue to fester." In his view, what are those real problems? How are colleges guilty of "duplicity and exploitiveness" in their dealings with student athletes?
3. Why don't gifted athletes go directly from high school to professional sports? Why are few college athletes likely to become pros?
4. How convincing is the evidence Barbash provides to support his case? How representative are his examples?
5. What would be the advantages of paying student athletes? Can you think of any disadvantages?
6. Explain the pun with which this essay concludes.

Suggestions for Writing

1. Argue for a change in the sports program at your school that would benefit either the program or the school.
2. Barbash claims that many schools have a "jock curriculum" that enables athletes to keep playing even if they are not learning anything important. Imagine a situation in which someone has asked you to identify the easiest courses at your own school. Then write an essay that would persuade that person to take more challenging courses.

SNOWED IN:
THE COCAINE BLIZZARD

Mark A. R. Kleiman

As you read this essay about cocaine, notice how Mark Kleiman shows the limitations of several policy options before making his own proposal. Consider why Kleiman employs this strategy. Consider also whether or not the author seems reliable. According to a note that accompanied the first publication of this essay in 1990, Kleiman is a lecturer in public policy at Harvard's John F. Kennedy School of Government who worked for the Justice Department between 1979 and 1983. Ask yourself whether this information influences your attitude toward his proposal or whether you can evaluate the author's credibility from the essay itself.

President George Bush, congressional Democrats, most big-city police chiefs, and the vast majority of Americans agree that it is both vital and feasible to stop the flow of cocaine from South America into the United States. Unfortunately, they're wrong. Nothing that happens in South America has any real chance of significantly reducing the cocaine problem in North America.

The mid-February [1990] "drug summit" in Cartagena was only the most recent media event promoting the fantasy theme of solving our drug problem offshore. Since the president's Oval Office address of last September applauding increased anti-cocaine efforts by the Colombian government, there has been a series of what the drug czar's latest strategy document calls "successes." The Colombian government "declared war" on the Medellín cartel. Several major South American dealers were indicted or extradited, and one was killed in a shoot-out with police. The Defense Department announced a billion dollar effort against drug smuggling. Manuel Noriega, reclassified from CIA asset to national menace when his drug-dealing activities came to light, moved his headquarters from the presidential palace in Panama City to the Metropolitan Correctional Center in Miami.

None of this, alas, had any perceptible effect on the U.S. cocaine market. A kilogram in Miami still costs about what it did a year ago (roughly $16,000), and retail crack markets continue to spread to new neighborhoods and new cities.

Some legislators have responded to this disappointing news by berating the administration for not doing enough to stop the drug flow, or doing the wrong things. But that criticism is misplaced; stopping the drug flow is like stopping the tide. Neither of the two goals of the "international supply reduction" strategy—creating a physical shortage of cocaine or increasing its import price enough to force consumption down—is achievable.

Consider the prospects for creating a long-term physical shortage,   5
by eradicating and seizing so much cocaine that U.S. demand can't be
satisfied. Cocaine isn't scarce and can't be made scarce. The State Department puts total production last year at 775 tons, more than triple current
U.S. consumption. If increased seizures or increased demand threatened a
shortage, farmers and refiners could always grow and process more
cocaine.

The attempt to create a short-term shortage is frustrated by the fact
that everyone in the cocaine business holds large inventories. In one recent
six-week period, U.S. domestic law enforcement agencies seized more
than forty tons of cocaine, about a two-month supply for the entire country. The vast bulk of that was concentrated in four large caches. Yet there
was no shortage of cocaine. There must be even larger inventories in South
America: the stuff is cheap to make, and no trafficker wants to be out of
stock when a customer calls.

Thus we can't create a shortage because Adam Smith° is more powerful than William Bennett°. That leaves us with the goal of increasing
prices. If more enforcement could impose very heavy costs on drug dealers, prices might rise enough to reduce abuse substantially — for drug
consumption, like consumption of anything else, does respond to price.
Even if some existing users will pay almost anything (most of them will
not), new users certainly won't. Unfortunately, there's no reason to believe
that anything done offshore could have much impact on domestic retail
prices.

Refined cocaine is only a raw material in the cocaine dealing business — and a cheap raw material at that. Of the five dollar retail price of a
rock of crack cocaine, only about fifty cents goes to growers, processors,
and importers. The rest — ninety percent of the total — is added after the
drug reaches the United States. That $4.50 in wholesale and retail markups
isn't much influencd by conditions in the Andes or by seizures on the high
seas or at points of entry. Even a doubling of import prices wouldn't much
change the drug scene as viewed from the streets of Los Angeles, New
York, or Washington.

Nor do any of the four currently fashionable approaches to increasing the price of cocaine imports — eradication, substitution, pre-emptive
buying, or interdiction — have any prospect of doubling import prices.
Eradication is cheap ($21 million) but largely futile: existing growers can
always grow more coca. That's just as true for techno-thriller approaches
such as releasing coca-eating caterpillars as for the more old-fashioned
chop-and-spray techniques. In addition, new growers can enter the market by opening new areas to cultivation; the Colombian lowlands and the

Adam Smith (1723–1790): A Scottish economist who formulated the laws of supply and demand.
William Bennett (b. 1943): Headed federal efforts to control drugs at the time this essay was first
published.

Amazon basin of Brazil have already been added to the Andean highlands as coca-growing regions because of eradication attempts and increased demand. Farther afield, Indonesia's role as the major supplier of coca for licit pharmaceutical cocaine between World War I and World War II shows that the range of *Erythroxylon coca* is not limited to South America. As long as the customer base is there, the financial awards of growing coca will assure that there will always be a supply to meet the demand despite any costs imposed by eradication efforts.

Crop substitution — offering coca growers incentives and technical assistance to grow non-drug crops — is another popular idea. Anything we can do to improve the ability of South American peasant farmers to earn an honest living is to be applauded, but providing alternatives isn't the same as reducing the supply of cocaine for the export trade.

Even at current prices, coca yields more revenue per hectare than any licit crop. Some farmers, given the choice, will leave the coca trade, but their greedier neighbors won't. And unfortunately, many of the technologies taught by crop-substitution experts are useful when applied to illicit as well as licit species. For instance, attempts in Thailand throughout the seventies to introduce drip irrigation and terrace farming to help farmers substitute rice for poppy led to the development of drip-irrigated, terrace-farmed poppy fields. By the same token, better roads built to encourage orange-growing make it that much easier to get coca to the airport.

Buying the coca crop, a perennial favorite despite a disastrous experience with Burmese opium in the sixties, sounds plausible only until someone asks what is to keep the farmers from growing twice as much coca and selling us half. Whatever the price announced for the official buy, refiners only have to offer to pay a little more to ensure their sources of supply. As both the European Community and the U.S. Department of Agriculture can testify, agricultural price supports are a reliable way to generate bumper crops. Buying refined cocaine instead of raw leaf runs into the same problem: somebody can always make more.

The fourth major international supply control strategy, and the one on which we now spend nearly $3 billion per year, is interdiction: capturing bulk drug shipments on their way north. The effectiveness of seizures in increasing price depends on how expensive it is for cocaine importers to replace the drugs lost to enforcement. For high-seas and port-of-entry seizures, replacing their merchandise costs them only about $2,000 per kilo — that is what cocaine sells for leaving the dock in Colombia. To this one must add the costs to importers of using more expensive smuggling techniques to avoid seizures. But it's hard to see how the replacement costs and additional smuggling expense associated with even a doubling of current interdiction efforts could make more than a few hundred million dollars' worth of impact on the $20 billion to $30 billion U.S. cocaine trade. That ratio of additional cost to current price suggests a price change of five percent or less: twenty-five cents added to the price of that five dollar rock.

It may seem incredible that in the high-tech nineties we can't keep drugs out of the country. But tens of thousands of vessels and vehicles and millions of people and heaven knows how many containers of everything from cars to blue jeans cross the U.S. border every month. It is obvious by now that we can't keep illegal aliens out, and an alien is substantially harder to hide than a kilogram of cocaine.

Since the value of a kilogram of cocaine goes from a couple of thou- 15 sand dollars as it leaves Colombia to more than $10,000 as it reaches the United States, individuals and organizations will expend ingenuity, time, money, and risk to get the powder in, as long as there are customers with money and a distribution system to deliver the drugs to them. Like Star Wars, interdiction is an offense-defense game that the defense is guaranteed to lose.

In fact, interdiction actually makes the situation worse in South America by forcing U.S. importers to buy more cocaine from Colombian exporters—the Medellín and Cali cartels and their competitors—to replace seized drugs. Every time we seize a kilogram of cocaine, someone in Colombia sells another kilogram to the importers. From the viewpoint of the South American drug lords, a kilogram seized is about as good as a kilogram snorted or smoked. Last year seizures accounted for about a quarter of all the cocaine shipped north.

If source control and interdiction won't work, what will? Legalization, the latest fad? Only if you either (1) imagine that making a product much more safe and convenient to buy and cutting its price by ninety percent won't have a huge impact on its consumption, or (2) don't care how many heavy crack users there are. (See "Crackdown" by James Q. Wilson and John J. DiIulio, Jr., *The New Republic,* July 10, 1989.) Biomedical research? Only if you think that the root of the national drug crisis is insufficient knowledge about neurotransmitter chemicals and receptor sites. Treatment and prevention? Maybe, if we knew more about how to do them.

The one area of anti-drug effort that now gets almost no federal money is the point of contact between the drug distribution system and the drug user: the dealer on the street. The size of the cocaine problem in a city or neighborhood depends not on the state of the world cocaine market, but on how many retail dealers choose to make that city or that neighborhood their marketplace and how blatantly they feel they can safely hawk their wares. That in turn depends partly on retail-level law enforcement (and hardly at all on foreign source control).

State and local governments have been pouring more and more resources—police, prosecutors, courts, and corrections—into enforcing the drug laws, mostly at the retail level. As a result, many local systems are choking on drug cases. Corrections capacity (cells and "alternatives" alike) is in particularly short supply; local systems are catching more drug dealers than they have room for. The federal government, which has provided lots of cheerleading but not much money, could usefully donate some of the billions it now spends failing to keep drugs out of the country to expanding local criminal-justice systems.

But all of the political pressures push the other way. The ACLU   20
[American Civil Liberties Union] doesn't like street-level enforcement because it means building more prisons. Police and prosecutors don't like it because chasing Mr. Big is more glamorous, less grubby, and safer. Republicans don't like it because it costs money and doesn't go bang. The president doesn't like it because it means spending federal revenues on state and local programs. Voters don't like it because it means putting a prison or halfway house in somebody's neighborhood. Against all of these disadvantages, increasing our capacity to punish retail drug dealers has a single advantage: some hope of actually reducing the impact of drug dealing on our lives.

Questions for Discussion

1. Why is a cocaine shortage unlikely to develop despite repeated government attempts to seize supplies?
2. What policies have been pursued in an attempt to reduce the amount of cocaine imported into the United States? Why is it that each of these policies has failed?
3. How could seizing drug shipments from South America benefit growers and exporters?
4. What does Kleiman propose the federal government do about illegal drug use? Why does he offer his proposal only after demonstrating what is wrong with current federal policy? Does he recognize that his proposal could encounter objections?
5. What does this argument reveal about the author's political values? In writing about the drug problem, does Kleiman seem to have any other concerns about the government?

Suggestions for Writing

1. Kleiman argues that dealers should be prosecuted more aggressively. What about drug users? Should using cocaine be against the law? If not, why not? If so, what should the penalty be? Write an essay persuading others to accept your views.
2. Write an essay designed to persuade worried taxpayers to support the construction of new prisons.

THE LANGUAGE OF POWER

Yolanda T. De Mola

> *Although bilingual education has existed in this country for more than a hundred years, it has provoked considerable controversy since 1968 when Congress passed legislation mandating special programs for students whose native language is not English. By offering instruction in both English and another language (often, but not always, Spanish), bilingual programs were intended to make education easier for students who could not understand English — and also to recognize that the United States is a multicultural nation. As you read "The Language of Power," note why De Mola objects to bilingual education even though she herself values more than one language.*

One of the more unproductive discussions I have had in my life took place in the lobby of a Madrid hotel in 1963. I was one of a group of Fulbright scholars, all teachers of Spanish from the United States, touring and studying in what was for some of us the land of our ancestors. A concierge remarked to me that there was no richer language in the world than his native Spanish. "Nowhere on earth can one find the nuances, the prolific lexicon of a Cervantes in his *Quixote*," he observed. Not so, I countered: "What you say may be true, but the blend of Latin and Anglo-Saxon has given English the largest vocabulary of any language in the world. In fact, the resonance, the vigor of English have caused it to replace French as the international language of diplomacy." Though I love both languages, as an American I felt compelled to uphold the primacy of English.

Today a somewhat more serious debate persists among educators, politicians and sociologists. It is a two-pronged polemic: Is bilingual education a help or a hindrance to Spanish-speaking children? Should English be made the official language of the United States? Both questions generate heated discussions and are no closer to resolution than when they were first raised some 20 years ago.

Alicia Coro, a native Cuban who has been director of Bilingual Education and Minority Affairs at the Department of Education in Washington, D.C., since September 1987, has a daughter who, in the early 1960's, was ready to start school. The child spoke no English whatsoever but did not have the option of enrolling in bilingual classes. Within a short time she was fluent in English. Today Mrs. Coro says: "If I had to make the decision now, I probably would not put her in a bilingual program." And she adds: "Some parents don't want their children in bilingual classes [because] they want them to progress in school and compete."

Perhaps today there are skilled bilingual teachers, but some 15 years ago I saw a man and a woman interviewed on television whose responses to the interviewer gave clear evidence that they were illiterate in two languages. At best, bilingual classes should be few and seen only as transitional rather than as a crutch to discourage maximum use of English. Far greater benefits might be reaped by the 1.5 million children with a limited knowledge of English if creative and intensive English programs were to be offered to them. Some 73 percent of the children whose English is limited are Hispanic. A much lower percentage of these, however, make the general academic progress that Asian children make who do not have the crutch of bilingual education.

In his provocative book *Hunger of Memory,* Richard Rodriguez writes: "Supporters of bilingual education today imply that students like me miss a great deal by not being taught in their family's language. What they seem not to recognize is that, as a socially disadvantaged child, I considered Spanish to be a private language. What I needed to learn in school was that I had the right and the obligation to speak the public language of *los gringos.* . . .

"Without question, it would have pleased me to hear my teachers address me in Spanish when I entered the classroom. But I would have delayed having to learn the language of public society. I would have evaded learning the great lesson of school, that I had a public identity."

It is regrettable that most children do not become fluent in the language of their parents or grandparents as well as English. Ours is probably the only world power whose citizens are not educated to be bilingual. Nevertheless, if one is to live and work in the United States, one must own the common language lest communication fail and we become a babel of misunderstanding. It is difficult enough to live with ethnic tensions without also losing the source of unity and comprehension — our public language. Perhaps it is the bridge that can enable us to become in reality "one nation under God."

With many others whose first language was not English, I am convinced today that its mastery is the fastest route out of the ghetto, the best formula for professional and personal success. Language is power and that power grows when one knows the dominant language well. Self-confidence comes to the child who can express clearly and accurately his or her thoughts and feelings. The danger of dropping out of school is also diminished.

The longer I observe the process of integration (not assimilation) of the Hispanic into our society, the more I am convinced that there are those in government, industry and, yes, even the church who have a vested interest in preventing the Hispanic from rising on the social and corporate ladder. The role of Lord or Lady Bountiful can be very congenial — the role of enabler perhaps less so. If signs in Spanish are taken down, the Hispanic will be challenged to learn the name of the product in English. An American living in Paris does not expect to see signs for commodities in English.

Recently, after a meeting with bilingual teachers and principals of District 10 in the Bronx, a member of a women's committee commented: "Despite the public relations and budgeting additions, the [bilingual] program is little more than a 'dumping ground' for kids with limited English proficiency." Why is it that only 8 percent of the students in the Bronx High School of Science, a school with rigorous entrance requirements, are Hispanic while Asians abound, in spite of their being numerically far fewer in New York City than the Latinos?

The movement to make English the official language of the United States is in no way a put-down of other languages or cultures. But it is the language used predominantly by the print and electronic media; it is the tongue in which government at every level is conducted. To be an effective citizen one ought to vote, and to do so intelligently one must be well informed. Candidates, of course, present the issues and outline their platforms in English.

Linda Chavez, former president of U.S. English as the Official Language of the Country, indicates that until that goal is achieved, legal empowerment for Hispanics is denied. She stresses that for social services, translators are always available for those (like the elderly) who do not yet use English well. In particular, Puerto Ricans who are citizens are not denied any rights because of their inability to speak English. Special interest groups who lobby for a bilingual nation (English and Spanish) fail to realize that such a posture is offensive to the millions whose second language is not Spanish. Let us indeed become a bilingual nation by learning well both English and the language of our ancestry or of our choice.

Many years ago my mother accompanied me, her oldest, to the first grade on the opening day of school. When she returned to the upper Manhattan school to take me home, the teacher said to her: "This child must be placed in kindergarten. All she can say in English is 'O.K.'" That was my earliest confrontation with the educational system. I do not recall having any problem picking up the dominant language easily and quickly. In time, English became my favorite subject; eventually it was my college major. My experience is not unique.

As long as we remain a polyglot society without one common linguistic system to unite us, fear of one another is perpetuated and ethnic prejudices endure.

Questions for Discussion

1. De Mola draws upon her own experience in paragraphs 1 and 13. Do these paragraphs help her argument? Do they leave her open to counterargument?
2. Does De Mola include any evidence to support her claim that bilingual education impedes academic progress?
3. What does De Mola mean when she makes a distinction between "integration" and "assimilation"? Why could someone be in favor of one but not the other?
4. Consider the analogy that De Mola makes in paragraph 9 between the use of Spanish in the United States and the use of English in Paris. How would an advocate of bilingualism respond to this comparison?

Suggestions for Writing

1. De Mola claims that mastering English is "the best formula for professional and personal success." If you believe that there are other subjects that are more important to learn, argue on behalf of one of them.
2. Can "the language of power" be acquired in American public schools? If you were disappointed or bored by English classes in high school, how could those classes have been improved? Write an argument on behalf of a specific change in the teaching of English.

DEATH AND JUSTICE: HOW CAPITAL PUNISHMENT AFFIRMS LIFE

Edward I. Koch

> *The following essay relies heavily upon refutation. Arguing on behalf of capital punishment, Edward Koch considers a number of arguments against the death penalty and tries to demolish them one by one. As you read, consider the advantages and disadvantages of this strategy. Be alert for appeals to ethos and pathos. Koch was mayor of New York City when he first published this essay in 1985. Does he expect readers to consider him a credible authority on this topic? And does he try to involve your emotions?*

Last December a man named Robert Lee Willie, who had been convicted of raping and murdering an eighteen-year-old woman, was executed in the Louisiana state prison. In a statement issued several minutes before his death, Mr. Willie said: "Killing people is wrong. . . . It makes no difference whether it's citizens, countries, or governments. Killing is wrong." Two weeks later in South Carolina, an admitted killer named Joseph Carl Shaw was put to death for murdering two teenagers. In an appeal to the governor for clemency, Mr. Shaw wrote: "Killing is wrong when I did it. Killing is wrong when you do it. I hope you have the courage and moral strength to stop the killing."

It is a curiosity of modern life that we find ourselves being lectured on morality by cold-blooded killers. Mr. Willie previously had been convicted of aggravated rape, aggravated kidnapping, and the murders of a Lousiana deputy and a man from Missouri. Mr. Shaw committed another murder a week before the two for which he was executed, and admitted mutilating the body of the fourteen-year-old girl he killed. I can't help wondering what prompted these murderers to speak out against killing as they entered the deathhouse door. Did their newfound reverence for life stem from the realization that they were about to lose their own?

Life is indeed precious, and I believe the death penalty helps to affirm this fact. Had the death penalty been a real possibility in the minds of these murderers, they might well have stayed their hand. They might have shown moral awareness before their victims died, and not after. Consider the tragic death of Rosa Velez, who happened to be home when a man named Luis Vera burglarized her apartment in Brooklyn. "Yeah, I shot her," Vera admitted. "She knew me, and I knew I wouldn't go to the chair."

During my twenty-two years in public service, I have heard the pros and cons of capital punishment expressed with special intensity. As a district leader, councilman, congressman, and mayor, I have represented constituencies generally thought of as liberal. Because I support the death penalty for heinous crimes of murder, I have sometimes been the subject of emotional and outraged attacks by voters who find my position reprehensible or worse. I have listened to their ideas. I have weighed their objections carefully. I still support the death penalty. The reasons I maintain my position can be best understood by examining the arguments most frequently heard in opposition.

1. The death penalty is "barbaric." Sometimes opponents of capital punishment horrify with tales of lingering death on the gallows, of faulty electric chairs, or of agony in the gas chamber. Partly in response to such protests, several states such as North Carolina and Texas switched to execution by lethal injection. The condemned person is put to death painlessly, without ropes, voltage, bullets, or gas. Did this answer the objections of death penalty opponents? Of course not. On June 22, 1984, the *New York Times* published an editorial that sarcastically attacked the new "hygienic" method of death by injection, and stated that "execution can never be made humane through science." So it's not the method that really troubles opponents. It's the death itself they consider barbaric.

Admittedly, capital punishment is not a pleasant topic. However, one does not have to like the death penalty in order to support it any more than one must like radical surgery, radiation, or chemotherapy in order to find necessary these attempts at curing cancer. Ultimately we may learn how to cure cancer with a simple pill. Unfortunately, that day has not yet arrived. Today we are faced with the choice of letting the cancer spread or trying to cure it with the methods available, methods that one day will almost certainly be considered barbaric. But to give up and do nothing would be far more barbaric and would certainly delay the discovery of an eventual cure. The analogy between cancer and murder is imperfect, because murder is not the "disease" we are trying to cure. The disease is injustice. We may not like the death penalty, but it must be available to punish crimes of cold-blooded murder, cases in which any other form of punishment would be inadequate and, therefore, unjust. If we create a society in which injustice is not tolerated, incidents of murder — the most flagrant form of injustice — will diminish.

2. No other major democracy uses the death penalty. No other major democracy — in fact, few other countries of any description — are plagued by a murder rate such as that in the United States. Fewer and fewer Americans can remember the days when unlocked doors were the norm and murder was a rare and terrible offense. In America the murder rate climbed 122 percent between 1963 and 1980. During that same period, the murder rate in New York City increased by almost 400 percent, and the statistics are even worse in many other cities. A study at M.I.T. showed that based on 1970 homicide rates a person who lived in a large American city ran a greater risk of being murdered than an American soldier in

World War II ran of being killed in combat. It is not surprising that the laws of each country differ according to differing conditions and traditions. If other countries had our murder problem, the cry for capital punishment would be just as loud as it is here. And I daresay that any other major democracy where 75 percent of the people supported the death penalty would soon enact it into law.

3. An innocent person might be executed by mistake. Consider the work of Hugo Adam Bedau, one of the most implacable foes of capital punishment in this country. According to Mr. Bedau, it is "false sentimentality to argue that the death penalty should be abolished because of the abstract possibility that an innocent person might be executed." He cites a study of the 7,000 executions in this country from 1893 to 1971, and concludes that the record fails to show that such cases occur. The main point, however, is this. If government functioned only when the possibility of error didn't exist, government wouldn't function at all. Human life deserves special protection, and one of the best ways to guarantee that protection is to assure that convicted murderers do not kill again. Only the death penalty can accomplish this end. In a recent case in New Jersey, a man named Richard Biegenwald was freed from prison after serving eighteen years for murder; since his release he has been convicted of committing four murders. A prisoner named Lemuel Smith, who, while serving four life sentences for murder (plus two life sentences for kidnapping and robbery) in New York's Green Haven Prison, lured a woman corrections officer into the chaplain's office and strangled her. He then mutilated and dismembered her body. An additional life sentence for Smith is meaningless. Because New York has no death penalty statute, Smith has effectively been given a license to kill.

But the problem of multiple murder is not confined to the nation's penitentiaries. In 1981, 91 police officers were killed in the line of duty in this country. Seven percent of those arrested in the cases that have been solved had a previous arrest for murder. In New York City in 1976 and 1977, 85 persons arrested for homicide had a previous arrest for murder. Six of these individuals had two previous arrests for murder, and one had four previous murder arrests. During those two years the New York police were arresting for murder persons with a previous arrest for murder on the average of one every 8.5 days. This is not surprising when we learn that in 1975, for example, the median time served in Massachusetts for homicide was less than two and a half years. In 1976 a study sponsored by the Twentieth Century Fund found that the average time served in the United States for first-degree murder is ten years. The median time served may be considerably lower.

4. Capital punishment cheapens the value of human life. On the contrary, it can be easily demonstrated that the death penalty strengthens the value of human life. If the penalty for rape were lowered, clearly it

10

would signal a lessened regard for the victims' suffering, humiliation, and personal integrity. It would cheapen their horrible experience, and expose them to an increased danger of recurrence. When we lower the penalty for murder, it signals a lessened regard for the value of the victim's life. Some critics of capital punishment, such as columnist Jimmy Breslin, have suggested that a life sentence is actually a harsher penalty for murder than death. This is sophistic nonsense. A few killers may decide not to appeal a death sentence, but the overwhelming majority make every effort to stay alive. It is by exacting the highest penalty for the taking of human life that we affirm the highest value of human life.

5. The penalty is applied in a discriminatory manner. This factor no longer seems to be the problem it once was. The appeals process for a condemned prisoner is lengthy and painstaking. Every effort is made to see that the verdict and sentence were fairly arrived at. However, assertions of discrimination are not an argument for ending the death penalty but for extending it. It is not justice to exclude everyone from the penalty of the law if a few are found to be so favored. Justice requires that the law be applied equally to all.

6. Thou Shalt Not Kill. The Bible is our greatest source of moral inspiration. Opponents of the death penalty frequently cite the sixth of the Ten Commandments in an attempt to prove that capital punishment is divinely proscribed. In the original Hebrew, however, the Sixth Commandment reads "Thou Shalt Not Commit Murder," and the Torah specifies capital punishment for a variety of offenses. The biblical viewpoint has been upheld by philosophers throughout history. The greatest thinkers of the nineteenth century — Kant, Locke, Hobbes, Rousseau, Montesquieu, and Mill — agreed that natural law properly authorizes the sovereign to take life in order to vindicate justice. Only Jeremy Bentham was ambivalent. Washington, Jefferson, and Franklin endorsed it. Abraham Lincoln authorized executions for deserters in wartime. Alexis de Tocqueville, who expressed profound respect for American institutions, believed that the death penalty was indispensable to the support of social order. The United States Constitution, widely admired as one of the seminal achievements in the history of humanity, condemns cruel and inhuman punishment, but does not condemn capital punishment.

7. The death penalty is state-sanctioned murder. This is the defense with which Messrs. Willie and Shaw hoped to soften the resolve of those who sentenced them to death. By saying in effect, "You're no better than I am," the murderer seeks to bring his accusers down to his own level. It is also a popular argument among opponents of capital punishment, but a transparently false one. Simply put, the state has rights that the private individual does not. In a democracy, those rights are given to the state by the electorate. The execution of a lawfully condemned killer is no more an act of murder than is legal imprisonment an act of kidnapping. If an individual forces a neighbor to pay him money under threat of punishment, it's called extortion. If the state does it, it's called taxation. Rights and responsibilities surrendered by the individual are what give the state its power to govern. This contract is the foundation of civilization itself.

Everyone wants his or her rights, and will defend them jealously. Not everyone, however, wants responsibilities, especially the painful responsibilities that come with law enforcement. Twenty-one years ago a woman named Kitty Genovese was assaulted and murdered on a street in New York. Dozens of neighbors heard her cries for help but did nothing to assist her. They didn't even call the police. In such a climate the criminal understandably grows bolder. In the presence of moral cowardice, he lectures us on our supposed failings and tries to equate his crimes with our quest for justice.

The death of anyone — even a convicted killer — diminishes us all. 15
But we are diminished even more by a justice system that fails to function. It is an illusion to let ourselves believe that doing away with capital punishment removes the murderer's deed from our conscience. The rights of society are paramount. When we protect guilty lives, we give up innocent lives in exchange. When opponents of capital punishment say to the state, "I will not let you kill in my name," they are also saying to murderers: "You can kill in your *own* name as long as I have an excuse for not getting involved."

It is hard to imagine anything worse than being murdered while neighbors do nothing. But something worse exists. When those same neighbors shrink back from justly punishing the murderer, the victim dies twice.

Questions for Discussion

1. Why does Koch begin his argument by quoting two convicted murderers? How does he expect readers to respond to Willie and Shaw?
2. What does Koch gain by revealing that he heard arguments about capital punishment during twenty-two years of public service?
3. Most of Koch's argument is devoted to showing why he disagrees with arguments that have been made against capital punishment. How convincing is his refutation of these arguments? Where is he most convincing? Where is he most vulnerable to counterargument?
4. If you proved that your opponents were wrong, would that be sufficient to prove that you were right? To what extent can a writer afford to rely upon refutation as a writing strategy?
5. Consider paragraph 9. Aside from the absence of the death penalty in New York, could there be any other factors accounting for the number

of repeat offenders? Why do you think murderers might be released after only a few years of imprisonment?

6. What does Koch mean by saying that "the victim dies twice" when murders are not punished?

Suggestions for Writing

1. Write an argument against capital punishment that will challenge at least two of Koch's points.
2. If you believe that violent crime is caused by problems such as poverty and drug abuse, argue on behalf of a specific reform that might reduce the murder rate.

GAYS IN ARMS

Jacob Weisberg

> *As its provocative title suggests, "Gays in Arms" addresses a question involving sexual preference — specifically, whether or not homosexual men and women should have the right to serve in the American military. Consider how Jacob Weisberg uses different types of data, such as examples and government documents, to make his case. Recognizing that he is taking a controversial stand on a topic that could make some readers feel uneasy, Weisberg anticipates and responds to a number of arguments that could be made against him. Note this strategy as you read, and ask yourself whether there are any arguments that the author has overlooked.*

The Air Force is looking for a few gay men. To be exact, it's been looking for 18 of them at its Carswell base in Tarrant County, Texas. This is the number of non-commissioned officers who have been implicated in "homosexual activity" in the past two months. Twelve have been discharged, and six more are currently "under investigation," according to Capt. Barbara Carr, a public affairs officer.

At a news conference last month in Fort Worth, one of the 12 described the hunt for the wicked witches of west Texas. In December 1989 an officer of the Air Force's Office of Special Investigations informed him that he had been named as part of a gay ring. His honorable discharge papers were already prepared and would be signed if he cooperated by naming other homosexuals. Otherwise, he would be court-martialed. After six hours of intermittent interrogation in a broom closet with a two-way mirror, the anonymous airman yielded five names, and ended his military career.

The outburst at Carswell is typical of the military's sporadic persecution of gays. For the most part enlisted homosexuals keep quiet, and although friends and commanding officers often know they are gay, most pass through the services without trouble. "Ninety-nine percent go through and do very well," says Sandra Lowe, an attorney with the Lambda Legal Defense and Education Fund. But now and again, either because someone proclaims his or her homosexuality openly or because an officer wants a purge, a dozen or so are exposed and quickly "released," as the Pentagon prefers to euphemize it. According to Department of Defense figures, about 1,400 are expelled in any given year, at a cost of some tens of millions of dollars in lost training.

Women are dismissed for homosexuality three times as often as men are, eight times as often in the Marine Corps. In 1988 agents of what columnist Jack Anderson calls the "notoriously overzealous" Naval Investigative Service (NIS) persuaded one female Marine to give them the names of 70 lesbians at the Parris Island, South Carolina, boot camp. Fourteen members of what the NIS calls a "nest" were discharged. Three who wouldn't name names did time in the brig for sodomy and "indecent acts."

One of those prosecuted at Parris Island was Capt. Judy Mead, a 12-year veteran of the Marines. Mead was brought before a board of officers on charges of conduct unbecoming an officer for having a "long-term personal relationship with a known lesbian." Although Mead was not charged with being gay herself, she once allegedly slept "in the same bed" with a civilian lesbian and was, on another occasion, "in the presence" of persons suspected to be lesbians. Mead protested she didn't know her friends were gay. One of the officers answered that her antenna should have gone up because her friends played softball and "looked homosexual." The panel recommended Mead for a less than honorable discharge. After a year of hearings and $16,000 in legal bills she was reinstated by a review board, but soon afterward she was passed over for a routine promotion despite her otherwise excellent service record.

Mead was acquitted because DOD policy doesn't explicitly prohibit association with homosexuals. That's about the only loophole. Under the Uniform Code of Military Justice, any homosexual act on or off duty is sufficient cause to warrant dismissal. Deeming even that too loose, the Pentagon issued a directive in 1982 that broadened the definition of homosexuality to include "a person, regardless of sex, who engages in, desires to engage in, or intends to engage in homosexual acts" — even if "acts" are never committed. This gives the armed forces the authority to terminate servicepersons at whim, on the flimsiest of evidence, for what are in essence thought-crimes. The most celebrated case of the moment is that of Joe Steffan, a naval cadet who stood near the top of his Annapolis class before he was expelled in 1987, two months before graduation, for telling friends he was gay. To date, the Navy has presented no evidence that Staffan ever practiced his preference.

In the wake of the Panama invasion, Americans are conducting a lively public debate on the difficult question of whether women should serve in combat. Opponents of letting women fight offer objections that are at least plausible. Most women do not meet objective standards of strength and endurance. There are reasons to suspect that sexually integrated units would not perform as effectively as traditional all-male ones. And so on. That is not to say that these objections are fully persuasive; women have never had a chance to disprove them in the U.S. armed services. Simply out of habit and prejudice, they are also denied many positions they could fill as well as men. In the case of homosexuals, however, the common justifications offered by defenders of the status quo do not make any practical or moral sense.

The arguments against letting gays serve are seldom stated. This is Pentagon policy: no official is allowed to defend the rules on the record. Spokesman Maj. Dave Super is only permitted to quote from an official statement that says "homosexuality is incompatible with military service." Beyond that he repeats that "the policy is the policy." A few months ago "Nightline" did a program on the Steffan case. Since the Navy was unwilling to provide a spokesperson, ABC had to settle for Representative Robert K. Dornan, who raved about sodomy and called homosexuality a mental illness. With supporters like Dornan, the DOD doesn't need opponents.

The last time the Pentagon elaborated its rules on homosexuals was in 1982, when the office of Secretary of Defense Caspar Weinberger promulgated this rationale:

> Homosexuality is incompatible with military service. The presence of such members adversely affects the ability of the Armed Forces to maintain discipline, good order, and morale; to foster mutual trust and confidence among the members; to ensure the integrity of the system of rank and command; to facilitate assignment and world-wide deployment of members who frequently must live and work under close conditions affording minimal privacy; to recruit and retain members of the military services; to maintain the public acceptability of military services; and, in certain circumstances, to prevent breaches of security.

This is a jambalaya justification, which tosses every remotely palatable argument in the pot. Consumed in a hurry, it almost tastes OK, but later proves indigestible.

Weinberger's last argument, that homosexuals are a security risk, is 10 the most familiar. It is also the least convincing. As the Navy's suppressed Crittenden report noted as far back as 1957: "The concept that homosexuals pose a security risk is unsupported by any factual data. Homosexuals are no more of a security risk, and in many cases are much less of a security risk, than alcoholics and those people with marked feelings of inferiority who must brag of their knowledge of secret information and disclose it to gain stature." Even if homosexuals were common targets for blackmail, the threat could be eliminated by allowing them out of the closet.

It is the Navy that is most preoccupied with the nexus of homosexuality and disloyalty. During its investigation of the exploded gun turret aboard the USS Iowa last year, the NIS put out a lurid story that Clayton Hartwig, one of 47 sailors who died in the explosion, had a "special relationship" with Kendall Truitt, who was the beneficiary of his $100,000 life insurance policy. There was simply not any evidence for this accusation against the two petty officers. A Congressional hearing later discovered a far more likely reason for the accident: gunpowder used in the 16-inch gun that blew up had destabilizd after being stored under improper conditions. The NIS may also have been responsible for the rumor that John Walker, of the Walker family spy ring, and Jerry Whitworth, another convicted Navy spy, were, in military parlance, "asshole buddies." There was no evidence that the two ever met.

Working backward through Weinberger's laundry list, the "public acceptability" argument is probably as close as the DOD comes to a legitimate worry. The fear is that some young men would be discouraged from volunteering if they knew they would be serving alongside homosexuals, and that parents would object to their boys serving in an unwholesome environment. The same line was taken against racial integration of the services before Harry S Truman accomplished it by executive order in 1948. In that case fears were largely unrealized, and there is every reason to think they are exaggerated today. Public tolerance for homosexuals is now higher than support for racial integration was 40 years ago. According to a recent Gallup Poll, 60 percent of the public believes that gays should be allowed in the military.

The public acceptability argument goes in a particularly vicious circle: gays are unacceptable because they are unacceptable. Straight soldiers will continue to fear and scorn homosexuals until they are forced to become acquainted with them on a routine basis. Of course, the admission of gays will no more eliminate homophobia than the integration of blacks cured racism. But irrational prejudices are bound to diminish over time if the isolation and ignorance they feed upon is ended.

The privacy argument is one that is viscerally felt by many who have served in the military. Soldiers and sailors say they don't want to be regarded with sexual interest when they are naked in common showers or asleep in common barracks. On "Nightline" Dornan compared allowing a homosexual in a barracks to "putting a man in a harem." The truth is that there are plenty of gays in the showers now. Most estimates put the number of male and female homosexuals in the branches of service at ten percent, mirroring the proportion in society at large. Denying this reality may make some straights more comfortable, but it doesn't make them invisible to those who may enjoy gazing at them. The unstated fear of some straights is that acknowledging the presence of homosexuals would free them to stare and proposition more openly and aggressively. But no one proposes to change rules about harassment or fraternization, which prohibit sexual advances and activity on duty.

When Weinberger notes the need to "ensure the integrity of the system of rank and command," he raises the specter that straights would refuse to take orders from homosexual commanders. This argument is again familiar from the time before racial integration. It was asserted then that no white soldier would take orders from a black commander. Some would not, and there were a few courts-martial for insubordination. But the overwhelming majority of whites faced the fact that even if they didn't like taking orders from blacks, they no longer had any choice about it. The same would happen with gays.

It is unclear why the Pentagon believes "mutual trust and confidence" would be undermined by homosexuals. One possible implication is that gays would be worried about personal relationships rather than about fighting, and would be less willing to make sacrifices for the group. But common sense and the example of ancient Greece suggest that male affection doesn't have to be Platonic to impel heroic deeds. Nor do mutual trust and confidence appear to have been shaken in West Germany, Italy, Sweden, Norway, Denmark, or the Netherlands, countries that allow gays to serve in their armies.

The argument heard most often today is that "discipline, good order, and morale" would suffer if homosexuals were allowed to fight alongside heteros. What's meant here is that the presence of sexual feelings would diminish the dynamic that binds men together and spurs them to fight and die. To be fair, the temper of a platoon that included open homosexuals would probably be different from that of one that didn't. But there is no reason to believe that it would be worse, that unit cohesion would suffer, or that the intangible but all-important process of bonding would fail to occur. The real fear, as Allan Berube, [in] *Coming Out Under Fire: Gay Men and Women in World War II . . .* puts it, is that "gays would taint bonding and camaraderie with homosexual overtones." Military units are rife with homosexual anxieties in the first place. Like those who make the shower argument, those who make the morale case seem to feel the heterosexual nature of exclusively male activities and situations can't be called into question. The open presence of gays would make the homoerotic elements of bonding undeniable. As Berube puts it: "There's a safety to their not being named."

Many of these points have been made by internal investigations that the Pentagon feels obliged to cover up. The most famous example is the Crittendon report. Though it recommended that the military continue to exclude homosexuals, the study's debunking of the security risk myth and its conclusion that homosexuals perform their duties as well as heterosexuals were enough to get it buried for 20 years, until it was subpoenaed in a court case in 1977.

The story replayed itself just last year, when a report titled "Nonconforming Sexual Orientations and Military Suitability" was mailed anonymously to the House Armed Services Committee. Written by Theodore Sarbin, a psychology professor at the University of California, Santa Cruz, and Capt. Kenneth Karols, a Navy doctor, for the DOD's Personnel Security Research and Education Center (PERSEREC) in Monterey, California, the study asserts that "the military cannot indefinitely isolate itself from the changes occurring in the wider society." It argues that the forces should view homosexuals as a non-ethnic minority group, rather than as deviants or criminals, and should do research to test the hypothesis that gays "can function appropriately in military units."

After receiving the report from Armed Services, Representatives 20 Gerry Studds and Pat Schroeder summoned Sarbin to a meeting on the Hill. They also invited Maynard Anderson, the Pentagon official who oversees PERSEREC. Anderson criticized the draft and said it was not ready to be released. Studds, who is gay, defended it. "When Gerry said he'd read it, Anderson went pale," Studds staffer Kate Dyer said. "Then he said I have a copy, and Anderson went paler. Then Gerry said he was going to release it to the press and Anderson went white."

Schroeder then asked if there were any other reports in the works bearing on the question of homosexuality. Anderson assured her there were not. A week later another document arrived in a plain wrapper: a PERSEREC report titled "Preservice Adjustment of Homosexual Military Accessions: Implications for Security Clearance Suitability." Its conclusion is that "homosexuals show preservice suitability-related adjustment that is as good or better than the average heterosexual." The report noted that its results "appear to be in conflict with the conceptions of homosexuals as unstable, maladjusted persons."

DOD's position is that neither report is finished. The Sarbin-Karols study was never even commissioned. The Pentagon says it asked for a report on whether homosexuals were reliable. Sarbin and Karols overstepped the bounds of their assignment by answering that they were *suitable*. "The entire effort, at least to date, is unfortunate," wrote Craig Alderman, Jr., Deputy Undersecretary of Defense for policy, in a memo to PERSEREC director Carson Eoyang. "Wholly aside from PERSEREC's lack of authority to conduct research into the military suitability area, we found [the report] to be technically flawed, to contain subject matter (Judeo-Christian precepts) which has no place in a Deparment of Defense publication." Eoyang memoed back that Alderman would not have objected if the report's conclusion had affirmed current policy. Sarbin has since rewritten the study limiting himself to the narrow question of security clearances. He said in a telephone interview that the report has been cleared for official release. But the Pentagon was unable to answer questions about its status.

Within the armed services, support for the policy appears to be weakening. Michael McIntyre, who interviewed officers for a 1980 thesis at the Naval Postgraduate School in Monterey, found that 92 percent of those he talked to did not think homosexuality should be grounds for discharge so long as it did not interfere with job performance. Still, the Joint Chiefs are not about to change of their own accord. "Don't expect them to come forward," says Lawrence Korb, a former Defense official now at the Brookings Institution. "The armed forces is not a social experiment."

Korb thinks the change eventually will be accomplished by legislative or executive action. But both avenues seem closed for the present. Studds says it would be counterproductive to press a bill in the House now, since it would have no chance of passage. "There is no way on earth Congress is going to take the initiative on this," he says. Of course, the simplest way to change the rules on gays would be by Presidential fiat, the way Harry Truman integrated the services in 1948. But then, George Bush is no Harry Truman.

Questions for Discussion

1. How did military policy toward gay people change in 1982? Do you see any ways in which the current policy could be abused?

2. What arguments are usually advanced to justify excluding gay people from military service?

3. What was the conclusion of the Crittenden report? Have more recent studies come to similiar conclusions? Why do you think the military suppresses these reports?

4. According to Weisberg, "Women are dismissed for homosexuality three times as often as men are, eight times as often in the Marine Corps." Why do you think this happens? Is it because there are a large number of female soldiers who are gay? Or is it because the military discriminates against women?

5. Does Weisberg provide any evidence that attitudes toward gay people in the military may be changing?

6. Consider the analogy made in paragraphs 12, 15, and 24. Given the purpose of this argument, why is it useful for Weisberg to compare racial integration with integration of people having different sexual preferences?

Suggestions for Writing

1. Weisberg has focused upon one way gay people are discriminated against. If you agree that homosexual men and women are "a non-ethnic minority group," do you think that they should be given legal protection from discrimination in employment or housing? Write an argument for or against making it illegal to deny a job or a home to someone because of his or her sexual preference.

2. If someone wants to volunteer to serve in the armed forces, should that person be accepted, or is the military justified in having standards regarding age and fitness? If you think there are people who should be denied the opportunity for military service, write an argument to justify the standards you would enforce.

THE DECLARATION
OF INDEPENDENCE

Thomas Jefferson

> *A time-honored way to organize an argument is to begin by presenting assumptions that provide a foundation for the argument that follows. Look closely at the assumptions with which Jefferson begins, and think about what they mean. Notice also Jefferson's language. Although "The Declaration of Independence" has become part of our national heritage, it began as a writing assignment that went through a number of different drafts. Before approving this document on July 4, 1776, Congress made twenty-four changes and deleted over three hundred words. As you read the final draft, ask yourself how you would respond if given the chance to edit Jefferson. Would you vote to adopt the declaration exactly as it stands, or would you recommend any changes?*

When in the course of human events, it becomes necessary for one people to dissolve the political bands which have connected them with another, and to assume among the powers of the earth, the separate and equal station to which the Laws of Nature and of Nature's God entitle them, a decent respect to the opinions of mankind requires that they should declare the causes which impel them to the separation.

We hold these truths to be self-evident, that all men are created equal, that they are endowed by their Creator with certain unalienable rights, that among these are life, liberty and the pursuit of happiness. That to secure these rights, governments are instituted among men, deriving their just powers from the consent of the governed. That whenever any form of government becomes destructive of these ends, it is the right of the people to alter or to abolish it, and to institute new government, laying its foundation on such principles and organizing its powers in such form, as to them shall seem most likely to effect their safety and happiness. Prudence, indeed, will dictate that governments long established should not be changed for light and transient causes; and accordingly all experience hath shown, that mankind are more disposed to suffer, while evils are sufferable, than to right themselves by abolishing the forms to which they are accustomed. But when a long train of abuses and usurpations, pursuing invariably the same object, evinces a design to reduce them under absolute despotism, it is their right, it is their duty, to throw off such government, and to provide new guards for their future security. Such has been the patient sufferance of these Colonies; and such is now the necessity which constrains them to alter their former systems of government. This history of the present King of Great Britain is a history of repeated injuries and usurpations, all having in direct object the establishment of an absolute tyranny over these States. To prove this, let facts be submitted to a candid world.

He has refused his assent to laws, the most wholesome and necessary for the public good.

He has forbidden his Governors to pass laws of immediate and pressing importance, unless suspended in their operation till his assent should be obtained; and when so suspended, he has utterly neglected to attend to them.

He has refused to pass other laws for the accommodation of large districts of people, unless those people would relinquish the right of representation in the legislature, a right inestimable to them and formidable to tyrants only.   5

He has called together legislative bodies at places unusual, uncomfortable, and distant from the depository of their public records, for the sole purpose of fatiguing them into compliance with his measures.

He has dissolved representative houses repeatedly, for opposing with manly firmness his invasions on the rights of the people.

He has refused for a long time, after such dissolutions, to cause others to be elected; whereby the legislative powers, incapable of annihilation, have returned to the people at large for their exercise; the State remaining in the meantime exposed to all the dangers of invasion from without and convulsions within.

He has endeavoured to prevent the population of these states; for that purpose obstructing the laws for naturalization of foreigners; refusing to pass others to encourage their migration hither, and raising the conditions of new appropriations of lands.

He has obstructed the administration of justice, by refusing his assent to laws for establishing judiciary powers.   10

He has made judges dependent on his will alone, for the tenure of their offices, and the amount and payment of their salaries.

He has erected a multitude of new offices, and sent hither swarms of officers to harass our people, and eat out their substance.

He has kept among us, in times of peace, standing armies without the consent of our legislatures.

He has affected to render the military independent of and superior to the civil power.

He has combined with others to subject us to a jurisdiction foreign to our constitution, and unacknowledged by our laws; giving his assent to their acts of pretended legislation: 15

For quartering large bodies of armed troops among us:

For protecting them, by a mock trial, from punishment for any murders which they should commit on the inhabitants of these States:

For cutting off our trade with all parts of the world:

For imposing taxes on us without our consent:

For depriving us in many cases of the benefits of trial by jury: 20

For transporting us beyond seas to be tried for pretended offences:

For abolishing the free system of English laws in a neighbouring

Province, establishing therein an arbitrary government, and enlarging its boundaries so as to render it at once an example and fit instrument for introducing the same absolute rule into these Colonies:

For taking away our Charters, abolishing our most valuable laws, and altering fundamentally the forms of our governments:

For suspending our own legislatures, and declaring themselves invested with power to legislate for us in all cases whatsoever.

He has abdicated government here, by declaring us out of his protection and waging war against us.   25

He has plundered our seas, ravaged our coasts, burnt our towns, and destroyed the lives of our people.

He is at this time transporting large armies of foreign mercenaries to complete the works of death, desolation and tyranny, already begun with circumstances of cruelty and perfidy scarcely paralleled in the most barbarous ages, and totally unworthy the head of a civilized nation.

He has constrained our fellow citizens taken captive on the high seas to bear arms against their country, to become the executioners of their friends and brethren, or to fall themselves by their hands.

He has excited domestic insurrections amongst us, and has endeavoured to bring on the inhabitants of our frontiers, the merciless Indian savages, whose known rule of welfare, is an undistinguished destruction of all ages, sexes, and conditions.

In every stage of these oppressions we have petitioned for redress in the most humble terms: our repeated petitions have been answered only by repeated injury. A prince whose character is thus marked by every act which may define a tyrant is unfit to be the ruler of a free people.   30

Nor have we been wanting in attention to our British brethren. We have warned them from time to time of attempts by their legislature to extend an unwarrantable jurisdiction over us. We have reminded them of the circumstances of our emigration and settlement here. We have appealed to their native justice and magnanimity, and we have conjured them by the ties of our common kindred to disavow these usurpations, which would inevitably interrupt our connections and correspondence. They too have been deaf to the voice of justice and consanguinity. We must, therefore, acquiesce in the necessity, which denounces our separation, and hold them, as we hold the rest of mankind, enemies in war, in peace friends.

We, therefore, the Representatives of the United States of America, in General Congress assembled, appealing to the Supreme Judge of the world for the rectitude of our intentions, do, in the name, and by authority of the good people of these Colonies, solemnly publish and declare, That these United Colonies are, and of right ought to be, Free and Independent States; that they are absolved from all allegiance to the British Crown, and that all political connection between them and the state of Great Britain, is and ought to be totally dissolved; and that as Free and Independent States, they have full power to levy war, conclude peace, contract alliances, establish commerce, and to do all other acts and things which Independent States may of right do. And for the support of this declaration, with a firm reliance on the protection of Divine Providence, we mutually pledge to each other our lives, our fortunes, and our sacred honor.

Questions for Discussion

1. What do you think Jefferson meant by "men" in paragraph 2? What does it mean to have "unalienable rights"? And what do you think "the pursuit of happiness" means?
2. Jefferson begins his argument with truths that he declares to be "self-evident." Do any of the statements in paragraph 2 strike you as open to dispute?
3. Of the various charges Jefferson makes against King George III, which do you think are the most serious?
4. How fairly has Jefferson treated Native Americans in this document?
5. Has Jefferson taken any steps to protect his fellow colonists from the charge that they were acting rashly in declaring independence?
6. Modern conventions governing capitalization differ from those that were observed in the eighteenth century. When first published, paragraph 32 of "The Declaration of Independence" began with a reference to the Representatives of the united States of America." Is there a difference between "united States of America" and "United States of America"?

Suggestions for Writing

1. Slavery was legal in this country for almost a hundred years after the Declaration of Independence, and women were not allowed to vote in national elections until 1920. Do you think that there are people living in this country today who still do not enjoy rights to "life, liberty, and the pursuit of happiness"? If so, write a "declaration of independence" in support of their rights.
2. According to Jefferson, George III was a tyrant guilty of "cruelty and perfidy scarcely paralleled in the most barbarous ages." Do research on George III, and then write an argument on his behalf.

6

Writing to Convey Information

Were you aware that the industrial revolution has given way to the information revolution? Today, every intelligent person needs to know how to acquire and report information. Ask yourself whether in the course of a single week you do any of the following: ask directions, consult the telephone book, look something up in a book, read a newspaper, check gasoline prices, or listen to a weather report. All of these efforts to acquire information are things people do every day. Information helps us negotiate the pathways of the world. And it also forms the basis for understanding that world. Clearly, we need to understand how to manage information.

What is information? One type of information consists of "facts": independently verifiable events, statistics, and statements — Peter Jennings was born in Canada; Angell Memorial Hospital in Boston had a $2 million deficit in 1988; 114 people were killed when a walkway collapsed in the Kansas City Hyatt Regency Hotel in 1981. That is how information exists outside of us. But information also exists in our minds; this type of information comes from being able to put facts together to make inferences. For example, it is a fact that Naperville, Illinois, had a population of 22,600 in 1970, 42,600 in 1980, and 83,000 in 1989. We can combine this information and infer that by the year 2000 Naperville will have a population well in excess of 150,000, since the population appears to be almost doubling every ten years. In short, information consists not only of facts but also of educated opinion and reasonable speculations. Our main concern, however, is with the way we transfer information from one mind to another. Though this can be a very complex process, we can say that the most powerful way to transfer information from one mind to another is through language—and specifically, by writing. That is what we are concerned with in this chapter.

FINDING A SUBJECT

Frequently, when you write to inform, you have been given an assignment by a professor at college or a supervisor at work. Term papers, laboratory reports, case studies, engineering and business reports, client interviews, medical histories, news stories, accident reports—a list of the kinds of informative writing you may be asked to do is practically endless. But when the subject for the report is assigned (or if you already know what you want to write about), your job has been made considerably easier.

If you must find your own subject, you would do well to consider three elements: what you are interested in, what you know the most about, and what you are good at. Almost any sport or hobby can be written about informatively. If you are an expert skier, for example, you can write a paper about what conditions to expect at various ski areas. Consider, also, whether there is a subject, such as the life of Ronald Reagan or Native American folklore, that you are interested in and have already read about. If so, you can probably write an informative paper on that subject without having to do additional research.

If you are expected to do some research on your subject, take advantage of this opportunity by choosing something you want to learn about. Perhaps some important discovery has recently been announced—for instance, a new development in cell biology suggests dinosaur DNA may be recoverable from insects fossilized in amber. You may be interested in learning more about an important theory or principle—such as strange attractors in chaos theory or the principle of artistic proportion.

Consider, also, the range of subjects included in this chapter: You may want to report upon the changing American scene, as Sam Bingham and Nicholas Lemann do. Perhaps, like Stephen Jay Gould, who wrote "Women's Brains," you are interested in natural phenomena, or you may want to profile a particular person, the way Elizabeth Kaye does in "Peter Jennings Gets No Self-respect." You may wish to describe a commercial process, as in "The Dark Side of Tomatoes" and "Inside Hallmark's Love

Machine." You can trace the history and function of a place, as John Sedgwick does with a veterinary hospital in "The Doberman Case." Or considering the length of "The Doberman Case" and "Stressed Out in Suburbia," you may want to summarize one of these articles — or something else that you have read — so that others can grasp its main points. There is almost no limit for possible topics except the limits imposed by how much you know, how much you want to learn, and how much time you have to write. If you can't think of anything you want to write about, review the techniques for discovering and focusing a subject explained earlier in this book (pp. 5–15).

ACQUIRING INFORMATION

Although writing to inform does not necessarily entail doing research, there may be times when you lack adequate information to finish the paper you want or need to write. Research can provide you with that information. There are many guides to research in print, and you will almost certainly find a chapter on how to do research if you own a rhetoric or a handbook. Teaching in detail the research strategies available for writers is beyond the scope of this introduction, but you should be aware of four basic principles.

1. Research is not limited to long, formal papers with lengthy bibliographies, such as a ten-page "research paper" due at the end of the semester. Writers often need to consult sources when working on shorter assignments prompted by a number of different motives for writing.
2. A good search strategy involves consulting different kinds of sources, including both books and articles and sometimes government documents and personal interviews. Don't get discouraged if you can't find a book on your topic, or if the periodicals you need have been checked out by someone else. Search for another kind of source.
3. Information that comes from sources should be documented according to one of the nationally recognized documentation styles, such as those recommended by the Modern Language Association, the American Psychological Association, or *The Chicago Manual of Style*.
4. Writers who use sources should be careful to remain in control of their material, incorporating information into their writing without letting a paper become a collection of undigested data from which the author's voice has disappeared.

When time is limited, you may find the information you need by simply consulting a general encyclopedia such as *Encyclopedia Americana* or *Encyclopaedia Britannica*. You may also consider using one of the specialized works that can be found in the reference collections of most libraries, such as the following:

> *Contemporary Authors*
> *Dictionary of American Biography*
> *Dictionary of American History*
> *Encyclopedia of Philosophy*
> *Encyclopedia of Religion*
> *Encyclopedia of World Literature in the 20th Century*
> *McGraw-Hill Encyclopedia of Science and Technology*
> *The Reader's Encyclopedia*

When time allows further reading, a library's main catalog will direct you to books on your subject within its collection. For recent information on specific topics you will often need to consult periodical literature (or material, like magazines and newspapers, that is published periodically). The most common index to periodical literature is *The Readers' Guide to Periodical Literature,* which can direct you to articles on your topic in approximately five hundred general circulation magazines, such as *Newsweek, Rolling Stone,* and *Scientific American.* For information in scholarly publications you will need to consult a specialized index such as one of the following:

> *Applied Science and Technology Index*
> *Art Index*
> *Biological and Agricultural Index*
> *Business Periodicals Index*
> *Education Index*
> *General Science Index*
> *Humanities Index*
> *Index Medicus*
> *Music Index*
> *Social Sciences Index*

Although a few journals are covered in more than one of these indexes, each of these resources will usually direct you to different listings. Many topics can be researched through more than one index, but it is essential to consider which indexes are most suitable for your topic. If you are looking for information on mandatory drug testing in the workplace, you will be able to find material through the *Business Periodicals Index* and the *Index Medicus* but not through the *Humanities Index* or the *Music Index*.

There is no reason to assume, however, that research must be confined to libraries. If you have ever wondered how food is prepared in a local fast-food restaurant, you might consider doing some field research — touring the facility, asking questions of employees, and then writing an informative behind-the-scenes report. Or if you are interested in writing a profile of someone, like Elizabeth Kaye's profile of Peter Jennings, you might interview that person and, perhaps, his or her associates.

When interviewing someone, you should always try to do some preliminary research before conducting the interview so that you will be able to ask knowledgeable questions. Always schedule an interview in advance, and prepare a list of questions that are broad enough to give someone room to discuss his or her thoughts but specific enough to find out what you need to know. Try to know your questions by heart, so that you can talk naturally with the person you are interviewing without stopping to find and read a question that you wrote down someplace. And if you want to use a tape recorder, you should always ask permission to do so.

WORKING WITH INFORMATION

As you plan your paper, keep in mind that achieving the goal of being factual and objective requires that you be able to handle information properly. You must know what is a fact and what an opinion, and you must be able to summarize information.

The scientific world accepts only facts that can be empirically verified — that is, tested in controlled environments — but most of us accept testimony and generally agreed beliefs as fact. For instance, suppose that while you are out for your daily walk, you see that the front window of the hardware store is broken. You notify the owners, and they tell you that someone smashed it with a crowbar. They believe that because the barber across the street says that he saw it happen. But maybe the barber is lying. The only scientifically acceptable fact in this account is that the window was broken. That someone hit it with a crowbar becomes more factual when another person in the vicinity also says he or she saw this happen. For most people two witnesses providing the same testimony would be sufficient evidence to establish how the window was broken, and even one source may be sufficient if that source is reliable.

Informative writing generally does not require the same level of factuality as is found in scientific reports (which are also writing to inform but for special audiences). Consider the following statement from Raymond Sokolov's "The Dark Side of Tomatoes."

> The sad fact is that you can't grow a tomato on the west coast of Mexico in January, pick it green, ship it three to four thousand miles, and expect it to be as good as a garden fruit in summer.

The *fact* that Sokolov refers to has become a fact because repeated experiences have shown that January tomatoes are not very flavorful, tomatoes picked green are not as flavorful as vine-ripened, and varieties that tolerate shipment over long distances are unnaturally firm. So inferences and opinions are acceptable as long as you do not pretend they are any-thing else.

As you gather information, you will probably find you need to condense that information. So you need to know how to summarize. A *summary* is a condensation of information that reports only the main points and omits all — or most — of the supporting information. For example, the following paragraphs appeared in a report in the San Jose *Mercury News* for June 25, 1991:

> PCR analysis was invented and patented in 1985 by scientists at the Cetus Corp. The instrument that amplifies trace quantities of DNA is about the size of a shoe box.
>
> By cyclically changing the temperature of the contents and by supplying various building-block chemicals, the device splits apart paired strands of corkscrew-shape DNA molecules and uses each strand as a template to create a new DNA segment.
>
> With each repetition of the procedure, the number of identical DNA segments is doubled, and trillions of copies can be manufac-tured rapidly. The result is that fragments of DNA formerly too small to analyze can be amplified easily for study.
>
> A feature of the system is that scientists can select any section of interest from a DNA molecule — typically a single set of genes — and amplify only that part.

Extracting the information from this report requires understanding what the report says and restating in your own words the information you consider to be important. Here is a summary of the above passage:

> PCR analysis amplifies trace amounts of DNA mechanically in a boxlike device that cycles temperature as it splits all or a selected part of the characteristic DNA pairs and combines them with building-block chemicals.

The summary reduces the length of the passage to a fourth its origi-nal size and includes what most readers would consider all the essentials. The name of the company that invented the gadget, the date it was in-vented, and its size are left out. So is information about the shape of DNA molecules and the information that split strands act as templates, that the segments are identical, that there can be trillions of them, and that re-searchers can specify which genes are amplified. Most readers will con-sider these details to be nonessential. However, people who are interested in knowing which company developed the device or the amount of recon-stituted DNA it can make will not find the summary above useful. Re-member that your purpose in summarizing and the audience for whom you are summarizing influence your decisions about what information to include.

Making these decisions is easier when you can analyze your subject to determine what its parts are. Analysis can also help you decide whether you have enough information and the space to present it in. *Analysis* is a systematic way of thinking about a subject so as to divide it into the elements of which it is made. This analysis must be done consistently on some logical basis—which is called the *basis for analysis.* You can use that basis to determine what the parts of the subject are, and then you can analyze the subsequent parts, each with its own basis. For example, history can be analyzed by examining it from a perspective of time, of place, of ideas, of economics, or of social customs. So you can work, for example, with information on the history of sixteenth-century Italian military weapons or on medieval social customs in England.

The opposite of analysis is classification. *Classification* is the thinking process whereby you consider a number of diverse items or pieces of information, looking for ways to group this bit with that and establish some order. Again, you must have some *basis for classification*—some principle by which you decide which things go in each group. Suppose you have a bin full of plastic "jewels" to sell. You need to price them, but it is a time-consuming task to put a price tag on each piece of plastic. But you certainly can make a sign that says,

Large	$3
Medium	$2
Small	$1

Or one that says,

Red	$3
Blue	$2
Green	$1

But you should not make a sign that says,

Red	$3
Medium	$2
Square	$1

Using more than one basis for classification creates confusion: How much does a medium-sized, square, red piece cost?

If you can't keep straight which thinking process is which, don't be concerned. Once you have accomplished a classification, it is hard to distinguish it from analysis, and they are often used in tandem. For instance, in Sedgwick's "The Doberman Case" Dr. Virginia Rentko collects information to try to see how she should treat the husky with pneumothorax.

> Generally, pneumothorax is due to long-term lung disease, such as bronchitis or asthma, but the husky showed no evidence of that. It can also result from being hit by a car, but that didn't seem likely either, because the husky's toenails were all intact. In a car accident, they usually get scraped up or ripped off in the dog's sudden skid

across the pavement. Abuse couldn't be ruled out, but that usually shows up as extreme skinniness. A dog who cowers in fear when a human reaches out a hand might also have been abused.

Dr. Rentko collects evidence, simultaneously analyzing a problem and fitting the evidence she collects to the analysis she is doing.

To take an easier example, suppose you look at an automobile and note that it has wheels, a body, a motor, a transmission, and so on; you have *analyzed* the automobile by dividing it into parts. Or you can look at all those parts of the automobile taken apart and lying on the garage floor and figure out that this part belongs to the motor, that one to the transmission, and so on — that is *classification*. Analysis involves taking things apart, and classification involves putting things together.

Elsewhere in this book you will find writers using analysis and classification to fulfill other motives for writing. And within this chapter you will notice that writing to inform often involves a number of other strategies. Some kinds of information require that you narrate events, as Sedgwick does to inform us about the Doberman; other kinds of information lend themselves to description — Elizabeth Kaye, for example, describes a number of things about Peter Jennings. Sometimes, a comparison is called for, as in Sokolov's piece on tomatoes; and other times, an author will search for causes or effects, as Lemann and Gould do. But in each case the motive for writing is to give the reader information about the subject, and the writer chooses whatever strategies will most efficiently accomplish that goal.

CONSIDERING YOUR AUDIENCE

When you write to inform, you must pay special attention to the interests and abilities of your audience if you are to offer the quality and quantity of information that is appropriate for your readers. When you write for general readers, you should not expect them to understand specialized vocabulary and advanced concepts. Consider the following excerpt from a college textbook for an introductory course in astronomy:

> Based on his determination that the sun was much larger than the earth, Aristarchus proposed that the sun was at rest and the earth moved around it in a yearly orbit. This *heliocentric* (sun-centered) model was opposed to the prevailing *geocentric* (earth-centered) model. The concept of a heliocentric universe was immediately challenged. If the earth moved in an orbit, the stars would appear to shift relative to one another, depending on the position of the earth in its orbit. This phenomenon, called *parallax*, was not observed. Aristarchus' reply to this objection was that the stars must be extremely far away, making any parallax shifts too small to notice. — *Thomas Michael Corwin and Dale G. Wachowiak*, The Universe: From Chaos to Consciousness, *246.*

The authors have considered their audience. They have not talked down to them, but they have recognized that vocabulary may be a problem. They have also presented a fairly difficult concept in a context that makes it easier to understand.

Compare that passage with one from Gilbert E. Satterthwaite's *Encyclopedia of Astronomy*, which also describes parallax but is directed to more sophisticated readers:

> The angle subtended at a heavenly body by a baseline of known length, usually designated P or π. It is of course directly related to the distance; the word has therefore come to be used by astronomers as synonymous with distance.
>
> The baseline used for nearer objects, such as the members of the solar system, is the equatorial radius of the earth; parallaxes determined on this basis are termed *geocentric parallaxes*. . . . For more distant objects, the baseline used is the semimajor axis of the Earth's orbit; these are termed *heliocentric parallaxes*. (305)

Think about how much and what kind of information you need to give your audience, but also consider how you will present it. For instance, Corwin and Wachowiak correctly realize that for beginners in astronomy they must create interest in the concept and that they must not give their readers more information than can be processed immediately. Later on in the text, when the students have acquired some expertise, the authors address parallax more technically, but still not as technically as Satterthwaite does. Satterthwaite's discussion goes on in considerable detail to discuss various kinds of parallaxes, but he can assume that his readers will be highly motivated to read his discussion and will have the knowledge to understand fine points, a different audience altogether from Corwin and Wachowiak's.

In general, there are two points to bear in mind when you are writing to inform:

- You are not informing readers if you tell them what they already know.
- You can inform readers about what they do not know only if you use language that they can understand.

SHAPING YOUR WRITING

Writing to inform need not always have a thesis; business reports, for instance, are frequently simple narrations of what has happened or text that exists mainly to link numbers in some meaningful way. But informative writing can benefit from having a thesis. When you do have a thesis, usually you will be wise to put it up front and indicate it clearly for your reader. Busy people appreciate having signals from the author that will alert them to the most important information and give them the opportunity to skim the rest. They also appreciate having some idea of the scope of the article. For instance, because of the way Nicholas Lemann opens his essay, readers know that he will contrast information about a modern suburb with preconceptions that many people have. This direction is established by the very first sentence: "I recently spent some time in Naperville, Illinois, because I wanted to see exactly how our familiar ideas about the suburbs have gotten out of date."

You can follow your introduction with background information that gives the reader a context into which to fit the rest of the report. Notice how Sam Bingham informs readers about Rocky Ford's past before reporting its current conflict with a Denver suburb. Arrange your points in an effective order. A good strategy is to save your most impressive or most startling facts until just before you conclude. Notice how Stephen Jay Gould presents increasingly disgraceful examples of faulty interpretation. It is also possible to present your most important information first — though that method can easily lead to an anticlimax. If there is more than one side to your subject, be sure to present them all — as Elizabeth Kaye does with her portrait of Peter Jennings.

Students are often advised to couch all their information in neutral, precise, objective language, because informing is supposed to be even-handed; but that does not mean that you should take all the zest out of your prose. Too much scientific and informative writing sounds as if it were produced by a machine. As the prose of Stephen Jay Gould reveals, though, you can write informatively and still let your own personality show through. Presenting information while still conveying a human voice helps readers remain interested in the information without damaging any of its value.

When you are finished, what do you do? Make clear to your reader that you are finished. Don't just stop. Sometimes you write a conclusion, sometimes not. Some essays don't require one. For example, very short essays usually do not have a formal conclusion, but they may end with an emphatic statement that signals that the end has come.

If you do decide to write a conclusion, you may proceed in a variety of ways. Let the writers in this chapter guide you about what to do. You may decide to use the most common kind of conclusion for an informative essay, which is one like Sokolov's. It recapitulates the points in a brief summary: "they show that the real obstacle to bringing decent domestic tomatoes to U.S. tables in the off-season is human greed and laziness, not bad science or gas." Or you might frame your essay by returning to a point you had made in your introduction, as Gould does when he concludes his essay by returning to a novel he had mentioned in his first paragraph. Or you might end with a quotation, as Elizabeth Kaye and Dennis Farney do. There really is no single way to end an informative essay. Notice what other writers do, and experiment with different strategies.

But however you choose to conclude your paper, remember that writing to inform springs from a need to communicate with others. However interested you may be in your topic, you will not be genuinely informative if you do not leave readers feeling at least a little more knowledgeable once they have read what you have written. The best way to judge how well you have succeeded in satisfying this purpose is to get your paper off your desk and let someone else read it.

A SHARE OF THE RIVER

Sam Bingham

Bingham sets the scene for "A Share of the River" in detail, describing the country around Rocky Ford, Colorado, and narrating the history of the town. As you read this essay, consider how the scene has changed as the result of various acts. Consider also why the information that Bingham reports could interest readers outside of Colorado.

The Rocky Ford irrigation ditch is an unpretentious excavation, no wider than a country road, fringed by weeds and spanned by cranky creosoted bridges too low to pass under without crawling on the cracked clay bottom. It meanders south from the Arkansas River and across the largely boarded-up streets of the town of Rocky Ford, a half-dead farming community about a hundred miles southeast of Aurora, Denver's largest suburb. Aurora people don't go there, and wouldn't notice the old irrigation work if they did.

Coming down Highway 50, a traveler sees instead the wreck of the American Crystal Sugar Company's huge redbrick Victorian beet mill and the barren fields that once supplied the Foxley & Company feedlots, in Ordway, before Foxley went broke. Rocky Ford once exported ten million cantaloupes a year to New York City alone. Now it has sunk so low in the food chain of the state economy that Aurora has bought most of the water that justified the town's existence.

"They paid about $22 million for a little more than half the water rights, but we haven't seen much of that in Rocky Ford," says Ron Aschermann, the last of four generations of Aschermanns to farm along the ditch. "It's hollowed out the valley. Without the water, the land is worthless. You can't farm it, and you can't tax it. Without the farming, you've got no business on Main Street. Without the tax base, you either go without schools and services or you assess what's left so high that even those who want to stay can't afford to."

Aschermann still grows onions, wheat, and a few acres of the once famous Rocky Ford cantaloupes on his land, but he speaks as if he were the last of the Arapaho, who were driven from the area a century ago. His son is studying real estate finance in Denver.

Over the last twenty years, the valley of the Arkansas has lost about a quarter of its 330,000 irrigated acres to the cities—Pueblo, Colorado Springs, and, finally, Aurora. As Aschermann says, "They're just rolling us up."

Rocky Ford is older than Aurora. It took its name from the spot where the Santa Fe Trail crossed the Arkansas River, the place where in 1833 an enterprising merchant named William Bent built the first white outpost in the territory, which came to be called Bent's Fort. After Bent and his successors killed off the beaver and the buffalo and the Indians, Rocky Ford succeeded to cattlemen and, ultimately, farmers. Led by an Illinois immigrant named George Washington Swink, farmers dug the first irrigation ditch on the Arkansas there in 1874, two years before Colorado became a state.

By the end of the century, there were dozens of small towns thriving along the Arkansas, digging ditches and tapping off the river. Each ditch was allocated a share of the river, and anyone who could prove he would put the water to beneficial use was allocated a share of the ditch. Shareholders controlled their interests through ditch companies: the Bessemer, the Catlin, the Amity Mutual, the Fort Lyon, the Las Animas, the High Line. The oldest ditches got first rights to the water in times of drought. Shares could be sold or traded at will, and the more senior the right the more it was worth.

Few people in communities on the Arkansas questioned the buying and bartering of ditch rights. And few in Rocky Ford sensed danger when the American Crystal Sugar Company bought up a majority of shares in the local ditch. American Crystal farmed thousands of acres of sugar beets in the area, and at its height, in the sixties, the mill employed a hundred men year-round, six hundred during the fall and winter harvest. America had stopped buying Cuban sugar, there was no grain embargo, and money flowed in Rocky Ford.

Then it ebbed away. Sugar prices fluctuated wildly in the seventies, and the days of easy credit gave way to the foreclosures of the farm crisis. The mill in Rocky Ford shut down in 1979, the last of six in the valley to die.

A year later, the people of Rocky Ford learned that an outfit called *10* the Resource Investment Group had bought the whole show. For $13 million, RIG got the mill, 4,100 acres of land, and fifty-four percent of the ditch company—112 cubic feet of water per second off the top of the Arkansas River. "You could tell from the name that they weren't interested in farming," Aschermann says, "but nobody around here could raise that kind of money."

The principal partners in RIG, John and Bill Bowlen, of Calgary, Alberta, had done better than most in oil and gas speculation, and they did well in water, too. In 1983, they signed a contract selling the water rights to Aurora for a profit of nine million dollars. "We're always looking for trends," said John Bowlen of the sale not long ago. "The direction of growth was clear. It was an opportunity and we took it." A few months after that, the Bowlen family bought the Denver Bronco NFL franchise.

Aschermann and the remaining minority shareholders in the Rocky Ford ditch went to court, joined by ditch companies up and down the Arkansas. They were worried not just about insuring their share of the water but also about the fate of the American Crystal land, which RIG still owned. The precedents were bad. In 1985, when the Foxley feedlot company sold a majority share in neighboring Colorado Canal to Colorado Springs, little was left behind on 30,000 acres but dust and weeds. Orville Tomky, a farmer who held on after Foxley left, said, "When someone sells, everyone has to jump in and spend to protect what's left. You've got to defend it 365 days of the year."

The farmers in Rocky Ford spent three years and $30,000 doing just that. In the end, they won the protection they sought, including a promise that RIG would restore natural prairie on the American Crystal land, which would no longer be irrigated; but RIG did so little to meet its requirements that three years later Aschermann et al. hauled both the company and Aurora back into court on a contempt charge. The judge fined the city and the speculators just two thousand dollars each, but he warned that further delay could cost them millions. Aurora, eager not to offend, has taken over the challenge.

Tom Griswold, utilities director for that city, is a vigorous blond man of forty-three. His office overlooks the 284 square miles of the Aurora planning area. Geographically, Aurora is arguably the largest city in the state. Denver exceeds it only because of having recently annexed a fifty-square-mile site just north of Aurora, on which it hopes to build the world's largest airport — one intended to turn the metro area into an international hub ("midway between Munich and Tokyo," say the promotional brochures). The population of Aurora grew from 74,974 to 232,800 between 1970 and 1985. "Since then, the oil bust has dropped us back a little," Griswold says, "but the new airport and completion of the beltway will set it off again. We're planning for about 430,000 by the year 2010, and the planning area, when it's built out, will support about 700,000."

He worries little about Rocky Ford. "I grew up on a hog farm in   15
Illinois myself," he said. "There's an attraction to that kind of life, but frankly if you go down to Rocky Ford you won't see any young people farming. There's no future in it anymore."

To put back the prairie, he's hired a thirty-seven-year-old former hog farmer named Gerry Knapp, whose great-grandfather broke ground along the Arkansas over a century ago. Knapp surveys his planting — grama grass, Western wheatgrass, galleta, and bluestem — with pride, and will tell visitors that the work is right on schedule. But the fact is, putting back is not as easy as plowing up. After a century of silt and salt from the river, after years of plows, fertilizers, herbicides, and pesticides, the land has changed, and nobody knows for sure whether the interplay of plants and soil life that kept the natural prairie alive can be re-created in the long term on the old fields of Rocky Ford.

When Griswold speaks of the long term, however, he speaks of Aurora. He looks at the map on his wall and then out the window at the snowy peaks beyond his densely paved landscape. "Oh, there's plenty of water out there," he says, "and it's inevitably going to flow to the cities. We have people in here every week offering us deals for water rights from one place or another. Some are more feasible than others, but one way or another we're going to get the water."

Questions for Discussion

1. How did Rocky Ford, Colorado, lose much of its water supply to a Denver suburb a hundred miles away? How has Rocky Ford changed in the last thirty years?
2. Why does Bingham take the trouble to report that Ron Aschermann's son is "studying real estate finance in Denver" and that the Bowlen family recently bought the Denver Broncos? Within the context of this article as a whole, what is the significance of this information? What does it lead you to conclude?
3. Consider the way Bingham portrays Tom Griswold. Is he good at his job? Does he have any limitations?
4. Bingham quotes Griswold three times in this article. Why do you think he chose the quotation in paragraph 17 for his conclusion?
5. Why is it that farmland cannot be easily restored to natural prairie?

Suggestions for Writing

1. Has your hometown changed since you were a child? If so, write an essay that will report how it once was and what it is like today. Pretend that you are a visiting journalist and include only those details that you could observe or learn from residents.
2. How does your town get its water supply, and how carefully is the quality of that supply maintained? Is it facing any long-term difficulties? Are there any plans for managing the water supply during a drought? Is there any danger of contamination through industrial or agricultural pollution? Interview a municipal authority and report on how the people in your community get their water and what risks, if any, they should be informed about.

THE DARK SIDE OF TOMATOES

Raymond Sokolov

You may think you already know all you need to know about tomatoes, but the following essay by food writer Raymond Sokolov contains information that may surprise you. As you read, notice how Sokolov conveys a human voice by expressing his own love for tomatoes. But be alert for information that you did not know. And as you appraise that information, try to distinguish between facts and opinion.

In a world riven by hate, greed, and envy, everyone loves tomatoes. I have never met anyone who didn't eat tomatoes with enthusiasm. Like ice cream, the whole, perfect, vine-ripened tomato is a universal favorite. The old-fashioned kind of tomato, not the hard-walled hybrids picked green, engineered to survive long truck rides, and ripened with gas on the way to market.

Real (as I will call vine-ripened, soft-walled, acid-flavored, summergrown) tomatoes are an article of faith, a rallying point for the morally serious, a grail. And the real tomato's acolytes are not some ragged little band of malcontents. They are us, brothers and sisters in tomatomania, converts to the first Western religion since the Stone Age to worship a plant.

Everyone I know seems to have his own story of how the scales fell from his palate as he tasted, really tasted, a real tomato for the first time. My own ecstatic rebirth as a tomatomane took place on a rail siding in some border no man's land between Yugoslavia and Greece in early August of 1960. After two days of sparse and dismal food on the old Simplon-Orient Express passing through Yugoslavia, I was able to buy a large red tomato from a boy hawking them to passengers waiting on the platform. I bit into one; juice spurted on my cheeks and tears almost mixed in. I still quiver when I recall that moment.

Such pure memories, reinforced each summer by new experiences with real tomatoes, have their dark side. They make us picky, unwilling to settle, or at least to settle happily, for false tomatoes. And so we become tomato bores, railing against square tomatoes without taste.

The Tom Paine of this rebellion is Thomas Whiteside, who attempted to get to the bottom of the dark lagoon of tomato industrialization in an exhaustively reported article in *The New Yorker* in 1977. It was Whiteside who spread the word about tomatoes picked green for durability and transportability from Florida. It was Whiteside who alerted *New Yorker* sophisticates to the existence of square tomatoes, hybridized by modern plant scientists to accommodate mechanical harvesting. And it was Whiteside who raised the consciousness of upper-middle-class America about artificial ripening of tomatoes induced by ethylene gas. 5

Of course, there were other tomato muckrakers out there building the almost complete consensus of intelligent consumers against the supermarket tomato. But an informal survey indicates that Whiteside was the crucial figure, the tomato Jeremiah behind whom a growing throng collected. All praise to him. He pointed to a great truth: the industrial tomato is a dud. Only corporate executives of tomato companies would disagree with that.

In attempting to think clearly about this matter, it is crucial to keep in mind that the tomato we hate is the one that we buy whole and raw to be consumed whole and raw. We are not talking about tomatoes produced for canning. This means that the square tomato is a red herring. The square tomato is not a tomato you and I can normally buy. It is aimed at the commercial canning market, where delicacy of texture and taste is of far less moment than it is for fresh tomatoes. In any case, I have never laid eyes on a square tomato and I doubt most tomato radicals have. So the square tomato is an illegitimate rallying point. Yes, it exists, and Gordie C. Hanna, of the University of California at Davis, did engineer the first cultivar suitable for machine harvesting, the VF 145, in the 1950s and 1960s. But to set up the VF 145 as an outrageous example of the perversion of science in the service of agronomic pelf would be a distortion.

So is the hate campaign against artificial ripening. The gas that growers use, in storage areas and in trucks hurtling northward, to set the process of ripening in motion is the same gas that tomatoes and many other plants produce in the normal course of natural ripening. This gas is ethylene. According to *Webster's New World Dictionary,* it is "a colorless, flammable gaseous hydrocarbon of the olefin series . . . with a disagreeable odor: it is obtained from natural or coal gas, by cracking petroleum, by the action of sulfuric or phosphoric acid on alcohol, etc., and is used as a fuel and anesthetic, in hastening the ripening of fruits and to form polyethylene."

To the eye of the scientophobe, that definition settles the argument. What could be worse than to asphyxiate tomatoes with the same poison that comes from air-polluting petroleum, puts people out on operating tables, and contributes to the degradation of the environment in the form of nonbiodegradable and unnecessary plastic packaging?

Yes, but ethylene per se is a benign natural organic substance. A ripe   10
apple exudes it into the air and will hasten the ripening of other fruits, including tomatoes. Not all chemicals are bad. It is the use we put them to that counts.

Yet there must be some explanation for those pale and tooth-resistant tomatoes. My theory was that a plant geneticist/villain had messed about with the genes of "normal" garden tomatoes and concocted a sturdier hybrid fit for long interstate trips in eighteen-wheeled tractor-trailers. That mad doctor of the plant labs deserved to be the target of a campaign of vilification as a traitor to his science and to humanity. I set out to find him.

Suspect No. 1 was the man who had hybridized Florida's infamous Walter tomato. The Walter won't ripen after picking until it has been gassed. And the Walter was the ancestor of the MH-1, a grower's dream developed by the University of Florida at Homestead. According to Whiteside, you could play catch with the MH-1 at twenty paces or let it fall from more than six feet without breaking the skin. The Walter and the MH-1 are not cannery tomatoes. They are for the table. They and tomatoes like them, from south Florida and from the state of Sinaloa in Mexico, are what make tomato lovers gnash their teeth and wish for a Senate select committee to expose the whole tasteless mess.

I was one of these people until I met Charles M. Rick, a retired professor of plant genetics at the University of California, Davis, known in his field as Mr. Tomato. Ruddy, lanky, white-haired, and white-bearded, Rick is a completely unabashed enthusiast for the achievements of tomato science as he has known it since his student days, which ended in 1940 with a Harvard doctorate.

Since then, he and his colleagues all over the world have capitalized on the extraordinary genetic malleability of the tomato to increase crop yields manyfold. Rick is not, however, an ethereal lab technician. Far from it. He is famous for trekking all over Peru in search of wild tomato strains that might enrich the gene pool of cultivated plants back home. He's a home gardener, too, and talks with enthusiasm about Burpee's Better Boy and another favorite variety, Caligrande, which he grows today because of its resistance to tobacco mosaic virus.

For the past six years, Rick has been assembling a tomato germ   15
plasm bank, a collection of 2,600 to 2,700 tomato lines in the form of seeds. When I was there, two women in his lab were extracting seeds from wild green tomatoes the size of gooseberries. Andean plants like these have been the source of "virtually all tomato disease resistance since the forties," he says.

Although Rick is the epitome of the modern tomato scientist, he is also in the great tradition of untutored green thumbs who long ago hybridized the red, fist-sized tomato we think of as normal from the tiny wild fruit nature gave to our pre-Columbian ancestors. By the time Cortés reached Mexico in 1519, cultivation had already produced tomatoes we would recognize today. Hybridization continued in Europe. All the garden tomatoes we love so much are the result of centuries of human meddling. Today's commercial varieties are no more artificial than the "normal" kind. And, if Rick is right, they are not categorically worse in quality.

"I don't think it's right to attribute poor market quality to breeding," he says. "That's a bunch of nonsense. Unbiased tests have been conducted — at Michigan State, for example — blind tastings of commercial varieties that were all vine-ripened. Most of the criticism is a reaction to what's happened to these tomatoes when they're grown in the off-season.

The sad fact is that you can't grow a tomato on the west coast of Mexico in January, pick it green, ship it three to four thousand miles, and expect it to be as good as a garden fruit in summer. Ethylene ripening is not the issue; it's the season, the low light in winter that hurts. And they add a greater handicap by picking them green and ripening them in transit. . . . I'm not sure the best tomato in the world would be a gem under those conditions."

He saw some possible hope in work being done on tomato ripening at a Davis biotechnology firm, Calgene Inc., which just received a patent for an alteration of tomato DNA. The change affects the function of the enzyme that causes softening of the fruit during the ripening process. By thwarting the enzyme, Calgene has created a tomato that stays firm longer, while ripening normally in other respects. In principle, the Calgene tomato could be picked mature instead of green, after it had developed flavor.

These are early reports, and the most optimistic prediction for the first retail sales of these tomatoes is two winters from now. Field tests are currently under way in Mexico. But in the meantime, the pressure of a $4 billion U. S. market for fresh tomatoes has finally convinced one bold and energetic New York family named Marcelli to take a great leap forward. This past winter, they were managing to deliver high-quality tomatoes to Manhattan restaurants and grocers. How do the Marcellis do what no one else seems able to manage? Simple. They let Florida tomatoes ripen on the vine. They truck them nonstop to New York. And they keep them cool, at 55 to 60 degrees, but don't refrigerate, which would degrade flavor.

"Real tomatoes," as the sticker on each one reads, are not up to the *20* supreme standard of summer garden fruit. And they are certainly expensive. But they show that the real obstacle to bringing decent domestic tomatoes to U.S. tables in the off-season is human greed and laziness, not bad science or gas.

Questions for Discussion

1. Consider the first four paragraphs of this article. Why does Sokolov devote so much space to expressing his feelings about tomatoes before reporting information on tomato breeding? Do you think this was a good writing decision?

2. Is there anything wrong with using ethylene to ripen tomatoes artificially?

3. How appetizing is a tomato that you can drop "more than six feet without breaking the skin"? Why are such tomatoes like the MH-1 being grown and sold?

4. If there are already over two thousand six hundred tomato lines, why would anyone try to collect or breed new ones? What are the benefits of tomato breeding?

5. What obstacles would have to be overcome before the quality of super-market tomatoes improved, especially during the off-season?

Suggestions for Writing

1. Investigate a commonly eaten food and report on how it is produced. Possibilities include not only the food that people buy in supermarkets but also the food products purchased in restaurants like McDonalds.
2. Interview a farmer, gardener, florist, or produce manager and report upon the problems that a person has to overcome in order to be successful.

PETER JENNINGS GETS NO SELF-RESPECT

Elizabeth Kaye

> *The following selection is an excerpt from a much longer profile of Peter Jennings that was first published in* Esquire. *Ask yourself why readers would be interested in acquiring information about Jennings — or about other people who appear regularly on television. As you read this profile of the popular news anchorman, notice how Elizabeth Kaye combines direct observation of Jennings with material she has collected from sources. Note the various pieces of information that Kaye provides, and consider how they combine to provide a history of Jennings's career as well as a sense of his character.*

As a child, he read nothing but comic books. He did no homework. He liked what was easy. He was eleven when he showed his eight-year-old sister how to smoke. "All you've got to do," he told her, "is breathe in."

He dropped out of school in the tenth grade. He was impetuous, cocky, accustomed to getting his way. His mother took to asking, "What's going to become of Pete?"

For years, Peter Jennings was embarrassed by his academic history. He avoided the subject. When he couldn't avoid it, he lied. He'd say he attended Carleton University in Ottawa. In fact, he'd gone to Carleton's night school for a week. These days, he's a featured speaker at colleges. He no longer lies. He's still embarrassed.

Now when his remarks are quoted in newspapers and journals, he'll read them, then say to himself, "There goes a product of no education." He doesn't like how he sounds. "I never sound nearly as sophisticated," he says, "as I'd like to be."

At times this amuses him. "Will you be doing this currently?" he *5* asks his executive producer one day. "Presently," Paul Friedman responds, and after that, Jennings's misuse of those words becomes a standing joke. He'll recall the day he decided that an Israeli assault on South Lebanon was too minor to be called an invasion. On the air, he called it an incursion. Then he said, "They've incurred before and they'll incur again."

One day, he details the gaps in his education. He's intent and serious as he says, "I never have ever read Proust." He smiles an instant later. "I've managed to live without it so far. But it hasn't been easy."

Still, he always laments that he hasn't studied literature or economics, that his spelling is poor, that he's unfamiliar with grammatical rules. "Because God graced me with a halfway decent set of pipes," he says, "the ability to talk to people, and a look, a demeanor, that is not distracting,

I've gotten away with bad grammar." He doesn't want to get away with things.

Years ago he determined to prove there was more to him than his trench coat. He was dashing, continental, prematurely aristocratic. He understood that his salient feature was not his mind. Ted Koppel met him in 1964. "Peter," he thought, "is enormously glamorous."

He used to believe that he could prove himself only by writing for *The Wall Street Journal* or *Time.* Five years ago he wrote his first piece. When it was published in *The Christian Science Monitor,* he sent it to his mother. "Look, Mother," he fancied himself saying, "your son is quite legitimate."

Now, in his desk, there's a half-finished article. It's a tongue-in-cheek   10
piece about how he's always asked to blurb books but never asked to review them. His wife, many of his colleagues and friends, have *written* books. "He's a little in awe of it," says his wife.

His own talents were demonstrated in other ways. He spent fifteen years proving them. By the time he was done he'd patrolled half the world and garnered respect from the kind of smart, tough writers he admired most. "His reporting from the Middle East was excellent," says David Halberstam. "It had intelligence, context, very little hype. His years overseas served him well. Now he gets things right."

Still, he feels lucky. Sometimes he feels unduly lucky.

Speaking of what qualifies him to be a network anchor, he'll say that, to him, his journalistic credentials are all that count. He'll also say, "Anybody who pretends they've got here on that — minus the cosmetic features — is kidding themselves."

And sometimes he'll think how ironic it is that his reward for establishing himself as more than a face and a voice is a job that makes so much of both.

Usually he's in a hurry. He doesn't walk: he strides at a pace familiar   15
to race walkers. He buries his hands in his trench-coat pockets. He's aware that the trench coat is still the emblem of his persona. Often he's characterized as the "urbane" or "sophisticated" anchor. To his abiding annoyance, he's also called the James Bond of broadcasting.

His trench coat is a London Fog. He swears he'll never wear a Burberry. It's been rumored at ABC that his clothes are bought at Caldor. In fact, he buys them in bulk twice a year from the London discount store where Mrs. Thatcher gets her underwear. He's always on the International Best-Dressed List. Several items in his wardrobe look better at a distance.

He walks to work each morning. People always stare at him. There are, he initially concluded, three ways to deal with it. Look at the ground, look the other way, look them in the eye. He's taken to saying, "Good morning." Afterward, he'll often think, "That was stupid. Maybe they didn't know me anyway."

As a rule, they know him. At a Washington hotel, the staff lines up to greet him. During inaugural week, that same hotel took reservations only from the Bush family, their secret-service contingent, Charlton Heston, and Jennings.

Lunching at the Plaza one day, he orders a red-caviar omelet. The waiter isn't certain that red caviar is available. He returns to say that "the lady downstairs" says she'll be pleased to get some for Peter Jennings. "What's her name?" asks Jennings. "May I write her a note?" He proceeds to do so. His handwriting, like his manner, is polished, elegant, graceful.

But while the star treatment pleases him, fame itself strikes him as 20 undignified, unseemly. "Sarah," he said to his sister after his mother gave his baby pictures to *People* magazine, "you must somehow tell Mother that she's not supposed to do that."

He's often complimented on his work. Usually he responds by saying, "You watch too much television." He disapproves of television. He loves working in it. "I think that's an ambivalence," he says, "that a lot of us have."

In his early years, he wouldn't get out of bed in the morning. This changed in his late teens, when he discovered what he calls "the joy of work." Now a piece of paper taped to his desk lamp reads: INDIFFERENCE IS NOT PART OF THE PROCESS — IT'S THE END OF IT. The caveat is unnecessary.

At home, when he hears a siren go off, he goes to the window. Wherever he goes, he makes interviews out of casual conversations. At parties, he'll hear an issue discussed, then come to the office demanding, "Why aren't we doing it?" "Walk me three blocks from anywhere," he'll say, "I guarantee you I'll find a story." He prides himself on sensing stories before they happen. "If I have a gift aside from, you know — my hair and my teeth — it is that," he says. "I don't know why."

When he was a reporter, his instincts often guided him to Asia or Africa or the Middle East, just before a situation ignited. But sometimes he'd be at home when his phone rang in the middle of the night to alert him to a guerilla raid, a hijacking. He liked nothing more than getting out the door and onto a plane. Like any passion, his had its price. He was forty-one when he married for the third time.

These days his wife is always taking the phone off the hook. He's 25 always putting it back on. "It's a little game we play," she says, "but Peter has never not answered the phone." He no longer goes off on every story. He's still inclined to.

On the road, he works twenty hours a day. He seems inexhaustible. In 1986 he goes to Manila for the elections. He travels with Mike Clemente, eighteen years his junior, then his writer and producer, still one of his closest friends. He sleeps two hours on the fourteen-hour overnight flight. He pores over briefing books until the plane lands at midnight. For the next six hours, they traverse the city, reporting, exploring. They assemble the show. Jennings broadcasts it at 8:30 in the morning. Afterward, Clemente goes to a chair and collapses. Jennings goes to the door. "Well," he says, "what are we going to do now?"

After returning from another trip, he invites a correspondent to his home for dinner. After the meal, Jennings sits on the couch, eyes reddened, nearly closing. "Why did he invite me over?" the correspondent thinks. "Why doesn't he just rest?" As Jennings talks, he slides lower on the couch. He lies down. He keeps talking until he passes out from exhaustion.

For relaxation, he'll sail his iceboat the length and breadth of frozen ponds. The boat screams along the opaque ice. It can tip over, but it can't stop. . . .

He admires moderation. It's never been his style. Courting a woman, he was madly in love or totally uninterested. Given a choice, he'd wear only black tie or no tie. He smoked too much for more than thirty years, then quit and never missed it.

For his work, he'll study for days and hours. "You think I've got it?" 30 he'll ask his researcher. "You think we're there?" When it comes to self-knowledge, he's less meticulous. "Who has time to be introspective?" he asks.

One day, he expresses anger at journalists who inaccurately portray him as "a weeper"; the next day he cries while being interviewed for *Rolling Stone.* Usually, when asked about his feelings, he repeats his wife's opinion. "On that," he'll say, "I defer to Kati." Similarly, in his dealings with others, he's both preternaturally thoughtful and blind.

In airports, he'll carry golf clubs for old men, and suitcases for elderly women. He's constantly writing letters to recommend friends for co-ops and jobs. At work, he buys a stool for the elevator operator to sit on. Five years ago, when cutbacks were instituted at ABC, he salvaged the job of his friend Charles Glass. Glass was taken hostage by Shiite terrorists the week Jennings's third marriage seemed about to collapse. Jennings spent hours pressuring the State Department, visiting the Syrian ambassador, trying to obtain Glass's release. He spent days comforting Glass's family at a time when he needed comforting. As a rule, he aspires to be no less benevolent. It doesn't always work out that way.

At times, he'll freeze colleagues with a look that suggests they need to be bathed. Thinking he's being polite, he'll be imperious. "Dare I say," he asks a correspondent, "that that sounds like the statement of a U.S. government official?"

To junior correspondents and producers, his approval is consequential. He'll work with them for hours, encouraging and teaching them. At other times, thinking he's being helpful, he'll offer a few pointed comments that prove to be devastating. "You're not a mean man," he's told by Paul Friedman, "but sometimes you say mean things."

Recently, he critiqued the work of someone else in the office. "Do 35 you realize," Friedman asked him afterward, "what you did to that poor person?" He replied, "You're kidding."

"I'm really surprised," he says later, "when I have this impact on people." . . .

His colleagues say he's a perfectionist. He doesn't like that term. He'll concede that he has exacting standards. The difference seems semantic.

Before a show, he's often buoyant. During the broadcast, his mood changes. "I'm terrible tonight, aren't I?" he'll ask Friedman during commercial breaks. "Peter," Friedman tells him, "you're being too hard on yourself."

One night he closes the broadcast with a piece about Jesse Jackson's campaign to change the moniker "blacks" to "African-Americans." He wants to say something before he signs off, but doesn't know what to say. He doesn't want to just say "good night." He says, "It's something for us all to think about." He looks authoritative as he says it. He thinks, "What a stupid thing to say."

After a show, he'll always ask, "How did we do? Was it all right?" 40
Like anyone, he enjoys praise. But the more established he becomes, the more he's learned to distrust it. He now equates criticism with the truth. Often, he seems almost eager to be criticized. "Good show," he'll be told. "Except for yours truly," he'll answer.

Friedman's begun to tell him that this can be a little tiring. . . .

He wonders at times if he expects too much. He expects the most from those who mean the most to him. His expectation of his wife, she says, "is that I always excel and be smarter than anybody." "Is that wrong?" he asks.

Kati Marton is dark-eyed, slender, chicly dressed. Soon after they met, he bought her boots at the most expensive shoemaker in Paris. "When I met her," he'll say, "she was wearing plastic boots from Philadelphia. Look at her now."

He's attuned to the details of women's appearance. He tells a pregnant woman, "You're carrying lower this time." When his assistant gets an unfortunate haircut, he'll say, "Playing bridge this week, are we?" He doesn't want Marton to look like every other New York woman. "He wants me to be more European, elegant," she says, "but it should be seamless, effortless."

Marton is the author of three books. In public, Jennings speaks 45
proudly of her skills and knowledge. In private, if she says something he deems unworthy of her, he'll tell her, "That was banal." Recently, after she discussed foreign policy at a dinner party, he told her, "I was so proud of you. You were so clear, so measured." . . .

He was born in Canada, raised first in Toronto, later in Ottawa. His mother's family had wealth. His father had position. He had good looks, ready charm. It's a combination that can lead to a self-indulgent youth, as it did in his case. He recalls himself as "a shlump," "a bit delinquent," "bone lazy." He suspects that he's never stopped compensating for it.

Always, he worshiped his father. He always describes him in the same way: "He was the most honorable man I ever met."

Charles Jennings was the first radio news broadcaster in Canada. Later, he was the general supervisor of programming for the Canadian Broadcasting Company. He believed that broadcasting should be a public service. His relish for life leavened a genteel Scottish-Protestant household.

The Jennings house was abrim with politicians, artists, musicians. "If you do what he does," his son quickly realized, "you meet interesting people." He was still a child when his father gave him his first lesson in broadcasting. He taught him how to describe the sky.

He entered his teens unchallenged, complacent. He'd already hosted   50
a radio show, called *Peter's Program*. He read news, played musical requests, was deluged with fan mail. He was ten at the time. Since then, he'd developed abundant self-regard, fine manners, and no discipline. "I got by," he'll say now, "on a fairly natural rhythm."

He played sports, made friends, courted many young women, lavished them with gifts and flowers. He fell madly in love with each of them, one at a time. At one of Canada's best schools he acquired additional polish and failing grades. He left school for good when he was seventeen. All he wanted, he told his father, was to be a broadcaster.

By then, his father had lost his campaign to prevent CBC television from taking ads. Broadcasting, he felt, now had more to do with internal politics than craft. He told his son to work in a bank for three years, hoping he'd change his mind. Canadian banks often hired the ne'er-do-well sons of the middle class.

Jennings worked in a bank. At twenty, he auditioned for the CBC. He passed the audition. The CBC had an antinepotism rule. He couldn't be hired.

"What the hell am I going to do?" he asked his father. His father got him an announcing job in Brockville, at the smallest, weakest station in Canada. Soon after that, he and his father began what he calls "this sort of almost relationship between equals."

Now, prospering in the commercial broadcasting his father fought   55
against, he donates hours to PBS, to charity work, to drives for literacy, drug education, the homeless. In these ways, he attempts to honor his father's commitment to public service. "But I'm paid vastly too much," he allows, "to consider myself a public servant."

Charles Jennings died in 1973. "I don't mean to sound plaintive," his son says of him now, "but I never met any one person who had better values. It doesn't even matter, he could have not been successful and I don't think I'd have cared very much."

But he would always care about making up for the impression he'd made as a lazy child. And he would never stop trying to prove to his father that he himself could succeed. . . .

In late January 1989 Jennings is in his New York office. On the back of the door, his reporter's trench coat hangs beside his anchorman's pinstripe jacket. Soon ABC News will lead the ratings. For the third year in a row Jennings will be cited as the best anchor by the *Washington Journalism Review*. Votes for him will exceed the combined vote for Rather and Brokaw. News organizations want their anchor to be liked, respected, trusted. Jennings is all three. He's also the anchor preferred by viewers with university degrees.

Now Jennings is on the phone, planning his trip to Korea and Japan. He's setting up several interviews. He quickly details what they'll be about. "I'll want to talk about Korean attitudes," he's saying, "about how they see Chinese-Japanese relations, about what they think of Japan as an emerging nation, about Korean-Japanese trade, about their view of the rapprochement of China and Japan in terms of the Deng-Gorbachev meeting, so I mean, it's a real quick-and-dirty. Obviously, I'll work around the clock."

He hangs up a minute later, jots down some notes, sets aside some *60* clippings. His glance moves to the windowsill. There, among many family pictures, is a photograph of a white-haired, smiling gentleman. Jennings looks at the picture. A long moment passes before he says, "I think I still — to a very great measure — want to impress my father."

Questions for Discussion

1. What has this article revealed about Peter Jennings's childhood? How did the circumstances under which he grew up help him get started in his profession? Did his childhood leave him with any disadvantages that he subsequently needed to overcome?
2. How has Jennings changed since he first became a correspondent?
3. Would you be willing to work for Peter Jennings? What would the advantages be? What would the disadvantages be?
4. How well does Jennings treat women?
5. Kaye includes several details about the way Jennings dresses. Why is his clothing worth reporting? What do you learn about him from the clothes he wears?
6. How does Jennings see himself? Does his sense of his self differ from the way others see him?
7. Think about what you have *not* learned from the material reprinted here. Is there any other information about Jennings that you would like to know?

Suggestions for Writing

1. Write a profile of someone who seems good at her job. Investigate her background, interview her, and, if possible, observe her as she works. Ask her colleagues about her. Then write a profile that will integrate the most informative quotations within an article tied together by writing of your own. Use narration and description where appropriate.

2. Do library research on a public figure, and write a short essay about that person's childhood. Be sure to reveal your sources and to write in your own words. Avoid relying upon a single source.

THE DOBERMAN CASE

John Sedgwick

The following essay offers an inside view of one of the country's best animal hospitals. Notice how Sedgwick develops more than one topic — telling the story of Thor the Doberman, Puppy the Labrador, and an unnamed husky, while also providing abundant information on the history, operation, and mission of Angell Memorial Hospital. As you read, think about why Sedgwick chose to write at such length. Consider how the various parts of this selection relate to one another and whether the subject is interesting enough to justify such extensive reporting.

The Doberman case begins suddenly, as emergencies always do. The veterinary ambulance — a van with "ON THE MOVE FOR ANIMALS" on its side — comes racing up with its lights flashing and horn honking to Angell Memorial Hospital's main entrance. Two attendants jump out, yank open the van's rear doors, and reach inside for a coffee-colored Doberman who lies on his side in the fetal position, his tongue drooping onto a green canvas stretcher.

With their pointed ears and fearsome reputations, Dobermans can look devilish, but this one seems almost angelic — all softness and vulnerability. According to the telephone report, he has been clubbed over the head with a hockey stick. Blood oozes out of his nostrils to form a sticky pool under his muzzle, and he is shivering.

"O.K., bud," one of the attendants says gently. "O.K."

The men lift the stretcher out of the ambulance and ease it onto a stainless-steel gurney that has been positioned on the sidewalk by two white-coated nurses. Then they briskly wheel the animal up the long cement ramp and through the sliding glass door. They hurry through the packed waiting room — where both animals and humans crane their necks to see what's coming through — and down a narrow fluorescent-lit hall and into the Intensive Care Unit, a large open room ringed with sixty cages for the hospital's sickest patients.

There the acrid smell of disinfectant mingles with the animals'   5 musky scents. Most of the patients lie flat on their sides with I.V. tubes running into a shaved leg, their faces limp with the weary, put-upon expression common to the extremely ill of all species. At a veterinary hospital, noise is usually a good sign: the barking dog is the one who is ready to go home. The I.C.U. is pretty quiet, except for the steady blip of the heart monitors and an occasional piercing whine from a husky in the corner. But, with all this suffering, the quietness has a keen edge.

From the outside, the only hint that Boston's Angell Memorial Hospital might be an animal hospital at all, let alone one of the finest animal hospitals in the world, is the small statue of a rearing horse in front, a 1915 monument to Angell's original clientele. Otherwise, the building looks like the Catholic seminary it used to be before Angell and its parent organization, the Massachusetts Society for the Prevention of Cruelty to Animals (M.S.P.C.A.), moved in from their original quarters in Boston's medical district fifteen years ago. It's a giant brick warehouse of a building in a run-down section of Boston's Jamaica Plain that has largely been abandoned to charitable institutions — a former orphanage called the Home for Little Wanderers is just up the street — and the poor. A small chapel still stands by the main building. A security guard patrols the parking lot, and the brick wall that surrounds the property is topped in places by barbed wire.

Inside, Angell might be mistaken for a regular hospital, or, as they say in the veterinary world, a human hospital. But it's a hospital that obviously doesn't want to get wrecked. The furniture is heavy and indestructible; the floors are all covered with washable linoleum instead of wall-to-wall carpeting; and there's a peculiar configuration to the waiting room — high baffles rise up between the seats to keep the animals from seeing each other and having a fit. At least, that's the idea. Actually, the animals usually lie down on the floor and poke their noses around the corners to see who else is there. The owners are the ones who are cut off. They sit in parallel, avoiding eye contact.

Now that the Doberman has passed, a panting Rottweiler is being soothed by his owner, an environmental sculptor, while "As the World Turns" goes unwatched on the television set over their heads. There is a three-inch gash on the side of the dog's face. "But you should see the beagle," the sculptor explains. An elderly woman in white double-knits peers anxiously into a plastic Sky Kennel at her cat, Petey, who hasn't urinated in three days. A man in hiking shoes stands by a large wire cage containing a litter of Newfoundland puppies, who tumble about like clothes in a dryer as they await their first checkup. And a glassy-eyed cocker spaniel stares vacantly out from the plump lap of his suburbanite mistress, who is afraid that the dog has glaucoma.

Forty-three thousand cases came through Angell's waiting room last year. Except for a pregnant goat who appeared for an emergency delivery, all were "small animals," meaning household pets. Of these, sixty percent were dogs and thirty percent cats. It's a puzzling ratio, given that cats have recently come to outnumber dogs nationally fifty-six million to fifty-three million, and there is no evidence that the ranking runs any differently in Boston. Nor are cat owners known to be indifferent to their pets' welfare. At Angell, the tender devotion of cat people typically overwhelms that of dog people. "They'll bring in a pillow and crystal dish for Fluffy," says one nurse in Angell's I.C.U. "But for the dog, it's 'O.K., here's Fido.'" Cats, however, are less demonstrative and presumed to be self-reliant. Also, the decision to invest in medical care is ultimately financial — dogs you have to pay for, cats you usually get for free. Finally, dogs are generally far better liked. According to one prominent poll, dogs are America's favorite animal, followed by the horse and the swan. The cat comes in twelfth, just after the elephant, the owl, and the turtle, but ahead of the ladybug.

It can be a rough world for house pets, and it is Angell's responsibility   *10* to repair the damage. Cats and dogs are hit by cars — cats generally taking the blow head on, dogs on the flank or rear. And they fall out of high-rises. With their nearly miraculous ability to spread their paws and stabilize themselves in mid-flight, cats land lightly. The most frequent injury is a broken jaw from smacking their mouths on the pavement. Dogs aren't as likely to fall, but when they do they drop like stones. Dogs are more prone to physical abuse. One mixed breed was hurled against a wall. (After his injuries were treated at Angell, the M.S.P.C.A. persuaded the owners to give him up, and he was adopted by Angell's chief of staff.) Another mongrel was doused with lighter fluid and set on fire. One German shepherd took four bullets in the chest to protect his owner from a burglar. And, of course, both species succumb to a range of diseases that all living creatures are prey to: tumors, cancers, infections, intestinal parasites. Cats even get a version of AIDS, the recently identified feline immuno-deficiency virus, which is transmitted to other cats by bite.

And then there are the remaining ten percent of cases, the ones that are neither dogs nor cats, which are designated "exotics," Angell's term for "other." Currently, a duck with lymphoma is swimming around a plastic bathtub in the exotics ward; a rabbit is in for hair balls; a couple of cockatiels are suffering seizures; and a box turtle is having its shell reconstructed after being pounced on by the family's black Labrador. Not too long ago, a cockfighting operation was broken up, and about fifty chickens were remanded to Angell. The nurses had never heard such clucking, but they did appreciate getting eggs from the hens in the morning. A boa constrictor came in one time after its owner discovered a gouge in its side and feared the mouse it had swallowed was trying to get out. (It wasn't.) And surgeons once removed three dollars in loose change from the stomach of a New England Aquarium seal.

To treat these problems, Angell's staff performs elaborate medical procedures that make one forget that the patient on the examining table is "just a pet." Angell does chemotherapy, open-heart surgery, radiation treatment, total hip replacement for victims of dysplasia, and cataract surgery; it even implants pacemakers, some of which the hospital obtains from undertakers to keep costs down.

There are about forty vets on Angell's staff, and they are an impressive group. Only about two thousand veterinarians graduate each year from the country's twenty-seven veterinary schools. Ten years ago, ten candidates competed for every position. That ratio fell steadily through the eighties, when potential vets were lured away by the promise of far higher incomes in business and law, and by decade's end it bottomed out at three applicants for every spot. Nevertheless, the students who do enter vet school are remarkably committed. When Tufts School of Veterinary Medicine polled its applicants to find out how long they had wanted to be vets, nearly all of them checked off the box that said "For as long as I can remember." Their interest was then usually confirmed by working with animals in a research laboratory, on a farm, or at a zoo.

While veterinarians are sometimes viewed as second-class physicians, the competition for veterinary school is actually stiffer than for medical school, whose ranks of applicants also thinned in the eighties. Because veterinary students have more than a dozen different species to master, their work load is noticeably heavier than medical students'. "We don't automatically get called Doctor, either," one Angell veterinarian grumbles, displaying a rare touch of rancor. "We don't get the M.D. plates, and we don't get our Wednesday afternoons off for golf." So why do they do it? "We're nuts," says another vet.

Actually, the individuals most likely to place vets in a separate medical category are "real" doctors, but even they come away from Angell questioning their assumptions. "It's not snobbery," says Dr. Gus Thornton, Angell's former chief of staff, who is now president of the M.S.P.C.A. "It's more like amazement. I remember a physician brought his dog in and I diagnosed the animal as having diabetes. The man was *aghast.* 'That's exactly the symptoms *my* patients have!' he told me. Physicians don't seem to understand that cancer is cancer, heart disease is heart disease, and diabetes is diabetes. The only difference is the package it comes in." 15

The current chief of staff, Dr. Paul Gambardella, describes Angell Memorial as both the Boston City and the Massachusetts General of the veterinary world. That is, it handles the blood-soaked emergency cases, like the Doberman, that come in at all hours from the surrounding neighborhood, and the more exotic referral cases from a wider geographical range. One couple flew their dog over from Paris on the Concorde after he had gotten into some rat poison. Other pets have come from Switzerland, the Virgin Islands, and New Brunswick, Canada. General Alfred Gray, Commandant of the Marine Corps, personally escorted his teacup poodle, Cozette, from Maryland to Angell by military plane for orthopedic work. Elvis Presley flew his Chow in from Graceland for treatment of kidney failure. And the late Josephine Lilly, a daughter-in-law of the pharmaceutical magnate Eli Lilly, used to deliver her pugs, Trig and Sootchi, here from Cape Cod in the backseat of the family Rolls-Royce Silver Cloud. The dogs were accompanied only by the chauffeur, who invariably amused the vets with his report on the animals' condition. "Well, the *cook* noticed . . ." he would begin, or "The *gardener* observed . . ." Mrs. Lilly was so impressed with the hospital's care that she helped Angell raise a million dollars to modernize its I.C.U. In return, the hospital allows her pugs to use a corner of the ward as their presidential suite whenever they come to visit.

Despite all this history, it still comes as a shock to push open the heavy door of the I.C.U. and find these shaggy four-legged creatures inside, where one expects humans to be: their little bodies lying on stainless steel, their legs swathed in white bandages, their chests wired to heart monitors. And the peculiarity is only reinforced by the matter-of-fact way the staff treats the animals, as if their presence were the most natural thing in the world.

And nowadays perhaps it is. Now that darkest Africa has become a kind of theme park and every trapped whale makes the evening news, the hospital is just another meeting point in the increasingly merged worlds of humans and animals. There are now 109 million cats and dogs in American homes, one for every citizen under thirty. (Yet Americans rank second to the French in terms of pet ownership per capita, and are trailed closely by the English and the Australians.) Americans spend $7 billion a year on pet food (twice the sum spent on baby food), and another $7 billion on veterinary care of the sort provided by Angell. Apparently, the money lavished on pets is a function of affluence. The poorest countries, like China and certain African nations, rank lowest in pet ownership; they are more likely to see cats and dogs as competitors for food (if not as food itself) than as companions.

Although pets have been a feature of elite society at least since the Egyptians (whose pharaohs showed a great fondness for cats) and the Romans (whose emperors preferred caged monkeys), pet ownership didn't infiltrate the middle classes until industrialism spread and agricultural predominance receded. In that transition, animals became bound to humans more by emotion than by function. Indeed, as a recent article on the American Kennel Club (AKC) in *The Atlantic* suggested, many breeds of dogs have now lost their functional capabilities entirely after years of being bred purely for appearance. Most sheepherding dogs, like Border collies and kelpies, can no longer keep track of sheep, and once useful breeds, like Irish setters, "are now so dumb," in the words of AKC critic Michael W. Fox, "they get lost on the end of their leash."

The emotional bond may have been man's essential connection with animals all along, a connection that was obscured by the exigencies of life on the farm. One gets a different feeling about animals if one has to milk them, brand them, feed them, and ultimately slaughter them — all for one's livelihood. The ethnologist Konrad Lorenz described humans' love for animals as a spillover of our instinctual love for babies. As a result, we generally prefer those animals that look most like babies. Specifically, according to Lorenz, we like a creature with "a relatively large head, predominance of the brain capsule, large and low-lying eyes, bulging cheek region, short and thick extremities, a springy, elastic consistency, and clumsy movement." This explains why we are more drawn to puppies and kittens than to full-grown dogs and cats, but it gives a pretty good account of why we like dogs and cats, too.

It also helps explain why pet owners lavish such expensive and high-technology care on their pets when they are sick. They see their pets as members of the family. At Angell, the staff shares this view. They routinely speak of ailing pets with words usually reserved for family. They call the animals "honey" or "sweetheart," and they refer to the owner as the pet's "mom" or "dad." They discuss their own pets' behavioral problems as though they were talking about Junior's troubles in kindergarten, and they put framed photographs of their animals on their desks where pictures of their children would normally go. They do this in a jokey, offhand manner, but they mean a lot by it.

Right now in the I.C.U., Dr. Deborah Cogan, a thirty-four-year-old internist on emergency duty, gives the stricken Doberman a tired, sorrowful look. It's 4:30 P.M. She has been at work since seven this morning, attending to so many sick and injured dogs and cats that she relies on a thick pack of index cards to keep them all straight. And she will be here until nine tonight, before the hour's drive to Salem, where she lives with her two cats, her shepherd-husky crossbreed, and her boyfriend, an aircraft engineer. When she arrives home, he'll probably tell her she's burning out, and she will numbly agree. But what can she do? "We're talking major love here," she says. When she was two years old, she refused to kiss a friend of the family, preferring to kiss the friend's dachshund instead. At six, she was already being asked by neighbors for veterinary advice. She started assembling a library of veterinary texts at seven, and at eleven she was subscribing to Cornell's catalog, because she knew she wanted to go to its veterinary school. Her course was set.

The Doberman's head is drooping over the edge of the stretcher, and blood from his nose is dribbling onto the floor. Cogan presses her stethoscope lightly against the dog's chest, then feels inside his rear thigh for a pulse. A Dalmation on an I.V. comes over to sniff the new patient, until he's escorted into his cage by a technician. Nearby, a blind spaniel whimpers quietly.

It is never easy to determine what is wrong with an animal who can't say where he hurts, but it is even harder when the animal is barely conscious. Lying in front of Cogan, the Doberman is darkness itself. She shines a penlight into the dog's eyes, as if to illuminate his mind. She is checking for brain damage: pupils that are jammed wide open or shut down to pinpoints are not encouraging sights. The penlight is weak and the room is bright, but Cogan is pleased to detect a flickering response to the light. Then she pries open the animal's jaws with a tongue depressor, wipes away the bloody slobber with a paper towel, and considers the dog's gums, which act as litmus paper for an animal's general condition. A rich pink is best, dull blue the worst. The dog's gums are pale pink. O.K. She can live with that. Dr. Cogan feels the animal's skull with her fingertips, trying to detect the extent of the damage. "He feels mushed over here," she tells the nurses. Under the skin, the dog's forehead is spongy with blood. "He's got some bleeding under his skull." She can feel the break with her fingertips, but the displacement — the gap between the broken bones — doesn't seem too severe. Surgical wiring probably won't be necessary. She'll need X-rays to decide the issue, however. "He's so out of it, we probably could do it without anesthesia," she says. Then she tells the nurses to put in an I.V. catheter.

"He's an attack dog, you know," Dr. Cogan reminds the nurses. "So watch your faces." At a veterinary hospital, one cannot be too careful, and nearly everyone at Angell has a scar to mark an occasion of misplaced trust. One vet has a scar between her eyes where she was greeted by a pit bull. "I thought he just banged my head," she says. "Then I reached up and felt the blood."

The nurses shave one of the Doberman's forelegs and scrub it down with an antiseptic solution, then warily insert the I.V. But the dog doesn't flinch. When a nurse draws back her hand, it is dark with blood and hair. "Oh, yum," she says, reaching for a towel.

The I.V. should help the blood circulation and limit the brain damage. Now Dr. Cogan is worried about something else. The dog's pulse hasn't matched up with his heartbeat, and through her stethoscope the beat itself sounds feeble and irregular. She hooks him up to a heart monitor, and the video screen confirms her anxieties. The graph should be as regular as the teeth on a handsaw, but these waves are spaced unevenly, and the curve of one beat doesn't always duplicate that of the next. Definite arrhythmia. Dobermans, like many large dogs, are prone to cardiomyopathy, or heart disease. Does this dog have heart disease on top of all his other problems? Or could the blow to the head have damaged the dog's heart, too?

Angell came into being in large part to protect victimized animals like the Doberman. It is run by the M.S.P.C.A. as part of the society's mission to ease the suffering of animals, but its work has recently been overshadowed by the astonishing surge of the animal rights movement. Once boldly modern, the M.S.P.C.A. has started to appear rather old-fashioned in these days when animal rights activists are raiding laboratories to release captive research animals, splattering paint on those who wear furs, demanding an end to meat eating (and even an end to pet owning), and crusading so broadly — and so effectively — that Congress now receives more mail on animal rights than on any other subject. Where once the M.S.P.C.A. had the animal welfare cause virtually to itself, a hundred advocacy groups have now taken it up — most prominently the Animal Liberation Front and People for the Ethical Treatment of

Animals (PETA) — with a combined membership estimated at ten million (although the hard-core activists probably number two million at most). The M.S.P.C.A. is grateful for the publicity that the movement has brought the cause, but it is careful to distance itself from the urban-guerrilla-style violence that has drawn much of that publicity. "We absolutely do not believe in any way in violent acts — the breaking and entering, the splattering of paint, the threat, all done in the name of animals," says Dr. Thornton, the M.S.P.C.A. president. "One of the biggest parts of my job is to keep telling people we don't rob and steal. We're here to protect animals." The society, he explains categorically, is "neither anti-vivisectionist nor vegetarian."

Angell pointedly conducts none of the animal-based research done by most teaching hospitals. While veterinarians as a group are rarely staunch animal rights advocates, since so many of them make their living performing the research the activists seek to ban, Angell veterinarians, working outside the lab, tend to be more liberal on the topic than most. Deborah Cogan is one of the few true radicals on the topic at Angell. She gave up eating meat ten years ago, eliminated fish a few months back, and is now considering an end to eggs and dairy products as well. "I just don't want that on my conscience," she says. She obtains her few makeup items from a special catalog that provides products that have not been tested on animals. She contributes to PETA, among several other like-minded organizations, and would like to see animal-based research drastically reduced if not done away with entirely. "Most research involves some really horrible experiments," she says. She cites one ballistics experiment that involved shooting cats in the head to determine the utility of giving different types of treatment after head injuries, and a sleep-deprivation test in which cats were forced to balance for hours on a tiny perch over a pool of water. "There are a million ridiculous experiments," she says. "I'd have to take each one on a case-by-case basis." She rarely proselytizes among her peers, however. "There are too many other things to do."

As part of its mission to provide care for animals, the M.S.P.C.A.   30 maintains three hospitals in the state, of which Angell is by far the largest. The society also runs eight animal shelters, publishes a bimonthly magazine called *Animals,* operates a pet cemetery, runs a law-enforcement division, and lobbies the government for the animal protection cause. Even though Angell's interests run counter in some ways to the society's formal goal of *prevention* of cruelty (since the animals are treated after the injury or illness has occurred), the hospital is by far the most illustrious of the M.S.P.C.A.'s operations, and the most expensive.

Although Angell charges market rates for its services, it runs a significant annual deficit that in 1988 came to $2 million out of a $15 million operating budget. The M.S.P.C.A. contributed a million from its $40 million endowment; the hospital made up the rest with its own fundraising.

Angell Memorial is named for George Thorndike Angell, the founder of the M.S.P.C.A., and although he never lived to see it, the hospital is an embodiment of his vision. A prominent Boston lawyer with a stern Yankee countenance, Angell was a legal partner of the noted abolitionist and Massachusetts politician Samuel Sewall. Born in 1823, Angell had a strong, if somewhat peculiar, sense of Victorian obligation to society. He warned people about the dangers of poisonous wallpaper, leaded pottery, and adulterated food. He was so concerned about premature burial that he campaigned vigorously for what might be called death insurance, to make sure that interment did not occur until decay had actually set in. He ventured into the field of animal welfare rather impetuously in the winter of 1868, when he read a report of a race between two horses from Boston to Worcester, a distance of some forty miles, after which both horses collapsed and died of exhaustion. He fired off an indignant letter to the Boston *Daily Advertiser* calling for fellow citizens to band together to prevent the repetition of this sort of outrage. Within hours of its publication he was the head of a new organization called the Massachusetts Society for the Prevention of Cruelty to Animals.

While drawing on the distinctively Boston style of philanthropy, the organization followed an international movement that had been started in 1824 by the Royal Society for the Prevention of Cruelty to Animals, and brought to the United States when Henry Bergh founded the American Society for the Prevention of Cruelty to Animals in New York in 1866. (All these groups predated any organizations concerned with the welfare of *children*. In fact, it was Bergh's A.S.P.C.A. that went on to found the first child advocacy group, the New York Society for the Prevention of Cruelty to Children, as an adjunct to its animal work. That occurred in 1874, when an A.S.P.C.A. agent discovered there were no laws to prevent the appalling abuse of a child known as Little Mary Ellen and argued before the court that children should at least be entitled to the same rights as animals. A Massachusetts society followed a year later.)

George Angell began by installing public drinking fountains for horses, then called for laws against blood sports — particularly dogfighting and cockfighting. But he soon realized that simple ignorance underlay most of the cruelty, and he designed an educational campaign to deepen the public's appreciation of animals. He took it upon himself to speak for the animals, largely because they couldn't speak for themselves. For this reason, he named the society's magazine *Our Dumb Animals,* and he filled it with inspiring animal stories. He got the Boston police to distribute the magazine throughout the city. Angell also brought out the first American edition of *Black Beauty,* which he termed "the *Uncle Tom's Cabin* of the horse," and, selling it at a steep discount, he made it a national best-seller. He also formed a children's humane association, something on the order of today's Cub Scouts and Brownies, called the Bands of Mercy, in which children gathered to sing the Band of Mercy hymn, recite the Band of

Mercy pledge ("I will try to be kind to all living creatures and try to protect them from cruel usage"), and dedicate themselves to the animal welfare cause.

Through these acts, Angell hoped to reap a double harvest, not only improving the lot of animals but also increasing mankind's sensitivity to its own species. He once noted that none of the inmates of a Boston prison had ever owned a dog or a cat as a child.

Quaint as his attitudes seem today, he left his mark on the animal world. When he died in 1909, thirty-eight cart horses, their bridles adorned with black rosettes, followed his casket to Mount Auburn Cemetery in Cambridge.

Angell Memorial Hospital was founded by George Angell's successor, Dr. Francis H. Rowley. It originally occupied a handsome brick building on Longwood Avenue, in the heart of Boston's medical district. The structure had majestic granite pillars that attested to the inherent high-mindedness of the veterinary enterprise. "The degree of civilization can be measured by the width of human sympathy," Harvard's president A. Lawrence Lowell declared at the dedication, using terms that foreshadow the animal rights movement. "In the primitive stages of civilization, as we know them, human sympathy does not extend beyond the tribe or little family. . . . Gradually, sympathy was enlarged from the tribe to the nation, from the nation to other nations, from other nations to all mankind, and from all mankind to animals. . . . This hospital is built to commemorate [the principle] that every creature capable of suffering is entitled to the sympathy of man."

Since this was still the horse-and-buggy age, the interior was designed with the needs of the city's workhorses in mind. It featured a "horse operating room," which contained a gigantic operating table, a recovery ward for horses, two stables, a covered courtyard for tying up horses outdoors, and a drinking trough out front. Some staff members feared that the popularity of the automobile in those early years might put Angell out of business. Indeed, Harvard University's School of Veterinary Medicine had closed in 1902 for precisely this reason. But the hospital was equipped with facilities for small animals as well, including a charming cat ward with wicker baskets atop each cage for the easy transportation of feline patients. And, as industrialism proceeded, companion animals replaced horses as Angell's main line of business.

In those early days, veterinary procedures had an improvised quality that seems unimaginable by the high-tech standards of today. Surgical dressings were sterilized in the oven of the gas stove in the upstairs kitchen. And the surgeons' clothes were so fragrant with ether and Lysol fumes that they sometimes caused pet owners to fall into a dead faint while their animals were being examined.

Still, Angell was quick to make use of the advances in human medicine developed at the hospitals around it, establishing its own firsts as well.

In 1935, Angell's Dr. C. Lawrence Blakely pioneered open-chest surgery for diaphragmatic hernia in dogs by using a bicycle pump to keep their injured lungs expanded during operations. In 1943 came the first use of aseptic surgery on small animals. In 1958, Angell researchers were the first to trace the spread of pansteatitis in cats to red-meat tuna. In 1965, they identified dangerous side effects of using medroxyprogesterone, a drug hormone, in canine birth control. And so on through 1975, when Dr. Susan Cotter, drawing on Angell's extensive pathology records, became the first person to identify the ways in which feline leukemia is transmitted.

In that year, Angell's work load had increased to the point where larger quarters were required, and the hospital moved out of its princely quarters and across the tracks, to the more forbidding part of town that one nurse calls Gotham City.

In mysteries like the Doberman case, the veterinarian often takes on the role of the detective, eagerly interviewing witnesses who might shed some light on the case. When Dr. Cogan hears that a couple of men are waiting to see her patient, she makes a point of seeing them. "I want to get everything I can," she says.

She meets them in a spare examination room painted a pleasant rose color. Standing by the stainless-steel examining table, the two men seem like rough characters. One is white and unshaven; he has on jeans with a belt buckle in the shape of a fire truck. The other is black and athletic-looking, and wears a Mets T-shirt. They work at the Always Open towing company in Dorchester, they tell her, and hand her a business card. "Wheel lift your troubles away," it says.

The Mets fan does most of the talking. He says the dog's name is Thor, he is about four years old, and he has been a guard dog at the towing company for the last few months. The dog belongs to the company's owner, Bobby Scandone. "You should see him," the Mets fan says with a laugh. "He's as big as four of us." Cogan makes a note on her clipboard. She would like to see him very much; there is a limit to how far she can go in treatment without a deposit from the owner. But she doesn't dwell on the financial considerations now.

"The dog's been in good health?" she asks, looking up. She doesn't 45 want to lead the men, but she needs to find out if there's any evidence of long-standing heart disease.

"Oh *yeah*," says the Mets fan, plainly amazed that anyone should even wonder.

Cogan asks how Thor got hurt, and they tell her that he had been tied up by the fence and "some guy" started pestering him. They warned him to leave the dog alone for his own good. "If you mess with Thor," the Mets fan told him, "you're history." They didn't know the man had a hockey stick. The dog started to growl, and the man hit him. "He gave

Thor one real good whack," the Mets fan says, "and Thor went down and that was it." The company secretary then called Angell.

The two men want to see Thor, but Dr. Cogan says it isn't possible right now. "Will he be in overnight?" the Mets fan asks.

"Definitely overnight," Dr. Cogan replies. Right now, she's figuring that he'll be lucky to be out in two weeks — if he ever recovers at all.

"You watch yourself around Thor, Doctor," says the Mets fan. "Don't put your face too close." Dr. Cogan smiles weakly and says goodbye. 50

Back in the I.C.U., Thor has returned from radiology and is lying down in one of the five larger cages, or "runs," along the far wall. Once again, he is curled up in the fetal position, trembling. The X-rays confirm what Cogan had thought: the skull fracture isn't too bad. They place the break over the dog's left sinus, which explains the blood running out his snout.

Out of hope as much as anything, Dr. Cogan tells a nurse to add a label to his cage: "Caution — Attack Dog, Will Bite."

Thor is only one of about forty animals in peril this afternoon in Angell's I.C.U.

Down that row of runs, the husky has started to croon again. A handsome, bushy-coated dog with the mismatched irises — one brown, one pale blue — that are characteristic of his breed, he lies unhappily on the floor, his head sheathed in an Elizabethan collar, a plastic cone that keeps him from gnawing at the bandages swathed tightly around his middle. Three nights back he came in barely able to breathe.

Dr. Virginia Rentko, a cheerful second-year resident with a thick mane of dark hair, was on duty when the husky arrived. She couldn't get a stethoscope on him, the dog was in such a state of anxiety. (His coat was so thick that it would have been difficult to hear anything anyway.) X-rays, however, showed a clear case of pneumothorax: air was leaking out of his lungs, through balloonlike pockets called blebs and bullae, and getting trapped inside his chest cavity, keeping his lungs from fully expanding. 55

Dr. Rentko plunged a syringe into the husky's chest to drain off the trapped air. But she filled up one syringe, then another and another; air was seeping into the animal's chest faster than the syringes could tap it off.

The next step was second only to yanking molars as Dr. Rentko's least favorite veterinary activity: she drove a sharp spike between the dog's ribs to implant a valve that would release all the trapped air. The dog was now so exhausted that Dr. Rentko needed to give him only a local anesthetic. While nurses held the husky down, she thrust the spike in through his leathery skin in what she terms a "controlled push" — careful not to push too hard and puncture the dog's lungs or, more disastrously, his heart. The spike went in like a knife. ("It's a weird sensation," she says.) She wrapped a bandage around the dog's chest to hold the valve in place, and attached the Elizabethan collar so he'd leave the bandage alone.

Dr. Rentko labeled the ailment "spontaneous pneumothorax," which is a way of saying she didn't have a clue how it came about. Generally, pneumothorax is due to long-term lung disease, such as bronchitis or asthma, but the husky showed no evidence of that. It can also result from being hit by a car, but that didn't seem likely either, because the husky's toenails were all intact. In a car accident, they usually get scraped up or ripped off in the dog's sudden skid across the pavement. Abuse couldn't be ruled out, but that usually shows up as extreme skinniness. A dog who cowers in fear when a human reaches out a hand might also have been abused.

Just the opposite with this husky. Far from retreating before Dr. Rentko, the dog was coming on too strong with her. He would try to bite her every time she came in. "He was trying to dominate me," she says. So she had to bully him right back. She put him on a short leash, took him outside the hospital, and told him to sit. To her surprise, he sat. And he heeled on the way back. There have been no further problems. Now she is concerned that perhaps she went a little far. "I think I'll go in there and love him up a little bit," Dr. Rentko says. The husky perks up — his mismatched eyes brighten — as the doctor comes near. She drives her hands into his thick fur. The husky croons.

The cage diagonally across from the husky is empty. It was occupied 60 just yesterday by a black Labrador named Puppy, something of a misnomer since the dog was actually eight years old. The owner, James Yuille, is a real estate developer from the fishing town of Gloucester, about an hour north of Boston. He and his wife, Nohora, had found the dog in Puerto Rico when he was eight months old. He had been about the only constant in their lives. "Of course," Yuille adds, "we have no children." Yuille had been sitting in the living room on Sunday night when Puppy suddenly yelped. Yuille looked up and saw that the dog's front leg had buckled under him as he ran across the floor. Yuille figured that Puppy had sprained a paw. He rushed to the dog and was reaching down to examine him when Puppy's other front leg buckled. Yuille grabbed the dog's chest to hold him up, and then his back legs gave way, too. "I thought, Jesus Christ," Yuille says, "the dog is having a heart attack." He rushed Puppy to his local veterinarian, who, completely mystified, referred him to Angell. Yuille sped to Boston with Puppy in his wife's lap. Ten minutes from the hospital, the dog started having seizures. Then he lost control of his muscles altogether and lay paralyzed in Nohora Yuille's lap. By the time they reached the hospital, Puppy was no longer breathing and his heart had stopped. "For all intents and purposes, the dog was dead," Yuille said. "There was no heartbeat, nothing."

Dr. Sheri Siegel, a quiet-spoken young intern with a Southern accent, was on emergency duty that time. She slapped a defibrillator paddle on the dog's chest to administer a mild electric shock and get his heart going again. Then she put him on a respirator to restore his breathing. She ran a myelogram to see if there were any lesions on his spine that would account for the paralysis. There was one lesion, but not the kind that would explain anything. Tick paralysis was another possibility, but there were no signs of tick infestation in Puppy's blood. "Basically," Dr. Siegel said, "what we've got is this huge mystery."

Yuille returned the next morning. Puppy was flat on his side in his cage, the respirator in his mouth, nearly motionless. The dog tried to perk up for his owner, though. He flapped his tail feebly, and strained to lift his head. Yuille opened the cage, ran a hand down Puppy's neck, and looked quizzically at the dog. "What? What?" he asked. "Speak to me, Puppy. Speak." Puppy opened his mouth, as if trying to answer, but no sounds came out. "That's a good dog," Yuille said sadly, and patted him some more.

When visiting hours in the I.C.U. were over, Yuille sat by himself in the waiting room, his head cradled in his hands.

That afternoon, Dr. Siegel saw that the dog was doing no better and brought the owner in to see Puppy one last time. The case was hopeless, she told him. Together, they decided to put the dog to sleep.

Into Puppy's I.V. catheter Dr. Siegel injected Fatal Plus, a lethal dose   65
of the anesthetic sodium pentobarbital, which works by anesthetizing the brain, then stopping the heart. In seconds, Puppy went limp. Neither Yuille nor the doctor said anything.

Since Yuille wanted to take the body with him back to Gloucester for burial, Dr. Siegel wrapped it up in brown plastic and wheeled it out on a gurney to the sidewalk. There Yuille took Puppy in his arms and placed him carefully in the back of his pickup truck. "Thanks," he said to Dr. Siegel as he turned back to her.

"Sorry," she replied. Then he drove off.

Humans haven't *always* provided care for the animals around them, but they have tried to do so for a surprisingly long time. More than 20,000 years ago, stone-age man appreciated the rudiments of animal physiognomy, even if it was only to know where to insert a spear into a tiger for the best effect. While the ancient Greeks are usually credited with the first significant advances in the treatment of animals, the Hindus of India, in keeping with their veneration of animals, were actually the first to describe the basic principles of veterinary medicine. They did so in their earliest scriptures, the Vedas of 1800 to 1200 B.C. In 250 B.C., the Indian king Asoka established hospitals for treating horses, elephants, cattle, game birds, and fish. The wardens there maintained basic hygiene and practiced fairly sophisticated surgical techniques, including the cauterization of wounds and the use of long tubes to direct medicines through the nose directly into the animal's stomach. Veterinary practice did not advance much further until the fourth century A.D., when the Byzantines described specific veterinary ailments, including fever, digestive disorders, and tetanus. Another millennium passed before the first true veterinary school was established. That occurred in Lyons, France, in 1762, after a plague wiped out half the country's cattle population. The veterinary movement swept across Europe, and in 1793 led to the foundation in London of the first modern veterinary hospital, or, as it was called, "hippiatric infirmary," after its primary patient, the horse. A decade later, a prominent London veterinarian named Delabere Blaine opened the first of Angell's historical antecedents, an Infirmary for Dogs, which offered, as he put it in an advertisement, "the most active and judicious treatment with every attention toward [the dogs'] health and comfort, on terms always moderate, but proportionate to the expense and trouble they occasion."

The Animal Medical Center in New York City was the first veterinary hospital in the United States. It was opened as the New York Women's League for Animals in 1914, a year ahead of Angell. Today it is the only other hospital in the United States that handles anything like the range of Angell's cases. The two institutions are holdovers from a time when animal hospitals provided every service necessary to healing the sick. Since then, veterinary medicine has followed the path of human medicine and split into two separate levels of care: local clinics for regular checkups and routine treatments, and teaching hospitals for major surgery. The result is that in most cities outside of Boston and New York, animals need to be driven a considerable distance — in Chicago, it's two hours — to the nearest teaching hospital for emergency care. Some animals, presumably, don't make it.

Why aren't there more Angells? One reason is cost. Paul Gambardella, Angell's chief of staff, says, "It would take one helluva pile of dough to do what we are doing." Estimates hover around the $40 million mark to found an animal hospital today. Angell is crammed with much of the same expensive equipment as human hospitals: defibrillators ($10,000 apiece), heart monitors ($4,000), oxygen chambers ($98,000). Indeed, the equipment may have come secondhand from those human hospitals, trickling down from human medicine the way much of the new clinical information does. About the only important piece of current technology that Angell does not yet possess is the CAT scan, and it has access to one at a local hospital on Saturday mornings. Angell also has to attract the personnel to cover all the major specialties: cardiology, ophthalmology, neurology, gastroenterology, anesthesiology, oncology, radiology, surgery, pathology, even psychology, in the form of a pet psychoanalyst who comes to the hospital once a week to deal with destructive behaviors. Though veterinarians routinely work for a fraction of a physician's salary, the personnel costs for so many people are substantial. Finally, any Angell must have a sufficient endowment to cover inevitable shortfalls.

But a darker factor is also at work in limiting the number of general hospitals for animals, namely the economic rivalry between the basic providers of veterinary care. Local veterinarians are understandably anxious about passing their clients along to a large hospital that can provide all the local veterinarians' services. To avoid potential conflicts, teaching hospitals have deliberately steered clear of the routine work — spayings, immunizations — that is any vet's bread and butter. How, then, is it possible for a general hospital like Angell to do everything and still get referrals? In large part because Angell has always been careful never to keep a referral case once the initial course of treatment is complete. History has its benefits.

While Angell's expenses are certainly high, they are nothing like those of human hospitals. By the standards of human medicine, its prices read like misprints: a day in its I.C.U., $150; a total hip replacement, $1,200; heart surgery, $800. Human hospitals run on the assumption that human life is of infinite value, and charge accordingly. Veterinary hospitals are forced to make a more conservative appraisal. Unlike human hospitals, animal hospitals rarely receive what are termed "third-party payments," the whatever-it-costs insurance-company payouts that have contributed to the wild escalation in the price of human medical care. (Currently, only one national insurance company, the Animal Health Insurance Agency, offers any sort of pet medical insurance. A catastrophic coverage plan costs $40 a year, has a $250 deductible, and pays up to $2,500 an incident. A comprehensive plan, for $97.50 a year, has a $50 deductible and pays a maximum of $1,000 per injury or illness. Among Angell's clients, there are few takers; pet owners would rather take their chances.) At Angell, nearly all payments are made directly out of the owner's pocket, by cash, check, MasterCard, Visa, or American Express. So the owner actually puts a price on his pet, and it's usually not that high. Paul Gambardella explains the situation this way: "As soon as John Q. Public says, 'The price is too much, I can't pay it,' that's when we go out of business." Additionally, euthanasia for animals is a legal and morally respectable option, so owners have a recourse when the costs of vital treatment start to soar, disturbing as it can be to a vet to see how quickly some owners choose to put their pets to sleep. And finally, Angell bills have not been inflated by malpractice insurance, for the simple reason that pets are legally considered personal property and therefore valued only at their cost — virtually eradicating any incentive for owners to sue.

To keep care affordable, Angell goes much shorter on staff than a human hospital. White-coated doctors do not clog its halls. During a routine operation, the surgeon will often go about his work alone, without so much as a single nurse to attend him. The vets also work cheap. Even though all Angell's veterinarians have completed college, four years of veterinary school, a year's internship, and two or three years of residency, they receive an annual salary of $50,000 tops, even while working between twelve and fourteen hours a day, six days a week. The secondhand equipment offers some savings, too. And, time being money, the course of veterinary treatment runs remarkably fast. The pets get better or they don't, but either way, they do it quickly. It is rare for a patient to remain at Angell for more than a week, and almost unheard of for one to stay a month. At Angell the current titleholder is believed to be Blanca, a spaniel hit by a bus; she resided at Angell for thirty-five days. She became so well known to the entire hospital staff that whenever she returns for treatment she makes a "grand tour" of the hospital to say hello to everyone.

But another thing speeds up the action at Angell: the hardy nature of the animals themselves. Many house pets might have been bred for the purpose of undergoing major surgery, and Angell's veterinarians continue to be impressed by the speed of their convalescence. Humans who have abdominal surgery are usually bedridden for a week or more. Pets who get spayed are typically up and about the next morning, and so frisky the chief danger is they'll pop their stitches. Animals simply don't dwell on their condition the way humans do, and, at least according to Gambardella, thinking about it appears only to prolong the ordeal.

Certainly Thor is responding promptly to treatment. He came in on a Wednesday afternoon. On Thursday morning, he was still pretty much dead out in an oxygen chamber, where he had been placed to make sure his brain received sufficient oxygen and because he had been suffering from seizures. That first night, Dr. Cogan had put him on a heart-stabilizing drug called digoxin for the heart arrhythmia, and by the next morning the monitor showed that his heartbeat had returned to normal. By the end of the day, he started to lift up his head and take notice of his surroundings. By Friday morning he began to lap a bit of water out of his water bowl. Dr. Cogan was ecstatic. "He's started to drink!" she exclaimed. That afternoon he was standing, although somewhat unsteadily. And when another dog sauntered by, he brought his nose close to give him a sniff. Dr. Cogan saw that, and the sight filled her with hope.

On Saturday night, Thor took a nip out of the night nurse. Dr. Cogan offered her condolences, but it cheered her, too. The Doberman was becoming himself again. By Monday, he was stalking about his cage, although he leaned noticeably to the left. Apparently, the vestibular region of his brain, which controls balance, had been hurt by the blow. The heartbeat remained normal, which Dr. Cogan couldn't begin to explain without running a lot more tests for which there was no money. On Tuesday, Dr. Cogan pronounced herself "really happy." Thor was eating, drinking, defecating, and urinating. There might be diminished brain function, but who knew? "It's not like he has to memorize the multiplication tables," she said. Thor was ready to go home.

Thor's "parents" came in to get him that night. Both are extremely large. Bobby Scandone has a scraggly beard and dark, curly hair, and his shoes lack shoelaces. Bobby's mother, Lucille Scandone, is nearly as large, but neater. The Scandones live together in blue-collar Winthrop, just north of Boston. Cogan had been apprehensive about them: "I wasn't sure they really cared about Thor. He was a biter, you know. I figured they thought he was just a junkyard dog." Now they sit together on a heavy wooden bench outside the waiting room. They have brought in yet another Dober-man, named Venus, who is slumped on the floor beside Lucille. Venus is here to see the neurologist for a few medical problems of her own. All her hair has fallen out, giving her skin an oddly porcine appearance, and she has lost control of her back legs.

Venus suddenly lets loose a flood of urine on the floor. "Now, *why* is she wetting like this?" Lucille asks.

"She's nervous, Ma," the son says. He seems nervous, too. He says it's the coffee he drank on the way over. More likely it's Thor. He hasn't seen the dog since Friday night, and he's worried about him.

"Oh, it's been awful the last few months with her," the mother goes on, referring to Venus. "God, I hope they don't put her to sleep," she says. "I'm not ready for that." She wrings her hands. "I'm very, very upset."

"It'll be all right, Ma," the son says, his eyes downcast.

The neurologist, Gillian Irving, wears lipstick and speaks with an English accent. She comes up, introduces herself, and leads Venus into the examining room. After a few minutes' examination, she diagnoses the dog as having a classic case of wobbler's disease, a degenerative disease of the spinal column. Cortisone should help, plus a harness to help lift her up onto her feet. "Oh, thank God," Lucille Scandone tells her son as they retreat to the waiting room. "I was sure she was going to make me put her to sleep." She smiles for the first time.

And then Dr. Cogan appears with Thor, who is straining powerfully on his leash. His toenails clack on the linoleum, and he draws strong huffing breaths. His ears are up, and his eyes are keen. He looks sleek and athletic, ready once again to terrorize all of Dorchester. "Hey, he looks good!" Bobby shouts. He takes the dog's leash, feels the dog pulling on it. In seconds, Thor is galloping for the door, hauling his three-hundred-pound master behind him. Bouncing lightly along behind him, Bobby might be filled with helium. "My *God!*" Bobby says. "He's got his strength back. I can't hold him!" Thor drags Bobby outside, down the ramp, and past the sculpture of the rearing horse out front. "Thaw! Thaw!" Bobby yells delightedly in his Boston accent. His mother and Venus follow. Dr. Cogan trails after all of them, worried as ever, yelling after Lucille to go easy on Venus's leash, not to put more pressure on the dog's spinal cord.

Bobby bends down to Thor and rubs him all over. "That's my boy," he says. "That's my boy." Then he looks up at Dr. Cogan, who is watching

80

proudly from the ramp, her hands stuffed in her coat pockets against the cool evening breeze. "Thanks, Doctor," he says.

"Sure thing," she says, smiling.   *85*

It is eight-fifteen. Another long day at Angell. Dr. Cogan thinks for a moment that maybe it *is* worth it after all. Then she heads back in to check on her other cases.

Questions for Discussion

1. Although this article is about Angell Memorial Hospital and the nature of veterinary medicine, the author chose to structure it around the story of a badly injured Doberman. What does the information about Thor contribute to the article as a whole?

2. Given the length of this article, the editors considered cutting the story of Puppy (paragraphs 60–67). Do you think that story could have been deleted? Or do you think eliminating Puppy's story could leave readers with a false impression?

3. What are the similarities between veterinary medicine and human medicine? What are the differences? How is a veterinary hospital like Angell different from a hospital for humans?

4. Although there are more cats than dogs in the United States, dogs receive veterinary care much more frequently. How does Sedgwick explain this?

5. According to this article, "surgeons once removed three dollars in loose change from the stomach of a New England Aquarium seal." How do you think it got there? What are the implications of this information?

6. Why do people have pets? Why would someone set a dog on fire?

7. Are there any conflicts between veterinarians and physicians? What does this article reveal about vets? Why would someone work more than twelve hours a day, six days a week, for a salary that is much less than most doctors earn?

8. Why are there relatively few hospitals like Angell in the United States? What kind of veterinary care would you be able to get for a seriously injured pet in your community?

Suggestions for Writing

1. Write an essay providing instructions for the care or training of an animal with which you have personal experience.

2. Visit your local humane society and report upon neglected or mistreated animals that have been brought there.

INSIDE HALLMARK'S LOVE MACHINE

Dennis Farney

The following article by a reporter for the Wall Street Journal *provides extensive information about the country's largest manufacturer of greeting cards. Notice how Farney begins by narrating an event that sets the scene for the rest of the piece. As you read, consider what it would be like to work for Hallmark. How does information about the workplace, or scene, relate to the act of creating greeting cards?*

Steve Finken's conference table is where the punch lines come to die.

It is 4 P.M. at Hallmark Cards Inc., decision time in one small corner of the world's largest greeting-card maker. Time for Mr. Finken's brainstorming session with writers for the Shoebox Greetings line, the kinkiest division of a well-scrubbed Midwestern company.

Each writer's quota is 50 knee-slappers a week, and the writers know that about 47 will be rejected by their droll and sardonic boss. Mr. Finken, running on snap judgments and gut instinct, is deciding the fate of ideas, one every 10 seconds.

He holds up a roughed-out birthday card and reads aloud:

"Even when you're old, we'll observe a moment of silence for your sagging flesh."   5

Titters all around. But Mr. Finken asks: "When would you send that? I don't know." Flip, into the reject pile.

The writers barely protest as Mr. Finken mows down their creations with enigmatic rejections.

"A bit of a stretch."

"Too many levels."

"Retailers will ponder."   10

It is hard to predict what will survive this process. "Happy birthday from all of us at the office," Mr. Finken reads. "Except the boss, who spit on the wall when asked to sign this."

Mr. Finken is tempted. But "spit on the wall? Make it 'spewed coffee from his nose,'" he suggests. The idea joins a small pile making the initial cut.

That's life in "the emotion business," as some Hallmarkers call it, and privately held Hallmark is the General Motors of emotion. It sculpts emotion, teases it into new shapes, embosses it, adds ribbons and saucy lines, and sells it for more than $2.5 billion a year. It makes 11 million greeting cards *a day*. In an era when people don't write and are often too busy to call, its products are a social glue that cements relationships.

"What we say is 'I love you,' 10,000 different ways," says Bobbie Burrow, who has spent 33 years writing Hallmark cards. Actually, she has written at least that many herself. Her husband stopped giving cards to her because the card he'd select kept turning out to be one she'd written.

"It kind of loses something, writing to yourself," she says with a   15
laugh. If pressed, Ms. Burrow can write a text in five minutes. Here's one
of her favorites:

> *There's a very special garden*
> *Where the flowers of friendship grow.*
> *It's nurtured by the kindness*
> *And concern that good friends show. . . .*
> *It's a place of peace and beauty*
> *Where bright new dreams can start —*
>
> *It's friendship's lovely garden*
> *And it blossoms in the heart.*

Such verses — sentiments with a floral scent — made Hallmark blos-
som. Its all-time best-selling card shows a cart full of purple pansies;
introduced in 1941 and still going strong, it has sold more than 25 million
copies.

Another flower, though, figured in one of the company's greatest
clunkers. This was the "Wunderflower" venture, a container carrying
both a greeting and dormant lily-of-the-valley bulbs. The bulbs began
sprouting, prematurely and by the thousands, on dealers' shelves. Hallmark took the blame and the loss.

But Hallmark is more than budding flowers and sentimental rhymes.
Seeking strategic investments and also to protect fellow Kansas City companies from hostile takeovers in recent years, it has bought into Payless
Cashways Inc., a home-improvement retailer, and Kansas City Southern
Industries Inc. It is struggling to salvage another diversification move,
control of the nation's largest Spanish-language communications company, but recently admitted the effort could fail. Despite appearances, it
is a highly competitive place, one that lives and dies on its ability to
identify social trends.

On the shelf for 1990:

- Divorce announcements. ("Because about 50% of all marriages
  end in divorce — and people need a way to communicate about it,"
  company literature explains.)
- "Reconciliation" cards tinged with guilt and remorse, about relationships turned bittersweet.
- Sympathy messages on the occasion of a pet's demise. (There are,
  Hallmark calculates, more U.S. households with pets than households with children.)
- Intimate cards, the most intimate in the company's history, offering 520 ways to say everything from "I love you" to "Let's work
  things out."
- Cards that harried parents too busy for heart-to-heart talks can
  slip behind a child's pillow.

Hallmark employs 20,500 people full time and 10,500 part time, and *20* it goes to great lengths to keep them cheery. The workers own one-third of the company. To keep them in touch with popular culture, Hallmark pays their way, on company time, to watch movies at the company-built Crown Center hotel and shopping complex. A man named Gordon MacKenzie skips around Hallmark's halls making sure people don't take themselves too seriously. His title is "Creative Paradox."

The company believes in old-fashioned service through 21,000 retail outlets, all but 175 or so independently owned. And it believes in public service: The Hall Family Foundations own the largest collection of Henry Moore sculptures in the U.S. and helped build an elegant sculpture garden for it at Kansas City's art museum.

It is dreadfully ironic, in view of all this paternalism, that when the company came into the national eye in the 1980s, it was associated with death, plagiarism and bare-knuckled legal tactics.

In 1981, an elevated walkway in the Kansas City Hyatt Regency Hotel — developed by Hallmark — collapsed, killing 114 people in a crush of concrete and steel. Well over 200 others were injured.

At the time, some wondered whether damage awards might over- whelm Hallmark's insurance coverage and cripple the company finan- cially. But Hallmark's lawyers exploited a rift in the plaintiffs' ranks and drove home a money-saving package settlement. The disaster ended up costing the company $120 million, all covered by insurance, according to a spokesman.

A few years later, Hallmark was accused by a small Colorado-based *25* card maker, Blue Mountain Arts, of plagiarizing no fewer than 83 Blue Mountain card designs and pressuring retailers to drop Blue Mountain. Blue Mountain portrayed Hallmark as a bully. "Like a pirate ship with a hundred guns, Hallmark's army of lawyers is trying to prove that might makes right," charged Bob Gall, Blue Mountain's general manager.

In 1988, after the Supreme Court let stand a preliminary injunction against selling the disputed cards, Hallmark settled. Hallmark admitted no wrongdoing but junked its offending line, destroying thousands of cards. Neither side will talk about monetary aspects of the settlement.

If these events left dents in Hallmark's corporate psyche, they hardly show. Over the years, however, the company has adapted to a world at variance with its own general good cheer.

During World War II, it sold a savage caricature of Adolf Hitler, Benito Mussolini and Emperor Hirohito strolling past a graveyard. In 1946, it sold a get-well card depicting an atom bomb. (It was a friendly bomb, though, "guaranteed to kill germs.") In 1972, during the Vietnam War, it sold a Christmas card featuring the peace symbol. And it's sold a coffee mug, intended for one liberated-but-cynical woman to send an- other, which read: "Men are only good for one thing. . . . And how important is parallel parking anyhow?"

Today, Hallmark inhabits a world where crack is sold on the streets not far from its elegant headquarters. A world of AIDS. A world of "blended families" — merged families that combine the fragments left over after several divorces.

"We're moving into uncharted waters," says Clar Evans. "People are   *30* living longer and thus playing ever more roles, and old social constraints are fading. Grandmothers can become sky divers. Life becomes almost a quick sketch."

At first blush, it might seem that all this change threatens Hallmark and its Norman Rockwell world. In fact, just the opposite is true. The more society atomizes — the more divorces, latchkey kids, sky-diving grandmothers and second careers — the more niches are created for greeting cards and greeting-card sales. "That" says Ms. Evans, "is where the money comes in."

That's also why Hallmark relies heavily on research, some of it computer-age scientific. The company uses focus groups and panel tests. It can take every card made in the past five years and analyze whether it sold and why or why not.

Down to the neighborhood level, Hallmark's experts know which kind of cards will sell best in which places. Engagement cards sell best in the Northeast, which is big on engagement parties. Birthday cards saying "Daddy" sell best in the South because even adult Southerners tend to call their fathers Daddy.

But even in the computer age, a surprising amount of research is seat-of-the-pants intuitive. Reading the comic pages, Hallmark President Irvine O. Hockaday, Jr., was struck by a startling, if temporary, personality change in Garfield the Cat. A recent sequence found the curmudgeonly Garfield uncharacteristically frightened and lonely. He actually hugged his owner.

"I'm going to write [cartoonist] Jim Davis and see what he was   *35* trying to do," Mr. Hockaday muses. "If Garfield is moving in that direction, maybe we're one step behind."

Hallmark looks for such research from all its employees. Step into the cubicle of artist Wendie Collins, a pixie of a woman described by a supervisor as "a 12-year-old at heart." You are awash in artifacts, including windup teeth that clack, beefcake photos, a Cary Grant cutout and a plastic-banana lamp — "my own toys," she says.

Ms. Collins initiated "Boo Bazaar," a line of cards and curios that includes everything needed for a Halloween party. She realized that adults were throwing more Halloween parties, not just for their children but for themselves.

Hallmark will consider almost any idea but won't accept just anything. Until late in his life, founder Joyce C. Hall headed the Okay Committee and personally approved each and every card. The committee is gone, but written taste guidelines help determine what goes out the door.

That gradually changes as society changes. Now, for example, Hallmark will depict a man and woman together in bed — but the woman is likely to be wearing the man's pajama top, not sexy lingerie. Explains a Hallmark photographer: "We don't do Victoria's Secret." That would never "reach the gate."

What does "reach the gate" defines the company's corporate image,   *40* an image that counts enormously in the card business.

For starters, 80% to 85% of Hallmark's customers are women. Most men don't buy cards if they can avoid it. Yet when they do, they tend to buy expensive ones — probably because they're feeling guilty.

Another anomaly of the market is that the $4.2 billion greeting-card industry is made up of three giants, a small second tier and at least 700 dwarfs. Hallmark is the giant among giants, with a market share it puts at 44%. Also sizable are two publicly held competitors, American Greetings Corp., with roughly a third of the market, and Gibson Greetings Inc., with about 10%.

A wild melee of dwarfs fight over crumbs that drop from the giants' table. The dwarfs include everything from New York's Metropolitan Museum of Art and missionary societies to hundreds of small "alternative card" operations. An alternative-card company is to Hallmark as a flea to an elephant. But a flea can still bite an elephant. Almost within the shadow of Hallmark headquarters, some Kansas City card shops love the alternatives and wouldn't think of stocking Hallmark.

"Oh, no," Cheryl White dismisses Hallmark with a laugh. She is co-owner of Classic Cards, about two miles away from Hallmark headquarters. Hallmark, even its Shoebox line, is too "mainstream," she says. "One of our best sellers right now is a set of earrings made from condoms," she explains. "It's so blatant!"

But Hallmark, dominating the broad middle of the market, isn't   *45* blatant. Why risk the corporate image? With divisions such as Shoebox as well as traditional cards that quote the Bible and 19th-century poets, the company edges out toward both the risque and the ultra-traditional ends of the market. Cautiously.

Today, Hallmark, like many other marketers, is focusing on the vast increase in working women. And like other marketers, it is finding an ambivalence tinged with guilt on the part of working mothers. Hallmark's response, launched early last year, is To Kids with Love.

Deirdre DeVey, who is product development manager for everyday cards, sees an even broader trend, a "return to romance." But that return takes many forms. Many Hallmark cards now seem to go two ways at once — a sentimental message on the cover, a zinger on the inside. One card, its cover all sweetness and modesty, shows a demure little figure saying in demure little letters: "Just a simple little card to say 'I love you.'" Inside, the message reads: "(Kinda makes you want to have sex, doesn't it?)"

Until about a year ago, most Hallmark cards communicated positive feelings. But then, the company began experimenting with "the reconciliation theme." Says Denise Johnson, who initiated the effort: "It's about that Gosh-I-Wish-Things-Could-Be-Better feeling." One Easter card, decorated with glowing tulips and spring flowers, says it this way:

Easter is a good time to put things behind us. . . .
That's why I want to let you know that I care about you,
And I hope this will be the start of better times for us.

This text, with its use of "I" and "you" and "us," responds to a fresh desire for emotional intimacy that Hallmark sees permeating society. As writer Barbara Loots puts it: "People want their card to be exactly their own—from me to you."

And that's what Hallmark is trying to produce in its Just How I Feel   50
line. Unveiled in mid-November after two years of work, Just How I Feel is the most thoroughly researched product in Hallmark's history. It contains some of the company's most intimate, personal cards, which try for a "me-to-you" feeling.

For example:

Anyone can love
When it's easy
But you continue to love
When I make it very difficult.
Thanks for loving me
No matter what.

Packed with "I's" and "you's" the 520 cards in the Just How I Feel line may be the ultimate embodiment of Hallmark's self-image as an enhancer and reinforcer of relationships. And the cards could stand as the ultimate embodiment of the Hallmark corporate strategy as well. As Sally Groves, the creative director for writing and editorial, puts it: "Fortunately, people still fall in love a lot. And when they hit bad times, well, we're there for them, too."

Questions for Discussion

1. In his introduction Farney describes Hallmark Cards Inc. as "a well-scrubbed" company. What do you think he means by this? What information supports this claim? Are there any kinds of greeting cards that Hallmark is unlikely to produce?
2. Why have changing times proved to be good business for Hallmark? What are some of the new products recently developed by Hallmark?
3. Consider the sample lyric included in paragraph 15. What does it illustrate?

4. What is it like to work for Hallmark? Would you be willing to work there?

5. How do sales patterns for greeting cards differ from one part of the country to another? What type of person buys the greatest number of cards?

6. According to this article, Hallmark sees itself "as an enhancer and reinforcer of relationships." Has any of the information included within this article led you to conclude that it is also a business?

7. Has the information reported in this article changed your attitude toward greeting cards? Would you be more or less likely to send a Hallmark card now that you know the company manufactures 11 million cards a day?

Suggestions for Writing

1. Draw upon your own work experience and write a behind-the-scenes report upon how a particular business operates.

2. Visit a local card store and study the alternatives that are available for Hallmark cards. Focus upon a particular type of card (such as birthday cards or anniversary cards). Then write an essay comparing or contrasting the cards produced by two different companies.

STRESSED OUT IN SUBURBIA

Nicholas Lemann

> *Nicholas Lemann is a regular contributor to the* Atlantic, *where this article first appeared. It focuses upon a changing scene, contrasting suburbia today with suburbia in the 1950s. As you read, think about what kind of person is likely to result from the kind of life fostered by these different scenes. Notice how Lemann draws upon a number of written sources without allowing these sources to dominate what he himself has to say.*

I recently spent some time in Naperville, Illinois, because I wanted to see exactly how our familiar ideas about the suburbs have gotten out of date. Naperville is thirty miles west of the Chicago Loop. It had 7,000 residents in 1950, 13,000 in 1960, 22,600 in 1970, and 42,600 in 1980, and just in this decade it has nearly doubled in population again, to 83,000 this year. Driving there from Chicago, you pass through the West Side ghetto, the site of riots in the late sixties, and then through a belt of older suburbs at the city limits. Just when the suburbs seem to be dying out, you arrive in Oak Brook, with its collection of new shopping malls and office towers. The seventeen-mile stretch from Oak Brook west through Naperville to the old railroad city of Aurora has the look of inexplicable development common to booming areas that were recently rural. Subdivisions back up onto cornfields. Mirrored-glass office parks back up onto convenience-store parking lots. Most of the trees are saplings.

The picture we have of middle-class life in the United States is essentially still set in the suburbs of the 1950s. The sheer volume of information available about the American middle class is greater for the 1950s than for any other period of our history, because there was then a tremendous outpouring of journalism, sociology, and fiction on the subject. The middle class seemed fascinating at the time: it was acquiring a new home, the suburbs, and a new economic base, the large bureaucratic business organization, and these were quickly becoming the dominant social forms in the country. Since the early sixties, suburbia has been taken more for granted.

The people who grew up in fifties suburbia now dominate the country culturally, and from them we are getting a second wave of interest in middle-class family life, which comes from their own involvement in it. Here, too, the basic idea is the fifties; people's concept of suburbia, like their concepts of summer and marriage, comes more from what they knew growing up than from what they've experienced themselves as adults. On television especially, constant references are made these days to the suburbs of the Baby Boom generation's youth as the proper locus of the American middle class. All subsequent developments seem slightly perfidious.

While we've been glorifying the suburbs of the fifties, the suburbs of the eighties have been evolving into places quite different. The most obvious change has been a political-economic one: in the fifties the suburbs were exclusively residential, but businesses have been moving to them over the past fifteen years, and this has broken the iron association of suburbs with commuting downtown. The fastest-growing kind of town in the country is one on the outer edge of a metropolitan area which has acquired an employment base. Christopher Leinberger and Charles Lockwood, writing in *The Atlantic* three years ago,° called these communities "urban villages," and there are also several other names for them, including "edge cities" and "technoburbs." The communities have cropped up all over the country — in Plano, Texas, and Tysons Corner, Virginia; the towns in the valleys surrounding the Los Angeles Basin and along the outer reaches of San Francisco Bay; New York satellites like Stamford, White Plains, and Princeton. Because we're fixated on the fifties, we don't have a good sense of what life is like in these places, which, if they're not yet typical of suburbia, certainly represent the direction in which suburbia is heading.

Our notion now of suburbia in the fifties is that it was essentially benign — sometimes gawky, often dull, but on the whole healthy and happy. But in the fifties themselves virtually everything written about the suburbs was negative, even alarmed. The indictment can be summed up in one word: conformity. Working for huge corporations, living in tract homes, surrounded by spookily similar neighbors, the new middle-class Americans had lost their feelings of pride, meaning, and identity. They wanted only to blend unobtrusively into a group.

The run of suburban literature began, roughly, with the publication of David Riesman's *The Lonely Crowd* (which is not explicitly about the suburbs, but set the tone) in 1950. The deservedly best-remembered of the many books about the suburbs by sociologists and journalists is William H. Whyte's *The Organization Man* (1956). There was also a flood of suburban fiction, of which the best-known works are probably the stories and novels of John Cheever and, because of its catch-phrase title, *The Man in the Gray Flannel Suit,* by Sloan Wilson. The suburbs took such a beating in most of these books that by 1967 the sociologist Herbert Gans was able to cast *The Levittowners* as an attack on the attackers of the new middle class. Gans argued convincingly that most of the critics of suburbia didn't know what they were talking about, and were animated by a snobbish distaste for the lower middle class. But the idea that suburban society was oriented toward the community at the expense of the individual is so widespread in the literature that there must have been something to it. Today nobody worries about conformity as a national issue, and nobody

writing in The Atlantic *three years ago:* See "How Business Is Reshaping America," October 1986: 43–52.

I met in Naperville mentioned it as a problem. The suburban psychological force that occasionally overwhelms people is not the need to fit in but the need to be a success.

The history of Naperville as an urban village begins in 1964, when AT&T decided to build a major facility there for its research division, Bell Labs, along the new Interstate 88. Before that, as the next-to-last stop on the Burlington & Northern line from Chicago, Naperville attracted some hardy long-distance commuters, but it was mainly an independent small town, with frame houses and streets laid out in a grid.

Bell Labs opened in 1966 and is still by far the largest employer in Naperville — 7,000 people work there, developing electronic switching systems, and another 3,000 work at a software development center in the neighboring town of Lisle. In 1969 Amoco moved its main research-and-development facility from the industrial town of Whiting, Indiana, to a site in Naperville along the interstate, near Bell Labs. Today more than 2,000 people work there. All through the seventies and eighties businesses have built low-slung, campus-style office complexes up and down I-88, which Governor James R. Thompson in 1986 officially subtitled "The Illinois Research and Development Corridor." There are now four big chain hotels on the five-mile stretch that runs through Lisle and Naperville. In Aurora, Nissan, Hyundai, and Toyota have all established distribution centers, and four insurance companies have set up regional headquarters.

In the fifties the force driving the construction of residential neighborhoods in the suburbs was that prosperity had given young married couples the means to act on their desire to raise children away from the cities. In the eighties in Naperville there is still some of this, but the real driving force is that so many jobs are there. Dozens of new residential subdivisions fan out in the area south of the office complexes and the old town center. In this part of town, whose land Naperville aggressively annexed, the school district has built three new elementary schools since 1984 and added to seven others. A new junior high school opened this fall, another one is under construction, and last spring the town's voters passed a bond issue to build another elementary school and additions to two high schools.

In *The Organization Man,* William Whyte was struck by how removed the place he studied — Park Forest, Illinois, the fifties equivalent of Naperville, brand-new and also thirty miles from the Loop — was from Chicago and from urban forms of social organization. Naperville is even more removed, mainly because downtown commuters are a small minority of the new residents. Nearly everybody in Park Forest worked in Chicago. Only five thousand people take the train from the Naperville station into Chicago every day; most people work in Naperville or in a nearby suburban town. The people I talked to in Naperville knew that

10

they were supposed to go into Chicago for the museums, theater, music, and restaurants, so they were a little defensive about admitting to staying in Naperville in their free time, but most of them do. Though Naperville has many white ethnics (and a few blacks and Asians), it has no ethnic neighborhoods. There are ethnic restaurants, but many of them are the kind that aren't run by members of that ethnic group. Naperville is politically conservative but has no Democratic or Republican organizations active in local politics. Nobody who can afford a house lives in an apartment. There are only a few neighborhood taverns. Discussions of Chicago focus on how much crime is there, rather than on the great events of municipal life.

Places like Naperville are often dismissed as examples of heedless sprawl, ugly and unplanned. The charge may be true of some places, but it is not of Naperville, which is extremely well run. A master plan precisely sets forth how the town is to grow, to the point when all its empty space is filled up. The downtown shops have been kept alive. There is an excellent new library, a brick walkway (built by volunteers) along the DuPage River in the center of town, and plenty of green space. City property taxes have been lowered in each of the past three years. Naperville represents not chaos but a conscious rejection of the pro-urban, anti-automobile conventions that prevail among planners.

In distancing itself from Chicago, Naperville has continued a trend that was already well under way in Whyte's Park Forest. Otherwise, most of the ways in which Naperville is different from Whyte's Park Forest and places like it were not predicted by the suburbia experts of the time.

Naperville is much more materially prosperous, and at the same time more anxious about its standard of living, than Park Forest was. The comparison isn't exact, because Park Forest was a middle-middle-class community dominated by people in their late twenties and early thirties; Naperville is more affluent and has a somewhat fuller age range. Nonetheless, since Naperville is the fastest-growing town in the area, it can fairly be said to represent the slice of American life that is expanding most rapidly right now, as Park Forest could in the fifties. The typical house in Park Forest cost $13,000 and had one story (the most expensive house there by far, where the developer lived, cost $50,000). The average house in Naperville costs $160,000, and the figure is higher in the new subdivisions. Plenty of new houses in town cost more than $500,000. Most of the new houses in Naperville have two stories; in fact, the small section of fifties and sixties suburbia in Naperville is noticeably more modest than the new housing.

In fifties suburbs the architecture was usually quite simple. In Naperville the new houses are flamboyantly traditional, with steeply pitched roofs, red-brick or stained-cedar exteriors (aluminum siding is banned in many of the subdivisions), leaded-glass windows, massive front doors, cathedral ceilings, fireplaces, gables, even turrets. The names of subdivisions and of house models often evoke European nobility: The Chateaux of La Provence, La Royale, The Golf Villas of White Eagle Club, The Country Manor, Charlemont IV. Whyte had chapters called "Classless-ness in Suburbia" and "Inconspicuous Consumption," and described the material ethos of Park Forest as quasi-socialist. Although in the fifties the average American, known to intellectuals as "mass man," was materially much better outfitted than he had been, the suburbs had become home to a wider range of people than they had been before the Second World War, and so seemed more democratic. Naperville is much made fun of in the neighboring communities as the home of snobs and yuppies.

Obviously one reason for the difference is that Park Forest in the   15
early fifties was only a very few years into the postwar boom, which left the middle class vastly better off than it had been before. Another is that the consumer culture was young and undeveloped in the fifties. Middle-class people today want to own things that their parents wouldn't have dreamed of.

The affluence of Naperville is also a by-product of what is probably the single most important new development in middle-class life since the fifties (and one almost wholly unanticipated in the fifties), which is that women work. Park Forest was an exclusively female town on weekdays; when Whyte wrote about the difficulty of being a "superwoman," he meant combining housework with civic and social life. In Naperville I heard various statistics, but it seems safe to say that most mothers of young children work, and the younger the couple, the likelier it is that the wife works. When *Business Week* did a big story on the "mommy track" last spring, it used a picture of a woman from Naperville. What people in Naperville seem to focus on when they think about working mothers is not that feminism has triumphed in the Midwest but that two-career couples have more money and less time than one-career couples.

In the classic suburban literature almost no reference is made to punishingly long working hours. The Cheever story whose title is meant to evoke the journey home at the end of the working day is called "The Five Forty-Eight," and its hero is taking that late a train only because he stopped in at a bar for a couple of Gibsons on the way from his office to Grand Central Station. In Naperville the word "stress" came up constantly in conversations. People felt that they had to work harder than people a generation ago in order to have a good middle-class life. In much of the rest of the country the idea holds sway that the middle class is downwardly mobile and its members will never live as well as their parents did. Usually this complaint involves an inexact comparison — the complainer is at an earlier stage in his career, works in a less remunerative field, or lives in a pricier place than the parents who he thinks lived better than he does. In Naperville, where most people are in business, it's more a case of people's material expectations being higher than their parents' than of their economic station being lower. A ranch-style tract house, a Chevrolet, and meat loaf for dinner will not do any more as the symbols of a realized dream. Also, a changed perception of the future of the country has helped create the sense of pressure in Naperville. Suburbanites of the fifties were confident of a constantly rising standard of living, level of education, and gross national product in a way that most Americans haven't been since about the time of the 1973 OPEC embargo. The feeling is that anyone who becomes prosperous has beaten the odds.

It is jarring to think of placid-looking Naperville as excessively fast-paced, but people there talk as if the slack had been taken out of life. They complain that between working long hours, traveling on business, and trying to stay in shape they have no free time. The under-the-gun feeling applies to domestic life as well as to work. It's striking, in reading the old suburban literature today, to see how little people worried about their children. Through many scenes of drunkenness, adultery, and domestic discord, the kids seem usually to be playing, oblivious, in the front yard. Today there is a national hyperawareness of the lifelong consequences of childhood unhappiness (hardly an issue of *People* magazine fails to make this point); the feeling that American children can coast to a prosperous adulthood has been lost; and the entry of mothers into the work force has made child care a constant worry for parents. The idea that childhood can operate essentially on autopilot has disappeared.

Teenagers in Naperville complain that they have nothing to do, but everyone else is overscheduled, including children. Day care adds a layer of complication to life: Naperville's booming day-care centers accept not only pre-school children but also children who need supervision after school, until their parents get home. The school system's buses drop some children off at day-care centers in the afternoon. Every neighborhood has stories about latchkey kids, too.

A constant round of activities has been organized for children. The Naperville park district, which carries out the traditional functions of a municipal recreation department, runs an elaborate sports program, which parents appreciate while slightly rueing the time they spend ferrying their kids to soccer games and swim meets. "Sometimes we wonder why our kids can't just get a baseball game together," one mother told me. In the elementary schools, as late as the early seventies all students went home for lunch. Now the schools have lunchrooms — and many special new programs, added in part because of lobbying by parents who expect a high level of service from the schools. In the mid-eighties, at the parents' request, the elementary schools added an hour a day of special "enrichment" programs for students with IQs over 125. The high schools added advanced-placement courses. School administrators and parents complain about the competitive atmosphere for students, in which an idyllic midwestern upbringing is a fading memory and it's painful to be average.

Adults in Naperville are competitive too. The people I talked to there were intensely aware of income distinctions within the community, a subject that rarely came up in books about the suburbs of a generation ago. The most direct blast of it that I got was in a meeting with a group of women who had just finished a parenting class taught by the elementary school system's social worker. The parenting class is part of a small culture of therapy that has sprung up in Naperville, in response partly to problems like divorce and drugs and partly to people's increased awareness of psychological well-being as an important issue in life. What seemed to be the real reason the women I met took the class was that they wanted affirmation of their decision not to work, which they felt had consigned them to a slightly lower status level than women with jobs. Their message was that they might have less money and prestige, but they were better parents.

Working mothers, they told me, buy off their children with copious gifts of new toys in place of maternal contact. They leave their children behind even on vacations, which are spent in expensive glamour spots. They sign their children up for a ceaseless round of overachieving activities, and then expect the full-time mothers to do all the carpooling. The neighborhood children are always hanging around the houses where the mothers are at home. Working mothers' children are kept up ridiculously late at night because that's the only time they see their parents. The mothers don't do volunteer work in the community. The litany ended with the inevitable coup de grace: "You wonder why they had kids."

The new houses in the subdivisions in Naperville clearly show an evolutionary adaptation of domestic architecture to customers who are busier than people used to be and more concerned with the fine gradations of status. The living and dining rooms are shrunken, vestigial spaces flanking the front hall. People entertain at home less and less because they don't have time to, and so they don't need these rooms. In Park Forest in the fifties (and in most of the suburban fiction of the time), the socializing was so constant — cocktail parties, dinner parties, teas, coffees, bridge-club gatherings — that Whyte found it a cause for concern, because it enforced conformity. In Naperville everybody says that the at-home party is dying. Instead, people go out to restaurants, which are almost completely absent from the mythology of fifties suburbia.

Kitchens are usually built open to a large family room in back, which is meant to contain the main household television set and which has taken up the space left by the shrinking of the living and dining rooms. This indicates that what cooking goes on must not be elaborate or messy enough to bother the family members sitting a few feet away. Other rooms in the houses show that people want to be reminded that they are winners. The bizarrely large and well-appointed master bathrooms that Philip Langdon wrote about in these pages last month° are common in

these pages last month: See "Glorified Bathrooms, *Atlantic,* October 1989: 102–108.

Naperville. Often there is a small "study" off to the side downstairs, designed to suggest brandy and cigars and meant to be available for use as a home office. A small but dramatic balcony overlooks the front hall or the family room in many houses.

Because of the placement of the family room, which often opens to   *25* an outdoor deck, the new houses in Naperville are oriented toward the back yard, which may be fenced. In the fifties most writers described the unfenced front yard as the locale for much of the children's outdoor life. This contributed to the intense feeling of community in suburban neighborhoods, which led to the joke, quoted by Whyte, that Park Forest was "a sorority house with kids." In Naperville it seems much more possible not to know your neighbors. All the subdivisions have homeowners' associations. These constitute organized politics, such as it is, in the new parts of Naperville. The mayor, Margaret Price (who herself started out as a homeowners'-association president), meets with them regularly. But some homeowners' associations take off as community organizations and others don't.

The most reliable connection between subdivision residents and the community is children. Adults meet through the children's activities. I often heard that new neighborhoods coalesce around new elementary schools, which have many parent-involving activities and are also convenient places to hold meetings. The churches (mostly Protestant and Catholic, but the town has places of worship for Jews and even Muslims) have made an effort to perform some of the same functions — there is always a new church under construction, and eight congregations are operating out of rented space. The Reverend Keith Torney, who recently left the First Congregational Church in Naperville, after eighteen years, for a pulpit in Billings, Montana, told me, "We try to create a community where people can acquire roots very quickly. We divided the congregation into twelve care groups. Each has twenty to thirty families. They kind of take over for neighbors and grandma — they bring the casserole when you're sick. People come here for a sense of warmth, for a sense that people care about you."

All these community-building efforts amount to swimming against the tide, though, because population mobility in the newer parts of Naperville is great. According to local lore, the average house in Naperville changes hands every three years — a turnover rate comparable to or higher than those Whyte and Gans found in Park Forest and Levittown, and they were entirely new communities, whereas Naperville has a large well-established area that presumably brings the average turnover down. Naperville has two school districts; in the one that covers the new subdivisions, new students make up more than a quarter of the enrollment every fall. And this kind of mobility is occurring at a time when corporate transfers, which were thought in the fifties to be the main reason people moved so much, are slightly in decline, because of a lessening in people's willingness to do whatever their employers want.

There isn't any hard information on where new Naperville residents come from or where departing ones go. Most of the people I met had moved to Naperville from elsewhere in the Chicago area, often from the inner-ring suburbs. They came there to be closer to their jobs along I-88, because the schools are good and the crime rate is low, and because Naperville is a place where the person who just moved to town is not an outsider but the dominant figure in the community. If they leave, it's usually because of a new job, not always with the same company; the amount of company-switching, and of entrepreneurship, appears to be greater today than it was in the fifties. Several of the new office developments in the area have the word *corporate* in their names. (I stayed in a hotel on Corporetum Drive.) Since the likes of AT&T and Amoco don't call attention to themselves in this way, the use of the word is probably a sign of the presence of new businesses. People's career restlessness, and companies' desire to appear regally established right away, are further examples of the main message I got from my time in Naperville: the suburbs and, by extension, middle-class Americans have gone from glorifying group bonding to glorifying individual happiness and achievement.

The bad side of this change in ethos should be obvious right now: Americans appear to be incapable of the social cohesion and the ability to defer gratification which are prerequisites for the success of major national efforts. But a good side exists too. Representations of middle-class life in the fifties are pervaded with a sense of the perils of appearing to be "different." William Whyte wrote a series of articles for *Fortune,* and the photographs that Dan Weiner took to illustrate them (which are included in *America Worked,* a new book of Weiner's photographs) communicate this feeling even more vividly than *The Organization Man* does: the suburban kaffeeklatsch and the executive's office come across as prisons. There can't be much doubt that the country is more tolerant now than it was then.

Much of the fifties literature, especially the fiction, is pervaded as well by a sense of despair. Of course, American intellectuals since about the time of the First World War have been trying to prove that middle-class life is empty, while most Americans have enthusiastically embraced it. Still, the dark side of suburbia was detected by so many observers that it's hard to believe they all just projected it from their own minds onto their subject matter.

The darkest of all the suburban novels is probably Richard Yates's *Revolutionary Road,* which was published in 1961 but is set in the summer of 1955, in "a part of western Connecticut." In theme *Revolutionary Road* is similar to the television show *thirtysomething:* well-educated young people who think of themselves as hip and liberal marry, have children, and

30

buy a house in the suburbs with the intention of retaining the ideals of their youth. In *Revolutionary Road* this endeavor leads inexorably to boozing, vicious quarreling, self-loathing, madness, and, ultimately, suicide. Frank, the husband, takes a meaningless job in the sales-promotion department of Knox Business Machines, purveyor of the Knox 500 Electronic Computer (computers were fifties intellectuals' favorite symbol of everything that was wrong with America). April, the wife, keeps getting pregnant, to her horror.

Frank and April are not updated versions of the Babbitts. On the contrary, they are determined *not* to be Babbitts:° they worry about conformity, listen to jazz, and struggle to understand Freud. So when they are destroyed, the message is not that they are victims of their own moral and cultural insensitivity but that the suburbs have no place for good people. To underscore the point, the minor character who, in occasional appearances, offers the most perceptive comments about Frank's and April's lives is an inmate of a mental hospital. It's only when Frank and April can summon the self-delusion to engage in dull, bourgeois husband-wife role-playing that they feel momentarily content. Intellectual honesty equals misery.

Frank and April's expectations are much lower materially than a similar couple's would be now. A novelist with Yates's talent for the damning detail surely would today have them acquiring lots of unnecessary and expensive trendy household items; in *Revolutionary Road* money is mentioned only rarely, and always in the context of necessities rather than luxuries. But then, Frank and April take it for granted that in every middle-class couple the man can find an easy and secure job that pays enough to support the whole family, and the woman can bear and raise healthy children.

Perhaps suburban life has become enough of a project to have filled in that old hollowness. Even the struggle against depression is much more of a busy-making activity than it used to be, thanks to the proliferation of therapies and support groups. Mortages are bigger, jobs are more demanding, parenthood is a stretch in every way. Who has time to peer into the abyss?

Questions for Discussion

1. What motivated Lemann to visit Naperville, Illinois? How does Naperville differ from a 1950s suburb like Oak Brook, Illinois?
2. What factors have led to the rapid growth of Naperville? How well is this "urban village" coping with development?
3. Why have so many people moved to Naperville? Why do you think the average house is sold to new owners every three years?

Babbitts: George and Myra Babbitt are a conventional middle-class couple satirized by Sinclair Lewis in *Babbit,* a novel published in 1922.

4. Why would someone living in Naperville complain of stress? Why would someone find it "painful to be average" there?

5. How has the design of a middle-class suburban home changed to reflect changing patterns of domestic life?

6. Lemann cites a number of other writers in this article, such as David Reisman, William H. Whyte, John Cheever, and Sloan Wilson. What do these citations contribute to the article? Does Lemann expect readers to be familiar with the works he draws upon?

7. From the information in this article, is suburban life getting better or worse?

Suggestions for Writing

1. Do you know of a suburb where you would be willing to live? If so, write an essay about what it is like to live there. Include specific information about population, stores, recreation, cultural facilities, and housing costs.

2. Read one of the books mentioned in this article and write a summary of its contents.

WOMEN'S BRAINS

Stephen Jay Gould

> *Stephen Jay Gould is a paleontologist who teaches at Harvard University and contributes a regular column to* Natural History. *In the following essay Gould reports information about a French scientist named Paul Broca who falsely concluded that women are less intelligent than men. As you read this essay, consider Gould's purpose in reporting the story of Broca's research. Consider also what this essay reveals about the nature of information.*

In the prelude to *Middlemarch,* George Eliot° lamented the unfulfilled lives of talented women:

> Some have felt that these blundering lives are due to the inconvenient indefiniteness with which the Supreme Power has fashioned the natures of women: if there were one level of feminine incompetence as strict as the ability to count three and no more, the social lot of women might be treated with scientific certitude.

Eliot goes on to discount the idea of innate limitation, but while she wrote in 1872, the leaders of European anthropometry were trying to measure "with scientific certitude" the inferiority of women. Anthropometry, or measurement of the human body, is not so fashionable a field these days, but it dominated the human sciences for much of the nineteenth century and remained popular until intelligence testing replaced skull measurement as a favored device for making invidious comparisons among races, classes, and sexes. Craniometry, or measurement of the skull, commanded the most attention and respect. Its unquestioned leader, Paul Broca (1824–80), professor of clinical surgery at the Faculty of Medicine in Paris, gathered a school of disciples and imitators around himself. Their work, so meticulous and apparently irrefutable, exerted great influence and won high esteem as a jewel of nineteenth-century science.

Broca's work seemed particularly invulnerable to refutation. Had he not measured with the most scrupulous care and accuracy? (Indeed, he had. I have the greatest respect for Broca's meticulous procedure. His numbers are sound. But science is an inferential exercise, not a catalog of facts. Numbers, by themselves, specify nothing. All depends upon what you do with them.) Broca depicted himself as an apostle of objectivity, a man who bowed before facts and cast aside superstition and sentimentality. He declared that "there is no faith, however respectable, no interest, however legitimate, which must not accommodate itself to the progress of human knowledge and bend before truth." Women, like it or not, had smaller brains than men and, therefore, could not equal them in intelli-

---

George Eliot: The pen name of English novelist Mary Ann Evans (1819–1880).

gence. This fact, Broca argued, may reinforce a common prejudice in male society, but it is also a scientific truth. L. Manouvrier, a black sheep in Broca's fold, rejected the inferiority of women and wrote with feeling about the burden imposed upon them by Broca's numbers:

> Women displayed their talents and their diplomas. They also invoked philosophical authorities. But they were opposed by *numbers* unknown to Condorcet or to John Stuart Mill. These numbers fell upon poor women like a sledge hammer, and they were accompanied by commentaries and sarcasms more ferocious than the most misogynist imprecations of certain church fathers. The theologians had asked if women had a soul. Several centuries later, some scientists were ready to refuse them a human intelligence.

Broca's argument rested upon two sets of data: the larger brains of men in modern societies, and a supposed increase in male superiority through time. His most extensive data came from autopsies performed personally in four Parisian hospitals. For 292 male brains, he calculated an average weight of 1,325 grams; 140 female brains averaged 1,144 grams for a difference of 181 grams, or 14 percent of the male weight. Broca understood, of course, that part of this difference could be attributed to the greater height of males. Yet he made no attempt to measure the effect of size alone and actually stated that it cannot account for the entire difference because we know, a priori, that women are not as intelligent as men (a premise that the data were supposed to test, not rest upon):

> We might ask if the small size of the female brain depends exclusively upon the small size of her body. Tiedemann has proposed this explanation. But we must not forget that women are, on the average, a little less intelligent than men, a difference which we should not exaggerate but which is, nonetheless, real. We are therefore permitted to suppose that the relatively small size of the female brain depends in part upon her physical inferiority and in part upon her intellectual inferiority.

In 1873, the year after Eliot published *Middlemarch,* Broca measured   5
the cranial capacities of prehistoric skulls from L'Homme Mort cave. Here he found a difference of only 99.5 cubic centimeters between males and females, while modern populations range from 129.5 to 220.7. Topinard, Broca's chief disciple, explained the increasing discrepancy through time as a result of differing evolutionary pressures upon dominant men and passive women:

> The man who fights for two or more in the struggle for existence, who has all the responsibility and the cares of tomorrow, who is constantly active in combating the environment and human rivals, needs more brain than the woman whom he must protect and nour-

ish, the sedentary woman, lacking any interior occupations, whose
role is to raise children, love, and be passive.

In 1879, Gustave Le Bon, chief misogynist of Broca's school, used
these data to publish what must be the most vicious attack upon women
in modern scientific literature (no one can top Aristotle). I do not claim
his views were representative of Broca's school, but they were published
in France's most respected anthropological journal. Le Bon concluded:

> In the most intelligent races, as among the Parisians, there are a large
> number of women whose brains are closer in size to those of gorillas
> than to the most developed male brains. This inferiority is so obvious
> that no one can contest it for a moment; only its degree is worth
> discussion. All psychologists who have studied the intelligence of
> women, as well as poets and novelists, recognize today that they
> represent the most inferior forms of human evolution and that they
> are closer to children and savages than to an adult, civilized man.
> They excel in fickleness, inconstancy, absence of thought and logic,
> and incapacity to reason. Without doubt there exist some distin-
> guished women, very superior to the average man, but they are as
> exceptional as the birth of any monstrosity, as, for example, of a
> gorilla with two heads; consequently, we may neglect them entirely.

Nor did Le Bon shrink from the social implications of his views. He
was horrified by the proposal of some American reformers to grant
women higher education on the same basis as men:

> A desire to give them the same education, and, as a consequence, to
> propose the same goals for them, is a dangerous chimera. . . . The
> day when, misunderstanding the inferior occupations which nature
> has given her, women leave the home and take part in our battles: on
> this day a social revolution will begin, and everything that maintains
> the sacred ties of the family will disappear.

Sound familiar?*

I have reexamined Broca's data, the basis for all this derivative pronouncement, and I find his numbers sound but his interpretation ill-
founded, to say the least. The data supporting his claim for increased
difference through time can be easily dismissed. Broca based his contention on the samples from L'Homme Mort alone — only seven male and six
female skulls in all. Never have so little data yielded such far ranging
conclusions.

In 1888, Topinard published Broca's more extensive data on the Parisian hospitals. Since Broca recorded height and age as well as brain size,

---

*When I wrote this essay, I assumed that Le Bon was a marginal, if colorful, figure. I
have since learned that he was a leading scientist, one of the founders of social psychology, and best known for a seminal study on crowd behavior, still cited today (*La
psychologie des foules,* 1895), and for his work on unconscious motivation.

we may use modern statistics to remove their effect. Brain weight decreases with age, and Broca's women were, on average, considerably older than his men. Brain weight increases with height, and his average man was almost half a foot taller than his average woman. I used multiple regression, a technique that allowed me to assess simultaneously the influence of height and age upon brain size. In an analysis of the data for women, I found that, at average male height and age, a woman's brain would weigh 1,212 grams. Correction for height and age reduces Broca's measured difference of 181 grams by more than a third, to 113 grams.

I don't know what to make of this remaining difference because I   10
cannot assess other factors known to influence brain size in a major way. Cause of death has an important effect: degenerative disease often entails a substantial diminution of brain size. (This effect is separate from the decrease attributed to age alone.) Eugene Schreider, also working with Broca's data, found that men killed in accidents had brains weighing, on average, 60 grams more than men dying of infectious diseases. The best modern data I can find (from American hospitals) records a full 100-gram difference between death by degenerative arteriosclerosis and by violence or accident. Since so many of Broca's subjects were elderly women, we may assume that lengthy degenerative disease was more common among them than among the men.

More importantly, modern students of brain size still have not agreed on a proper measure for eliminating the powerful effect of body size. Height is partly adequate, but men and women of the same height do not share the same body build. Weight is even worse than height, because most of its variation reflects nutrition rather than intrinsic size — fat versus skinny exerts little influence upon the brain. Manouvrier took up this subject in the 1880s and argued that muscular mass and force should be used. He tried to measure this elusive property in various ways and found a marked difference in favor of men, even in men and women of the same height. When he corrected for what he called "sexual mass," women actually came out slightly ahead in brain size.

Thus, the corrected 113-gram difference is surely too large; the true figure is probably close to zero and may as well favor women as men. And 113 grams, by the way, is exactly the average difference between a 5 foot 4 inch and a 6 foot 4 inch male in Broca's data. We would not (especially us short folks) want to ascribe greater intelligence to tall men. In short, who knows what to do with Broca's data? They certainly don't permit any confident claim that men have bigger brains than women.

To appreciate the social role of Broca and his school, we must recognize that his statements about the brains of women do not reflect an isolated prejudice toward a single disadvantaged group. They must be weighed in the context of a general theory that supported contemporary social distinctions as biologically ordained. Women, blacks, and poor people suffered the same disparagement, but women bore the brunt of Broca's argument because he had easier access to data on women's brains. Women were singularly denigrated but they also stood as surrogates for other disenfranchised groups. As one of Broca's disciples wrote in 1881: "Men of the black races have a brain scarcely heavier than that of white woman." This juxtaposition extended into many other realms of anthropological argument, particularly to claims that, anatomically and emotionally, both women and blacks were like white children — and that white children, by the theory of recapitulation, represented an ancestral (primitive) adult stage of human evolution. I do not regard as empty rhetoric the claim that women's battles are for all of us.

Maria Montessori did not confine her activities to educational reform for young children. She lectured on anthropology for several years at the University of Rome, and wrote an influential book entitled *Pedagogical Anthropology* (English edition, 1913). Montessori was no egalitarian. She supported most of Broca's work and the theory of innate criminality proposed by her compatriot Cesare Lombroso. She measured the circumferences of children's heads in her schools and inferred that the best prospects had bigger brains. But she had no use for Broca's conclusions about women. She discussed Manouvrier's work at length and made much of his tentative claim that women, after proper correction of the data, had slightly larger brains than men. Women, she concluded, were intellectually superior, but men had prevailed heretofore by dint of physical force. Since technology has abolished force as an instrument of power, the era of women may soon be upon us: "In such an epoch there will really be superior human beings, there will really be men strong in morality and in sentiment. Perhaps in this way the reign of women is approaching, when the enigma of her anthropological superiority will be deciphered. Woman was always the custodian of human sentiment, morality and honor."

This represents one possible antidote to "scientific" claims for the constitutional inferiority of certain groups. One may affirm the validity of biological distinctions but argue that the data have been misinterpreted by prejudiced men with a stake in the outcome, and that disadvantaged groups are truly superior. In recent years, Elaine Morgan has followed this strategy in her *Descent of Woman,* a speculative reconstruction of human prehistory from the woman's point of view — and as farcical as more famous tall tales by and for men. 15

I prefer another strategy. Montessori and Morgan followed Broca's philosophy to reach a more congenial conclusion. I would rather label the whole enterprise of setting a biological value upon groups for what it is: irrelevant and highly injurious. George Eliot well appreciated the special tragedy that biological labeling imposed upon members of disadvantaged groups. She expressed it for people like herself — women of extraordinary talent. I would apply it more widely — not only to those whose dreams are flouted but also to those who never realize that they may dream — but I cannot match her prose. In conclusion, then, the rest of Eliot's prelude to *Middlemarch*:

> The limits of variation are really much wider than anyone would imagine from the sameness of women's coiffure and the favorite love stories in prose and verse. Here and there a cygnet is reared uneasily among the ducklings in the brown pond, and never finds the living stream in fellowship with its own oary-footed kind. Here and there is born a Saint Theresa, foundress of nothing, whose loving heart-beats and sobs after an unattained goodness tremble off and are dispersed among hindrances instead of centering in some long-recognizable deed.

Questions for Discussion

1. Why do you think Mary Ann Evans chose to publish under a man's name? And why do you think Gould chose to open and close his article with references to one of her books?
2. When reporting the accomplishments of the French scientist Paul Broca, Gould declares that data were carefully collected and that the numbers are reliable. But he then observes, "Numbers, by themselves, specify nothing. All depends upon what you do with them." How was Broca misled by his numbers? What did he fail to take into account?
3. What does Gould mean when he supports the claim that "women's battles are for all of us"?
4. What is the significance of Gould's footnote?
5. This article includes several long quotations. Are they all necessary? Which had the most impact upon you?

Suggestions for Writing

1. Gould's essay demonstrates, among other things, how women have been victimized by false assumptions made by men. Write a report about discrimination against women in school, in sports, or in the workplace.
2. Do research on either George Eliot or Paul Broca and report, in your own words, upon what she or he accomplished. Be sure to reveal your sources, and try to consult at least one work written by the person you are investigating.

7

Writing to Explain Something

You just backed your new car into the trailer hitch on your uncle's truck, so you are going to have to talk to the insurance adjuster. Yesterday, you told your boss that you liked her new dress because it made her look thinner, and then you had to spend some time clearing up the misunderstanding. This morning, when you helped your neighbor install his new sound system, you had to put the directions into words he could understand. And right after that, your brother called to ask you how to set up a spreadsheet on the computer. Sounds as if you've had some explaining to do.

In other words, you've had to make people understand something outside of themselves. But each of these situations involves a different kind of explaining:

What it is — clarify your remark to your boss.
What it means — interpret the directions.
Why it is — justify your claim to the insurance company.
How it is done — show how to set up a spreadsheet.

Clarifying and *interpreting* involve telling what something is and what it means. *Justifying* involves giving reasons, that is, telling why; and *showing how* involves analyzing a process. Each of these kinds of explanation can be given independently or in combination with any of the others.

Suppose you are asked on a midterm exam in earth science to explain why there is a big desert between the Sierra Nevada and the Rockies. You may profit by considering the four kinds of explaining. You can *clarify* the question by describing what a desert is; for example, "A desert is a place where there is very little annual rainfall." Then you can *interpret* that statement by noting some of the implications: "Only a few very hardy plants that have adapted well to going without water can grow in deserts; and animals that require large supplies of water, like mammals, generally avoid deserts." You can *justify* — give reasons for — your interpretation: "All the rain falls on the western slope, and there is none left for the valley." And you can *show how* air collects moisture over the ocean and moves inland as clouds that rise over the coastal mountains and encounter cooler air, which causes the moisture to condense and fall as rain on the western slope.

THINKING ABOUT PURPOSE

When your intent is to clarify, you should describe what something is and distinguish it from other things that may be similar. When your intent is to interpret, you need to point out what words imply — or what a knowledgeable audience can infer from them. To do so, you may need to *paraphrase,* which means putting someone else's words into words of your own (usually words that can be more easily understood by your audience), or you may need to fill gaps where another writer has assumed knowledge that some readers do not possess. When your intent is to justify, you must give reasons or evidence that can help people understand why something happened. And when your intent is to show how, you need to describe how something happens or teach how something is done.

You will find examples of these strategies within the essays included in this chapter. Consider, for example, the first selection, Mona Melanson's "Beat the Butterflies." To teach readers how to do something — in this case, how to give a good interview when one is looking for a job — Melanson offers ten steps that can lead to the successful completion of this process. She begins her advice with a justification — why bother? — and presents each step that job candidates need to take to polish their interviewing skills and get over being nervous. Stressing the importance of thinking out strategies before actually appearing for the interview, Melanson presents activities for the job candidate to perform sequentially, seven of which should be completed before the interview begins. She has moved beyond providing information on job interviews (such as the length of the average interview or the number of interviews usually conducted when a new position is filled); she is teaching a process that readers should be able to employ. This element of deliberate instruction is one way in which writing to explain differs from writing to inform.

But these two motives are so closely related that it can be difficult, at times, to distinguish between them. Think of writing to explain simply as an extension of writing to inform. Explanations require the use of information for a purpose that goes beyond increasing the knowledge of readers. The discussion of writing to convey information in Chapter 6 is pertinent to explanation, however, and you may benefit from reviewing that chapter before you attempt to write to explain.

The principal difference between providing information and giving an explanation is that explanation assumes that information cannot speak for itself. When writing to inform, you may be content to present a profile c f someone without offering any explanation about why that person is the way he is — although the information provided might inspire readers to draw certain conclusions for themselves. Writing about that same individual when your motive is to explain, you have the responsibility to account for that person's nature. Or to compare two essays that offer a behind-the-scenes report, the article by Dennis Farney in Chapter 6 offers much information about Hallmark, but the author does not expect us to do anything specific with that information — such as buying fewer cards from Hallmark. The information might prove to be of use to some readers, but it exists simply because knowledge can be satisfying even when it does not have practical applications. In Jessica Mitford's article in this chapter, information on embalming is shaped into an explanation designed to make readers reject a process they might otherwise take for granted. Writing to explain can thus be defined as writing to inform with an element of writing to persuade within it: You are providing information that can change a reader's behavior, belief, or perception. That change is not insisted upon — as it is in writing to persuade — but it is suggested by the explanation.

In some cases the recommended change will be readily apparent: If readers follow Mona Melanson's advice on how to interview for a job, they will almost certainly change the way they approach interviews. In other cases the change may be only implied: By explaining the death of Benny Paret, Norman Cousins suggests the need for reforming professional boxing; and by explaining the nature and aim of fiction, Flannery O'Connor is attempting to change what readers expect of writers.

FINDING A SUBJECT

When looking for a subject, consider the courses you are taking. If you are enrolled in an American history course, you might explain what manifest destiny is or how the United States became involved in Vietnam. If you prefer to focus on scientific matters and you're enrolled in physics, you can explain how the "butterfly effect" works or what a "strange attractor" is in chaos theory. Perhaps neither social studies nor science interests you; try explaining how jazz originated or how to prepare a canvas for painting. For a literature course you might explain what the characteristics of an epic are, or you might analyze a sonnet so that its meaning is clear.

Notice that none of these suggestions seem to have a place for you to express how you feel about them. Explaining involves your mind rather than your heart—though it is often important to explain your emotions to others. And although a reader will almost always enjoy a well-written explanation, entertainment is not its primary motive. This does not mean, however, that explanation needs to be dry. Both Jessica Mitford and Flannery O'Connor incorporate humor into explanations, and both convey a strong voice that makes their explanations lively.

If your courses don't provide a sufficiently varied menu for you to discover something you think you can explain well, examine your extracurricular interests. Do you enjoy sports? If so, you might explain how to tack a sailboat, how to throw a curve ball, or how to lift weights. If you like to travel, you could explain how to get the best air fares or how to camp out in British Columbia. Think about something that has piqued your curiosity recently, such as why the paper in books gets yellow and falls apart as the books age. Whatever you enjoy or are vitally interested in will very likely offer many subjects that can be explained with care and enthusiasm. Sometimes called *process analysis,* essays of this sort take one of two forms. You can explain something by showing how it is done (as Jessica Mitford does when writing about embalming) or by teaching how to do it (as Mona Melanson does when writing about job interviews).

When you have selected your subject, you're ready to plan what you want to say about it. One useful way to prepare for writing an explanation is to make a list of what you already know about your subject. Analyze the subject quickly to see what its main divisions are, and then quickly list the subtopics that develop those main points. When you have a preliminary list, decide whether you already know enough or whether you need to do some research to be able to explain to a reader what it is and why it is important.

As soon as you have begun to get an idea of the size and complexity of your subject, start narrowing and focusing so that your writing will not be full of undeveloped generalizations. Find a small enough part of your subject to explain thoroughly in a relatively brief essay. You may find it easier to do this by thinking about the people who would be interested in reading your explanation (in addition to your classmates and your teacher). You may also wish to think about how these people happened to come across your essay: If it were to be published, what magazine might they have found it in? What do readers of that magazine usually expect to learn? Writing to explain is so closely linked to audience that it is artificial to talk about topics without thinking of readers.

Once you have identified a tentative topic, you should test your choice before proceeding. Ask yourself: "Will I be explaining something that my readers probably do not understand?" If the answer is yes, then you know that you are about to engage in meaningful communication. If you discover that the answer is no (as it would be, for example, if you set out to teach college students how to make a peanut butter and jelly sandwich), then look for another topic.

CONSIDERING YOUR AUDIENCE

When you are writing to explain, you must be exceptionally careful to consider the needs of your audience. You may have had the experience of trying to follow directions for making some computer software operate properly, only to discover that the person who wrote the manual assumed you would know more about computers than you do. A frequent error in such writing is to use *jargon* — specialized language that cannot be easily understood by readers who lack expertise in that field. Another common error is to omit an important step. Probably everyone has had the experience of trying to follow directions for putting together some object and finding the directions so complicated, so illogical, and so confusing that they are useless. But different kinds of readers need different kinds of help with information. When you get ready to write, make a realistic appraisal of who your readers are, what they know, and what they need to be told. Remember that when writing to explain, you are not simply providing information; you are making a conscious effort to help readers make sense of information that calls for clarification, interpretation, justification, or demonstration.

H. Paul Grice's four rules for conversation guide the handling of information so that clear communication can take place. They can also help writers decide what to tell and how to tell it when using information for explanation. Grice pointed out that the information in a conversation should observe the rules of quantity, quality, relevance, and manner.

To observe the rule of *quantity,* you need to give your readers enough information so that they can understand what you want them to know and so that there are no gaps to impede their understanding. An example may help clarify that point. If you arrive in Denton, Texas, and ask at a service station for directions to get to the senior high school, and the attendant says only, "Go downtown and make a sharp right," you will probably soon be lost. You need more information. But you don't need to be told the name of every street between the service station and the one you should turn onto, either. So the rule of quantity demands that your reader have enough information, but not too much. How much is enough depends to a great degree upon your reader and your purpose. Norman Cousins illustrates this principle nicely; he gives the reader only enough background information to understand the point he makes, and he assumes that the reader has little knowledge of prizefighting. A person who knew more about prizefighting would probably need more information to be convinced of Cousins's point. Or consider the selection by Jessica Mitford; it may give you more information about embalming than you want to know, but the volume of information that she provides is essential for her purpose.

The rule of *quality* dictates that you give correct, accurate information. If you are told to turn left and you should have turned right, you will not find your destination. Or if you are told to turn right at the third street rather than the second, you might not find your way as easily as if you went down the second street. The attendant correctly told you to turn right but inaccurately specified the third street. Writers occasionally find it necessary to adjust the degree of correctness and accuracy to accommodate the needs of readers. Suppose that you are driving a semitrailer when you ask directions to the senior high. Hadn't the attendant better notice that and give you directions to go down streets that don't have tree limbs hanging over them? This can be a tricky point to manage, but Pat Mora handles it deftly: She gives Gabriela enough information to understand the nature of writing, but she avoids references that would confuse a child. Writing on a similar topic for a more sophisticated audience, Flannery O'Connor makes allusions to writers and theologians that a child would not recognize.

The rule of *relevance* means that the information you get when you ask directions to the senior high school should tell you exactly how to get there, not something else, such as "Gee, that's a good school, but it's eight o'clock at night." Readers expect to find the information that you promise. In the attendant's response to the question for directions, the quality of the school and the hour are irrelevant. However, if the driver was wearing a tuxedo, the attendant might notice and volunteer directions to the gym where a dance was being held, which is on the opposite side of the campus from the visitors' parking. The hour is still irrelevant, but a man in a tuxedo might appreciate directions to the building where a dance was being held. Although writing about the nature and aim of fiction, Flannery O'Connor also comments upon writing classes because her original audience consisted of college students and teachers. For this audience her comments are relevant, but an audience of publishers would find them irrelevant.

Finally, the rule of *manner* means that accurate information should be offered clearly and confidently. For instance, you probably want to feel sure that the person who gives you directions really knows where your destination is, so you would be uncomfortable if that person fidgeted and hemmed and hawed and wouldn't look you in the eye while giving you directions. Similarly, if a child on foot were asking directions, someone responding to that request should adjust the relevance and manner of the information. Pat Mora begins her letter to Gabriela with friendly references to Gabriela's mother, mint chocolate chip ice cream, and "buying a new red sweater at the mall." References such as these are designed to put

Mora's original audience at ease. Or to take a different example, Mona Melanson doesn't risk alienating her audience by preaching; instead, she gives her suggestions in a friendly but nevertheless professional manner well suited for college students but not for children.

As you ponder what information to offer your readers and how to present it, you should also consider the proper quantity for those readers, how the characteristics of your readers might affect the quality and relevance of the information you give, and how you can suit the manner of your presentation not only to the material but also to your reader. If you think carefully about these things, your explanations will be clear and useful.

BEAT THE BUTTERFLIES

Mona Melanson

> *As you read the following article, which first appeared in the* Wall Street Journal, *consider how Mona Melanson goes beyond giving the sort of conventional advice most readers have already heard repeatedly: Dress neatly for interviews, and be sure to be on time. Note any suggestions that make sense to you, and ask yourself whether Melanson's explanation could help you get a job.*

Whether it's your first, 15th or 100th job interview, it's likely to be nerves city — and with good reason. A drop-dead resume and sparkling cover letter are great preliminaries, but meeting face-to-face puts you on the spot, live and in living color. Like it or not, that's usually what makes or breaks your candidacy.

Vying for that all-important first job generally means competing in two different events: the 20-minute "tell-me-about-yourself" on-campus sprint, and the marathon on-site interview, often involving three or more company representatives.

In either case, the following 10-step process should help you fine-tune your interviewing style. Thorough preparation won't guarantee job offers, but it will help you beat the butterflies. And in job interviews, poise is the name of the game.

ON YOUR MARK, GET SET

Step 1: Ask yourself how well you fit the job for which you're interviewing. You're going to be grilled about your skills, education, motivation, accomplishments, strengths and weaknesses. Beneath these formalities is the interviewer's basic question: "Why should I hire you for this job?"

To keep your answers on target, take the time beforehand to create a   5
"match-up" list. On a sheet of paper, label one column "Job Qualifications Specified." Beside it, create several other columns with headings such as "Education and Training," "Extracurricular Activities," "Summer/Part-time Jobs" and "Volunteer/Community Service."

Gather data from as many sources as possible to fill each column. Specific job requirements are best explored via past graduates who work for the company. Your placement office staff should be able to provide names. In addition, some companies provide recruiting materials that detail entry-level jobs.

Under the other headings, jot down items gleaned from your teachers' evaluations of projects, term papers or exams. If you've had summer or part-time work, summarize positive comments from your bosses, co-workers, customers or clients. Above all, emphasize extracurriculars that demonstrate interpersonal, communication, organizational, technical, sales or leadership skills. Not all learning takes place in the classroom.

Step 2: Select the items from each column that most closely match the job requirements. List these on a separate sheet of paper, leaving enough room to expound on your contributions or accomplishments.

Whenever possible, express your results in terms that can be measured: dollars, percentages, ratios or hours saved. Examples: "I was part of a group of six volunteers who worked nights and weekends for four months to raise $25,000 for the homeless shelter" or "I worked as a summer temporary file clerk along with two others. We prepared more than 1,000 files for storage in five weeks. Our manager told us that our efforts led to a 20% increase in the department's productivity before the end of the summer."

Step 3: Review these selected accomplishments and pick three to five   *10* that fit the job and the company. These are the items you want to highlight in interviews. Beware of the parrot syndrome, however. Over-rehearsing can lead to a presentation that's too slick or stilted.

"Don't try to anticipate and memorize your responses to all the questions you think you might be asked in an interview," says Addie Johnson, manager of college relations at Bank of America. "Qualifying for a job is not like trying out for a part in a movie. Be yourself and answer each question in your own natural style."

Step 4: Based on your research, draft a half dozen or so questions to ask the interviewer. You need to know if the job meets your criteria and if the company will be a suitable place to start your career. The interview should be a two-way exchange of information.

Student job seekers often fail to ask about the unit's or department's objectives. Questions to consider: What are the department's goals for this year? What progress is the group making toward these goals? If hired, how would my work contribute to achieving these goals? Such questions show a level of interest that recruiters like to see.

Other areas to explore include the working environment, amount of customer contact, cross-training opportunities, work schedules (is flextime available?) and prospects for advancement. A topic to avoid: benefits.

"It's natural for job applicants to want to know 'What's in this job   *15* for me?'" says Ms. Johnson. She recommends asking for "written information about benefits at the close of the interview rather than in the main part of the meeting."

Step 5: Stage a number of "dress rehearsals" with someone else—a roommate, a friend, a teacher or a staff person in your school's placement office. Give your mock-interviewer a list of questions you think you'll be asked and request that she add some of the toughest ones she's faced.

As you respond, practice weaving into the conversation your main selling points (see step 3 above). Cover each area as appropriate: how your college course work qualifies you to do the job; the relevance of your outside activities or work experience; why you want this type of work.

This is an excellent time to hone your listening skills. Wait for the mock-interviewer to finish each question or statement before you speak; fight the tendency to shoot off the first idea that pops into your mind.

After each trial run, have your partner critique the quality and delivery of your answers: Did you go off on tangents, or were you unnecessarily terse? Did you say "uh-huh" or "y'know," use slang or malaprops? Did you speak so softly that she had trouble hearing you — or so loudly that you were almost shouting? How much confidence did you project?

Body language is equally critical. A firm handshake is appropriate *20* at the beginning and end of the meeting. Make eye contact, but don't overdo it. You don't have to stare at the interviewer the whole time.

T-MINUS 24 HOURS . . .

Step 6: On the day before a scheduled interview, select neat, comfortable clothes that look businesslike and won't distract the interviewer. Plan to look your best.

Don't underestimate the value of getting a good night's sleep. This isn't the time to pull an all-night interview cram session. Being well rested keeps you alert and enthusiastic; you'll listen better and feel more confident about your answers.

Step 7: D-day. Make sure you arrive early. While waiting for your appointment, do what some athletes do as part of their warm-up routine. Visualize the first few moments of greeting the interviewer. Relax and take a few deep breaths, then create a scene in which you are listening, smiling and answering the questions with ease. Review the key company- and job-specific points you want to bring out.

Step 8: Once the interview has begun, take time to listen to every question and to think carefully about your answer. As noted above, interviewers complain that many college applicants answer questions incorrectly or incompletely simply because they don't hear what's really being asked.

A tip: "Rephrase part of each question you're asked as part of the *25* beginning of the answer you give," suggests Ms. Johnson. "This technique also gives you more time to formulate your responses."

Be straightforward in talking about your strengths and weaknesses. If you're good at something, don't be afraid to say so. Statements such as "I've been told by my professors that I express myself well in writing" or "One of my strengths in using spreadsheet software is accuracy, even under tight deadlines" are appropriate. By the same token, avoid self-putdowns.

PARTING THOUGHTS

Step 9: At the close of the meeting, thank the interviewer for the opportunity to discuss your qualifications. Before you shake hands, it's fully acceptable to ask something like, "When may I expect to hear from you about your decision?"

Step 10: Immediately after the interview, write two notes. The first is a thank-you/follow-up note to the interviewer, reinforcing the reasons why you feel you could perform well on that job. As a courtesy, again express your appreciation for being asked to interview.

The second note is to yourself. While the experience is fresh in your mind, evaluate how you handled the interview. Write down the interviewers' questions and your responses. Reviewing these comments and impressions will help refine your skills for your next interview.

Questions for Discussion

1. Melanson describes the first job as "all-important." Do you agree with her, or do you think she is putting too much emphasis upon the first job?
2. Why is it important for job seekers to ask questions of interviewers?
3. Did you learn any tips from this essay that you had not already heard elsewhere?
4. Does Melanson guarantee that her system will produce good results?
5. Consider the sequence of steps in this article. Are they arranged in a sensible pattern? Was it necessary to label them as steps?

Suggestions for Writing

1. Interview a personnel officer and report his or her views of what makes a job candidate seem attractive and what is likely to lead to elimination from further consideration.
2. Check with the Placement Office at your school and prepare a report on which majors seem to enjoy the highest rate of job placement and which the lowest.

SHOUTING "FIRE!"

Alan M. Dershowitz

> *Americans have often been told that freedom of speech doesn't mean being able to shout "Fire!" in a crowded theater. But where does that expression come from, and what exactly does it mean? As you read this essay, notice how Alan Dershowitz, a professor of law at Harvard University, clarifies and interprets a common expression by locating it within an historical context. Note that according to Oliver Wendell Holmes, "the character of every act depends upon the circumstances in which it is done." Consider how Dershowitz himself uses the interrelationship of act and scene when making his explanation.*

When the Reverend Jerry Falwell learned that the Supreme Court had reversed his $200,000 judgment against *Hustler* magazine for the emotional distress that he had suffered from an outrageous parody, his response was typical of those who seek to censor speech: "Just as no person may scream 'Fire!' in a crowded theater when there is no fire, and find cover under the First Amendment, likewise, no sleazy merchant like Larry Flynt should be able to use the First Amendment as an excuse for maliciously and dishonestly attacking public figures, as he has so often done."

Justice Oliver Wendell Holmes's classic example of unprotected speech — falsely shouting "Fire!" in a crowded theater — has been invoked so often, by so many people, in such diverse contexts, that it has become part of our national folk language. It has even appeared — most appropriately — in the theater: in Tom Stoppard's play *Rosencrantz and Guildenstern Are Dead* a character shouts at the audience, "Fire!" He then quickly explains: "It's all right — I'm demonstrating the misuse of free speech." Shouting "Fire!" in the theater may well be the only jurisprudential analogy that has assumed the status of a folk argument. A prominent historian recently characterized it as "the most brilliantly persuasive expression that ever came from Holmes's pen." But in spite of its hallowed position in both the jurisprudence of the First Amendment and the arsenal of political discourse, it is and was an inapt analogy, even in the context in which it was originally offered. It has lately become — despite, perhaps even because of, the frequency and promiscuousness of its invocation — little more than a caricature of logical argumentation.

The case that gave rise to the "Fire!"-in-a-crowded-theater analogy — *Schenck* v. *United States* — involved the prosecution of Charles Schenck, who was the general secretary of the Socialist Party in Philadelphia, and Elizabeth Baer, who was its recording secretary. In 1917 a jury found Schenck and Baer guilty of attempting to cause insubordination among soldiers who had been drafted to fight in the First World War. They and other party members had circulated leaflets urging draftees not to "submit to intimidation" by fighting in a war being conducted on behalf of "Wall Street's chosen few." Schenck admitted, and the Court found, that the intent of the pamphlets' "impassioned language" was to "influence" draftees to resist the draft. Interestingly, however, Justice Holmes noted that nothing in the pamphlet suggested that the draftees should use unlawful or violent means to oppose conscription: "In form at least [the pamphlet] confined itself to peaceful measures, such as a petition for the repeal of the act" and an exhortation to exercise "your right to assert your opposition to the draft." Many of its most impassioned words were quoted directly from the Constitution.

Justice Holmes acknowledged that "in many places and in ordinary times the defendants, in saying all that was said in the circular, would have been within their constitutional rights." "But," he added, "the character of every act depends upon the circumstances in which it is done." And to illustrate that truism he went on to say,

> The most stringent protection of free speech would not protect a man in falsely shouting fire in a theater, and causing a panic. It does not even protect a man from an injunction against uttering words that may have all the effect of force.

Justice Holmes then upheld the convictions in the context of a war-time draft, holding that the pamphlet created "a clear and present danger" of hindering the war effort while our soldiers were fighting for their lives and our liberty.   5

The example of shouting "Fire!" obviously bore little relationship to the facts of the Schenck case. The Schenck pamphlet contained a substantive political message. It urged its draftee readers to *think* about the message and then—if they so chose—to act on it in a lawful and nonviolent way. The man who shouts "Fire!" in a crowded theater is neither sending a political message nor inviting his listener to think about what he has said and decide what to do in a rational, calculated manner. On the contrary, the message is designed to force action *without* contemplation. The message "Fire!" is directed not to the mind and the conscience of the listener but, rather, to his adrenaline and his feet. It is a stimulus to immediate *action,* not thoughtful reflection. It is—as Justice Holmes recognized in his follow-up sentence—the functional equivalent of "uttering words that may have all the effect of force."

Indeed, in that respect the shout of "Fire!" is not even speech, in any meaningful sense of that term. It is a *clang* sound—the equivalent of setting off a nonverbal alarm. Had Justice Holmes been more honest about his example, he would have said that freedom of speech does not protect a kid who pulls a fire alarm in the absence of a fire. But that obviously would have been irrelevant to the case at hand. The proposition that pulling an alarm is not protected speech certainly leads to the conclusion that shouting the word *fire* is also not protected. But the core analogy is the nonverbal alarm, and the derivative example is the verbal shout. By cleverly substituting the derivative shout for the core alarm, Holmes made it possible to analogize one set of words to another — as he could not have done if he had begun with the self-evident proposition that setting off an alarm bell is not free speech.

The analogy is thus not only inapt but also insulting. Most Americans do not respond to political rhetoric with the same kind of automatic acceptance expected of schoolchildren responding to a fire drill. Not a single recipient of the Schenck pamphlet is known to have changed his mind after reading it. Indeed, one draftee, who appeared as a prosecution witness, was asked whether reading a pamphlet asserting that the draft law was unjust would make him "immediately decide that you must erase the law." Not surprisingly, he replied, "I do my own thinking." A theatergoer would probably not respond similarly if asked how he would react to a shout of "Fire!"

Another important reason why the analogy is inapt is that Holmes emphasizes the factual falsity of the shout "Fire!" The Schenck pamphlet, however, was not factually false. It contained political opinions and ideas about the causes of the war and about appropriate and lawful responses to the draft. As the Supreme Court recently reaffirmed (in *Fallwell* v. *Hustler*), "The First Amendment recognizes no such thing as a 'false' idea." Nor does it recognize false opinions about the causes of or cures for war.

A closer analogy to the facts of the Schenck case might have been provided by a person's standing outside a theater, offering the patrons a leaflet advising them that in his opinion the theater was structurally unsafe, and urging them not to enter but to complain to the building inspectors. That analogy, however, would not have served Holmes's argument for punishing Schenck. Holmes needed an analogy that would appear relevant to Schenck's political speech but that would invite the conclusion that censorship was appropriate. 10

Unsurprisingly, a war-weary nation — in the throes of a know-nothing hysteria over immigrant anarchists and socialists — welcomed the comparison between what was regarded as a seditious political pamphlet and a malicious shout of "Fire!" Ironically, the "Fire!" analogy is nearly all that survives from the Schenck case; the ruling itself is almost certainly not good law. Pamphlets of the kind that resulted in Schenck's imprisonment have been circulated with impunity during subsequent wars.

Over the past several years I have assembled a collection of instances — cases, speeches, arguments — in which proponents of censorship have maintained that the expression at issue is "just like" or "equivalent to" falsely shouting "Fire!" in a crowded theater and ought to be banned, "just as" shouting "Fire!" ought to be banned. The analogy is generally invoked, often with self-satisfaction, as an absolute argument-stopper. It does, after all, claim the high authority of the great Justice Oliver Wendell Holmes. I have rarely heard it invoked in a convincing, or even particularly relevant, way. But that, too, can claim lineage from the great Holmes.

Not unlike Falwell, with his silly comparison between shouting "Fire!" and publishing an offensive parody, courts and commentators have frequently invoked "Fire!" as an analogy to expression that is not an automatic stimulus to panic. A state supreme court held that "Holmes's aphorism . . . applies with equal force to pornography" — in particular to the exhibition of the movie *Carmen Baby* in a drive-in theater in close proximity to highways and homes. Another court analogized "picketing . . . in support of a secondary boycott" to shouting "Fire!" because in both instances "speech and conduct are brigaded." In the famous Skokie case one of the judges argued that allowing Nazis to march through a city where a large number of Holocaust survivors live "just might fall into the same category as one's 'right' to cry fire in a crowded theater."

Outside court the analogies become even more badly stretched. A spokesperson for the New Jersey Sports and Exposition Authority complained that newspaper reports to the effect that a large number of football players had contracted cancer after playing in the Meadowlands — a stadium atop a landfill — were the "journalistic equivalent of shouting fire in a crowded theater." An insect researcher acknowledged that his prediction that a certain amusement park might become roach-infested "may be tantamount to shouting fire in a crowded theater." The philosopher Sidney Hook, in a letter to *The New York Times* bemoaning a Supreme Court decision that required a plaintiff in a defamation action to prove that the offending statement was actually false, argued that the First Amendment does not give the press carte blanche to accuse innocent persons "any more than the First Amendment protects the right of someone falsely to shout fire in a crowded theater."

Some close analogies to shouting "Fire!" or setting off an alarm are, [15] of course, available: calling in a false bomb threat; dialing 911 and falsely describing an emergency; making a loud, gunlike sound in the presence of the President; setting off a voice-activated sprinkler system by falsely shouting "Fire!" In one case in which the "Fire!" analogy was directly to the point, a creative defendant tried to get around it. The case involved a man who calmly advised an airline clerk that he was "only here to hijack the plane." He was charged, in effect, with shouting "Fire!" in a crowded theater, and his rejected defense — as quoted by the court — was as follows: "If we built fire-proof theaters and let people know about this, then the shouting of 'Fire!' would not cause panic."

Here are some more-distant but still related examples: the recent incident of the police slaying in which some members of an onlooking crowd urged a mentally ill vagrant who had taken an officer's gun to shoot the officer; the screaming of racial epithets during a tense confrontation; shouting down a speaker and preventing him from continuing his speech.

Analogies are, by their nature, matters of degree. Some are closer to the core example than others. But any attempt to analogize political ideas in a pamphlet, ugly parody in a magazine, offensive movies in a theater, controversial newspaper articles, or any of the other expressions and actions catalogued above to the very different act of shouting "Fire!" in a crowded theater is either self-deceptive or self-serving.

The government does, of course, have some arguably legitimate bases for suppressing speech which bear no relationship to shouting "Fire!" It may ban the publication of nuclear-weapon codes, of information about troop movements, and of the identity of undercover agents. It may criminalize extortion threats and conspiratorial agreements. These expressions may lead directly to serious harm, but the mechanisms of causation are very different from that at work when an alarm is sounded. One may also argue — less persuasively, in my view — against protecting certain forms of public obscenity and defamatory statements. Here, too, the mechanisms of causation are very different. None of these exceptions to the First Amendment's exhortation that the government "shall make no law . . . abridging the freedom of speech, or of the press" is anything like falsely shouting "Fire!" in a crowded theater; they all must be justified on other grounds.

A comedian once told his audience, during a stand-up routine, about the time he was standing around a fire with a crowd of people and got in trouble for yelling "Theater, theater!" That, I think, is about as clever and productive a use as anyone has ever made of Holmes's flawed analogy.

Questions for Discussion

1. What was the political context that led Oliver Wendell Holmes to make his famous remark about shouting fire in a crowded theater?
2. Why does Dershowitz believe that the fire analogy was inappropriate for the Schenck case? Why does he conclude that it was "not only inapt but also insulting"?
3. How important is the word *falsely* in the quotation from Holmes in paragraph 4? Would Holmes approve of calling "Fire" when there is a fire? How would he respond to someone who calls "Fire" out of a sincere but mistaken belief that there is a fire?
4. According to Dershowitz, what types of speech might the government have legitimate reason to suppress?
5. How convincing is the alternative analogy offered by Dershowitz in paragraph 10?
6. What evidence does Dershowitz offer to support his claim that the Holmes ruling "is almost certainly not good law"?

Suggestions for Writing

1. Take a commonly used expression (such as "You can't teach an old dog new tricks," or "Don't throw the baby out with the bath water") and explain what it means. Try to define circumstances for which the expression would be both appropriate and inappropriate.

2. Research a Supreme Court decision involving censorship, abortion, gun control, or capital punishment. Then explain why the Court reached its decision and what the implications of that decision are for the future.

WHO KILLED BENNY PARET?

Norman Cousins

> *The following essay is one of the many columns Norman Cousins wrote when he was editor of the* Saturday Review. *It was inspired by the 1963 death of a boxer named Benny Paret. Cousins explains that there is more to Paret's death than simply the blow that killed him; he explains the reasons behind the event. As you read this essay, notice how Cousins distinguishes the immediate cause from a number of underlying causes. Notice also the detail Cousins uses to convey the immediacy of the fight scene, and consider what that detail accomplishes. How is it related to Cousins's purpose?*

Sometime about 1935 or 1936 I had an interview with Mike Jacobs, the prize-fight promoter. I was a fledgling reporter at that time; my beat was education but during the vacation season I found myself on varied assignments, all the way from ship news to sports reporting. In this way I found myself sitting opposite the most powerful figure in the boxing world.

There was nothing spectacular in Mr. Jacobs' manner or appearance; but when he spoke about prize fights, he was no longer a bland little man but a colossus who sounded the way Napoleon must have sounded when he reviewed a battle. You knew you were listening to Number One. His saying something made it true.

We discussed what to him was the only important element in successful promoting — how to please the crowd. So far as he was concerned, there was no mystery to it. You put killers in the ring and the people filled your arena. You hire boxing artists — men who are adroit at feinting, parrying, weaving, jabbing, and dancing, but who don't pack dynamite in their fists — and you wind up counting your empty seats. So you searched for the killers and sluggers and maulers — fellows who could hit with the force of a baseball bat.

I asked Mr. Jacobs if he was speaking literally when he said people came out to see the killer.

"They don't come out to see a tea party," he said evenly. "They come out to see the knockout. They come out to see a man hurt. If they think anything else, they're kidding themselves." 5

Recently, a young man by the name of Benny Paret was killed in the ring. The killing was seen by millions; it was on television. In the twelfth round, he was hit hard in the head several times, went down, was counted out, and never came out of the coma.

The Paret fight produced a flurry of investigations. Governor Rockefeller was shocked by what happened and appointed a committee to assess the responsibility. The New York State Boxing Commission decided to find out what was wrong. The District Attorney's office expressed its concern. One question that was solemnly studied in all three probes concerned the action of the referee. Did he act in time to stop the fight? Another question had to do with the role of the examining doctors who certified the physical fitness of the fighters before the bout. Still another question involved Mr. Paret's manager; did he rush his boy into the fight without adequate time to recuperate from the previous one?

In short, the investigators looked into every possible cause except the real one. Benny Paret was killed because the human fist delivers enough impact, when directed against the head, to produce a massive hemorrhage in the brain. The human brain is the most delicate and complex mechanism in all creation. It has a lacework of millions of highly fragile nerve connections. Nature attempts to protect this exquisitely intricate machinery by encasing it in a hard shell. Fortunately, the shell is thick enough to withstand a great deal of pounding. Nature, however, can protect man against everything except man himself. Not every blow to the head will kill a man — but there is always the risk of concussion and damage to the brain. A prize fighter may be able to survive even repeated brain concussions and go on fighting, but the damage to his brain may be permanent.

In any event, it is futile to investigate the referee's role and seek to determine whether he should have intervened to stop the fight earlier. That is not where the primary responsibility lies. The primary responsibility lies with the people who pay to see a man hurt. The referee who stops a fight too soon from the crowd's viewpoint can expect to be booed. The crowd wants the knockout; it wants to see a man stretched out on the canvas. This is the supreme moment in boxing. It is nonsense to talk about prize fighting as a test of boxing skills. No crowd was ever brought to its feet screaming and cheering at the sight of two men beautifully dodging and weaving out of each other's jabs. The time the crowd comes alive is when a man is hit hard over the heart or the head, when mouthpiece flies out, when the blood squirts out of his nose or eyes, when he wobbles under the attack and his pursuer continues to smash at him with pole-axe impact.

Don't blame it on the referee. Don't even blame it on the fight   *10* managers. Put the blame where it belongs — on the prevailing mores that regard prize fighting as a perfectly proper enterprise and vehicle of entertainment. No one doubts that many people enjoy prize fighting and will miss it if it should be thrown out. And that is precisely the point.

Questions for Discussion

1. Why does Cousins begin this essay with five paragraphs narrating a conversation he had almost thirty years before the death of the fighter that motivated him to write? What does Mike Jacobs contribute to the essay that follows? And why does Cousins make a point of revealing that the conversation had taken place many years earlier?

2. How successful is the transition between paragraphs 5 and 6?
3. What causes contributed to the death of Benny Paret? What does Cousins believe to have been the real cause?
4. Consider the last sentence in paragraph 9. Why does Cousins include so many details within a single sentence? How has Cousins constructed the sentence to make it read smoothly despite its length?
5. What is Cousins's purpose in explaining the death of Benny Paret? Does this explanation imply an argument?
6. Has boxing changed since 1963, when this essay was first published? Or do you think it is still possible for a fighter to die in the ring?

Suggestions for Writing

1. Are athletes abused in other sports? If so, explain the problem that concerns you and describe its effects.
2. People often complain that there is too much violence on television, but violence (like sex) always seems to draw a large number of viewers. Write an essay explaining why people enjoy watching violence.

EMBALMING IN THE U.S.A.

Jessica Mitford

> *The child of an upper-class English family, Jessica Mitford settled in the United States and studied American customs with a critical eye. The following selection is an excerpt from the best known of her works,* The American Way of Death *(1963). Consider how Mitford clarifies embalming by comparing it to other procedures with which readers are likely to be more familiar. Consider why Mitford goes into so much detail, and note how these details make you feel.*

Embalming is indeed a most extraordinary procedure, and one must wonder at the docility of Americans who each year pay hundreds of millions of dollars for its perpetuation, blissfully ignorant of what it is all about, what is done, how it is done. Not one in ten thousand has any idea of what actually takes place. Books on the subject are extremely hard to come by. They are not to be found in most libraries or bookshops.

In an era when huge television audiences watch surgical operations in the comfort of their living rooms, when, thanks to the animated cartoon, the geography of the digestive system has become familiar territory even to the nursery school set, in a land where the satisfaction of curiosity about almost all matters is a national pastime, the secrecy surrounding embalming can, surely, hardly be attributed to the inherent gruesomeness of the subject. Custom in this regard has within this century suffered a complete reversal. In the early days of American embalming, when it was performed in the home of the deceased, it was almost mandatory for some relative to stay by the embalmer's side and witness the procedure. Today, family members who might wish to be in attendance would certainly be dissuaded by the funeral director. All others, except apprentices, are excluded by law from the preparation room.

A close look at what does actually take place may explain in large measure the undertaker's intractable reticence concerning a procedure that has become his major *raison d'être*. Is it possible he fears that public information about embalming might lead patrons to wonder if they really want this service? If the funeral men are loath to discuss the subject outside the trade, the reader may, understandably, be equally loath to go on reading at this point. For those who have the stomach for it, let us part the formaldehyde curtain. . . .

The body is first laid out in the undertaker's morgue — or rather, Mr. Jones is reposing in the preparation room — to be readied to bid the world farewell.

The preparation room in any of the better funeral establishments has the tiled and sterile look of a surgery, and indeed the embalmer-restorative   5 artist who does his chores there is beginning to adopt the term "derma-surgeon" (appropriately corrupted by some mortician-writers as "demi-surgeon") to describe his calling. His equipment, consisting of scalpels, scissors, augers, forceps, clamps, needles, pumps, tubes, bowls and basins, is crudely imitative of the surgeon's as is his technique, acquired in a nine- or twelve-month post-high-school course in an embalming school. He is supplied by an advanced chemical industry with a bewildering array of fluids, sprays, pastes, oils, powders, creams, to fix or soften tissue, shrink or distend it as needed, dry it here, restore the moisture there. There are cosmetics, waxes and paints to fill and cover features, even plaster of Paris to replace entire limbs. There are ingenious aids to prop and stabilize the cadaver: a Vari-Pose Head Rest, the Edwards Arm and Hand Positioner, the Repose Block (to support the shoulders during the embalming), and the Throop Foot Positioner, which resembles an old-fashioned stocks.

Mr. John H. Eckels, president of the Eckels College of Mortuary Science, thus describes the first part of the embalming procedure: "In the hands of a skilled practitioner, this work may be done in a comparatively short time and without mutilating the body other than by slight incision — so slight that it scarcely would cause serious inconvenience if made upon a living person. It is necessary to remove all the blood, and doing this not only helps in the disinfecting, but removes the principal cause of disfigurements due to discoloration."

Another textbook discusses the all-important time element: "The earlier this is done, the better, for every hour that elapses between death and embalming will add to the problems and complications encountered. . . ." Just how soon should one get going on the embalming? The author tells us, "On the basis of such scanty information made available to this profession through its rudimentary and haphazard system of technical research, we must conclude that the best results are to be obtained if the subject is embalmed before life is completely extinct — that is, before cellular death has occurred. In the average case, this would mean within an hour after somatic death." For those who feel that there is something a little rudimentary, not to say haphazard, about this advice, a comforting thought is offered by another writer. Speaking of fears entertained in early days of premature burial, he points out, "One of the effects of embalming by chemical injection, however, has been to dispel fears of live burial." How true; once the blood is removed, chances of live burial are indeed remote.

To return to Mr. Jones, the blood is drained out through the veins and replaced by embalming fluid pumped in through the arteries. As noted in *The Principles and Practices of Embalming,* "every operator has a favorite injection and drainage point — a fact which becomes a handicap only if he fails or refuses to forsake his favorites when conditions demand it." Typical favorites are the carotid artery, femoral artery, jugular vein, subclavian vein. There are various choices of embalming fluid. If Flextone is used, it will produce a "mild, flexible rigidity. The skin retains a velvety softness, the tissues are rubbery and pliable. Ideal for women and children." It may be blended with B. and G. Products Company's Lyf-Lyk tint, which is guaranteed to reproduce "nature's own skin texture . . . the velvety appearance of living tissue." Suntone comes in three separate tints: Suntan; Special Cosmetic Tint, a pink shade "especially indicated for young female subjects"; and Regular Cosmetic Tint, moderately pink.

About three to six gallons of a dyed and perfumed solution of formaldehyde, glycerin, borax, phenol, alcohol and water is soon circulating through Mr. Jones, whose mouth has been sewn together with a "needle directed upward between the upper lip and gum and brought out through the left nostril," with the corners raised slightly "for a more pleasant expression." If he should be bucktoothed, his teeth are cleaned with Bon Ami and coated with colorless nail polish. His eyes, meanwhile, are closed with flesh-tinted eye caps and eye cement.

The next step is to have at Mr. Jones with a thing called a trocar. This 10 is a long, hollow needle attached to a tube. It is jabbed into the abdomen, poked around the entrails and chest cavity, the contents of which are pumped out and replaced with "cavity fluid." This is done, and the hole in the abdomen sewed up, Mr. Jones's face is heavily creamed (to protect the skin from burns which may be caused by leakage of the chemicals), and he is covered with a sheet and left unmolested for a while. But not for long — there is more, much more, in store for him. He has been embalmed, but not yet restored, and the best time to start restorative work is eight to ten hours after embalming, when the tissues have become firm and dry.

The object of all this attention to the corpse, it must be remembered, is to make it presentable for viewing in an attitude of healthy repose. "Our customs require the presentation of our dead in the semblance of normality . . . unmarred by the ravages of illness, disease or mutilation," says Mr. J. Sheridan Mayer in his *Restorative Art*. This is rather a large order since few people die in the full bloom of health, unravaged by illness and unmarked by some disfigurement. The funeral industry is equal to the challenge: "In some cases the gruesome appearance of a mutilated or disease-ridden subject may be quite discouraging. The task of restoration may seem impossible and shake the confidence of the embalmer. This is the time for intestinal fortitude and determination. Once the formative work is begun and affected tissues are cleaned or removed, all doubts of success vanish. It is surprising and gratifying to discover the results which may be obtained."

The embalmer, having allowed an appropriate interval to elapse, returns to the attack, but now he brings into play the skill and equipment of sculptor and cosmetician. Is a hand missing? Casting one in plaster of Paris is a simple matter. "For replacement purposes, only a cast of the back of the hand is necessary; this is within the ability of the average operator and is quite adequate." If a lip or two, a nose or an ear should be missing, the embalmer has at hand a variety of restorative waxes with which to model replacements. Pores and skin texture are simulated by stippling with a little brush, and over this cosmetics are laid on. Head off? Decapitation cases are rather routinely handled. Ragged edges are trimmed, and head joined to torso with a series of splints, wires and sutures. It is a good idea to have a little something at the neck — a scarf or high collar — when time for viewing comes. Swollen mouth? Cut out tissue as needed from inside the lips. If too much is removed, the surface contour can easily be restored by padding with cotton. Swollen necks and cheeks are reduced by removing tissue through vertical incisions made down each side of the neck. "When the deceased is casketed, the pillow will hide the suture incisions . . . as an extra precaution against leakage, the suture may be painted with liquid sealer."

The opposite condition is more likely to be present itself — that of emaciation. His hypodermic syringe now loaded with massage cream, the embalmer seeks out and fills the hollowed and sunken areas by injection. In this procedure the backs of the hands and fingers and the under-chin area should not be neglected.

Positioning the lips is a problem that recurrently challenges the ingenuity of the embalmer. Closed too tightly, they tend to give a stern, even disapproving expression. Ideally, embalmers feel, the lips should give the impression of being ever so slightly parted, the upper lip protruding slightly for a more youthful appearance. This takes some engineering, however, as the lips tend to drift apart. Lip drift can sometimes be remedied by pushing one or two straight pins through the inner margin of the lower lip and then inserting them between the two front upper teeth. If Mr. Jones happens to have no teeth, the pins can just as easily be anchored in his Armstrong Face Former and Denture Replacer. Another method to maintain lip closure is to dislocate the lower jaw, which is then held in its new position by a wire run through holes which have been drilled through the upper jaws at the midline. As the French are fond of saying, *il faut souffrir pour être belle.*

If Mr. Jones has died of jaundice, then the embalming fluid will very 15 likely turn him green. Does this deter the embalmer? Not if he has intestinal fortitude. Masking pastes and cosmetics are heavily laid on, burial garments and casket interiors are color-correlated with particular care, and Jones is displayed beneath rose-colored lights. Friends will say, "How *well* he looks." Death by carbon monoxide, on the other hand, can be rather a good thing from the embalmer's viewpoint: "One advantage is the fact that this type of discoloration is an exaggerated form of a natural pink coloration." This is nice because the healthy glow is already present and needs but little attention.

The patching and filling completed, Mr. Jones is now shaved, washed and dressed. Cream-based cosmetic, available in pink, flesh, suntan, brunette and blonde, is applied to his hands and face, his hair is shampooed and combed (and, in the case of Mrs. Jones, set), his hands manicured. For the horny-handed son of toil special care must be taken; cream should be applied to remove ingrained grime, and the nails cleaned. "If he were not in the habit of having them manicured in life, trimming and shaping is advised for better appearance — never questioned by kin."

Jones is now ready for casketing (this is the present participle of the verb "to casket"). In this operation his right shoulder should be depressed slightly "to turn the body a bit to the right and soften the appearance of lying flat on the back." Positioning the hands is a matter of importance, and special rubber positioning blocks may be used. The hands should be cupped slightly for a more lifelike, relaxed appearance. Proper placement of the body requires a delicate sense of balance. It should lie as high as possible in the casket, yet not so high that the lid, when lowered, will hit the nose. On the other hand, we are cautioned, placing the body too low "creates the impression that the body is in a box."

Jones is next wheeled into the appointed slumber room where a few last touches may be added — his favorite pipe placed in his hand or, if he was a great reader, a book propped into position. (In the case of little Master Jones a Teddy bear may be clutched.) Here he will hold open house for a few days, visiting hours 10 A.M. to 9 P.M.

Questions for Discussion

1. Why do you think it was once customary for a relative to witness an embalming? After reading this essay, would you be willing to return to this custom?
2. What is the distinction between "dermasurgeon" and "demisurgeon" in paragraph 5?
3. Why does Mitford identify the corpse as "Mr. Jones"?
4. Consider Mitford's diction in this essay. What is the effect of using French instead of simply saying "reason for being" *(raison d'être)* or "it is necessary to suffer in order to be beautiful" *(il faut souffrir pour être belle)*? Where does Mitford make fun of the language used in the funeral industry? Are any of her word choices designed to make embalming seem unattractive?
5. According to this selection, the reason so much is done to a corpse is to make it presentable for viewing. Open-casket funerals are common in the United States but rare in many other countries. Why do you think this custom is popular here? Does the custom justify the procedure Mitford describes?

Suggestions for Writing

1. Identify an option to embalming and explain what it would involve.
2. Explain another process (such as the process of getting married) for which a large industry stands to profit.

HOW LEAN PRODUCTION
CAN CHANGE THE WORLD

James P. Womack, Daniel T. Jones, and Daniel Roos

Womack, Jones, and Roos make a staggering claim that indicates their explanation has a persuasive dimension. The title of this article immediately establishes that the authors will do more than report information. As you read, be alert for the various types of explanation the authors employ. You will find that they clarify what lean production means by distinguishing it from mass production, they show how it is done, and they justify their claim that it can change the world. When you finish reading, ask yourself whether this explanation is convincing.

In the spring of 1950, a young Japanese engineer named Eiji Toyoda set out on a three-month pilgrimage to Ford Motor Company's River Rouge plant in Detroit. The enterprise his family had founded, the Toyota Motor Company, had just suffered through a disastrous collapse in sales and a lengthy strike, and Toyoda knew the company needed help. In its 13 years of existence, it had produced a total of 2,685 cars; Ford's Rouge plant, world citadel of mass production, was pouring out 7,000 in a single day.

Eiji Toyoda studied every inch of the Ford facility, pinpointing what he described as "some possibilities" for increasing manufacturing efficiency back home. But it was not long before Toyoda and his production genius, Taiichi Ohno, concluded that mass production was not the answer, for their company or their country. A more basic change was required. Out of that decision, over the last four decades, has emerged a fundamentally new approach to industrial production that has enabled Japan to achieve its current economic eminence and will, we believe, eventually transform virtually every industry around the world.

Just as the mass-production principles pioneered by Henry Ford and General Motors' Alfred Sloan swept away the age of craft production after World War I, so the ideas of Toyoda and Ohno are today chipping away at the foundations of mass production. We call their system "lean" production because it uses less of everything than a comparable mass-production operation: half the human effort in the factory, half the manufacturing space, half the investment in tools, half the engineering hours to develop a new product. Lean production is built not simply on technical insight but on a precisely defined set of relationships that extends far beyond the factory floor to encompass designers, suppliers and customers.

In the course of a $5 million, five-year study of the international auto industry, conducted at the Massachusetts Institute of Technology, we discovered, as expected, that the most efficient companies were Japanese.

The surprise was this: because American manufacturers have been shutting down their most inefficient plants and adopting lean production techniques, the best American-owned auto plants in North America are now more productive than the average Japanese auto plant — and are very nearly equal in quality.

In other words, the revolution is spreading, and it will change the world. In its time, mass production altered the kinds of products the consumer could buy, the fate of individual companies, the global economic balance and the very nature of work. We expect that lean production will do nothing less. 5

Henry Ford knew how to deal with customers. He left them to the dealers. And he knew how to handle the dealers, too: Keep them small and isolated, financially independent of the company but under a binding contract to sell only your cars. Make them build up their inventories to make sure there will be enough cars on hand for walk-in customers.

It was a marvelous arrangement if you were a mass-production car maker. For one thing, you received full payment from your dealers at the shipping dock but bought your parts and raw materials on consignment. What's more, you could keep your assembly line going even when sales dipped — the dealers had to buy what you made. Henry Ford also knew how to handle those dealers who balked at having Model T's stuffed down their throats in a recession. He canceled their franchises.

In many ways, the American dealership system has hardly changed at all since Ford's day. The needs of the factory still come first; dealers and customers are expected to make any necessary accommodations. It is some measure of the disparity between mass production and lean production that, in Japan, the whole system begins with and is totally geared to the needs of dealers and customers.

Consider the typical American car dealer; we have visited dozens like him in the course of our research. He runs a small business — 47 percent of the 25,000 dealers are on a single lot — and the inventory he maintains is still far bigger than he wants. Effectively, he operates a parking lot on which sits a vast array of new cars gathering grime and running up interest costs. He is constantly doing battle with the car maker's marketing division, which is devoted to selling all of the company's models to maintain steady production back at the factory. Thus the dealer often finds that his only chance to order a popular model depends on his willingness to accept one that is unpopular.

The sales people in auto showrooms work on individual commissions and are primarily skilled at getting the best deal for themselves and their boss. We have been continually amazed at just how little they know about their products — for example, the salesperson who praised the fuel economy of four-cylinder engines while showing us a V-6. Once the haggling over price is done and a deal is struck, the customer usually never 10 sees the salesperson again — specialists take over the details of financing, warranty and service.

It all looks very different in Japan, from the relationship between dealer and producer (mutually supportive) to the marketing approach (dealers sell cars door to door).

The Japanese car company divides its distribution function among a number of nationwide "channels," each of which sells a portion of the company's product range. One of Toyota's channels, for instance, is called Corolla, and its lineup includes not just the Corolla but the Camry, the Celica and other models.

The Corolla channel sells its cars through 78 dealer firms, each of which operates from about 17 different sites. The channel owns 20 percent of the dealerships outright and has a stake in others, although most dealerships are financially independent. The 30,400 employees of the channel sell about 635,000 cars and trucks a year.

At each Corolla dealership, the sales staff is organized into teams of seven or eight people who are trained in all aspects of the job. Every day starts and ends with a team meeting. When sales lag, the team puts in extra hours, and when sales lag to the point that the factory no longer has enough orders to sustain full output, production personnel can be transferred into the sales system.

Team members draw up a profile of every household within the   15
geographic area around the dealership, then periodically make their rounds — after first calling for an appointment. During these visits the sales representative updates the household profile: How many cars of what age does each family have? What makes of car with what features? How many children are there in the household and what use does the family make of its cars? When does the family think it will need to replace its cars?

Based on the answers, and the Corolla channel's range of products, the sales person suggests the most appropriate specifications for a new vehicle. Should the family members actually be in the market, the details of what they want in a car will be thoroughly discussed. The final order, which typically includes a complete financing package, trade-in on the old car and insurance, would be handled by the same sales agent, who is trained to provide one-stop service.

The prime objective of Japanese dealers is not simply a one-shot sale but a long-term relationship with their customers, and that must rest on the customers' feeling that they are part of the Corolla "family," where they are treated well and charged a fair price. Brand loyalty is the goal. In the United States, there is little such loyalty: repurchase of the same make of car falls from about 30 percent for those above age 56 down to 13 percent for those under age 25. In Japan, brand switching is far less frequent.

The purchase of a car is only the beginning. It is clearly understood that the dealer will fix any problems the owner encounters with the car at no cost to the owner—even after the end of the formal warranty. Should the owner have trouble with his insurance company over an accident claim, the dealer will do battle for him, and a car will be made available while the owner's car is being repaired. The sales agent will call the owner regularly, updating his files on the family, so that he knows when to ask whether the son leaving for college or the daughter taking her first job will need a car. The agent will also send the owner a birthday card each year, or a condolence card in case of a death in the family.

It is often said in Japan that the only way to escape your car sales agent is to leave the country. In fact, an increasing number of Japanese buyers, particularly younger people in big cities, prefer going to buy their car at the showroom.

The dealership, of course, is very different from its American counterpart. In Japan, there are only three or four demonstrator models on hand. Since most cars are manufactured to order, there is no need for vast parking areas for unsold vehicles. Moreover, there is no battle over the walk-in customer: the sales team is paid on a group commission. 20

The primary purpose of the dealer's service area is to prepare vehicles for the Ministry of Transport inspections. The first inspection must be passed when the car is three years old; thereafter, the process becomes more frequent and more demanding. For example, by about the seventh year the entire brake system will probably be targeted for replacement, whether or not it is functioning normally.

The inspection system has a huge and beneficent impact on the Japanese automotive industry, providing citizens with a strong incentive to buy a new car. Indeed, most Japanese do so, in good times and in bad.

The chance to custom-order your car, routine in Japan, has become relatively rare in the United States, where special orders substantially slow down the production process. But, one might ask, how can Japanese factories be so efficient when their production schedules continue to be subject to the whims of customers' special orders?

One explanation can be found in those questions the sales staff asks customers. The answers are carefully studied to provide clues to changing customer tastes. During the entire period when new cars destined for sale through the Corolla channel are being designed, staff members from the channel are sent out on loan to development teams to contribute what they have learned about customers' needs and attitudes.

At the factory, executives make an educated guess as to how different models, colors and the like will sell; then they establish a production schedule. The object is to get the right combinations going down the line to match actual demand—the right proportion of high-specification cars, for example, which take a little longer to make than low-specification cars. 25

The Japanese "build" schedule is more accurate at the start than its Western counterparts; it is also revised far more frequently as the dealers pick up and communicate customer feedback. Corrections and adjustments can be made quickly: at any one time, the whole distribution network contains just three weeks' supply of finished units, compared to two months' supply in the United States.

The Japanese companies are well aware of one important weakness in their system — the high cost of their sales approach, particularly the door-to-door selling. The companies believe that the most promising solution lies in the area of information technology, and they are working on it.

The first thing one encounters on entering a Corolla dealership today is an elaborate computer display. Each Corolla owner has a membership card that can be inserted in the unit just as one would insert a bank card in a cash machine. On the screen appears all the information the company has about the owner's household, and he is invited to check it over and enter any corrections and new information. The system then makes suggestions about the models most appropriate to the household's needs, with prices included. The customer can also access data bases on everything from car insurance to parking permits (many Japanese cities require possession of a permit before one may buy a car). At this point, if the owner is seriously interested in buying, he or she can approach the sales desk and discuss the particulars with the members of the sales team.

The Japanese auto companies hope that this way of selling cars represents the wave of the future. (Indeed, they expect that at some point the customer will be able to tap into these data bases on his home computer or television screen.) The customer who buys from the showroom will still have his own sales representative, someone who will stay in touch with him and whom he can contact in case of problems. But the showroom purchase leaves the sales force with much more time to devote to "conquest" sales — those to motorists who have been buying other brands. The overall goal: to reduce the cost of selling the average new car while maintaining up-to-date information on customers and holding their loyalty.

In the United States today, there is much discussion of the inadequacies of the American automotive distribution system. So many customers, car companies and dealers are unhappy. Suggestions for a solution have focused on new formats for dealers — creating publicly owned dealer chains or separating the sales and service functions. The Japanese success suggests that the problem should be examined in a much broader context, in which distribution is an integral part of a customer-focused lean-production system.

And the clock is ticking. The Japanese have not applied their lean *30* distribution approach to the United States market because of the many weeks that pass between the production of an auto in Japan and its delivery to a dealer in, say, Peoria, Ill. "The system makes no sense unless cars are built to order and delivered almost immediately," a Japanese auto executive told us. Then he added, "We can do this only as we develop a complete top-to-bottom manufacturing system in North America and Europe by the end of the 1990's."

CRAFT VS. MASS

In 1894, Evelyn Henry Ellis, a wealthy member of the English Parliament, set out to buy a car. He didn't go to a car dealer—there were none. Instead, he visited the noted Paris machine-tool company of Panhard et Levassor. There he found in place an archetypical craft-production factory where skilled, multifaceted workers were turning out a few hundred cars a year.

Many of the components in the cars from Panhard were produced at individual machine shops scattered throughout Paris. Trouble was, the parts were created without benefit of a standard gauging system, so when the mismatched components arrived at Panhard's final assembly hall, a cadre of skilled fitters had to take over. They would file the first two parts until they fit together perfectly, then file the third part until it fit the first two, continuing that way until the whole vehicle was complete. That process produced what is known as "dimensional creep"—the dimensions of the finished cars differed significantly, though all were being built to the same blueprints.

In June 1895, when he drove the 56 miles from Southampton to his country home in his new handmade Panhard, Evelyn Ellis made history. He was the first person to drive an automobile in England, and his car ended up in the Science Museum in London.

Yet craft production had its substantial drawbacks. Costs were high and did not drop when manufacturing volume increased; that meant only the rich could afford cars. Consistency and reliability were elusive. And the small, individual craft shops could not pursue the kind of systematic research that would lead to major technological advances.

Within a few decades, the mass-production techniques pioneered by Henry Ford would all but banish the craft system from the auto industry. The key to the new approach was the complete interchangeability of parts and the simplicity of attaching them to each other. Ford insisted that the same gauging system be used for every component, thereby eliminating the filing and fitting that led to dimensional creep. To speed up the assembly process, he assigned each worker only a single task, to be performed from a station beside a moving assembly line. Similarly, he made machine tools to handle just one task, avoiding the downtime inherent in craft production, as machinists readjusted tools to do a variety of tasks. Thus untrained, inexpensive labor replaced high-cost, skilled labor; and Ford found that the more cars he made, the lower the cost per car, and the lower the price he could charge the public.

With the assembly floor now occupied by very narrowly focused workers, Ford hired battalions of indirect workers for tasks that assemblers and machine-shop foremen had handled in craft shops. The newcomers included machine-tool repairmen and quality inspectors and the so-called rework men, who patched up defective cars at the end of the assembly line. Since the new assemblers were neither equipped nor motivated to suggest ways to improve efficiency, more layers of indirect workers were hired, including industrial engineers and manufacturing engineers and product engineers.

Ford and his rival, William Durant, the founder of General Motors, succeeded very well in applying mass-production principles in the factory, but neither could efficiently organize or manage his huge engineering-manufacturing-marketing complex. That was the achievement of Alfred Sloan, Durant's successor. Sloan created decentralized divisions, managed objectively and "by the numbers" from a relatively small corporate head-quarters. He thought it both unnecessary and inappropriate for senior managers to know much about the details of operating each division. If the periodic reports on sales, market share and profit showed that performance was poor, it was time to change the general manager.

To operate his revamped company, Sloan effectively invented the professions of financial manager and marketing specialist, complementing the engineering specialists, so that every functional area of the auto company would have its dedicated experts. The division of labor was now complete, and the American mass-production giants were ready to conquer the world.

By 1955, the Big Three — Ford, G.M. and Chrysler — dominated car markets abroad. But times were changing. Mass production was now firmly established in Europe, and compact cars from the Continent were beginning to steal some of the American market. And at Toyota, Taiichi Ohno was developing an entirely new way of making cars.

MASS VS. LEAN

In 1946, the Japanese government, with American prompting, im- *40* posed severe restrictions on the ability of company owners to dismiss their employees. The balance of power shifted dramatically from the companies to the workers. At Toyota, four years later, the union won a remarkable agreement that remains the standard in the Japanese auto industry. Under its terms, employees were guaranteed lifetime employment and a pay scale steeply graded by seniority rather than by specific job function. For their part, the employees agreed to be flexible as to their work assignments and committed to helping the company find new and better ways of increasing efficiency.

Seniority-based wages virtually guaranteed that most employees would remain with Toyota, since a worker who joined another company would start with zero seniority and take a huge pay cut. It became clear to Ohno that the workers were now as much or more of a long-term fixed cost as the company's machinery. So it made sense to continuously enhance their skills and to gain the benefit of their knowledge and experience as well as their brawn.

Ohno had decided that the mass-production system was rife with waste. The armies of engineering and production specialists, for example, added no value to the car; he thought that the assembly workers could be trained to do most of the specialists' work — and could do it better because of their direct acquaintance with conditions on the line.

So Ohno organized workers into teams, gave them a place on the assembly line and told them to decide together how best to perform the necessary operations. Instead of a foreman, who simply watched over his crew, each team was given a leader who had his own share of assembly tasks, including filling in for absentees. Bit by bit, Ohno added to the teams' responsibilities: housekeeping, minor tool repair, quality checking. He also set aside time for the team to come up with ways to improve the process.

In the mass-production companies, factory managers were generally graded on two criteria, yield and quality. Yield was the number of cars actually produced in relation to the scheduled number, and quality referred to the state of the product when it reached the shipping dock. Managers knew that stopping the line for whatever reason spelled big trouble because the loss of minutes and cars would have to be made up with expensive overtime at the end of the shift. Moreover, letting cars go down the line with a misaligned part was no problem, because such mistakes could be fixed in the rework area — beyond the assembly line but ahead of the quality checker at the shipping dock. Thus was born the "move the metal" mentality of the mass-production auto companies. A yield of 90 percent was taken as a sign of good management.

In striking contrast to the mass-production plant, where only the senior assembly-line manager could stop the line, Ohno placed a red handle at every work station and instructed workers to stop the whole line immediately if a problem emerged that they could not resolve. He had no patience with factories where errors were treated as random events, to be repaired and forgotten. Ohno taught the workers to trace every error systematically back to its cause and to devise a fix so that it would never occur again.

At first, the new Toyota production line stopped all the time, and the workers became discouraged. But, gradually, the number of errors began to drop. Toyota's assembly plants now have virtually no rework areas and perform almost no rework, while mass-production plants devote 20 percent of plant area and 25 percent of total work hours to fixing their mistakes. In Toyota plants, where every worker can halt the line, yields approach 100 percent, and the line practically never stops.

SUPPLY

For all the attention it receives, the automotive assembly plant accounts for only about 15 percent of the total manufacturing process. The rest is devoted to the design and fabrication of the 10,000 discrete parts that make up the unimaginably complicated modern car. For any one vehicle, that job is accomplished by hundreds of suppliers, some of them divisions of the assembler, some of them independent operators. General Motors relies on in-house suppliers for 70 percent of its needs; Toyota, for only 27 percent.

In a mass-production company, suppliers have traditionally been called in after all the plans for a new model are complete. The suppliers are handed precise engineering drawings and asked to make bids. ("What will be the cost per steering wheel for 400,000 steering wheels per year?") The assembler sets a quality target (the allowable number of defective parts per thousand) and a once- or twice-a-week delivery schedule. For parts that require new capital investment by the supplier, the contract will usually be for a year's duration — less for parts that are already in production for other models.

But the suppliers know from long experience that none of the real rules are written into the bid. They know that it often takes a bid below cost to win the contract. What makes that feasible is the rich potential: follow-on business for a new model can often extend for 10 years, not to mention the market for replacement parts. And there exists a long tradition of annual upward cost adjustments, even though the winning supplier will almost certainly be reducing production costs as it gains experience in producing the part — the so-called learning curve.

The relationship between mass-production suppliers and assemblers $_{50}$ has been marked by mutual suspicion and distrust. The suppliers jealously guard information about their operations from the assemblers, lest it reveal the size of their profits. Even after a supplier has been selected to make a part, assemblers routinely line up alternate suppliers so the companies can be played against each other in the years to come. If the new model fails to sell as expected, a supplier may be dumped for a lower bidder.

To be sure that enough parts are on hand to meet sudden changes in demand, suppliers build up huge, expensive inventories. Because of the arms-length relationship between supplier and assembler, the two do not cooperate to reduce the number of defective parts.

To counteract such problems, and respond to a surge in demand, during the 1950's Toyota turned the mass-production supply system on its head. The company divided its suppliers into separate tiers with different responsibilities. First-tier suppliers were each assigned a major component such as car seats or the electrical system; the first-tier supplier would in turn call on second-tier companies to provide individual parts or subsystem components. In many cases, the second-tier firms developed a third level of suppliers.

Toyota only dealt directly with the first-tier companies, which were selected immediately after the decision to develop a new model. These suppliers became an integral part of the product-development team and were handed, not engineering specifications as in the mass-production system, but performance specifications. For example, a first-tier supplier was told to design a set of brakes that would stop a 2,200-pound car going 60 miles per hour in the space of 200 feet, and do it 10 times in succession without fading. The space within which the brakes had to fit was specified, as was the price: $40 a set. A prototype was to be delivered to Toyota for testing. If it worked, a production order would be awarded.

Today, the leading Japanese lean producers work directly with fewer than 300 first-tier suppliers on a development project; mass-production plants, by contrast, have up to 2,500 suppliers to contend with. More significantly, lean assemblers such as Toyota expect their suppliers to share information about their operations. This is accomplished, in part, at meetings of first-tier and second-tier supplier associations, where advances in manufacturing techniques are discussed. The sharing is furthered by the presence at first-tier plants of Toyota design engineers, who observe and take part in production planning for the new model.

In other words, in contrast to the secrecy built into the mass-production system, lean assemblers are privy to the most sensitive information about their suppliers' operations, including costs and quality levels. That is possible because the relationship between assembler and supplier, and among suppliers, is cooperative rather than competitive. Cooperation is enhanced by the fact that both desire a long-term, stable relationship; an assembler will occasionally drop a supplier but only, as an assembler's purchasing agent told us, "when we think they have given up." And the relationship is helped along by the assembler's taking equity stakes in his supplier companies, which in turn often have substantial holdings of each other's stock.

After the lean assembler establishes a target price for a new model, the assembler and suppliers jointly work backward to determine how the vehicle can be made for that price while allowing a reasonable profit for all parties. The assembler is well aware of the learning curve that will lower suppliers' costs. Any cost savings initiated by a supplier, beyond those anticipated in the contract, go to the supplier alone. This is the principal mechanism in the lean-supply system for achieving rapid and continuous improvement in the production process.

The single most inspired facet of lean supply was another contribution of Toyota's Taiichi Ohno: the just-in-time system. In essence, it held that new parts should only be produced to meet an immediate need; when a container bearing a particular part returned empty from the assembler, that was the signal to the supplier to turn out more parts. The system eliminated practically all inventories. It also meant that one small kink could bring the whole operation to a halt. In Ohno's view, that was the charm of the idea — it removed all safety nets and focused every worker on anticipating problems and solving them. In the endless quest for perfection, the risk was worth it.

PURSUING PERFECTION

That quest suggests a most striking disparity between mass production and lean production. Mass producers set limited goals — an acceptable number of defects, a maximum level of inventories. To do better, they argue, would cost too much or exceed inherent human capabilities. Lean producers, on the other hand, set their sights on perfection: continually declining costs, zero defects, zero inventories.

They never reach the promised land, but they have achieved a success that is carrying lean production beyond the shores of Japan. The system will require some major changes in our ideas about work. A key objective of lean production is to push responsibility far down the organizational ladder. Responsibility means freedom to control one's job — a big plus — but it also increases the pressure to avoid mistakes, and hence raises the stress level.

We are accustomed to thinking of our careers in terms of a climb *60* toward ever higher levels of technical proficiency in an ever narrower area of specialization, accompanied by responsibility for ever larger numbers of subordinates. The career path in lean production leads to a continuous broadening of one's professional skills, and they are applied in a team setting rather than in a rigid hierarchy. There is a cost, however. The better you are at teamwork, the less you may know about a narrow specialty you might take with you to another employer or use to start a new business.

In many ways, lean production combines the best features of both craft production and mass production — the ability to reduce costs per unit, dramatically improve quality and quickly respond to consumers' desires, while at the same time providing employees with ever more challenging work. The final limits of the system are not yet known, and its diffusion is still at an early stage — about where mass production was in the early 1920's. Lean production will not be quickly or painlessly embraced. Yet in the end, we believe, it will supplant mass production and the remaining outposts of craft production in all areas of industrial endeavor and become the standard global production system of the 21st century. As a result, the world will be a different and better place.

Questions for Discussion

1. The authors of this article claim that they were not surprised to discover that Japanese auto companies were the most efficient in the world. But what else did they discover?

2. How does the American system of car dealerships favor mass production carmakers?

3. How are new cars sold in Japan? What are the advantages of this system? Are there any disadvantages?

4. What government policies have favored the auto industry in Japan?

5. Why do the authors devote several paragraphs to showing how mass production replaced craft production? Would their focus be stronger if they had limited themselves to contrasting mass production with lean production? If they needed to discuss all three types of production, should they have discussed them in the order in which they were developed?

6. What made mass production successful for over forty years? Why did it ultimately begin to lose out to lean production? What are the advantages of lean production?

7. How do mass production companies and lean production companies differ in their relations with suppliers?

8. The authors predict, "Lean production will not be quickly or painlessly embraced," but they conclude that it will eventually become standard and that this will make the world "a different and better place." What difficulties will American companies need to overcome if they shift to lean production? Do you agree that the shift will be worth the trouble?

Suggestions for Writing

1. Drawing upon your own experience with cars, explain why some cars are more likely to break down than others.

2. If you have ever held a job that made you dread going to work, explain how working conditions affected your morale.

A LETTER TO GABRIELA,
A YOUNG WRITER

Pat Mora

Pat Mora is a writer. She is also Hispanic. Her open letter to Gabriela explains what Mora thinks it means to be both. As you read this selection, pay particular attention to Mora's sense of audience. Note references that show that Mora was writing to a young girl. But consider also that Mora published this letter in English Journal, *a periodical read by thousands of English teachers. Think about why Mora chose to share this letter with teachers, and look for any points indicating that she had this additional audience in mind when she wrote.*

Dear Gabriela,

Your mother tells me that you have begun writing poems and that you wonder exactly how I do it. Do you perhaps wonder why I do it? Why would anyone sit alone and write when she could be talking to friends on the telephone, eating mint chocolate chip ice-cream in front of the television, or buying a new red sweater at the mall?

And, as you know, I like people. I like long, slow lunches with my friends. I like to dance. I'm no hermit, and I'm not shy. So why do I sit with my tablet and pen and mutter to myself?

There are many answers. I write because I'm a reader. I want to give to others what writers have given me, a chance to hear the voices of people I will never meet. Alone, in private. And even if I meet these authors, I wouldn't hear what I hear along with the page, words carefully chosen, woven into a piece unlike any other, enjoyed by me in a way no other person will, in quite the same way, enjoy them. I suppose I'm saying that I love the privateness of writing and reading. It's delicious to curl into a book.

I write because I'm curious. I'm curious about me. Writing is a way of finding out how I feel about anything and everything. Now that I've left the desert where I grew up, for example, I'm discovering how it feels to walk on spongy fall leaves and to watch snow drifting *up* on a strong wind. I notice what's around me in a special way because I'm a writer. It's like radar, like the keen listening and looking of Indiana Jones when he walks into the jungle loud with parrots and monkeys. So I notice my world more, and then I talk to myself about it on paper. Writing is my way of saving my feelings.

I write because I believe that Mexican Americans need to take their rightful place in American literature. We need to be published and to be studied in schools and colleges so that the stories and ideas of our people won't quietly disappear. Although I'm happy when I finish the draft of a poem or story, deep inside I always wish I wrote better, that I could bring more honor and attention to, for example, the *abuelitas* I write about. The mix of sadness and pleasure occurs often in life, doesn't it, Gabriela?

Although we don't discuss it often because it's depressing, our people have been and sometimes still are viewed as inferior. Maybe you have already felt hurt when someone by a remark or odd look said to you: you're not like us, you're not one of us, speaking Spanish is odd, your family looks funny.

Some of us decide we don't want to be different. We don't want to be a part of a group that is often described as poor and uneducated. I remember feeling that way. I spoke Spanish at home to my grandmother and aunt, but I didn't always want my friends at school to know that I spoke Spanish. I didn't like myself for feeling that way. I sensed it was wrong, but I didn't know why. Now, I know.

I know that the society we live in and the shows and ads we see all affect us. It's not easy to learn to judge others fairly, not because of the car they drive, the house they live in, the church they attend, the color of their skin, the language they speak at home. It takes courage to face the fact that we all have ten toes, get sleepy at night, get scared in the dark. Some families, some cities, some states, and even some countries foolishly convince themselves that they're better than others. And then they teach their children this ugly lie. It's like a weed with burrs and stickers that pricks people.

How are young women who are Afro American, Asian American, Native American, Hispanics, or members of all the other ethnic groups supposed to feel about themselves? Some are proud of their cultural roots. But commercials are also busy trying to convince us that our car, clothes, and maybe even our family aren't good enough. It's so hard in 1990 to be your self, your many interesting selves, because billboards and magazine ads tell you that beautiful is being thin, maybe blonde, and rich, rich, rich. No wonder we don't always like ourselves when we look in the mirror.

Some people like crossword puzzles, and some like jigsaw puzzles. My writing is my puzzle. I write because I like playing with words.

There are no secrets to good writing. Read. Listen. Write. Read. Listen. Write. You learn to write well by reading wonderful writing and by letting those words and ideas become part of your blood and bones. But life is not all books. You become a better writer by listening — to your self and to all the colors, shapes, and sounds around you. Listen with all of your senses. Listen to the wrinkles on your *tia's* face.

Writers write. They don't just talk about writing just as dancers don't just talk about dancing. They do it because they love it and because they want to get better and better. They practice and practice to loosen up just as you practiced and practiced when you were learning to talk. And because you practiced, you don't talk the way you did when you were three.

Do you know the quotation that says that learning to write is like learning to ice-skate? You must be willing to make a fool of yourself. Writers are willing to try what they can't do well so that one day they can write a strong poem or novel or children's book.

After a writer gains some confidence, writers begin to spend more *15* and more time revising just as professional ice-skaters create and practice certain routines until they have developed their own, unique style. You probably don't like rewriting now. I didn't either until a few years ago.

How or why a book or poem starts varies. Sometimes I hear a story I want to save, sometimes it's a line, or an idea. It would be as if you saw someone dance and you noticed a step or some special moves and for a few days you didn't actually try the steps but off and on you thought about them. Maybe you even feel the moves inside you. And then one day you just can't stand it any more and you turn on the music and begin to experiment. You don't succeed right away, but you're having fun even while you're working to get the rhythm right. And slowly you loosen up, and pretty soon you forget about your feet and arms and you and the music are just moving together. Then the next day you try it again, and maybe alter it slightly.

My pen is like that music. Usually I like to start in a sunny spot with a yellow, lined tablet and a pen. I have a number of false starts like you did dancing. I'm working but having fun. Alone. The first line of a poem is sometimes a hard one because I want it to be an interesting line. It may be the only line a reader will glance at to decide whether to read the whole piece. I'm searching for the right beginning. I play a little game with myself. (This game works with any kind of writing.) I tell myself to write any line no matter how bad or dull, since I can later throw it away. If I sit waiting for the perfect line, I might never write the poem. I'm willing to make a fool of myself. So I start, usually slowly. I write a few lines, read them aloud, and often start again. I keep sections I like and discard the uninteresting parts. The next day I read my work and try to improve it. I'm trying to pull out of myself the poem or story that's deep inside.

It's important, Gabriela, not to fall in love with the words you write. Pick your words or phrases, and then stand back and look at your work. Read it out loud.

You and I are lucky to be writers. So many women in history and even today who could be much better writers than I am have not had that private pleasure of creating with words. Maybe their families think writing is a waste of time, maybe they don't believe in themselves, maybe they have to work hard all day and then have to cook and clean and take care of their children at night, maybe they've never been taught to read and write.

I hope that you develop pride in being Mexican American and that *20* you discover what you have to say that no one else can say. I hope that you continue writing, Gabriela.

Questions for Discussion

1. What is the effect of using a letter as a way of writing an essay on writing? Where does Mora show that she is writing for a young girl? What keeps this "letter" from being limited to an audience of one?

2. Why does Mora write? Which of her reasons seem most important to her? Which seem most important to you?

3. What does Mora mean when she writes, "It takes courage to face the fact that we all have ten toes, get sleepy at night, get scared in the dark." Why would any of these admissions take courage?

4. Mora states that writers must be willing to make fools of themselves. What does she mean?

5. Consider the analogy that Mora makes in paragraph 13 between dancing and writing. Does this analogy reflect the way you are motivated to write?

6. Mora cautions Gabriela "not to fall in love with the words you write." Wouldn't you expect a writer to love her own words? What is the reason for keeping some distance between yourself and your work?

Suggestions for Writing

1. Write a letter to a friend explaining how to survive in college. Direct your letter to someone specific, but imagine that person wanting to pass the letter around after she or he has read it.

2. Explain what you do when you write a paper. Consider the circumstances that make your writing come fairly easily and the circumstances that can make writing difficult.

THE NATURE AND AIM OF FICTION
Flannery O'Connor

Flannery O'Connor was a novelist and short story writer; she was also a Catholic and a southerner — a background that influenced much of her work. This essay was originally a lecture given in response to an invitation to talk to college students about writing fiction. As you read it, analyze O'Connor's conception of who a writer is and what a writer does — and how the sort of writing she admires differs from that in the average best-seller. Consider whether O'Connor's explanation of what it means to write fiction could help you write essays. If you enjoy O'Connor's voice or are interested by her ideas, think about reading some of her fiction, beginning with the stories collected in A Good Man Is Hard to Find.

I understand that this is a course called "How the Writer Writes," and that each week you are exposed to a different writer who holds forth on the subject. The only parallel I can think of to this is having the zoo come to you, one animal at a time; and I suspect that what you hear one week from the giraffe is contradicted the next week by the baboon.

My own problem in thinking what I should say to you tonight has been how to interpret such a title as "How the Writer Writes." In the first place, there is no such thing as THE writer, and I think that if you don't know that now, you should by the time such a course as this is over. In fact, I predict that it is the one thing you can be absolutely certain of learning.

But there is a widespread curiosity about writers and how they work, and when a writer talks on this subject, there are always misconceptions and mental rubble for him to clear away before he can even begin to see what he wants to talk about. I am not, of course, as innocent as I look. I know well enough that very few people who are supposedly interested in writing are interested in writing well. They are interested in publishing something, and if possible in making a "killing." They are interested in seeing their names at the top of something printed, it matters not what. And they seem to feel that this can be accomplished by learning certain things about working habits and about markets and about what subjects are currently acceptable.

If this is what you are interested in, I am not going to be of much use to you. I feel that the external habits of the writer will be guided by his common sense or his lack of it and by his personal circumstances; and that these will seldom be alike in two cases. What interests the serious writer is not external habits but what Maritain° calls, "the habit of art"; and he

---

Maritain: Jacques Maritain (1882–1973), a French theologian and philosopher.

explains that "habit" in this sense means a certain quality or virtue of the mind. The scientist has the habit of science; the artist, the habit of art.

Now I'd better stop here and explain how I'm using the word *art*.   5
Art is a word that immediately scares people off, as being a little too grand. But all I mean by art is writing something that is valuable in itself and that works in itself. The basis of art is truth, both in matter and in mode. The person who aims after art in his work aims after truth, in an imaginative sense, no more and no less. St. Thomas° said that the artist is concerned with the good of that which is made; and that will have to be the basis of my few words on the subject of fiction.

Now you'll see that this kind of approach eliminates many things from the discussion. It eliminates any concern with the motivation of the writer except as this finds its place inside the work. It also eliminates any concern with the reader in his market sense. It also eliminates that tedious controversy that always rages between people who declare that they write to express themselves and those who declare that they write to fill their pocketbooks, if possible.

In this connection I always think of Henry James.° I know of no writer who was hotter after the dollar than James was, or who was more of a conscientious artist. It is true, I think, that these are times when the financial rewards for sorry writing are much greater than those for good writing. There are certain cases in which, if you can only learn to write poorly enough, you can make a great deal of money. But it is not true that if you write well, you won't get published at all. It is true that if you want to write well and live well at the same time, you'd better arrange to inherit money or marry a stockbroker or a rich woman who can operate a type-writer. In any case, whether you write to make money or to express your soul or to insure civil rights or to irritate your grandmother will be a matter for you and your analyst, and the point of departure for this dis-cussion will be the good of the written work.

The kind of written work I'm going to talk about is story-writing, because that's the only kind I know anything about. I'll call any length of fiction a story, whether it be a novel or a shorter piece, and I'll call anything a story in which specific characters and events influence each other to form a meaningful narrative. I find that most people know what a story is until they sit down to write one. Then they find themselves writing a sketch with an essay woven through it, or an essay with a sketch woven through it, or an editorial with a character in it, or a case history with a moral, or some other mongrel thing. When they realize that they aren't writing stories, they decide that the remedy for this is to learn something that they refer to as the "technique of the short story" or "the technique of the novel." Technique in the minds of many is something rigid, something

---

St. Thomas: St. Thomas Aquinas (c. 1225–1274), a Catholic philosopher and theologian.
Henry James: An American novelist and critic (1843–1916), and an author of more than forty books.

like a formula that you impose on the material; but in the best stories it is something organic, something that grows out of the material, and this being the case, it is different for every story of any account that has ever been written.

I think we have to begin thinking about stories at a much more fundamental level, so I want to talk about one quality of fiction which I think is its least common denominator — the fact that it is concrete — and about a few of the qualities that follow from this. We will be concerned in this with the reader in his fundamental human sense, because the nature of fiction is in large measure determined by the nature of our perceptive apparatus. The beginning of human knowledge is through the senses, and the fiction writer begins where human perception begins. He appeals through the senses, and you cannot appeal to the senses with abstractions. It is a good deal easier for most people to state an abstract idea than to describe and thus re-create some object that they actually see. But the world of the fiction writer is full of matter, and this is what the beginning fiction writers are very loath to create. They are concerned primarily with unfleshed ideas and emotions. They are apt to be reformers and to want to write because they are possessed not by a story but by the bare bones of some abstract notion. They are conscious of problems, not of people, of questions and issues, not of the texture of existence, of case histories and of everything that has a sociological smack, instead of with all those concrete details of life that make actual the mystery of our position on earth.

The Manicheans separated spirit and matter. To them all material *10* things were evil. They sought pure spirit and tried to approach the infinite directly without any mediation of matter. This is also pretty much the modern spirit, and for the sensibility infected with it, fiction is hard if not impossible to write because fiction is so very much an incarnational art.

One of the most common and saddest spectacles is that of a person of really fine sensibility and acute psychological perception trying to write fiction by using these qualities alone. This type of writer will put down one intensely emotional or keenly perceptive sentence after the other, and the result will be complete dullness. The fact is that the materials of the fiction writer are the humblest. Fiction is about everything human and we are made out of dust, and if you scorn getting yourself dusty, then you shouldn't try to write fiction. It's not a grand enough job for you.

Now when the fiction writer finally gets this idea through his head and into his habits, he begins to realize what a job of heavy labor the writing of fiction is. A lady who writes, and whom I admire very much, wrote me that she had learned from Flaubert° that it takes at least three activated sensuous strokes to make an object real; and she believes that this is connected with our having five senses. If you're deprived of any of

Flaubert: Gustave Flaubert (1821–1880), a French novelist.

them, you're in a bad way, but if you're deprived of more than two at once, you almost aren't present.

All the sentences in *Madame Bovary* could be examined with wonder, but there is one in particular that always stops me in admiration. Flaubert has just shown us Emma at the piano with Charles watching her. He says, "She struck the notes with aplomb and ran from top to bottom of the keyboard without a break. Thus shaken up, the old instrument, whose strings buzzed, could be heard at the other end of the village when the window was open, and often the bailiff's clerk, passing along the high-road, bareheaded and in list slippers, stopped to listen, his sheet of paper in his hand."

The more you look at a sentence like that, the more you can learn from it. At one end of it, we are with Emma and this very solid instrument "whose strings buzzed," and at the other end of it we are across the village with this very concrete clerk in his list slippers. With regard to what happens to Emma in the rest of the novel, we may think that it makes no difference that the instrument has buzzing strings or that the clerk wears list slippers and has a piece of paper in his hand, but Flaubert had to create a believable village to put Emma in. It's always necessary to remember that the fiction writer is much less *immediately* concerned with grand ideas and bristling emotions than he is with putting list slippers on clerks.

Now of course this is something that some people learn only to 15 abuse. This is one reason that strict naturalism is a dead end in fiction. In a strictly naturalistic work the detail is there because it is natural to life, not because it is natural to the work. In a work of art we can be extremely literal, without being in the least naturalistic. Art is selective, and its truthfulness is the truthfulness of the essential that creates movement.

The novel works by a slower accumulation of detail than the short story does. The short story requires more drastic procedures than the novel because more has to be accomplished in less space. The details have to carry more immediate weight. In good fiction, certain of the details will tend to accumulate meaning from the story itself, and when this happens, they become symbolic in their action.

Now the word *symbol* scares a good many people off, just as the word *art* does. They seem to feel that a symbol is some mysterious thing put in arbitrarily by the writer to frighten the common reader — sort of a literary Masonic grip that is only for the initiated. They seem to think that it is a way of saying something that you aren't actually saying, and so if they can be got to read a reputedly symbolic work at all, they approach it as if it were a problem in algebra. Find x. And when they do find or think they find this abstraction, x, then they go off with an elaborate sense of satisfaction and the notion that they have "understood" the story. Many students confuse the *process* of understanding a thing with understanding it.

I think that for the fiction writer himself, symbols are something he uses simply as a matter of course. You might say that these are details that, while having their essential place in the literal level of the story, operate in depth as well as on the surface, increasing the story in every direction.

I think the way to read a book is always to see what happens, but in a good novel, more always happens than we are able to take in at once, more happens than meets the eye. The mind is led on by what it sees into the greater depths that the book's symbols naturally suggest. This is what is meant when critics say that a novel operates on several levels. The truer the symbol, the deeper it leads you, the more meaning it opens up. To take an example from my own book, *Wise Blood*, the hero's rat-colored automobile is his pulpit and his coffin as well as something he thinks of as a means of escape. He is mistaken in thinking that it is a means of escape, of course, and does not really escape his predicament until the car is destroyed by the patrolman. The car is a kind of death-in-life symbol, as his blindness is a life-in-death symbol. The fact that these meanings are there makes the book significant. The reader may not see them but they have their effect on him nonetheless. This is the way the modern novelist sinks, or hides, his theme.

The kind of vision the fiction writer needs to have, or to develop, in order to increase the meaning of his story is called anagogical vision, and that is the kind of vision that is able to see different levels of reality in one image or one situation. The medieval commentators on Scripture found three kinds of meaning in the literal level of the sacred text: one they called allegorical, in which one fact pointed to another; one they called tropological, or moral, which had to do with what should be done; and one they called anagogical, which had to do with the Divine life and our participation in it. Although this was a method applied to biblical exegesis, it was also an attitude toward all of creation, and a way of reading nature which included most possibilities, and I think it is this enlarged view of the human scene that the fiction writer has to cultivate if he is ever going to write stories that have any chance of becoming a permanent part of our literature. It seems to be a paradox that the larger and more complex the personal view, the easier it is to compress it into fiction.

People have a habit of saying, "What is the theme of your story?" and they expect you to give them a statement: "The theme of my story is the economic pressure of the machine on the middle class" — or some such absurdity. And when they've got a statement like that, they go off happy and feel it is no longer necessary to read the story.

Some people have the notion that you read the story and then climb out of it into the meaning, but for the fiction writer himself the whole story is the meaning, because it is an experience, not an abstraction.

Now the second common characteristic of fiction follows from this, and it is that fiction is presented in such a way that the reader has the sense that it is unfolding around him. This doesn't mean he has to identify himself with the character or feel compassion for the character or anything like that. It just means that fiction has to be largely presented rather than

20

reported. Another way to say it is that though fiction is a narrative art, it relies heavily on the element of drama.

The story is not as extreme a form of drama as the play, but if you know anything about the history of the novel, you know that the novel as an art form has developed in the direction of dramatic unity.

The major difference between the novel as written in the eighteenth century and the novel as we usually find it today is the disappearance from it of the author. Fielding, for example, was everywhere in his own work, calling the reader's attention to this point and that, directing him to give his special attention here or there, clarifying this and that incident for him so that he couldn't possibly miss the point. The Victorian novelists did this, too. They were always coming in, explaining and psychologizing about their characters. But along about the time of Henry James, the author began to tell his story in a different way. He began to let it come through the minds and eyes of the characters themselves, and he sat behind the scenes, apparently disinterested. By the time we get to James Joyce, the author is nowhere to be found in the book. The reader is on his own, floundering around in the thoughts of various unsavory characters. He finds himself in the middle of a world apparently without comment.

But it is from the kind of world the writer creates, from the kind of character and detail he invests it with, that a reader can find the intellectual meaning of a book. Once this is found, however, it cannot be drained off and used as a substitute for the book. As the late John Peale Bishop° said: "You can't say Cézanne painted apples and a tablecloth and have said what Cézanne painted." The novelist makes his statements by selection, and if he is any good, he selects every word for a reason, every detail for a reason, every incident for a reason, and arranges them in a certain time-sequence for a reason. He demonstrates something that cannot possibly be demonstrated any other way than with a whole novel.

Art forms evolve until they reach their ultimate perfection, or until they reach some state of petrifaction, or until some new element is grafted on and a new art form made. But however the past of fiction has been or however the future will be, the present state of the case is that a piece of fiction must be very much a self-contained dramatic unit.

This means that it must carry its meaning inside it. It means that any abstractly expressed compassion or piety or morality in a piece of fiction is only a statement added to it. It means that you can't make an inadequate dramatic action complete by putting a statement of meaning on the end of it or in the middle of it or at the beginning of it. It means that when you write fiction you are speaking *with* character and action, not *about* character and action. The writer's moral sense must coincide with his dramatic sense.

John Peale Bishop: An American essayist and poet (1892–1944).

It's said that when Henry James received a manuscript that he didn't like, he would return it with the comment, "You have chosen a good subject and are treating it in a straightforward manner." This usually pleased the person getting the manuscript back, but it was the worst thing that James could think of to say, for he knew, better than anybody else, that the straightforward manner is seldom equal to the complications of the good subject. There may never be anything new to say, but there is always a new way to say it, and since, in art, the way of saying a thing becomes a part of what is said, every work of art is unique and requires fresh attention.

It's always wrong of course to say that you can't do this or you can't do that in fiction. You can do anything you can get away with, but nobody has ever gotten away with much. *30*

I believe that it takes a rather different type of disposition to write novels than to write short stories, granted that both require fundamentally fictional talents. I have a friend who writes both, and she says that when she stops a novel to work on short stories, she feels as if she has just left a dark wood to be set upon by wolves. The novel is a more diffused form and more suited to those who like to linger along the way; it also requires a more massive energy. For those of us who want to get the agony over in a hurry, the novel is a burden and a pain. But no matter which fictional form you are using, you are writing a story, and in a story something has to happen. A perception is not a story, and no amount of sensitivity can make a story-writer out of you if you just plain don't have a gift for telling a story.

But there's a certain grain of stupidity that the writer of fiction can hardly do without, and this is the quality of having to stare, of not getting the point at once. The longer you look at one object, the more of the world you see in it; and it's well to remember that the serious fiction writer always writes about the whole world, no matter how limited his particular scene. For him, the bomb that was dropped on Hiroshima affects life on the Oconee River, and there's not anything he can do about it.

People are always complaining that the modern novelist has no hope and that the picture he paints of the world is unbearable. The only answer to this is that people without hope do not write novels. Writing a novel is a terrible experience, during which the hair often falls out and the teeth decay. I'm always highly irritated by people who imply that writing fiction is an escape from reality. It is a plunge into reality and it's very shocking to the system. If the novelist is not sustained by a hope of money, then he must be sustained by a hope of salvation, or he simply won't survive the ordeal.

People without hope not only don't write novels, but what is more to the point, they don't read them. They don't take long looks at anything, because they lack the courage. The way to despair is to refuse to have any kind of experience, and the novel, of course, is a way to have experience.

The lady who only read books that improved her mind was taking a safe course — and a hopeless one. She'll never know whether her mind is improved or not, but should she ever, by some mistake, read a great novel, she'll know mighty well that something is happening to her. . . .

You may think from all I say that the reason I write is to make the reader see what I see, and that writing fiction is primarily a missionary activity. Let me straighten this out.   35

Last spring I talked here, and one of the girls asked me, "Miss O'Connor, why do you write?" and I said, "Because I'm good at it," and at once I felt a considerable disapproval in the atmosphere. I felt that this was not thought by the majority to be a highminded answer; but it was the only answer I could give. I had not been asked why I write the way I do, but why I write at all; and to that question there is only one legitimate answer.

There is no excuse for anyone to write fiction for public consumption unless he has been called to do so by the presence of a gift. It is the nature of fiction not to be good for much unless it is good in itself.

A gift of any kind is a considerable responsibility. It is a mystery in itself, something gratuitous and wholly undeserved, something whose real uses will probably always be hidden from us. Usually the artist has to suffer certain deprivations in order to use his gift with integrity. Art is a virtue of the practical intellect, and the practice of any virtue demands a certain asceticism and a very definite leaving-behind of the niggardly part of the ego. The writer has to judge himself with a stranger's eye and a stranger's severity. The prophet in him has to see the freak. No art is sunk in the self, but rather, in art the self becomes self-forgetful in order to meet the demands of the thing seen and the thing being made. . . .

St. Thomas called art "reason in making." This is a very cold and very beautiful definition, and if it is unpopular today, this is because reason has lost ground among us. As grace and nature have been separated, so imagination and reason have been separated, and this always means an end to art. The artist uses his reason to discover an answering reason in everything he sees. For him, to be reasonable is to find, in the object, in the situation, in the sequence, the spirit which makes it itself. This is not an easy or simple thing to do. It is to intrude upon the timeless, and that is only done by the violence of a single-minded respect for the truth.

It follows from all this that there is no technique that can be discovered and applied to make it possible for one to write. If you go to a school   40
where there are classes in writing, these classes should not be to teach you how to write, but to teach you the limits and possibilities of words and the respect due them. One thing that is always with the writer — no matter how long he has written or how good he is — is the continuing process of learning how to write. As soon as the writer "learns to write," as soon as he knows what he is going to find, and discovers a way to say what he knew all along, or worse still, a way to say nothing, he is finished. If a

writer is any good, what he makes will have its source in a realm much larger than that which his conscious mind can encompass and will always be a greater surprise to him than it can ever be to his reader.

I don't know which is worse — to have a bad teacher or no teacher at all. In any case, I believe the teacher's work should be largely negative. He can't put the gift into you, but if he finds it there, he can try to keep it from going in an obviously wrong direction. We can learn how not to write, but this is a discipline that does not simply concern writing itself but concerns the whole intellectual life. A mind cleared of false emotion and false sentiment and egocentricity is going to have at least those road-blocks removed from its path. If you don't think cheaply, then there at least won't be the quality of cheapness in your writing, even though you may not be able to write well. The teacher can try to weed out what is positively bad, and this should be the aim of the whole college. Any discipline can help your writing: logic, mathematics, theology, and of course and particularly drawing. Anything that helps you to see, anything that makes you look. The writer should never be ashamed of staring. There is nothing that doesn't require his attention.

We hear a great deal of lamentation these days about writers having all taken themselves to the colleges and universities where they live decorously instead of going out and getting firsthand information about life. The fact is that anybody who has survived his childhood has enough information about life to last him the rest of his days. If you can't make something out of a little experience, you probably won't be able to make it out of a lot. The writer's business is to contemplate experience, not to be merged in it.

Questions for Discussion

1. Consider the analogy with which O'Connor opens her essay. What reason could she have for beginning with a comparison that makes writers seem like animals in a zoo?
2. What do you think O'Connor means when she insists that "there is no such thing as THE writer"?
3. O'Connor claims that "very few people who are supposedly interested in writing are interested in writing well." Does this seem true to you? Why would anyone interested in writing *not* be interested in writing well?
4. How does O'Connor define *habit, art, symbol,* and *vision?*
5. In paragraph 13 O'Connor quotes two sentences from *Madame Bovary,* a nineteenth-century novel. What are these sentences meant to illustrate?
6. How has fiction changed since the eighteenth century? What is the difference between writing a novel and writing a short story?

7. Does O'Connor expect people to read nothing but great works of fiction?

8. Are any of O'Connor's comments on the writing of fiction relevant to the writing of nonfiction?

9. According to O'Connor, what is the role of a writing teacher? Have you ever benefited from a writing teacher in a way that O'Connor does not recognize?

Suggestions for Writing

1. Summarize what you have learned so far about writing, and write an essay explaining the nature and aim of *non*fiction.

2. Draw upon your knowledge of music, sports, or crafts and define what makes work successful in any one of these fields.

8

Writing to Evaluate Something

When you are trying to decide whether you want to buy a wool sweater or a cotton one, when you bet your brother that your school will win the game this weekend, when you decide which dictionary to buy or make a decision to vote for a particular candidate — when you do any of these things, you are *evaluating*. Evaluating is something everyone does every day. It means thinking critically and trying to make intelligent choices. It can also involve trying to influence others to accept your judgments, especially if you have put them in writing.

Evaluation requires that you determine the nature or the quality of what you are judging. For instance, if you decide to consume less caffeine, that judgment addresses the nature of caffeine. Or perhaps you purchase a name brand lawn mower rather than a store brand to assure yourself that you will have a reliable, well-made machine; in this situation your concern is with quality. Evaluation also means determining importance or worth. For example, you have a thousand things to do before the weekend, and you know you can't get them all done; so you decide to spend your time on the most important ones. You are concerned with worth in the sense of benefit if you decide that a course in art history would be more useful to you as an architecture major than a course in music history; and worth in the sense of price is the question if you were to purchase precious metals — ounce for ounce, gold is worth more than silver.

But evaluation is also a persuasive act. In the above examples you are persuading yourself. However, there will be plenty of times when your evaluation must persuade someone else: Which supplier should you recommend to your employer? What should you say when asked to write a letter of recommendation? Whose opinion should prevail when a couple disagree about which of two apartments to rent? Addressing situations like these means you have to apply what you have already learned about persuasion: how to define your assumptions, make inferences, respond to opposition, and draw conclusions.

When writing an evaluation, you also need to assure your readers that you have the credentials to make judgments about the subject you are addressing. Persuading your readers that you know what you're talking about is a large part of persuading your readers to accept your evaluation. The more your readers think you know about your subject, the more likely they are to follow your advice. But no matter how knowledgeable you may be, try not to sound as if you have a monopoly on good advice. People can take a perverse pleasure in not following the advice of a critic who seems arrogant. Consider how Mark Twain just barely avoids the charge of arrogance in his essay on James Fenimore Cooper. Much of Twain's credibility results from his own reputation as a master of the craft of fiction; but he also disposes the reader to agree with his attack on Cooper by allowing his trademark folksy tone to show through. Thinking, "This person who seems so unpretentious couldn't possibly be an ill-tempered, arrogant boor," the reader acquits Twain and finds Cooper guilty as charged. Like Twain, you can often benefit from sounding engaging as well as knowledgeable. Although the extent to which you allow your personality to come through will depend upon your rhetorical situation, evaluations are seldom impersonal.

PLANNING YOUR ESSAY

When you are ready to choose a subject for evaluation, consider what you have some experience and knowledge of as well as what you are interested in. If you are knowledgeable about a subject, you will usually have a good idea of what criteria people generally use when evaluating that subject. This knowledge will help you focus on the concerns your evaluation should cover if it is to satisfy the needs of readers. For example, if you recently bought a stationary bicycle for home use and think that your written evaluation of the available models will help others decide which one to buy, make sure you don't base your evaluation only on which bicycle is cheapest. Readers also need to know what they are getting for their money. Report what you know about features such as mileage counters and tension adjustment; then discuss how well different bikes perform and how likely they are to hold up under use. Otherwise, a reader may wind up with a bicycle that was cheap because it lacked important features or because it was difficult to use.

If you have the time to do research, writing an evaluation can be an excellent way to prepare for a decision you need to make. Thus, if you are planning to buy a stationary bicycle but do not understand the differences among various models, you can use evaluation as a way to decide what to buy. Careful shoppers go through this process routinely. They may visit a number of stores, question salespeople and friends who have experience with the product, and — if the purchase is large — go to the library and consult one or more of the magazines available for consumers. Writing an evaluation of a product you expect to purchase is a way of discovering and reporting the results of this process.

Evaluation, of course, is not limited to comparative shopping. Other situations require other types of research. But whatever your subject, you should examine what kind of information you have about it and assess whether you have to do research. Information is essential, because you must support your evaluation with specific evidence. When evaluating a novel by James Fenimore Cooper, Mark Twain supported the claims he makes with evidence from the novel. When evaluating the functioning of justice in a case involving child abuse, Dorothy Rabinowitz researched that case by studying court records and conducting numerous interviews. Evidence in an evaluation of your own might come directly from personal experience. Or if, like Bruce Catton, you want to evaluate important historical figures, then you will probably need to read extensively if you have not already done so. Choose evidence judiciously according to your understanding of your subject, and be sure that you have enough.

A good way to begin an evaluation is to think about your subject analytically, using one of the strategies discussed in Chapter 6 (see pp. 235–38). Here is a four-step process for using analysis to plan an evaluation:

1. Divide your subject by identifying its major components. For example, if you are evaluating a restaurant, you might address atmosphere, service, food, and prices. Or if you are evaluating an essay, you can evaluate it according to content, style, and organization.
2. Consider what information you have (or can obtain) to discuss the divisions you have identified.
3. Ask yourself which of these divisions are most likely to be important to readers, and consider whether you have overlooked any important part of your subject your readers would probably

want information about. Unless you are writing for your own benefit, eliminate any division that seems to be a personal interest unlikely to concern other readers.

4. Decide whether to discuss all important divisions that you have identified or to focus only upon one if you have enough information about it and feel sure that you would be focusing upon something important. An evaluation of a restaurant, for example, can be limited to a discussion of its food (although you would probably end up subdividing that subject somehow — according to appetizers, entrees, and desserts or according to selection, presentation, and taste).

When planning an evaluation, you should also consider how strongly you feel about your subject. Some people believe that you should always write about something you have a real investment in, because your enthusiasm will enhance the liveliness of your writing. Others think this course of action leads to a one-sided evaluation. If you've just bought a new car and are crazy about it, you probably lack the objectivity you need to evaluate it fairly. But if you've driven the car for a year and you still love it, you probably have enough objectivity to see its flaws as well as its virtues and can execute a balanced judgment. One of the strengths of Dorothy Rabinowitz's evaluation is the balance she provides: For instance, although she strongly champions the defendant in the case she reviews, she doesn't ignore that person's errors in judgment. At the other extreme, Mark Twain finds no redeeming features in Cooper's *Deerslayer;* he uses humor to cloak the imbalance.

DEFINING YOUR CRITERIA

Effective, accurate evaluations are not the result of whim; they are based on standards that most people agree with, that the authority of the writer bolsters, or that can be independently verified. Evaluation requires you to make the criteria you use for judging absolutely clear — as Twain does when he provides a list of eighteen "rules governing literary art," or as Ruth Dorgan does when she begins her essay on "Jack and the Beanstalk" by revealing the principles she brings to evaluating literature: "examine the text closely and give evidence for any thesis." Both Twain and Dorgan apply criteria that many people would agree with — and the criteria can be verified by questioning a representative sample of readers. The criteria involve something more than Twain's or Dorgan's personal preferences. Criteria that can be verified by anyone who cares to check are considered external. Such tangible qualities as size and price are clearly external. Anyone can verify your judgment that a Whippersnapper lawn mower at 18 inches and 25 pounds is a better buy for an arthritic gardener than a Lawndozer at 22 inches and 70 pounds. All that person has to do is recognize two basic assumptions you made: Arthritic persons require maneuverable mowers; light, small machines are more maneuverable than large, heavy ones.

Nora Ephron uses an internal criterion for judging *People* magazine. The reader can't test it; Ephron never states it. She implies it by stating her appraisal: *People* is "a potato chip. A snack. Empty calories." Her criterion is also implicit in every piece of evidence she uses to criticize *People*. Internal criteria are subjective and a matter of the evaluator's judgment, and as such, they can be risky to use. The persuasiveness of your judgment depends largely on your being able to ensure that your readers will recognize your special expertise. Ephron relies upon her expertise, but she also protects her judgment by hedging it. By praising *People* for doing what it said it would do, she is able to deliver a telling blow at the same time that she ensures that the reader will see her as fair-minded:

> I do read it. I read it in the exact way its editors intend me to—straight through without stopping. I buy it in airline terminals, and I find that if I start reading it at the moment I am seated on the Eastern shuttle, it lasts until shortly before takeoff.

Criteria should also be appropriate for your audience. Suppose your criterion for evaluating a magazine for novice computer users is that each issue should include a new shortcut for software developers. Your criterion is inappropriate for your audience because someone learning how to use a computer is unlikely to develop new software. If you base your judgment of stocks on which ones will double your money fastest, your standard is inappropriate for advising widows and orphans, whose primary interest in stocks is a safe income. As another example, consider "Unlike a Virgin" by Luc Sante, which originally appeared in *The New Republic,* a magazine of political and social commentary. Holding many of the same beliefs as Sante, subscribers to *The New Republic* probably approved of his evaluation of Madonna as an opportunist with limited talent. But readers of *Cosmopolitan* or *Money* may find this evaluation based upon criteria that they do not agree with. As a final example, if you are evaluating local housing for an audience of single students who want to party, you will not want to rate housing higher because playgrounds and day-care facilities are available; whereas that information can be vital for married couples. You should set criteria you think your readers will agree with — or at least will not reject.

Examine your criteria and ask yourself if they justify the evaluation you plan to make. You may be furious at one of the local apartment complexes for charging you two months' rent as a deposit because you have a pet, but your sense of having been victimized is not necessarily a legitimate criterion for giving that complex a negative rating in your guide to local housing. You would be much better off simply stating the policy; perhaps other prospective tenants would not object to such a high deposit—may even approve of it. Base your evaluation of the apartment complex on more objective criteria. For example, what is the rent per square foot? Are the apartments furnished? What appliances are included? Is there a fireplace? What kind of storage is available? Does the rent include access to swimming pools and party facilities? Have there been complaints about how the complex is maintained? What about late-payment policies?

You also need to consider the kind of evidence that will persuade your audience to accept your evaluation. If you want the single students on campus to accept your negative evaluation of the apartment complex that has the high pet deposit, you might consider investigating management's policies about parties, whether guests can use the pool, and how management handles summer sublets. If the policies are strict in these ways, single students should be informed; and the students will probably elect to rent elsewhere, even though there is a grand party room, every unit has a fireplace, and the rent is not out of line. You should offer evidence according to what you think your readers expect to find out and how knowledgeable they are. It is rare that any subject will elicit the kind of universal agreement that will permit you to use the same criteria and information for all audiences.

Readers expect to find enough information to reconstruct the reasoning you used to arrive at your evaluation. Be sure to provide adequate information for readers unfamiliar with the subject you are evaluating. When readers are unfamiliar with a subject that is complex, a thorough and persuasive evaluation can take many pages—as you will see when you read "From the Mouths of Babes." But whatever the level of expertise your audience possesses, you are responsible for making sure they understand the information you give them and the criteria that led you to report that information.

ORGANIZING YOUR ESSAY

However you choose to proceed, you should state your judgment clearly and place it prominently. It is the main point of your essay and, depending upon other decisions you have made, may appear near the beginning or the end of your writing. Generally, it is useful to put it both places. That way, you prepare your readers for the conclusion you will draw, and the evidence you present is clearly in support of your evaluation. It is usually wise to show your readers that you have considered both the strengths and the weaknesses of your subject. To do so, many writers have chosen to adapt the pattern of classical oration (see pp. 20–21) for evaluations:

- Present your subject. (This discussion includes any background information, description, acknowledgment of weaknesses, and so forth.)
- State your criteria. (If your criteria are controversial, be sure to justify them.)
- Make your judgment. (State this as clearly and emphatically as possible.)
- Give your reasons. (Be sure to present good evidence for each reason.)
- Refute opposing evaluations. (Let your reader know you have given thoughtful consideration to opposing views, when such views exist.)
- State your conclusion. (You may restate or summarize your judgment.)

Notice that the refutation comes near the end, after the judgment is well established. An alternative strategy is to refute opposing evaluations early in the essay; this strategy can be especially effective when opposing views are already widely held and you intend to advance a new point of view. Recognizing views that your audience may already hold can, in this case, clear the way for a fresh evaluation. This is the strategy that Mark Twain used when writing about Cooper at a time when Cooper was much praised.

Consider how you can most advantageously present your subject. Make use of appropriate techniques for developing ideas: for instance, you might look at the subject historically — employing a great deal of narrative and cause-and-effect technique — as Rabinowitz does, or you can make a comparative judgment as Catton does. Comparative judgments focus on similarities, and contrastive judgments focus on differences, but the two can be — and often are — combined. In any comparison you must find a point of similarity between what you are evaluating and another item, and this similarity should be significant. There is little purpose in evaluating two identical stationary bicycles, for instance, but a reader will be interested in a comparison between bicycles made by different companies. If the items being compared are essentially different, but they show some point of similarity, you are probably dealing with an *analogy*. Note carefully the points of similarity or difference; they will be your basis for comparison.

As you work your way through your comparison, present your evidence in an organized way. People generally find it useful to see one of two common patterns of organization: subject by subject or point by point. Bruce Catton uses both in "Grant and Lee." For instance, he first contrasts Grant and Lee by focusing on one general and describing him, then turning to and describing the other. Next, he addresses their similarities point by point. Both strategies have advantages and disadvantages. The subject approach has the advantage of not making frequent switches between the items compared. However, if the comparison is long or complicated, keeping a whole subject in mind can become difficult. The point-by-point method is a good choice if you have many points of comparison, but it can give the impression of disorderliness if it moves too rapidly between items.

Comparison and contrast are by no means limited to evaluations; elsewhere in this book you will find writers using these strategies for other motives. But comparison and contrast are especially useful for evaluation because placing two subjects alongside each other can lead to a better understanding of each — and often help you decide whether one is superior. If offered two different jobs, both of which seem attractive, you can probably clarify which is preferable by carefully comparing them.

It would be a mistake, however, to assume that evaluation must always lead to a rating of some sort. Although criticism usually leads to a judgment regarding quality or worth, it is ultimately concerned with improving our understanding of whatever is being evaluated. In this chapter R. Jackson Wilson provides the clearest example of how evaluation can be a type of explanation. Discussing an engraving of Walt Whitman, Wilson begins by offering his judgment; he calls the engraving "superb." He then goes on to interpret the engraving, for the judgment makes sense only if readers can understand the interpretation behind the judgment. Similarly, Ruth Dorgan judges that the giant is the true hero of "Jack and the Beanstalk"; most of her essay is devoted to explaining how she arrived at this judgment. A critic reviewing a book or movie in a newspaper is expected to give the work an overall rating, because that is what newspaper readers most want to know: Is this work worth reading or seeing? (For information on reviewing, see pp. 474–75.) But evaluation isn't always a matter of getting people to do (or not do) something. Sometimes, it's simply devoted to getting people to see something that they might otherwise miss. Judgment, in this case, may be implicit. Understanding that there is more to something than we had realized can lead us to reappraise our valuation of that subject.

As we have seen before, motives for writing can overlap. An explanation may be necessary to persuade readers to accept a particular judgment. The selections that follow were chosen to give you a sense of different types of evaluation. As you read them, try to evaluate the extent to which each succeeds in accomplishing what it sets out to do.

JACK THE GIANTMUGGER

Ruth Dorgan

Ruth Dorgan teaches English at the University of Wisconsin, Stevens Point. Note how Dorgan begins by stating external criteria; however, be alert for any additional criteria that she does not state but that are reflected in her defense of a giant who is usually seen as a villain. As you read Dorgan's essay, think about how it offers a fresh point of view. Consider whether you could surprise readers with an unconventional response to another well-known work, be it a fairy tale, a novel, or a film.

My five-year-old son is very fond of a folk tale dear to the hearts of adults and children alike. It is a story about the little guy who makes good, the weakling who outsmarts the strong man; it is Horatio Alger and David and Goliath; it is the American Dream; it is "Jack and the Beanstalk." I had read this story to my older son many times, usually thinking about something else. But the other day I started paying attention to what the story said, something I urge my college English students to do all the time, and I realized that Jack is the most overrated hero in children's literature and that the giant has been misunderstood and maligned. In short, Jack is a shiftless, irresponsible wastrel who turns to thieving when he has ruined his poor mother and himself, and the giant is an outcast who bothers no one — except Englishmen who come to rob him — spends his time looking at beautiful things and listening to music and is victimized by his wife, opportunists and a world that does not love difference.

Another thing I ask my literature students to do is examine the text closely and give evidence for any thesis they propose. The text of "Jack and the Beanstalk" provides ample evidence to support my thesis. At the beginning of the tale, Jack's mother is in despair because she has no money left and no goods to sell, only a cow. She sends Jack to market to sell the cow and he trades her for a handful of colorful beans which delight his whimsical nature. His mother is, of course, furious and flings the beans out the window. Jack retires to his room ashamed and hungry. In the morning a huge beanstalk has sprung up outside the window and Jack climbs out of the land of the prosaic and ordinary into the land of the different and extraordinary, where he does such damage with his shallow mind and greedy nature that all the king's men could not restore its peace and stark beauty.

The giant looks like a monster, moves like a leviathan, shouts like a berserk. But he is at heart solitary and esthetic. He lives in his remote land, counting his gold, listening to his harp and watching his little hen lay eggs — when he is not being betrayed by his wife. Is he a miser? I think not; he is a lover of beauty, and he lives handsomely: The food is plentiful, at any rate. And he owns beautiful things like the little harp, which, it is significant to note, loves him. (The harp calls out, "Wake, my master, wake!" when Jack steals it on his final raid.) Is he a cannibal? ("I'll grind his bones to make my bread!" he roars.) No, he is a ranter and a bellower who is so easily fooled that he could never find his victim.

The giant, nevertheless, has serious faults. He does bellow and threaten, and his wife is afraid of him—but not so afraid that she doesn't trick him twice, and with that old female chauvinist philosophy: the way to man's heart. And so she stuffs him with food and he is content. He roars at his little hen, too: "Lay!" She lays. So he is a male chauvinist. I don't know a man who isn't (even my five-year-old who speaks of Mommy's kitchen, Mommy's washing machine). The giant thinks that females are to serve him and be commanded. That is a serious fault but a common one.

But what about his threats against Englishmen (and they are exclusively against Englishmen). Obviously he is a Celtic giant; no one but the Irish hate the English so much. And what kind of supernatural beings do the Irish revere and respect? The little people. In a land where littleness is cherished the giant was bound to find himself an outcast. Giants are rare enough, but an Irish giant—that is unheard of.

And so he established himself in a remote land and made a very satisfactory life for himself, if not for his wife. (Male chauvinists believe that every woman is willing to say with Ruth, "Whither thou goest, I will go.") He had room and privacy to stomp around and roar (as it is the nature of giants to do) until he was tired, and then sit and look at and listen to all his lovely things. But Jack fixed all that.

The first time Jack invaded the giant's land, he stole a bag of gold. Perhaps we might excuse him for this: He needed it and the giant had more. But when he went back the second time he took a source of endless wealth: the obliging little hen. The story says, "Then Jack and his mother wanted for nothing in all the world." Then why did he climb the beanstalk a third time? It was a gratuitous, mischievous, destructive thing to do. He took the last treasure the giant had: the little harp that soothed the giant's outcast soul. Jack had no need of it. He hardly seems like the type to love music; he just loves to take things. When the giant naturally pursued, Jack called for his mother to bring the hatchet. And like every mother who wants to help her son succeed at his trade, she ran to help. Together they killed the giant "dead as a stone from that day to this." A good day's work: ego satisfying and highly profitable. They congratulate each other; they eat heartily. Starting with a handful of beans, they have made it big. This is called, I think, free enterprise.

But my heart is with the giant. He was big and ugly and loud and, above all, different, but still he had found refuge in a hostile world and made some kind of life for himself. And then small-minded Jack came climbing the beanstalk. People like Jack do not understand what is different from themselves: Freaks of any kind are fair game. And people like

Jack never stop until they have done as much mischief and destruction as they can. Jack succeeds and the giant is destroyed. That's the way it usually happens, but I don't have to like it, and it is time Jack the Giantkiller is exposed for what he is: Jack the Giantmugger. A giant is a very rare thing. Jack is waiting on every street corner to rob you blind.

Questions for Discussion

1. Where does Dorgan first state her thesis? What evidence does she offer for its support?
2. According to Dorgan, the giant is victimized by "a world that does not love difference." What does it mean to be "different"? Is Dorgan making a comment about life that goes beyond how to interpret a fairy tale?
3. In paragraphs 4 and 6 Dorgan writes about female and male chauvinists. Do the attitudes she describes still seem recognizable twenty years after this essay was first published?
4. What does Jack represent for Dorgan? Why does he disappoint her?
5. How does Dorgan account for the shortcomings of the character who is, in her evaluation, the most attractive in "Jack and the Beanstalk?"

Suggestions for Writing

1. Reread a fairy tale or children's book and ask yourself whether it contains any values that a child is unlikely to perceive. Then, evaluate at least one of the characters in that work, offering evidence that will show others why you see that character as you do.
2. Dorgan writes that her new understanding of "Jack and the Beanstalk" came from doing what she urges her students to do: paying attention to what a story says, examining the text closely, and providing evidence to support a thesis. How well has she fulfilled the goals she sets in paragraphs 1 and 2? Read "Jack and the Beanstalk," and then write an evaluation of "Jack the Giantmugger."

PEOPLE MAGAZINE

Nora Ephron

> *Nora Ephron is a journalist and novelist. You may be familiar with her work if you saw* Heartburn, *the film made of the novel Ephron wrote about her marriage to* Washington Post *writer Carl Bernstein. Before you read her essay on* People *magazine, try to examine a copy of this magazine, if you are not already familiar with it. When you finish reading, decide whether Ephron's evaluation has reinforced your own impression or led you to reconsider how you feel about* People. *Note that Ephron wrote this evaluation in 1975.*

The people over at *People* get all riled up if anyone suggests that *People* is a direct descendant of anything at all. You do not even have to suggest that it is; the first words anyone over there says, *insists,* really, is that *People* is *not* a spin-off of the *Time* "People" section (which they are right about), and that it is *not* a reincarnation of *Life* (which they are, at least in part, wrong about). *People,* they tell you, is an original thing. Distinctive. Different. Unto itself. They make it sound a lot like a cigarette.

People was introduced by Time Inc. a year ago, and at last reports it was selling 1,250,000 copies a week, all of them on newsstands. It is the first national weekly that has been launched since *Sports Illustrated* in 1954, and it will probably lose some three million dollars in its first year, a sum that fazes no one at Time Inc., since it is right on target. *Sports Illustrated* lost twenty-six million in the ten years before it turned the corner, and *People* is expected to lose considerably less and turn the corner considerably quicker. There is probably something to be said for all this—something about how healthy it is for the magazine business that a thing like this is happening, a new magazine with good prospects and no nudity that interests over a million readers a week—but I'm not sure that I am the person who is going to say it. *People* makes me grouchy, and I have been trying for months to figure out why. I do read it. I read it in the exact way its editors intend me to—straight through without stopping. I buy it in airline terminals, and I find that if I start reading it at the moment I am seated on the Eastern shuttle, it lasts until shortly before takeoff. This means that its time span is approximately five minutes longer than the *New York Post* on a day with a good Rose Franzblau column, and five minutes less than *Rona Barrett's Gossip,* which in any case is not available at the Eastern shuttle terminal in La Guardia Airport.

My problem with the magazine is not that I think it is harmful or dangerous or anything of the sort. It's almost not worth getting upset about. It's a potato chip. A snack. Empty calories. Which would be fine, really—I like potato chips. But they make you feel lousy afterward too.

People is a product of something called the Magazine Development Group at Time Inc., which has been laboring for several years to come up with new magazines and has brought forth *Money* and two rejected dummy magazines, one on photography, the other on show business. The approach this group takes is a unique one in today's magazine business: Most magazines tend to be about a sensibility rather than a subject, and tend to be dominated not by a group but by one editor and his or her concept of what that sensibility is. In any event, the idea for *People* — which was a simple, five-word idea: let's-call-a-magazine-*People* — started kicking around the halls of Time Inc. a couple of years ago. Some people, mainly Clare Boothe Luce,° think it originated with Clare Boothe Luce; others seem to lean toward a great-idea-whose-time-has-come theory, not unlike the Big Bang, and they say that if anyone thought of it at all (which they are not sure of), it was Andrew Heiskell, Time Inc.'s chairman of the board. But the credit probably belongs, in some transcendental way, to Kierkegaard, who in 1846 said that in time, all anyone would be interested in was gossip.

From the beginning, *People* was conceived as an inexpensive maga-   5
zine — cheap to produce and cheap to buy. There would be a small staff. Low overhead. Stringers. No color photographs except for the cover. It was intended to be sold only on newsstands — thus eliminating the escalating cost of mailing the magazine to subscribers and mailing the subscribers reminders to renew their subscriptions. It was clear that the magazine would have to have a very strong appeal for women; an increasing proportion of newsstands in this country are in supermarkets. Its direct competitor for rack space at the check-out counter was the *National Enquirer*. A pilot issue of the magazine, with Richard Burton and Elizabeth Taylor on the cover, was produced in August, 1973, and test-marketed in seven cities, and it is the pride of the Time Inc. marketing department that this was done in the exact way Procter & Gamble introduces a new toilet paper. When Malcolm B. Ochs, marketing director of the Magazine Development Group at Time Inc., speaks about *People,* he talks about selling "packaged goods" and "one million units a week" and "perishable products." This sort of talk is not really surprising — I have spent enough time around magazine salesmen to know they would all be more comfortable selling tomatoes — but it is nonetheless a depressing development.

The second major decision that was arrived at early on was to keep the stories short. "We always want to leave people wishing for more," says Richard B. Stolley, *People's* managing editor. This is a perfectly valid editorial slogan, but what Stolley does not seem willing to admit is the reason for it, which is that *People* is essentially a magazine for people who

---

Clare Boothe Luce: An American writer and political activist (1903–1987), wife of publisher Henry R. Luce, the founder of *Time* magazine.

don't like to read. The people at *People* seem to believe that people who read *People* have the shortest attention spans in the world. *Time* and *Life* started out this way too, but both of them managed to rise above their original intentions.

The incarnation of *Life* that *People* most resembles is not the early era, where photographs dominated, nor even the middle-to-late period, when the photography and journalism struck a nice balance, but the last desperate days, when Ralph Graves was trying to save the magazine from what turned out to be its inevitable death. This is not the time to go into Graves's most serious and abhorrent editorial decision, which was to eliminate the *Life* Great Dinners series; what I want to talk about instead is his decision to shorten the articles. There are people over at the Time-Life Building, defenders of Graves, who insist he did this for reasons of economy—there was no room for long pieces in a magazine that was losing advertising and therefore editorial pages—but Graves himself refuses to be so defended. He claims he shortened the articles because he believes in short articles. And the result, in the case of *Life,* was a magazine that did nothing terribly well.

People has this exact quality—and I'm not exactly sure why. I have nothing against short articles, and no desire to read more than 1500 words or so on most of the personalities *People* profiles. In fact, in the case of a number of those personalities—and here the name of Telly Savalas springs instantly to mind—a caption would suffice. I have no quarrel with the writing in the magazine, which is slick and perfectly competent. I wouldn't mind if *People* were just a picture magazine, if I could at least see the pictures; there is an indefinable something in its art direction that makes the magazine look remarkably like the centerfold of the *Daily News.* And I wouldn't even mind if it were a fan magazine for grownups—if it delivered the goods. But the real problem is that when I finish reading *People,* I always feel that I have just spent four days in Los Angeles. *Women's Wear Daily* at least makes me feel dirty; *People* makes me feel that I haven't read or learned or seen anything at all. I don't think this is what Richard Stolley means when he says he wants to leave his readers wanting more: I tend to be left feeling that I haven't gotten anything in the first place. And even this feeling is hard to pinpoint; I am looking at a recent issue of *People,* with Hugh Hefner on the cover, and I can't really say I didn't learn anything in it: On page 6 it says that Hefner told his unauthorized biographer that he once had a homosexual experience. I didn't actually know that before reading *People,* but somehow it doesn't surprise me.

Worst of all—yes, there is a worst of all—I end up feeling glutted with celebrity. I stopped reading movie magazines in the beauty parlor a couple of years ago because I could not accommodate any more information about something called the Lennon Sisters. I had got to the point where I thought I knew what celebrity was—celebrity was anyone I would stand up in a restaurant and stare at. I had whittled the list down to Marlon

Brando, Mary Tyler Moore and Angelo "Gyp" DeCarlo, and I was fairly happy. Now I am confronted with *People,* and the plain fact is that a celebrity is anyone *People* writes about; I know the magazine is filling some nameless, bottomless pit of need for gossip and names, but I haven't got room in my life for so many lights.

People's only serious financial difficulty at this point is in attracting   10 advertisers, and one of the reasons the people at *People* think they are having trouble doing so is that their advertisers don't know who the *People* reader is. Time Inc. has issued a demographic survey which shows that *People's* readers are upscale, whatever that means, and that 48 percent of them have been to college. I never believe these surveys — *Playboy* and *Penthouse* have them, and theirs show that their readers are mainly interested in the fine fiction; in any case, I suspect that *People's* real problem with advertisers is not that they don't know exactly who's reading the magazine, but that they know exactly who's reading it. In one recent issue there are three liquor ads — for Seagram's Seven Crown, Jim Beam and a bottled cocktail called the Brass Monkey, all of them brands bought predominantly by the blue-collar middle class. It's logical that these brands would buy space in *People* — liquor companies can't advertise on television. But any product that could would probably do better to reach non-readers through the mass-market women's magazines, which at least sit around all month, or on television itself.

"The human element really is being neglected in national reporting," says Richard Stolley. "The better newspapers and magazines deal more and more with events and issues and debates. The human beings caught up in them simply get squelched. If we can bring a human being out of a massive event, then we've done what I want to do." I don't really object to this philosophy — I'm not sure that I agree with it, but I don't object to it. But it seems a shame that so much of the reporting of the so-called human element in *People* is aimed at the lowest common denominator of the also-so-called human element, that all this coverage of humanity has to be at the expense of the issues and events and ideas involved. It seems even sadder that there seems to be no stopping it. *People* is the future, and it works, and that makes me grouchiest of all.

Questions for Discussion

1. Why does *People* magazine make Nora Ephron feel "grouchy"?
2. How was *People* developed? Why was it assumed that it would have to appeal to women?
3. Where in this essay does Ephron try to be fair to *People*?
4. How does Ephron define "celebrity"? Has *People* changed what this word means? How long is such status likely to last? Which of the "celebrities" mentioned in this essay are familiar to you?

5. What does Ephron reveal about herself in the course of writing about *People*? What else doesn't she like? What do you think it would take to please her?

Suggestions for Writing

1. Choose an easily obtainable newspaper or magazine. Study at least three issues carefully. Then write an evaluation of it. Consider whether it is informative, entertaining, and well designed.
2. Study the ads in a recent issue of *People* and try to determine whether advertisers have by now decided what type of people read *People*. Compare your conclusions with the claims Ephron makes in paragraphs 6 and 10.

UNLIKE A VIRGIN

Luc Sante

> *As a rule, it's a good idea to keep an open mind when you read an evaluation — even if you are already familiar with its subject. If you have ever seen or heard Madonna, you may have your own opinion of her as a singer and actress. Consider what criteria your opinion is based upon, and think about whether your criteria differ from Luc Sante's. Note that Sante emphasizes agency, the means through which Madonna became successful. Think about whether this emphasis is appropriate or whether an evaluation should focus strictly upon a performer's work.*

After two or three months of ceaseless barrage upon the American continent, the winds of Madonna have shifted and besieged Europe. Not that the American public is likely to banish her from memory for even a second, especially since The Movie is playing in every minimall and multiplex and is still being considered from every angle in Sunday supplements throughout the land, and The Album is prominently on display in retail outlets of every demographic. The Tour, however, has left these shores, taking with it the unilateral media saturation that brought Madonna into every room of every house and caused her to hover in the periphery, at least, of every consciousness. Is there anyone, at large or in stir, who does not know the details of Madonna's latest look, with its kewpie-doll ponytail and dominatrix affectations, its nose-cone brassieres and pin-striped suits with breast slits? Or of her stage show, complete with tubular-breasted males, wriggling mermen, and a kickline of Dick Tracies?

Of course, Madonna dwells among us at most times, and her presence is felt in record shops and T-shirt boutiques and on MTV and in the sheets and rags that draw all their material from speculation on the hidden lives of celebrities. But in this late-century version of the dog-and-pony show, her face and body and the attributes of her legend appeared on and in every general-interest magazine and newspaper and magazine-format television program, her name was heard as a reference and a figure of speech in the routines of comedians, the banter of TV news co-anchors, the fulminations of media moralists, in bar-talk and gym-talk and water-cooler-talk and supermarket-line-talk. In the night sky of the American imagination, Madonna looms.

For the time being, at least. Will she endure as a figure to color forever our idea of fame, to become the little picture accompanying the definition of "media star" in the illustrated dictionaries of the future? Will she enter the domain of clip-art imagery as a badly printed blob on shopping bags and paper place mats whose muddy outlines are nevertheless as instantly recognizable as those of the Marilyn of the dress-flipping-up-over-steam-vent or the Brando of the peaked cap and motorcycle jacket?

Such, after all, is her ambition. Madonna is not out for mere money or mere glory; even less is she in pursuit of the perfect beat or the sublime hook. It is not for her to achieve international respect and then disappear into genteel privacy in Switzerland or New Mexico, to define a song or a movie role and then suffer that title's parenthetical accompaniment of her name in every printed citation. She does not want to make her pile and cut out — she does not want to cut out. Madonna wants to conquer the unconscious, to become indelible.

She has already taken steps toward this end. There is, for example, 5 the matter of the single name, which in America is usually an abbreviation conferred by the public over time as an accolade and a sign of affection. Madonna has taken the shortcut of lopping it off herself. And there is the image. In her canny way Madonna realized that in this day and age success results less often from imposing a spectacular figure on the public than from erecting a screen upon which the public can project its own internal movies. So she invented herself as a mutable being, a container for a multiplicity of images. She could be anything, with only the one unchanging grace note: the mole just above her lip.

Madonna Louise Veronica Ciccone hails from Michigan, came to New York in the late 1970's or early '80s, studied dance, hung out heavily, began her career as a photographer's model (some mildly dirty pictures from this period surfaced a few years ago, and some of the tabloids were weak-minded enough to think they could make a scandal out of them), appeared in a small role in at least one low-grade exploitation movie, and then began making a name as a "track singer" (a lost term from that brief interregnum between live performance and the total electronic environment, referring to vocalists who appeared in clubs singing to taped accompaniment).

On the New York club scene she appears to have gone from decorative nobody to new face on the rise in a sort of Ruby Keeler minute. She persuaded Mark Kamins, a deejay at Danceteria, the club of that hour, to produce a song for her ("Everybody"), then persuaded Seymour Stein, the godfather of New York "new wave," to issue it on his Sire Records label, and it hit the charts. In those days (1982), when Reaganism was still young, dance-party records made by ambitious white semi-bohemians might be viewed as artistic and even political statements merely by virtue of their genre. By eschewing rock-n-roll jingoism in favor of bass out front, wide backbeat, and lyrics that in essence always said, "Let's everybody party down," they made a gesture of calling out to the whole world, especially to its third part. It was a year or two before this stance became generic.

So it was that Madonna's early records, blasting out over such stations as WBLS in New York, stations that were then just beginning to be referred to by the demographic euphemism "urban contemporary," sounded like more than mere product. The very simple lyrics of her second 45, "Holiday" ("We should take a holiday, some time to cele-brate . . ."), had a utopian flavor, however soft. Her voice, with its nasal tough-girl inflection by Ronnie Spector out of Minnie Mouse and related by blood or marriage to the throw-down quality exuded by such chan-teuses as Teena Marie and Evelyn "Champagne" King, made the invita-tion sound uncompromising, almost brave. After three or four hits in succession, Madonna was a downtown singer with proven crossover ability.

Still, the likelihood of her achieving any further distinction seemed remote. Madonna, however, was not one to accept any predetermined view of her career. She immediately raised the stakes, and in rapid order began advancing one marketing theme after another, in the process re-vealing that while she had a small talent as a pop singer, as an image strategist she possessed something approaching genius. Her first order of business was to jettison the appealing but limited waif look featured on the cover of her eponymous first album, to replace its whisper with a shout. For this purpose she initiated a hostile takeover of the sartorial repertoire of her older rival Cyndi Lauper, an original who had taken the hippie-punk scavenger aesthetic to an extreme point and assembled herself as a living collage of old and new styles, clashing colors, mismatched fabrics, accessories contrived from the most unlikely objects.

Madonna, of course, was no original; she was, like her role model 10 David Bowie, a magpie with a flair for highlighting the critical elements of the styles she appropriated. She dispensed with the self-mockery im-plicit in Lauper's presentation and zeroed in on its fetishistic sexual aspect. Hence the bras-as-outerwear, the "Boy Toy" belt buckles, the junk jewelry by the pound. The look titillated boys of all ages, while teenage girls found in it a form of rebellion that could be safely assumed and doffed outside parental ken, since it involved nothing drastic or irreversible. The look instantly propelled Madonna into the national image bank. She had taken her first beachhead.

A measure of the success of this image was that it lasted much longer in the consciousness of the public than it did in Madonna's own career. Its early crudity can be assessed in her "Virgin Tour" video, which shows her looking askew and even a bit chunky, missing notes and flailing around on stage, but evidently learning on the job. This, however, was her live show. At the same time, she was displaying a precocious understanding of the nascent power of the video clip, becoming one of the first pop stars to issue songs that were inseparably entwined with the visual imagery of their MTV illustrations in the minds of consumers.

Her first successful salvo in this direction was "Like a Virgin." "Should go over big in Italy," quipped a friend of mine at the time; sure enough, the video was shot in Venice, and it contained the first glimmers of her now-trademark Catholic-transgression sideline. Of course, it also possessed all of the grace of a "Girls of the Adriatic" *Playboy* feature, along with the patented MTV significance-trigger of staggering slo-mo; but it can be said to have made its point. Her follow-up was "Material Girl," which may have sounded a bit like Carmen Miranda. What everybody noticed, however, was the video, in which Madonna shamelessly reinvented the wheel, lifting wholesale Marilyn's courtroom dance sequence from *Gentlemen Prefer Blondes* and flushing it of its satire. Subtlety, Madonna well knew, butters no parsnips in the pop marketplace. "Material Girl" was crass, vulgar, obvious, charmless, and virtually definitive of the grasping zeitgeist of 1984. It was, naturally, her biggest hit to date, and probably remains so.

Around the same time she was fortunate enough to be handed an opportunity well beyond her own contrivance. Susan Seidelman, a little-known but enterprising filmmaker apprenticing, as Madonna had, in the Manhattan bohemia career institute, cast her in *Desperately Seeking Susan* as the mystery woman of the title. The film was halting, turgid, and as instantly irrelevant as any Gidget vehicle. But in its tame exploitation of the downtown-scene mystique it somehow rang the safe-rebellion chime for millions of middle-class youth. Madonna was ideally suited to her role, which called for her to look sultry and jaded and not say a whole lot. The movie earned many times its budget, its title entered the catchphrase arsenal of headline writers everywhere, and Madonna emerged from the experience having attained a new rung of celebrity, along with a reputation, soon shown to be utterly unfounded, as a major box-office attraction.

The rest, as they say, is history. She married the troubled Sean Penn and succeeded in profiting from his bad press, appeared in a couple of cinematic bombs (*Shanghai Surprise* and *Who's That Girl?*, in case you've forgotten) that did not leave her terribly scathed, issued many song-and-video packages that each involved a new look and a new attempt at a veneer of meaning, made a stab at artistic respectability by appearing in a sub-par David Mamet play, raised middle-American hackles with further Catholic-transgression affectations in the "Like a Prayer" video and with a mock-Sapphic Mutt-and-Jeff talk-show routine with Sandra Bernhard, promptly began being seen with Warren Beatty in as many simultaneous locations as Saint Anthony of Padua, and then embarked on an entirely new round of publicity with The Tour, The Movie, and The Album.

This dawn broke in early spring, as the tour started in Japan and   15
immediately began spinning off magazine spreads. The stage show looked scary in these pictures, a late-modernist casino spectacular involving elements from the Cabaret Voltaire, Salvador Dali's 1939 World's Fair show, *A Clockwork Orange,* Ken Russell movies, and the Alternative Miss World pageant. Madonna's hairstyle, for which she acknowledged the influence of the mid-1960s "Tressy" doll (you squeezed her stomach and pulled an

endless lock through a hole in the top of her head), at the same time suggested styles current on late-night cable-TV commercials for Dial-a-Mistress. The Jean-Paul Gaultier outfits were similarly daunting, redolent of Brunhilde and Attack of the Amazons and the homey-sinister allure of the 1950s bondage accoutrements immortalized in those little books published by Irving Klaw. Has she gone too far this time? you were supposed to ask.

The show itself was a wink and a nudge, a dance number and a blackout routine. Indeed, in its erotic display it was probably one of the most traditional stage shows to follow the circuit since everybody stopped wondering who killed burlesque. The degree of sexuality present in its set pieces was entirely allusive, twice-removed, and all but obliterated by the massive inverted commas that enclosed every aspect of the production. As a spiritual heir to Barnum, Madonna was in essence executing her version of the sign he famously put up reading "This Way to the Egress," which lured scores of people with active imaginations and small vocabularies right out the door.

For the record: she mock-kicked her female dancers around the stage while insulting them and complaining about the New York attitude (or at least that was the line at the Nassau Coliseum), mimed sodomizing various parties (though you would have missed the allusion had you been thinking Ziegfeld), allowed herself to be mock-ravished by male dancers gotten up as eunuchs during a faux-Oriental version of "Like a Virgin" and by an unseen diety while she struck ecstasy-of-Saint-Teresa poses during "Like a Prayer." There was also a song (included on the current album) whose lyrics and production number were devoted to spanking. Oh, yes, and there were those male dancers adorned with breasts that flopped like so many pairs of flaccid phalli while her own set looked like armor-plated projectiles.

There might be said to be a recurring theme here. If truth be told, Madonna herself does not precisely exude sexuality. What she exudes is more like will, iron self-discipline, and, of course, punctuality, that courtesy of monarchs. In her "Ciao, Italia" video, decked out in various gymnastic outfits and body-pumping to the screams of tens of thousands in a soccer stadium in Turin, Madonna looks perfectly able to make the trains run on time.° (Do not mistake this for an ethnic slur: her last name could just as easily be O'Flanagan and the setting Oslo or Kalamazoo.) Between the teasing simulation of carnality and the real passion for efficiency lies Madonna's bona fide erotic territory.

All the sexual imagery in the show, behind its rococo and vaudeville trappings, was single-mindedly fixated on power and its representations. The reason that Madonna does not possess much intrinsic sexual appeal,

---

to make the trains run on time: Before World War II Benito Mussolini, Fascist dictator of Italy, was much praised for making Italian trains run on time.

in spite of having raided the symbolic vanity cases of every icon from Harlow to Deitrich to Hayworth to Monroe (and throwing in Elvis for good measure), is that she lacks any trace of vulnerability, a quality that, it should be noted, is essential to the charms of both sexes. Pout and pant and writhe though she might, Madonna is not sexually convincing because her eyes do not register. They are too busy watching the door.

If, at this point there is any aspect of Madonna's act that seems independent of calculations, it is her preoccupation with the Catholic mysteries. Just such treading of the line between sacred and profane in the "Like a Prayer" video, you will recall, curtailed her lucrative career as a Pepsi-Cola spokesmodel. It seems there was this thing that happened between her and (apparently) Saint Martin de Porres, and then she acquired a case of stigmata, and then . . . Somehow various people took offense at this rather conventional set of images straight out of the Symbolist fakebook and put pressure on her corporate sponsors to suppress a commercial that by all accounts (it was broadcast exactly once) featured a very different, rather family-oriented story-line, even though it was set to the same tune as the video. This incident did not, however, prevent Madonna from including in her stage show a routine suggesting a musical-comedy version of *The Devils of Loudun,* complete with candles, crosses, stained glass, censers, and dancers garbed in mini-cassocks. While it makes for natural theater and automatic naughtiness, and comes equipped with a rich vocabulary of props, costumes, and buzzwords, it is also, how shall we say, parochial, an odd liability for one attempting so earnestly to cover as broad a consumer base as possible.

Perhaps the whiff of scandal accounts for the gusto with which Madonna throws herself into the exploitation of sacerdotal iconography. During her tour in Toronto, plainclothes cops put in an appearance, apparently following up a complaint of lewdness, and although they took no action, Madonna's parent company, Warner Bros., took the incident and ran with it, generating even more publicity from a non-case of censorship manqué. This occurred, with superb commercial timing, within a week of a more serious occasion: the action by the Broward County (Florida) sheriff's office to ban sales and performances of 2 Live Crew's witless but entirely traditional party record. A week or two after that, the National Endowment for the Arts chose to disregard the advice of its own nominating panel and withheld funds from four performance artists whose very earnest and noncommercial work happens to address the concerns of sexual minorities. Meanwhile, in Italy, Madonna succeeded in garnering more publicity from condemnations of her act by religious authorities, and their disapproval either affected ticket sales or provided a cover for sluggish trade. Presumably, Madonna is now free to title her next opus *Like a Martyr.*

And what of the other two legs of Madonna's media-assault troika? The album, *I'm Breathless,* is a departure for her, although not necessarily a very good idea. It functions as a sort of subsidiary sound track tie-in to *Dick Tracy,* and three of the songs included are featured in the movie. The whole is therefore imbued with a 1930s pastiche quality (all except "Vogue," which is fairly generic dance music but possesses considerably more vigor than any of the other tracks). But the current idea of what the 1930s sounded like bears about the same relation to the real thing as the kind of music that is played by men wearing straw boaters and candy-striped shirts and is called "Dixieland" bears to New Orleans jazz.

Whatever interest the songs might themselves contain is disfigured by an excess of cute fillips, the sort of fripperies that at the time were restricted to novelty records. The three songs appearing in the movie are by Stephen Sondheim, which is fine if you happen to share that kind of taste, although it should be pointed out that his penchant for chromatic eccentricities does no favor to Madonna, whose limited vocal equipment is inadequate to the task at hand. As yet another attempt to expand her horizons, this move by Madonna seems ill-advised, as it neither bears her triumphantly into a new area nor capitalizes on her actual strengths — but the thing currently sits at No. 4 on the charts, so who is to say?

The impossibility of second-guessing the vagaries of the American public is emphasized by the appearance of *Dick Tracy,* a film graced by moments of enormous pictorial beauty that otherwise lurches woodenly along — a Red Grooms construction devised by computer or committee — and yet is the hit movie of the summer. Madonna plays one of the four principal roles not calling for grotesque facial prostheses, although Breathless Mahoney is an animated graphic with all the soul of a rubber stamp. Madonna's job is to look, once again, sultry and jaded. Unfortunately she has been given entirely too much to say, and even though her lines consist of strung-together femme fatale clichés sampled and resequenced from somebody's memory of the works of Mae West, poor Madonna does not manage even a cartoonish conviction. She simply utters, and the lines fall from her mouth and drop on the floor. "I was wondering what a girl had to do to get arrested," she says, with the same inflection she might use to convey her intention of seeing if the mail has arrived.

Madonna, then, is a bad actress, a barely adequate singer, a graceless   25
dancer, a boring interview subject, a workmanlike but uninspired (co-) songwriter, and a dynamo of hard work and ferocious ambition. She has thus far been brilliant at imposing herself on the attention of the world, but there is no telling how long she can keep it up. Her pool of ideas, derived from a diligent study of iconology, is limited. There are only so many more myths she can recut to her fit. Her ability to titillate will wane with time; there is a certain age past which pop stars need to affect a serious demeanor or else find another line of work, and perhaps *I'm Breathless,* for all its many teases, represents a rehearsal for this eventuality, a record made for people who stay home at night.

Actually, it is entirely possible that Madonna will be able to coast from wild youth into eminence without an inordinate amount of exertion. To judge by the audience at her recent stage shows, the largest part of her constituency is made up of teenage girls who may not think she's a genius but admire her as a workhorse and a career strategist (and because she scares teenage boys). To these consumers she is already a fixture, who may ultimately be accorded the sort of permanent landmark status currently enjoyed by enigmas like Bob Hope. For the remainder of the public, much of Madonna's success to date has resulted from her function as a ready-made, albeit a very self-willed readymade. If other decades possessed their blond bombshell superstars, is it not fitting that the present era should have one of its own? From this perspective, Madonna is a star the way Ivory is a soap and Broadway is a street. But while endurance comes naturally to statues, it requires speed and fluidity of humans, and in ever increasing amounts. Madonna cannot afford to sleep.

Questions for Discussion

1. How did Madonna rise to fame? According to this review of her career, what are her principal abilities?
2. Who have been the greatest influences upon Madonna?
3. What type of audience is most responsive to Madonna, and why does she appeal to them? Is this essay written for them?
4. Why does Sante find Madonna objectionable? Where does he summarize his evaluation of her?
5. What does Sante mean when he writes, "Madonna cannot afford to sleep?"

Suggestions for Writing

1. Write an evaluation of another popular performer. If space or time is limited, focus your evaluation on a specific album, video, or film.
2. If you feel that Sante has been too harsh on Madonna, defend her performance in one of the works cited in this review of her career.

A MAN WATCHING

R. Jackson Wilson

Wilson evaluates the engraving of Walt Whitman by first placing it in the context in which it appeared — a copy of a photograph printed as the frontispiece of a book of Whitman's poetry. Consider whether Wilson's assessment is based on internal or external criteria and whether making this evaluation requires any special knowledge the average reader does not have. As you read, think about whether art criticism can help readers appreciate a work more fully.

On the first left-hand page of the 1855 edition of *Leaves of Grass* was a superb engraving, made from a daguerreotype. Readers were left to suppose that it must be a picture of the author, a visual token for the name, Walt Whitman, that was mysteriously missing from the title page at the right. The picture is of a man watching. It is a smallish picture, at least in relation to the trim size of the book. In part, this was necessary because engraving needed to be condensed enough so that the lines and hatchings did not show too plainly. But the requirements of technology were perfectly consistent with the writer's esthetic purpose. Situating the picture on a much larger blank page was obviously meant to heighten an effect of solitude and separation, as though this figure of a man were self-imposed on elemental space.

The parabola — defined only by a careful arc in the shading around the legs — is an implicit peephole, and was part of a very skillful attempt to control the effect of looking in such a way that the line of sight is unidirectional, and travels from the figure, through the page, to the reader, as if the viewer is not so much seeing the man as being watched by him. One of the poet's eyes is nearly hidden in the shadow, but this only calls attention the more strongly to the other eye. There is also a rather emphatic suggestion that this figure cannot do anything *but* look. His dress — the open shirt, the rumpled trousers, the soft hat — is vaguely like a workingman's, an artisan's perhaps — or, more accurately, a bohemian version of artisanal garb. But his stance argues, plainly, that work is the remotest of possibilities. Hands and fingers, which might do something, are kept sedulously out of sight, touching only his own body. Legs and feet, which might have suggested that he had come from somewhere to stand behind this aperture, and at some point would surely leave it, are cropped. He is not just a man watching; he is a man whose nature is to watch. The following year, in a prose sketch, Whitman would describe the figure himself, and rather well, as a "rough-looking man," with a "careless, lounging gait. Walt Whitman, the sturdy, self-conscious, microcosmic prose-poetical author of that incongruous hash of mud and gold — 'Leaves of Grass.'"

Questions for Discussion

1. A daguerreotype was an early form of the photograph. Is it significant that the engraving of Whitman was made from a daguerreotype? Would your response to this picture change if you were told that it was made by an artist sketching from life or from imagination?
2. What is the technical explanation for the size of the figure in proportion to the page? Why does Wilson believe that these proportions are appropriate for the poet?
3. According to Wilson, the figure shown is "not just a man watching; he is a man whose nature is to watch." What is the difference?
4. Wilson's evaluation of this "superb engraving" suggests that it was appropriate for the context in which it originally appeared. From your study of this picture, and Wilson's comments about it, what would you expect Whitman's poetry to be like?

Suggestions for Writing

1. Evaluate one of the photographs reprinted on pages 382–86. Look closely at the photo you choose, explain the details of its composition, and appraise its quality.
2. Choose a photograph you like of someone you know well. Write an essay that will help make other people see the photo through your eyes.

GRANT AND LEE:
A STUDY IN CONTRASTS

Bruce Catton

> *Bruce Catton was a well-regarded historian of the Civil War. To evaluate the two most important generals of that war, Catton contrasts their origins, their manner, and what they came to represent. As you read, observe the way Catton brings information about their backgrounds and about the men themselves to bear upon his judgment of them. But ask yourself whether Catton supplies sufficient evidence to support his evaluation.*

When Ulysses S. Grant and Robert E. Lee met in the parlor of a modest house at Appomattox Court House, Virginia, on April 9, 1865, to work out the terms for the surrender of Lee's Army of Northern Virginia, a great chapter in American life came to a close, and a great new chapter began.

These men were bringing the Civil War to its virtual finish. To be sure, other armies had yet to surrender, and for a few days the fugitive Confederate government would struggle desperately and vainly, trying to find some way to go on living now that its chief support was gone. But in effect it was all over when Grant and Lee signed the papers. And the little room where they wrote out the terms was the scene of one of the poignant, dramatic contrasts in American history.

They were two strong men, these oddly different generals, and they represented the strengths of two conflicting currents that, through them, had come into final collision.

Back of Robert E. Lee was the notion that the old aristocratic concept might somehow survive and be dominant in American life.

Lee was tidewater Virginia, and in his background were family, culture, and tradition . . . the age of chivalry transplanted to a New World which was making its own legends and its own myths. He embodied a way of life that had come down through the age of knighthood and the English country squire. America was a land that was beginning all over again, dedicated to nothing much more complicated than the rather hazy belief that all men had equal rights and should have an equal chance in the world. In such a land Lee stood for the feeling that it was somehow of advantage to human society to have a pronounced inequality in the social structure. There should be a leisure class, backed by ownership of land; in turn, society itself should be keyed to the land as the chief source of wealth and influence. It would bring forth (according to this ideal) a class of men with a strong sense of obligation to the community; men who lived not to gain advantage for themselves, but to meet the solemn obligations which had been laid on them by the very fact that they were privileged. From them the country would get its leadership; to them it could look for the higher values — of thought, of conduct, of personal deportment — to give it strength and virtue.

Lee embodied the noblest elements of this aristocratic ideal. Through him, the landed nobility justified itself. For four years, the Southern states had fought a desperate war to uphold the ideals for which Lee stood. In the end, it almost seemed as if the Confederacy fought for Lee; as if he himself was the Confederacy . . . the best thing that the way of life for which the Confederacy stood could ever have to offer. He had passed into legend before Appomattox. Thousands of tired, underfed, poorly clothed Confederate soldiers, long since past the simple enthusiasm of the early days of the struggle, somehow considered Lee the symbol of everything for which they had been willing to die. But they could not quite put this feeling into words. If the Lost Cause, sanctified by so much heroism and so many deaths, had a living justification, its justification was General Lee.

Grant, the son of a tanner on the Western frontier, was everything Lee was not. He had come up the hard way and embodied nothing in particular except the eternal toughness and sinewy fiber of the men who grew up beyond the mountains. He was one of a body of men who owed reverence and obeisance to no one, who were self-reliant to a fault, who cared hardly anything for the past but who had a sharp eye for the future.

These frontier men were the precise opposites of the tidewater aristocrats. Back of them, in the great surge that had taken people over the Alleghenies and into the opening Western country, there was a deep, implicit dissatisfaction with a past that had settled into grooves. They stood for democracy, not from any reasoned conclusion about the proper ordering of human society, but simply because they had grown up in the middle of democracy and knew how it worked. Their society might have privileges, but they would be privileges each man had won for himself. Forms and patterns meant nothing. No man was born to anything, except perhaps to a chance to show how far he could rise. Life was competition.

Yet along with this feeling had come a deep sense of belonging to a national community. The Westerner who developed a farm, opened a shop, or set up in business as a trader, could hope to prosper only as his own community prospered — and his community ran from the Atlantic to the Pacific and from Canada down to Mexico. If the land was settled, with towns and highways and accessible markets, he could better himself. He saw his fate in terms of the nation's own destiny. As its horizons expanded, so did his. He had, in other words, an acute dollars-and-cents stake in the continued growth and development of his country.

And that, perhaps, is where the contrast between Grant and Lee becomes most striking. The Virginia aristocrat, inevitably, saw himself in relation to his own region. He lived in a static society which could endure

10

almost anything except change. Instinctively, his first loyalty would go to the locality in which that society existed. He would fight to the limit of endurance to defend it, because in defending it he was defending everything that gave his own life its deepest meaning.

The Westerner, on the other hand, would fight with an equal tenacity for the broader concept of society. He fought so because everything he lived by was tied to growth, expansion, and a constantly widening horizon. What he lived by would survive or fall with the nation itself. He could not possibly stand by unmoved in the face of an attempt to destroy the Union. He would combat it with everything he had, because he could only see it as an effort to cut the ground out from under his feet.

So Grant and Lee were in complete contrast, representing two diametrically opposed elements in American life. Grant was the modern man emerging; beyond him, ready to come on the stage, was the great age of steel and machinery, of crowded cities and a restless burgeoning vitality. Lee might have ridden down from the old age of chivalry, lance in hand, silken banner fluttering over his head. Each man was the perfect champion of his cause, drawing both his strengths and his weaknesses from the people he led.

Yet it was not all contrast, after all. Different as they were — in background, in personality, in underlying aspiration — these two great soldiers had much in common. Under everything else, they were marvelous fighters. Furthermore, their fighting qualities were really very much alike.

Each man had, to begin with, the great virtue of utter tenacity and fidelity. Grant fought his way down the Mississippi Valley in spite of acute personal discouragement and profound military handicaps. Lee hung on in the trenches at Petersburg after hope itself had died. In each man there was an indomitable quality . . . the born fighter's refusal to give up as long as he can still remain on his feet and lift his two fists.

Daring and resourcefulness they had, too; the ability to think faster   *15* and move faster than the enemy. These were the qualities which gave Lee the dazzling campaigns of Second Manassas and Chancellorsville and won Vicksburg for Grant.

Lastly, and perhaps greatest of all, there was the ability, at the end, to turn quickly from war to peace once the fighting was over. Out of the way these two men behaved at Appomattox came the possibility of a peace of reconciliation. It was a possibility not wholly realized, in the years to come, but which did, in the end, help the two sections to become one nation again . . . after a war whose bitterness might have seemed to make such a reunion wholly impossible. No part of either man's life became him more than the part he played in this brief meeting in the McLean house at Appomattox. Their behavior there put all succeeding generations of Americans in their debt. Two great Americans, Grant and Lee — very different, yet under everything very much alike. Their encounter at Appomattox was one of the great moments of American history.

Questions for Discussion

1. Although this essay is focused upon two individuals, we get little specific information about them. Catton says nothing of their age, education, physical appearance, or personal habits. Instead, he treats them as symbols. According to his evaluation of these men, what did each symbolize?
2. Does Catton express a preference for either Grant or Lee? How sympathetic is he to these two men? Is he at all critical of them?
3. According to Catton, "the little room" in which Grant and Lee signed the papers that effectively ended the Civil War contributed to a moving "scene" in which "a great chapter in American life came to a close, and a great new chapter began." Why would a small room in a modest house be an appropriate setting for this act? How would the scene differ if it had taken place on the battlefield, at Grant's headquarters, or in the White House?
4. How would this essay change if Catton had decided to emphasize the similarities between Grant and Lee, comparing them instead of contrasting them?
5. Consider the organization of this essay. After devoting three paragraphs to Lee, Catton devotes three paragraphs to Grant. He then devotes a fourth paragraph to Lee and a fourth paragraph to Grant before discussing both of them together in each of the last five paragraphs. Was this a good plan? Or should Catton have located what is now paragraph 10 in the place of what is now paragraph 7?

Suggestions for Writing

1. Compare or contrast two individuals of similar stature in order to show what they represent or why one is preferable to the other.
2. Do research on either Grant or Lee and write a report upon that general's major shortcomings.

FENIMORE COOPER'S LITERARY OFFENSES

Mark Twain

During the first half of the nineteenth century James Fenimore Cooper was regarded as a great American novelist. During the second half of that century Mark Twain emerged as a great novelist, but he was originally perceived by critics as little more than a popular humorist. As you read the following attack upon Cooper, who was dead by the time Twain wrote this essay, ask yourself what motivated this negative evaluation. Consider how it affects you. Does Twain's evaluation convince you that Cooper is not worth reading, or does it lead you to wonder whether Cooper could possibly be as bad as Twain claims?

The Pathfinder and The Deerslayer stand at the head of Cooper's novels as artistic creations. There are others of his works which contain parts as perfect as are to be found in these, and scenes even more thrilling. Not one can be compared with either of them as a finished whole.

The defects in both of these tales are comparatively slight. They were pure works of art. — *Prof. Lounsbury.*

The five tales reveal an extraordinary fulness of invention.

. . . One of the very greatest characters in fiction, Natty Bumppo. . . .

The craft of the woodsman, the tricks of the trapper, all the delicate art of the forest, were familiar to Cooper from his youth up. — *Prof. Brander Matthews.*

Cooper is the greatest artist in the domain of romantic fiction yet produced by America. — *Wilkie Collins.*

It seems to me that it was far from right for the Professor of English Literature in Yale, the Professor of English Literature in Columbia, and Wilkie Collins to deliver opinions on Cooper's literature without having read some of it. It would have been much more decorous to keep silent and let persons talk who have read Cooper.

Cooper's art has some defects. In one place in *Deerslayer,* and in the restricted space of two-thirds of a page, Cooper has scored 114 offenses against literary art out of a possible 115. It breaks the record.

There are nineteen rules governing literary art in the domain of romantic fiction—some say twenty-two. In *Deerslayer* Cooper violated eighteen of them. These eighteen require:

1. That a tale shall accomplish something and arrive somewhere. But the *Deerslayer* tale accomplishes nothing and arrives in the air.

2. They require that the episodes of a tale shall be necessary parts of the tale, and shall help to develop it. But as the *Deerslayer* tale is not a tale, and accomplishes nothing and arrives nowhere, the episodes have no rightful place in the work, since there was nothing for them to develop.

3. They require that the personages in a tale shall be alive, except in the cases of corpses, and that always the reader shall be able to tell the corpses from the others. But this detail has often been overlooked in the *Deerslayer* tale.

4. They require that the personages in a tale, both dead and alive, shall exhibit a sufficient excuse for being there. But this detail also has been overlooked in the *Deerslayer* tale.

5. They require that when the personages of a tale deal in conversation, the talk shall sound like human talk, and be talk such as human beings would be likely to talk in the given circumstances, and have a discoverable meaning, also a discoverable purpose, and a show of relevancy, and remain in the neighborhood of the subject in hand, and be interesting to the reader, and help out the tale, and stop when the people cannot think of anything more to say. But this requirement has been ignored from the beginning of the *Deerslayer* tale to the end of it.

6. They require that when the author describes the character of a personage in his tale, the conduct and conversation of that personage shall justify said description. But this law gets little or no attention in the *Deerslayer* tale, as Natty Bumppo's case will amply prove.

7. They require that when a personage talks like an illustrated, gilt-edged, tree-calf, hand-tooled, seven-dollar Friendship's Offering in the beginning of a paragraph, he shall not talk like a negro minstrel in the end of it. But this rule is flung down and danced upon in the *Deerslayer* tale.

8. They require that crass stupidities shall not be played upon the reader as "the craft of the woodsman, the delicate art of the forest," by either the author or the people in the tale. But this rule is persistently violated in the *Deerslayer* tale.

9. They require that the personages of a tale shall confine themselves to possibilities and let miracles alone; or, if they venture a miracle, the author must so plausibly set it forth as to make it look possible and reasonable. But these rules are not respected in the *Deerslayer* tale.

10. They require that the author shall make the reader feel a deep interest in the personages of his tale and in their fate; and that he shall make the reader love the good people in the tale and hate the bad ones. But the reader of the *Deerslayer* tale dislikes the

good people in it, is indifferent to the others, and wishes they would all get drowned together.

11. They require that the characters in a tale shall be so clearly defined that the reader can tell beforehand what each will do in a given emergency. But in the *Deerslayer* tale this rule is vacated.

In addition to these large rules there are some little ones. These require that the author shall

12. *Say* what he is proposing to say, not merely come near it.
13. Use the right word, not its second cousin.
14. Eschew surplusage.
15. Not omit necessary details.
16. Avoid slovenliness of form.
17. Use good grammar.
18. Employ a simple and straightforward style.

Even these seven are coldly and persistently violated in the *Deerslayer* tale.

Cooper's gift in the way of invention was not a rich endowment; but such as it was he liked to work it, he was pleased with the effects, and indeed he did some quite sweet things with it. In his little box of stage-properties he kept six or eight cunning devices, tricks, artifices for his savages and woodsmen to deceive and circumvent each other with, and he was never so happy as when he was working these innocent things and seeing them go. A favorite one was to make a moccasined person tread in the tracks of the moccasined enemy, and thus hide his own trail. Cooper wore out barrels and barrels of moccasins in working that trick. Another stage-property that he pulled out of his box pretty frequently was his broken twig. He prized his broken twig above all the rest of his effects, and worked it the hardest. It is a restful chapter in any book of his when somebody doesn't step on a dry twig and alarm all the reds and whites for two hundred yards around. Every time a Cooper person is in peril, and absolute silence is worth four dollars a minute, he is sure to step on a dry twig. There may be a hundred handier things to step on, but that wouldn't satisfy Cooper. Cooper requires him to turn out and find a dry twig; and if he can't do it, go and borrow one. In fact, the Leather Stocking Series ought to have been called the Broken Twig Series.

I am sorry there is not room to put in a few dozen instances of the delicate art of the forest, as practiced by Natty Bumppo and some of the other Cooperian experts. Perhaps we may venture two or three samples. Cooper was a sailor — a naval officer; yet he gravely tells us how a vessel, driving toward a lee shore in a gale, is steered for a particular spot by her skipper because he knows of an *undertow* there which will hold her back against the gale and save her. For just pure woodcraft, or sailorcraft, or whatever it is, isn't that neat? For several years Cooper was daily in the society of artillery, and he ought to have noticed that when a cannon-ball strikes the ground it either buries itself or skips a hundred feet or so; skips again a hundred feet or so — and so on, till finally it gets tired and rolls. Now in one place he loses some "females" — as he always calls women — in the edge of a wood near a plain at night in a fog, on purpose to give Bumppo a chance to show off the delicate art of the forest before the reader. These mislaid people are hunting for a fort. They hear a cannon-blast, and a cannon-ball presently comes rolling into the wood and stops at their feet. To the females this suggests nothing. The case is very different with the admirable Bumppo. I wish I may never know peace again if he doesn't strike out promptly and *follow the track* of that cannon-ball across the plain through the dense fog and find the fort. Isn't it a daisy? If Cooper had any real knowledge of Nature's ways of doing things, he had a most delicate art in concealing the fact. For instance: one of his acute Indian experts, Chingachgook (pronounced Chicago, I think), has lost the trail of a person he is tracking through the forest. Apparently that trail is hopelessly lost. Neither you nor I could ever have guessed out the way to find it. It was very different with Chicago. Chicago was not stumped for long. He turned a running stream out of its course, and there, in the slush in its old bed, were that person's moccasin-tracks. The current did not wash them away, as it would have done in all other cases — no, even the eternal laws of Nature have to vacate when Cooper wants to put up a delicate job of woodcraft on the reader.

We must be a little wary when Brander Matthews tells us that Cooper's books "reveal an extraordinary fulness of invention." As a rule, I am quite willing to accept Brander Matthews's literary judgments and applaud his lucid and graceful phrasing of them; but that particular statement needs to be taken with a few tons of salt. Bless your heart, Cooper hadn't any more invention than a horse; and I don't mean a high-class horse, either; I mean a clothes-horse. It would be very difficult to find a really clever "situation" in Cooper's books, and still more difficult to find one of any kind which he has failed to render absurd by his handling of it. Look at the episodes of "the caves"; and at the celebrated scuffle between Maqua and those others on the table-land a few days later; and at Hurry Harry's queer water-transit from the castle to the ark; and at Deerslayer's half-hour with his first corpse; and at the quarrel between Hurry Harry and Deerslayer later; and at — but choose for yourself; you can't go amiss.

If Cooper had been an observer his inventive faculty would have worked better; not more interestingly, but more rationally, more plausibly. Cooper's proudest creations in the way of "situations" suffer noticeably from the absence of the observer's protecting gift. Cooper's eye was splendidly inaccurate. Cooper seldom saw anything correctly. He saw nearly all things as through a glass eye, darkly. Of course a man who cannot see the commonest little every-day matters accurately is working at a disadvantage when he is constructing a "situation." In the *Deerslayer* tale Cooper has a stream which is fifty feet wide where it flows out of a lake; it presently narrows to twenty as it meanders along for no given reason, and yet when a stream acts like that it ought to be required to explain itself. Fourteen pages later the width of the brook's outlet from the lake has suddenly shrunk thirty feet, and become "the narrowest part of the stream." This shrinkage is not accounted for. The stream has bends in it, a sure indication that it has alluvial banks and cuts them; yet these bends are only thirty and fifty feet long. If Cooper had been a nice and punctilious observer he would have noticed that the bends were oftener nine hundred feet long than short of it.

Cooper made the exit of that stream fifty feet wide, in the first place, for no particular reason; in the second place, he narrowed it to less than twenty to accommodate some Indians. He bends a "sapling" to the form of an arch over this narrow passage, and conceals six Indians in its foliage. They are "laying" for a settler's scow or ark which is coming up the stream on its way to the lake; it is being hauled against the stiff current by a rope whose stationary end is anchored in the lake; its rate of progress cannot be more than a mile an hour. Cooper describes the ark, but pretty obscurely. In the matter of dimensions "it was little more than a modern canal-boat." Let us guess, then, that it was about one hundred and forty feet long. It was of "greater breadth than common." Let us guess, then, that it was about sixteen feet wide. This leviathan had been prowling down bends which were but a third as long as itself, and scraping between banks where it had only two feet of space to spare on each side. We cannot too much admire this miracle. A low-roofed log dwelling occupies "two-thirds of the ark's length" — a dwelling ninety feet long and sixteen feet wide, let us say — a kind of vestibule train. The dwelling has two rooms — each forty-five feet long and sixteen feet wide, let us guess. One of them is the bedroom of the Hutter girls, Judith and Hetty; the other is the parlor in the daytime, at night it is papa's bedchamber. The ark is arriving at the stream's exit now, whose width has been reduced to less than twenty feet to accommodate the Indians — say to eighteen. There is a foot to spare on each side of the boat. Did the Indians notice that there was going to be a tight squeeze there? Did they notice that they could make money by climbing down out of that arched sapling and just stepping aboard when the ark scraped by? No, other Indians would have noticed these things, but Cooper's Indians never notice anything. Cooper thinks they are marvelous creatures for noticing, but he was almost always in error about his Indians. There was seldom a sane one among them.

The ark is one hundred and forty feet long; the dwelling is ninety feet long. The idea of the Indians is to drop softly and secretly from the arched sapling to the dwelling as the ark creeps along under it at the rate of a mile an hour, and butcher the family. It will take the ark a minute and a half to pass under. It will take the ninety-foot dwelling a minute to pass under. Now, then, what did the six Indians do? It would take you thirty years to guess, and even then you would have to give it up, I believe. Therefore, I will tell you what the Indians did. Their chief, a person of quite extraordinary intellect for a Cooper Indian, warily watched the canal-boat as it squeezed along under him, and when he had got his calculations fined down to exactly the right shade, as he judged, he let go and dropped. And *missed the house!* That is actually what he did. He missed the house, and landed in the stern of the scow. It was not much of a fall, yet it knocked him silly. He lay there unconscious. If the house had been ninety-seven feet long he would have made the trip. The fault was Cooper's, not his. The error lay in the construction of the house. Cooper was no architect.

There still remained in the roost five Indians. The boat has passed   10
under and is now out of their reach. Let me explain what the five did — you would not be able to reason it out for yourself. No. 1 jumped for the boat, but fell in the water astern of it. Then No. 2 jumped for the boat, but fell in the water still farther astern of it. Then No. 3 jumped for the boat, and fell a good way astern of it. Then No. 4 jumped for the boat, and fell in the water *away* astern. Then even No. 5 made a jump for the boat — for he was a Cooper Indian. In the matter of intellect, the difference between a Cooper Indian and the Indian that stands in front of the cigar-shop is not spacious. The scow episode is really a sublime burst of invention; but it does not thrill, because the inaccuracy of the detail throws a sort of air of fictitiousness and general improbability over it. This comes of Cooper's inadequacy as an observer.

The reader will find some examples of Cooper's high talent for in-accurate observation in the account of the shooting-match in *The Pathfinder.*

> A common wrought nail was driven lightly into the target, its head having been first touched with paint.

The color of the paint is not stated — an important omission, but Cooper deals freely in important omissions. No, after all, it was not an important omission; for this nailhead is *a hundred yards from* the marksmen, and could not be seen by them at that distance, no matter what its color might be. How far can the best eyes see a common house-fly? A hundred yards? It is quite impossible. Very well; eyes that cannot see a house-fly that is a hundred yards away cannot see an ordinary nail head at that distance, for the size of the two objects is the same. It takes a keen eye to see a fly or a nail-head at fifty yards — one hundred and fifty feet. Can the reader do it?

The nail was lightly driven, its head painted, and game called. Then the Cooper miracles begin. The bullet of the first marksman chipped an edge of the nail-head; the next man's bullet drove the nail a little way into the target — and removed all the paint. Haven't the miracles gone far enough now? Not to suit Cooper; for the purpose of this whole scheme is to show off his prodigy, Deerslayer-Hawkeye-Long-Rifle-Leather-Stocking-Pathfinder-Bumppo before the ladies.

> "Be all ready to clench it, boys!" cried out Pathfinder, stepping into his friend's tracks the instant they were vacant. "Never mind a new nail; I can see that, though the paint is gone, and what I can see I can hit at a hundred yards, though it were only a mosquito's eye. Be ready to clench!"
>
> The rifle cracked, the bullet sped its way, and the head of the nail was buried in the wood, covered by the piece of flattened lead.

There, you see, is a man who could hunt flies with a rifle, and command a ducal salary in a Wild West show today if we had him back with us.

The recorded feat is certainly surprising just as it stands; but it is not surprising enough for Cooper. Cooper adds a touch. He has made Pathfinder do this miracle with another man's rifle; and not only that, but Pathfinder did not have even the advantage of loading it himself. He had everything against him, and yet he made that impossible shot; and not only made it, but did it with absolute confidence, saying, "Be ready to clench." Now a person like that would have undertaken that same feat with a brick-bat, and with Cooper to help he would have achieved it, too.

Pathfinder showed off handsomely that day before the ladies. His very first feat was a thing which no Wild West show can touch. He was standing with the group of marksmen, observing — a hundred yards from the target, mind; one Jasper raised his rifle and drove the center off the bull's-eye. Then the Quartermaster fired. The target exhibited no result this time. There was a laugh "It's a dead miss," said Major Lundie. Pathfinder waited an impressive moment or two; then said, in that calm, indifferent, know-it-all way of his, "No, Major, he has covered Jasper's bullet, as will be seen if anyone will take the trouble to examine the target."

Wasn't it remarkable! How *could* he see that little pellet fly through the air and enter that distant bullet-hole? Yet that is what he did; for nothing is impossible to a Cooper person. Did any of those people have any deep-seated doubts about this thing? No; for that would imply sanity, and these were all Cooper people.

> The respect for Pathfinder's skill and for his *quickness and accuracy of sight* [the italics are mine] was so profound and general, that the instant he made this declaration the spectators began to distrust their own opinions, and a dozen rushed to the target in order to ascertain the fact. There, sure enough, it was found that the Quartermaster's bullet had gone through the hole made by Jasper's, and that, too, so accurately as to require a minute examination to be certain of the

15

circumstance, which, however, was soon clearly established by discovering one bullet over the other in the stump against which the target was placed.

They made a "minute" examination; but never mind, how could they know that there were two bullets in that hole without digging the latest one out? for neither probe nor eyesight could prove the presence of any more than one bullet. Did they dig? No; as we shall see. It is the Pathfinder's turn now; he steps out before the ladies, takes aim, and fires.

But, alas! here is a disappointment; an incredible, an unimaginable disappointment — for the target's aspect is unchanged; there is nothing there but that same old bullet-hole!

"If one dared to hint at such a thing," cried Major Duncan, "I should say that the Pathfinder has also missed the target!"

As nobody had missed it yet, the "also" was not necessary; but never mind about that, for the Pathfinder is going to speak.

"No, no, Major," said he, confidently, "that *would* be a risky declaration. I didn't load the piece, and can't say what was in it; but if it was lead, you will find the bullet driving down those of the Quartermaster and Jasper, else is not my name Pathfinder."
A shout from the target announced the truth of this assertion.

Is the miracle sufficient as it stands? Not for Cooper. The Pathfinder speaks again, as he "now slowly advances towards the stage occupied by the females":

"That's not all, boys, that's not all; if you find the target touched at all, I'll own to a miss. The Quartermaster cut the wood, but you'll find no wood cut by that last messenger."

The miracle is at last complete. He knew — doubtless *saw* — at the distance of a hundred yards — that his bullet had passed into the hole *without fraying the edges*. There were now three bullets in that one hole — three bullets embedded processionally in the body of the stump back of the target. Everybody knew this — somehow or other — and yet nobody had dug any of them out to make sure. Cooper is not a close observer, but he is interesting. He is certainly always that, no matter what happens. And he is more interesting when he is not noticing what he is about than when he is. This is a considerable merit.

The conversations in the Cooper books have a curious sound in our modern ears. To believe that such talk really ever came out of people's mouths would be to believe that there was a time when time was of no value to a person who thought he had something to say; when it was the custom to spread a two-minute remark out to ten; when a man's mouth was a rolling-mill, and busied itself all day long in turning four-foot pigs

of thought into thirty-foot bars of conversational railroad iron by atten-
uation; when subjects were seldom faithfully stuck to, but the talk wandered all around and arrived nowhere; when conversations consisted
mainly of irrelevancies, with here and there a relevancy, a relevancy with
an embarrassed look, as not being able to explain how it got there.

Cooper was certainly not a master in the construction of dialogue.
Inaccurate observation defeated him here as it defeated him in so many
other enterprises of his. He even failed to notice that the man who talks
corrupt English six days in the week must and will talk it on the seventh,
and can't help himself. In the *Deerslayer* story he lets Deerslayer talk the
showiest kind of book-talk sometimes, and at other times the basest of
base dialects. For instance, when someone asks him if he has a sweetheart,
and if so, where she abides, this is his majestic answer:

> "She's in the forest—hanging from the boughs of the trees, in a
> soft rain—in the dew on the open grass—the clouds that float about
> in the blue heavens—the birds that sing in the woods—the sweet
> springs where I slake my thirst—and in all the other glorious gifts
> that come from God's Providence!"

And he preceded that, a little before, with this: 25

> "It consarns me as all things that touches a fri'nd consarns a
> fri'nd."

And this is another of his remarks:

> "If I was Injin born, now, I might tell of this, or carry in the scalp
> and boast of the expl'ite afore the whole tribe; or if my inimy had
> only been a bear"

—and so on.

We cannot imagine such a thing as a veteran Scotch Commander-in-
Chief comporting himself in the field like a windy melodramatic actor,
but Cooper could. On one occasion Alice and Cora were being chased by
the French through a fog in the neighborhood of their father's fort:

> *"Point de quartier aux coquins!"* cried an eager pursuer, who seemed
> to direct the operations of the enemy.
> "Stand firm and be ready, my gallant 60ths!" suddenly exclaimed
> a voice above them; "wait to see the enemy; fire low, and sweep the
> glacis."
> "Father! father!" exclaimed a piercing cry from out the mist; "it is
> I! Alice! thy own Elsie! spare, O! save your daughters!"
> "Hold!" shouted the former speaker, in the awful tones of parental
> agony, the sound reaching even to the woods, and rolling back in
> solemn echo. "'Tis she! God has restored me my children! Throw
> open the sally-port; to the field, 60ths, to the field! pull not a trigger,
> lest ye kill my lambs! Drive off these dogs of France with your steel!"

Cooper's word-sense was singularly dull. When a person has a poor ear for music he will flat and sharp right along without knowing it. He keeps near the tune, but it is *not* the tune. When a person has a poor ear for words, the result is a literary flatting and sharping; you perceive what he is intending to say, but you also perceive that he doesn't *say* it. This is Cooper. He was not a word-musician. His ear was satisfied with the *approximate* word. I will furnish some circumstantial evidence in support of this charge. My instances are gathered from half a dozen pages of the tale called *Deerslayer*. He uses "verbal," for "oral"; "precision," for "facility"; "phenomena," for "marvels"; "necessary," for "predetermined"; "unsophisticated," for "primitive"; "preparation," for "expectancy"; "rebuked," for "subdued"; "dependent on," for "resulting from"; "fact," for "condition"; "fact," for "conjecture"; "precaution," for "caution"; "explain," for "determine"; "mortified," for "disappointed"; "meretricious," for "factitious"; "materially," for "considerably"; "decreasing," for "deepening"; "increasing," for "disappearing"; "embedded," for "enclosed"; "treacherous," for "hostile"; "stood," for "stooped"; "softened," for "replaced"; "rejoined," for "remarked"; "situation," for "condition"; "different," for "differing"; "insensible," for "unsentient"; "brevity," for "celerity"; "distrusted," for "suspicious"; "mental imbecility," for "imbecility"; "eyes," for "sight"; "counteracting," for "opposing"; "funeral obsequies," for "obsequies."

There have been daring people in the world who claimed that Cooper could write English, but they are all dead now — all dead but Lounsbury. I don't remember that Lounsbury makes the claim in so many words, still he makes it, for he says that *Deerslayer* is a "pure work of art." Pure, in that connection, means faultless — faultless in all details — and language is a detail. If Mr. Lounsbury had only compared Cooper's English with the English which he writes himself — but it is plain that he didn't; and so it is likely that he imagines until this day that Cooper's is as clean and compact as his own. Now I feel sure, deep down in my heart, that Cooper wrote about the poorest English that exists in our language, and that the English of *Deerslayer* is the very worst that even Cooper ever wrote.

I may be mistaken, but it does seem to me that *Deerslayer* is not a *30* work of art in any sense; it does seem to me that it is destitute of every detail that goes to the making of a work of art; in truth, it seems to me that *Deerslayer* is just simply a literary *delirium tremens*.

A work of art? It has no invention; it has no order, system, sequence, or result; it has no lifelikeness, no thrill, no stir, no seeming of reality; its characters are confusedly drawn, and by their acts and words they prove that they are not the sort of people the author claims that they are; its humor is pathetic; its pathos is funny; its conversations are — oh! indescribable; its love-scenes odious; its English a crime against the language.

Counting these out, what is left is Art. I think we must all admit that.

Questions for Discussion

1. Why does Twain preface his essay with quotes from two prominent professors and an important English novelist?
2. Consider the eighteen rules that Twain provides for "literary art." Do any of them overlap? Which seem the most important to you? Are the last seven really "little ones"? Which of these rules is appropriate for nonfiction?
3. Why is it important for writers to be good observers? Why does Twain believe that Cooper "seldom saw anything correctly"? Does he persuade you that this is so?
4. Twain points out that Cooper always called women "females." What is the difference between these two words? Why would anyone find it objectionable to call a woman a female?
5. Consider the second sentence in paragraph 6. Do you detect a shift in diction at some point in this sentence? Do you think it was deliberate? What is its effect?
6. According to Twain, what is wrong with Cooper's dialogue? How useful are the examples he provides?
7. Cooper had been dead for forty-four years when Twain wrote this essay, and Twain later went on to write another essay attacking Cooper. What would motivate someone to make a detailed and sustained attack upon a dead writer?

Suggestions for Writing

1. Use Twain's criteria to evaluate a novel that you have recently read.
2. Read *Deerslayer* and evaluate how fairly Twain has treated Cooper.

FROM THE MOUTHS OF BABES TO A JAIL CELL

Dorothy Rabinowitz

> *Demonstrating how evaluation can be applied to the administration of justice, the following essay discusses a case involving child abuse — a subject that can inspire strong feelings that obscure clear thinking. Since the essay is fairly long, you may find it useful to take notes as you read. Look for the author's judgment and the evidence she provides to support it. Try also to define the criteria Rabinowitz has used in judging the trial of a young woman charged with 131 counts of sexual abuse.*

On August 2, 1988, Margaret Kelly Michaels, then twenty-six years old, was sentenced by a New Jersey judge to forty-seven years in prison. It was as harsh a sentence as any judge in this country is likely to mete out for a crime involving neither drugs nor murder, but it was not nearly harsh enough for most of those assembled in the courtroom that day at the Essex County Court House in Newark. She faced, according to those moved to carefully calculate such things (and there were many on hand), an imprisonment of no fewer than 730 years. Three months earlier, Michaels had been convicted on 115 (of an alleged 131) counts of sexual abuse against twenty children, ranging in age from three to five. Each of the children had been in her charge at the Wee Care Day Nursery, an exclusive preschool in the suburban community of Maplewood, New Jersey, about twenty miles from New York City; each of the crimes was said to have been committed during regular school hours at the nursery, essentially a few rented rooms in the basement and on the second and third floors of the town's large Episcopal church; each day during the seven months she worked as a teacher's aide and then as a teacher at Wee Care, from September 1984 to April 1985, Kelly Michaels, according to the prosecutors, raped and assaulted them with knives, forks, a wooden spoon, and Lego blocks. The prosecution maintained that she had been able to do all this unnoticed by her fellow teachers, by school administrators, by parents and other visitors to the school, and unnoticed as well by anyone working for the church or attending services at the church — that is to say, unnoticed for nearly 150 school days by any adult. Unnoticed, and on a daily basis, Michaels had also, according to the prosecutors, licked peanut butter off the children's genitals, played the piano in the nude, and made them drink her urine and eat a "cake" of her feces. For 150 school days, not a single child ever said so much as a single word about any of these crimes because — again according to the prosecution — Kelly Michaels had forced them to keep at least 115 terrible secrets.

Although monstrous in its allegations, the case against Kelly Michaels was as much a work of the prosecution's feverish imagination as a construction of the law. A substantial body of evidence suggests that Kelly Michaels was convicted of crimes she did not commit. Her story deserves telling in some detail because the circumstances that resulted in her arrest, trial, and imprisonment bespeak a condition of national hysteria not unlike the hysteria that seized the Massachusetts Bay Colony in the seventeenth century during the excitements of the Salem witch trials. If Kelly Michaels was unjustly convicted, it is because we live in an age of trial by accusation. Our society, at the moment, is quick to condemn anybody and everybody charged, on the flimsiest of evidence, with the crimes of abusing or molesting children. In the interest of a higher virtue (i.e., protecting the children), a credulous public and a sensationalist press stand willing to cast aside whatever civil liberties or constitutional rights obstruct the judgment of heaven.

At the time of Kelly Michaels's conviction, I was working for WWOR–TV, New Jersey's largest television station. I reported and wrote commentaries about the media for the station's evening news program, and because the Michaels case was one of the biggest local stories, I had followed it for months. From the beginning, I found something strange about the state's case—something incomprehensible in the many counts of abuse, in the large number of children allegedly victimized, in the highly improbable circumstances in which Kelly Michaels was said to have accomplished the molestation of half the children in the school. I found no less strange the reactions of my colleagues to my casually voiced doubts to the effect that the case against Kelly Michaels was as rotten as last week's fish. Youngish journalists who prided themselves on their skepticism—types who automatically sniffed with suspicion at any and every pronouncement by a government official—were outraged by the merest suggestion that the state's charges against Kelly Michaels lacked credibility. In late July 1988, just before Michaels's sentence was to be handed down, I told one of the station's news managers that I planned to do a commentary on the media coverage of the trial. *The Village Voice* had published a lengthy story on the case by journalist Debbie Nathan that raised critical questions about the press coverage. The story provided, I thought, the perfect opportunity to raise certain, by now deeply nagging, questions of my own about this case.

"Forget it," the news managers informed me. This meant, in translation: This news organization is not prepared to air doubts about the trial of one of the most despised defendants ever convicted in a New Jersey court—a child molester.

Shortly after Kelly Michaels's sentencing, I decided to go back and research the history of this case, beginning with the first allegations made against her in the spring of 1985. In the course of my research, I read through trial materials and interviewed most of the leading participants: the investigators, prosecutors, judge, and parents, as well as the convicted defendant herself. What emerged at the end of that research was not only the story of a young woman whom I believe to have been falsely accused and unjustly condemned but also an understanding of the ways in which the laws can be made to sustain the decrees of fear and superstition. In almost every detail, the prosecution of Kelly Michaels replicated the prosecution of similar cases being brought against alleged child molesters everywhere in the United States. The accused tend to be teachers, camp counselors, and members of "sex rings." The cases almost always rely on only the testimony of small children; and this testimony invariably comes to involve more and more victims, who describe more and more bizarre, cruel, and lurid acts. All the cases also make extensive use of child-abuse "specialists" and "investigators," who insist that parents, prosecutors, and jurors must—in a phrase whispered frequently at such trials and even affixed to posters and buttons—*believe the children*. As proof of the prevailing doctrine, Essex County Assistant Prosecutor Glenn Goldberg, who tried the state's case against Kelly Michaels, kept a BELIEVE THE CHILDREN button pinned to his office bulletin board.

By and large, this commandment has been obeyed. People everywhere in the country have believed. Believed almost anything and everything told to them by witnesses under the age of six. Believed tales as fantastic as any fairy story ever told by the Brothers Grimm. In Sequim, Washington, investigators listened attentively as children in a local preschool charged that they had been taken by a teacher to graveyards and forced to witness animal sacrifices. In Chicago, children told sympathetic authorities of how they were made to eat a boiled baby. A Memphis preschool teacher, Frances Ballard, was acquitted of terrorizing children into watching her put a bomb in a hamster and exploding it, and of fifteen other charges no less fantastic; but, in a trial to rival those of the Salem witches, she was convicted of kissing the genitals of a four-year-old boy.

The most sensational case of child abuse reached its denouement on January 18 of this year, when a jury in Los Angeles acquitted Ray Buckey and his mother, Peggy McMartin Buckey, on fifty-two counts—this after deliberating for nine weeks over evidence presented in the course of thirty-three months at a trial that cost the taxpayers of California an estimated $15 million. Buckey, a teacher at the Virginia McMartin Preschool (founded by his grandmother) in Manhattan Beach, a well-to-do seaside city that is a part of greater Los Angeles, was said by the children to have stuck silverware in their anuses, taken them on visits to cemeteries, and killed a horse with a baseball bat. The parent who first came forth after believing her son, a woman named Judy Johnson, died in 1986 of an alcohol-related illness; not long after her initial charge against Buckey of child sodomy, she made a similar allegation against an AWOL marine, claiming that he also had sodomized the family dog.

The prosecution of Kelly Michaels took place in the midst of a national hysteria about the crimes of child abuse that, by the spring of 1985, had become as virulent and as contagious as the Asian flu. Kelly Michaels left the Wee Care Day Nursery on April 26, 1985, in order to accept a better-paying job in the nearby town of East Orange, New Jersey. Four days later, on April 30, one of her former students, a four-year-old boy whom I will call Terry Weldon,* inadvertently set in motion her transformation into an object of revulsion. His mother had taken him to his pediatrician for a checkup, and a nurse began to take his temperature by putting a thermometer in his rectum. Terry played quietly for a half-minute or so and then said, "That's what my teacher does to me at nap time at school." When the nurse asked him what he meant, he answered, "Her takes my temperature." His nap-time monitor was Kelly Michaels.

Kelly Michaels had not come to Maplewood from Pittsburgh, where she was raised, to teach preschoolers. Nor, for that matter, had she come east to settle in Maplewood. She loved the theater and wanted to be an actress. She was pretty in a traditional, American-girl sort of way, with a dimply smile and eyes, as even her childhood photos show, that knew how to meet a camera lens. She was voted "best actress" of her high school, St. Benedict's Academy, and went on to major in theater at Seton Hill, a Catholic women's college near Pittsburgh. In the summer of 1984, then just a few credits shy of her B.A., she took up the offer of a college friend who had invited her to share an efficiency apartment in a poor, mostly black neighborhood in East Orange. For the time being, East Orange was as close as she could get to Manhattan's theaters and drama schools.

Up to this point, she had lived with her parents, John and Marilyn   10
Michaels, and her four sisters and brothers in a pleasant, woodsy, middle-class section of Pittsburgh called White Oak Heights. Her early life had been, from all evidence, a happy one as the eldest child of a close-knit family. They were a talkative, bookish lot, given to heated debate on art and politics, which might explain Kelly Michaels's rather extraordinary command of the language — a faintly formal, old-fashioned eloquence that made her seem, at times, the child of another era.

When I met Kelly Michaels for the first time, in the dark visitors' cubicle at the women's prison in Clinton, New Jersey, two months after her sentencing, she still retained some of the wholesome look I had seen in her school photographs. Her shock at the accusations brought against her were still as fresh in her mind as at the moment when she was first questioned in 1985. Her gift for language allowed her to express not only rage at her accusers but also an intellectual scorn for the absurdity of their charges. On several subsequent occasions when I spoke to her, she never failed to voice her amazement that a jury had believed the charges. "To watch these witnesses, these prosecutors with their details — and none of it had ever happened," she once told me. "Yet, all these people were coming up to the stand to give descriptions of what never happened."

*All the names of the Wee Care preschoolers and of their parents have been changed.

After arriving in East Orange, Michaels began looking for work. She answered a number of want ads, including one for a teacher's aide. She had never worked in the child-care field, but the director of the nursery was impressed with her. She was subsequently hired by Wee Care (the pay was about four dollars an hour) and began work there in September. Her mother, Marilyn, told me last year, when I visited her in White Oak Heights, that she had teased Kelly when she called to say she had begun working at a preschool. Be careful, she told her daughter, look at what is happening in Los Angeles to those teachers in the McMartin case.

Within a month at Wee Care, Kelly Michaels was promoted to teacher. She had impressed her supervisors and appeared to be popular with the three-year-olds whose class she took charge of and with the other children whom she supervised during nap time. Following days that she stayed home sick, children would run to greet her — a fact the prosecution would not deny but rather pointed to as evidence that Michaels "was an actress" and that "child abusers are very clever people." Michaels liked the children and their parents too, but the salary proved impossible to live on. When she went home for Christmas, her parents told me, she said she planned to leave Wee Care and return to Pittsburgh. John Michaels, to his bitter regret, urged her to be responsible and finish out the year. Kelly Michaels returned to Wee Care but did not finish out the year; she left two months before the school was to close for the summer in order to take the job in East Orange.

Ten days after Terry Weldon's checkup, Essex County Investigator Richard Mastrangelo and Maplewood Detective Sergeant John Noonan knocked on the door of the apartment Kelly Michaels shared with her friend Cynthia. Terry Weldon's mother, upon arriving home after his examination, had fixed her son lunch and then phoned the doctor to talk about the temperature-taking incident. The doctor advised her to call the state child-protective agency, the Division of Youth and Family Services (DYFS). Her call was referred to the agency's Institutional Abuse Unit, which contacted the Child Abuse Unit of the Essex County prosecutor's office, which agreed to initiate an investigation. We have now in this country a vastly increased number of child-protection agencies and experts. This is largely a result of the passage in 1979 of the Federal Child Abuse Act, which dramatically increased funds available to states and localities for such agencies and experts. Funds begat staffs, which grew, as did their zeal.

On May 2, Terry's mother — the wife of a Maplewood police officer and the daughter of a prominent Essex County judge — brought him to the Essex County prosecutor's office in Newark, where he was questioned by the head of the office's Child Abuse Unit, Assistant Prosecutor Sara Sencer, now Sara McArdle. She happened to live in Maplewood. 15

McArdle questioned Terry, handing to him during the interview what is called, by child-abuse experts, an "anatomically correct" doll —

that is, a rag doll that has an anus and genitalia. On the basis of what the child does with — and to — such a doll, investigators like McArdle say they can conclude whether and what type of abuse is likely to have occurred. Under questioning by McArdle, according to a prosecutor's report, Terry Weldon stuck his finger in the doll's rectum.

Terry also told McArdle that two other boys had had their temperature taken. Both were questioned. The boys seemed to know nothing about temperature-taking, but one of them, according to McArdle, said Michaels had touched his penis. Then a fourth allegation was made: The Weldons had notified Wee Care director Arlene Spector of their son Terry's story, and Spector, in turn, had notified the members of the school board. Under repeated questioning from his father, a board member — with the father telling him "he was his best friend and that he could tell him anything" (this from the prosecutor's office report) — another boy said that Michaels had touched his penis with a spoon. A decision was made to bring Kelly Michaels in for questioning.

The two investigators who arrived at Kelly Michaels's apartment on the morning of May 6 found only one bed in the apartment, and this, Michaels later said, at once attracted their attention. She said they exchanged sly and significant glances. She was told she was not under arrest and did not need a lawyer but that she was under investigation and would she please come to the prosecutor's office for questioning. Once there, she waived her *Miranda* rights and spent several hours insisting that the allegations were unfounded and that she was innocent. About temperature-taking, she explained that teachers took it by placing plastic strips on the children's foreheads. She was urged to take a lie-detector test and did; she passed. Two and a half years later, at Michaels's trial, the county prosecutors prevented the results of this polygraph from being admitted into evidence, basing their objection on a state law stipulating that any person submitting to a police lie-detector test must first sign an agreement authorizing future use of the results. Michaels, who had never before been brought into a police station, knew nothing of this requirement; nor did the detectives questioning her see fit to mention it.

She was driven home, and, shaken though she was at the end of this day, she remembers reaching the conclusion that it must all have been some kind of bizarre misunderstanding. In one sense it was: The jury eventually rejected the charge that she had taken Terry Weldon's temperature rectally — the very charge that provoked the entire investigation: anal penetration of the boy. But, as is invariably true in these cases, the first accusation was followed by more accusations — many more.

No one examining the scores of such child sexual-abuse cases can 20 fail to be struck by the way in which, in almost every instance, an initial accusation leads to others and still others — and on and on, until the charges number in the hundreds. At one point during the McMartin case, the police announced they had thirty-six suspects and had uncovered as many as 1,200 alleged victims of sexual abuse. An investigation begun in Jordan, Minnesota, at about the same time that Judy Johnson first made her allegations about Ray Buckey, followed a similar — if even stranger — pattern.

There, a case was opened after a woman named Christine Brown alleged that her daughter had been sexually abused by James Rud, a trash collector and a neighbor in the trailer park where she and her daughter lived. Other children in the trailer park were questioned, and some acknowledged that they, too, had been victimized — by Christine Brown. She was charged soon after with eighteen counts of criminal sexual activity. A mother of five with little money, Brown approached her older sister and brother-in-law, Helen and Tom Brown (the shared surname is coincidental), for help, and they agreed to mortgage their house to post Christine's bail. Two months later, the prosecutor in the case, Kathleen Morris, had Tom and Helen arrested for child abuse, and they spent five days in jail. Several dozen local residents met at City Hall to protest the arrests, among them an automobile painter named Bob Bentz, his wife, Lois, and a local policeman, Greg Myers. Not long after, all three were arrested on charges of child abuse, along with Myers's wife and a married couple who had driven the Browns home from jail.

In nearly all such cases, the allegations and the numbers of suspects begin to mount only after the entry of investigators and of representatives of child-abuse agencies. It is these experts who convince parents and children alike that the number of abuses and abusers is virtually limitless — beyond their imagination.

On May 15, 1985, nine days after Kelly Michaels had been brought in for questioning, Wee Care convened a meeting of parents. The school had sent out a letter on May 8, informing the parents that a former employee of the school was being investigated "regarding serious allegations made by a child," and while this prompted a flurry of phone calls by parents to the school, no other allegations against Michaels emerged. The prosecutor's office was set to wrap up its case — based on the allegations made by Terry Weldon and the two boys who alleged Michaels touched their penis — and present it to a grand jury. But the Wee Care board thought it best that the parents be informed about abuse by an expert, in this instance, Peg Foster, a social worker who codirected a Sexual Assault Unit at a Newark hospital.

On the evening of May 15, Foster told the assembled parents a number of things they had never heard before. She told them that sexual abuse is not unusual. She told them that, although she could point to no hard evidence — because no such evidence exists — she believed that one in three children in the United States has had an "inappropriate sexual experience" by the time he or she reaches the age of eighteen. She encouraged the parents to take their children to their pediatricians to check for physical injury. She told them to go home and begin checking their sons and daughters carefully for genital soreness — and also for nightmares, biting, spitting, bed-wetting, masturbation, or for what might be construed in any way as sexual behavior, or, for that matter, for any sort of noticeable changes in behavior. She did not tell them, of course, that the "symptoms" are for many children a normal part of development.

On May 22, the state's Division of Youth and Family Services — the agency that Terry Weldon's mother had first contacted — initiated its own investigation. The agency had allowed the county prosecutor's office to have the first chance at the case, but by law its staff was required to undertake its own inquiry. That afternoon, a DYFS social worker named Lou Fonolleras made his first of many visits to Wee Care and conducted his first of many interviews with the school's children. It was Fonolleras, a roundish man of thirty-four with a B.A. in psychology, who played the crucial role in building the case against Kelly Michaels.

Something of the state of mind that Fonolleras brought to his work is perhaps revealed in his official report of his first day at Wee Care. Describing the large, stone-faced church's many nooks and crannies, he noted that these would make ideal hiding places for child molesters. In his report, he described the school as a "pedophile's paradise." But no child he interviewed that first day told him that he or she had been abused by Kelly Michaels, or by anyone else. Two days after Fonolleras's visit to Wee Care, the county prosecutor's office brought its case to the grand jury, and the grand jury, agreeing that the state had a case, handed up an indictment. On June 12, Kelly Michaels was arrested and charged with six counts of abuse; she pleaded innocent to all charges. She was taken to the county jail, where she was confined in protective custody.

Fonolleras continued to suspect that there was more to the Wee Care case than six counts of abuse. When I met with him more than two years later, he explained that despite the denials of abuse voiced by the children he had talked with that day in May, he had glimpsed clues in "the children's body language," and that "you can't go by what they *say*" — though, of course, he himself eventually did just that. On June 6, he returned to Wee Care at the behest of a parent who, following instructions, had noticed her son behaving strangely. During the course of this interview, Fonolleras has said, he learned of the "pile-up" game. The "pile-up" is said to have worked this way: During nap time in a basement classroom, Kelly Michaels would march her students upstairs to a third-floor choir room, place kitchen utensils on the floor, and make the children strip and, once naked, roll around together.

In the days that followed, Fonolleras conducted interviews with other Wee Care children, bringing to these meetings not only crayons and paper but knives and forks and spoons. Remarkably, he made no tape recordings of these interviews, nor did he keep his written records. At the Michaels trial, he told the court that he had destroyed all the notes he took at these initial meetings because, at the time, he saw no reason to save them. He was not at this time gathering evidence for a criminal prosecution — although, as it turned out, there would have been no prosecution, beyond the six initial charges, had not Fonolleras, moved by what he heard in these unrecorded interviews, raised the specter of widespread child abuse. During my conversation with him, he explained that the only way to understand his technique of eliciting testimony about child abuse was to know what the children had told him in the very first interviews — the records of which, of course, he had thrown away.

Sometime in mid-June, Fonolleras called the county prosecutor's office with the suggestion that it might want to look further into the Wee Care case. The prosecutor's office and the DYFS agreed to launch a joint investigation and also brought in Peg Foster, who had earlier instructed the Wee Care parents on what she believed to be the symptoms of child abuse. For two months — during July and August of 1985 — this investigative team talked with the Wee Care staff and with parents, and also recorded interviews with the children. These interviews, it is important to understand, are not like those that might take place between two adults. Listening to tapes of the interviews, one might be struck by how little the children actually confided on their own and also by the wholly fantastical nature of so much of what they did say. Most of the children were confused, had nothing to say, or flatly denied that anything had happened to them. It was also clear that what a child actually *said* during the questioning often carried little weight with the investigators. If a child persisted in denying that anything had been done to him or her, Fonolleras or another investigator would typically write: "At this time Hugh denied victimization. It should be noted [that] during the interview, Hugh was victimizing an anatomically correct doll."

As a rule, the children were given knives and forks and then asked to show — on an anatomically correct doll — where Kelly had hurt them. On the tapes that I heard, a child's first response more often than not was to poke the doll in the eye or the neck or a knee. Invariably, the listener then hears the voice of Fonolleras, urging, "Where else? Uh-huh, where else?" After a succession of "where else?" responses, the child winds up poking at a penis, or a vagina, or an anus. Here, the "where elses" stop. Later, Fonolleras's official report typically would note how a child "described" the penetration of her vagina or his anus.   30

Fonolleras was quick to praise those who confirmed his suspicions: "Boy, you're doing so good." But he was stern with those who responded with firm or frequent noes. Here is Fonolleras with one tiny recalcitrant: "If you don't help me, I'm going to tell your friends that you not only don't want to help *me* but you won't help *them.*"

What follows is part of a transcript of an interview with Luke, age four, conducted by Fonolleras and Essex County Investigator Richard Mastrangelo.

Fonolleras: A lot of other kids have helped us since we saw you last.

Luke: I don't have to. No!

Fonolleras: Did we tell you Kelly is in jail?

Luke: Yes, my mother already told me.

Fonolleras [indicating Mastrangelo]: Did I tell you this is the guy who arrested her, put her in there? Don't you want to ask us any questions?

Luke: No!

Fonolleras at this point handed Luke an anatomically correct doll, then proceeded with his questioning.

Fonolleras: What color did Kelly have down there? Brown like her head? Did she have hair under her arm?

Luke: My daddy do.

At this point, Luke began to shriek, and there are indications that he was kicking Fonolleras. Fonolleras offered him a piece of cake and asked him if he would like to see Investigator Mastrangelo's badge. Mastrangelo then said to Luke, "So your penis was bleeding?" Luke laughed.

Fonolleras [taking a new tack]: Did Kelly play "Jingle Bells" with clothes on?

Luke [screaming now]: No, I saw her penis! I peed on her!

Fonolleras: You peed on her?

Luke: No, she peed on me!

At this time Luke told Fonolleras that he wanted to stop. But Fonol-   35
leras urged him to continue. He asked more questions about Luke's penis, about whether he put it in Kelly's mouth.

Fonolleras: Whose mouth did you have to put your penis in?

Luke: Nobody.

Fonolleras: Did anybody kiss your penis?

Luke: No. I want to go home.

Fonolleras: Did she put this fork in your bottom? Yes or no.

Luke: I forgot.

Fonolleras: Did she do anything else to your bottom?

Luke: That's all she did.

There followed a series of "I forgot" and "I don't know" responses. Finally, tiredly, Luke said, "Okay, okay, I'll try to remember." He then said — in an obviously playful, make-believe tone — "She put that in my heinie."

Fonolleras: The fork!

Luke [shrieking]: Yes!

There were more questions, and more noes from Luke. Fonolleras then said, in a disappointed tone, "I thought you were going to help me." The session ends with Luke shouting, "It's all lies!"

If the parents of the Wee Care children harbored any doubts about these interviews and the resulting abuse charges, they kept those doubts to themselves. One Wee Care parent, grateful for the kindness Kelly Michaels had shown his child, did write to express his faith in her innocence. Still, the months of group meetings with investigators and other parents eroded his faith. At the trial, this father took the stand as a vocal witness for the prosecution.

As the investigations progressed, it became amply clear that some of the parents took as true every word of the stories of abuse they began hearing from their children. One mother explained (to a grand jury) how her four-and-a-half-year-old son had told her that Kelly had stuck a spoon and a pencil in his ear, that her aide, Brenda Sopchak, had given him a "truth drink," that Kelly had begged the aide not to call the police, that she had told the little boys she would cut them in pieces and throw them away so the mothers couldn't find them again.

Asked if she thought her son might have been fantasizing, the mother, a school board member, answered, "No." He was, she further explained, "merely recounting what had happened during the day." 40

If Kelly Michaels's fellow teachers harbored doubts about her guilt, they, too — with one notable exception — kept these doubts largely to themselves. There were children, it appears, who had told investigators that other teachers had been present when they were being molested by Kelly. Some of the children named every teacher in the school. This would explain the clear eagerness to please in the answers some teachers gave during their grand jury testimony. Before being questioned herself, Kelly Michaels's classroom aide, Brenda Sopchak, was played a tape of a child accusing *her*. She now began to remember things: Michaels's suspiciously even temper, how she seemed to be in a daydreamlike state at times, and the like. Another teacher testified that Kelly wore no underpants under her jeans. Only Wee Care's head teacher, Diane Costa, remained unwaveringly supportive of Kelly Michaels, whom she described as a "model teacher." But Costa herself was indicted on the charge of failing to report child abuse, which meant that she could not testify at Michaels's trial without placing herself under the threat of prosecution. The indictment effectively silenced the one authoritative voice capable of undermining the state's case.

After closing for the summer, Wee Care did not reopen in September 1985. Only the members of the investigative team returned from time to time to the classrooms. Assessing their months of research, these investigators claimed that Kelly Michaels had, in her seven months at the school, sexually abused the entire Wee Care student body, fifty-one children. Two more grand juries were convened, and in December, Kelly Michaels was indicted on 235 counts of abuse against thirty-one children.

The trial of Kelly Michaels began on June 22, 1987. (One of the Wee Care families had moved out of Maplewood, and others had chosen not to expose their children to the rigors of a jury trial; as a result, the charges against Kelly Michaels now numbered 163.) Because the Michaels family had run out of money, Kelly Michaels was defended by a team of "pool attorneys" appointed by New Jersey's Office of the Public Defender. Pool attorneys are not salaried employees of the state but free-lancers permitted to pick and choose among available cases. Michaels's case went unassigned for four months: It would seem that many of these lawyers were reluctant to take on a case that looked as though it would drag on for months, or to defend a woman accused of sexually assaulting, among others, the grandson of a prominent local judge. (The judge, as it turned out, was the first witness called by the prosecution.)

Harvey Meltzer and Robert Clark, the defense attorneys eventually assigned to the case, believed their client to be innocent. They hoped to base their defense on logistics and common sense — on the contention that no one could have abused children sexually in every corner of the school without anybody else finding out about it.

The prosecutors, for their part, knew their hopes lay in the emotional *45* nature of the case. Lacking material evidence, the prosecutors sought to stir outrage — and, of course, to convince the jurors that they should simply *believe the children.*

They needed some sort of facsimile evidence, and in the summer of 1985, months before the 235-count indictment against Michaels was handed up, they began instructing Wee Care parents in the preparation of charts and diaries detailing the "symptoms" of abuse — the bed-wetting, nightmares, changes in behavior, and so on — that they had first learned of at the meeting at Wee Care in mid-May of that year. During my interviews at the prosecutor's office in the winter of 1988, I saw huge stacks of these charts. One of the more noteworthy symptoms of abuse listed on the charts was "child won't eat peanut butter." The children's lack of appetite for peanut butter, the prosecutors contended, was proof of the charge made by the children that Michaels had spread peanut butter on their genitals and then licked it off. Sometimes it was peanut butter alone, but sometimes — as the testimony evolved in ever more elaborate detail — it was peanut butter and jelly.

I met that winter as well with a number of Wee Care parents who were eager to tell me all the significant changes they had noticed in their children, in particular their suddenly sexualized behavior. Each time I was told a new detail — how a child grabbed his father's genitals or talked about kissing penises — I inquired when this kind of behavior or talk had begun. Invariably I was told, "Just after disclosure." That is, not after Kelly Michaels is said to have begun sexually molesting the children, in the fall of 1984, but after the parents were told, in the spring of 1985, to look for portents and signs.

One mother told me, "My daughter was all over my husband. She had turned into a little five-year-old whore!"

I asked her when this behavior had begun.

"After disclosure." *50*

Disclosure, like so many other quasi-legalisms that support the accusations of child abuse, became a household word among the Wee Care parents. It never occurred to the mother in question or to any of the other mothers with whom I spoke that the hypersexuality of their children might have to do not with Kelly Michaels but with the exhaustive questioning, and lurid disclosures, to which they were subjected by investigators and by their parents. (There were parents, I learned, who kept separate charts listing suspicious behavior they began to remember having occurred prior to disclosure. But not one of these parents had found the behavior unusual enough *at the time* to consult a pediatrician or ask a Wee Care teacher about it.)

The charts were useful not only to the prosecution. They also provided some parents with a way of explaining all types of problems they had with their children. That their children had been molested at school now served to explain *everything*. As one parent said, "Everything my husband and I had passed off as just some phase our child was going through, we could look back on and say, 'Now, *now* we could understand why.'" Other parents cited the molestation as the cause of their marital breakup. No matter what else might be going on at home, parents held that their children's problems stemmed from abuse at Wee Care.

In court, the charts aided the parents in their testimony and perhaps aided Judge William Harth in his decision to allow such testimony. In a similar case, a higher state court in New Jersey subsequently ruled as inadmissible — as hearsay — the testimony of parents on the subject of what their children told them. Michaels's lawyer Harvey Meltzer requested a mistrial based on this ruling, which was handed down after the prosecution had presented its case. The judge refused to grant the mistrial. Instead, he instructed the jury to disregard some twenty charges based on hearsay; but he did not give the instruction until much later, just prior to the jury's deliberation. Thus, the jurors had been allowed to listen for months to hearsay that at the last moment they were told to erase from their minds.

In Judge Harth's courtroom, the parent-plaintiffs were treated with unstinting consideration for their every concern, particularly the concern for anonymity. The guarantee of anonymity, of course, encourages the multiplication of charges and accusations. To the privacy of the parents and children Judge Harth accorded something akin to sacred status, while the name of the accused — like that of the accused and their families at similar tribunals across the nation — was emblazoned in headlines, irremediably tarnished.

To protect the Wee Care families' anonymity, the judge strictly cur-   55
tailed the amount of investigation into their backgrounds he would allow defense attorneys. To protect that anonymity, the judge sealed the trial transcript. Nor were the children required to testify in open court. They testified in the judge's chambers, and their testimony was shown to the jury on closed-circuit TV — a not uncommon arrangement at such child-

abuse trials. Judge Harth also refused to allow the defense psychologists to examine the children, as the prosecution doctors had been able to do. These children (who had, in fact, been analyzed and counseled for some two years prior to the trial) would, the judge said, be too traumatized to answer questions by a second set of psychologists. The defense argued in vain that *its* psychologists must have a chance to determine whether the children were, in fact, traumatized, but the judge held firm. It was a decision that violated the most fundamental principle of due process — the principle that both sides must be heard in a courtroom. Not even a cardinal principle of the justice system was a match, apparently, for the revered status accorded alleged victims of child abuse.

At the trial the children's testimony, given after two and a half years of preparation and training, was rich in detail, a startling difference from the earlier denials and bewilderment recorded during the investigative phase. One witness was Luke, who had shouted "It's all lies!" at Fonolleras's questions. Mindful of this taped outburst, prosecutor Sara McArdle asked Luke whether he hadn't meant he was *hoping* it was all lies. This time he didn't disappoint his interrogator: Yes, the child answered, he had been hoping it was all lies.

Still, even now there were child witnesses who continued to change stories, midtestimony, or to deny that anything had happened. One child told the court that Kelly forced him to push a sword into her rectum. A lengthy and earnest colloquy then took place, between the attorneys and the judge, as to whether the child was saying *sword* or *saw*. After he had pushed the sword, or saw, into his teacher's rectum, the boy told the court, she told him to take it out.

"What did Kelly say when you took the sword out?" the child was then asked.

"She said, 'Thank you.'"

Brad Greene told the court that Kelly threatened to turn him into a mouse — that, in fact, she *had* turned him into a mouse for a little while during a plane trip to visit his grandmother. Child witness Celine Mauer said that she had been "tractored" by Kelly; that is, been abused, with other children, inside a tractor. Indeed, the prosecutors went to some trouble to substantiate this claim — bringing a representative of the Maplewood street maintenance department to confirm that a tractor had been parked in the vicinity of the school.

Who would have believed any of this? Surely no reasonable adult, no jury. Yet it was offered as evidence. Thanks to the current zeal to prosecute child abusers, strange new rules have come to obtain at these trials according to which the witnesses need not be credible all the time. These rules did not obtain at the McMartin trial, at which jurors rejected the children's stories, but it did obtain at the trial of Kelly Michaels. Prosecutor Glenn Goldberg advised the jury at the outset that it was not necessary to believe everything the children said. Where child abuse is concerned, the prosecutor told them, "there is no physical evidence. Is the jury going to be able to understand this?"

In effect, the prosecutor asked the jurors if they could bring themselves to forget certain values with which they had been imbued as citizens of a democracy, values such as the importance of evidence in a criminal trial, and if they could suspend their belief in the Constitution in the interest of protecting children. As the verdict proved, they could.

Perhaps the most important witness for the prosecution was not a child or a parent but Bronx psychologist Eileen Treacy. An article in *New York* magazine later revealed that the curriculum vitae of this particular child-abuse "expert" exaggerated her credentials. The article also cited a ruling by a New Jersey judge, Mark Epstein, in a similar child-abuse case. That ruling declared, "The most damning witness [against the prosecution] was Eileen Treacy. . . . Ms. Treacy's questioning gently but surely led [the child] where Ms. Treacy wanted to take him." The judge was convinced, he said, that Treacy would have been able to elicit the same accusations from children who had *not* been abused.

If a child said emphatically that nothing had happened, the denial, Treacy explained, was the very proof that the abuse *had* taken place. In this expert's view, all friendship or affection shown by teacher to child signified an effort to seduce. At the Michaels trial, Treacy testified that the Wee Care students were "the most traumatized group of children" she had ever seen. She explained the trauma by referring to the theories of Suzanne Sgroi, a pediatrician and the discoverer of the Child Sex Abuse Syndrome. According to Dr. Sgroi, the syndrome develops in a number of phases. There is the "engagement phase," during which time the abuser seduces the child into the activity. This is followed by the "secrecy phase," the "suppression phase," and so on; and Treacy explained each of them to the jury. "Proof of the suppression stage," she said, "is the succession of no, no, no answers." When one child, during testimony, expressed concern for Michaels, this demonstrated "that she [the child] had a relationship with Kelly, and that fits into the engagement phase."

Treacy, it should be said, did not limit herself to interpretations based on the theories of Dr. Sgroi. In one of the abuse diaries, a parent had noted that her child no longer liked tuna fish. This, Treacy pointed out to the jurors, was significant. "It's well known," she said, "that the smell of tuna fish is similar to the odor of vaginal excretions." In the winter of 1988, when I visited Treacy in her office in the Bronx, I remarked on the many children's drawings on the walls. She told me that if I looked closely at the drawings, I would "see how obvious *hands* are in all their pictures." The predominance of hands, she explained, was a strong sign that the children who drew these pictures had been molested.

To encounter Treacy's Kafkaesque testimony is to understand how a jury managed to find the accused in this case guilty, however improbable

65

the evidence. The abuse expert, a psychologist, had in effect told the jury that they must suspend all rational belief if they were to understand the abuse the children had suffered. It was a world in which no meant yes, black meant white. Yet, the jury was told, they must believe its premises, believe the children, or else be counted guilty of betraying these young victims.

The principal witness for the defense was Dr. Ralph Underwager, an avowed opponent of the child-abuse investigators' techniques, their reliance on dolls and children's drawings, and their insistence on finding child abuse whether or not any took place. At the Michaels trial, Dr. Underwager said, "The child is interrogated and desperately is trying to figure out what are the *rules,* what's wanted of me by this powerful adult before me? The child says no, Kelly's clothes were *on,* when the interrogators want the response 'Her clothes were *off.*' And what happens? The interviewer doesn't stop, doesn't *believe* the child, *repeats* the question. It just tells the child: What you told me before isn't enough. It isn't right. It's not what I want . . ." His testimony said, in effect, that nothing had happened to the Wee Care children except the visits of the investigators. The Wee Care parents I talked to vehemently agreed that, of everybody on the defense side, the person they hated the most was Dr. Underwager.

Defense attorneys Clark and Meltzer made the decision early not to present character witnesses to testify on Kelly Michaels's behalf. Such a witness may be asked anything under cross-examination, and what the attorneys feared most was the discovery that Michaels had been involved in two brief homosexual love affairs. Kelly Michaels refers to the liaisons as nothing more than youthful experiments, but the defense lawyers reasoned that the prosecution would seek to make a damaging connection between her sexual history and the criminal acts with which she was charged.

(Prosecutor Goldberg sought to nourish this view by close textual analysis of a Bob Dylan song that Kelly Michaels had copied into her roll book. The lyrics include the lines "Your lover who just walked out the door/Has taken all his blankets from the floor." The prosecutor, who has an undergraduate major in psychology, told the jury that the song was very significant, that it was an extremely important clue to Kelly Michaels's secret life as a sexual criminal. The Wee Care children, he told the jury, "slept on blankets and mats.")

With no character witnesses called — no old classmates, friends, 70 neighbors, or teachers to color in, with stories and comments, the outline of a normal life — the jurors saw only the Kelly Michaels of the Wee Care case, the abuser of children so luridly portrayed in the testimony.

For the jurors who doubted that one woman could commit so many awful crimes, Assistant Prosecutor Sara McArdle reminded them in her summation that Adolf Hitler, "one man," had persecuted not a "little school" but the "entire world" — "Jews, Gypsies, Czechs, and blacks."

Blacks, of course, were not among Hitler's victims, but many of the jurors were black.

Bearing in mind, perhaps, that prosecutorial excess is one of the grounds relevant to an appeal, prosecutor McArdle later vehemently denied any intentional parallel between the defendant and Adolf Hitler. She went on to say that she could not imagine that anyone could read anything untoward into this simple historical analogy. Thus, the prosecution, which had vested so much faith in a lack of appetite for peanut butter, and which divined damning proofs of guilt in Bob Dylan lyrics in a roll book, now disdained as fanciful any notion that a comparison to Hitler might be something other than a neutral reference.

It took the jury thirteen days to reach its verdict that Michaels was guilty of 115 counts of abuse. Meltzer requested that the court consider granting his client bail pending appeal. The judge turned down the request: Michaels, he said, was a danger to the community. He said, "I just cannot forget the children."

But a three-member appellate panel agreed that, because of the legal questions the trial raised, Kelly Michaels should be granted bail pending appeal. Among the questions the judges doubtless had in mind was the defendant's constitutional right to face her accusers — denied in this trial, as in many of the other trials involving children's hearsay testimony.

News that Kelly Michaels might get bail raised storms of protest 75 from the Wee Care parents. The prosecutors appealed. Local politicians, declaring themselves outraged, joined them. The parents marched and picketed. One mother, weeping, told reporters that when she had informed her child that Kelly had been convicted, the child had said, "Now I'm safe." "What do I tell her *now*? Now, my daughter's *not* safe!" The state's highest court, in short order, vacated the bail decision.

In the days immediately following the end of the McMartin trial and the acquittal of Ray Buckey and his mother, the *Los Angeles Times* published an analysis of the press coverage of the case. The headline above the first installment in the series could as easily have been affixed to analyses of the Michaels trial: WHERE WAS SKEPTICISM IN MEDIA? PACK JOURNALISM AND HYSTERIA MARKED . . . COVERAGE. . . . FEW JOURNALISTS STOPPED TO QUESTION THE BELIEVABILITY OF THE PROSECUTION'S CHARGES.

During the trial, stories began leaking from the prosecutor's office suggesting that Kelly Michaels had herself been sexually abused by her parents. The stories were widely circulated among reporters covering the case. One of them, a television reporter, told me of stories she had heard that Kelly Michaels's mother had molested her and sent her nude photographs of herself; and of how Kelly Michaels's father — who, the story went, also molested his daughter — had called Wee Care every day to make sure that she was initiating the children in the practices of pederasty.

Such stories were not broadcast or printed. Still, they had enormous impact on the press, for they meshed nicely with current dogma — and the press is nothing if not up on the latest dogma — which holds that children who are molested become molesters themselves. The rumors that Kelly Michaels had been sexually abused by her parents thus counted heavily in persuading many reporters that she was guilty. In turn, these reporters, subtly and sometimes not so subtly, conveyed their belief to their readers and viewers.

Of course, the newspapers and the TV stations no longer concern themselves with Kelly Michaels, who will not come up before a parole board for twelve more years. When she does come up for parole, the Wee Care parents have vowed they will be there to see that it is denied. Her attorney is moving ahead with an appeal. In the meantime, Kelly Michaels sits in her small cell at the women's prison in Clinton, New Jersey, where the Wee Care parents are determined to keep her.

The Wee Care Day Nursery closed down in the aftermath of the   *80* investigation; the former Wee Care students, it would appear, thereafter went to another sort of school: one in which they were instructed, by child-agency investigators and by prosecutors, in the details of the sex crimes supposedly committed against them. Perhaps the worst thing about the long investigation and trial is that — however unfounded the charges — the child witnesses grow up having internalized the belief that they have been the victims of hideous sexual abuse. No one who saw them will soon forget the frenzied faces of thirteen- and fourteen-year-old former McMartin pupils in the hours following the verdict. These adolescents had spent their last six years — fully half their lives — instructed in the faith that they had been subjected, at ages four and five, to unspeakable sexual horrors; this belief they had come to hold as the defining truth of their lives and identities. It is not surprising that these children should have wept and raved when the verdict was handed down denying all that they believed in.

Believe the children is the battle cry of the child-abuse militants, who hold as an article of faith that a pederast lurks behind every door and blackboard. But child after child repeatedly said that Kelly Michaels had done nothing — and they had *not* been believed. The prosecutors had brought experts to court to testify that children denying abuse should not be believed. *Believe the children* apparently means — to those raising the rallying cry — believe the children *only* if they say they have been molested. "To believe a child's *no* is simplistic," prosecutor McArdle had told the jury.

The scores of investigations and trials of alleged child molesters, undertaken in the name of a good — protecting children — have irreparably shattered lives and reputations. It is not an unfamiliar pattern in our history. We are a society that, every fifty years or so, is afflicted by some paroxysm of virtue — an orgy of self-cleansing through which evil of one kind or another is cast out. From the witch-hunts of Salem to the communist hunts of the McCarthy era to the current shrill fixation on child abuse, there runs a common thread of moral hysteria. After the McCarthy era, people would ask: But how could it have happened? How could the presumption of innocence have been abandoned wholesale? How did large and powerful institutions acquiesce as congressional investigators ran roughshod over civil liberties — all in the name of the war on communists? How was it possible to believe that subversives lurked behind every library door, in every radio station, that every two-bit actor who had ever belonged to the wrong political organization posed a threat to the nation's security?

Years from now people doubtless will ask the same questions about our present era — a time when the most improbable charges of abuse find believers; when it is enough only to be accused by anonymous sources to be hauled off to the investigators; a time when the hunt for child abusers has become a national pathology.

Questions for Discussion

1. According to Rabinowitz, how plausible were the charges against Kelly Michaels? What do you think of these charges?
2. Why did Rabinowitz decide to research and publish this article after Michaels had been imprisoned? Why does she go into so much detail? Does the Michaels case have national implications?
3. Consider the analogy Rabinowitz makes in paragraph 2 between child abuse cases and the Salem witch trials. Upon what similarities does this analogy depend? Are there any significant differences between the two?
4. Rabinowitz draws repeated attention to the motto *believe the children*. Is there anything wrong with believing children? What happens when children are not believed? Did the investigators and prosecutors in the Michaels case believe what children told them?
5. What role has the federal government played in influencing how child abuse cases are treated?
6. Why did defense attorneys refrain from calling character witnesses to testify on Michaels's behalf? Do you think this was a wise decision?
7. What is your impression of Lou Fonolleras?
8. How fairly was Kelly Michaels treated in court?

Suggestions for Writing

1. Drawing upon the information reported in this article, write an evaluation in your own words of the case against Kelly Michaels.
2. How well does justice function in your own community? Are people treated equally by the law? Write an evaluation of a branch of municipal or state government with which you have had personal experience.

9

Writing to Explore an Idea

These days, there always seems to be more to do than there is time to do it in. Efficiency, we are told, is a virtue. "Just do it," an advertisement for running shoes harangued; and indeed, we always seem to be running, one way or another. In writing, too, we have been offered models of efficiency: Put the thesis first so that your reader can quickly find the main points; pare down to the leanest language you can produce; don't be wordy; get to the point. Efficiency is important. We wouldn't ever get anything done without some of it. But efficiency, carried to an extreme, can extinguish thinking entirely and replace it with doing. There would be no time to explore an idea, to contemplate, to reflect, to play with alternatives, to think of a better solution.

Exploring an idea is, in the best sense of the word, thinking, and it has both a critical and a creative aspect. Critical thinking is traditionally associated with logic, analysis, and problem solving — with, above all else, trying to prove something. Creative thinking is often associated with the arts, for it is characterized by experimentation and a spirit of inquiry that is sympathetic to ambiguity. If critical thinking usually follows a series of steps to a carefully defined conclusion, creative thinking can play with possibilities without necessarily reaching a conclusion. Its purpose is to find things out rather than to prove anything in particular. But these two types of thinking complement each other. Although each can be pursued independently, they become powerful when fused together. Exploring the teaching of science, Lewis Thomas — a distinguished physician and hospital administrator — tries to imagine a new approach to science education in which the critical and the creative are joined:

> But maybe, just maybe, a new set of courses dealing systematically with ignorance in science will take hold. The scientists might discover in it a new and subversive technique for catching the attention of students driven by curiosity, delighted and surprised to learn that science is . . . an "endless frontier." The humanists, for their part, might take considerable satisfaction in watching their scientific colleagues confess openly to not knowing everything about everything. And the poets, on whose shoulders the future rests, might, late nights, thinking things over, begin to see some meanings that elude the rest of us.

In addition to illustrating an ideal in which criticism and creativity are joined, as science becomes a type of poetry, this passage shows Thomas exploring an idea. Although there is a persuasive dimension to his work, he has not committed himself to making a sustained argument. He is, instead, conveying a sense of thinking aloud — or in print, as happens to be the case. Note that he uses *might* three times and *maybe* twice. He does not pause to explain why the future rests upon the shoulders of poets — leaving readers to reflect upon that thought for themselves. And rather than dwelling upon facts, he seems to delight in the idea that scientists do not know everything.

If you like to think things over late at night, like the poets Thomas imagines, you may have felt that your mind was freely ranging, stopping here and there on an interesting point or image, and moving on to something else. And it may occasionally question and probe, sift and select, as you work deeper into the idea. Generally, that kind of thinking is unstructured, but lack of formal structure does not make it pointless. Associating one idea with another may take you far from where you began, and it may not take you to a predetermined destination to which every turn of the road has led efficiently, but it should take you some place worth being.

For example, suppose that riding down the highway, you notice a gnarled tree far away in a field. Wondering about why the tree is so gnarled can lead you to ponder the forces that may have caused the tree to grow crooked. But as you think about the tree, you realize that it is beautiful because of its flaw, and that leads you to begin thinking about how a beautiful flaw is important, that anything perfect is not interesting, and so on. Richard Selzer engages in this kind of thinking when he meditates on his visit to a slaughterhouse. The visit reminds him of Yale, where he will judge architectural designs for a model slaughterhouse; that experience in turn leads him to imagine an ideal slaughterhouse. The essay does not have a thesis, but it is unified by the spirit of inquiry and Selzer's strong voice as a writer. Writing with a voice very different from Selzer's, Jane Goodall also moves from one idea to another, taking advantage of the flexibility exploration allows. Remembering a chimpanzee named Lucy leads Goodall to think of a book written by the man who raised this chimp, and that leads her to recall her experience with other scientists and her own education before moving on to a recognition that flows from the culmination of these different thoughts.

Every idea that has contributed to the development of our civilization is the product of both critical and creative thinking. Art and philosophy, to be sure, are creative, but so are science and technology. Everyone knows about Benjamin Franklin and the kite with which he is supposed to have discovered electricity, and we have all heard the story that Newton recognized gravity as a force after an apple dropped on his head. (Newton's own version was that he began thinking about gravity after watching an apple fall in his orchard, some twenty years before he published his famous book on the laws of gravity.) Technology can also result from creative thinking. The personal computer resulted from the creative thinking of a teenager (Steve Jobs) working in his garage. Similar creative episodes are responsible for Edison's light bulb, Bell's telephone, and Marconi's radio.

Creative thinking is something everyone can do, and everyone should get in the habit of encouraging creative thoughts. Although there are no rules for how to do that, knowing the conditions that favor creative ideas may help. First, creative thoughts occur most often when people have plenty of information. Newton had already developed calculus when he was prompted to figure out why things fall to earth. Alexander Fleming was already a chemist when he noticed the peculiar healing effect of certain molds. The more you know, the more likely you are to understand that the world is a strange and wonderful place. The second element necessary to creative thinking is the ability to reflect upon information until you reach a new insight. When Newton saw the apple fall, he was prepared and ready to think about why. As Lewis Thomas notes, in the sciences today "it is required that the most expert and sophisticated minds be capable of changing course — often with a great lurch — every few years." Although some element of luck is often involved, creativity results from the prepared mind's reception of new ideas. Fleming's discovery of penicillin illustrates the third step: He noticed. Often, though, even prepared minds need time to incubate ideas. Fleming realized he had noticed something important only after a period of time for reflection. He used his eyes to see and his mind to wonder.

You are probably thinking that exploring is akin to self-discovery, and that is true; but whereas the similarities are striking, the differences are crucial. Through self-discovery you can see what the world makes of you, and through exploration you can pursue what you make of the world. Whereas self-discovery turns the mind inward to a contemplation of the self, exploring turns the mind outward toward a perception of the world. And just as you can write as an act of self-discovery, so you can write as an act of exploration. It's a good idea to try all of the permutations of this process — the interior and the exterior, the creative and the critical.

In exploration, writing is the record of the mind at work. Thinking is often chaotic and messy work, but some of your best ideas will come if you have your mind open to the free play of ideas without worrying too much about where your ideas are taking you. Enjoying this freedom does not mean, however, that you can simply put all your random thoughts on paper and call the result an exploratory essay. Creative explorations frequently lack a point — or have several. They may even backtrack, contradict themselves, and wander. Writing to explore expresses your curiosity and your scope of inquiry. But the final version of your exploration should be unified by a sense that it has been a quest and by a consistent voice that makes that quest your own. Look at Russell Baker's "Completely Different." Seemingly chaotic, Baker's exploration is decidedly expressive. It represents his playing with the idea of difference, which allows him to associate other ideas — miniaturizing, advertising, saving time — which he also addresses, pulling all the ideas into an essay that is — well, completely different. But strange as this essay may seem at first glance, it nevertheless has coherence. And although it does not insist upon a specific thesis, it does lead readers to think along certain lines.

Writing a critical exploration, however, has a few more conventions than writing a creative one. The writer is responsible for presenting a thesis and making sure that the other elements of the essay adhere to it; this form is sometimes referred to as *closed*. Some critical explorations, like Gloria Naylor's or Lewis Thomas's, display a thesis early and ratify that thesis in the development (also called *exposition*, from the Latin *ponere*, "to place, to set," and *ex*, "out"). These essays are less open in form than Jane Goodall's, Richard Selzer's, or Russell Baker's. And there are other options: A critical exploration may pose and answer a question or state and solve a problem. For these options you can use any of the patterns of arrangement (or any combination of these patterns) illustrated elsewhere in this book: narration, description, process, division, comparison and contrast, cause and effect. Or you can use the pattern illustrated in the essays by James Fallows, Gloria Naylor, and Joseph Epstein: the extended definition.

Of these three essays Epstein's is the most closed in form. Although his essay shows imagination and wit, it also incorporates nearly all the strategies traditionally recommended for an essay of definition. To define *vulgarity,* Epstein does the following:

- Contrasts it with words with which it might be confused.
- Defines the word through negation, or showing what it does not mean.
- Provides examples.
- Traces the history of the word.
- Quotes a dictionary.

Along the way, he seems to have a good time, and he conveys the sense that he needs to write the essay to find out what *vulgarity* means — as opposed to setting out to make a specific point. Nevertheless, his essay is fairly conventional in form.

Like Epstein, James Fallows also uses examples. His essay "Land of Plenty" is about *sodai gomi,* Japanese for "bulky garbage," as he explains in his opening paragraph. But he then offers a surprising definition of this term: "*sodai gomi* in its literal sense is a . . . serious trial for my family." Although he defines *sodai gomi* and explains why it exists, Fallows seems primarily interested in exploring how he feels about this practice. Examples are also important for Gloria Naylor's definition of *nigger* in "Mommy, What Does 'Nigger' Mean?" Like Fallows, she draws principally upon her own experience when defining a term, rather than turning to a dictionary or using one of the other strategies employed by Epstein.

Epstein, Fallows, and Naylor show that definition can take different forms. The main advantage of exploration is that it gives writers the flexibility to experiment with forms, adopting strategies that work for them and avoiding a predetermined pattern that dictates what must happen in any given paragraph. Both Fallows and Naylor choose to include narration within their essays; Fallows also uses some cause-and-effect division, and Naylor employs division. But this doesn't mean they had to use those strategies; it just means that they found it convenient to do so. Similarly, writers with other motives may choose to use definition. If, for example, you want to persuade people to support gun control, it will be wise for you to define what you mean by *gun control.*

We have discussed definition in this chapter because three of the writers in the selections that follow happen to use it, not because it is limited to exploration alone. But words embody ideas; and when searching for an idea to explore in an essay of your own, you might begin with a word you would like to understand better.

CONSIDERING YOUR AUDIENCE

Addressing your audience for an exploration is much the same as addressing your audience for informing, explaining, or persuading. Your goal in an exploration is either to invite the reader to journey with you or to convince your readers to accept an answer or solution you have proposed — or even to adjust their perspective to match yours. So although you will need to imagine your audience afresh with each exploration, some considerations will remain constant: Because people participate in intellectual journeys at different speeds, you will want to consider pacing for whatever audience you have. You also need to consider whether your readers are inexperienced; if they are, they may not be able to cope with material that is too demanding or unconventional. So you will always need to adjust the scope and density of your writing according to who you expect your audience will be. When possible, try thinking of your exploration as a conversation you are having with a friend. That means you can risk much more in a creative exploration, partly because your intimate audience is trustworthy, and partly because you need not try to convince anyone. There will be no refutation, no attack. And as the risks are greater, so are the potential rewards: originality of expression and a heightened awareness of what the world offers.

Be aware that when you write a creative exploration, you are expecting your readers to make an effort to understand your writing — even if it involves logical leaps and topical pirouettes. You venture into unknown territories and your readers follow; but once there, readers may reach conclusions that you did not anticipate. Because your writing does not rule out widely ranging interpretations, your readers will interpret your writing in numerous ways. Because they are encouraged to interpret what you say, readers feel invited to participate in your exploration and, perhaps, to begin their own. They are watching you watch yourself think. And this experience will encourage them to think for themselves.

SHAPING YOUR ESSAY

Revising and editing are essential, of course, if you want your exploration to be readable. If you recall the process you employed for "re-seeing" several of your earlier papers, you will understand the kinds of things that need to be removed and the kinds of things that can be left in, what needs to be connected and what needs to be restated. But as you edit your exploration, retain as much of its spontaneity as you can. Keeping in mind that exploring an idea is like conversing with a reader, make your tone friendly and informal.

Playing with ideas for their own sake can be fun, and it usually has a personal dimension. With the exception of "Completely Different," all of the works in this chapter employ the first person, the "I" that helps convey the sense of an individual human mind at play. In exploration you can demonstrate that you have given your reader your trust, and when you do that, you can expect trust in return. Notice the sense of play with which Fallows discusses his scavenging or with which Joseph Epstein describes his Uncle Jake. Both Fallows and Epstein share their feelings and solicit yours in return: They invite you to participate in the feelings and the fun.

Notice, too, that Jane Goodall and Gloria Naylor also share their feelings as they explore ideas, but their moods are more serious. Playing with ideas does not necessarily make writers feel playful.

Perhaps the greatest challenge in writing to explore an idea is knowing when to stop. The nature of this motive allows for considerable freedom and experimentation. The essays in this chapter show a range from the very unconventional open form displayed by Russell Baker's "Completely Different" to the much more critical and closed forms represented by Lewis Thomas and Gloria Naylor. Not too surprisingly, the endings of these pieces are consistent with how open or closed they are. James Fallows takes advantage of the open form of the exploratory essay to conclude his piece with an imaginary conflict. Richard Selzer's "How to Build a Slaughterhouse" is an intriguing mixture of open and closed forms, mingling what amounts to a narrative reporting of what goes on in a slaughterhouse with a mystic journey to an ideal slaughterhouse Selzer creates. Selzer achieves closure to this essay with an encapsulation — an account of his visit to a butcher shop — but that visit is open to multiple interpretations, almost as if it were the conclusion to a work of fiction. Joseph Epstein closes his exploration of *vulgar* with a rallying cry that reflects his point of view. Gloria Naylor ends her essay by returning to a reminiscence that she began with and that illustrates the point she has been making. Having offered a solution to the problem of how to teach science, Lewis Thomas concludes with a restatement of the rationale for adopting his solution.

Judge the kind of ending you need to give your essay according to whether it is primarily creative or critical, open or closed. Then, supply the kind of ending your audience will expect. Remember that you don't have to have a formal conclusion, but you do need to give your reader a sense of completion.

Lewis Carroll's Red Queen confessed that she often entertained six contradictory ideas before breakfast. As you begin to explore ideas on your own, be aware that recognizing contradictions and incongruities can lead to new perceptions. But how you think and what you think about is ultimately up to you. No one should insist that you change ideas that you truly hold sacrosanct; similarly, no one should insist that you adhere to an idea you have explored thoroughly and found inadequate for you. Making that kind of choice for yourself is a basic human right, and writing to explore is an important tool for exercising that right. When you argue about ideas, you have the responsibility to make a well-defined position clear. But when you explore ideas, you are free to find out what you think — and that can be a great adventure.

THE MIND OF THE CHIMPANZEE

Jane Goodall

> *Jane Goodall has lived and worked with chimpanzees for over thirty years. The following selection begins with her looking into the eyes of a chimpanzee and wondering "what was going on behind them." As you read, consider how Goodall's exploration involves both noticing details about animals and reflecting upon what those details mean. Consider also how noticing and reflecting led Goodall to new insights. Ask yourself what Goodall learned about chimpanzees and the conventions of scientific discourse.*

Often I have gazed into a chimpanzee's eyes and wondered what was going on behind them. I used to look into Flo's, she so old, so wise. What did she remember of her young days? David Greybeard had the most beautiful eyes of them all, large and lustrous, set wide apart. They somehow expressed his whole personality, his serene self-assurance, his inherent dignity — and, from time to time, his utter determination to get his way. For a long time I never liked to look a chimpanzee straight in the eye — I assumed that, as is the case with most primates, this would be interpreted as a threat or at least as a breach of good manners. Not so. As long as one looks with gentleness, without arrogance, a chimpanzee will understand, and may even return the look. And then — or such is my fantasy — it is as though the eyes are windows into the mind. Only the glass is opaque so that the mystery can never be fully revealed.

I shall never forget my meeting with Lucy, an eight-year-old home-raised chimpanzee. She came and sat beside me on the sofa and, with her face very close to mine, searched in my eyes — for what? Perhaps she was looking for signs of mistrust, dislike, or fear, since many people must have been somewhat disconcerted when, for the first time, they came face to face with a grown chimpanzee. Whatever Lucy read in my eyes clearly satisfied her for she suddenly put one arm round my neck and gave me a generous and very chimp-like kiss, her mouth wide open and laid over mine. I was accepted.

For a long time after that encounter I was profoundly disturbed. I had been at Gombe° for about fifteen years then and I was quite familiar with chimpanzees in the wild. But Lucy, having grown up as a human child, was like a changeling, her essential chimpanzeeness overlaid by the various human behaviours she had acquired over the years. No longer purely chimp yet eons away from humanity, she was man-made, some other kind of being. I watched, amazed, as she opened the refrigerator and various cupboards, found bottles and a glass, then poured herself a gin

---

Gombe: Gombe National Park in Tanzania.

and tonic. She took the drink to the TV, turned the set on, flipped from one channel to another then, as though in disgust, turned it off again. She selected a glossy magazine from the table and, still carrying her drink, settled in a comfortable chair. Occasionally, as she leafed through the magazine she identified something she saw, using the signs of ASL, the American Sign Language used by the deaf. I, of course, did not understand, but my hostess, Jane Temerlin (who was also Lucy's "mother"), translated: "That dog," Lucy commented, pausing at a photo of a small white poodle. She turned the page. "Blue," she declared, pointing then signing as she gazed at a picture of a lady advertising some kind of soap powder and wearing a brilliant blue dress. And finally, after some vague hand movements — perhaps signed mutterings — "This Lucy's, this mine," as she closed the magazine and laid it on her lap. She had just been taught, Jane told me, the use of the possessive pronouns during the thrice weekly ASL lessons she was receiving at the time.

The book written by Lucy's human "father," Maury Temerlin, was entitled *Lucy, Growing Up Human.* And in fact, the chimpanzee is more like us than is any other living creature. There is close resemblance in the physiology of our two species and genetically, in the structure of the DNA, chimpanzees and humans differ by only just over one per cent. This is why medical research uses chimpanzees as experimental animals when they need substitutes for humans in the testing of some drug or vaccine. Chimpanzees can be infected with just about all known human infectious diseases including those, such as hepatitis B and AIDS, to which other non-human animals (except gorillas, orangutans and gibbons) are immune. There are equally striking similarities between humans and chimpanzees in the anatomy and wiring of the brain and nervous system, and — although many scientists have been reluctant to admit to this — in social behaviour, intellectual ability, and the emotions. The notion of an evolutionary continuity in physical structure from pre-human ape to modern man has long been morally acceptable to most scientists. That the same might hold good for mind was generally considered an absurd hypothesis — particularly by those who used, and often misused, animals in their laboratories. It is, after all, convenient to believe that the creature you are using, while it may react in disturbingly human-like ways, is, in fact, merely a mindless and, above all, unfeeling, "dumb" animal.

When I began my study at Gombe in 1960 it was not permissible — at least not in ethological circles — to talk about an animal's mind. Only humans had minds. Nor was it quite proper to talk about animal personality. Of course everyone knew that they *did* have their own unique characters — everyone who had ever owned a dog or other pet was aware of that. But ethologists, striving to make theirs a "hard" science, shied away from the task of trying to explain such things objectively. One respected ethologist, while acknowledging that there was "variability between individual animals," wrote that it was best that this fact be "swept under the carpet." At that time ethological carpets fairly bulged with all that was hidden beneath them.

How naive I was. As I had not had an undergraduate science education I didn't realize that animals were not supposed to have personalities, or to think, or to feel emotions or pain. I had no idea that it would have been more appropriate to assign each of the chimpanzees a number rather than a name when I got to know him or her. I didn't realize that it was not scientific to discuss behaviour in terms of motivation or purpose. And no one had told me that terms such as *childhood* and *adolescence* were uniquely human phases of the life cycle, culturally determined, not to be used when referring to young chimpanzees. Not knowing, I freely made use of all those forbidden terms and concepts in my initial attempt to describe, to the best of my ability, the amazing things I had observed at Gombe.

I shall never forget the response of a group of ethologists to some remarks I made at an erudite seminar. I described how Figan, as an adolescent, had learned to stay behind in camp after senior males had left, so that we could give him a few bananas for himself. On the first occasion he had, upon seeing the fruits, uttered loud, delighted food calls: whereupon a couple of the older males had charged back, chased after Figan, and taken his bananas. And then, coming to the point of the story, I explained how, on the next occasion, Figan had actually suppressed his calls. We could hear little sounds, in his throat, but so quiet that none of the others could have heard them. Other young chimps, to whom we tried to smuggle fruit without the knowledge of their elders, never learned such self-control. With shrieks of glee they would fall to, only to be robbed of their booty when the big males charged back. I had expected my audience to be as fascinated and impressed as I was. I had hoped for an exchange of views about the chimpanzee's undoubted intelligence. Instead there was a chill silence, after which the chairman hastily changed the subject. Needless to say, after being thus snubbed, I was very reluctant to contribute any comments, at any scientific gathering, for a very long time. Looking back, I suspect that everyone was interested, but it was, of course, not permissible to present a mere "anecdote" as evidence for anything.

The editorial comments on the first paper I wrote for publication demanded that every *he* or *she* be replaced with *it,* and every *who* be replaced with *which.* Incensed, I, in my turn, crossed out the *its* and *whichs* and scrawled back the original pronouns. As I had no desire to carve a niche for myself in the world of science, but simply wanted to go on living among and learning about chimpanzees, the possible reaction of the editor of the learned journal did not trouble me. In fact I won that round: the paper when finally published did confer upon the chimpanzees the dignity of their appropriate genders and properly upgraded them from the status of mere "things" to essential Being-ness.

However, despite my somewhat truculent attitude, I did want to learn, and I was sensible of my incredible good fortune in being admitted to Cambridge. I wanted to get my PhD, if only for the sake of Louis Leakey° and the other people who had written letters in support of my admission. And how lucky I was to have, as my supervisor, Robert Hinde. Not only because I thereby benefitted from his brilliant mind and clear thinking, but also because I doubt that I could have found a teacher more suited to my particular needs and personality. Gradually he was able to cloak me with at least some of the trappings of a scientist. Thus although I continued to hold to most of my convictions — that animals had personalities; that they could feel happy or sad or fearful; that they could feel pain; that they could strive towards planned goals and achieve greater success if they were highly motivated — I soon realized that these personal convictions were, indeed, difficult to prove. It was best to be circumspect — at least until I had gained some credentials and credibility. And Robert gave me wonderful advice on how best to tie up some of my more rebellious ideas with scientific ribbon. "You can't *know* that Fifi was jealous," he admonished on one occasion. We argued a little. And then: "Why don't you just say *If Fifi were a human child we would say she was jealous.*" I did.

It is not easy to study emotions even when the subjects are human. I   10
know how I feel if I am sad or happy or angry, and if a friend tells me that he is feeling sad, happy or angry, I assume that his feelings are similar to mine. But of course I cannot know. As we try to come to grips with the emotions of beings progressively more different from ourselves the task, obviously, becomes increasingly difficult. If we ascribe human emotions to non-human animals we are accused of being anthropomorphic — a cardinal sin in ethology. But is it so terrible? If we test the effect of drugs on chimpanzees because they are biologically so similar to ourselves, if we accept that there are dramatic similarities in chimpanzee and human brain and nervous system, is it not logical to assume that there will be similarities also in at least the more basic feelings, emotions, moods of the two species?

In fact, all those who have worked long and closely with chimpanzees have no hesitation in asserting that chimps experience emotions similar to those which in ourselves we label pleasure, joy, sorrow, anger, boredom and so on. Some of the emotional states of the chimpanzee are so obviously similar to ours that even an inexperienced observer can understand what is going on. An infant who hurls himself screaming to the ground, face contorted, hitting out with his arms at any nearby object, banging his head, is clearly having a tantrum. Another youngster, who gambols around his mother, turning somersaults, pirouetting and, every so often, rushing up to her and tumbling into her lap, patting her or pulling her hand towards him in a request for tickling, is obviously filled with *joie de vivre*. There are few observers who would not unhesitatingly

---

Louis Leakey: British archaeologist and anthropologist (1903–1972), born in Kenya.

ascribe his behaviour to a happy, carefree state of well-being. And one cannot watch chimpanzee infants for long without realizing that they have the same emotional need for affection and reassurance as human children. An adult male, reclining in the shade after a good meal, reaching benignly to play with an infant or idly groom an adult female, is clearly in a good mood. When he sits with bristling hair, glaring at his subordinates and threatening them, with irritated gestures, if they come too close, he is clearly feeling cross and grumpy. We make these judgements because the similarity of so much of a chimpanzee's behaviour to our own permits us to empathize.

It is hard to empathize with emotions we have not experienced. I can imagine, to some extent, the pleasure of a female chimpanzee during the act of procreation. The feelings of her male partner are beyond my knowledge — as are those of the human male in the same context. I have spent countless hours watching mother chimpanzees interacting with their infants. But not until I had an infant of my own did I begin to understand the basic, powerful instinct of mother-love. If someone accidentally did something to frighten Grub, or threaten his well-being in any way, I felt a surge of quite irrational anger. How much more easily could I then understand the feelings of the chimpanzee mother who furiously waves her arms and barks in threat at an individual who approaches her infant too closely, or at a playmate who inadvertently hurts her child. And it was not until I knew the numbing grief that gripped me after the death of my second husband that I could even begin to appreciate the despair and sense of loss that can cause young chimps to pine away and die when they lose their mothers.

Empathy and intuition can be of tremendous value as we attempt to understand certain complex behavioural interactions, provided that the behaviour, as it occurs, is recorded precisely and objectively. Fortunately I have seldom found it difficult to record facts in an orderly manner even during times of powerful emotional involvement. And "knowing" intuitively how a chimpanzee is feeling — after an attack, for example — may help one to understand what happens next. We should not be afraid at least to try to make use of our close evolutionary relationship with the chimpanzees in our attempts to interpret complex behaviour.

Questions for Discussion

1. Within the course of this selection, Goodall reflects upon her acceptance by a chimpanzee named Lucy, the similarities of chimps to humans, the conventions of scientific discourse, the nature of emotion, and the importance of empathy. Are these topics related, or does Goodall seem to wander off the point? Does this selection have a thesis?
2. Why does Goodall introduce such concerns as "good manners," "gentleness," and "arrogance" in her opening paragraph?

3. Why have some scientists been reluctant to believe that animals experience different emotions? Why is it convenient for humans to believe that we alone have minds?

4. Goodall reveals in paragraph 6 that she did not have an undergraduate education in science. Was this a liability or an asset in her early work with chimps?

5. Why was Goodall snubbed at the first scientific conference she attended? What does she mean when she writes of "the trappings of a scientist" and "scientific ribbon"?

6. On what evidence does Goodall base her claim that chimpanzees and human beings are closely related? Why does she urge people not to be afraid to explore this relationship? Why would anyone be afraid to do so?

Suggestions for Writing

1. Write an essay exploring what it means to be an animal. Do animals ever have virtues that human beings may lack? What would it be like to be a cat or a dog for a day?

2. To what extent can we gauge how people are feeling from the way they act? Are somersaults necessarily a sign of happiness? Or do people sometimes disguise the way they feel? Write an essay exploring the reasons why someone might want to keep other people from knowing how he or she feels.

LAND OF PLENTY

James Fallows

> *Have you ever been tempted to retrieve something that someone else is throwing away? This is a temptation James Fallows faced when living in Japan and finding all sorts of interesting things neatly piled for trash removal. Fallows, who writes regularly about Asia for the* Atlantic *and the* Wall Street Journal, *explores what Japanese garbage says about Japan. As you read, consider what you can learn about people from what they throw away and what they decide to keep. Ask yourself how Americans and Japanese compare when it's time to put out the trash.*

On *sodai gomi* nights in Japan we learn what kind of people we are. *Sodai gomi,* which rhymes with "oh my homey," means "bulky garbage." It's sometimes used colloquially to describe husbands who have retired from the salaryman life and now spend their time around the house. That *sodai gomi* problem may be a strain on Japanese families, but *sodai gomi* in its literal sense is a more serious trial for my family.

Three nights a week the residents of our neighborhood in Yokohama deposit their household trash at specified areas on the street corners. It's wrapped in neat bundles, it looks like gifts, it disappears at dawn. For two or three nights near the end of each month they bring out the *sodai gomi.* These are articles no longer wanted around the house and too big for normal trash collection. Big garbage can really be big: I've seen sofas, refrigerators, bookcases, chairs, bed frames, vacuum cleaners, an acetylene welding tank, a motorcycle, and numerous television sets.

Sodai gomi exists for two reasons. One is the small size of the typical Japanese house, with its lack of attic, cellar, garage, or spare room. When a new TV comes in, the old one must go out. (This also applies to cars. To buy a new one, you have to prove to the government that you have a place to park it, which for most people means getting rid of the old car. I can't figure out what happens to the old cars: they're certainly not on the roads, and so far I haven't seen one in a *sodai gomi* pile.)

The other reason is the Japanese desire for freshness and purity. No one here really enjoys using something that has passed through other people's hands. My Japanese friends seem to feel about buying a second-hand radio, lamp, or table the way I'd feel about buying someone else's socks. There is a "recycle shop" in our neighborhood that sells used clothes and toys at cut rates. Presumably someone must buy there, since it's still in business, but usually shoppers seem to scoot by in embarrassment, as if it were a Frederick's of Hollywood shop. Whenever I'm listening to the Far East Network, the U.S. military's radio station, and hear an ad for a garage sale, I realize that the American soldiers are unusual not just because they have garages but also because they can sell their old possessions rather than throw them out.

Our first *sodai gomi* night came shortly after we moved into our ₅
current house. It cut into our hearts in a way none of our neighbors could
have known. For one thing, we had no furniture, silverware, or other
household belongings, because everything except the clothes in our suitcases was making a five-week sea journey up from our last house, in
Malaysia. We had also just come from a culture with a wholly different
approach to used goods. Malaysia is a land of tropical abundance, but no
one throws anything away. Just before leaving we had auctioned off every
spare item in the house, from frying pans and mosquito nets to half-used
rolls of Scotch tape. Several customers were enthusiastically bidding for
the shirts my sons had on. It was painful to go from that world to one in
which we didn't have any household goods, couldn't bring ourselves to
buy the overpriced new ones in the store — and then saw heaps of clean,
new-looking merchandise just sitting on the street.

You can see where I am leading. It was not in us to resist. We had
quickly tired of eating, sitting, relaxing, studying, and performing all
other indoor activities on the floor, without tables or chairs, while waiting
for our ship to come in. "Set the floor, please, boys," my wife would call
at dinner time. I lay sprawled on my stomach in front of my computer
keyboard, attempting to type while resting my weight on my elbows,
trying to cheer myself with mental images of Abe Lincoln sprawled before
the fire as a boy. Then one evening, as we trudged home at twilight from
the train station, we saw two replenished-looking *sodai gomi* piles. In one
was a perfectly nice plastic lawn chair, in the other an ordinary low Japanese tea table. You couldn't use both of these at the same time — if you sat
in the lawn chair, you'd be too high to reach down to the table comfortably. But if we had the table we could at least eat without bending over to
reach plates of food on the floor, which made me feel like a husky eating
its chow.

We were in a crowd, of course, when we first saw the *sodai gomi*. We
were too confused and timid to grab anything from the pile just then. But
that night I sat in our kitchen, peering through our window toward the
sodai gomi at the end of the street. The door to a *juku,* or cram school, was
near the piles. The last group of teenage students left there around eleven.
After midnight the trains from Tokyo become much less frequent: I could
depend on intervals of fifteen or twenty minutes between clumps of sala-
rymen teetering drunkenly from the station toward home. The street
looked bare at 12:30, so I made my move. The next morning we placed
our breakfast dishes on our table, and I read the morning paper while
luxuriating in my full-length lawn chair.

It was two more days before the *sodai gomi* collectors came. In those
two nights we laid in as many provisions as we decently could. A shiny
new bell for one son's bicycle, a small but attractive wooden cupboard, a
complete set of wrenches and screwdrivers in a metal toolbox, a Nauga-
hyde-covered barstool, a lacquer serving tray. If I didn't already know

English, I would probably have taken the four large boxes containing four dozen tape cassettes from the Advanced Conversational English series. My son walked in the door one day, said "Guess what?" and presented a black-and-white TV. In self-defense I should point out that everything except a few rusty wrenches looked perfectly clean, whole, and serviceable. In any other culture you'd never believe these things were being thrown out.

That was last summer; we've learned a lot since then. We realize that *sodai gomi* is part of a larger cycle, in which it's important to give as well as receive. So when our household shipment arrived, we gave the lawn chair back to the pile — and later we bought a new color TV and gave back the black-and-white one. We've learned that we're not alone in our secret practice. Last month I met an American writer who lives on the outskirts of Tokyo. I admired the leather notebook he was carrying and asked him where he got it. "You'll never believe this . . . ," he said. We've learned that some Japanese, too, overcome their squeamishness about secondhand material. When I'm up late at night, I sometimes catch a glimpse of the *sodai gomi* area — a more disinterested glimpse, now that our house is furnished — and see a van cruising back and forth, checking it out. In the morning the choicest items are gone.

And I've learned where I'll draw the line. As the only foreigners in   10
our neighborhood, we are laughably conspicuous. People must know that we're skimming the *sodai gomi,* but if we do our best to be discreet about it, operating in the dead of night, everyone can pretend not to notice and we bring no shame upon our kind. Late one night, on the way home from the train station, I saw two handsome wooden bookcases sitting by a lamppost. I thought of the books piled on our floor, I looked around me quickly, and I happily picked up one bookcase with both arms.

It was fifteen minutes before I could get back for the other — only to find that it wasn't there. Twenty yards down the street I saw a hunched, shuffling figure. An old wino in a filthy overcoat, with a crippled left leg, was laboriously dragging the bookcase away toward his lair. Within seconds I was heading home again, looking as if I'd never dream of wrestling a bum for a bookcase. But I know what first flashed through my mind when I saw my treasure disappear: "I can take this guy!"

Questions for Discussion

1. According to Fallows, *sodai gomi* means "bulky garbage," but it is also "part of a larger cycle." What does *sodai gomi* reveal about life in Japan, and what are its unwritten rules?
2. Why are the Japanese reluctant to take or purchase secondhand goods? What would the Japanese probably think of the typical American garage sale?
3. Why does Fallows wait until after midnight before making his first

raid upon the *sodai gomi* pile? How would you describe his relation to neighbors at the time he wrote this essay?

4. Describing his initial response to the *sodai gomi* pile, Fallows writes, "It cut into our hearts in a way none of our neighbors could have known." Would this essay help them to understand? Or is it written only for American readers?

5. What is the purpose of this essay? Is Fallows interested in defining an aspect of life in Japan or an aspect of American character? Why does it conclude with an imaginary conflict between the author and a crippled alcoholic?

Suggestions for Writing

1. Define a foreign or ethnic custom that you have witnessed or experienced, and explore what it reveals about the culture from which it comes.

2. Are new things always better than old things? Write an essay exploring the advantages of auctions, garage sales, or thrift shops.

"MOMMY, WHAT DOES 'NIGGER' MEAN?"

Gloria Naylor

> *Gloria Naylor is a novelist who grew up in New York City. In the following essay Naylor draws upon a painful childhood memory to explore a complex term — whose meaning changes depending upon the rhetorical situation: who is using the word, upon what occasion, for what purpose, and to what audience. As you read, consider what the various uses of nigger reveal about the author's heritage as a black American. And ask yourself what this essay says about the nature of language.*

Language is the subject. It is the written form with which I've managed to keep the wolf away from the door and, in diaries, to keep my sanity. In spite of this, I consider the written word inferior to the spoken, and much of the frustration experienced by novelists is the awareness that whatever we manage to capture in even the most transcendent passages falls far short of the richness of life. Dialogue achieves its power in the dynamics of a fleeting moment of sight, sound, smell and touch.

I'm not going to enter the debate here about whether it is language that shapes reality or vice versa. That battle is doomed to be waged whenever we seek intermittent reprieve from the chicken and egg dispute. I will simply take the position that the spoken word, like the written word, amounts to a nonsensical arrangement of sounds or letters without a consensus that assigns "meaning." And building from the meanings of what we hear, we order reality. Words themselves are innocuous; it is the consensus that gives them true power.

I remember the first time I heard the word "nigger." In my third-grade class, our math tests were being passed down the rows, and as I handed the papers to a little boy in back of me, I remarked that once again he had received a much lower mark than I did. He snatched his test from me and spit out that word. Had he called me a nymphomaniac or a necrophiliac, I couldn't have been more puzzled. I didn't know what a nigger was, but I knew that whatever it meant, it was something he shouldn't have called me. This was verified when I raised my hand, and in a loud voice repeated what he had said and watched the teacher scold him for using a "bad" word. I was later to go home and ask the inevitable question that every black parent must face — "Mommy, what does 'nigger' mean?"

And what exactly did it mean? Thinking back, I realize that this could not have been the first time the word was used in my presence. I was part of a large extended family that had migrated from the rural South after World War II and formed a close-knit network that gravitated around my maternal grandparents. Their ground-floor apartment in one of the buildings they owned in Harlem was a weekend mecca for my immediate family, along with countless aunts, uncles and cousins who brought along assorted friends. It was a bustling and open house with assorted neighbors and tenants popping in and out to exchange bits of gossip, pick up an old quarrel or referee the ongoing checkers game in which my grandmother cheated shamelessly. They were all there to let down their hair and put up their feet after a week of labor in the factories, laundries and shipyards of New York.

Amid the clamor, which could reach deafening proportions — two   5 or three conversations going on simultaneously, punctuated by the sound of a baby's crying somewhere in the back rooms or out on the street — there was still a rigid set of rules about what was said and how. Older children were sent out of the living room when it was time to get into the juicy details about "you-know-who" up on the third floor who had gone and gotten herself "p-r-e-g-n-a-n-t!" But my parents, knowing that I could spell well beyond my years, always demanded that I follow the others out to play. Beyond sexual misconduct and death, everything else was considered harmless for our young ears. And so among the anecdotes of the triumphs and disappointments in the various workings of their lives, the word "nigger" was used in my presence, but it was set within contexts and inflections that caused it to register in my mind as something else.

In the singular, the word was always applied to a man who had distinguished himself in some situation that brought their approval for his strength, intelligence or drive:

"Did Johnny really do that ?"

"I'm telling you, that nigger pulled in $6,000 of overtime last year. Said he got enough for a down payment on a house."

When used with a possessive adjective by a woman — "my nigger" — it became a term of endearment for husband or boyfriend. But it could be more than just a term applied to a man. In their mouths it became the pure essence of manhood — a disembodied force that channeled their past history of struggle and present survival against the odds into a victorious statement of being: "Yeah, that old foreman found out quick enough — you don't mess with a nigger."

In the plural, it became a description of some group within the   10 community that had overstepped the bounds of decency as my family defined it: Parents who neglected their children, a drunken couple who fought in public, people who simply refused to look for work, those with excessively dirty mouths or unkempt households were all "trifling niggers." This particular circle could forgive hard times, unemployment, the occasional bout of depression — they had gone through all of that themselves — but the unforgivable sin was lack of self-respect.

A woman could never be a "nigger" in the singular, with its connotation of confirming worth. The noun "girl" was its closest equivalent in that sense, but only when used in direct address and regardless of the gender doing the addressing. "Girl" was a token of respect for a woman. The one-syllable word was drawn out to sound like three in recognition of the extra ounce of wit, nerve or daring that the woman had shown in the situation under discussion.

"G-i-r-l, stop. You mean you said that to his face?"

But if the word was used in a third-person reference or shortened so that it almost snapped out of the mouth, it always involved some element of communal disapproval. And age became an important factor in these exchanges. It was only between individuals of the same generation, or from an older person to a younger (but never the other way around), that "girl" would be considered a compliment.

I don't agree with the argument that use of the word nigger at this social stratum of the black community was an internalization of racism. The dynamics were the exact opposite: the people in my grandmother's living room took a word that whites used to signify worthlessness or degradation and rendered it impotent. Gathering there together, they transformed "nigger" to signify the varied and complex human beings they knew themselves to be. If the word was to disappear totally from the mouths of even the most liberal of white society, no one in that room was naïve enough to believe it would disappear from white minds. Meeting the word head-on, they proved it had absolutely nothing to do with the way they were determined to live their lives.

So there must have been dozens of times that the word "nigger" was   15
spoken in front of me before I reached the third grade. But I didn't "hear" it until it was said by a small pair of lips that had already learned it could be a way to humiliate me. That was the word I went home and asked my mother about. And since she knew that I had to grow up in America, she took me in her lap and explained.

Questions for Discussion

1. What two motives led Naylor to become a writer?
2. How does Naylor describe her family background? Why is it relevant to the question she is exploring in this essay?
3. How many different meanings of *nigger* does Naylor provide in this essay? Why is it that the word can only be understood by the context in which it is used and the inflection with which it is spoken? What elements of the situation described in paragraph 3 alerted Naylor to the use of a "bad word" before the teacher confirms that she had been insulted?
4. What does Naylor mean when she writes that some people consider the use of *nigger* by blacks to be "an internalization of racism"? Why does she believe that it shows the opposite?

5. Consider the final paragraph of this essay. What does the last sentence imply?

Suggestions for Writing

1. Identify another word that can be either insulting or affectionate depending upon how it is used. Explore what the varied meanings of your term reveal about the people who use it.
2. According to an expression known to many children, "Sticks and stones can break your bones, but words can never hurt you." Is this true? Write an essay exploring the extent to which words can cause injury.

HOW TO BUILD A SLAUGHTERHOUSE

Richard Selzer

> *Richard Selzer teaches surgery at Yale, where he was invited to judge architectural designs for a slaughterhouse — an invitation that led him to visit a slaughterhouse already in operation. Consider what the visit evokes for Selzer and why he chose to write about it. As you read, consider what this essay says about the nature of architecture. But be alert for other concerns. Aside from architecture, what else is Selzer exploring in this essay?*

It is May and, for whatever reason, I have been invited to serve on a jury that is to pass judgment on the final projects of a group of candidates for the degree of Master of Architecture at Yale University. But I am not an architect. I am a surgeon. Nor do I know the least thing about buildings, only that, like humans, they are testy, compliant, congenial, impertinent. That sort of thing. When I am faced with blueprints and drawings-to-scale, which are the lingua franca of architecture, something awful happens to the left half of my brain. It shrinks, or dessicates, collapses, and I fall into a state of torpor no less profound than that of the Andean hummingbird when it is confronted with mortal danger. Sadly, my acceptance of such an invitation by the Yale School of Architecture is just another example of the kind of imposturage of which otherwise honest men and women are capable.

The charge that has been given the students is to design and build an abattoir. It is understood that prior to this undertaking they have, as a class, made a field trip to a slaughterhouse in the New Haven area. For months afterward they have been working toward this date. It is two days before we are all to meet for the examination in the seventh floor "pit" at the School of Architecture. But if I cannot know what they know of buildings, at least I can have seen what they have seen, and so I telephone the owner of the slaughterhouse on the outskirts of New Haven, the one that the students visited months before. "Yes," he says, "by all means." His voice is genial, welcoming.

It will be no great shock, I think. A surgeon has grown accustomed to primordial dramas, organic events involving flesh, blood, and violence. But before it is done this field trip to a slaughterhouse will have become for me a descent into Hades, a vision of life that perhaps it would have been better never to know.

In a way, it is the last place on earth that seems appropriate to the mass slaying of creatures. Just another grinding truck stop off Route 1 in North Haven, Connecticut, with easy access for large vehicles and, nearby, an old cemetery tossing in the slow upheaval of resurrection. It is 7:00 A.M. Outside, another truck rumbles into the corral.

THERMOKING is the word painted on both sides of the huge open-   5
sided car filled with cattle. Each cow has a numbered tag punched through
an ear. Outside, the enclosure is already ridiculous with lambs. What a
sinister probability this truck gives out. Inside it, the cows are, for the
most part, silent until one lifts its head and moos wildly. Now another
joins in, and another, until the whole compound resounds with the terrible
vocabulary of premonition.

The building itself is low and squat — a single story only, made of
cement blocks and corrugated metal and prestressed concrete. Behind it is
a huge corral. Such a building does not command but neither does it skulk.
It carries out its business in secret and decides what you will see, hides
from you what it chooses. If only I can come upon it — the undiscovered
heart of this place that I know, must believe, is here. Does this building
breathe? Has it a pulse? It must.

Now the gate at the rear of the truck is opened. The cattle mill about
like bewildered children until, prodded from behind, they move sightless
and will-less down the ramp and into a gated pen as if in sleep through an
incurable dream. Here they come, slowly, their hooves weighted down
with reluctance. The wooden floor of the entryway is scarred, packed and
beaten. The hooves, staggering, thump the timbers. There is a quick
lateral skid on manure. It is the sound of those skidding hooves that,
months later, you will hear while waiting in line at the bank or getting a
haircut.

The cowherd urges them on. They seem afraid of displeasing him.
With gentle callings and whistles he inveigles them into the pen. I keep
my gaze on a pair of mourning doves waddling among the droppings
until, threatened by a hoof, one takes to the air with a muted small whis-
tling of its wings. The other follows in a moment. Against a nearby fence
a row of fiery tulips spurts. Into the narrow passageway the cattle go single
file, crowding at the mouth of it, bumping into each other, clopping
sidewise so as not to lose their place. It's as if, once having passed through
that gate, they would be safe. As if what lay ahead were not extinction but
respite, and there were not, just ahead, death bobbing like clover in a
pasture, but life. Only the first two or three begin to suspect. One after
the other these lift their heads at the sound of the stunning gun. But there
is the sweet assuaging voice of the cowherd and the laughter of the men
inside to draw them on.

The one at the van shies as she encounters some hard evidence. She
balks, stops, the others press against her until, with a toss of her horns,
she throws her new knowledge down before the herd, like an impediment.
Without warning (do I imagine it?) the leaves on the trees at the periphery of the corral begin to siffle, the grass to stir. Tails rise as if in a wind.
Ears and flanks shiver in a cold blast. As abruptly, all is still. But I see it
has not been the wind, only death that has swept across the corral and
whooshed away.

Inside, the men are waiting. All are dressed in identical uniforms — overalls, ankle-length rubber aprons, high rubber boots and orange plastic hard hats. The hooks, tracks, scales, tables and trays have an air of brutal metallic strength; there are no windows nor anything made of wood. The room echoes like a gymnasium. From somewhere too far off to be heard clearly, a silken radio voice announces the morning news. Something about a famine in Ethiopia . . . There is the smell of cowhide and tobacco. One of the men clicks over the multitude in the pen. " . . . six, eight, ten, fourteen . . ." he counts. "Plus one hundred sixty. Jesus! a day's work."

The Process begins. There is a muffled whump from the stunning pen, like the firing of a mortar shell. A body arches, the tail blown forward between quivering legs. She goes down, folding on all fours at once, something from which the air has been let out. They drag her a foot or two to the hoist. A chain is placed about one hind leg and the winch activated. A moment later she is aloft above the Killing Oval — a kind of theater with a centrally slanting stone floor and a drain at the lowest point. As she hangs upside down, her coat seems a bit loose, shabby, with all the points and angles of her skeleton showing. The throat slitter is ready. It is clear that he is the star. Enisled in his oval space, alone there with his cattle who, one at a time, stretch out their necks to him, he shines beneath his hard hat. He is blond; his eyes blue knife blades; hefty; a side of beef himself, though not at all fat. No part of him shakes with the thrust. Still, if physiognomy is any hint of character, he has found his rightful place. The eyes boil from her head; saliva drips from her limp tongue. Up on his toes for the sticking, and oh those chicory-blue eyes. For just so long as the blade needs to burrow into the neck — one second, two — the pudgy hand of the man grasps the ear of the cow, then lets go. He is quick with the knife, like a robin beaking a worm from the ground. The slit is made just beneath the mandible, the knife moved forward and back and with-drawn. In this manner the jugular vein and carotid artery are severed. The larynx, too, is cut through. He has a kind of genius. His movements are streamlined, with no doubt about them. How different from my own surgery where no single move but is plucked at by hesitation.

In the abattoir there is gradation of rank, at the bottom of which hierarchy is the hoser, often the newest member of the group. Only after a long education to the hose will he be formally instructed in the art of stunning and hoisting. Then on to bunging, decapitation, amputation of the hooves, gutting, skinning, and, if his dream is to be realized, killing, which is at the pinnacle. In this, it is not unlike the surgical residency training program at Yale. Never mind.

The stunner turns their brains off like spigots; the slitter turns on the faucet of their blood which squirts in a forceful splash toward the stone floor. For a moment the cows are still, megaliths, then a mooing, flailing, kicking as the effect of the stunning wears off. Now and then the slitter must step out of the way of a frantic hoof. It takes so long until all movement stops! As the bleeding slackens the hose is used and the business dilutes into wateriness. The hose flogs across unblinking eyes; it is a storm of weeping. I am tempted to reach out, I am that close, and lift a velvet lip, finger a horn, but I do not. There is rebuke implicit in such acts.

"Two hundred and fifty gallons of water per second," the hoser tells me. It does not occur to me to doubt him. I peer through the scrim of blood and water to the stunning pen where the next cow has just been felled. It is in the stunning pen that the animals seem most exposed, with no tiny shield of leaves, no small tangle of brambles, such as any captured thing is entitled to hide behind. And all the while the flat mooing of the already-slit, a hollow blare pulled up and out from their cavernous insides that stops abruptly and has no echo. And the howl of the stunned. Now there is a throatful of hot vowel if ever you heard it.

Each cow is impaled at the groin on a ceiling hook and detached   15 from the hoist to make room for the next. These ceiling hooks are on tracks and can be pushed along from station to station. A second hook is used in the other groin. A light touch sends the splayed animal sliding on the rack like a coat in a factory. Already there is a second cow bleeding from the hoist, and the third has been stunned. The efficiency of the men is a glittering, wicked thing. They are synchronous as dancers and for the most part as silent. It is their knives that converse, gossip, press each other along. The smallest faltering of one would be felt at once by each of the others. There would be that slackening which the rest would have to take up. But now and then they laugh, always at each other, something one of them has said. One of them is always the butt. It does you good to hear this chaffing. I see that without laughter the thing could not be done. They are full of merriment, like boys. Or like gods, creating pain and mirth at the same time. A dozen times a day, the hoser, who is younger than the rest and a little simple, I am told, turns his hose on one of the other men who roars with outrage. Everyone else dies of laughter, then rises again, redder in the face. What are their minds like? Bright and light and shadowless, I think. Disinfected.

There is a sequence to it: stun, hoist, slit, hose, bung, behead, amputate and gut. Each step in the process is carried out by one man at his station. The cattle are slid from one to the other on the racks. What a heat! What an uproar! Already the sink and scales, all the ghastly furniture of this place retreats into far corners and I see nothing but the cattle. At one end of the room the heads are lined up on a folding rack, such as might otherwise be used to dry clothes. Tranquillity has been molded into their mouths. The once swiveling lips are still; the brown eyes opaque. Here they are axed open and the brains examined by the inspector.

"What are you looking for?" I ask him. With scissors and forceps he cuts into the base of one brain.

"Pus, spots, lumps," he says. I peer over his shoulder and see instead at the back of the cow's eyes all the black and white of her tribe puddled there. At the base of her brain a sloping pasture, green with, here and there, a savory buttercup to which all of her life she had lowered her muzzle. And in her throat, pockets of retained lowing which I think to hear escaping even as he prods the tissue with his forceps.

The beheader is not yet twenty. When he turns to see who is spying there, his smile is hesitant and shy. Around his waist a chain belt holds a bone-handled sharpener and a spare knife. He flashes his wrist and there is the quick hiss of the blade against the rasp. Later he will show me his knife, let me heft it, turn, flip, feint.

"Nice?" he asks me.

"Nice," I say. "Nice." Abruptly, he kneels to his work. He might be   20
giving first aid to the victim of an accident. Not Judith at the nape of Holofernes nor Salome working her way through the gorge of John the Baptist was more avid than this youth who crouches over his meat like a lion, his blade drinking up blood.

The first slitter has been replaced by another. This one is Italian. His hair is thick and black with just a spot of russet like the flash of a fox's tail. His shoulder is jaunty, his cheek shadowed by eyelashes as he sinks the knife. It is less a stab than a gesture, delicate and powerful, the thrust of a toreador. Against the tang of his knife, the loaded artery pops, and the whole of the cow's blood chases the blade from the premises. I see the slow wavelike pulse of the slitter's jugular vein. Once he laughs out loud. The sound is sudden and unexpected. I turn to watch the mirth emerging from so much beauty of lips and teeth and throat. At eye level a posthumous hoof flexes, extends, flexes again.

All at once, a calf, thinking, I suppose, to escape, wallops through the half-open gate of the stunning pen and directly into the Killing Oval. She is struck on the flank by a bloodfall from the hoist. Her eyes are shining pits of fear. The men view this with utmost seriousness. Immediately two of them leave their tasks and go to capture the miscreant, one by the tail, the other by an always handy ear, and they wrestle the calf back into the pen to wait her turn. Now here is no Cretan bull dance with naked youths propelled by the power of horns, but an awkward graceless show, as the calf robs them of their dignity. They slide on the floor, lose their balance. At last calm is restored. Half an hour later, writhen and giving up the ghost, the calf has her turn. So, there is a predetermined schedule, an immutable order. Why?

". . . nine, ten, eleven, twelve. One dozen." Someone is counting a cluster of impaled and hanging calves. They are like black-and-white curtains ungirt, serious. The men part them with the backs of their hands in order to pass through. They are not just dead; they are more than dead, as though never alive. Beyond, trays of steaming guts; another rack of heads, all clot and teeth. Each head is tagged with the number of its carcass, just so each plastic bag of viscera. Should a beast be found diseased in any part, the inspector discards the whole of it. The men do not wear gloves but plunge boldly into the swim. Are they in a kind of stupor of blood? Oddly spellbound by the repetition of their acts? Perhaps it is the efficiency of the Process which blinds them. I think of the wardens of Auschwitz. At the final station, barrels of pelts. For leather, for rugs.

"A guy in New Jersey buys them," the skinner tells me.   25

I see that one of the slit and hoisted continues to writhe, and all at once she gives a moo less through her clotted muzzle than from the gash in her neck. It is a soft call straight to my heart. And followed by little thirsty whispers.

"It's still mooing," I say.

"Oh, that," says the slitter.

"How can that be?" I ask. "The larynx has been severed. Hear that?" He cocks his head. There is a soft sucking sigh from the veal cluster farther on, as though someone were turning over in his sleep.

"They do that sometimes," he explains, "even that long after they've   30 been cut." There is an absolute absence of any madness in him which might explain, mollify, soften. He is entirely cool, reserved, intent.

But today they have not been able to kill them all. Some will have to wait overnight in the corral. Thirty minutes after the command has been given to stop, everything in the slaughterhouse is neat and tidy, as much as rinsing and scrubbing can make it so. The tools have been scraped clean; the planks scoured and freshly swept. When it is all done, the beheader snatches a hose from the youngest, the one who is simple, and sprays him in the crotch. Another joins in the play. How young even the older ones look now. They are eager to go home, where I should think them the gentlest of men. This slaughterhouse is a place one leaves wanting only to make love. In the courtyard my nose is feathered by the smell of fresh air. Overhead a gull blows by, beaking at the sky. From my car I see a cow swing her muzzle at a fly, lash with her tail and fall still. On the roof, along the eaves, doves mourn.

In the morning I arrive just before the men. I wait for them to come. Soon they do. One of them has brought a little dog, a terrier, who scampers along, bouncing sideways and snapping high-pitched chunks out of the silent air. The sight of the dog tickles the men, each of whom stops to pet or scratch. "You, Fritzie," they say, and growl, "little pecker." Now the building awakens, accepting clatter and water gushing into its basins. It begins again.

For two days my new colleagues and I watch and listen as the twelve students present their models, their blueprints. Never, never have there been abattoirs more clever, more ingenious than the abattoirs of Yale. For ease of access the "Plants" are unequaled. Railroad sidings, refrigerated trucks contiguous at one end, attached meat markets. It is all there. And inside, disposable plastic troughs for collecting the blood, fluorescent lighting, air purification, marvelously efficient stunning rooms. "Here," they say, pointing, "is where they are stunned." And, "I have placed the killing alcove here." The faces of the students do not change; they do not tremble at the reenactment of Purgatory. Rather, a cool, calm correctness is what they own. Like the slaughterers, the students have grown used to the awful facts; what concerns them is the efficiency of the process. When they speak of the butchers, they commend their technique. And so do I. So do I. And if ever I should wish to own an abattoir, I would be wise to choose any one of these student architects to make it for me. But there is another abattoir that concerns me now. It is the real abattoir that lies just beneath the abattoir these architects and I have seen.

•   •   •

In the design and building of an abattoir one must remember that once it was that the animals were the gods. Slaughtering was then no mere step in the business of meat preparation but an act charged with religious import and carried out in a temple. The altar was sprinkled with blood. The flame of animal life partook of the sacred and could be extinguished only by the sanction of religion. But, you say, what can architecture do in the face of slaughter? Beauty and spirit stop at the first splash of blood. Better to settle for efficiency. But efficiency gives way before the power of the mythic imagination. And so we shall try:

First, the location. No grinding truck stop on the highway, but a   *35* cool glade at the foot of a ridge with, beyond, another ridge and another. Some place beautifully remote, I think, on a small elevation from which the sky and the sun might be consulted. Yet not so high as to be seen silhouetted against heaven from the sea. That is for temples and light-houses. Nor ought it to be easily seen from any road but must be out of sight, like certain sanatoria, oracular pools, surgical operating rooms. A place without vista, turned in upon itself. And hidden by trees. The gods always play where there are trees that invite mist to their branches. I should build it in a grove, then, to benefit from the resident auspicious deities. And yes, trees, not so much to lend mystery and darkness as for compan-ionship, to bear witness. Let a vivid spring leap nearby with water that is cold and delicious. To listen to its quick current is tantamount to bathing in its waters. Just so simply are ablutions performed. Hand-scooped from the stream, such water will, if drunk at certain susceptible times of the day—twilight and dawn—summon visitations, induce dreams. Pulled up into the throats of the doomed beasts, it will offer them peace, make them ready.

At this place let there be equal parts of sun and shade and at night the cold exaltation, the lambent flood of moonlight. And no nearby houses, for the shadow of this place must not fall across the dwellings of human beings. Killing of any kind has its contagious aspects. Place it thus and the abattoir becomes a god—distant, dignified, lofty, silent. Gaunt and stark until the beasts are ushered in. Only then does its blood begin to flow. Only then is the building warmed and colored, completed. Made human. Such a building is a presence. I would want anyone looking at my abattoir for the first time to fall under its spell, to believe it particularly his as well—there would be that certain tilt of a roof, the phantom shadow of leaves cruising over tile. One glance at such a site and you will say as Oedipus said at Colonus: "As for this place, it is clearly a holy one."

David, it is reported in the Bible, purchased a threshing floor from Araunah the Jebusite upon which to build the altar of his temple.° Alas, the Jebusites are no more, and neither are their threshing floors to be found in the land. Even so, I would use stone for the floor, roughhewn granite quarried nearby, granite that will wash black in the rain, turn gold in the setting sun. Granite with beveled edges cut to fit neatly, the gaps between to be filled with mortar. Brick too is permissible since the elements of earth and fire are combined to form it. Brick is earth which has gone through fire. It is sacrificial. None of this will be understood by those who see but a stone in a stone, a brick in a brick. It is in the precise placement and the relationship of these materials that their sacramental quality lies. The roofs of the inner passageway will be of slate raftered with the bisected trunks of oak trees upon which strips of bark have been left. These trees should be felled in October, for in the spring all of the power of the tree is devoted to the making of leaves. In the fall the wood is more compressed and solidified. Oak is preferred above all others, as much for its strength and resistance to water as for the news whispered by its leaves that nothing is annihilated; there is only change and the return of matter to a former state. Stone, brick and wood, then. The earth has been burnt; the stone has been cut from its place; the tree has been felled; and all three rise in the form of the abattoir. Yet their texture must survive. The memory of the original tree, clay, earth, stone, is made permanent by the form in which each is made. The builder with his hand and his eyes must do justice to the talent and potential of the material. Nor are these materials passive but offer their own obstacles and tendencies.

Centrally, there is to be a vast open atrium flanked by columns whose capitals are carved as the horned heads of beasts. Everything must reflect the cattle. They are the beating heart of the place. So let there be columns and an unroofed atrium. As nobody can live without the ample to-and-fro of air, so will the building be dead that does not permit the internal play of abundant air. Between the columns of the atrium place lustral stone basins in which water from the stream may be collected for the washing of hands. Columns too, for avenues of light that in the company of the breeze and the high fountain will rinse the air of reek.

The building faces east to receive the morning sun in which it is best for the men to work. There are to be no steps in any part of the abattoir, only timbered ramps curved like those of a ziggurat along which the animals are led up to the porch or vestibule. This antechamber measures in cubits twenty by twenty. (The cubit being the length of the forearm from elbow to fingertips.) It is the function of this room to separate the profane world from the sacred area which is the atrium. In order to enter the atrium the cattle must pass in single file beneath an arch. It is well

David, . . . , temple: See the second book of Samuel 24:18–25.

known that to pass through an archway is to be changed forever in some way. Who is to say that such a passage does not purify these beasts, make them ready to die? The atrium itself is vast, measuring in cubits sixty long, forty wide, and thirty high. As I have said, it is roofless in order to receive the direct rays of the sun. Nor has it any walls on either side but open colonnades. To the rear of the atrium is a third and smaller room where the men take their rest. Inside, the corridors, vestibule and resting room must be brilliant with light from wall lamps and skylights. Shadows are dangerous in an abattoir. They make you think. There is to be no rebirth here, as we know it. It is a place for endings, where residue is hosed away and no decay permitted.

Let us dwell upon the interior of the building. If a stable has the odor 40 of manure, why, that is fitting to the stable. The smell increases the stableness of the building, confirms it in its role as the dwelling place for beasts. Just so is the odor of fresh-spilled blood apt for an abattoir. You would not expect perfume. Still, I would be grateful for the sacred smell of sawdust or straw — for the sake of the cattle, to conceal it from them. Blood has no smell, you say? And it is true that there is no odor of it in the operating room. But I think that to catch the whiff of blood is a talent beyond human olfaction. Tigers smell blood and hunt it down precisely. And sharks who, having shed a single drop of their own blood, will devour themselves. Are you certain that domestication blunts the noses of these animals? No, compassion dictates that we separate the about-to-be-slain from those crossing over. Listen! The stones ring with hooves. And in a corner of the atrium, the sawdust is roiled where one of them has floundered, the cloven hoofprints brimming with red shavings. And no reek in the air.

When, as happens, they cannot all be slain in one day, the cattle are led at dusk from the clearing in front of the abattoir down to a narrow tortuous path lined by thick shrubbery. It is the same path by which they left the world at dawn. Here and there the path forks, suggesting a labyrinth. Such a serpiginous route emphasizes the immense apartness of the abattoir. They are ushered into a pasture at some remove where they spend the night in a world cast in frost and moonlight. Stay with them through these hallucinated hours white as foam and filled with heightened meaning. Be there just before dawn, waiting. Long before you see them you will hear the sound of their lips pulling at the grass of the pasture. Ah, there! Look! The first one — all white, breasting the mist, then coming clear of it, like a nymph stepping out of the woods.

Now they are led back to the slaughterhouse. I hear the soothing murmur of the herder making his sweet deceit. "Come along now, ladies. Be polite. No need to crowd. It's all the same in the end." A moo interrupts.

"Hush, now." Again the labyrinthine path must be navigated. In the early morning the climate of the place is that of a cellar — cool and cavernous. There are the pillars caught in the very act of rising. There is the sibilance of insects and a throbbing of frogs. The mist rises and soon there are drifting veils of water and sunlight, something piney in the air. Pious the feet that pace the stone floor of the atrium. The heads of the men are covered with small capulets. Prayers are recited. One of them holds the knife up to the sunlight, then turns to examine its larger shadow upon the floor. Any nick or imperfection that might cause suffering to the animal is thereby magnified and corrected before the beast is led to it. At the last moment the blade is smeared with honey for sweetness and lubrication. All the energy of the place emanates from the edge of that knife blade. It is a holy object, a radiant thing. In the dazzling sunlight it is like a silver thorn to be laid upon the willing neck of the beast.

But a cow is not much, you argue. A cow is not beautiful as a trout, say, is beautiful. A trout—made of river water, and speckled stone, and tinted by the setting sun. Nor are cows rare, as peacocks are rare, or certain blue butterflies. These cattle bring with them no paraphernalia of the past. They have none. I tell myself that. For a cow, the sun that rises each day is a brand-new sun, not the one that set the day before and rose the day before that. Humans are the only ones afflicted with a past. But then I think of the many-cattled pastures of my childhood in the milk-drenched upper counties of New York State. I close my eyes and see again a herd upon a green slope. There! One lifts her dripping muzzle to stare at a trusted human being. Nonsense, you say, to deplore this slaughter when with each footstep we erase whole histories. Besides, they do it humanely. What! Would you rescue them? Burst upon the scene with a machine gun and order the animals to be loaded on the truck and driven away? To the country, to the middle of the meadow, and set them free?

I know, I know. But to one who watches from the periphery, there seems no place for this event in human experience. 45

Hypocrite, you say, why don't you give up meat instead of professing all this outrage?

Give up meat! Oh, no, I couldn't do that, I have eaten meat all of my life. Besides, vegetarianism seems to me a kind of national atonement, an act of asceticism like the fasting that is done during Lent or on Yom Kippur.

So. We are all meat eaters here. The desire for meat is too deeply seated in us. As deeply seated as the desire for romance. The difference between those butchers and you is that they do not come to the abattoir each day with their hearts gone fluid with emotion. They have no patience with the duplicity of sentiment.

It is the next day, and already the event is too far away for grief or pity. How quickly the horror recedes. I pass the butcher shop whose window is neatly arranged with parts of meat labeled shank, loin, T-bone. For a long time I stand gazing at the display. For one fleeting instant it occurs to me that this window full of meat is less than dead, that, at a given signal, the cut-up flesh could cast off its labels and cellophane

wrappers and reassemble, seek out its head and hooves, fill with blood
and *be* again. But the thought passes quickly as it came.

"Is the veal fresh?" I ask the butcher. 50

Slaughtered yesterday," the man says. "Can't be much fresher than
that."

"Let me have a pound and a half of the scallopini," I tell him. "Nice
and thin, and give it a good pounding."

Questions for Discussion

1. In his third paragraph Selzer writes that his visit to the slaughterhouse
   was "a descent into Hades, a vision of life that perhaps it would have
   been better never to know." Yet in paragraph 31 he writes, "This
   slaughterhouse is a place one leaves wanting only to make love." Is this
   a contradiction? Does Selzer know how he feels about the slaughterhouse he visited?
2. Once Selzer has visited the slaughterhouse, what motivates him to
   return the following day?
3. This essay includes many details that do not relate directly to the design
   of a slaughterhouse. What is the significance of the mourning doves
   and tulips in paragraph 8, the radio announcement in paragraph 10, and
   the dog in paragraph 32?
4. What does Selzer mean when, writing about the slitter, he comments,
   "if physiognomy is any hint of character, he has found his rightful
   place"? Where else does Selzer describe the slitter? How would you
   describe his attitude toward them?
5. In paragraph 15 Selzer writes, "The efficiency of the men is a glittering,
   wicked thing." Why "glittering" and why "wicked"? How does Selzer
   want the work of a slaughterhouse to proceed?
6. How are the architecture students at Yale like the men who work in the
   slaughterhouse? What does Selzer imply about the surgical residency
   program at Yale?
7. What would be the effect of deleting from this essay the description
   Selzer provides in paragraphs 34–43 of his ideal slaughterhouse? Would
   anything be lost?
8. Consider the last four paragraphs of this essay. Why does Selzer buy
   veal slaughtered on the same day he had visited the slaughterhouse?
   Why does he instruct the butcher to "give it a good pounding"?

Suggestions for Writing

1. According to Richard Selzer, "We are all meat eaters here." Literally,
   this sentence makes no sense, since some people are vegetarians. In
   what sense, then, are we all meat eaters? Write an essay exploring what
   it means to be an eater of meat.
2. Write an imaginative description of an ideal hospital, dormitory, or
   shopping mall.

THE ART OF TEACHING SCIENCE

Lewis Thomas

A physician and medical educator, Lewis Thomas writes about science from a point of view that nonscientists often find refreshing. In the following essay, which was first published in the New York Times, *Thomas explores why science is too important to be left to scientists. As you read, consider how Thomas tries to make science attractive to people who prefer the humanities. Think of the science classes that you have taken, and ask yourself whether you would have found more pleasure in the sort of teaching that Thomas envisions.*

Everyone seems to agree that there is something wrong with the way science is being taught these days. But no one is at all clear about when it went wrong or what is to be done about it. The term "scientific illiteracy" has become almost a cliché in educational circles. Graduate schools blame the colleges; colleges blame the secondary schools; the high schools blame the elementary schools, which, in turn, blame the family.

I suggest that the scientific community itself is partly, perhaps largely, to blame. Moreover, if there are disagreements between the world of the humanities and the scientific enterprise as to the place and importance of science in a liberal-arts education and the role of science in 20th-century culture, I believe that the scientists are themselves responsible for a general misunderstanding of what they are really up to.

During the last half-century, we have been teaching the sciences as though they were the same collection of academic subjects as always, and — here is what has really gone wrong — as though they would always be the same. Students learn today's biology, for example, the same way we learned Latin when I was in high school long ago: first, the fundamentals; then, the underlying laws; next, the essential grammar and, finally, the reading of texts. Once mastered, that was that: Latin was Latin and forever after would always be Latin. History, once learned, was history. And biology was precisely biology, a vast array of hard facts to be learned as fundamentals, followed by a reading of the texts.

Furthermore, we have been teaching science as if its facts were somehow superior to the facts in all other scholarly disciplines — more fundamental, more solid, less subject to subjectivism, immutable. English literature is not just one way of thinking; it is all sorts of ways; poetry is a moving target; the facts that underlie art, architecture and music are not really hard facts, and you can change them any way you like by arguing about them. But science, it appears, is an altogether different kind of learning: an unambiguous, unalterable and endlessly useful display of data that only needs to be packaged and installed somewhere in one's temporal lobe in order to achieve a full understanding of the natural world.

And, of course, it is not like this at all. In real life, every field 5 of science is incomplete, and most of them — whatever the record of accomplishment during the last 200 years — are still in their very earliest stages. In the fields I know best, among the life sciences, it is required that the most expert and sophisticated minds be capable of changing course — often with a great lurch — every few years. In some branches of biology the mind-changing is occurring with accelerating velocity. Next week's issue of any scientific journal can turn a whole field upside down, shaking out any number of immutable ideas and installing new bodies of dogma. This is an almost everyday event in physics, in chemistry, in materials research, in neurobiology, in genetics, in immunology.

On any Tuesday morning, if asked, a good working scientist will tell you with some self-satisfaction that the affairs of his field are nicely in order, that things are finally looking clear and making sense, and all is well. But come back again on another Tuesday, and the roof may have just fallen in on his life's work. All the old ideas — last weeks' ideas in some cases — are no longer good ideas. The hard facts have softened, melted away and vanished under the pressure of new hard facts. Something strange has happened. And it is this very strangeness of nature that makes science engrossing, that keeps bright people at it, and that ought to be at the center of science teaching.

The conclusions reached in science are always, when looked at closely, far more provisional and tentative than are most of the assumptions arrived at by our colleagues in the humanities. But we do not talk much in public about this, nor do we teach this side of science. We tend to say instead: These are the facts of the matter, and this is what the facts signify. Go and learn them, for they will be the same forever.

By doing this, we miss opportunity after opportunity to recruit young people into science, and we turn off a good many others who would never dream of scientific careers but who emerge from their education with the impression that science is fundamentally boring.

Sooner or later, we will have to change this way of presenting science. We might begin by looking more closely at the common ground that science shares with all disciplines, particularly with the humanities and with social and behavioral science. For there is indeed such a common ground. It is called bewilderment. There are more than seven times seven types of ambiguity in science, all awaiting analysis. The poetry of Wallace Stevens is crystal clear alongside the genetic code.

One of the complaints about science is that it tends to flatten every-   10
thing. In its deeply reductionist way, it is said, science removes one mystery after another, leaving nothing in the place of mystery but data. I have even heard this claim as explanation for the drift of things in modern art and modern music: Nothing is left to contemplate except randomness and senselessness; God is nothing but a pair of dice, loaded at that. Science is linked somehow to the despair of the 20th-century mind. There is almost nothing unknown and surely nothing unknowable. Blame science.

I prefer to turn things around in order to make precisely the opposite case. Science, especially 20th-century science, has provided us with a glimpse of something we never really knew before; the revelation of human ignorance. We have been accustomed to the belief, from one century to another, that except for one or two mysteries we more or less comprehend everything on earth. Every age, not just the 18th century, regarded itself as the Age of Reason, and we have never lacked for explanations of the world and its ways. Now, we are being brought up short. We do not understand much of anything, from the episode we rather dismissively (and, I think, defensively) choose to call the "big bang," all the way down to the particles in the atoms of a bacterial cell. We have a wilderness of mystery to make our way through in the centuries ahead. We will need science for this but not science alone. In its own time, science will produce the data and some of the meaning in the data, but never the full meaning. For perceiving real significance when significance is at hand, we will need all sorts of brains outside the fields of science.

It is primarily because of this need that I would press for changes in the way science is taught. Although there is a perennial need to teach the young people who will be doing the science themselves, this will always be a small minority. Even more important, we must teach science to those who will be needed for thinking about it, and that means pretty nearly everyone else — most of all, the poets, but also artists, musicians, philosophers, historians and writers. A few of these people, at least, will be able to imagine new levels of meaning which may be lost on the rest of us.

In addition, it is time to develop a new group of professional thinkers, perhaps a somewhat larger group than the working scientists and the working poets, who can create a discipline of scientific criticism. We have had good luck so far in the emergence of a few people ranking as philosophers of science and historians and journalists of science, and I hope more of these will be coming along. But we have not yet seen specialists in the fields of scientific criticism who are of the caliber of the English literary and social critics F. R. Leavis and John Ruskin or the American literary critic Edmund Wilson. Science needs critics of this sort, but the public at large needs them more urgently.

I suggest that the introductory courses in science, at all levels from grade school through college, be radically revised. Leave the fundamentals, the so-called basics, aside for a while, and concentrate the attention of all students on the things that are not known. You cannot possibly teach quantum mechanics without mathematics, to be sure, but you can describe the strangeness of the world opened up by quantum theory. Let it be known, early on, that there are deep mysteries and profound paradoxes revealed in distant outline by modern physics. Explain that these can be approached more closely and puzzled over, once the language of mathematics has been sufficiently mastered.

At the outset, before any of the fundamentals, teach the still imponderable puzzles of cosmology. Describe as clearly as possible, for the youngest minds, that there are some things going on in the universe that lie still beyond comprehension, and make it plain how little is known. *15*

Do not teach that biology is a useful and perhaps profitable science; that can come later. Teach instead that there are structures squirming inside each of our cells that provide all the energy for living. Essentially foreign creatures, these lineal descendants of bacteria were brought in for symbiotic living a billion or so years ago. Teach that we do not have the ghost of an idea how they got there, where they came from, or how they evolved to their present structure and function. The details of oxidative phosphorylation and photosynthesis can come later.

Teach ecology early on. Let it be understood that the earth's life is a system of interdependent creatures, and that we do not understand at all how it works. The earth's environment, from the range of atmospheric gases to the chemical constituents of the sea, has been held in an almost unbelievably improbable state of regulated balance since life began, and the regulation of stability and balance is somehow accomplished by the life itself, like the autonomic nervous system of an immense organism. We do not know how such a system works, much less what it means, but there are some nice reductionist details at hand, such as the bizarre proportions of atmospheric constituents, ideal for our sort of planetary life, and the surprising stability of the ocean's salinity, and the fact that the average temperature of the earth has remained quite steady in the face of at least a 25 percent increase in heat coming in from the sun since the earth began. That kind of thing: something to think about.

Go easy, I suggest, on the promises sometimes freely offered by science. Technology relies and depends on science these days, more than ever before, but technology is far from the first justification for doing research, nor is it necessarily an essential product to be expected from science. Public decisions about the future of technology are totally different from decisions about science, and the two enterprises should not be tangled together. The central task of science is to arrive, stage by stage, at a clearer comprehension of nature, but this does not at all mean, as it is sometimes claimed to mean, a search for mastery over nature.

Science may someday provide us with a better understanding of ourselves, but never, I hope, with a set of technologies for doing something or other to improve ourselves. I am made nervous by assertions that human consciousness will someday be unraveled by research, laid out for close scrutiny like the workings of a computer, and then — and *then . . . !* I hope with some fervor that we can learn a lot more than we now know about the human mind, and I see no reason why this strange puzzle should remain forever and entirely beyond us. But I would be deeply disturbed by any prospect that we might use the new knowledge in order to begin doing something about it — to improve it, say. This is a different matter from searching for information to use against schizophrenia or dementia, where we are badly in need of technologies, indeed likely one day to be sunk without them. But the ordinary, everyday, more or less normal human mind is too marvelous an instrument ever to be tampered with by anyone, science or no science.

The education of humanists cannot be regarded as complete, or even *20* adequate, without exposure in some depth to where things stand in the various branches of science, particularly, as I have said, in the areas of our ignorance. Physics professors, most of them, look with revulsion on assignments to teach their subject to poets. Biologists, caught up by the enchantment of their new power, armed with flawless instruments to tell the nucleotide sequences of the entire human genome, nearly matching the physicists in the precision of their measurements of living processes, will resist the prospect of broad survey courses; each biology professor will demand that any student in his path master every fine detail within that professor's research program.

The liberal-arts faculties, for their part, will continue to view the scientists with suspicion and apprehension. "What do the scientists want?" asked a Cambridge professor in Francis Cornford's wonderful "Microcosmographia Academica." "Everything that's going," was the quick answer. That was back in 1912, and scientists haven't much changed.

But maybe, just maybe, a new set of courses dealing systematically with ignorance in science will take hold. The scientists might discover in it a new and subversive technique for catching the attention of students driven by curiosity, delighted and surprised to learn that science is exactly as the American scientist and educator Vannevar Bush described it: an "endless frontier." The humanists, for their part, might take considerable satisfaction in watching their scientific colleagues confess openly to not knowing everything about everything. And the poets, on whose shoulders the future rests, might, late nights, thinking things over, begin to see some meanings that elude the rest of us. It is worth a try.

I believe that the worst thing that has happened to science education is that the fun has gone out of it. A great many good students look at it as slogging work to be got through on the way to medical school. Others are turned off by the premedical students themselves, embattled and bleeding for grades and class standing. Very few recognize science as the high adventure it really is, the wildest of all explorations ever taken by human beings, the chance to glimpse things never seen before, the shrewdest maneuver for discovering how the world works. Instead, baffled early on, they are misled into thinking that bafflement is simply the result of not having learned all the facts. They should be told that everyone else is baffled as well—from the professor in his endowed chair down to the platoons of postdoctoral students in the laboratories all night. Every important scientific advance that has come in looking like an answer has turned, sooner or later—usually sooner—into a question. And the game is just beginning.

If more students were aware of this, I think many of them would decide to look more closely and to try and learn more about what *is* known. That is the time when mathematics will become clearly and unavoidably recognizable as an essential, indispensable instrument for engaging in the game, and that is the time for teaching it. The calamitous loss of applied mathematics from what we might otherwise be calling higher education is a loss caused, at least in part, by insufficient incentives for learning the subject. Left by itself, standing there among curriculum offerings, it is not at all clear to the student what it is to be applied to. And there is all of science, next door, looking like an almost-finished field reserved only for chaps who want to invent or apply new technologies. We have had it wrong, and presented it wrong to class after class for several generations.

An appreciation of what is happening in science today, and how great   25
a distance lies ahead for exploring, ought to be one of the rewards of a liberal-arts education. It ought to be good in itself, not something to be acquired on the way to a professional career but part of the cast of thought needed for getting into the kind of century that is now just down the road. Part of the intellectual equipment of an educated person, however his or her time is to be spent, ought to be a feel for the queernesses of nature, the inexplicable thing, the side of life for which informed bewilderment will be the best way of getting through the day.

Questions for Discussion

1. Where is the blame for "scientific illiteracy" usually put? Where does Thomas believe that at least part of the blame belongs?
2. Why does Thomas believe that science is mysterious and exciting?
3. Thomas claims that the teaching of science often leaves students feeling that science is boring. Is this true of your own education in science? How does he think science should be taught? Would you welcome the changes he proposes in this essay?
4. Why is it important for people in other fields to study science? Why not leave science to the scientists?
5. In paragraph 22 Thomas claims that the future rests upon the shoulders of poets. What do you think he means by this?
6. In exploring the nature of science and science education, Thomas has implied an argument. How would the essay probably change if Thomas wanted to emphasize that argument?

Suggestions for Writing

1. What is your least favorite subject? Write an essay exploring the reasons that have led you to feel that way.
2. Write an essay exploring what poets could contribute to science.

WHAT IS VULGAR?

Joseph Epstein

The following essay was first published in The American Scholar, *the journal of Phi Beta Kappa. You will find that it contains many references that Epstein expected his original audience to understand, but you will also find that it includes humor, personal experience, and strongly expressed opinions. If you think it is surprising that someone would write at such length about a single word, ask yourself why being alert to* vulgarity, *as Epstein defines it, has implications for both our daily lives and American culture as a whole.*

What's vulgar? Some people might say that the contraction of the words *what* and *is* itself is vulgar. On the other hand, I remember being called a stuffed shirt by a reviewer of a book of mine because I used almost no contractions. I have forgotten the reviewer's name but I have remembered the criticism. Not being of that category of writers who never forget a compliment, I also remember being called a racist by another reviewer for observing that failure to insist on table manners in children was to risk dining with Apaches. The larger criticisms I forget, but, oddly, these goofy little criticisms stick in the teeth like sesame seeds. Yet that last trope — is it, too, vulgar? Ought I really to be picking my teeth in public, even metaphorically?

What, to return to the question in uncontractioned form, is vulgar? Illustrations, obviously, are wanted. Consider a relative of mine, long deceased, my father's Uncle Jake and hence my grand-uncle. I don't wish to brag about bloodlines, but my Uncle Jake was a bootlegger during Prohibition who afterward went into the scrap-iron — that is to say, the junk — business. Think of the archetypal sensitive Jewish intellectual faces: of Spinoza,° of Freud,° of Einstein,° of Oppenheimer.° In my uncle's face you would not have found the least trace of any of them. He was completely bald, weighed in at around two hundred fifty pounds, and had a complexion of clear vermilion. I loved him, yet even as a child I knew there was about him something a bit — how shall I put it? — outsized, and I refer not merely to his personal tonnage. When he visited our home he generally greeted me by pressing a ten- or twenty-dollar bill into my hand — an amount of money quite impossible, of course, for a boy of nine or ten, when what was wanted was a quarter or fifty-cent piece. A

Spinoza: Benedict (1632–1677), a Dutch philosopher. *Freud:* Sigmund (1856–1939), the Austrian founder of psychoanalysis. *Einstein:* Albert (1879–1955), a German-born physicist who formulated theories of relativity. *Oppenheimer:* J. Robert (1904–1967), an American physicist who opposed the government's decision to develop the hydrogen bomb.

widower, he would usually bring a lady-friend along; here his tastes ran to Hungarian women in their fifties with operatic bosoms. These women wore large diamond rings, possibly the same rings, which my uncle may have passed from woman to woman. A big spender and a high roller, my uncle was an immigrant version of the sport, a kind of Diamond Chaim Brodsky.

But to see Uncle Jake in action you had to see him at table. He drank whiskey with his meal, the bottle before him on the table along with another of seltzer water, both of which he supplied himself. He ate and drank like a character out of Rabelais.° My mother served him his soup course, not in a regular bowl, but in a vessel more on the order of a tureen. He would eat hot soup and drink whiskey and sweat — my Uncle Jake did not, decidedly, do anything so delicate as perspire — and sometimes it seemed that the sweat rolled from his face right into his soup dish, so that, toward the end, he may well have been engaged in an act of liquid auto-cannibalism, consuming his own body fluids with a whiskey chaser.

He was crude, certainly, my Uncle Jake; he was coarse, of course; gross, it goes without saying; uncouth, beyond question. But was he vulgar? I don't think he was. For one thing, he was good-hearted, and it somehow seems wrong to call anyone vulgar who is good-hearted. But more to the point, I don't think that if you had accused him of being vulgar, he would have known what the devil you were talking about. To be vulgar requires at least a modicum of pretension, and this Uncle Jake sorely lacked. "Wulgar," he might have responded to the accusation that he was vulgar, "so vat's dis wulgar?"

To go from persons to things, and from lack of pretension to a   5 mountain of it, let me tell you about a house I passed one night, in a neighborhood not far from my own, that so filled me with disbelief that I took a hard right turn at the next corner and drove round the block to make certain I had actually seen what I thought I had. I had, but it was no house — it was a bloody edifice!

The edifice in question totally fills its rather modest lot, leaving no backyard at all. It is constructed of a white stone, sanded and perhaps even painted, with so much gray-colored mortar that, even though it may be real, the stone looks fake. The roof is red. It has two chimneys, neither of which, I would wager, functions. My confidence here derives from the fact that nothing much else in the structure of the house seems to function. There is, for example, a balcony over a portico — a portico held up by columns — onto which the only possible mode of entry is by pole vault. There is, similarly, over the attached garage, a sun deck whose only access appears to be through a bathroom window. The house seems to have been built on the aesthetic formula of functionlessness follows formlessness.

Rabelais: François (1494?–1553?), a French humorist who in *Gargantua* describes a giant with an enormous appetite.

But it is in its details that the true spirit of the house emerges. These details are not minuscule, and neither are they subtle. For starters, outside the house under the portico, there is a chandelier. There are also two torch-shaped lamps on either side of the front door, which is carved in a scallop pattern, giving it the effect of seeming the back door to a much larger house. Along the short walk leading up to this front door stand, on short pillars, two plaster of paris lions — gilded. On each pillar, in gold and black, appears the owner's name. A white chain fence, strung along poles whose tops are painted gold, spans the front of the property; it is the kind of fence that would be more appropriate around, say, the tomb of Lenin. At the curb are two large cars, sheets of plastic covering their grills; there is also a trailer; and, in the summer months, a boat sits in the short drive-way leading up to the garage. The lawn disappoints by being not Astro-Turf but, alas, real grass. However, closer inspection reveals two animals, a skunk and a rabbit, both of plastic, in petrified play upon the lawn — a nice, you might almost say a finishing, touch. Sometimes, on long drives or when unable to sleep at night, I have pondered upon the possible decor of this extraordinary house's den and upon the ways of man, which are various beyond imagining.

You want vulgar, I am inclined to exclaim, I'll show you vulgar: The house I have just described is vulgar, patently, palpably, pluperfectly vulgar. Forced to live in it for more than three hours, certain figures of refined sensibility — Edith Wharton° or Harold Acton° or Wallace Stevens° — might have ended as suicides. Yet as I described that house, I noted two contradictory feelings in myself: how pleasant it is to point out someone else's vulgarity, and yet the fear that calling someone else vulgar may itself be slightly vulgar. After all, the family that lives in this house no doubt loves it; most probably they feel that they have a real showplace. Their house, I assume, gives them a large measure of happiness. Yet why does my calling their home vulgar also give me such a measure of happiness? I suppose it is because vulgarity can be so amusing — other people's vulgarity, that is.

Here I must insert that I have invariably thought that the people who have called me vulgar were themselves rather vulgar. So far as I know I have been called vulgar three times, once directly, once behind my back, and once by association. In each instance the charge was intellectual vulgarity: On one occasion a contributor to a collection of essays on contemporary writing that I once reviewed called me vulgar because I didn't find anything good to say about this book of some six hundred pages; once an old friend, an editor with whom I had had a falling out over politics, told another friend of mine that an article I had written seemed to him vulgar; and, finally, having patched things up with this friend and having begun

Edith Wharton: An American novelist (1862–1937), whose first book was *The Decoration of Houses. Harold Acton:* British art critic (1904–), historian, and author of *Memoirs of an Aesthete* and other works. *Wallace Stevens:* American poet (1879–1955).

to write for his magazine again, yet a third friend asked me why I allowed my writing to appear in that particular magazine, when it was so patently — you guessed her, Chester — vulgar.

None of these accusations stung in the least. In intellectual and academic life, vulgar is something one calls people with whom one disagrees. Like having one's ideas called reductionist, it is nothing to get worked up about — certainly nothing to take personally. What would wound me, though, is if word got back to me that someone had said that my manners at table were so vulgar that it sickened him to eat with me, or that my clothes were laughable, or that taste in general wasn't exactly my strong point. In a novel whose author or title I can no longer remember, I recall a female character who was described as having vulgar thumbs. I am not sure I have a clear picture of vulgar thumbs, but if it is all the same, I would just as soon not have them.

I prefer not to be thought vulgar in any wise. When not long ago a salesman offered to show me a winter coat that, as he put it, "has been very popular," I told him to stow it — if it has been popular, it is not for me. I comb my speech, as best I am able, of popular phrases: You will not hear an unfundamental "basically" or a flying "whatever" from these chaste lips. I do not utter "bottom line"; I do not mutter "trade-off." I am keen to cut myself out from the herd, at least when I can. In recent years this has not been difficult. Distinction has lain in plain speech, plain dress, clean cheeks. The simple has become rococo, the rococo simple. But now I see that television anchormen, hairdressers, and other leaders in our society have adopted this plainer look. This is discomfiting news. Vulgar is, after all, as vulgar does.

Which returns us yet again to the question: What is vulgar? *The Oxford English Dictionary,* which provides more than two pages on the word, is rather better at telling us what vulgar was than what it is. Its definitions run from "1. The common or usual language of a country; the vernacular. *Obs.*" to "13. Having a common and offensively mean character; coarsely commonplace; lacking in refinement or good taste; uncultured, ill-bred." Historically, the word vulgar was used in fairly neutral description up to the last quarter of the seventeenth century to mean and describe the common people. Vulgar was common but not yet contemned. I noted such a neutral usage as late as a William Hazlitt° essay of 1818, "On the Ignorance of the Learned," in which Hazlitt writes: "The vulgar are in the right when they judge for themselves; they are wrong when they trust to their blind guides." Yet, according to the *OED,* in 1797 the *Monthly Magazine* remarked: "So the word *vulgar* now implies something base and groveling in actions."

From the early nineteenth century on, then, vulgar has been purely pejorative, a key term in the lexicon of insult and invective. Its currency

William Hazlitt: An English essayist and critic (1778–1830).

as a term of abuse rose with the rise of the middle class; its spread was tied to the spread of capitalism and democracy. Until the rise of the middle class, until the spread of capitalism and democracy, people perhaps hadn't the occasion or the need to call one another vulgar. The rise of the middle class, the spread of capitalism and democracy, opened all sorts of social doors; social classes commingled as never before; plutocracy made possible almost daily strides from stratum to stratum. Still, some people had to be placed outside the pale, some doors had to be locked — and the cry of vulgarity, properly intoned, became a most effective Close Sesame.

Such seems to me roughly the social history of the word vulgar. But the history of vulgarity, the thing itself even before it had a name, is much longer. According to the French art historian Albert Dasnoy, aesthetic vulgarity taints Greek art of the fourth and third centuries B.C. "An exhibition of Roman portraits," Dasnoy writes, "shows that, between the Etruscan style of the earliest and the Byzantine style of the latest, vulgarity made its first full-blooded appearance in the academic realism of imperial Rome." Vulgarity, in Dasnoy's view, comes of the shock of philosophic rationalism, when humankind divests itself of belief in the sacred. "Vulgarity seems to be the price of man's liberation," he writes, "one might even say, of his evolution. It is unquestionably the price of the freeing of the individual personality." Certainly it is true that one would never think to call a savage vulgar; a respectable level of civilization has to have been reached to qualify for the dubious distinction of being called vulgar.

"You have surely noticed the curious fact," writes *Valéry*,° "that a   *15* certain *word,* which is perfectly clear when you hear or use it in *everyday* speech, and which presents no difficulty when caught up in the rapidity of an ordinary sentence, becomes mysteriously cumbersome, offers a strange resistance, defeats all efforts at definition, the moment you withdraw it from circulation for separate study and try to find its meaning after taking away its temporary function." Vulgar presents special difficulties, though: While vulgarity has been often enough on display — may even be a part of the human soul that only the fortunate and the saintly are able to root out — every age has its own notion of what constitutes the vulgar. Riding a bicycle at Oxford in the 1890s, Max Beerbohm° reports, "was the earmark of vulgarity." Working further backward, we find that Matthew Arnold° frequently links the word vulgar with the word hideous and hopes that culture "saves the future, as one may hope, from being vulgarized, even if it cannot save the present." "In Jane Austen's novels," Lionel Trilling° writes, "vulgarity has these elements: smallness of mind, insufficiency of awareness, assertive self-esteem, the wish to devalue, especially to devalue the human worth of other people." Hazlitt found vulgarity in

---

Valéry: Paul (1871–1945), a French poet and literary critic.   *Max Beerbohm:* An English critic, novelist, and caricaturist (1872–1956).   *Matthew Arnold:* An English poet and critic (1822–1888). *Lionel Trilling:* An American critic and educator (1905–1975).

false feeling among "the herd of pretenders to what they do not feel and to what is not natural to them, whether in high or low life."

Vulgarity, it begins to appear, is often in the eye of the beholder. What is more, it comes in so many forms. It is so multiple and so complex — so multiplex. There are vulgarities of taste, of manner, of mind, of spirit. There are whole vulgar ages — the Gilded Age in the United States, for one, at least to hear Mark Twain and Henry Adams° tell it. (Is our own age another?) To compound the complication there is even likeable vulgarity. This is vulgarity of the kind that Cyril Connolly° must have had in mind when he wrote, "Vulgarity is the garlic in the salad of life." In the realm of winning vulgarity are the novels of Balzac,° the paintings of Frans Hals,° some of the music of Tchaikovsky° (excluding the cannon fire in the 1812 Overture, which is vulgarity of the unwinning kind).

Rightly used, profanity, normally deemed the epitome of vulgar manners, can be charming. I recently moved to a new apartment, and the person I dealt with at the moving company we employed, a woman whose voice had an almost strident matter-of-factness, instructed me to call back with an inventory of our furniture. When I did, our conversation, starting with my inventory of our living room, began:

"One couch."

"One couch."

"Two lamp tables, a coffee table, a small gateleg table."   20

"Four tables."

"Two wing chairs and an occasional chair."

"Three chairs.

"One box of bric-a-brac."

"One box of shit."   25

Heavy garlic of course is not to every taste; but then again some people do not much care for endive. I attended city schools, where garlic was never in short supply and where profanity, in proper hands, could be a useful craft turned up to the power of fine art. I have since met people so well-mannered, so icily, elegantly correct, that with a mere glance across the table or a word to a waiter they could put a chill on the wine and indeed on the entire evening. Some people have more, some less, in the way of polish, but polish doesn't necessarily cover vulgarity. As there can be diamonds in the rough, so can there be sludge in the smooth.

It would be helpful in drawing a definitional bead on the word vulgar if one could determine its antonym. But I am not sure that it has an antonym. Refined? I think not. Sophisticated? Not really. Elegant? Nope. Charming? Close, but I can think of charming vulgarians — M. Rabelais, please come forth and take a bow. Besides, charm is nearly as difficult to

---

Henry Adams: An American historian and writer (1838–1918), great grandson of John Adams. *Cyril Connolly:* An English author and journalist (1903–1974).   *Balzac:* Honoré de (1799–1850), a French novelist.   *Frans Hals:* A Dutch painter (1581–1666).   *Tchaikovsky:* Peter (1840–1893), a Russian composer.

define as vulgarity. Perhaps the only safe thing to be said about charm is that if you think you have it, you can be fairly certain that you don't.

If vulgarity cannot be defined by its antonym, from the rear so to say, examples may be more to the point. I once heard a friend describe a woman thus: "Next to Sam Jensen's prose, she's the vulgarest thing in New York." From this description, I had a fairly firm sense of what the woman was like. Sam Jensen is a writer for one of the newsmagazines; each week on schedule he makes a fresh cultural discovery, writing as if every sentence will be his last, every little movie or play he reviews will change our lives — an exhibitionist with not a great deal to exhibit. Sam Jensen is a fictitious name — made up to protect the guilty — but here are a few sentences that he, not I, made up:

> The great Victorian William Morris combined a practical socialism with a love for the spirit of the King Arthur legends. What these films show is the paradox democracy has forgotten — that the dream of Camelot is the ultimate dream of freedom and order in a difficult but necessary balance.

> The screenplay by Michael Wilson and Richard Maibaum is not from an Ian Fleming novel; it's really a cookbook that throws Roger Moore as Bond into these action recipes like a cucumber tossed into an Osterizer. Osterization is becoming more and more necessary for Moore; he's beginning to look a bit puckered, as if he's been bottled in Bond.

From these sentences — with their false paradoxes, muffed metaphors, obvious puns, and general bloat — I think I can extrapolate the woman who, next to this prose, is the vulgarest thing in New York. I see teeth, I see elaborate hairdo, much jewelry, flamboyant dress, a woman requiring a great deal of attention, who sucks up most of the mental oxygen in any room she is in — a woman, in sum, vastly overdone.

Coming at things from a different angle, I imagine myself in session with a psychologist, playing the word association game. "Vulgar," he says, "quick, name ten items you associate with the word vulgar." "Okay," I say, "here goes:

1. Publicity
2. The Oscar awards
3. The Aspen Institute for Humanistic Studies
4. Talk shows
5. Pulitzer Prizes
6. Barbara Walters
7. Interviews with writers
8. Lauren Bacall
9. Dialogue as an ideal
10. Psychology."

This would not, I suspect, be everyone's list. Looking it over, I see that, of the ten items, several are linked with one another. But let me inquire into what made me choose the items I did.

Ladies first. Barbara Walters seems to me vulgar because for a great 30 many years now she has been paid to ask all the vulgar questions, and she seems to do it with such cheerfulness, such competence, such amiable insincerity. "What did you think when you first heard your husband had been killed?" she will ask, just the right hush in her voice. "What went on in your mind when you learned that you had cancer, now for the third time?" The questions that people with imagination do not need to ask, the questions that people with good hearts know they have no right to ask, these questions and others Barbara Walters can be depended upon to ask. "Tell me, Holy Father, have you never regretted not having children of your own?"

Lauren Bacall has only recently graduated to vulgarity, or at least she has only in the past few years revealed herself vulgar. Hers is a double vulgarity: the vulgarity of false candor — the woman who, presumably, tells it straight — and the vulgarity provided by someone who has decided to cash in her chips. In her autobiography, Miss Bacall has supposedly told all her secrets; when interviewed on television — by, for example, Barbara Walters — the tack she takes is that of the ringwise babe over whose eyes no one, kiddo, is going to pull the cashmere. Yet turn the channel or page, and there is Miss Bacall in a commercial or advertisement doing her best to pull the cashmere over ours. Vulgar stuff.

Talk shows are vulgar for the same reason that Pulitzer Prizes and the Aspen Institute for Humanistic Studies are vulgar. All three fail to live up to their pretensions, which are extravagant: talk shows to being serious, Pulitzer Prizes to rewarding true merit, the Aspen Institute to promoting "dialogue" (see item 9), "the bridging of cultures," "the interdisciplinary approach," and nearly every other phony shibboleth that has cropped up in American intellectual life over the past three decades.

Publicity is vulgar because those who seek it — and even those who are sought by it — tend almost without exception to be divested of their dignity. You have to sell yourself, the sales manuals used to advise, in order to sell your product. With publicity, though, one is selling only oneself, which is different. Which is a bit vulgar, really.

The Oscar awards ceremony is the single item on my list least in need of explanation, for it seems vulgar prima facie. It is the air of self-congratulation — of, a step beyond, self-adulation — that is so splendidly vulgar about the Oscar awards ceremony. Self-congratulation, even on good grounds, is best concealed; on no grounds whatever, it is embarrassing. But then, for vulgarity, there's no business like show business.

Unless it be literary business. The only thing worse than false mod- 35 esty is no modesty at all, and no modesty at all is what interviews with writers generally bring out. "That most vulgar of all crowds the literary," wrote Keats presciently — that is, before the incontestable evidence came in with the advent and subsequent popularity of what is by now that staple of the book review and little magazine and talk show, the interview with the great author. What these interviews generally come down to is an invitation to writers to pontificate upon things for which it is either unseemly for them to speak (the quality of their own work) or upon which they are unfit to judge (the state of the cosmos). Roughly a decade ago I watched Isaac Bashevis Singer,° when asked on a television talk show what he thought of the Vietnam War, answer, "I am a writer, and that doesn't mean I have to have an opinion on everything. I'd rather discuss literature." Still, how tempting it is, with an interviewer chirping away at your feet, handing you your own horn and your own drum, to blow it and beat it. As someone who has been interviewed a time or two, I can attest that never have I shifted spiritual gears so quickly from self-importance to self-loathing as during and after an interview. What I felt was, well, vulgar.

Psychology seems to me vulgar because it is too often overbearing in its confidence. Instead of saying, "I don't know," it readily says, "unresolved Oedipus complex" or "manic-depressive syndrome" or "identity crisis." As with other intellectual discoveries before (Marxism) and since (structuralism), psychology acts as if it is holding all the theoretical keys, but then in practice reveals that it doesn't even know where the doors are. As an old *Punch* cartoon once put it, "It's worse than wicked, my dear, it's vulgar."

Reviewing my list and attempting to account for the reasons why I have chosen the items on it, I feel I have a firmer sense of what I think vulgar. Exhibitionism, obviousness, pretentiousness, self-congratulation, self-importance, hypocrisy, overconfidence — these seem to me qualities at the heart of vulgarity in our day. It does, though, leave out common sense, a quality which, like clarity, one might have thought one could never have in overabundance. (On the philosophy table in my local bookstore, a book appeared with the title *Clarity Is Not Enough;* I could never pass it without thinking, "Ah, but it's a start.") Yet too great reliance on common sense can narrow the mind, make meager the imagination. Strict common sense abhors mystery, seldom allows for the attraction of tradition, is intolerant of questions that haven't any answers. The problem that common sense presents is knowing the limits of common sense. The too commonsensical man or woman grows angry at anything that falls outside his or her common sense, and this anger seems to me vulgar.

Vulgarity is not necessarily stupid but it is always insensitive. Its insensitivity invariably extends to itself: The vulgar person seldom knows that he is vulgar, as in the old joke about the young woman whose fiancé reports to her that his parents found her vulgar, and who, enraged, responds,

Isaac Bashevis Singer: A Polish-born (1904–1991) American writer of fiction, who received the Nobel Prize for literature in 1978.

"What's this vulgar crap?" Such obvious vulgarity can be comical, like a nouveau riche man bringing opera glasses to a porno film, or the Chicago politician who, while escorting the then ruling British monarch through City Hall, supposedly introduced him to the assembled aldermen by saying, "King, meet the boys." But such things are contretemps merely, not vulgarity of the insidious kind.

In our age vulgarity does not consist in failing to recognize the fish knife or to know the wine list but in the inability to make distinctions. Not long ago I heard a lecture by a Harvard philosophy professor on a Howard Hawks movie, and thought, as one high reference after another was made in connection with this low subject, "Oh, Santayana,° 'tis better you are not alive to see this." A vulgar performance, clearly, yet few people in the audience of professors and graduate students seemed to notice.

A great many people did notice, however, when, in an act of singular 40 moral vulgarity, a publisher, an editor, and a novelist recently sponsored a convicted murderer for parole, and the man, not long after being paroled, murdered again. The reason for these men speaking out on behalf of the convict's parole, they said, was his ability as a writer: His work appeared in the editor's journal; he was to have a book published by the publisher's firm; the novelist had encouraged him from the outset. Distinctions — crucial distinctions — were not made: first, that the man was not a very good writer, but a crudely Marxist one, whose work was filled with hatreds and half-truths; second, and more important, that, having killed before, he might kill again — might just be a pathological killer. Not to have made these distinctions is vulgarity at its most vile. But to adopt a distinction new to our day, the publisher, the editor, and the novelist took responsibility for what they had done — responsibility but no real blame.

Can an entire culture grow vulgar? Matthew Arnold feared such might happen in "the mechanical and material civilisation" of the England of his day. Vladimir Nabokov° felt it already had happened in the Soviet Union, a country, as he described it, "of moral imbeciles, of smiling slaves and poker-faced bullies," without, as in the old days, "a Gogol, a Tolstoy, a Chekhov in quest of that simplicity of truth [who] easily distinguished the vulgar side of things as well as the trashy systems of pseudo-thought." Moral imbeciles, smiling slaves, poker-faced bullies — the curl of a sneer in those Nabokovian phrases is a sharp reminder of the force that the charge of "vulgar" can have as an insult — as well as a reminder of how deep and pervasive vulgarity can become.

But American vulgarity, if I may put it so, is rather more refined. It is also more piecemeal than pervasive, and more insidious. Creeping vulgarity is how I think of it, the way Taft° Republicans used to think of

---

Santayana: George (1863–1952), an American poet and philosopher. *Vladimir Nabokov:* An American novelist and poet (1899–1977), born and raised in Russia. *Taft:* Robert A. (1889–1953), a U.S. senator from Ohio, a spokesperson for Republican conservatives and an unsuccessful presidential candidate.

creeping socialism. The insertion of a science fiction course in a major university curriculum, a television commercial by a once-serious actor for a cheap wine, an increased interest in gossip and trivia that is placed under the rubric Style in our most important newspapers: So the vulgar creeps along, while everywhere the third- and fourth-rate — in art, in literature, in intellectual life — is considered good enough, or at any rate highly interesting.

Yet being refined — or at least sophisticated — American vulgarity is vulnerable to the charge of being called vulgar. "As long as war is regarded as wicked," said Oscar Wilde, "it will always have its fascination. When it is looked upon as vulgar, it will cease to be popular." There may be something to this, if not for war then at least for designer jeans, French literary criticism, and other fashions. The one thing the vulgar of our day do not like to be called is vulgar. So crook your little finger, purse your lips, distend your nostrils slightly as you lift your nose in the air the better to look down it, and repeat after me: *Vulgar! Vulgar! Vulgar!* The word might save us all.

Questions for Discussion

1. What is the function of Uncle Jake in this essay? What does Epstein mean when he describes him as "outsized"?
2. Why would anyone enjoy calling someone or something vulgar? What could be considered vulgar about doing so?
3. What is vulgar about the house described in paragraphs 6 and 7?
4. How does Epstein present himself in this essay? Does he ever make fun of himself? What's the point of mentioning things that he has forgotten — as he does in paragraphs 1 and 10?
5. *Rococo* describes a style of architecture and decoration that involves elaborate ornamentation; it was fashionable in Europe during the early eighteenth century. What do you think Epstein means when, writing about contemporary America, he observes, "The simple has become rococo, the rococo simple"?
6. Why do you think Epstein waited until almost midway through his essay before devoting a paragraph to reporting what a dictionary says about *vulgar*? How well would paragraph 12 work as an introduction for this essay?
7. How can it be useful to understand the meaning of vulgarity? What does Epstein mean when he writes, "The word might save us all"?

Suggestions for Writing

1. Draw up your own list of five items or people that could be considered vulgar according to the definition set forth in this essay. Discuss each of your choices so that readers can understand why they are on your list.
2. Reread paragraph 37 and then write an essay exploring the limits of common sense.

COMPLETELY DIFFERENT

Russell Baker

In his Pulitzer Prize–winning autobiography Growing Up, *Russell Baker recalls how his career as a writer began with a high school essay on spaghetti that he wrote primarily for his own pleasure and that would "violate all the rules of formal composition I'd learned in school." As you read the following essay, originally one of Baker's columns in the* New York Times, *you will find that he is still breaking rules. If you have ever been told to avoid writing an incomplete sentence or a series of short paragraphs, think about what Baker achieves by violating these rules.*

This is all new.

It is completely different.

You have never experienced anything like it.

Now that you are experiencing it you will never be the same again.

You will be all new. 5

You will be completely different.

You will never want to experience the old experiences again.

Everything that is old has been discarded to create a completely different experience.

Long sentences have been.

Discarded. 10

Everything has been completely miniaturized.

Thought. Soap. "King Lear." Liver spots on the backs of hands. Travel time. Sunsets. Spin-dry cycles. Headaches.

All are now reduced to their absolute essentials.

All miniaturized.

This is a revolutionary new concept. 15

It will give you twice as much time as your old unrevolutionary new concept.

You will be twice as dynamic.

You will enjoy endless hours.

You will stay younger twice as fast.

Here is what the critics say: 20

"Since experiencing the revolutionary new concept I have become twice as irresistible to women" — Mr. B. T. of Houma, La.

"— a dynamic new route to newness. . . . I never knew what 'King Lear' could be until I saw it performed without commas or punctuation marks" — Mrs. C. J. of Rochester, N. Y.

You will also smell newer.

Why is this extraordinary advance in newness vital to success?

Because we live in today's world. 25

Today's world is completely different.

Today's world is all new.

Today's world requires people who are completely different.

It requires people who are all new.

We have all seen people who live in yesterday's world.

Are those people fun people?

Dynamic people?

When you open their doors do you smell an exciting new fresh-from-the-factory new-people smell?

With a hidden camera we interviewed a typical scrubwoman.

Note that these pictures show her seated before two boxes.

She cannot see the labels visible to you.

Note that one box is labeled "New Completely Different Person."

The other is labeled "Old Unchanged Person."

We will now run the tape.

"Mrs. Hummell, you are a weary 67-year-old scrubwoman who spends long nights alone on her knees in this empty building. We ask you to study these two boxes and tell us which box contains the sort of person you would prefer to keep you company through the night."

"Easy. That box right there."

"Now, you, Mrs. Hummel, have chosen the box labeled — unbeknownst to you — 'New Completely Different Person.' Tell me why you did not pick this other box labeled 'Old Unchanged Person.'"

"Because it looked too heavy to carry around all night."

"Let's open both boxes and look."

Notice Mrs. Hummel's expression as the "Old Unchanged Person" box is opened and a 135-pound woman emerges and asks her to spend an hour walking on the beach watching a sunset.

Notice that Mrs. Hummel recoils.

Mrs. Hummel recoils because the woman is not new.

She does not have new-woman smell.

She has not miniaturized the liver spots on the backs of her hands.

She does not propose living dynamically, but instead speaks in the exhausting rhythms of this particular sentence, with its antiquated commas and cumbersomely involuted grammatical structure, thereby making it all too evident that she is incapable of living dynamically by getting right to the point, a fact which is driven home by her suggestion that they spend an entire hour watching a sunset, thus consuming precious time that could be used to have her wrinkles surgically removed and the dull soap glaze banished from her hair by application of a new, completely different shampoo.

Note, by contrast, how delighted Mrs. Hummel looks when the box labeled "New Completely Different Person" is opened.

Yes, the figure emerging is a 10-ounce man.

He has been reduced to the absolute essentials of newness.

Mrs. Hummel can keep him in her apron pocket throughout the night. She can remove him when she wishes to inhale his exciting new smell.

He will tell her without commas how to have twice as much time for   *55*
dynamic living by watching a sunset in 15 seconds.

Mrs. Hummel will never be the same again.

Questions for Discussion

1. What idea is Baker exploring in this essay? How does the form of the essay suit his topic?
2. In paragraphs 9 and 10 Baker claims that long sentences have been discarded, yet he writes an exceptionally long sentence in paragraph 50. What is the function of that long sentence? Could it have appeared any earlier in the essay?
3. Baker comments on commas in paragraphs 22 and 55. In what sense is the comma significant? What would its elimination signal? Where does Baker use commas?
4. What type of language is Baker satirizing in this essay?
5. Consider the last three paragraphs. What do they reveal about Baker's values?

Suggestions for Writing

1. If the world seems very different from when you were a child, write an essay exploring what is being lost and what is being gained.
2. Are people becoming smaller, like the "New Completely Different Person" in Mrs. Hummel's apron pocket? Write an essay exploring what it means to be a small person.

10

Writing to Understand Reading

Everyone has had the experience of trying to read something that is difficult to understand. But another type of reading experience is even more common: thinking that we understand what we have read when there are actually dozens of points we have passed right over. Although people read in different ways, and much is still unknown about reading, we do know that a dozen people reading the same text are likely to see and remember a dozen different versions. With so many words printed on any page, the eye is unlikely to give equal attention to every line. Readers may agree about what a text seems to say overall, or they may disagree strongly. But whether they agree or disagree, they will have reached their conclusions by different routes.

When reading, many people skip over words or allusions that they do not understand, and they do it so routinely that they sometimes don't realize that they are doing it. They are also likely to pause at different points — to answer the phone, take a sip of coffee, or simply rest their eyes. These pauses can influence which parts of a text are remembered most clearly. Moreover, reading triggers specific associations for each reader derived from his or her own personal experience. We all bring our own unique experiences, personality, and knowledge of the world to any text we read. To a significant degree, we *create* the meaning we derive from reading.

Most critics now agree that there is no single way to interpret a text that is, somehow, the correct interpretation. This principle can yield results that are both liberating and enriching, since freeing readers to explore individual responses can add to the overall understanding of what a text can mean. Twelve people reading the same text can offer twelve different responses, all of them valuable. However, some responses to a text will be more illuminating than others if more time and care have been invested in them.

One of the best ways of testing your understanding of a text — and improving upon that understanding — is to write about what you read. Whether you are summarizing the information a work includes, evaluating the author's achievement, or exploring the ideas that have been raised, writing about reading requires you to think about the text. This usually means returning to the text and studying it carefully. To illustrate how writing can lead to a better understanding of reading, this chapter will focus upon writing about literature as it has been traditionally defined: fiction, drama, and poetry. Some critics define literature more broadly to include everything available in print. Whatever your own definition of literature, you can apply most of the techniques discussed here to almost anything you read.

RECOGNIZING WAYS TO APPROACH A TEXT

Like most types of writing, writing about literature can take a variety of different forms.

- You can *summarize* a work by briefly stating its key points.
- You can *review* a work by identifying its strengths and weaknesses.
- You can *explicate* a work by providing a line-by-line explanation of what a work means and how it achieves that meaning.
- You can *analyze* a work by discussing one or more of its parts.

The approach that you take should be determined by your rhetorical situation. Your instructor may assign a specific approach, or you may need to decide for yourself which approach best suits your audience and the material you will be writing about.

Summarizing is useful when a work is long, tells a story, offers information, or makes an argument. When writing about literature, you are more likely to find yourself needing to summarize a novel, story, or play than a poem. Summary can stand alone as a separate assignment, but more often it is part of a paper that then goes on to either evaluate or analyze the work summarized. As a general rule, you should write summary only if you have been specifically asked to do so or if you believe that your audience may not be familiar with the work you want to discuss. An audience that has read the work recently might ask, "Why are you telling me this? I know it already." On the other hand, an audience unfamiliar with the work may have trouble following your discussion of it without benefit of a brief summary. For this reason a writer reviewing a new book in a newspaper will usually include some summary along with evaluation. You, too, may have occasion to summarize a work that you want to examine critically. Be cautious, however: Some writers drift into writing summary because they find it easier to retell a story than to interpret it. When choosing to write a summary, make sure that your choice is deliberate, that it serves a clear purpose, that it covers the main points, and that it is as short as you can make it. (For additional information on summary, see pp. 20 and 236.)

Reviewing, like summarizing (which it often includes), makes the most sense when the work is unfamiliar to your audience. Both summaries and reviews attempt to provide a sense of the book as a whole; but whereas summaries limit themselves to content and try to be neutral, reviews also consider quality and offer judgments. In addition to providing a brief summary of the work, a reviewer will usually identify its theme and sometimes compare it with other works by the author that might already be known by the audience. (This is especially likely in reviews of a newly published book by a well-known author.)

At the heart of any review, however, is the reviewer's evaluation of the work's merit. Is the work original or predictable, thorough or superficial? These are among the questions a reviewer may address, offering at least one piece of evidence (such as a short quotation) that will support each opinion. Readers expect these opinions, since one of the principal reasons for reading a review is to decide whether or not you want to read the book. The extent to which readers are influenced by a review often depends upon the degree to which they trust the reviewer's judgment — either because they are already familiar with the reviewer or simply because the reviewer writes so well that she seems to be a credible authority. The review itself is unlikely to make an extensive argument, since it attempts to accomplish several goals within little space. Most book reviews average no more than a thousand words. That might sound like a long assignment if you are staring at a blank sheet of paper or computer screen with no idea what to write about, but it's very little space when you consider all that a reviewer is expected to cover.

An explication also attempts to cover an entire work, but in this case the emphasis is on explaining the work rather than summarizing its content or appraising its quality. If you choose to explicate a work, you have the responsibility to explain the function and meaning of everything within it. Consequently, explication is usually reserved for short works, especially poems (or excerpts, such as an important speech within a longer work). If you think you might wish to offer a line-by-line explication of *War and Peace,* you had better reserve the next several years of your life. On the other hand, the explication of a poem like "Pied Beauty" may well be the best way of understanding the work's meaning.

When you are looking for topics for writing about literature, analysis offers the greatest range of possibilities, for it opens up room for multiple interpretations of different parts of a work. Analyzing a work requires you to recognize its parts (see pp. 236–38). Many works have ready-made divisions within them. A novel is usually divided into chapters (and sometimes groups of chapters); a play, into acts and scenes. A short story might consist of two or three separate scenes, and a poem might be divided into stanzas. For such cases you can choose to write about one of these divisions — limiting yourself, for example, to the chapter in which Huckleberry Finn pretends to be a girl or to the suicide scene in *Romeo and Juliet.* But there are many other ways of dividing a work of literature. Analytical papers may be written on the following features:

- The role of a story within the story
- The significance of a specific dialogue
- The portrayal of one of the characters
- The setting, and why it is appropriate for what happens within the work
- The theme, or central idea, that the work conveys to you
- The use of figurative language or symbolism to convey more than one meaning
- A pattern of imagery that establishes a particular mood
- The organization of the work, and why it is structured as it is

Each of these possibilities can be modified depending upon your interests, the needs of your readers, and the nature of the text. You may decide to broaden or narrow your focus. For example, you may decide to contrast two characters if you have the space to do so and if doing so will be more illuminating than analyzing a single character. Or you may focus on one of several symbols that you have identified if you have much to say about it and relatively little to say about the others. But whatever part of the whole you select for analysis, you should try to make your analysis of that part contribute to your readers' understanding of the work as a whole.

PREPARING TO WRITE

On some occasions you may feel motivated to write about something immediately after you have read it. In fact, a good way to improve both your reading and your writing is to keep a journal devoted specifically to recording responses to what you read. The entries in a reading journal will typically include brief summaries that can help you when reviewing for exams, comments evaluating the strengths and weaknesses of the material, questions that you'd like to raise during class discussion of the assignment, and reflections of your own that were inspired along the way.

Even if you do not keep a reading journal on a regular basis, you should try to honor any impulse to write about what you read. If you sometimes wish that you had more to say when people discuss their reading, you are especially likely to benefit from getting something down on paper whenever you feel stimulated by a particular assignment. Imagine yourself having the chance to talk with the author of the material you've read. What would you praise? What would you ask about? And what, if anything, would you complain about? Sometimes, it's hard to find the words to get such a conversation started; but once you've started, you've increased the likelihood of touching on something that can lead to a better understanding of the work.

When you are assigned an out-of-class paper about literature, there are a number of things you can do to make sure that you'll have something to say when you begin to write.

1 *Note your preliminary response.* The first step in writing to understand reading is defining your preliminary response. If you have the option of choosing to write about one of several works, ask yourself which inspired the strongest reaction. Which did you like best and which the least? If you are required to write about a specific work, you can modify this question by asking yourself which aspects of the work appealed to you and which did not. Discovering a text (or part of a text) that you enjoyed can help you write a good paper, since you will be writing about material that you are willing to spend time with. On the other hand, good papers can also result from writing about reading that you definitely did *not* like if you enjoy trying to persuade others to agree with you: Consider how much fun Mark Twain must have had demolishing *The Deerslayer* in "Fenimore Cooper's Literary Offenses" (Chapter 8). In either case you are writing about material you have a clear response to, and this is usually easier than starting with material you have no particular feelings about one way or the other.

2. *Reread the work you have chosen to write about.* Once you know what work you will be writing about, the next step is to reexamine that work. Although you may not be able to reread an entire novel (or other long work), you should always be able to reread a story, poem, or play before writing an out-of-class paper about it. As you do so, annotate the work by marking key passages and making marginal notations as questions and ideas occur to you. You may have already annotated the text during your initial reading, but you are almost certain to notice new dimensions of the text as you reread. Be sure to look up any words or *allusions* that you passed over on your initial reading, and be alert for the repetition of words or ideas. Deliberate repetition often signals a way of better understanding

a text. You might ask yourself, for example, why "Abalone, Abalone, Abalone" is not simply titled "Abalone," or you might note the repeated references to Mrs. Dietrich's drinking in "Shopping." You should also note any pattern of related references, such as a number of different references to the weather or to clothing. Most importantly, you should reconsider your preliminary response to the work. If you had enjoyed reading it at first, how well does it hold up on another reading? Can you identify specific parts that gave you pleasure? If you are writing about a text that you initially disliked, are you coming to like it better as you spend more time with it? Or are you coming to a clearer understanding of why you find the text objectionable?

3. *Ask yourself questions about the work.* You should not feel as if you must understand every dimension of the text as you are reading it. Ideas will continue to occur to you after you have reread the work if you continue to think about it. Asking yourself questions is a good way to keep these thoughts coming. For example, you can use the pentad (pp. 13–14) to ask yourself such questions as "How does the setting of this work relate to what happens within it?" Or "What act is most central to this work, and who is responsible for it?" Moving beyond the pentad, you might ask: "Why has this work been arranged in the order in which it appears? Why does it begin and end where it does?" Or "Is anything inconsistent in this work? Are there changes that are not accounted for or any departures from what seems to be the main idea?" You can ask yourself questions like these whenever you have a few minutes that you can devote to your own thoughts. Some of the best ideas in your paper may result from answering a question you were thinking about as you walked across campus, washed some dishes, or stood in line at the post office. Preparing to write a paper about literature means making yourself imaginatively and intellectually engaged by the work you are going to write about. Make your mind receptive to ideas by frequently turning your thoughts to the work during the period between receiving the assignment and writing your first draft.

4. *Test your choice.* If you think actively about a work that inspired a strong response, you will probably generate more than one possible topic for writing. At this point you should evaluate these topics for their appropriateness. For instance, some topics may be too narrow and others too broad if you have been asked to write an essay of a specified length. You should also think about your audience's potential interest in the topic. Even if you write best when imagining a broader audience, ask yourself what you know about your instructor. How would she or he respond to a paper that seemed to do nothing more than restate points that had already been made in class? On the other hand, how receptive would your instructor be to a paper that challenged the views set forth in a class lecture? These are questions that have to be settled on an individual basis. But as a general rule, good writers are willing to take chances, and most instructors welcome a paper with fresh ideas as long as those ideas have been well thought out and well supported.

5. *Define your thesis.* Once you have decided upon the topic for your paper, you will know what parts of the literary work require additional study and which parts you will not need to discuss. But having a topic is not the same as having a thesis. Your topic identifies the aspect of the text that you will be writing about; your thesis is the central idea you intend to convey about that topic. Although your thesis may occur to you immediately after your initial reading, you will often know your topic before you feel certain about your thesis. If writing a paper about "Lullaby," for example, you may decide to write on the role of nature in that story, but you then need to decide what you believe that role to be.

6. *Gather your evidence.* A thesis requires support. When interpreting or evaluating literature, think of yourself as writing a type of argument requiring evidence for whatever you claim. Although knowing something of the historical context in which a work was written can often add to your understanding of it, the data supporting your claim should usually come from the text itself. (An exception is a research paper in which evidence comes from a number of sources. But even in this case much of the evidence will still normally come from the text that generated the topic.) Think critically about the evidence you discover, and be prepared to search again for additional support if necessary. Be careful at this stage not to ignore anything that seems to conflict with what you hope to prove. Considering apparent contradictions can prompt you to anticipate objections from your reader and thus help you strengthen your argument. Or you may decide that you need to revise your thesis so that it more accurately reflects your evidence.

WRITING THE PAPER

If you have considered your audience, chosen your topic, defined your thesis, and gathered evidence to support it, your next challenge is to decide how to organize your material.

Some papers take their pattern of organization from the work that is being written about. If you are explicating a poem, for example, you can go through it line by line in the order in which the lines appear. If you are writing a character analysis, you can trace the character's development throughout the work. And if you are discussing a theme or the use of a specific literary device, you can present your evidence in the order in which it appeared in the text. At times, however, you may wish to have more flexibility, moving around in the work from point to point. Instead of tracing a character's development from the beginning of a work to the end, you can organize your analysis in paragraphs or sections devoted to the character's various personality traits, arranging your material in whatever order best suits your purpose. Or instead of writing a line-by-line explication of a poem, you can organize an explication to focus on various dimensions such as imagery, metaphor, and rhyme, one by one.

But whatever your preliminary plan, you should be prepared to modify it if drafting generates good ideas that you didn't realize you had until you started to write. When writing about literature, you may very well find yourself arguing a position that is different from what you had originally planned — or you may find that you have much to say about what you expected to be a minor point in your paper, in which case you need to reconsider your focus. Discoveries like these are a normal part of the writing process, and they can be both illuminating and fun. Remember that you are writing to understand reading, not writing to honor an outline.

Because you cannot understand fully and exactly what you want to say until you have finished drafting a paper, revision is essential. Although there is nothing wrong with drafting a paper that ends up arguing something different from the thesis with which it begins, there is something wrong with handing it in. When revising a paper about literature, be sure to ask yourself if you wrote what you intended. You may need to revise your thesis, make serious cuts, or introduce evidence to support unsupported claims.

Here are a few additional points to keep in mind when revising a paper about literature.

- Consider how well the introduction and conclusion relate to the paper. Ask yourself if you introduced any ideas that you failed to pursue or came to a conclusion that seems unrelated to your original thesis.

- Double check to make sure that you have supported any claims you make and that you have not overlooked anything important.

- Think about how well you have responded to the needs of your audience. Have you summarized material that didn't need to be summarized, or failed to summarize material your audience may not have read? Have you explained any unusual words or references that readers may not understand? On the other hand, have you insulted the intelligence of readers by identifying a reference they would certainly know?

- Consider how you sound. When writing a paper about literature, you are assuming the role of a teacher trying to help others to a better understanding of the work. Try not to sound apologetic by overusing phrases like "in my opinion," for they will diminish your authority as a writer. But be careful not to go to the other extreme and sound contemptuous of anyone who might disagree with you. Strive for a tone that sounds thoughtful, confident, and reasonable. You should sound as if you believe what you are writing and want others to believe it too, but you should not sound as if you believe that you alone are right.

- When considering how you sound, reexamine the number and length of any quotations within the paper. Quotations are often necessary for supporting claims, but some quotations may be longer than they have to be, and too many quotations can keep your own voice from reaching readers. Remember that *you* are the writer of your paper; quotations should be subordinate to what *you* have to say. If your own words seem to do little more than link quotations together, you will need to become more actively involved in the paper. Keep quotations as short as possible, and be sure to weave them smoothly into what you are saying, making their significance clear.

- Observe the conventions appropriate for writing about literature:

A. Use the present tense (sometimes called "the literary present") for writing about what happens in a work of fiction, drama, or poetry.

When Mrs. Dietrich and her daughter go shopping, they see a woman who disturbs them.

B. Identify writers initially by their full name — William Shakespeare, Joyce Carol Oates — and subsequently by their last name, regardless of gender: Shakespeare and Oates, not William or Ms. Oates.

C. Unless you are given other instructions, follow the guidelines for documentation recommended by the Modern Language Association. These are covered in full in the *MLA Handbook for Writers of Research Papers* by Joseph Gibaldi and Walter S. Achtert. Here are a few rules that are needed most frequently in writing about literature.

  1. When the author of a work is clearly revealed in the paper, simply provide a page reference (without an abbreviation for page) within parentheses immediately after the second quotation mark but before the final punctuation for the sentence.

  Oates describes the morning as having "a metallic cast to the air" (486).

  2. Add the author's last name immediately before the page reference when the source of the quotation is not otherwise clear.

  According to this reasoning, word play "reflects real paradoxes in the nature of the world itself" (Burke 56).

  3. When quoting from a play that is divided into acts, scenes, and line numbers, identify quotes with these three numbers (separated by periods) rather than with a page reference.

Iago warns Othello that jealousy is a "green–eyed monster" (3.3.167).

4. When quoting from a poem, provide references to line numbers (without an abbreviation for line). Use a slash to indicate line divisions when quoting two or three lines. (As with a prose quotation, set off longer quotations by indenting ten spaces from the left margin.)

One of the most difficult questions this poem raises is what the speaker means by saying, "I live between the heron and the wren, / Beasts of the hill and serpents of the den" (5–6).

After you have revised your paper, you will, of course, still need to edit it — refining your style and making any necessary changes in grammar, punctuation, and spelling. But as you make these final changes, you can feel confident about what you have written if you know that you have looked closely at a work of literature, chosen a clearly defined approach for writing about it, and supported any claims that you made. Such a paper will reveal a serious effort to understand what another writer has created.

ABALONE, ABALONE, ABALONE

Toshio Mori

Born in California, Toshio Mori writes short stories that draw upon his Japanese heritage. The following story, which is very short, has only two characters and a very simple plot. But like many longer stories, it has what is often called a "turning point"—a moment in the story when a character changes as the result of something that has happened. Be alert for the turning point as you read this story, and consider whether or not the change is beneficial. It may help you to know that an abalone is a type of large mollusk found in warm seas. Its flesh is eaten, and its ornamental shell is a source of mother-of-pearl.

Before Mr. Abe went away I used to see him quite often at his nursery. He was a carnation grower just as I am one today. At noontime I used to go to his front porch and look at his collection of abalone shells.

They were lined up side by side against the side of his house on the front porch. I was curious as to why he bothered to collect them. It was a lot of bother polishing them. I had often seen him sit for hours on Sundays and noon hours polishing each one of the shells with the greatest of care. Of course I knew these abalone shells were pretty. When the sun strikes the insides of these shells it is something beautiful to behold. But I could not understand why he continued collecting them when the front porch was practically full.

He used to watch for me every noon hour. When I appeared he would look out of his room and bellow, "Hello, young man!"

"Hello, Abe-*san*," I said. "I came to see the abalone shells."

Then he came out of the house and we sat on the front porch. But he did not tell me why he collected these shells. I think I have asked him dozens of times but each time he closed his mouth and refused to answer. 5

"Are you going to pass this collection of abalone shells on to your children?" I said.

"No," he said. "I want my children to collect for themselves. I wouldn't give it to them."

"Why?" I said. "When you die?"

Mr. Abe shook his head. "No. Not even when I die," he said. "I couldn't give the children what I see in these shells. The children must go out for themselves and find their own shells."

"Why, I thought this collecting hobby of abalone shells was a simple affair," I said. 10

"It is simple. Very simple," he said. But he would not tell me further.

For several years I went steadily to his front porch and looked at the beautiful shells. His collection was getting larger and larger. Mr. Abe sat and talked to me and on each occasion his hands were busy polishing shells.

"So you are still curious?" he said.

"Yes," I said.

One day while I was hauling the old soil from the benches and replacing it with new soil I found an abalone shell half buried in the dust between the benches. So I stopped working. I dropped my wheelbarrow and went to the faucet and washed the abalone shell with soap and water. I had a hard time taking the grime off the surface.

After forty minutes of cleaning and polishing the old shell it became interesting. I began polishing both the outside and the inside of the shell. I found after many minutes of polishing I could not do very much with the exterior side. It had scabs of the sea which would not come off by scrubbing and the surface itself was rough and hard. And in the crevices the grime stuck so that even with a needle it did not become clean.

But on the other side, the inside of the shell, the more I polished the more lustre I found. It had me going. There were colors which I had not seen in the abalone shells before or anywhere else. The different hues, running berserk in all directions, coming together in harmony. I guess I could say they were not unlike a rainbow which men once symbolized. As soon as I thought of this I thought of Mr. Abe.

I remember running to his place, looking for him. "Abe-*san!*" I said when I found him. "I know why you are collecting the abalone shells!"

He was watering the carnation plants in the greenhouse. He stopped watering and came over to where I stood. He looked me over closely for awhile and then his face beamed.

"All right," he said. "Do not say anything. Nothing, mind you. When you have found the reason why you must collect and preserve them, you do not have to say anything more."

"I want you to see it, Abe-*san*," I said.

"All right. Tonight," he said. "Where did you find it?"

"In my old greenhouse, half buried in the dust," I said.

He chuckled. "That is pretty far from the ocean," he said, "but pretty close to you."

At each noon hour I carried my abalone shell and went over to Mr. Abe's front porch. While I waited for his appearance I kept myself busy polishing the inside of the shell with a rag.

One day I said, "Abe-*san,* now I have three shells."

"Good!" he said. "Keep it up!"

"I have to keep them all," I said. "They are very much alike and very much different."

"Well! Well!" he said and smiled.

That was the last I saw of Abe-*san*. Before the month was over he sold his nursery and went back to Japan. He brought his collection along and thereafter I had no one to talk to at the noon hour. This was before I discovered the fourth abalone shell, and I should like to see Abe-*san* someday and watch his eyes roll as he studies me whose face is now akin to the collectors of shells or otherwise.

Questions for Discussion

1. How do you picture the narrator of this story? How old is he? What is he like at the beginning of the story? Is he the same at the end? If not, how does he change, and where does this change begin?
2. Why does Mr. Abe refuse to discuss his collection of abalone shells? Why doesn't he plan to leave his collection to his children?
3. The act of polishing an abalone shell would seem to be very simple. But is it as simple as it seems? Why is it worth doing?
4. This story begins and ends with references to Mr. Abe going away, and paragraphs 8–9 mention his eventual death. What does this sense of passing away contribute to the story?
5. How do you interpret the title of this story? Could someone understand the title without reading the story?

Suggestions for Writing

1. Describe the setting of "Abalone, Abalone, Abalone," and explain why it is appropriate for what happens in this story.
2. A symbol is something that means both what it is and something more than it is. The rainbow (mentioned in paragraph 17) has been used as a symbol for new beginnings. If you think the abalone shell stands for something else, write an essay explaining what it symbolizes and how you came to this conclusion.

SHOPPING

Joyce Carol Oates

> *Bumper stickers, in recent years, have featured slogans such as "Born to shop" and "When the going gets tough, the tough go shopping." For many Americans shopping has become an important ritual — and the mall a type of second home. In the following story Joyce Carol Oates uses a Saturday morning trip to the mall as a way to reveal character and conflict. The characters are an upper-middle-class woman and her seventeen-year-old daughter. As you read, try to understand why these characters conflict. The author of many novels and collections of short stories, Joyce Carol Oates teaches writing at Princeton.*

An old ritual, Saturday morning shopping. Mother and daughter. Mrs. Dietrich and Nola. Shops in the village, stores and boutiques at the splendid Livingstone Mall on Route 12. Bloomingdale's, Saks, Lord & Taylor, Bonwit's, Neiman-Marcus: and the rest. Mrs. Dietrich would know her way around the stores blindfolded but there is always the surprise of lavish seasonal displays, extraordinary holiday sales, the openings of new stores at the Mall like Laura Ashley, Paraphernalia. On one of their Mall days Mrs. Dietrich and Nola would try to get there at midmorning, have lunch around 1 P.M. at one or another of their favorite restaurants, shop for perhaps an hour after lunch, then come home. Sometimes the shopping trips were more successful than at other times but you have to have faith, Mrs. Dietrich tells herself. Her interior voice is calm, neutral, free of irony. Ever since her divorce her interior voice has been free of irony. You have to have faith.

Tomorrow morning Nola returns to school in Maine; today will be a day at the Mall. Mrs. Dietrich has planned it for days. At the Mall, in such crowds of shoppers, moments of intimacy are possible as they rarely are at home. (Seventeen-year-old Nola, home on spring break for a brief eight days, seems always to be *busy,* always out with her *friends* — the trip to the Mall has been postponed twice.) But Saturday, 10:30 A.M., they are in the car at last headed south on Route 12, a bleak March morning following a night of freezing rain, there's a metallic cast to the air and no sun anywhere in the sky but the light hurts Mrs. Dietrich's eyes just the same. "Does it seem as if spring will ever come? — it must be twenty degrees colder up in Maine," she says. Driving in heavy traffic always makes Mrs. Dietrich nervous and she is overly sensitive to her daughter's silence, which seems deliberate, perverse, when they have so little time remaining together — not even a full day.

Nola asks politely if Mrs. Dietrich would like her to drive and Mrs. Dietrich says no, of course not, she's fine, it's only a few more miles and maybe traffic will lighten. Nola seems about to say something more, then

thinks better of it. So much between them that is precarious, chancy —
but they've been kind to each other these past seven days. Mrs. Dietrich
loves Nola with a fierce unreasoned passion stronger than any she felt for
the man who had been her husband for thirteen years, certainly far
stronger than any she ever felt for her own mother. Sometimes in weak
despondent moods, alone, lonely, self-pitying, when she has had too much
to drink, Mrs. Dietrich thinks she is in love with her daughter — but
this is a thought she can't contemplate for long. And how Nola would
snort in amused contempt, incredulous, mocking — "Oh *Mother!*" — if she
were told.

Mrs. Dietrich tries to engage her daughter in conversation of a harmless sort but Nola answers in monosyllables, Nola is rather tired from so
many nights of partying with her friends, some of whom attend the local
high school, some of whom are home for spring break from prep
schools — Exeter, Lawrenceville, Concord, Andover, Portland. Late
nights, but Mrs. Dietrich doesn't consciously lie awake waiting for Nola
to come home: they've been through all that before. Now Nola sits beside
her mother looking wan, subdued, rather melancholy. Thinking her private thoughts. She is wearing a bulky quilted jacket Mrs. Dietrich has
never liked, the usual blue jeans, black calfskin boots zippered tightly to
mid-calf. Mrs. Dietrich must resist the temptation to ask, "Why are you
so quiet, Nola? What are you thinking?" They've been through all that
before.

Route 12 has become a jumble of small industrial parks, high-rise   5
office and apartment buildings, torn-up landscapes — mountains of raw
earth, uprooted trees, ruts and ditches filled with muddy water. There is
no natural sequence to what you see — buildings, construction work, lev-
eled woods, the lavish grounds owned by Squibb. Though she has driven
this route countless times, Mrs. Dietrich is never quite certain where the
Mall is and must be prepared for a sudden exit. She remembers getting
lost the first several times, remembers the excitement she and her friends
felt about the grand opening of the Mall, stores worthy of serious shopping at last. Today is much the same. No, today is worse. Like Christmas
when she was a small child, Mrs. Dietrich thinks. She'd hoped so badly
to be happy she'd felt actual pain, a constriction in her throat like crying.

"*Are* you all right, Nola? — you've been so quiet all morning," Mrs.
Dietrich asks, half-scolding. Nola stirs from her reverie, says she's fine, a
just perceptible edge to her reply, and for the remainder of the drive there's
some stiffness between them. Mrs. Dietrich chooses to ignore it. In any
case she is fully absorbed in driving — negotiating a tricky exit across two
lanes of traffic, then the hairpin curve of the ramp, the numerous looping
drives of the Mall. Then the enormous parking lot, daunting to the inexperienced, but Mrs. Dietrich always heads for the area behind Lord &
Taylor on the far side of the Mall, Lot D; her luck holds and she finds a
space close in. "Well — we made it," she says, smiling happily at Nola.

Nola laughs in reply — what does a seventeen-year-old's laughter *mean?* — but she remembers, getting out, to lock both doors on her side of the car. The smile Nola gives Mrs. Dietrich across the car's roof is careless and beautiful and takes Mrs. Dietrich's breath away.

The March morning tastes of grit with an undercurrent of something acrid, chemical; inside the Mall, beneath the first of the elegant brass-buttressed glass domes, the air is fresh and tonic, circulating from invisible vents. The Mall is crowded, rather noisy — it *is* Saturday morning — but a feast for the eyes after that long trip on Route 12. Tall slender trees grow out of the mosaic-tiled pavement, there are beds of Easter lilies, daffodils, jonquils, tulips of all colors. Mrs. Dietrich smiles with relief. She senses that Nola too is relieved, cheered. It's like coming home.

The shopping excursions began when Nola was a small child but did not acquire their special significance until she was twelve or thirteen years old and capable of serious, sustained shopping with her mother. This was about the time when Mr. Dietrich moved out of the house and back into their old apartment in the city — a separation, he'd called it initially, to give them perspective — though Mrs. Dietrich had no illusions about what "perspective" would turn out to entail — so the shopping trips were all the more significant. Not that Mrs. Dietrich and Nola spent very much money — they really didn't, *really* they didn't, when compared to friends and neighbors.

At seventeen Nola is shrewd and discerning as a shopper, not easy to please, knowledgeable as a mature woman about certain aspects of fashion, quality merchandise, good stores. Her closets, like Mrs. Dietrich's, are crammed, but she rarely buys anything that Mrs. Dietrich thinks shoddy or merely faddish. Up in Portland, at the Academy, she hasn't as much time to shop but when she is home in Livingstone it isn't unusual for her and her girlfriends to shop nearly every day. Like all her friends she has charge accounts at the better stores, her own credit cards, a reasonable allowance. At the time of their settlement Mr. Dietrich said guiltily that it was the least he could do for them — if Mrs. Dietrich wanted to work part-time, she could (she was trained, more or less, in public relations of a small-scale sort); if not, not. Mrs. Dietrich thought, It's the most you can do for us too.

Near Bloomingdale's entrance mother and daughter see a disheveled woman sitting by herself on one of the benches. Without seeming to look at her, shoppers are making a discreet berth around her, a stream following a natural course. Nola, taken by surprise, stares. Mrs. Dietrich has seen the woman from time to time at the Mall, always alone, smirking and talking to herself, frizzed gray hair in a tangle, puckered mouth. Always wearing the same black wool coat, a garment of fairly good quality but shapeless, rumpled, stained, as if she sleeps in it. She might be anywhere   10 from forty to sixty years of age. Once Mrs. Dietrich saw her make menacing gestures at children who were teasing her, another time she'd seen the woman staring belligerently at *her*. A white paste had gathered in the corners of her mouth. . . . "My God, that poor woman," Nola says. "I didn't think there were people like her here—I mean, I didn't think they would allow it."

"She doesn't seem to cause any disturbance," Mrs. Dietrich says. "She just sits—Don't stare, Nola, she'll see you."

"You've seen her here before? Here?"

"A few times this winter."

"Is she always like that?"

"I'm sure she's harmless, Nola. She just *sits*."   15

Nola is incensed, her pale blue eyes like washed glass. "I'm sure *she's* harmless, Mother. It's the harm the poor woman has to endure that is the tragedy."

Mrs. Dietrich is surprised and a little offended by her daughter's passionate tone but she knows enough not to argue. They enter Bloomingdale's, taking their habitual route. So many shoppers!—so much merchandise! Nola speaks of the tragedy of women like that woman—the tragedy of the homeless, the mentally disturbed—bag ladies out on the street—outcasts of an affluent society—but she's soon distracted by the busyness on all sides, the attractive items for sale. They take the escalator up to the third floor, to the Juniors department where Nola often buys things. From there they will move on to Young Collector, then to New Impressions, then to Petites, then one or another boutique and designer—Liz Claiborne, Christian Dior, Calvin Klein, Carlos Falchi, and the rest. And after Bloomingdale's the other stores await, to be visited each in turn. Mrs. Dietrich checks her watch and sees with satisfaction that there's just enough time before lunch but not *too* much time. She gets ravenously hungry, shopping at the Mall.

Nola is efficient and matter-of-fact about shopping, though she acts solely upon instinct. Mrs. Dietrich likes to watch her at a short distance—holding items of clothing up to herself in the three-way mirrors, modeling things she thinks especially promising. A twill blazer with rounded shoulders and blouson jacket, a funky zippered jumpsuit in white sailcloth, a pair of straight-leg Evan-Picone pants, a green leather vest: Mrs. Dietrich watches her covertly. At such times Nola is perfectly content, fully absorbed in the task at hand; Mrs. Dietrich knows she isn't thinking about anything that would distress her. (Like Mr. Dietrich's betrayal. Like Nola's difficulties with her friends. Like her difficulties at school—as much as Mrs. Dietrich knows of them.) Once, at the Mall, perhaps in this very store in this very department, Nola saw Mrs. Dietrich watching her and walked away angrily and when Mrs. Dietrich caught up with her she said, "I can't stand it, Mother." Her voice was choked and harsh, a vein prominent in her forehead. "Let me go. For Christ's sake will you let me go."

Mrs. Dietrich didn't dare touch her though she could see Nola was trembling. For a long terrible moment mother and daughter stood side by side near a display of bright brash Catalina beachwear while Nola whispered, "Let me go. *Let me go.*"

Difficult to believe that girl standing so poised and self-assured in front of the three-way mirror was once a plain, rather chunky, unhappy child. She'd been unpopular at school. Overly serious. Anxious. Quick to tears. Aged eleven she hid herself away in her room for hours at a time, reading, drawing pictures, writing little stories she could sometimes be prevailed upon to read aloud to her mother, sometimes even to her father, though she dreaded his judgment. She went through a "scientific" phase a while later—Mrs. Dietrich remembers an ambitious bas-relief map of North America, meticulous illustrations for "photosynthesis," a pastel drawing of an eerie ball of fire labeled "Red Giant" (a dying star?) which won a prize in a state competition for junior high students. Then for a season it was stray facts Nola confronted them with, often at the dinner table. Interrupting her parents' conversation to say brightly: "Did you know that Nero's favorite color was green?—he carried a giant emerald and held it up to his eye to watch Christians being devoured by lions." And once at a large family gathering: "Did you know that last week downtown a little baby's nose was chewed off by rats in his crib?—a little *black* baby?" Nola meant only to call attention to herself but you couldn't blame her listeners for being offended. They stared at her, not knowing what to say. What a strange child! What queer glassy-pale eyes! Mr. Dietrich told her curtly to leave the table—he'd had enough of the game she was playing and so had everyone else.

Nola stared at him, her eyes filling with tears. Game?   20

When they were alone Mr. Dietrich said angrily to Mrs. Dietrich: "Can't you control her in front of other people, at least?" Mrs. Dietrich was angry too, and frightened. She said "I *try.*"

They sent her off aged fourteen to the Portland Academy up in Maine and without their help she matured into a girl of considerable beauty. A heart-shaped face, delicate features, glossy red-brown hair scissor-cut to her shoulders. Five feet seven inches tall, weighing less than one hundred pounds—the result of constant savage dieting. (Mrs. Dietrich, who has weight problems herself, doesn't dare to inquire as to details. They've been through that already.) Thirty days after they'd left her at the Portland Academy Nola telephoned home at 11:00 P.M. one Sunday giggly and high telling Mrs. Dietrich she adored the school she adored her suite mates she adored most of her teachers particularly her riding instructor Terri, Terri the Terrier they called the woman because she was so fierce, such a character, eyes that bore right through your skull, wore belts with the most amazing silver buckles! Nola loved Terri but she wasn't *in* love—there's a difference!

Mrs. Dietrich broke down weeping, *that* time.

Now of course Nola has boyfriends. Mrs. Dietrich has long since given up trying to keep track of their names. There is even one "boy" — or young man — who seems to be married: who seems to be, in fact, one of the junior instructors at the school. (Mrs. Dietrich does not eavesdrop on her daughter's telephone conversations but there are things she cannot help overhearing.) Is your daughter on the Pill? the women in Mrs. Dietrich's circle asked one another for a while, guiltily, surreptitiously. Now they no longer ask.

But Nola has announced recently that she loathes boys — she's fed   25
up.

She's never going to get married. She'll study languages in college, French, Italian, something exotic like Arabic, go to work for the American foreign service. Unless she drops out of school altogether to become a model.

"Do you think I'm fat, Mother?" she asks frequently, worriedly, standing in front of the mirror twisted at the waist to reveal her small round belly which, it seems, can't help being round: she bloats herself on diet Cokes all day long. "Do you think it *shows*?"

When Mrs. Dietrich was pregnant with Nola she'd been twenty-nine years old and she and Mr. Dietrich had tried to have a baby for nearly five years. She'd lost hope, begun to despise herself, then suddenly it happened: like grace. Like happiness swelling so powerfully it can barely be contained. I can hear its heartbeat! her husband exclaimed. He'd been her lover then, young, vigorous, dreamy. Caressing the rock-hard belly, splendid white tight-stretched skin. Mr. Dietrich gave Mrs. Dietrich a reproduction on stiff glossy paper of Dante Gabriel Rossetti's *Beata Beatrix,* embarrassed, apologetic, knowing it was sentimental and perhaps a little silly but that was how he thought of her — so beautiful, rapturous, pregnant with their child. She told no one but she knew the baby was to be a girl. It would be herself again, reborn and this time perfect.

"Oh, Mother — isn't it *beautiful*?" Nola exclaims.

It is past noon. Past twelve-thirty. Mrs. Dietrich and Nola have made   30
the rounds of a half-dozen stores, traveled countless escalators, one clothing department has blended into the next and the chic smiling saleswomen have become indistinguishable and Mrs. Dietrich is beginning to feel the urgent need for a glass of white wine. Just a glass. "Isn't it beautiful? — it's *perfect*," Nola says. Her eyes glow with pleasure, her smooth skin is radiant. As Nola models in the three-way mirror a queer little yellow-and-black striped sweater with a ribbed waist, punk style, mock-cheap, Mrs. Dietrich feels the motherly obligation to register a mild protest, knowing that Nola will not hear. She must have it and will have it. She'll wear it a few times, then retire it to the bottom of a drawer with so many other novelty sweaters, accumulated since sixth grade. (She's like her mother in that regard — can't bear to throw anything away.)

"*Isn't* it beautiful?" Nola demands, studying her reflection in the mirror.

Mrs. Dietrich pays for the sweater on her charge account.

Next, they buy Nola a good pair of shoes. And a handbag to go with them. In Paraphernalia, where rock music blasts overhead and Mrs. Dietrich stands to one side, rather miserable, Nola chats companionably with two girls — tall, pretty, cutely made up — she'd gone to public school in Livingstone with, says afterward with an upward rolling of her eyes, "God, I was afraid they'd latch on to us!" Mrs. Dietrich has seen women friends and acquaintances of her own in the Mall this morning but has shrunk from being noticed, not wanting to share her daughter with anyone. She has a sense of time passing ever more swiftly, cruelly.

She watches Nola preening in a mirror, watches other shoppers watching her. My daughter. Mine. But of course there is no connection between them — they don't even resemble each other. A seventeen-year-old, a forty-seven-year-old. When Nola is away she seems to forget her mother entirely — doesn't telephone, certainly doesn't write. It's the way all their daughters are, Mrs. Dietrich's friends tell her. It doesn't *mean* anything. Mrs. Dietrich thinks how when she was carrying Nola, those nine long months, they'd been completely happy — not an instant's doubt or hesitation. The singular weight of the body. A trancelike state you are tempted to mistake for happiness because the body is incapable of thinking, therefore incapable of anticipating change. Hot rhythmic blood, organs, packed tight and moist, the baby upside down in her sac in her mother's belly, always present tense, always *now*. It was a shock when the end came so abruptly but everyone told Mrs. Dietrich she was a natural mother, praised and pampered her. For a while. Then of course she'd had her baby, her Nola. Even now Mrs. Dietrich can't really comprehend the experience. *Giving birth. Had a baby. Was born.* Mere words, absurdly inadequate. She knows no more of how love ends than she knew as a child, she knows only of how love begins — in the belly, in the womb, where it is always present tense.

The morning's shopping has been quite successful but lunch at La Crêperie doesn't go well for some reason. La Crêperie is Nola's favorite Mall restaurant — always amiably crowded, bustling, a simulated sidewalk café with red-striped umbrellas, wrought-iron tables and chairs, menus in French, music piped in overhead. Mrs. Dietrich's nerves are chafed by the pretense of gaiety, the noise, the openness onto one of the Mall's busy promenades where at any minute a familiar face might emerge, but she is grateful for her glass of chilled white wine. She orders a small tossed salad and a creamed-chicken crepe and devours it hungrily — she *is* hungry. While Nola picks at her seafood crepe with a disdainful look. A familiar scene: mother watching while daughter pushes food around on her plate. Suddenly Nola is tense, moody, corners of her mouth downturned. Mrs. Dietrich wants to ask, What's wrong? She wants to ask, Why are you unhappy? She wants to smooth Nola's hair back from her forehead, check to see if her forehead is overly warm, wants to hug her close, hard. Why, why? What did I do wrong? Why do you hate me?

Calling the Portland Academy a few weeks ago Mrs. Dietrich suddenly lost control, began crying. She hadn't been drinking and she hadn't known she was upset. A girl unknown to her, one of Nola's suite mates, was saying, "Please, Mrs. Dietrich, it's all right, I'm sure Nola will call you back later tonight, or tomorrow, Mrs. Dietrich? — I'll tell her you called, all right? — Mrs. Dietrich?" as embarrassed as if Mrs. Dietrich had been her own mother.

How love begins. How love ends.

Mrs. Dietrich orders a third glass of wine. This is a celebration of sorts isn't it? — their last shopping trip for a long time. But Nola resists, Nola isn't sentimental. In casual defiance of Mrs. Dietrich she lights up a cigarette — yes, Mother, Nola has said ironically, since *you* stopped smoking *everybody* is supposed to stop — and sits with her arms crossed, watching streams of shoppers pass. Mrs. Dietrich speaks lightly of practical matters, tomorrow morning's drive to the airport, and will Nola telephone when she gets to Portland to let Mrs. Dietrich know she has arrived safely?

Then with no warning — though of course she'd been planning this all along — Nola brings up the subject of a semester in France, in Paris and Rouen, the fall semester of her senior year it would be; she has put in her application, she says, and is waiting to hear if she's been accepted. She smokes her cigarette calmly, expelling smoke from her nostrils in a way Mrs. Dietrich thinks particularly coarse. Mrs. Dietrich, who believed that particular topic was finished, takes care to speak without emotion. "I just don't think it's a very practical idea right now, Nola," she says. "We've been through it haven't we? I — "

"I'm going," Nola says.   40

"The extra expense, for one thing. Your father — "

"If I get accepted, I'm going."

"Your father — "

"The hell with him too."

Mrs. Dietrich would like to slap her daughter's face. Bring tears to   45
those steely eyes. But she sits stiff, turning her wine glass between her fingers, patient, calm, she's heard all this before; she says, "Surely this isn't the best time to discuss it, Nola."

Mrs. Dietrich is afraid her daughter will leave the restaurant, simply walk away, that has happened before and if it happens today she doesn't know what she will do. But Nola sits unmoving; her face closed, impassive. Mrs. Dietrich feels her quickened heartbeat. Once after one of their quarrels Mrs. Dietrich told a friend of hers, the mother too of a teenage daughter, "I just don't know her any longer, how can you keep living with someone you don't know?" and the woman said, "Eventually you can't."

Nola says, not looking at Mrs. Dietrich: "Why don't we talk about it, Mother?"

"Talk about what?" Mrs. Dietrich asks.

"You know."

The semester in France? Again?"   50

"No."

"What, then?"

"You *know*."

"I don't know, really. Really!" Mrs. Dietrich smiles, baffled. She feels the corners of her eyes pucker white with strain.

Nola says, sighing, "How exhausting it is."   55

"How *what*?"

"How exhausting it is."

"What is?"

"You and me — "

"What?"   60

"Being together — "

"Being together how — ?"

"The two of us, like this — "

"But we're hardly ever together, Nola," Mrs. Dietrich says.

Her expression is calm but her voice is shaking. Nola turns away,   65
covering her face with a hand, for a moment she looks years older than her age — in fact exhausted. Mrs. Dietrich sees with pity that her daughter's skin is fair and thin and dry — unlike her own, which tends to be oily — it will wear out before she's forty. Mrs. Dietrich reaches over to squeeze her hand. The fingers are limp, ungiving. "You're going back to school tomorrow, Nola," she says. "You won't come home again until June 12. And you probably will go to France — if your father consents."

Nola gets to her feet, drops her cigarette to the flagstone terrace and grinds it beneath her boot. A dirty thing to do, Mrs. Dietrich thinks, considering there's an ashtray right on the table, but she says nothing. She dislikes La Crêperie anyway.

Nola laughs, showing her lovely white teeth. "Oh, the hell with him," she says. "Fuck Daddy, right?"

They separate for an hour, Mrs. Dietrich to Neiman-Marcus to buy a birthday gift for her elderly aunt, Nola to the trendy new boutique Pour Vous. By the time Mrs. Dietrich rejoins her daughter she's quite angry, blood beating hot and hard and measured in resentment, she has had time to relive old quarrels between them, old exchanges, stray humiliating memories of her marriage as well, these last-hour disagreements are the cruelest and they are Nola's specialty. She locates Nola in the rear of the boutique amid blaring rock music, flashing neon lights, chrome-edged mirrors, her face still hard, closed, prim, pale. She stands beside another teenage girl looking in a desultory way through a rack of blouses, shoving the hangers roughly along, taking no care when a blouse falls to the floor.

As Nola glances up, startled, not prepared to see her mother in front of her, their eyes lock for an instant and Mrs. Dietrich stares at her with hatred. Cold calm clear unmistakable hatred. She is thinking, Who are *you*? What have I to do with *you*? I don't know *you*, I don't love *you*, why should I?

Has Nola seen, heard? — she turns aside as if wincing, gives the blouses a final dismissive shove. Her eyes look tired, the corners of her mouth downturned. Anxious, immediately repentant, Mrs. Dietrich asks if she has found anything worth trying on. Nola says with a shrug, "Not a thing, Mother."

On their way out of the Mall Mrs. Dietrich and Nola see the dishev- 70
eled woman in the black coat again, this time sitting prominently on a concrete ledge in front of Lord & Taylor's busy main entrance. Shopping bag at her feet, shabby purse on the ledge beside her. She is shaking her head in a series of annoyed twitches as if arguing with someone but her hands are loose, palms up, in her lap. Her posture is unfortunate — she sits with her knees parted, inner thighs revealed, fatty, dead white, the tops of cotton stockings rolled tight cutting into the flesh. Again, streams of shoppers are making a careful berth around her. Alone among them Nola hesitates, seems about to approach the woman — Please don't, Nola! please! Mrs. Dietrich thinks — then changes her mind and keeps on walking. Mrs. Dietrich murmurs isn't it a pity, poor thing, don't you wonder where she lives, who her family is, but Nola doesn't reply. Her pace through the first door of Lord & Taylor is so rapid that Mrs. Dietrich can barely keep up.

But Nola's upset. Strangely upset. As soon as they are in the car, packages and bags in the backseat, she begins crying.

It's childish helpless crying, as though her heart is broken. But Mrs. Dietrich knows it isn't broken, she has heard these very sobs before. Many times before. Still she comforts her daughter, embraces her, hugs her hard, hard. A sudden fierce passion. Vehemence. "Nola honey. Nola dear, what's wrong, dear, everything will be all right, dear," she says, close to weeping herself. She would embrace Nola even more tightly except for the girl's quilted jacket, that bulky L. L. Bean thing she has never liked, and Nola's stubborn lowered head. Nola has always been ashamed, crying, frantic to hide her face. Strangers are passing close by the car, curious, staring. Mrs. Dietrich wishes she had a cloak to draw over her daughter and herself, so that no one else would see.

Questions for Discussion

1. Reread the first two paragraphs of this story. Do they contain any signs of unhappiness or trouble?
2. Why are Mrs. Dietrich and her daughter silent in the car? Why do they feel they have to be careful about what they say to one another? How would you describe their relationship?

3. What is the significance of the title of this story? What are the characters shopping for? What does Mrs. Dietrich hope to experience by shopping with her daughter? What motivates Nola to go along? Why are they relieved to arrive at the mall?

4. What does the woman in the black coat represent? Why do the other shoppers try to avoid her? How do Mrs. Dietrich and Nola differ in their response to her?

5. What does the story reveal about Mr. Dietrich?

6. Why do we never learn Mrs. Dietrich's first name? What does this story suggest about her life from the glimpse of it we are allowed to see?

7. In paragraph 47 Nola abruptly asks, "Why don't we talk about it, Mother?" What is she referring to?

8. Why is Nola crying at the end of the story?

Suggestions for Writing

1. From whose point of view is "Shopping" told? Write an essay explaining how this is established and what influence it has upon your response to the story.

2. Compare Nola and Mrs. Dietrich. Despite their differences, how are they alike?

LULLABY

Leslie Marmon Silko

> *Born in New Mexico, Leslie Silko writes fiction that draws upon her heritage as a Native American. As you read the following story, pay particular attention to the scene. Note details about the landscape and the weather, and consider the relationship between the characters and the land. Consider what the story reveals about Native American culture, but consider also whether the story raises any concerns of universal significance.*

The sun had gone down but the snow in the wind gave off its own light. It came in thick tufts like new wool — washed before the weaver spins it. Ayah reached out for it like her own babies had, and she smiled when she remembered how she had laughed at them. She was an old woman now, and her life had become memories. She sat down with her back against the wide cottonwood tree, feeling the rough bark on her back bones; she faced east and listened to the wind and snow sing a high-pitched Yeibechei° song. Out of the wind she felt warmer, and she could watch the wide fluffy snow fill in her tracks, steadily, until the direction she had come from was gone. By the light of the snow she could see the dark outline of the big arroyo a few feet away. She was sitting on the edge of Cebolleta Creek, where in the springtime the thin cows would graze on grass already chewed flat to the ground. In the wide deep creek bed where only a trickle of water flowed in the summer, the skinny cows would wander, looking for new grass along winding paths splashed with manure.

Ayah pulled the old Army blanket over her head like a shawl. Jimmie's blanket — the one he had sent to her. That was a long time ago and the green wool was faded, and it was unraveling on the edges. She did not want to think about Jimmie. So she thought about the weaving and the way her mother had done it. On the tall wooden loom set into the sand under a tamarack tree for shade. She could see it clearly. She had been only a little girl when her grandma gave her the wooden combs to pull the twigs and burrs from the raw, freshly washed wool. And while she combed the wool, her grandma sat beside her, spinning a silvery strand of yarn around the smooth cedar spindle. Her mother worked at the loom with yarns dyed bright yellow and red and gold. She watched them dye the yarn in boiling black pots full of beeweed petals, juniper berries, and sage. The blankets her mother made were soft and woven so tight that rain rolled off them like birds' feathers. Ayah remembered sleeping warm on cold windy nights, wrapped in her mother's blankets on the hogan's sandy floor.

The snow drifted now, with the northwest wind hurling it in gusts. It drifted up around her black overshoes — old ones with little metal buckles.

Yeibechei: A Navajo song of healing.

She smiled at the snow which was trying to cover her little by little. She could remember when they had no black rubber overshoes; only the high buckskin leggings that they wrapped over their elkhide moccasins. If the snow was dry or frozen, a person could walk all day and not get wet; and in the evenings the beams of the ceiling would hang with lengths of pale buckskin leggings, drying out slowly.

She felt peaceful remembering. She didn't feel cold any more. Jimmie's blanket seemed warmer than it had ever been. And she could remember the morning he was born. She could remember whispering to her mother, who was sleeping on the other side of the hogan,° to tell her it was time now. She did not want to wake the others. The second time she called to her, her mother stood up and pulled on her shoes; she knew. They walked to the old stone hogan together, Ayah walking a step behind her mother. She waited alone, learning the rhythms of the pains while her mother went to call the old woman to help them. The morning was already warm even before dawn and Ayah smelled the bee flowers blooming and the young willow growing at the springs. She could remember that so clearly, but his birth merged into the births of the other children and to her it became all the same birth. They named him for the summer morning and in English they called him Jimmie.

It wasn't like Jimmie died. He just never came back, and one day a   5
dark blue sedan with white writing on its doors pulled up in front of the boxcar shack where the rancher let the Indians live. A man in a khaki uniform trimmed in gold gave them a yellow piece of paper and told them that Jimmie was dead. He said the Army would try to get the body back and then it would be shipped to them; but it wasn't likely because the helicopter had burned after it crashed. All of this was told to Chato because he could understand English. She stood inside the doorway holding the baby while Chato listened. Chato spoke English like a white man and he spoke Spanish too. He was taller than the white man and he stood straighter too. Chato didn't explain why; he just told the military man they could keep the body if they found it. The white man looked bewildered; he nodded his head and he left. Then Chato looked at her and shook his head, and then he told her, "Jimmie isn't coming home anymore," and when he spoke, he used the words to speak of the dead. She didn't cry then, but she hurt inside with anger. And she mourned him as the years passed, when a horse fell with Chato and broke his leg, and the white rancher told them he wouldn't pay Chato until he could work again. She mourned Jimmie because he would have worked for his father then; he would have saddled the big bay horse and ridden the fence lines each day, with wire cutters and heavy gloves, fixing the breaks in the barbed wire and putting the stray cattle back inside again.

hogan: A traditional Navajo dwelling made of logs and mud, with a door facing east.

She mourned him after the white doctors came to take Danny and Ella away. She was at the shack alone that day they came. It was back in the days before they hired Navajo women to go with them as interpreters. She recognized one of the doctors. She had seen him at the children's clinic at Cañoncito about a month ago. They were wearing khaki uniforms and they waved papers at her and a black ball-point pen, trying to make her understand their English words. She was frightened by the way they looked at the children, like the lizard watches the fly. Danny was swinging on the tire swing on the elm tree behind the rancher's house, and Ella was toddling around the front door, dragging the broomstick horse Chato made for her. Ayah could see they wanted her to sign the papers, and Chato had taught her to sign her name. It was something she was proud of. She only wanted them to go, and to take their eyes away from her children.

She took the pen from the man without looking at his face and she signed the papers in three different places he pointed to. She stared at the ground by their feet and waited for them to leave. But they stood there and began to point and gesture at the children. Danny stopped swinging. Ayah could see his fear. She moved suddenly and grabbed Ella into her arms; the child squirmed, trying to get back to her toys. Ayah ran with the baby toward Danny; she screamed for him to run and then she grabbed him around his chest and carried him too. She ran south into the foothills of juniper trees and black lava rock. Behind her she heard the doctors running, but they had been taken by surprise, and as the hills became steeper and the cholla cactus were thicker, they stopped. When she reached the top of the hill, she stopped to listen in case they were circling around her. But in a few minutes she heard a car engine start and they drove away. The children had been too surprised to cry while she ran with them. Danny was shaking and Ella's little fingers were gripping Ayah's blouse.

She stayed up in the hills for the rest of the day, sitting on a black lava boulder in the sunshine where she could see for miles all around her. The sky was light blue and cloudless, and it was warm for late April. The sun warmth relaxed her and took the fear and anger away. She lay back on the rock and watched the sky. It seemed to her that she could walk into the sky, stepping through clouds endlessly. Danny played with little pebbles and stones, pretending they were birds eggs and then little rabbits. Ella sat at her feet and dropped fistfuls of dirt into the breeze, watching the dust and particles of sand intently. Ayah watched a hawk soar high above them, dark wings gliding; hunting or only watching, she did not know. The hawk was patient and he circled all afternoon before he disappeared around the high volcanic peak the Mexicans called Guadalupe.

Late in the afternoon, Ayah looked down at the gray boxcar shack with the paint all peeled from the wood; the stove pipe on the roof was rusted and crooked. The fire she had built that morning in the oil drum stove had burned out. Ella was asleep in her lap now and Danny sat close to her, complaining that he was hungry; he asked when they would go to the house. "We will stay up here until your father comes," she told him, "because those white men were chasing us." The boy remembered then and he nodded at her silently.

If Jimmie had been there he could have read those papers and ex-   *10*
plained to her what they said. Ayah would have known then, never to sign them. The doctors came back the next day and they brought a BIA°policeman with them. They told Chato they had her signature and that was all they needed. Except for the kids. She listened to Chato sullenly; she hated him when he told her it was the old woman who died in the winter, spitting blood; it was her old grandma who had given the children this disease. "They don't spit blood," she said coldly. "The whites lie." She held Ella and Danny close to her, ready to run to the hills again. "I want a medicine man first," she said to Chato, not looking at him. He shook his head. "It's too late now. The policeman is with them. You signed the paper." His voice was gentle.

It was worse than if they had died: to lose the children and to know that somewhere, in a place called Colorado, in a place full of sick and dying strangers, her children were without her. There had been babies that died soon after they were born, and one that died before he could walk. She had carried them herself, up to the boulders and great pieces of the cliff that long ago crashed down from Long Mesa; she laid them in the crevices of sandstone and buried them in fine brown sand with round quartz pebbles that washed down the hills in the rain. She had endured it because they had been with her. But she could not bear this pain. She did not sleep for a long time after they took her children. She stayed on the hill where they had fled the first time, and she slept rolled up in the blanket Jimmie had sent her. She carried the pain in her belly and it was fed by everything she saw: the blue sky of their last day together and the dust and pebbles they played with; the swing in the elm tree and broomstick horse choked life from her. The pain filled her stomach and there was no room for food or for her lungs to fill with air. The air and the food would have been theirs.

She hated Chato, not because he let the policeman and doctors put the screaming children in the government car, but because he had taught her to sign her name. Because it was like the old ones always told her about learning their language or any of their ways: it endangered you. She slept alone on the hill until the middle of November when the first snows came. Then she made a bed for herself where the children had slept. She did not lie down beside Chato again until many years later, when he was sick and shivering and only her body could keep him warm. The illness came after the white rancher told Chato he was too old to work for him anymore,

BIA: U.S. Bureau of Indian Affairs.

and Chato and his old woman should be out of the shack by the next afternoon because the rancher had hired new people to work there. That had satisfied her. To see how the white man repaid Chato's years of loyalty and work. All of Chato's fine-sounding English talk didn't change things.

It snowed steadily and the luminous light from the snow gradually diminished into the darkness. Somewhere in Cebolleta a dog barked and other village dogs joined with it. Ayah looked in the direction she had come, from the bar where Chato was buying the wine. Sometimes he told her to go on ahead and wait; and then he never came. And when she finally went back looking for him, she would find him passed out at the bottom of the wooden steps to Azzie's Bar. All the wine would be gone and most of the money too, from the pale blue check that came to them once a month in a government envelope. It was then that she would look at his face and his hands, scarred by ropes and the barbed wire of all those years, and she would think, this man is a stranger; for forty years she had smiled at him and cooked his food, but he remained a stranger. She stood up again, with the snow almost to her knees, and she walked back to find Chato.

It was hard to walk in the deep snow and she felt the air burn in her lungs. She stopped a short distance from the bar to rest and readjust the blanket. But this time he wasn't waiting for her on the bottom step with his old Stetson hat pulled down and his shoulders hunched up in his long wool overcoat.

She was careful not to slip on the wooden steps. When she pushed   *15* the door open, warm air and cigarette smoke hit her face. She looked around slowly and deliberately, in every corner, in every dark place that the old man might find to sleep. The bar owner didn't like Indians in there, especially Navajos, but he let Chato come in because he could talk Spanish like he was one of them. The men at the bar stared at her, and the bartender saw that she left the door open wide. Snowflakes were flying inside like moths and melting into a puddle on the oiled wood floor. He motioned to her to close the door, but she did not see him. She held herself straight and walked across the room slowly, searching the room with every step. The snow in her hair melted and she could feel it on her forehead. At the far corner of the room, she saw red flames at the mica window of the old stove door; she looked behind the stove just to make sure. The bar got quiet except for the Spanish polka music playing on the jukebox. She stood by the stove and shook the snow from her blanket and held it near the stove to dry. The wet wool smell reminded her of new-born goats in early March, brought inside to warm near the fire. She felt calm.

In past years they would have told her to get out. But her hair was white now and her face was wrinkled. They looked at her like she was a spider crawling slowly across the room. They were afraid; she could feel the fear. She looked at their faces steadily. They reminded her of the first time the white people brought her children back to her that winter. Danny had been shy and hid behind the thin white woman who brought them. And the baby had not known her until Ayah took her into her arms, and then Ella had nuzzled close to her as she had when she was nursing. The blonde woman was nervous and kept looking at a dainty gold watch on her wrist. She sat on the bench near the small window and watched the dark snow clouds gather around the mountains; she was worrying about the unpaved road. She was frightened by what she saw inside too: the strips of venison drying on a rope across the ceiling and the children jabbering excitedly in a language she did not know. So they stayed for only a few hours. Ayah watched the government car disappear down the road and she knew they were already being weaned from these lava hills and from this sky. The last time they came was in early June, and Ella stared at her the way the men in the bar were now staring. Ayah did not try to pick her up; she smiled at her instead and spoke cheerfully to Danny. When he tried to answer her, he could not seem to remember and he spoke English words with the Navajo. But he gave her a scrap of paper that he had found somewhere and carried in his pocket; it was folded in half, and he shyly looked up at her and said it was a bird. She asked Chato if they were home for good this time. He spoke to the white woman and she shook her head. "How much longer?" he asked, and she said she didn't know; but Chato saw how she stared at the boxcar shack. Ayah turned away then. She did not say good-bye.

She felt satisfied that the men in the bar feared her. Maybe it was her face and the way she held her mouth with teeth clenched tight, like there was nothing anyone could do to her now. She walked north down the road, searching for the old man. She did this because she had the blanket, and there would be no place for him except with her and the blanket in the old adobe barn near the arroyo. They always slept there when they came to Cebolleta. If the money and the wine were gone, she would be relieved because then they could go home again; back to the old hogan with a dirt roof and rock walls where she herself had been born. And the next day the old man could go back to the few sheep they still had, to follow along behind them, guiding them, into dry sandy arroyos where sparse grass grew. She knew he did not like walking behind old ewes when for so many years he rode big quarter horses and worked with cattle. But she wasn't sorry for him; he should have known all along what would happen.

There had not been enough rain for their garden in five years; and that was when Chato finally hitched a ride into the town and brought back brown boxes of rice and sugar and big tin cans of welfare peaches. After that, at the first of the month they went to Cebolleta to ask the postmaster for the check; and then Chato would go to the bar and cash it. They did this as they planted the garden every May, not because anything would survive the summer dust, but because it was time to do this. The journey passed the days that smelled silent and dry like the caves above the canyon with yellow painted buffaloes on their walls.

He was walking along the pavement when she found him. He did not stop or turn around when he heard her behind him. She walked beside him and she noticed how slowly he moved now. He smelled strong of woodsmoke and urine. Lately he had been forgetting. Sometimes he called her by his sister's name and she had been gone for a long time. Once she had found him wandering on the road to the white man's ranch, and she asked him why he was going that way; he laughed at her and said, "You know they can't run that ranch without me," and he walked on determined, limping on the leg that had been crushed many years before. Now he looked at her curiously, as if for the first time, but he kept shuffling along, moving slowly along the side of the highway. His gray hair had grown long and spread out on the shoulders of the long overcoat. He wore the old felt hat pulled down over his ears. His boots were worn out at the toes and he had stuffed pieces of an old red shirt in the holes. The rags made his feet look like little animals up to their ears in snow. She laughed at his feet; the snow muffled the sound of her laugh. He stopped and looked at her again. The wind had quit blowing and the snow was falling straight down; the southeast sky was beginning to clear and Ayah could see a star.

"Let's rest awhile," she said to him. They walked away from the road   20
and up the slope to the giant boulders that had tumbled down from the red sandrock mesa throughout the centuries of rainstorms and earth tremors. In a place where the boulders shut out the wind, they sat down with their backs against the rock. She offered half of the blanket to him and they sat wrapped together.

The storm passed swiftly. The clouds moved east. They were massive and full, crowding together across the sky. She watched them with the feeling of horses — steely blue-gray horses startled across the sky. The powerful haunches pushed into the distances and the tail hairs streamed white mist behind them. The sky cleared. Ayah saw that there was nothing between her and the stars. The light was crystalline. There was no shimmer, no distortion through earth haze. She breathed the clarity of the night sky; she smelled the purity of the half moon and the stars. He was lying on his side with his knees pulled up near his belly for warmth. His eyes were closed now, and in the light from the stars and the moon, he looked young again.

She could see it descend out of the night sky: an icy stillness from the edge of the thin moon. She recognized the freezing. It came gradually, sinking snowflake by snowflake until the crust was heavy and deep. It had the strength of the stars in Orion, and its journey was endless. Ayah knew that with the wine he would sleep. He would not feel it. She tucked the blanket around him, remembering how it was when Ella had been with her; and she felt the rush so big inside her heart for the babies. And she sang the only song she knew to sing for babies. She could not remember if she had ever sung it to her children, but she knew that her grandmother had sung it and her mother had sung it:

> The earth is your mother,
>   she holds you.
> The sky is your father,
>   he protects you.
> Sleep,
> sleep.
> Rainbow is your sister,
>   she loves you.
> The winds are your brothers,
>   they sing to you.
> Sleep,
> sleep.
> We are together always
> We are together always
> There never was a time
> when this
> was not so.

Questions for Discussion

1. The first four sentences of this story include references to snow, wool, babies, and memories. Why are these references important for the story that follows?
2. Why does Ayah smile at the snow in paragraph 3? How would you describe her relationship to nature?
3. How had Ayah lost her children? What loss was the hardest for her to bear? Why?
4. What is the role of Jimmie in this story? Why does Silko emphasize that Jimmie had provided the blanket that shelters his mother?
5. Why are the men in the bar afraid of Ayah when she comes looking for Chato?
6. What does this story reveal about the relationship between Native Americans and Anglo-Americans? How do Ayah and Chato differ in their expectations about how they will be treated?
7. What happens at the end of this story? If Ayah recognizes that she and Chato are freezing, why does she let it happen?

Suggestions for Writing

1. Write an essay explaining why Ayah and Chato die in the cold. Where do you put the responsibility for their death?
2. Interpret the lullaby with which this story concludes, and explain how understanding the lullaby can help readers understand the story.

OFF FROM SWING SHIFT

Garrett Hongo

A common misconception about poetry, especially among people who do not read it, is that poetry is supposed to be about a limited number of subjects — like love and nature — that are, somehow, "poetic." Another common misconception is that poetry must be beautiful and inspirational. Experienced readers recognize that poetry, like fiction and drama, is about life in all its fullness and complexity. As you read the following poem, try to understand what the speaker is saying about his father's life.

Late, just past midnight,
freeway noise from the Harbor
and San Diego leaking in
from the vent over the stove,
and he's off from swing shift at Lear's.   5
Eight hours of twisting circuitry,
charting ohms and maximum gains
while transformers hum
and helicopters swirl
on the roofs above the small factory.   10
He hails me with a head-fake,
then the bob and weave
of a weekend middleweight
learned at the Y on Kapiolani
ten years before I was born.   15

The shoes and gold London Fogger
come off first, then the easy grin
saying he's lucky as they come.
He gets into the slippers
my brother gives him every Christmas,   20
carries his Thermos over to the sink,
and slides into the one chair at the table
that's made of wood and not yellow plastic.
He pushes aside stacks
of *Sporting News* and *Outdoor Life,*   25
big round tins of Holland butter cookies,
and clears a space for his elbows, his pens,
and the *Racing Form's* Late Evening Final.

His left hand reaches out,
flicks on the Sony transistor   30
we bought for his birthday
when I was fifteen.

The right ferries in the earphone,
a small, flesh-colored star,
like a tiny miracle of hearing,   *35*
and fits it into place.
I see him plot black constellations
of figures and calculations
on the magazine's margins,
alternately squint and frown   *40*
as he fingers the knob of the tuner
searching for the one band
that will call out today's results.

There are whole cosmologies
in a single handicap,   *45*
a lifetime of two-dollar losing
in one pick of the Daily Double.

Maybe tonight is his night
for winning, his night
for beating the odds   *50*
of going deaf from a shell
at Anzio still echoing
in the cave of his inner ear,
his night for cashing in
the blue chips of shrapnel still grinding   *55*
at the thickening joints of his legs.

But no one calls
the horse's name, no one
says Shackles, Rebate, or Pouring Rain.
No one speaks a word.   *60*

Questions for Discussion

1. What is a "swing shift"? In what sense is the man in the poem "off" from swing shift?
2. The first word in this poem is "Late." What does this suggest to you? Does it have a double meaning?
3. What contrast provides the focus for the opening stanza?
4. Consider lines 44–45. What does "handicap" mean within this context? How can there be "whole cosmologies/in a single handicap"? Does line 44 relate to any other lines in the poem?
5. What is the effect of repeating "no one" in lines 57–60?
6. Why are the horses named "Shackles," "Rebate," and "Pouring Rain"?

Suggestions for Writing

1. Describe the man who is the focus of this poem. What is his life like?
2. An *image* is a detail that appeals to one of our senses; it is usually something that we can visualize (such as "big round tins of Holland butter cookies"), but it can also be something we can hear, taste, or smell. Identify the images used in this poem, and explain what they suggest.

BLACK HAIR

Gary Soto

Some readers find poetry difficult because they try to read it as quickly as they read prose. Poetry usually needs to be read more slowly — and more than once — because poets try to convey meaning through language that has been compressed. "Black Hair" comes from a collection of poems that Gary Soto wrote about his family and friends. As you read it, note the details that the speaker provides about himself. But in addition to noting what the poem states, think about what else you can learn from it. Reread the poem, and consider what individual words suggest. Then try to reconstruct the story of the speaker's life.

At eight I was brilliant with my body.
In July, that ring of heat
We all jumped through, I sat in the bleachers
Of Romain Playground, in the lengthening
Shade that rose from our dirty feet.   5
The game before us was more than baseball.
It was a figure — Hector Moreno
Quick and hard with turned muscles,
His crouch the one I assumed before an altar
Of worn baseball cards, in my room.   10

I came here because I was Mexican, a stick
Of brown light in love with those
Who could do it — the triple and hard slide,
The gloves eating balls into double plays.
What could I do with 50 pounds, my shyness,   15
My black torch of hair, about to go out?
Father was dead, his face no longer
Hanging over the table or our sleep,
And mother was the terror of mouths
Twisting hurt by butter knives.   20

In the bleachers I was brilliant with my body,
Waving players in and stomping my feet,
Growing sweaty in the presence of white shirts.
I chewed sunflower seeds. I drank water
And bit my arm through the late innings.   25
When Hector lined balls into deep
Center, in my mind I rounded the bases
With him, my face flared, my hair lifting
Beautifully, because we were coming home
To the arms of brown people.   30

Questions for Discussion

1. Explain the opening line of this poem. Does it conflict with lines 11 and 15?
2. Why does the speaker watch baseball?
3. What does Hector Moreno represent? Is his first name significant?
4. What does it mean to be hurt by "butter knives"? Who is being hurt in lines 19–20?

Suggestions for Writing

1. Black hair is mentioned only once in this poem, but the title suggests that it is important. Can you explain line 16? Interpret the meaning of "torch," and explain why it could be "about to go out." Then explain the reference to hair in line 28. In your opinion, what does hair represent in the poem?
2. Discuss the last two lines of this poem. What does it mean to come "home/To the arms of brown people"? Does "Black Hair" offer any insight into what it means to be Hispanic?

SONNET 116

William Shakespeare

> *A sonnet is a fourteen-line poem, following a fixed rhythm and rhyme scheme. Each line consists of five units, called feet, and each foot consists of an unaccented syllable followed by an accented syllable. An English or Shakespearean sonnet consists of three* quatrains *(groups of four lines); in each quatrain the first line rhymes with the third and the second with the fourth. These twelve lines are followed by a* couplet, *which is a single pair of rhymed lines. As you read the following sonnet, notice that some of the rhymes are stronger than others. Consider whether perfect rhymes are important in poetry. And ask yourself if this poem provides an accurate definition of love.*

Let me not to the marriage of true minds
Admit impediments. Love is not love
Which alters when it alteration finds,
Or bends with the remover to remove:
Oh, no! it is an ever-fixéd mark,   5
That looks on tempests and is never shaken;
It is the star to every wandering bark,
Whose worth's unknown, although his height be taken.
Love's not Time's fool, though rosy lips and cheeks
Within his bending sickle's compass come;   10
Love alters not with his brief hours and weeks,
But bears it out even to the edge of doom.
If this be error and upon me proved,
    I never writ, nor no man ever loved.

Questions for Discussion

1. According to this poem, what is the basis of true love?
2. Is there any ambiguity within the first two lines? What does it mean to admit impediments (as in the Marriage Service: "If any of you know any just cause or just impediment why these persons should not be joined together . . .")?
3. Why is "Time" associated with a "bending sickle's compass"? What effect does Time's sickle have upon "rosy lips and cheeks"? What effect does Time have upon love as it is defined by this poem?
4. Consider lines 13–14. How strongly do they affirm the definition of love offered in lines 2–12?

Suggestions for Writing

1. Paraphrase what this poem says about love, and explain why you agree or disagree with this conception of love.
2. Contrast the view of love conveyed in this poem with the view conveyed by "Living in Sin."

LIVING IN SIN

Adrienne Rich

Although she has written several volumes of prose, Adrienne Rich is best known for her poetry, much of which reflects a feminist point of view. As you read the following poem, try to picture its scene — a small apartment. Understanding how the scene differs from what the woman in the poem expected may help you understand what is troubling her. But consider also how the woman differs from the man she is living with. Ask yourself if you have learned something about this woman that her partner does not seem to know.

She had thought the studio would keep itself;
no dust upon the furniture of love.
Half heresy, to wish the taps less vocal,
the panes relieved of grime. A plate of pears,
a piano with a Persian shawl, a cat   5
stalking the picturesque amusing mouse
had risen at his urging.
Not that at five each separate stair would writhe
under the milkman's tramp; that morning light
so coldly would delineate the scraps   10
of last night's cheese and three sepulchral bottles;
that on the kitchen shelf among the saucers
a pair of beetle-eyes would fix her own —
envoy from some village in the moldings . . .
Meanwhile, he, with a yawn,   15
sounded a dozen notes upon the keyboard,
declared it out of tune, shrugged at the mirror,
rubbed at his beard, went out for cigarettes;
while she, jeered by the minor demons,
pulled back the sheets and made the bed and found   20
a towel to dust the table-top,
and let the coffee-pot boil over on the stove.
By evening she was back in love again,
though not so wholly but throughout the night
she woke sometimes to feel the daylight coming   25
like a relentless milkman up the stairs.

Questions for Discussion

1. What is the setting of this poem like? What had the woman in the poem expected it to be like? What images lead you to these impressions?
2. Why do the stairs "writhe" under "the milkman's tramp"? Why is the milkman reintroduced in line 26? Does he represent anything besides a milk delivery?

3. What are "minor demons"? How can they be distinguished from "major demons"?

4. How do you imagine the future life of the woman in the poem?

5. What does the title mean? Is it ironic?

Suggestions for Writing

1. Contrast the man and the woman in this poem, and explain why that contrast is worth understanding.

2. Both "Living in sin" and "Off from Swing Shift" evoke a sense of disappointed expectations. Compare the two poems, and then explain how they differ.

NANI

Alberto Rios

> *Born in Nogales, Arizona, Alberto Rios is a poet and short story writer who draws upon a heritage that includes both Spanish and English. As you read the following poem, consider the relationship between the speaker and his grandmother. Try to understand how they differ from each other and how the speaker feels about the difference between them.*

Sitting at her table, she serves
the sopa de arroz° to me   rice soup
instinctively, and I watch her,
the absolute *mamá,* and eat words
I might have had to say more   5
out of embarrassment. To speak,
now-foreign words I used to speak,
too, dribble down her mouth as she serves
me albóndigas.° No more   spiced meatballs
than a third are easy to me.   10
By the stove she does something with words
and looks at me only with her
back. I am full. I tell her
I taste the mint, and watch her speak
smiles at the stove. All my words   15
make her smile. Nani° never serves   granny
herself, she only watches me
with her skin, her hair. I ask for more.
I watch the *mamá* warming more
tortillas for me. I watch her   20
fingers in the flame for me.
Near her mouth, I see a wrinkle speak
of a man whose body serves
the ants like she serves me, then more words
from more wrinkles about children, words   25
about this and that, flowing more
easily from these other mouths. Each serves
as a tremendous string around her,
holding her together. They speak
nani was this and that to me   30
and I wonder just how much of me
will die with her, what were the words
I could have been, was. Her insides speak
through a hundred wrinkles, now, more
than she can bear, steel around her,   35
shouting, then, What is this thing she serves?

She asks me if I want more.
I own no words to stop her.
Even before I speak, she serves.

Questions for Discussion

1. What is the speaker of this poem like? How does he differ from Nani?
2. Why is Spanish used in lines 2 and 9: "sopa de arroz" and "albóndigas"? Could you understand these lines without understanding Spanish? Why isn't Spanish used more extensively in the poem?
3. Why does the speaker ask for more food when he is full? Is the speaker full in more than one sense?
4. How could part of the speaker die when Nani dies?
5. Consider lines 33–36. What is it that steels around Nani? Why does Rios use such a vague word as "thing"? In your opinion, what is the "thing" that Nani serves?

Suggestions for Writing

1. What does this poem say about language? Discuss how it reveals a conflict between different cultures and different generations.
2. Four key words are repeated throughout this poem: *serves, speak, words,* and *watch*. Choose two of these and explain why they are important in the poem.

POWER

Audre Lorde

Audre Lorde published her first poem when she was still in high school —
a poem that her teachers didn't like but that nevertheless appealed to the
editors of a national magazine. She has said that she began to write poetry
"when I couldn't find the poems to express the things I was feeling." As you
read "Power," ask yourself what kind of feeling it expresses.

The difference between poetry and rhetoric
is being
ready to kill
yourself
instead of your children.   5

I am trapped on a desert of raw gunshot wounds
and a dead child dragging his shattered black
face off the edge of my sleep
blood from his punctured cheeks and shoulders
is the only liquid for miles and my stomach   10
churns at the imagined taste while
my mouth splits into dry lips
without loyalty or reason
thirsting for the wetness of his blood
as it sinks into the whiteness   15
of the desert where I am lost
without imagery or magic
trying to make power out of hatred and destruction
trying to heal my dying son with kisses
only the sun will bleach his bones quicker.   20

The policeman who shot down a 10-year-old in Queens
stood over the boy with his cop shoes in childish blood
and a voice said "Die you little motherfucker" and
there are tapes to prove that. At his trial
this policeman said in his own defense   25
"I didn't notice the size or nothing else
only the color," and
there are tapes to prove that, too.

Today that 37-year-old white man with 13 years of police forcing
has been set free   30
by 11 white men who said they were satisfied
justice had been done
and one black woman who said
"They convinced me" meaning

they had dragged her 4'10" black woman's frame   *35*
over the hot coals of four centuries of white male approval
until she let go the first real power she ever had
and lined her own womb with cement
to make a graveyard for our children.

I have not been able to touch the destruction within me.   *40*
But unless I learn to use
the difference between poetry and rhetoric
my power too will run corrupt as poisonous mold
or lie limp and useless as an unconnected wire
and one day I will take my teenaged plug   *45*
and connect it to the nearest socket
raping an 85-year-old white woman
who is somebody's mother
and as I beat her senseless and set a torch to her bed
a greek chorus will be singing in 3/4 time   *50*
"Poor thing. She never hurt a soul. What beasts they are."

Questions for Discussion

1. This poem opens with a startling statement about the difference between poetry and rhetoric, and it returns to this difference in lines 41–43. How could poetry lead to killing oneself, and how could rhetoric lead to killing children?
2. Lines 6–20 describe a disturbing dream that becomes easier to understand after we read the events described in lines 21–39. Why is there a dead child in the dream? How would the poem change if the dream came after the two stanzas about the policeman?
3. What do the words quoted in the third stanza reveal? Why does the speaker twice mention that there are tapes to prove what the policeman said?
4. According to the speaker of the poem, why did a black woman serving on a jury agree to set the policeman free?
5. What lines in the poem relate to the title?
6. Does the speaker intend to rape an 85-year-old white woman? If not, how could this ever happen? Do you see any irony in line 51?

Suggestions for Writing

1. *Tone* describes the way a writer sounds. How would you describe the tone of "Power"? Discuss how it compares with the tone of "Black Hair."
2. Define in your own words the difference between poetry and rhetoric. According to your definition, is "Power" poetry or rhetoric?

ULYSSES

Alfred, Lord Tennyson

> *A dramatic monologue is a poem in which a single speaker addresses a silent but identifiable audience, revealing his or her character. In the following poem the speaker is Ulysses—the Roman name for the hero of Homer's* Odyssey. *The poem portrays Ulysses in old age, after he has returned home from the adventures described by Homer and grown restless to set sail again. As you read "Ulysses," consider the character of the speaker and what this poem says about "roaming with a hungry heart." Tennyson was poet laureate of England from 1850 to 1892.*

It little profits that an idle king,
By this still hearth, among these barren crags,
Matched with an aged wife, I mete and dole
Unequal laws unto a savage race,
That hoard, and sleep, and feed, and know not me.   5
I cannot rest from travel: I will drink
Life to the lees: all times I have enjoyed
Greatly, have suffered greatly, both with those
That loved me, and alone; on shore, and when
Thro' scudding drifts the rainy Hyades   10
Vexed the dim sea. I am become a name;
For always roaming with a hungry heart
Much have I seen and known: cities of men
And manners, climates, councils, governments,
Myself not least, but honored of them all;   15
And drunk delight of battle with my peers,
Far on the ringing plains of windy Troy.
I am a part of all that I have met;
Yet all experience is an arch wherethro'
Gleams that untravelled world, whose margin fades   20
For ever and for ever when I move.
How dull it is to pause, to make an end,
To rust unburnished, not to shine in use!
As tho' to breathe were life. Life piled on life
Were all too little, and of one to me   25
Little remains: but every hour is saved
From that eternal silence, something more,
A bringer of new things; and vile it were
For some three suns to store and hoard myself,
And this gray spirit yearning in desire   30
To follow knowledge like a sinking star,
Beyond the utmost bound of human thought.
    This is my son, mine own Telemachus,

To whom I leave the sceptre and the isle —
Well-loved of me, discerning to fulfil   35
This labor, by slow prudence to make mild
A rugged people, and thro' soft degrees
Subdue them to the useful and the good.
Most blameless is he, centered in the sphere
Of common duties, decent not to fail   40
In offices of tenderness, and pay
Meet adoration to my household gods,
When I am gone. He works his work, I mine.
    There lies the port; the vessel puffs her sail:
There gloom the dark broad seas. My mariners,   45
Souls that have toiled, and wrought, and thought with me —
That ever with a frolic welcome took
The thunder and the sunshine, and opposed
Free hearts, free foreheads — you and I are old;
Old age hath yet his honor and his toil;   50
Death closes all; but something ere the end,
Some work of noble note, may yet be done,
Not unbecoming men that strove with Gods.
The lights begin to twinkle from the rocks:
The long day wanes: the slow moon climbs: the deep   55
Moans round with many voices. Come, my friends,
'T is not too late to seek a newer world.
Push off, and sitting well in order smite
The sounding furrows; for my purpose holds
To sail beyond the sunset, and the baths   60
Of all the western stars, until I die.
It may be that the gulfs will wash us down:
It may be we shall touch the Happy Isles,
And see the great Achilles, whom we knew.
Tho' much is taken, much abides; and tho'   65
We are not now that strength which in old days
Moved earth and heaven, that which we are, we are:
One equal temper of heroic hearts,
Made weak by time and fate, but strong in will
To strive, to seek, to find, and not to yield.   70

Questions for Discussion

1. To whom is Ulysses speaking in this poem?
2. Why has Ulysses decided to abdicate? What motivates his decision to
   go back to sea?
3. Consider lines 19–21. What do they say about the nature of experience?
4. How does Ulysses characterize his son Telemachus?

5. Does Ulysses recognize that there are any risks to undertaking an adventure in old age? Does he recognize that he has any limitations?

Suggestions for Writing

1. Write a description of Ulysses as portrayed in this poem. Is he an admirable character? Consider how he sees himself, but consider also whether there is anything that he does not recognize but that is implied by his speech.
2. Drawing upon what you have learned from this poem, write an essay that would justify your decision to either stay at home or join Ulysses on his search for "a newer world."

PIED BEAUTY

Gerard Manley Hopkins

> *A Jesuit priest who was sensitive to natural beauty and the rhythm of language, Gerard Manley Hopkins wrote poems that seemed startlingly modern when first published in 1918 — twenty-nine years after his death. Read this poem aloud, enjoying how it sounds. Then reread it, thinking about how it is constructed and what it means. You might find it helpful to know that* pied *means having patches of two or more colors. Consider whether it reminds you of any other words.*

Glory be to God for dappled things —
   For skies of couple-color as a brinded cow;
      For rose-moles all in stipple upon trout that swim;
Fresh-firecoal chestnut-falls; finches' wings;
   Landscape plotted and pieced — fold, fallow and plow;   *5*
      And all trades, their gear and tackle and trim.

All things counter, original, spare, strange;
   Whatever is fickle, freckled (who knows how?)
      With swift, slow; sweet, sour; adazzle, dim;
He fathers-forth whose beauty is past change: *10*
            Praise him.

Questions for Discussion

1. What are "dappled things," and why does the poem suggest that we should be thankful for them?
2. Where is rhyme used in this poem?
3. Explain line 9. What does "fathers-forth" mean, and how can beauty be "past change"?
4. Is there anything "counter, original, spare, strange" about this poem?

Suggestions for Writing

1. *Alliteration* describes the repetition of an initial consonant sound; *assonance* describes the repetition of sound within syllables. Discuss the role of alliteration and assonance in "Pied Beauty."
2. Discuss the images in lines 2–5, and explain how they relate to the poem's title.

TRIFLES

Susan Glaspell

> *If you have ever read a story called "A Jury of Her Peers," you will recognize the plot of* Trifles. *Susan Glaspell based that story upon the following play, which she wrote in 1916. According to Glaspell, both the play and the story were inspired by an experience she had while working for a newspaper in Des Moines, Iowa. As you read the play, try to imagine how lonely and isolated a midwestern farm could be before the introduction of electricity, radio, and television. Consider how the men in the play treat the women. Be sure to read the stage instructions, and note how the women change when the men are offstage.*

Scene: *The kitchen is the now abandoned farmhouse of* JOHN WRIGHT, *a gloomy kitchen, and left without having been put in order — unwashed pans under the sink, a loaf of bread outside the bread-box, a dish-towel on the table — other signs of incompleted work. At the rear the outer door opens and the* SHERIFF *comes in followed by the* COUNTY ATTORNEY *and* HALE. *The* SHERIFF *and* HALE *are men in middle life, the* COUNTY ATTORNEY *is a young man; all are much bundled up and go at once to the stove. They are followed by the two women — the* SHERIFF's *wife first; she is a slight wiry woman, a thin nervous face.* MRS. HALE *is larger and would ordinarily be called more comfortable looking, but she is disturbed now and looks fearfully about as she enters. The women have come in slowly, and stand close together near the door.*

COUNTY ATTORNEY: *(rubbing his hands)* This feels good. Come up to the fire, ladies.

MRS. PETERS: *(after taking a step forward)* I'm not — cold.

SHERIFF: *(unbuttoning his overcoat and stepping away from the stove as if to mark the beginning of official business)* Now, Mr. Hale, before we move things about, you explain to Mr. Henderson just what you saw when you came here yesterday morning.

COUNTY ATTORNEY: By the way, has anything been moved? Are things just as you left them yesterday?

SHERIFF: *(looking about)* It's just the same. When it dropped below zero last night I thought I'd better send Frank out this morning to make a fire for us — no use getting pneumonia with a big case on, but I told him not to touch anything except the stove — and you know Frank.

COUNTY ATTORNEY: Somebody should have been left here yesterday.

SHERIFF: Oh — yesterday. When I had to send Frank to Morris Center for that man who went crazy — I want you to know I had my hands full yesterday. I knew you could get back from Omaha by today and as long as I went over everything here myself —

COUNTY ATTORNEY: Well, Mr. Hale, tell just what happened when you came here yesterday morning.

HALE: Harry and I had started to town with a load of potatoes. We came along the road from my place and as I got here I said, "I'm going to see if I can't get John Wright to go in with me on a party telephone." I spoke to Wright about it once before and he put me off, saying folks talked too much anyway, and all he asked was peace and quiet — I guess you know about how much he talked himself; but I thought maybe if I went to the house and talked about it before his wife, though I said to Harry that I didn't know as what his wife wanted made much difference to John —

COUNTY ATTORNEY: Let's talk about that later, Mr. Hale. I do want to talk about that, but tell now just what happened when you got to the house.

HALE: I didn't hear or see anything; I knocked at the door, and still it was all quiet inside. I knew they must be up, it was past eight o'clock. So I knocked again, and I thought I heard somebody say, "Come in." I wasn't sure, I'm not sure yet, but I opened the door — this door *(indicating the door by which the two women are still standing)* and there in that rocker — *(pointing to it)* sat Mrs. Wright.

(They all look at the rocker.)

COUNTY ATTORNEY: What — was she doing?

HALE: She was rockin' back and forth. She had her apron in her hand and was kind of — pleating it.

COUNTY ATTORNEY: And how did she — look?

HALE: Well, she looked queer.

COUNTY ATTORNEY: How do you mean — queer?

HALE: Well, as if she didn't know what she was going to do next. And kind of done up.

COUNTY ATTORNEY: How did she seem to feel about your coming?

HALE: Why, I don't think she minded — one way or other. She didn't pay much attention. I said, "How do, Mrs. Wright it's cold, ain't it?" And she said, "Is it?" — and went on kind of pleating at her apron. Well, I was surprised; she didn't ask me to come up to the stove, or to set down, but just sat there, not even looking at me, so I said, "I want to see John." And then she — laughed. I guess you would call it a laugh. I thought of Harry and the team outside, so I said a little sharp: "Can't I see John?" "No," she says, kind o' dull like. "Ain't he home?" says I. "Yes," says she, "he's home." "Then why can't I see him?" I asked her, out of patience. "Cause he's dead," says she. "*Dead*?" says I. She just nodded her head, not getting a bit excited, but rockin' back and forth. "Why — where is he?" says I, not knowing what to say. She just pointed upstairs — like that *(himself pointing to the room above)*. I got up, with the idea of going up there. I walked from there to here — then I says, "Why, what did he die of?" "He died of a rope round his neck," says she, and just went on pleatin' at

her apron. Well, I went out and called Harry. I thought I might —
need help. We went upstairs and there he was lyin' —

COUNTY ATTORNEY: I think I'd rather have you go into that upstairs,
where you can point it all out. Just go on now with the rest of the
story.

HALE: Well, my first thought was to get that rope off. It looked . . .
(stops, his face twitches) . . . but Harry, he went up to him, and he
said, "No, he's dead all right, and we'd better not touch anything."
So we went back down stairs. She was still sitting that same way.
"Has anybody been notified?" I asked. "No," says she unconcerned.
"Who did this, Mrs. Wright?" said Harry. He said it business-like —
and she stopped pleatin' of her apron. "I don't know," she says. "You
don't *know*?" says Harry. "No," says she. "Weren't you sleepin' in
the bed with him?" says Harry. "Yes," says she, "but I was on the
inside." "Somebody slipped a rope round his neck and strangled him
and you didn't wake up?" says Harry. "I didn't wake up," she said
after him. We must 'a looked as if we didn't see how that could be,
for after a minute she said, "I sleep sound." Harry was going to ask
her more questions but I said maybe we ought to let her tell her story
first to the coroner, or the sheriff, so Harry went fast as he could to
Rivers' place, where there's a telephone.

COUNTY ATTORNEY: And what did Mrs. Wright do when she knew
that you had gone for the coroner?

HALE: She moved from that chair to this one over here *(pointing to a small
chair in the corner)* and just sat there with her hands held together and
looking down. I got a feeling that I ought to make some conversation, so I said I had come in to see if John wanted to put in a
telephone, and at that she started to laugh, and then she stopped and
looked at me — scared. *(the* COUNTY ATTORNEY, *who has had his
notebook out, makes a note)* I dunno, maybe it wasn't scared. I wouldn't
like to say it was. Soon Harry got back, and then Dr. Lloyd came,
and you, Mr. Peters, and so I guess that's all I know that you don't.

COUNTY ATTORNEY: *(looking around)* I guess we'll go upstairs first —
and then out to the barn and around there. *(to the* SHERIFF*)* You're
convinced that there was nothing important here — nothing that
would point to any motive.

SHERIFF: Nothing here but kitchen things.

(The COUNTY ATTORNEY, *after again looking around the kitchen, opens
the door of a cupboard closet. He gets up on a chair and looks on a shelf.
Pulls his hand away, sticky.)*

COUNTY ATTORNEY: Here's a nice mess.

(The women draw nearer.)

MRS. PETERS: *(to the other woman)* Oh, her fruit; it did freeze. *(to the*

LAWYER) She worried about that when it turned so cold. She said the fire'd go out and her jars would break.

SHERIFF: Well, can you beat the women! Held for murder and worryin' about her preserves.

COUNTY ATTORNEY: I guess before we're through she may have something more serious than preserves to worry about.

HALE: Well, women are used to worrying over trifles.

(The two women move a little closer together.)

COUNTY ATTORNEY: *(with the gallantry of a young politician)* And yet, for all their worries, what would we do without the ladies? *(the women do not unbend. He goes to the sink, takes a dipperful of water from the pail and pouring it into a basin, washes his hands. Starts to wipe them on the roller-towel, turns it for a cleaner place)* Dirty towels! *(kicks his foot against the pans under the sink)* Not much of a housekeeper, would you say, ladies?

MRS. HALE: *(stiffly)* There's a great deal of work to be done on a farm.

COUNTY ATTORNEY: To be sure. And yet *(with a little bow to her)* I know there are some Dickson county farmhouses which do not have such roller towels.

(He gives it a pull to expose its length again.)

MRS. HALE: Those towels get dirty awful quick. Men's hands aren't always as clean as they might be.

COUNTY ATTORNEY: Ah, loyal to your sex, I see. But you and Mrs. Wright were neighbors. I suppose you were friends, too.

MRS. HALE: *(shaking her head)* I've not seen much of her of late years. I've not been in this house — it's more than a year.

COUNTY ATTORNEY: And why was that? You didn't like her?

MRS. HALE: I liked her all well enough. Farmers' wives have their hands full, Mr. Henderson. And then —

COUNTY ATTORNEY: Yes — ?

MRS. HALE: *(looking about)* It never seemed a very cheerful place.

COUNTY ATTORNEY: No — it's not cheerful. I shouldn't say she had the homemaking instinct.

MRS. HALE: Well, I don't know as Wright had, either.

COUNTY ATTORNEY: You mean that they didn't get on very well?

MRS. HALE: No, I don't mean anything. But I don't think a place'd be any cheerfuller for John Wright's being in it.

COUNTY ATTORNEY: I'd like to talk more of that a little later. I want to get the lay of things upstairs now.

(He goes to the left, where three steps lead to a stair door.)

SHERIFF: I suppose anything Mrs. Peters does'll be all right. She was to take in some clothes for her, you know, and a few little things. We left in such a hurry yesterday.

COUNTY ATTORNEY: Yes, but I would like to see what you take, Mrs. Peters, and keep an eye out for anything that might be of use to us.

MRS. PETERS: Yes, Mr. Henderson.

(*The women listen to the men's steps on the stairs, then look about the kitchen.*)

MRS. HALE: I'd hate to have men coming into my kitchen, snooping around and criticising.

(*She arranges the pans under sink which the* LAWYER *had shoved out of place.*)

MRS. PETERS: Of course it's no more than their duty.

MRS. HALE: Duty's all right, but I guess that deputy sheriff that came out to make the fire might have got a little of this on. (*gives the roller towel a pull*) Wish I'd thought of that sooner. Seems mean to talk about her for not having things slicked up when she had to come away in such a hurry.

MRS. PETERS: (*who has gone to a small table in the left rear corner of the room, and lifted one end of a towel that covers a pan*) She had bread set.

(*Stands still.*)

MRS. HALE: (*eyes fixed on a loaf of bread beside the bread-box, which is on a low shelf at the other side of the room. Moves slowly toward it*) She was going to put this in there. (*picks up loaf, then abruptly drops it. In a manner of returning to familiar things*) It's a shame about her fruit. I wonder if it's all gone. (*gets up on the chair and looks*) I think there's some here that's all right, Mrs. Peters. Yes—here; (*holding it toward the window*) this is cherries, too. (*looking again*) I declare I believe that's the only one. (*gets down, bottle in her hand. Goes to the sink and wipes it off on the outside*) She'll feel awful bad after all her hard work in the hot weather. I remember the afternoon I put up my cherries last summer.

(*She puts the bottle on the big kitchen table, center of the room. With a sigh, is about to sit down in the rocking-chair. Before she is seated realizes what chair it is; with a slow look at it, steps back. The chair which she has touched rocks back and forth.*)

MRS. PETERS: Well, I must get those things from the front room closet. (*she goes to the door at the right, but after looking into the other room, steps back*) You coming with me, Mrs. Hale? You could help me carry them.

(*They go in the other room; reappear,* MRS. PETERS *carrying a dress and skirt,* MRS. HALE *following with a pair of shoes.*)

MRS. PETERS: My, it's cold in here.

(She puts the clothes on the big table, and hurries to the stove.)

MRS. HALE: *(examining the skirt)* Wright was close. I think maybe that's why she kept so much to herself. She didn't even belong to the Ladies Aid. I suppose she felt she couldn't do her part, and then you don't enjoy things when you feel shabby. She used to wear pretty clothes and be lively, when she was Minnie Foster, one of the town girls singing in the choir. But that—oh, that was thirty years ago. This all you was to take in?

MRS. PETERS: She said she wanted an apron. Funny thing to want, for there isn't much to get you dirty in jail, goodness knows. But I suppose just to make her feel more natural. She said they was in the top drawer in this cupboard. Yes, here. And then her little shawl that always hung behind the door. *(opens stair door and looks)* Yes, here it is.

(Quickly shuts door leading upstairs.)

MRS. HALE: *(abruptly moving toward her)* Mrs. Peters?

MRS. PETERS: Yes, Mrs. Hale?

MRS. HALE: Do you think she did it?

MRS. PETERS: *(in a frightened voice)* Oh, I don't know.

MRS. HALE: Well, I don't think she did. Asking for an apron and her little shawl. Worrying about her fruit.

MRS. PETERS: *(starts to speak, glances up, where footsteps are heard in the room above. In a low voice)* Mr. Peters says it looks bad for her. Mr. Henderson is awful sarcastic in a speech and he'll make fun of her sayin' she didn't wake up.

MRS. HALE: Well, I guess John Wright didn't wake when they was slipping that rope under his neck.

MRS. PETERS: No, it's strange. It must have been done awful crafty and still. They say it was such a—funny way to kill a man, rigging it all up like that.

MRS. HALE: That's just what Mr. Hale said. There was a gun in the house. He says that's what he can't understand.

MRS. PETERS: Mr. Henderson said coming out that what was needed for the case was a motive; something to show anger, or—sudden feeling.

MRS. HALE: *(who is standing by the table)* Well, I don't see any signs of anger around here. *(she puts her hand on the dish towel which lies on the table, stands looking down at table, one half of which is clean, the other half messy)* It's wiped to here. *(makes a move as if to finish work, then turns and looks at loaf of bread outside the breadbox. Drops towel. In that voice of coming back to familiar things.)* Wonder how they are finding things upstairs. I hope she had it a little more red-up° up there. You know,

red-up: Readied up; orderly.

it seems kind of *sneaking*. Locking her up in town and then coming out here and trying to get her own house to turn against her!

MRS. PETERS: But Mrs. Hale, the law is the law.

MRS. HALE: I s'pose 'tis. *(unbuttoning her coat)* Better loosen up your things, Mrs. Peters. You won't feel them when you go out.

(MRS. PETERS takes off her fur tippet,° goes to hang it on hook at back of room, stands looking at the under part of the small corner table.)

MRS. PETERS: She was piecing a quilt.

(She brings the large sewing basket and they look at the bright pieces.)

MRS. HALE: It's log cabin pattern. Pretty, isn't it? I wonder if she was goin' to quilt it or just knot it?

(Footsteps have been heard coming down the stairs. The SHERIFF enters followed by HALE and the COUNTY ATTORNEY.)

SHERIFF: They wonder if she was going to quilt it or just knot it!

(The men laugh, the women look abashed.)

COUNTY ATTORNEY: *(rubbing his hands over the stove)* Frank's fire didn't do much up there, did it? Well, let's go out to the barn and get that cleared up.

(The men go outside.)

MRS. HALE: *(resentfully)* I don't know as there's anything so strange, our takin' up our time with little things while we're waiting for them to get the evidence. *(she sits down at the big table smoothing out a block with decision)* I don't see as it's anything to laugh about.

MRS. PETERS: *(apologetically)* Of course they've got awful important things on their minds.

(Pulls up a chair and joins MRS. HALE at the table.)

MRS. HALE: *(examining another block)* Mrs. Peters, look at this one. Here, this is the one she was working on, and look at the sewing! All the rest of it has been so nice and even. And look at this! It's all over the place! Why, it looks as if she didn't know what she was about!

(After she has said this they look at each other, then start to glance back at the door. After an instant MRS. HALE has pulled at a knot and ripped the sewing.)

MRS. PETERS: Oh, what are you doing, Mrs. Hale?

MRS. HALE: *(mildly)* Just pulling out a stitch or two that's not sewed very good. *(threading a needle)* Bad sewing always made me fidgety.

---

tippet: A scarf for covering the neck and sometimes the shoulders.

MRS. PETERS: *(nervously)* I don't thing we ought to touch things.

MRS. HALE: I'll just finish up this end. *(suddenly stopping and leaning forward)* Mrs. Peters?

MRS. PETERS: Yes, Mrs. Hale?

MRS. HALE: What do you suppose she was so nervous about?

MRS. PETERS: Oh—I don't know. I don't know as she was nervous. I sometimes sew awful queer when I'm just tired. *(MRS. HALE starts to say something, looks at MRS. PETERS, then goes on sewing)* Well I must get these things wrapped up. They may be through sooner than we think. *(putting apron and other things together)* I wonder where I can find a piece of paper, and string.

MRS. HALE: In that cupboard, maybe.

MRS. PETERS: *(looking in cupboard)* Why, here's a bird-cage. *(holds it up)* Did she have a bird, Mrs. Hale?

MRS. HALE: Why, I don't know whether she did or not—I've not been here for so long. There was a man around last year selling canaries cheap, but I don't know as she took one; maybe she did. She used to sing real pretty herself.

MRS. PETERS: *(glancing around)* Seems funny to think of a bird here. But she must have had one, or why would she have a cage? I wonder what happened to it.

MRS. HALE: I s'pose maybe the cat got it.

MRS. PETERS: No, she didn't have a cat. She's got that feeling some people have about cats—being afraid of them. My cat got in her room and she was real upset and asked me to take it out.

MRS. HALE: My sister Bessie was like that. Queer, ain't it?

MRS. PETERS: *(examining the cage)* Why, look at this door. It's broke. One hinge is pulled apart.

MRS. HALE: *(looking too)* Looks as if someone must have been rough with it.

MRS. PETERS: Why, yes.

(She brings the cage forward and puts it on the table.)

MRS. HALE: I wish if they're going to find any evidence they'd be about it. I don't like this place.

MRS. PETERS: But I'm awful glad you came with me, Mrs. Hale. It would be lonesome for me sitting here alone.

MRS. HALE: It would, wouldn't it? *(dropping her sewing)* But I tell you what I do wish, Mrs. Peters. I wish I had come over sometimes when *she* was here. I— *(looking around the room)*—wish I had.

MRS. PETERS: But of course you were awful busy, Mrs. Hale—your house and your children.

MRS. HALE: I could've come. I stayed away because it weren't cheerful—and that's why I ought to have come. I—I've never liked this place. Maybe because it's down in a hollow and you don't see the road. I dunno what it is, but it's a lonesome place and always was. I wish I had come over to see Minnie Foster sometimes. I can see now — *(shakes her head)*

MRS. PETERS: Well, you mustn't reproach yourself, Mrs. Hale. Somehow we just don't see how it is with other folks until — something comes up.

MRS. HALE: Not having children makes less work — but it makes a quiet house, and Wright out to work all day, and no company when he did come in. Did you know John Wright, Mrs. Peters?

MRS. PETERS: Not to know him; I've seen him in town. They say he was a good man.

MRS. HALE: Yes — good; he didn't drink, and kept his word as well as most, I guess, and paid his debts. But he was a hard man, Mrs. Peters. Just to pass the time of day with him — *(shivers)* Like a raw wind that gets to the bone. *(pauses, her eye falling on the cage)* I should think she would 'a wanted a bird. But what do you suppose went with it?

MRS. PETERS: I don't know, unless it got sick and died.

(She reaches over and swings the broken door, swings it again, both women watch it.)

MRS. HALE: You weren't raised round here, were you? *(*MRS. PETERS *shakes her head)* You didn't know — her?

MRS. PETERS: Not till they brought her yesterday.

MRS. HALE: She — come to think of it, she was kind of like a bird herself — real sweet and pretty, but kind of timid and — fluttery. How — she — did — change. *(silence; then as if struck by a happy thought and relieved to get back to everyday things)* Tell you what, Mrs. Peters, why don't you take the quilt in with you? It might take up her mind.

MRS. PETERS: Why, I think that's a real nice idea, Mrs. Hale. There couldn't possibly be any objection to it, could there? Now, just what would I take? I wonder if her patches are in here — and her things.

(They look in the sewing basket.)

MRS. HALE: Here's some red. I expect this has got sewing things in it. *(brings out a fancy box)* What a pretty box. Looks like something somebody would give you. Maybe her scissors are in here. *(Opens box. Suddenly puts her hand to her nose)* Why — *(*MRS. PETERS *bends nearer, then turns her face away)* There's something wrapped up in this piece of silk.

MRS. PETERS: Why, this isn't her scissors.

MRS. HALE: *(lifting the silk)* Oh, Mrs. Peters — it's —

*(*MRS. PETERS *bends closer.)*

MRS. PETERS: It's the bird.

MRS. HALE: *(jumping up)* But, Mrs. Peters — look at it! It's neck! Look at its neck! It's all — other side *to.*

MRS. PETERS: Somebody — wrung — its — neck.

(Their eyes meet. A look of growing comprehension, of horror. Steps are heard outside. MRS. HALE *slips box under quilt pieces, and sinks into her chair. Enter* SHERIFF *and* COUNTY ATTORNEY. MRS. PETERS *rises.)*

COUNTY ATTORNEY: *(as one turning from serious things to little pleasantries)* Well ladies, have you decided whether she was going to quilt it or knot it?

MRS. PETERS: We think she was going to — knot it.

COUNTY ATTORNEY: Well, that's interesting, I'm sure. *(seeing the birdcage)* Has the bird flown?

MRS. HALE: *(putting more quilt pieces over the box)* We think the — cat got it.

COUNTY ATTORNEY: *(preoccupied)* Is there a cat?

*(*MRS. HALE *glances in a quick covert way at* MRS. PETERS.*)*

MRS. PETERS: Well, not *now.* They're superstitious, you know. They leave.

COUNTY ATTORNEY: *(to* SHERIFF PETERS, *continuing an interrupted conversation)* No sign at all of anyone having come from the outside. Their own rope. Now let's go up again and go over it piece by piece. *(they start upstairs)* It would have to have been someone who knew just the —

*(*MRS. PETERS *sits down. The two women sit there not looking at one another, but as if peering into something and at the same time holding back. When they talk now it is in the manner of feeling their way over strange ground, as if afraid of what they are saying, but as if they cannot help saying it.)*

MRS. HALE: She liked the bird. She was going to bury it in that pretty box.

MRS. PETERS: *(in a whisper)* When I was a girl — my kitten — there was a boy took a hatchet, and before my eyes — and before I could get there — *(covers her face an instant)* If they hadn't held me back I would have — *(catches herself, looks upstairs where steps are heard, falters weakly)* — hurt him.

MRS. HALE: *(with a slow look around her)* I wonder how it would seem never to have had any children around. *(pause)* No, Wright wouldn't like the bird — a thing that sang. She used to sing. He killed that, too.

MRS. PETERS: *(moving uneasily)* We don't know who killed the bird.

MRS. HALE: I knew John Wright.

MRS. PETERS: It was an awful thing was done in this house that night,

Mrs. Hale. Killing a man while he slept, slipping a rope around his neck that choked the life out of him.

MRS. HALE: His neck. Choked the life out of him.

(Her hand goes out and rests on the bird-cage.)

MRS. PETERS: *(with rising voice)* We don't know who killed him. We don't *know*.

MRS. HALE: *(her own feeling not interrupted)* If there'd been years and years of nothing, then a bird to sing to you, it would be awful — still, after the bird was still.

MRS. PETERS: *(something within her speaking)* I know what stillness is. When we homesteaded in Dakota, and my first baby died — after he was two years old, and me with no other then —

MRS. HALE: *(moving)* How soon do you suppose they'll be through, looking for the evidence?

MRS. PETERS: I know what stillness is. *(pulling herself back).* The law has got to punish crime, Mrs. Hale.

MRS. HALE: *(not as if answering that)* I wish you'd seen Minnie Foster when she wore a white dress with blue ribbons and stood up there in the choir and sang. *(a look around the room)* Oh, I *wish* I'd come over here once in a while! That was a crime! That was a crime! Who's going to punish that?

MRS. PETERS: *(looking upstairs)* We mustn't — take on.

MRS. HALE: I might have known she needed help! I know how things can be — for women. I tell you, it's queer, Mrs. Peters. We live close together and we live far apart. We all go through the same things — it's all just a different kind of the same thing. *(brushes her eyes, noticing the bottle of fruit, reaches out for it)* If I was you, I wouldn't tell her her fruit was gone. Tell her it *ain't*. Tell her it's all right. Take this in to prove it to her. She — she may never know whether it was broke or not.

MRS. PETERS: *(takes the bottle, looks about for something to wrap it in; takes petticoat from the clothes brought from the other room, very nervously begins winding this around the bottle. In a false voice)* My, it's a good thing the men couldn't hear us. Wouldn't they just laugh! Getting all stirred up over a little thing like a — dead canary. As if that could have anything to do with — with — wouldn't they *laugh*!

(The men are heard coming down stairs.)

MRS. HALE: *(under her breath)* Maybe they would — maybe they wouldn't.

COUNTY ATTORNEY: No, Peters, it's all perfectly clear except a reason for doing it. But you know juries when it comes to women. If there was some definite thing. Something to show — something to make a story about — a thing that would connect up with this strange way of doing it —

(The women's eyes meet for an instant. Enter HALE *from outer door.)*

HALE: Well, I've got the team around. Pretty cold out there.

COUNTY ATTORNEY: I'm going to stay here a while by myself. *(to the* SHERIFF*)* You can send Frank out for me, can't you? I want to go over everything. I'm not satisfied that we can't do better.

SHERIFF: Do you want to see what Mrs. Peters is going to take in?

(The LAWYER *goes to the table, picks up the apron, laughs.)*

COUNTY ATTORNEY: Oh, I guess they're not very dangerous things the ladies have picked out. *(Moves a few things about, disturbing the quilt pieces which cover the box. Steps back)* No, Mrs. Peters doesn't need supervising. For that matter, a sheriff's wife is married to the law. Ever think of it that way, Mrs. Peters?

MRS. PETERS: Not—just that way.

SHERIFF: *(chuckling)* Married to the law. *(moves toward the other room)* I just want you to come in here a minute, George. We ought to take a look at these windows.

COUNTY ATTORNEY: *(scoffingly)* Oh, windows!

SHERIFF: We'll be right out, Mr. Hale.

*(*HALE *goes outside. The* SHERIFF *follows the* COUNTY ATTORNEY *into the other room. Then* MRS. HALE *rises, hands tight together, looking intensely at* MRS. PETERS, *whose eyes make a slow turn, finally meeting* MRS. HALE*'s. A moment* MRS. HALE *holds her, then her own eyes point the way to where the box is concealed. Suddenly* MRS. PETERS *throws back quilt pieces and tries to put the box in the bag she is wearing. It is too big. She opens box, starts to take bird out, cannot touch it, goes to pieces, stands there helpless. Sound of a knob turning in the other room.* MRS. HALE *snatches the box and puts it in the pocket of her big coat. Enter* COUNTY ATTORNEY *and* SHERIFF.*)*

COUNTY ATTORNEY: *(facetiously)* Well, Henry, at least we found out that she was not going to quilt it. She was going to—what is it you call it, ladies?

MRS. HALE: *(her hand against her pocket)* We call it—knot it, Mr. Henderson.

(CURTAIN)

Questions for Discussion

1. Consider the kitchen in which *Trifles* takes place. Why is it a fitting scene for the play?
2. What is the most important act that takes place on stage? What important acts have taken place before the play begins?
3. Describe the marriage between the Wrights. What lines first led you to this impression?

4. What does the Sheriff reveal about himself when he says, "Nothing here but kitchen things"? And "Well, can you beat the women! Held for murder and worryin' about her preserves"?

5. According to Mrs. Hale, "women are used to worrying over trifles." Does your response to this line change as the play unfolds?

6. Why do Mrs. Hale and Mrs. Peters conceal the dead canary? What motivates them to sympathize with Mrs. Wright?

7. How do you read the final line of this play? Does it have a meaning the men do not understand?

Suggestions for Writing

1. Compare and contrast Mrs. Hale and Mrs. Peters.

2. What does *Trifles* say about women and the way they are treated by men? Explain.

ACKNOWLEDGMENTS

JANE GOODALL, "The Mind of the Chimpanzee," from *Through a Window: My Thirty Years with the Chimpanzees of Gombe*. Copyright © 1990 by Soko Publications Limited. Reprinted by permission of Houghton Mifflin Company.

ELLEN GOODMAN, "In the Male Direction," from *Keeping in Touch*. Copyright © 1985 by The Washington Post Company. Reprinted by permission of Summit Books, a division of Simon & Schuster, Inc.

STEPHEN JAY GOULD, "Women's Brains," from *The Panda's Thumb, More Reflections in Natural History* by Stephen Jay Gould. Reprinted by permission of W. W. Norton & Company, Inc. Copyright © 1980.

DAVID GROFF, "Taking the Test," from *Wigwag*, June 1990. Reprinted by permission.

GARRETT HONGO, "Off From Swing Shift." Copyright © 1982 by Garrett Kaoru Hongo. Reprinted from *Yellow Light*, Wesleyan University Press, by permission of University Press of New England.

ELIZABETH KAYE, "Peter Jennings Gets No Self-Respect." Reprinted from *Esquire*, September 1989, with permission.

MARTIN LUTHER KING, JR., "I Have a Dream." Reprinted by permission of Joan Daves Agency. Copyright © 1963 by Martin Luther King, Jr.

MARK A. R. KLEIMAN, "Snowed In," *New Republic*, April 23, 1990. Reprinted by permission.

EDWARD I. KOCH, "Death and Justice: How Capital Punishment Affirms Life." Reprinted from *The New Republic*, 1985.

NICHOLAS LEMANN, "Stressed Out in Suburbia." Reprinted from *The Atlantic*, November, 1988.

PRIMO LEVI, "The Last Christmas of the War" from *Moments of Reprieve*. Copyright © 1979, 1981, 1982, 1983, 1985 by Summit Books. Translation copyright © 1981, 1985 by Guilio Einaudi, editore S.p.a. Reprinted by permission of Summit Books, a division of Simon & Schuster, Inc.

AUDRE LORDE, "Power," from *The Black Unicorn* by Audre Lorde, reprinted with the permission of W. W. Norton & Company, Inc. Copyright © 1978 by Audre Lorde.

MONA MELANSON, "Beat the Butterflies," from *National Business Employment Weekly*, Fall 1989. Reprinted by permission of Bank of America.

BARBARA MELLIX, "From Outside, In" originally appeared in *The Georgia Review*, Volume XLI, No. 2 (Summer 1987), © 1987 by The University of Georgia, © 1987 by Barbara Mellix. Reprinted by permission of Barbara Mellix and *The Georgia Review*.

ANDREW MERTON, "About Men: When Father Doesn't Know Best." Copyright © 1990 by The New York Times Company. Reprinted by permission.

JESSICA MITFORD, "Embalming in the U.S.A.," from *The American Way of Death*. Reprinted by permission of Jessica Mitford. All rights reserved. Copyright © 1963, 1978 by Jessica Mitford.

PAT MORA, "A Letter to Gabriela, a Young Writer," from *English Journal*, September 1990. Copyright 1990 by the National Council of Teachers of English. Reprinted by permission.

TOSHIO MORI, "Abalone, Abalone, Abalone" from *The Chauvinist and Other Stories*. Reprinted by permission of the Estate of Toshio Mori and Asian American Studies Center, UCLA.

GLORIA NAYLOR, "Mommy, What Does 'Nigger' Mean?" from "Hers" column, February 20, 1986 in *The New York Times*. Copyright © 1986 by The New York Times Company. Reprinted by permission.

JOYCE CAROL OATES, "Shopping," from *Ms. Magazine*, March 1987.

FLANNERY O'CONNOR, "The Nature and Aim of Fiction" from *Mystery and Manners*. Copyright © 1969 by the Estate of Mary Flannery O'Connor. Reprinted by permission of Farrar, Straus and Giroux, Inc.

GEORGE ORWELL, "A Hanging," from *Shooting an Elephant and Other Essays*. Copyright © 1950 by Sonia Brownell Orwell and renewed 1978 by Sonia Pitt-Rivers, reprinted by permission of Harcourt Brace Jovanovich, Inc. and Martin Secker & Warburg Ltd.

GEOFFREY NORMAN, "Gators," from *Esquire Magazine,* October, 1980.

ANNA QUINDLEN, "A Baseball Wimp," from *Living Out Loud.* Copyright © 1987 by Anna Quindlen. Reprinted by permission of Random House, Inc.

DOROTHY RABINOWITZ, "From the Mouths of Babes to a Jail Cell," *Harper's Magazine,* May, 1990.

ADRIENNE RICH, "Living in Sin," reprinted from *The Factor of a Doorframe, Poems Selected and News, 1950–1984* by Adrienne Rich, by permission of W. W. Norton & Company, Inc. Copyright 1984 by Adrienne Rich. Copyright 1975, 1978 by W. W. Norton & Company, Inc. Copyright 1981 by Adrienne Rich.

ALBERTO RIOS, "Nani," from *Whispering to Fool the Wind,* The Sheep Meadow Press, 1982. Reprinted by permission of the author.

RICHARD RODRIGUEZ, *Hunger of Memory.* Copyright © 1982 by Richard Rodriguez. Reprinted by permission of David R. Godine, Publisher, Inc.

ANDREW A. ROONEY, "Old Friends." Reprinted with permission of Atheneum Publishers, an imprint of Macmillan Publishing Company, from *And More By Andy Rooney* by Andrew A. Rooney. Copyright © 1982 by Essay Productions, Inc.

MIKE ROYKO, "Farewell to Fitness," *Chicago Tribune,* 1980. Reprinted by permission of Tribune Media Service.

SCOTT RUSSELL SANDERS, "Grub," from *Wigwag,* June, 1990. Reprinted by permission.

LUC SANTE, "Unlike a Virgin," from *The New Republic,* August 20 and 27, 1990. Reprinted by permission.

MARILYN SCHIEL, "Levi's." Copyright © 1991 by Marilyn Schiel.

JOHN SEDGWICK, "The Doberman Case," from *Wigwag,* June 1990. Reprinted by permission.

RICHARD SELZER, "How to Build a Slaughterhouse," from *Taking the World in for Repairs.* Reprinted by permission of Georges Borchardt, Inc. for the author. Copyright © 1986 by Richard Selzer.

RAYMOND SOKOLOV, "Square, Gassed Tomatoes and Other Modern Myths." With permission from *Natural History,* July 1989. Copyright the American Museum of Natural History, 1989.

GARY SOTO, "Black Hair." Reprinted from *Black Hair* by Gary Soto, by permission of the University of Pittsburgh Press. © 1985 by Gary Soto.

JUDY SYFERS, "I Want a Wife." Copyright © 1971 by Judy Syfers. Reprinted by permission.

STEVE TESICH, "An Amateur Marriage." Reprinted from *The New York Times Magazine,* September 23, 1984.

LEWIS THOMAS, "The Art of Teaching Science," from *The New York Times Magazine,* 1982.

CALVIN TRILLIN, "Literally." Excerpted from his book entitled *Uncivil Liberties,* published by Tickner & Fields. Copyright © 1982 by Calvin Trillin.

ALICE WALKER, "Am I Blue?" from *Living Word.* Copyright © 1986 by Alice Walker. Reprinted by permission of Harcourt Brace Jovanovich, Inc.

JACOB WEISBERG, "Gays in Arms." Reprinted from *New Republic,* February 19, 1990.

RANDALL WILLIAMS, "Daddy Tucked the Blanket," from *The New York Times,* July 10, 1975. Copyright © 1975 by The New York Times Company. Reprinted by permission.

JACKSON R. WILSON, "A Man Watching," from *Figures of Speech: American Writers and the Literary Marketplace from Benjamin Franklin to Emily Dickinson.* Copyright © 1990 by Jackson R. Wilson. Reprinted by permission of Alfred A. Knopf, Inc.

INDEX TO THE READINGS
BY RHETORICAL STRATEGY (MODE)

Analysis

Argument

GLOSSARY

Act In Kenneth Burke's **pentad,** the event, what the **agent** does, what happened; also, one of the main divisions of a drama

Agency In Kenneth Burke's **pentad,** how the **act** was performed, the means by which the event happened

Agent In Kenneth Burke's **pentad,** the one who performs the **act,** the actor; usually a person, but occasionally an inanimate or abstract entity

Alliteration The repetition of initial consonant sounds

Allusion A reference to something or someone outside of the work, usually a literary or historical character, place, or event

Analogy An extended comparison of two similar but unrelated things using the familiar to explain the unfamiliar, the simple to explain the complex

Analysis Dividing a whole into its parts

Anaphora A word or phrase repeated for rhetorical effect at the beginning of consecutive sentences or clauses

Assonance Repetition of vowel sounds, especially of initial vowels

Brainstorming A technique for generating ideas by recording thoughts for a specific period of time

Causal Chain Interlinked causes and effects in which what happens causes something else to happen, which in turn becomes the cause generating another effect, and so on

Cause and Effect A rhetorical strategy in which a writer explains why something happened or what its results were; one of the classical topics for exploring an idea

Ceremonial Speech Speech to move an audience generally sympathetic to the speaker's position, usually to mark an occasion such as a funeral or political gathering

Claim What you are trying to prove, the idea you are arguing

Classical Topics Ways of thinking about a subject so as to discover what to say about it; ways to explore an idea

Classification Sorting things into categories based on some specific similarity

Comparison & Contrast Noting similarities and/or differences between ideas or objects; two of the classical topics for exploring an idea

Context All of the circumstances in which an act of writing occurs — for example, such environmental stimuli as past events, current attitudes, and so on — which influence meaning and understanding

Couplet A stanza containing two lines which usually rhyme

Criterion A standard for judgment (plural is *criteria*)
    internal: a personal, nonverifiable standard for judgment
    external: a standard upon which a number of people would agree

Data In argument, the facts and information used to support a claim

Deduction A kind of reasoning that begins with a generalization, includes a related specific fact, and leads to a conclusion which fits both

Definition A rhetorical strategy in which the essential nature or the meaning of a thing is explained; one of the classical topics for exploring an idea

Description A rhetorical strategy that focuses on a writer's sensory experience of a subject; one of the classical topics for exploring an idea

Discovery Draft A written exploration of a subject in an effort to develop a thesis

Division A rhetorical strategy which examines a subject by breaking it into its parts

Drafting Writing words on a page to express oneself, inform others, or persuade someone of something

Dramatism Kenneth Burke's theory which features the dynamic interactions of the elements of a text; see also **pentad**

Enthymeme A deductive argument in which either the generalization or the specific fact is unstated; see also **deduction**

Ethos The quality in the writing that impresses the reader with the authority and sense of the writer

Example A rhetorical strategy that makes its point by the use of facts or anecdotes to illustrate an idea

Explication An explanation of the function and meaning of everything in a particular literary work or part of a work

Figurative Language The use of words in an imaginative sense
    simile: a comparison using *like* or *as* of two dissimilar things
    metaphor: a comparison of two dissimilar things without using a connective such as *like* or *as*
    imagery: imaginative representation using evidence perceived through the senses

Foot In poetry, a single unit of meter containing a particular arrangement of accented and unaccented syllables

Freewriting A way of developing ideas by writing down thoughts on a particular subject as they occur

Identification Kenneth Burke's term for the means by which people overcome differences that exist between them

Imagery See **figurative language**

Induction Reasoning to reach a conclusion based on the significance of a series of examples or other evidence

Jargon Language used by insiders as a shortcut in discussions and usually not readily understood by others; technical slang

Journalist's Questions Questions answered in the lead of an effective newspaper story: who, what, when, where, why, and how.

Logical Fallacies Conclusions resulting from errors in reasoning

Logic, Substantive A method of reasoning that uses claims, data, warrants, and qualifiers to come to a conclusion

Logos The appeal of the thought and expression in the text to the rational abilities of the reader

Mapping A graphical way to discover ideas for writing by distributing topics over a sheet of paper and linking them to show relationships

Memoir An account of remembered events

Metaphor See **figurative language**

Motive A need or desire that occasions writing; a purpose, an intention, a rationale for writing

Narration A rhetorical strategy recounting events, usually in a chronological sequence; telling a story

Occasion The circumstances and conditions under which writing occurs including time, place, and attitudes — the context

Paraphrase Restating a passage in different words that convey the same meaning

Pathos The writer's appeal to the reader's emotions, beliefs, attitudes, and values

Pentad Kenneth Burke's analysis of the dramatic component of writing; see also **act, agency, agent, purpose, scene**

Persona The social, literary, psychological, or cultural "mask" or personality that a writer constructs for himself or herself; also, a character in a novel, short story, or drama

Premise The underlying value or belief that one assumes as a given truth at the beginning of an argument

Process The steps necessary to accomplish something, as, for instance, the *writing process;* also, a rhetorical strategy for explaining how to do something

Proposition The point to be demonstrated in an argument

Purpose An element of the **pentad;** why the **agent** performed the **act**

Qualifiers Terms such as *probably* or *unless* that protect an argument from unforeseen exceptions

Quatrain A four-line stanza, rhymed or unrhymed

Ratio In Kenneth Burke's **pentad,** the dynamic interaction of elements of a text — e.g., **act** and **scene, agent** and **scene** — which enriches the reader's understanding

Refutation Evidence or proof that an argument is false or erroneous

Review An evaluation of an unfamiliar text which offers both a sense of the text and a judgment on quality

Revision Re-seeing and reworking a draft of one's writing, noting in particular matters of audience, purpose, completeness, coherence, and unity

Rhetoric The study of principles leading toward the skillful and effective use of language; the analysis of the interaction among idea, text, and language

Rhyme A correspondence in the final sounds of two (or more) words

Scene An element of the **pentad;** *where* and *when* the **agent** performed the **act**

Sonnet A poem containing fourteen lines each of which contains five units, called feet, and each foot consists of an unaccented syllable followed by an accented syllable; the lines are rhymed in three four-line segments and a couplet, or two four-line segments and a six-line sestet, and the rhyme scheme reflects the development of the thought

Subject What the writing is about; the general area addressed

Substantive Logic See **logic, substantive**

Summary A condensation of a work presenting only the major point or points

Syllogism The main scheme of deductive argument in which a major premise and a minor premise combine to form a conclusion

Symbol The use of one thing to represent something else which it resembles in some way

Thesis The point to be made about the **topic**

Topic The specific part of the **subject** to be developed

Topoi A Greek word for the strategies useful for presenting convincing arguments; see also **classical topics**

Valid Follows the conventions of logic, although not necessarily true (if, for instance, the reasoner has begun with a false assumption)

Warrant An explanation, based on evidence (*backing*), that shows why a claim follows from the data

INDEX OF AUTHORS AND TITLES